CW01021736

HELP FROM BRUSSELS

THE PACE GUIDE TO EC GRANTS AND OTHER ASSISTANCE

by

CHARLES BIDWELL

Solicitor, Member of the Institute of Public Affairs Government Relations Group

PUBLIC AFFAIRS CONSULTANTS EUROPE LIMITED

Published in Great Britain 1994 by Public Affairs Consultants Europe Limited
3 Chiltern Business Centre, Garsington Road, Oxford OX4 5NG
Telephone: 0865 770099 Fax 0865 770011

ISBN: 1 897988 01 X

By the same author:
Maastricht and the UK
An Introduction to the European Union

Printed by Eyre & Spottiswoode Limited in Margate, Kent, England.

Contents

Foreword

by

The Right Honourable Sir Leon Brittan, QC
VICE-PRESIDENT OF THE
COMMISSION OF THE EUROPEAN COMMUNITIES

I am happy to be able to commend the "PACE Guide to EC Grants and Other Assistance". The Community is a major source of funds for use in many areas: in support of regional and industrial development; of education and training; of environmental protection; of overseas technical and development aid; and for many other purposes. I regard it as essential that information about the opportunities available should be as widely spread as possible. The "PACE Guide to EC Grants" is a useful tool for all those who need and use such grants.

Preface

It is difficult to calculate precise figures but, by our calculations, including expenditure on the European Agricultural Guidance and Guarantee Fund (EAGGF), the total sums distributed in EC Grants and under Other Assistance Programmes during the calendar year 1993 will have been in the region of BECU 62 (62 billion ECU): up from BECU 54 in 1992. The 1994 figure is expected to be in the region of BECU 70. If one excludes EAGGF expenditure, which is the biggest single item in the EC budget, amounting to 48.8% of total expenditure in 1993, the figures for the three years would be BECU 26, 30 and 32.

The criteria for gaining access to EC funds are not only stringent and complicated but vary from programme to programme and from year to year. Some accept and process applications throughout the year, whereas others call for applications at irregular intervals, normally with very tight time limits. There are no common standards except that incorrect or incomplete applications, or those which miss a deadline either for the initial application or for any stage during the evaluation process, are automatically discarded.

A browser might comment on the amount of detail in this book about the institutions, policies and legislative processes of the Communities, and on the references to the Coal and Steel Community and EURATOM. We make no apology for this. The European Community - in the singular since 1976 and a constituent part of the European Union since All Saints Day (1 November) 1993 - is so very different from the national administrations in the various Member States that it is essential, before becoming involved with it, to develop a good understanding of what it is all about, what it is trying to achieve and the restraints and difficulties it faces. For almost every programme, demand substantially outstrips supply. Applications are evaluated on merit, and choices have to be made. Time spent getting into the Community way of thinking so that you can present the type of proposition that the administrators really want is, in our experience, time well spent and dramatically increases the chances of success. It can also save the time and cost of presenting hopeless cases and the consequent frustration of having them rejected.

This book has been written as a result of repeated requests for information about EC grants programmes and the policies under which they are operated. It is aimed principally at British and Irish readers but much of the information is equally relevant to readers in other countries, both inside and outside the Community since the importance of the EC as both an economic and now a political bloc is steadily increasing and this trend can be expected to continue. The facts stated are believed to be correct as at the end of October, when it was assumed - now thankfully correctly - that the Maastricht Treaty would have been ratified by all Member States before our publication date.

The 175-odd programmes included in this book are being constantly updated or abandoned and new ones introduced. It will be noted that some of the programmes included have already been discontinued; and these have been included because they could be either resuscitated in their original form or included in new programmes at any time. Readers who want to be advised of changes in the programmes as and when they happen can register for the PACE continuous updating service as set out in Appendix 8.

My thanks go to everybody who has helped me in preparing and publishing this book, and this must include the administrators of the various programmes who supplied us with information and answered questions with good humour and understanding. Those who helped me are too numerous to mention individually but their help has all the same been invaluable.

Special tribute must be paid to Vian Bakir who did so much invaluable research and without whose hard work it would never have seen the light of day; to Diana Weir for her editing and indexing work, to Lesley Thomas for formatting, re-formatting and further re-formatting the whole work and guiding me through computer induced despondency, and to my family for their forbearance whilst I have been getting more and more bad tempered as the originally planned book of 200 pages has had to stretch to 730 odd pages to get all the information in!

Lastly, any and all mistakes or omissions are my sole responsibility. Readers are recommended to check all information for themselves before investing time or funds in preparing or pursuing applications based on information contained in this book. Under no circumstances will PACE or I be liable for direct, indirect, special, incidental or consequential damages arising out of any such mistakes or omissions.

Charles Bidwell
Oxford; March 1994

Chapter 1

The Rationale of EC Grants

Few speeches have changed the course of history.

At 4 pm on 9 May 1950, Robert Schuman, the French Foreign Minister, prefaced his press conference in the Salon de l'Horloge at the Quai d'Orsay by saying:

> "It is no longer a time for words, but for a bold constructive act. France has acted, and the consequences of her action may be immense. We hope they will. She has acted essentially in the course of peace. For peace to have a real chance, there must first be one Europe. ... France is taking the first decisive step to rebuild Europe by inviting Germany to play its part. This will transform the situation in Europe. This will open the door to other joint activities inconceivable hitherto. One Europe will emerge from all this; one Europe that is firmly united and solidly built; one Europe where living standards will rise as a result of the pooling of production and the expansion of markets leading to lower prices ..."

The speech that followed, now universally known as the Schuman Declaration, defines a set of principles, which remain the guiding philosophy of the Community to this day:

> "World peace cannot be safeguarded without the making of creative efforts proportionate to the dangers which threaten it.
>
> The contribution which an organised and living Europe can bring to civilisation is indispensable to the maintenance of peaceful relations.
>
> One Europe will not be made all at once, or according to a single plan. It will be built through concrete achievements which first create a de facto solidarity. The coming together of the nations of Europe requires the elimination of the age-old opposition of France and Germany. Any action taken must in the first place concern these two countries."

The first "concrete achievement" proposed was to place Franco-German coal and steel production under a common High Authority, whose decisions would be binding on all countries that joined, and legally enforceable. The members of the High Authority, although appointed by the national governments of the Member States, would be independent figures responsible to the Community as a whole and not just to the national governments which had appointed them.

The pooling of coal and steel production should immediately "provide for the setting up of common foundations for economic development as a first stage in the federation of Europe. ..."

The intention was clear: Schuman was not proposing a new technical arrangement subject to the haggling of negotiators, but stretching out a hand to Germany offering equal partnership in a new entity which would, as a first step, assume responsibility for the joint management of the two countries' coal and steel industries and act as a catalyst for the establishment of a wider European federation.

They had to move quickly if the French initiative, immediately transformed into a Franco-German initiative by the enthusiastic support of Konrad Adenauer, the German Chancellor, was to achieve any practical results. On 20 June 1950, France convened an Inter-Governmental Conference which was held in Paris and chaired by Jean Monnet, who had been largely responsible for both the concept and the content of the Schuman Declaration. The invitations were accepted by the three Benelux countries and Italy as well as Germany, but declined by the UK which considered that its interests would be best served by its "Special Relationship" with the United States and its links with the Commonwealth.

Monnet summed up the purpose of the meeting by saying, "We are here to undertake a common task - not to negotiate for our national advantage, but to seek it in the advantage of all. Only if we eliminate from our debates any particularist feelings shall we reach a solution. In so far as we, gathered here, can change our methods, the attitude of all Europeans will likewise gradually change."

The Conference fine-tuned the basic concepts. It was determined that the new organisation should break away from the shortcomings of traditional inter-governmental agencies, which had been hampered by insistence on unanimity, national control of the purse-strings, and an executive subordinated to national representatives. The powers and independence of the High Authority were recognised as being central to the proposal. At the suggestion of the Netherlands, a Council of Ministers was added to represent the Member States. A Parliamentary Assembly and a Court of Justice completed the institutional structure, the effectiveness of which can be judged by its continued existence virtually unchanged today, some forty-three years later.

The treaty establishing the European Coal and Steel Community (ECSC), the Treaty of Paris, was signed on 18 April 1951 and quickly ratified by the six Member States. The High Authority opened for business in Luxembourg on 10 August 1952 with Jean Monnet, "the father of European Unity", as its first president.

Following the philosophy of the Schuman Declaration, the idea of a European Political Community was strongly advocated at this early stage. As a first move, the Member States proposed bringing their armed forces together into a European Defence Community. This was however rejected by an alliance of Gaullists and Communists in the French Parliament in August 1954. Despite this disappointment, the Foreign Ministers of the six ECSC countries decided at the Messina conference in June 1955 to expand the principles established by the ECSC into a common market covering their countries. On 25 March 1957 they signed two further treaties in Rome: the Treaty Establishing the European Atomic Energy Community (EURATOM) and the Treaty Establishing the European Economic Community (normally referred to as the Treaty of Rome).

These were the three already existing Communities that Denmark, Ireland and the UK joined with effect from 1 January 1973, followed by Greece in 1981 and Portugal and Spain in 1986. Norway, which had negotiated terms at the same time as Ireland and the UK, withdrew its application after a referendum which voted against membership by 51% to 49%.

The three Communities, one de facto if not yet de jure, shared the same basic objectives expressed in the recitals to the three treaties: "to create one organised and vital Europe", "to lay the foundations of an ever closer union among the peoples of Europe", and to combine their efforts to "contribute ... to the prosperity of their peoples". This unity of purpose was recognised in the resolution of the European Parliament of 16 February 1976, which proposed that the three Communities should be designated "the European Community".

The legal system created by the European Community (EC) has become an established component of the legal and political lives of the Member States. Each year, on the basis of the Community Treaties (which can be defined as "Traités de Cadre" or Framework Treaties - treaties setting out the aims to be achieved as broad general principles whilst leaving it to the institutions that they establish to supply the details), Regulations, Directives, Decisions and Opinions are issued which vitally affect the workings of the Member States and the lives of their people.

Although the Treaties themselves have had to be amended by subsequent acts and treaties, notably the Single European Act and the Treaty on European Union, the basic philosophies and core objectives of the Community have changed little over the years. The amendments have been necessary to enable the Community to take in areas of activity where the need for Community-wide action was not initially foreseen or where changes have been necessary to accommodate changing circumstances. Attempts have also been made to address the perceived "democratic deficit" and make the Community appear less remote and more relevant to daily life.

These core objectives, as last amended by the Treaty on European Union, are as follows:

Article 2
"The Community shall have as its task by establishing a common market and an economic and monetary union and by implementing the common policies or activities referred to in Articles 3 and 3a, to promote throughout the Community a harmonious and balanced development of economic activities, sustainable and non-inflationary growth respecting the environment, a high degree of convergence of economic performance, a high level of employment and of social protection, the raising of the standard of living and quality of life, and economic and social cohesion and solidarity among Member States."

Article 3

"For the purposes set out in Article 2, the activities of the Community shall include:

a) the elimination, as between Member States, of customs duties and quantitative restrictions on the import and export of goods, and of all other measures having equivalent effect;

b) a common commercial policy;

c) an internal market characterised by the abolition, as between Member States, of obstacles to the free movement of goods, persons, services and capital;

d) measures concerning the entry and movement of persons in the internal market as provided for in Article 100c;

e) a common policy in the sphere of agriculture and fisheries;

f) a common policy in the sphere of transport;

g) a system ensuring that competition in the internal market is not distorted;

h) the approximation of the laws of the Member States to the extent required for the functioning of the common market;

i) a policy in the social sphere comprising a European Social Fund;

j) the strengthening of economic and social cohesion;

k) a policy in the sphere of the environment;

l) the strengthening of the competitiveness of Community industry;

m) the promotion of research and technological development;

n) encouragement for the establishment and development of trans-European networks;

o) a contribution to the attainment of a high level of health protection;

p) a contribution to education and training of quality and to the flowering of the cultures of the Member States;

q) a policy in the sphere of development co-operation;

r) the association of overseas countries and territories in order to increase trade and promote jointly economic and social development;

s) a contribution to the strengthening of consumer protection;

t) measures in the spheres of energy, civil protection, and tourism."

It is apparent that the objective is to create a united, fair and prosperous Community, reflecting Schuman's statement that "for peace to have a real chance there must be one Europe". There could not be one Europe if there were prosperous regions and poverty-stricken ones, decaying industries leading to mass unemployment without any hope of renewal, or domination of the Community by any Member State or of any sector of it by vested interests capable of abusing a dominant position.

It was a crucial part of the philosophy of Monnet and the other founding fathers that the Community should not be dependent on the annual allocations of finance from the purse of the Member States but should have its own independent sources of funding, even if in the final analysis the funds came out of the pockets of the citizens of the Member States.

It is for the purpose of achieving these objectives that the EC provides Grants and Other Assistance using its Own Funds as defined in the Treaty. The success of programmes is judged by how well they achieve the objectives of the Treaty, and new programmes are constantly being designed to improve performance.

Chapter 2

The Legal Basis of the European Community

The factor which distinguishes the European Community from earlier efforts to create a united Europe is that it is a community freely entered into by the various Member States, with the full knowledge of what was in the treaties and of the philosophy behind the treaties. It works not by means of force or domination, but simply by means of the rule of law. Law is now doing what for centuries "blood and iron" have failed to do. After all, the only unity that can be expected to last is that based on freely made associations. This unity is founded on fundamental values such as freedom and equality, and is protected and translated into reality by the rule of law. That is the thesis underlying the Treaties that created the Community.

Every social organisation has a constitution, which defines its structure, and lays down rules and procedures for its management. The constitution of the EC is not contained in one comprehensive document, but arises from the totality of rules and fundamental values by which the authority of the Community is exercised within the limits prescribed for it. This arises in the first instance from the founding treaties, as qualified and interpreted in the secondary legislation produced by the institutions of the Community, in accordance with the powers granted to them by the Treaties; and finally from the rules of procedure and precedents that have been established over the years.

The Community structure bears some resemblance to the constitutional order of a sovereign state, as is apparent from the list of tasks entrusted to it. These are not the narrowly circumscribed technical tasks commonly assumed by international organisations, but fields of competence which, taken as a whole, form some of the essential attributes of statehood. Under the ECSC Treaty the Community is competent for the Community-wide administration of the coal and steel industries, which play key roles in the national economies of the Member States. The European Atomic Energy Community (EURATOM) has common tasks to perform in research and development, and the subsequent utilisation of atomic energy for peaceful purposes. These two Communities aim at the closer interlocking of specific sectors of the economy (so-called "economic integration").

The task of the Economic Community, as set out in Article 2 of the original Treaty, was "by establishing a common market and progressively approximating the economic policies of Member States, to promote throughout the Community a harmonious development of economic activities, a continuous and balanced expansion, an increase in stability, an accelerated raising of the standard of living and closer relations between the States belonging to it."

It was obvious from the start that the Community had to be given sufficient jurisdiction over specific matters to achieve these objectives. Initially, the implementation of these objectives was limited to matters like ensuring the free movement of goods, free movement of workers, freedom of establishment, freedom to provide services, freedom of capital movements, agricultural matters, transport policy, social policy and competition. Other aspects of State sovereignty, such as defence, diplomacy, education and culture, were however withheld from the Community but, as European integration has continued, it has become necessary for the Member States to keep adding new spheres of Community competence, so that the nature of the Community is ever evolving.

The similarities between the Community order and that of a sovereign state become even more apparent if we consider the extent of the powers given to the Community institutions to enable them to perform the tasks entrusted to the Community. In general, the founding treaties do not confer sweeping powers on the institutions to take all measures they might consider necessary to achieve the objectives of the Treaties but, in each chapter, lay down strictly-defined limitations of the powers within which they can act - the principle of specific attribution of powers. This method has been chosen by Member States in order to ensure that the renunciation of their own powers in favour of Community action can be more easily monitored and controlled.

However, these points of resemblance between the Community order and the national order of a sovereign state do not suffice to confer on the EC the legal character of a "state". Sovereign powers have only been conferred on the EC's institutions within the limited spheres mentioned, and those institutions have not been given any power to increase their competence merely by their own decisions. Thus the EC lacks the universal jurisdiction characteristic of a state, such as the power to create for itself new fields of competence. It cannot therefore turn itself into the "centralised super state" portrayed in many quarters in the UK. It cannot even turn itself into a "federal state" as properly defined and understood in most Member States. According to the Oxford Dictionary, "federal" means "of or pertaining to, or of the nature of, that form of government in which two or more states constitute a political unity whilst remaining independent as to their internal affairs; of or pertaining to the political unity so constituted (1977) ... united in a league, allied (1867)". The very opposite of a centralised state in fact!

It is difficult to define the EC in institutional terms. It is far from being a "United States of Europe" with a strong central authority represented by an elected president and a powerful congress. Nor, on the other hand is it a vague assemblage of states which delegate certain powers, or a kind of international organisation endowed with technical powers. It is a unique hybrid institution lying somewhere between these two extremes and its exact position is not only difficult to pin down in general terms but, as it is constantly evolving to reflect the changing demands made on it by the Member States, its position within the ranging from spectrum a United States of Europe to a vague assemblage of states keeps shifting.

As emphasised in the Maastricht Treaty, the EC represents an endeavour to weld the Member States into "an ever closer union" and it is thus in a state of constant development. The Member States which make up the Community have very wide variations in traditions and cultures both within their own boundaries and from the other Member States. Some of them are rather artificial creations put together as matters of expediency; some came into being as sovereign states relatively recently but, they all have in common a genuine commitment to democracy, peace and prosperity - both within their own jurisdictions and in the Community as a whole - and a desire to see a united Europe. It is only to be expected that disagreements will arise from time to time, not only about priorities and how to achieve "ever closer union", but about timetables and other technical matters. Advances towards union are made when Member States realise that they cannot meet the challenges to democracy, peace and economic progress on their own. This continuous development, made up of advances followed by periods of consolidation and even retreat, makes it hard to analyse the Community as a political and legal institution, for the very word "institution" suggests a highly specific, almost rigid, framework.

Chapter 3

The Institutions of the European Community

A thorough knowledge of how the Community works, how it thinks and what it is trying to achieve is invaluable to everybody who wants to deal with it. It is totally different from dealing with the national governments of the Member States, or the Federal Government in Washington or inter-governmental agencies like the UN. Its unique institutional structure sets it apart from more traditional international organisations, and the institutions complement each other, each having a part to play in the decision-making process. In accepting the Treaties of Paris and Rome which set the Communities up, Member States relinquish a measure of their "national sovereignty" to them, representing as they do both national and shared interests: Monnet's national advantage in the advantage of all.

Article 4 of the Treaty of Rome, as amended by the Maastricht Treaty, states that the tasks entrusted to the Community are to be carried out by:

- a European Parliament,
- a Council,
- a Commission,
- a Court of Justice, and
- a Court of Auditors.

The Council and the Commission are to be assisted by an Economic and Social Committee and a Committee of the Regions, acting in an advisory capacity.

Article 4a states that a European System of Central Banks (ESCB) and a European Central Bank (ECB) are to be established in accordance with the procedures laid down in the Treaty. Article 4b establishes the European Investment Bank (EIB). Of these institutions, only the Court of Justice and the Parliament, or Assembly as it was originally called, were from the outset common to all three Communities. This was provided for in a Convention between the original six Member States, signed at the same time as the Rome Treaties. The process of creating common institutions was completed in July 1967 by the Treaty Establishing a Single Council and a Single Commission of the European Communities (the "Merger Treaty"), and any lingering doubts were finally dispelled by Article C of the Maastricht Treaty, which says; The Union shall be served by a single institutional framework."

These institutions and the others which have grown up over the years are examined in more detail below.

The Council

In EURATOM and the Economic Communities the Council is the supreme legislative body, taking the most important political decisions of the Community. Under Article 145 of the EECT, it is responsible for co-ordinating the economic policies of the Member States. In the ECSC it is an endorsing body that has to deal only with a few, especially important decisions.

Initially, the Council was made up of Foreign Ministers of the Member States and was a cohesive body, able to give direction to the Community. As the Community's competence increased however, so did the range of Council activities. Hence, over the 1960s and 1970s the Council became multi-headed, with important decisions being taken not only by the General Affairs Council of Foreign Ministers, but by other Councils such as the Council of Finance Ministers (ECOFIN), the Agricultural Council and, now, councils covering most spheres in which governments are involved. The ECOFIN ministers and the agricultural Ministers meet monthly, but the others meet only on a need-to-meet basis, with a minimum of once in each presidency.

As time went by and the Community grew bigger, ministers - including Foreign Ministers no longer formed the close friendships which existed in the initial stages and sessions came to be dominated by haggling among Member States, each trying to secure the best deal for their country.

It is in the Council that the individual interests of the Member States and the Community interest are balanced and reconciled. Although the Member States' interests are given precedence in the Council, the members of the Council are at the same time obliged to take into account the objectives and needs of the EC as a whole. The Council is a Community institution and not an inter-governmental conference. Consequently, it is not the lowest common denominator between the Member States that is sought in the Council's deliberations, but the highest possible between the Community and the Member States.

The Council adopts EC legislation - Regulations, Directives and Decisions - and therefore possesses ultimate controlling authority, since proposed Regulations and Directives only become law if the Council so agrees. Although it is, as such, the Community's legislative body in certain areas specified by the Single European Act and the Maastricht Treaty, it shares the function with the European Parliament. The Council and Parliament also have joint control over the EC's budget. Financially, the Council adopts international agreements negotiated by the Commission.

Article 151 states that "A committee consisting of the permanent Representatives of the Member States shall be responsible for preparing the work of the Council and for carrying out the tasks assigned to it by the Council".

This committee, known as COREPER, which is in turn assisted by committees of civil servants from the appropriate national ministries, will have discussed in advance the matters with which the Council is due to deal. If COREPER reaches an unanimous agreement on any matter, that matter is adopted by the Council without any further deliberation. Other matters are discussed by the Council in order to reach agreement. The Council is also assisted by a Secretariat-General based in Brussels. This is relatively small and its functions appear to be limited to providing backup services for the Council members.

Article 148 of the EEC Treaty distinguishes between decisions adopted unanimously, by a simple majority (where each State has one vote) and by a qualified majority (where 54 votes out of a total of 76 are required and votes are weighted so that the larger States exert a greater influence). Where a qualified majority is required, votes are distributed as follows: France, Germany, Italy and the United Kingdom have ten votes each, Spain has eight, Belgium, Greece, the Netherlands and Portugal each have five, Denmark and Ireland each have three, and Luxembourg, two. When the Council acts on a proposal that does not emanate from the Commission, 54 votes and the support of eight Member States are both necessary.

The importance of majority voting is not so much that it prevents the smaller states from blocking important decisions as they could, as a rule, be brought into line by political pressure. The real benefit is that it makes it possible to outvote the larger Member States which would normally withstand such pressure. This principle therefore contributes to the equality of Member States and consequently must be regarded as a cornerstone of the EC's constitution.

However, despite this intrinsically well-balanced approach, the political importance of the majority principle has in practice remained small. The reason for this dates back to 1965 when France, afraid that its vital interests were being threatened in proposals for changing the financing of the Common Agricultural Policy (CAP), completely blocked decision-making in the Council for more than six months by making a unanimous decision impossible by boycotting Council meetings. This was know as "the policy of the empty chair" and was not resolved until the "Luxembourg Agreement" of 29 January 1966 which states that, in the case of matters where very important interests of one or more countries are at stake, the Council will endeavour, within a reasonable time, to reach solutions that can be adopted by all the members of the Council while respecting these particular interests as well as those of the Community as a whole. The French delegation emphasised that it considered that in such cases the discussion must be continued until "unanimous agreement" was reached. The Luxembourg Agreement provides no solution for cases where reaching unanimity proves impossible, but confines itself to stating that a divergence of views on this point still exists among the Member States. Although the Agreement therefore succeeded in ending the deadlock in the Council, it also in practice spelt a threat to the very principle of majority voting. It provides no criteria for determining within the Council what constitutes "a very important interest" and appears to leave this decision solely to the Member State concerned. In effect any Member State could demand unanimity for any major decision in the Council which means that each Member State in practice retains a right of veto.

This situation, which detracted from the decision-making ability of the Council, was considerably improved when qualified majority voting was introduced by the Single European Act (SEA). Most legislation, particularly that relating to the functioning of the internal market, was to be dealt with by a qualified majority. Unanimity was only required on issues of fundamental importance, such as the accession of a new Member State, amendments to the Treaties or the launching of a new common policy, the approximation of laws covering fiscal provisions, the free movement of persons and the rights and interests of employed persons. An abstention by any member present in person or represented does not prevent the adoption of acts which require unanimity. Qualified majority voting has been further extended by the Maastricht Treaty, as will be seen in Chapter 5 on the legislative process.

One of the criticisms frequently levelled at the EC and particularly at the Council, is that too many decisions affecting the lives of millions of ordinary people are taken behind closed doors: in other words, there is not enough "transparency" in the decision-making process. When the Council meets, it does so in a dual capacity: part of the time it is meeting in its capacity as the executive branch of the EC "government" and part of the time, in its function as part of the legislative process, as one of the chambers of the EC legislature, alongside the European Parliament and the Commission. It always meets in closed session, which is obviously necessary when acting in its executive capacity, but there is growing pressure on the Council to hold the legislative parts of its meetings in public. At the Edinburgh summit in December 1992, EC Heads of State or Government took a first step in this direction when they took the decision to televise some formal sessions of the Council. They also agreed that the Council would have its seat in Brussels but would hold its meetings in April, June and October in Luxembourg.

The European Council

As European affairs became more important in the political life of the Member States, it became clear that there was a need for the national leaders to meet on a regular basis and the European Council evolved from the regular meetings of Heads of State or Government and their Foreign Ministers. The decision was taken at the Paris Summit in December 1974 to put these meetings on a regular footing and formalise the procedure: the objective of the meetings was to discuss important issues confronting the EC in general rather than detail. The title for these meetings, the European Council, was then adopted and the arrangement was formalised by the Single European Act in 1986, which recognised the position of the European Council as the supreme EC body for political co-operation.

Initially it met three times a year, but now it meets at the end of each presidency to receive a report of progress during the out-going presidency and to consider policy in its widest terms. Special meetings are called under the Article 147 procedure when necessary. The President of the Commission now attends in his/her own right.

Thanks to its high-profile membership and its dramatic debates, the European Council soon hit the headlines as a launching-pad for major political initiatives and as a forum for settling controversial issues blocked at ministerial level. The European Council also deals with current international issues through European Political Co-operation (EPC), a mechanism devised to allow Member States to align their diplomatic positions and present a united front.

The Maastricht Treaty confirms the pivotal role of the European Council in the EC's development by specifying that "the European Council shall provide the Union with the necessary impetus for its development and shall define the general political guidelines thereof". (Article D, Title I)

The chapter on the Common Foreign and Security Policy in the Maastricht Treaty reinforces the European Council's role of political leadership and strategy formation by giving it responsibility for establishing "general guidelines".

The European Council has not sought to assume the formal law-making role of the Council of Ministers. It simply would not have the time, so it tends to produce communiqués designed to provide the basis for proposals which can then be inserted into the EC decision-making machinery.

The Presidency

The Presidency is extremely influential since "the Council shall meet when convened by its president on his own initiative, or at the request of one of its members or of the Commission." It also sets the agendas for Council meetings and the various Councils are chaired by the representative from the Member State holding the Presidency.

Title V of the Maastricht Treaty assigns a vital role for the Presidency in representing the Union in matters coming within the Common Foreign and Security Policy, and in implementing common measures. (Article J.5).

The Presidency of the Council rotates among the governments of the Member States, changing every six months as set out in Article 146, (which is set out in Appendix 5). It follows that topics considered important by one Presidency can get pushed forward but then downgraded by its successor to whom they are of little interest. To ensure greater continuity and also as a form of backup when taking difficult decisions on behalf of the Community, the Troika system has grown up, consisting of the Presidency, the previous Presidency and the next one, meeting to discuss common problems and also forming joint delegations to external meetings. The Troika is given formal recognition in the Provisions on a Common Foreign and Security Policy introduced by the Maastricht Treaty.

The presidency also briefs the European Parliament after each meeting of the European Council.

The European Parliament

Although the powers of the European Parliament have been extended with successive constitutional reforms of the EC, the expansion of these powers has not matched the pace of the transfer of authority from individual countries to the EC. As a result, a "democratic deficit" has arisen. National governments have given up control over executive powers they have transferred to the EC, but corresponding rights of control have not been given to the European Parliament. Other criticisms of the degree of democracy in the EC have centred on the lack of openness in the way EC decisions are taken and on the perceived inadequacy in the accountability of the Commission. Some of these problems were addressed in the Single European Act and Maastricht Treaty, but further reforms are envisaged when the structures are reviewed by the Inter-Governmental Conference scheduled for 1996. The logical extension of the Parliament's powers would be to give it total powers of supervision and control over the Commission which, in accordance with the Monnet philosophy, is not answerable to the national parliaments of the individual Member States.

The precursor of the European Parliament, the Assembly set up by the European Coal and Steel Community in 1952, was a purely consultative body with delegates appointed by the Member States. This cautious start was necessary because a Parliament elected by direct universal suffrage would have been unacceptable to the parliamentarians of the Member States and they would immediately have seen it as a rival. Since then, the Parliament's democratic legitimacy has increased with its election by direct universal suffrage in accordance with a Council Decision of 20 September 1976. Since June 1979, elections for the European Parliament have been held every five years, the next one is in June 1994, when 240 million electors will elect 567 MEPs.

Article 138(3) of the EECT provides that the Parliament “shall draw up proposals for elections ... in accordance with a uniform procedure in all Member States (and) the Council shall acting unanimously ... lay down the appropriate provisions which it shall recommend to Member States for adoption”. This has not yet happened and is unlikely to happen before the June 1994 elections.

Currently, the Parliament has 518 seats. The four most populous countries (France, Germany, Italy and the UK) each have 81 seats, Spain 60, the Netherlands 25, Belgium, Greece and Portugal 24, Denmark 16, Ireland 15 and Luxembourg has six. Since German unification, 18 observers from the eastern Länder have been taking part in the Parliament's proceedings.

It was agreed at the Edinburgh Summit that, from the 1994 elections, membership would be increased to 567, allocated as follows: Luxembourg six, Ireland 15, Denmark 16, Belgium, Greece and Portugal 25, Netherlands 31, Spain 64, France, Italy and UK 87, and Germany 99. The Home Secretary decided that five of the UK's additional six seats should be go to England and one to Wales, and a boundary commission was appointed to draw up new constituencies. The length of time between the original decision to increase the number of seats taken in December 1992, the setting up of the boundary commission, and the implementation of the report submitted in the middle of September has been the cause of considerable discontent amongst the opposition parties.

Article 138a of the Maastricht Treaty says, "Political parties at European level are important as a factor for integration within the Union. They contribute to forming a European awareness and to expressing the political will of the citizens of the Union". The Liberal Federation is to discuss becoming a European Political Party formation later this year but, as usual in their dealings with the EC, the Tories find themselves in an ambiguous position. They have to face both ways at once: inwards to placate their more jingoistic back benchers, and outwards to avoid causing undue offence to the

European Peoples' Party (EPP) with whom they have sat in the Parliament since May 1992. Although sitting with the EPP, a grouping consisting basically of Christian Democrats, they have always been at great pains to emphasise that they do not belong to it. They have even gone so far as to denounce the Athens Declaration drawn up by the EPP Congress in November 1992, which might make negotiations about any form of future co-operation after the June elections fraught with uncertainty.

The biggest groups in the current Parliament are: Socialists 198; European Peoples' Party (including the English Conservatives) 162; and Liberal and Democratic Reformist Group 46. Egon Klepsch, the German Christian Democrat, has been President of the Parliament since January 1992.

It was announced at the Edinburgh Summit that the Parliament's seat would be in Strasbourg, where the 12 monthly plenary sessions would continue to be held: additional plenary sessions and the meetings of the various committees which do so much of the detailed work would be held in Brussels and the General Secretariat would remain in Luxembourg. This announcement took MEPs by surprise, as there had been no consultations with them and they considered that not only was this peripatetic existence, which causes the packing up of crates of papers and the mass migration of MEPs and officials disruptive and wasteful, but it was incompatible with the treaties and the natural prerogatives of a Parliament elected by direct, universal suffrage, and deserving the right to determine its own working methods in order to fulfil its functions as efficiently as possible. Besides, there is a magnificent new building in Brussels designed specifically for the Parliament, whilst when it meets in Strasbourg it has to borrow the Council of Europe building which anyway will not be large enough to accommodate the new MEPs from the countries which have already applied to join! It was considered a deliberate attempt to stop the Parliament becoming too powerful.

The Parliament provides a democratic forum for debate. It has a watchdog function, exercising the advisory and supervisory powers conferred upon it by Treaty, and plays an increasingly important part in the legislative process. It meets the democratic criterion of transparency, or openness: like legislatures in all democratic countries, the European Parliament is an open institution. Plenary sessions of the Parliament are in public, as are many of its committee meetings. The Parliament and its committees also organise public hearings on topical issues.

The Single European Act established a procedure with two readings in Parliament and two in Council. Known as the co-operation procedure (defined in Article 7 of the SEA), it gave the Parliament a bigger say in a wide range of policy areas most particularly all matters referring to the completion of the single market. Thus, for the first time, the Parliament, with increased powers to amend legislation, was given a genuine and meaningful role in the legislative process. Thus today, the Parliament shares the legislative function with the Council: it has a hand in the drafting of Directives and Regulations, proposing amendments which it invites the Commission to take into account.

The SEA made international co-operation and association agreements and all subsequent enlargements of the EC subject to the Parliament's assent. The Maastricht

Treaty requires that the Parliament's assent should be required for the uniform electoral procedure and Union citizenship.

The 1975 Budgetary Treaty gave the Parliament the right of co-decision alongside the Council over the EC's annual budget. The budget is prepared by the Commission: it then passes backwards and forwards between the Council and the Parliament as the two arms of the budgetary authority. While the Council's opinion prevails on "compulsory expenditure", largely relating to the CAP, the Parliament has the last word on "non-compulsory expenditure", which it can alter within the limits set by the Treaty. It can adopt the budget or reject it, as it has done in the past, causing the whole procedure to start again from scratch. It is learning, as did the House of Commons in the sixteenth and seventeenth centuries, to use its budgetary powers to gain influence over policy matters.

The Maastricht Treaty further increases the Parliament's powers by introducing a process of "co-decision" for all legislation concerning areas like the free movement of workers, research and development policy, the environment, health, education, consumer protection, culture and trans-European networks. It may now reject the Council's common position and halt the legislative process, provided that an absolute majority of MEPs are in favour and the conciliation procedure (described in Chapter 5) has failed. In other words, the Parliament has the final veto in these policy areas.

The Parliament's democratic control over the Commission and its President is limited under the Treaty so that it may only:

- "request the Commission to submit any appropriate proposal on matters on which it considers that a Community act is required ..." (Article 138b);
- "set up a temporary Committee of Inquiry to investigate ... alleged contraventions or maladministration in the implementation of Community law ..." (Article 138c);
- "force the whole Commission to resign if it passes a motion of censure by a two-thirds majority (Article 144)"; and
- "approve, en masse, the nominations for the Commission and the President at the start of their mandate, which is increased from four to five years from 1995, coinciding with the parliamentary term". (Article 158). It does not however, have the power to influence the choice of candidates or to veto any one particular candidate.

The Parliament also comments and votes on the Commission's programme each year and monitors implementation of the common policies, relying for its information on reports produced by the Court of Auditors. It also monitors the day-to-day management of these policies by means of oral and written questions to the Council and the Commission. Foreign Ministers, who are responsible for European Political Co-operation, also answer MEPs' questions and brief them on action taken in response to the Parliament's resolutions on international relations and human rights.

Citizens of the Union also have the right to petition the Parliament (Article 138d), and an ombudsman will be appointed by Parliament to follow up complaints (Article 138e).

However, despite all these powers, the democratic credentials of the EC are still in question. The mere existence of a parliament cannot satisfy the fundamental requirements of a democratic constitution that all public authority must emanate from the people. That calls not only for transparency in the decision-making process but also for representativeness in the decision-making institutions. In this respect the present organisation of the EC leaves something to be desired, and it can rightly be described as a still "underdeveloped democracy".

Although the Parliament's decision-making powers in the legislative process are limited, it is generally consulted by the legislative decision-making organ - the Council - on all important matters, even when not required to by the Treaties. The outcome of such consultations is not binding on the Council and they often only have any impact if the Commission successfully advocates the Parliament's views in the Council.

The Parliament's overall position in the institutional structure is still thoroughly unsatisfactory, which in turn detracts from the EC's democratic credentials. It exercises only symbolically the functions that can reasonably be expected of a true parliament in a real parliamentary democracy. Above all, it does not elect a government because no government in the normal sense exists at EC level. Instead, the functions analogous to government provided for in the Treaties are performed by the Council and the Commission. The Parliament has no powers of supervision over the Council, which is subject to parliamentary control only in so far as each of its members is subject to the control of his national parliament as a national minister.

Despite its deficiencies and the absolutely deplorable attendance records of some MEPs from all Member States and all parties, it provides the European forum par excellence, acting as a melting-pot for the political and national sensibilities of a community of 370 million people. It frequently calls for new policies to be launched and for existing ones to be developed or altered. The Crocodile Group's draft Treaty on European Union, adopted in 1984, was the catalyst which finally set the Member States on the road to the SEA: it called for the convening of the Inter-Governmental Conferences on political union and economic and monetary union which led to the Maastricht Treaty. The run-up to the 1996 Inter-Governmental Conference on the structure of the Community will undoubtedly see demands for ever greater powers.

The Commission

The Commission is the key institution of the EC and acts in a dual role: in its capacity as "Custodian of the Treaties" it has to make decisions on policy matters concerning their implementation, and, as the Community's executive, it carries out and enforces adopted Community policy. There were originally three Commissions, one for each Community, but they were merged into a single Commission by the Merger Treaty on 1 July 1967.

The Members of the Commission, currently 17 (two each for France, Germany, Italy, Spain, and the UK, and one each for the remaining seven countries) must be nationals of the Member States. They are generally former senior Cabinet Ministers and are appointed by the Member States by "common accord" for a term of four years, extended to five by the Maastricht Treaty, which also makes their appointment en bloc subject to the approval of the European Parliament. Jaques Delors has been President of the Commission since 1985 and his term of office lasts until 1994. He is assisted by six Vice-Presidents and, like all the other Commissioners, he also has responsibilities for administration within designated Directorates-General. There is a commitment in the Maastricht Treaty to examine the size of the Commission (Declaration 15) and the larger states might lose the right to appoint two Commissioners.

Under Article 157(2), "The Members of the Commission shall, in the general interests of the Community, be entirely independent in the performance of their duties ... they shall neither seek nor take instructions from any government or from any other body. ... Each Member State undertakes to seek to respect this principle and not to seek to influence the members of the Commission in the performance of their tasks."

The entire Commission can be forced to resign en bloc by a vote of censure in the Parliament supported by a two-thirds majority, although this has yet to happen. Individual Commissioners, on the other hand, can only be dismissed by the Court of Justice, either on grounds of serious misconduct or because they no longer fulfil the conditions required for the performance of their duties.

The Commission is backed by a civil service, based in Brussels and Luxembourg. It consist of 23 departments called Directorates-General, which are set out in Appendix 3. At the last count there were 13,484 officials (Eurocrats) in the Commission, and, contrary to popular myth, this number (which has remained reasonably stable over the years) compares favourably - from the tax-payer's point of view - with the staffing levels of national government departments. The Eurocrats are recruited from the Member States and the under-representation of the UK is notorious. Among the 4,357 in the administrative grade, there are 724 French citizens, 624 Germans, 530 Belgians, and only 511 Britons. Each Commissioner has a personal cabinet consisting of a handful of trusted advisers normally from their own country: the sole exception to the practice of mixing nationalities throughout the Commission.

The status of the Eurocrats is interesting in that they are not true bureaucrats carrying out the orders of their political masters. Article 155 states, "In order to ensure the proper functioning and development of the common market, the Commission shall:

- ensure that the provisions of this Treaty and the measures taken by the institutions pursuant thereto are applied;
- formulate recommendations or deliver opinions on matters dealt with in this Treaty, if it expressly so provides or if the Commission considers it necessary;
- have its own power of decision and participate in the shaping of measures taken by the Council and by the European Parliament in the matter provided for in this Treaty.

This obligation to originate policy means that they are obliged to take political decisions in the broadest sense of the word in accordance with the Monnet philosophy of seeking advantage for all.

Further in accordance with the Monnet philosophy, the Commission enjoys financial autonomy and can, in theory, spend its budget as it sees fit, unlike the secretariats of conventional international organisations. Representing the Community interest as a whole and taking no instructions from individual Member States, it enjoys a great deal of independence in performing its duties, which can be summarised as follows.

i As the guardian of the Treaties, it ensures that Regulations and Directives adopted by the Council are properly implemented. It can bring a case before the Court of Justice to ensure that this is done. So far, the Commission has performed its role as guardian of the Treaties very effectively. For instance, if, after the adoption of a harmonisation measure by a qualified majority, a Member State deems it necessary to apply national provisions on the grounds of major needs such as public policy, public security or public health, or on grounds relating to the protection of the environment or the working environment, it must notify the Commission of those provisions. The Commission will then satisfy itself that they are not a device for arbitrary discrimination or a disguised barrier to intra-Community trade. If so, the matter may be dealt with by the Court of Justice.

ii Closely connected with the role of guardian of the Treaties is the task of defending the EC's interests. As a matter of principle, the Commission may serve no interests other than those of the Community. It must constantly endeavour, in what often prove to be difficult negotiations within the Council, to make the EC interest prevail and seek compromise solutions that take account of that interest. In doing so, it also plays the role of mediator between the Member States - a role for which, by virtue of its neutrality, it is particularly suited and qualified.

iii The Commission is the motive power behind EC policy. It is the starting point for every Community action, as it is the Commission that has to present proposals and drafts of EC legislation to the Council - referred to as the Commission's right of initiative. It is not free to choose its own activities, but is obliged to act if the Community interest so requires. The Council may also ask the Commission to draw up a proposal. Under the ECSC Treaty the Commission also has law making powers. In certain circumstances these are subject to the assent of the Council, which enables it to overrule Commission measures. Article J.9 of the Maastricht Treaty gives the Commission the right "to be fully associated with the work carried out in the Common Foreign and Security Policy field". This was considered necessary because trade and aid policies, which have always been Commission responsibilities, are inseparably bound up with political relations with other countries.

iv Lastly, the Commission also has its executive function. Classic examples of this are the implementation of the EC budget, enforcing competition policy and the administration of the protective clauses contained in the Treaties and secondary legislation. Much more extensive than these "primary" executive powers are the "derived" powers devolved on the Commission by the Council. These essentially involve adopting the detailed rules required to implement Council decisions. In the final analysis however, most of the implementation of EC policy has to be done by the Member States themselves. They have to implement Directives into their own national legal systems, monitor the application of the national implementing measures and punish non-compliance as appropriate under their own domestic procedures. This solution, enshrined in the Treaties, has the advantage that the "foreign" reality of the EC system is brought closer into domestic reality through the workings of the more familiar national system.

Federalists, whether in the true meaning of the word or the corrupted meaning which is becoming current in the UK, see the Commission as the embryo of a European government, accountable to a bicameral parliamentary system consisting of the European Parliament and a Senate which will replace the Council as we know it today. This is the logical conclusion of the quest for "ever closer union amongst the peoples of Europe".

The European Court of Justice

A system will endure only if its rules are respected and obeyed and are seen to be respected and obeyed. As Lord Hewart put it, "It is not merely of some importance but it is of fundamental importance that justice should not only be done, but should manifestly and undoubtedly be seen to be done." If common rules in a community of states were to be subject only to the interpretation and enforcement of the national courts they could be interpreted and applied differently from one State to another. The fundamental principle of the uniform application of EC law in all Member States would thus be jeopardised. These considerations led to the establishment of a Community Court of Justice as soon as the ECSC was created.

The European Court of Justice (ECJ), based in Luxembourg, consists of 13 judges assisted by six Advocates-General, all appointed for a six-year term by common agreement among the Member States. They are chosen from persons whose independence is beyond doubt and who possess the qualifications required for appointment to the highest judicial offices in their own countries, or who are jurisconsults of recognised competence.

The Court has two main functions.

The first function is to give its opinion on the correct interpretation or the validity of EC provisions when asked to do so by the national court of a Member State. If a question of this kind is raised in a case before a court or tribunal against whose decision there is no appeal, the Court of Justice must be asked to give a preliminary ruling. Article 177 gives the Court the jurisdiction to give preliminary rulings by which it exercises a form of advisory function that is legally binding. The following are examples of matters on which preliminary rulings may be given:

i clarification of the meaning and scope of the provisions of the Treaties or of Council and Commission Regulations;

ii identification of the national law referred to in any particular provision of EC law;

iii determination of the period of validity of a Community rule;

iv decisions on the legal acts or legal measures falling respectively under EC law or under national law;

v determination of the question of whether EC rules are self-sufficient or require to be supplemented by provisions of national law; and

vi examination of the validity of EC legal acts.

It is to be expected that applications will be made under Article 177 to define the application of "the principle of subsidiarity" as defined in Article 3b of the Treaty and the limits within which it and "action ... necessary to achieve the objectives of this Treaty" are to apply.

The second main function of the Court is to check the laws enacted by the EC institutions for compatibility with the Treaties. This judicial function of the Court is very important, and embraces the following types of proceedings.

i Actions against States that fail to fulfil their obligations under the Treaties or under EC law. Such actions may be initiated by the Commission or by another Member State; in practice, it is usually the Commission that takes the initiative. The Court examines the case and decides whether there has been an infringement of the relevant Treaty. If it finds that an infringement has occurred, the State is bound to take immediate steps to comply with the Court's judgement.

ii In the context of the Court's jurisdiction to examine the validity of the acts of the EC institutions, an action may be brought on the ground of failure to act or for the annulment of action taken by an institution. Actions on the ground of failure to act may be brought against the Council or the Commission if either institution fails to take a decision that is mandatory under the Treaty or a legal instrument based on the Treaty.

iii Actions concerning disputes involving the non-contractual liability of the EC.

iv Proceedings seeking a review of the fines the Commission is permitted to impose in the case of certain infringements of EC law. In these cases, the Court acts as a court of appeal which has the right either to annul the fines or to increase or reduce them.

v Actions concerning disputes between the EC and its officials or their successors in title.

vi Finally, the Court acts as a court of arbitration when this jurisdiction is expressly conferred upon it by the particular contract concerned.

The Court's judgements and interpretations are gradually building up a body of case-law applicable Community-wide. In Chapter 4 we deal in greater detail with the conflict between Community law and the national law of the Member States: in Community law, the ECJ's rulings take precedence over those of national courts and it has therefore played a decisive role in shaping the EC as we know it today. For instance, one of the essential aims of the Treaty is the improvement of living conditions in Europe but, in its preamble, it says only in an incidental and sketchy manner that such improvement can be achieved solely by safeguarding and developing human rights and fundamental freedoms. The Court therefore had to decide whether or not it was competent when an EC citizen complained to it about the application of the Treaty on grounds of the violation of human rights. The Court was faced with this decision when a disabled war veteran complained that he was obliged to prove his identity in order to buy reduced-price "Christmas butter". He was told that such identification was necessary in order to prevent abuses and ensure that only those entitled to this privilege benefited. However, the person in question regarded having to give his name when others did not as degrading and humiliating, conflicting with human dignity and the principle of equality. He complained to the Court, which ruled in his favour (Siauder judgement, 12 November 1969). The Court's decision, therefore, was that respect for fundamental rights is part of the general principles of the EC which it has a duty to uphold.

A few years later, this principle was more clearly stated in a case involving the democratic tradition of the Member States:

"The Court could not uphold measures incompatible with fundamental rights recognised and protected by the Constitutions of the Member States (and with) international treaties for the protection of human rights of which they are signatories." (Nold v Commission judgement, 14 May 1974). Although it went largely unnoticed at the time, it set a precedent so that a few years later it no longer seemed out of place to promote the European Union as based on fundamental rights, especially those of freedom, equality and social justice set out in the preamble to the SEA.

The independence of the Court is beyond doubt, since there are two procedural arrangements which protect it from pressure from Member States' governments. The first is that, although hearings are in public, the deliberations of the judge are in secret. Secondly, judges can only be removed from office by a unanimous vote of their colleagues to the effect that they are no longer capable of carrying out their functions.

Actions can be brought to the Court in one of two ways: either the action is started before the Court itself, or it is started before a national court and a question on interpretation or validity of Community law is referred by that court to the European Court. Applicants in direct actions may be Community institutions, Member States or natural or legal persons. Different rules apply according to the nature of the action. The Court has always had almost impossible demands on its time, so the SEA empowered the Council to set up a Court of First Instance with responsibility for certain classes of action. On 24 October 1988, the lower court was established with jurisdiction in actions relating to the Staff Regulations of the Communities, competition law, anti-dumping law and matters covered by the ECSC Treaty.

The European Court of Justice has no connection with the European Court of Human Rights (ECHR) based in Strasbourg, whose function is to act as the final court of appeal in cases affecting human rights and whose members are determined by the Council of Europe's parliamentary assembly.

The Court of Auditors

The Court of Auditors was set up by Budgetary Treaty on 22 July 1975. Before the Maastricht Treaty it was a something of a Cinderella body, but the Maastricht Treaty, in recognition of its importance, elevated its status to make it the fifth Institution of the Community. It has 12 members (formerly nine), appointed by the Council after consultations with the European Parliament, for six year terms and is based in Brussels and Luxembourg.

Its role is to check that revenue is received, that expenditure is incurred "in a lawful and regular manner" and that the EC's financial affairs are properly managed. This includes examination of ECSC borrowing and lending operations, projects financed through contributions from Member States undertaken in co-operation with associated developing countries, and monitoring the revenue and expenditure of EC bodies such as the European Centre for the Development of Vocational Training in Berlin and the European Foundation for the Improvement of Living and Working Conditions in Dublin.

The Court's findings are set out in annual reports, which are drawn up at the end of each financial year and published in the Official Journal of the European Communities. It is hoped that it will carry greater clout with its new enhanced status.

The Economic and Social Committee (ECOSOC)

In EEC and EURATOM matters, the Council and the Commission are assisted by the Economic and Social Committee (ECOSOC), which acts in an advisory capacity. It consists of 189 members representing employers, workers and various interests such as agriculture, transport, trade, small enterprises, the professions and consumers. France, Germany, Italy and the UK have 24 members each, Spain 21, Belgium, Greece, the Netherlands and Portugal 12 each, Denmark and Ireland nine each, and Luxembourg five. The members are selected for four-year terms by the Council from lists submitted by Member States.

ECOSOC is a consultative body. Its Opinions were originally confined to specific issues stipulated by the Treaties or to proposals referred by the Council or the Commission. Since 1972, however, it has had the right to take up issues on its own initiative. In 1986 the SEA consolidated its role in the tighter co-operation procedure set up between the various EC institutions for the purpose of devising and implementing common policies in the furtherance of European Union. In practical terms this has substantially boosted the number of Opinions issued every year by the Committee from seven in 1960 to nearly 180 in 1989. In the vast majority of cases, ECOSOC reaches a consensus on Commission proposals, despite the fact that initial positions often differ widely.

ECOSOC Opinions are interesting on several counts. For instance, they help the Commission to ascertain what impact its proposals are likely to have - particularly on those most directly concerned - and what amendments may be necessary to enlist wider support. Commission departments also have to tackle a wide range of specific issues and, here again, ECOSOC can provide valuable technical expertise. Lastly, ECOSOC's

Own-Initiative Opinions and Information Reports are of particular importance since they cover subjects neglected or ignored by the institutions. ECOSOC material frequently prompts the Commission to table relevant proposals.

The standard procedure for obtaining an ECOSOC Opinion is as follows:

i requests for Opinions are forwarded to the Chairman of ECOSOC, usually from the Council but sometimes from the Commission;

ii after consultations with Section Chairmen, ECOSOC's Bureau decides which Section is to be responsible for the preparatory work;

iii the Section sets up a Study Group (usually 12 strong) and appoints a Rapporteur who is assisted by experts (usually four);

iv on the basis of the Study Group's work, the Section adopts an opinion by a simple majority and forwards it to ECOSOC's Chairman;

v after considering the Section's Opinion, ECOSOC adopts its opinion by a simple majority at a Plenary Session;

vi this Opinion is sent to the Council, the Commission and the European Parliament and is also published in the Official Journal of the European Communities.

As a result of its composition and its political and technical terms of reference, ECOSOC exerts a strong influence on the EC's decision-making process.

The Committee of the Regions

The Committee of the Regions was set up by the Maastricht Treaty with responsibility for representing the regional and local authorities in the EC. It is modelled on the Economic and Social Committee and has 189 members, ranging from 24 each for the large Member States to six for Luxembourg. The members are appointed by the Council for four year terms on the basis of proposals from Member States. No rules were laid down concerning the qualifications of nominees and, in the UK, it has consistently been the view of the opposition parties in the House of Commons that they should be elected local councillors. This has been refused by the Government who are determined to retain complete freedom to appoint their own nominees. The Committee's role in the legislative process is purely advisory. It will be consulted by the Council and the Commission and may submit its own opinion on matters where it believes that specific regional interests are involved.

The Consultative Committee

In matters relating to the European Coal and Steel Community, the Commission is assisted by a Consultative Committee, which has 96 members representing, in equal numbers, producers, workers, consumers and dealers in the coal and steel industries. They may not be bound by any mandate or instructions from the organisations which nominated them. This Committee must be consulted before decisions are taken on a large number of subjects and it can also submit opinions on its own initiative.

The European Investment Bank

As a financing agency for the "balanced and steady development" of the common market, the EC has at its disposal the European Investment Bank (EIB), whose shareholders are the Member States. The EIB provides loans and guarantees in all economic sectors to promote the development of less developed regions, to modernise or convert undertakings or create new jobs and to assist projects of common interest to several Member States. The EIB also lends funds to countries which are associated with the EC or have co-operation agreements with it, and handles loans made in the context of economic aid to Poland and Hungary.

The European Monetary Institute (EMI)

The European Monetary Institute is to be established in the second stage of Economic and Monetary Union (EMU), which is scheduled to begin on 1 January 1994, and will consist of the governors of the central banks of the Member States. The EMI will be responsible for developing EMU through stage two. More specifically, the role of the EMI will be:

- to strengthen co-operation among the national central banks and co-ordination of monetary policies;
- to monitor the European Monetary System;
- to facilitate the use of the ECU and oversee its development, including the functioning of the ECU clearing system; and
- to prepare for stage three of EMU.

The European System of Central Banks (ESCB)

The EMU chapters in the Maastricht Treaty will create an independent European System of Central Banks, consisting of the European Central Bank and the central banks of the Member States. The ESCB will be set up before stage three of EMU and will replace the EMI. The primary objective of the ESCB will be to maintain price stability. The basic tasks of the ESCB will be:

- to define and implement EC monetary policy;
- to conduct foreign exchange operations;
- to hold and manage official foreign reserves of Member States (Member States can still hold foreign exchange working balances); and
- to promote smooth operation of payment systems.

Chapter 4

EC Legislation

There are four sources of Community Law:

1. the primary source in the Treaties as amended from time to time;
2. the secondary legislation made by the Institutions of the EC pursuant to the Treaties;
3. international agreements to which the EC is a party; and
4. the complete jurisprudence of the European Court.

1. PRIMARY LAW

The primary source of EC law is the founding Treaties, the European Coal and Steel Community Treaty (the Treaty of Paris), the EURATOM and Economic Community Treaties (the Treaties of Rome) as signed by the Member States, together with the various protocols and annexes attached to them, and their later additions and amendments. This primary law is mainly confined to setting out the objectives of the Communities, establishing their mechanisms and laying down timetables by which these objectives are to be achieved. They set up institutions for the task of filling out the constitutional skeleton in the interest of the Communities as a whole and confer on them the necessary legislative and administrative powers to do so. Since the Merger Treaty in 1967 the term European Community has been used to embrace all three communities.

2. SECONDARY LEGISLATION

Secondary legislation is made by the Community institutions, under the powers conferred upon them by the Treaties, in line with the procedures outlined in Chapter 5. A new legislative system had to be devised from scratch when the Community was set up, and it had to be decided not only what sort of legislative acts should be adopted but the effects which these various types of acts should have. In view of the Monnet philosophy of the independence of the Institutions, they had to be able to align the disparate economic, social and, not least, environmental conditions in the various Member States, effectively without having to depend constantly on the goodwill of the Member States. On the other hand, they were not to interfere in the domestic systems of law more than was absolutely necessary to achieve the objectives of the Community. The EC legislative system is therefore based on the principle that, where the same arrangement should apply in all Member States, national arrangements must be replaced by Community legislation, but, where this is not necessary, due account must be taken of the existing legal orders in the Member States - the "doctrine of subsidiarity" which, even if not codified until the Maastricht Treaty, had in principle existed from the beginning.

Against this background, a range of tools was developed which allowed the EC institutions to work on the national legal systems in varying measures. The first, most drastic action is the replacement of national rules by EC rules. Secondly, there are Community rules by which the EC institutions act only indirectly on the Member States' legal systems. Thirdly, measures may be taken which affect only a defined or identifiable addressee, in order to deal with a particular case. Lastly, provision was made for measures which have no binding force on either the Member States or the citizens of the EC.

These basic categories of legislative measure are to be found in all three Treaties. The actual forms they take and their titles differ between the earliest ECSC Treaty and the two later ones, the EEC and EURATOM Treaties. The former makes provision for only three types of legislative act - Decisions, Recommendations and Opinions (Article 14); but the latter two provide for five forms - Regulations, Directives, Decisions, Recommendations and Opinions (Articles 189 EECT and 161 EURATOM). The pattern was changed because it was recognised that the forms developed for the ECSC would not adequately meet the needs of the broader-based Communities. The new titles were intended to avoid the conceptual shortcomings in the earlier Treaty, but still cause considerable confusion in dealing with the ECSC.

In the EEC and EURATOM Treaties, non-binding measures are called Recommendations or Opinions, but under the ECSC Treaty only the term "Opinions" is used. Unhappily, under the ECSCT "Recommendations" are binding legislative measures, corresponding to Directives in the EEC and EURATOM Treaties. EEC and EURATOM Recommendations urge the addressees to adopt or refrain from a particular form of behaviour: Opinions are used where the EC institutions are called upon to state a view on a current situation or specific event in the EC or Member States.

The real significance of non-binding Recommendations and Opinions is political and moral. In providing for measures of this kind, the draftsmen of the Treaties assumed that, given the prestige of EC institutions and their broader view and wide knowledge of conditions beyond the national framework, those concerned would voluntarily comply with Recommendations made to them. These non-binding acts are not adopted by the legislative procedure described below, but are simply issued by a single EC institution.

In the EEC and EURATOM Treaties, the main binding legislative measures are Regulations, Directives and Decisions, each of which has different consequences both as to the method of their incorporation into the jurisprudence of the EC and the individual Member States and in terms of the legal effects flowing from them.

Regulations

Regulations are the legislative measures which enable the EC institutions to encroach furthest on the domestic legal systems of the Member States (and are called "General Decisions" in the ECSC Treaty).

A Regulation, according to Article 189, "shall have general application. It shall be binding in its entirety and directly applicable in all Member States". They are published in the Official Journal of the European Communities L Series and enter into force either on the day specified in them or, in the absence of any specified date, on the twentieth day following their publication. They are self-executing in the legal orders of the individual Member States and need no national implementing measure to bring them into effect. In certain cases, Regulations affect the rights and obligations of individuals and may be relied upon before national courts.

Regulations are used when required by the Treaty, either specifically or when necessary to regulate the market as a whole. Taking examples from agriculture: Article 38(1) EECT states, "The common market shall extend to agriculture and trade in agricultural products" and Article 38(4) "The operation and development of the common market for agricultural products must be accompanied by the establishment of a common agricultural policy among the Member States". This policy statement in the Treaty clearly envisages that agricultural market goods will be traded not just inside one Member State, in which domestic rules apply, but between buyers and sellers in different Member States; the market can only operate smoothly if common rules are in force throughout the territory of the EC. This requires central joint management for the EC as a whole, as the measures needed for the operation of the market have to take effect directly in all Member States. Only a Regulation could do this.

The purpose and effect of the ECSCT General Decision is clearly illustrated by the way in which the Commission intervenes in the EC steel market. The crisis which had been smouldering in the iron and steel industry since 1975 got worse in 1980 and became the worst crisis since the war. There was a collapse in the demand for steel both in the EC and on the world market, which led to a substantial fall in prices in the EC even though production costs were rising. European steel producers' financial position deteriorated to the point where it was feared that there would be lasting damage to the steel industry, which would have been a major blow to the achievement of the objectives of the ECSCT as set out in Article 3, particularly the achievement of an orderly EC market and the improvement of workers' living and working conditions. This dangerous situation required direct adjustment of steel output, binding on all steel firms, in order to restore the balance of supply and demand on the steel market, an ECSC Decision was the only instrument available to provide the necessary measures, binding and actually applied in all Member States and by all steel firms equally.

Directives

The second binding EC legislative measure is the Directive, or Recommendation in the ECSC Treaty.

A Directive, according to Article 189, "shall be binding, as to the result to be achieved, upon each Member State to which it is addressed, but shall leave the national authorities the choice of form and methods."

The reasoning behind the format of the Directive is that it allows Community intervention in the domestic legal and economic structures of the Member States in a less obtrusive form, by allowing them to take account of their own special domestic circumstances when implementing EC rules. The draftsmen of the Treaties took the view that the Member States were the best judges of how their own individual requirements could best be reconciled with the far-reaching changes in national systems needed to implement the Treaties. The format also reflects a second guiding principle: the desire to achieve the relevant measure of unity where necessary whilst preserving the multiplicity of the national and regional characteristics within the Member States.

As Directives and ECSC Recommendations are not self-executing, they require legislative measures - Acts of Parliament, Statutory Instruments or Parliamentary or Executive decrees - to introduce them into the domestic legislation of the various Member States, according to their own respective national legislative processes. Directives provide the usual method for the "harmonisation" process or achieving the "approximation of laws" as, for example, under Article 100 EECT, in which inconsistencies between the various national legal or administrative rules are ironed out; they are also used for aligning the economic policy of the Member States.

This latitude in the implementation of Directives has in itself given rise to anomalies. It has been the practice in most Member States to implement Directives in a minimalist way, introducing the lowest standard permissible under the Directive. The UK on the other hand has consistently adopted a maximalist approach and implemented Directives more stringently than required by the Directive itself. The Prime Minister, John Major, announced in answer to journalists' questions at the end of the Edinburgh Summit that the policy of "gold-plating" as it is called was to be reviewed, but evidence of any changes is still awaited.

Except when an ECSC Recommendation is addressed directly to an EC firm, Directives and ECSC Recommendations do not confer direct rights and duties on EC citizens, as they are addressed solely to the Member States. Rights and duties are only acquired when the Directive or Recommendation has been incorporated into domestic law by the Member States, but this point is of no practical importance as long as the Member States comply with their obligations. If the directive is mis-implemented or not implemented at all however, citizens of a Member State may be disadvantaged. The ECJ has refused to allow this and has ruled that in such cases EC citizens can invoke the Directive or Recommendation directly. This is applicable only if two conditions have been met: the time stipulated in the Directive for its incorporation into national law has expired and the relevant provision of the Directive is worded clearly enough to leave the Member States with no discretion to determine the effect of the measures to be taken.

Directives are normally published in the Official Journal and take effect upon notification to the State or States to which they are addressed. The date for implementation of the provisions of the directive into national law is always stated.

Decisions

The third category of EC legislative measures consists of EEC or EURATOM Decisions and ECSC Individual Decisions. Decisions are binding in their entirety on those to whom they are addressed and do not need to be incorporated into the national legal system to take effect. The Council or the Commission may address a Decision to a Member State authorising it, for example, to derogate from a certain rule of EC law. Decisions addressed to individuals or companies are most commonly found in those areas where the Commission has a role in regulating business practices, such as competition law, state aids and anti-dumping. As with Directives, there is no Treaty requirement that they be published, although as a rule they are. They take effect upon notification to those to whom they are addressed.

3. INTERNATIONAL AGREEMENTS TO WHICH THE EC IS A PARTY

International Agreements to which the EC is a party fall into three categories. Firstly there are agreements made by the Community within the treaty-making jurisdiction given to it by the Treaties, like the agreements reached with the ACP countries or CEEC. Secondly, there are hybrid agreements in which the subject matter falls partly within the jurisdiction of the EC and remains partly with the individual Member States, like the Co-operation and Association Agreements; and, thirdly, there are agreements concluded prior to the Treaties, such as GATT, which have been assumed by the EC by way of succession. The rules relating to and the differences between these types of international agreements are beyond the scope of this book.

4. THE COMPLETE JURISPRUDENCE OF THE EUROPEAN COURT

This includes not only the Court's decisions, but its general principles and opinions expressed concerning matters of Community Law. Over the years it has built up a reputation for independence and fairness which is universally respected. Preliminary rulings made under the Article 177 procedures have been welcomed and it has seldom been accused of either unreasonably refusing to hear an application or interfering unnecessarily with the domestic courts of the Member States. This leads to the vital question of conflicts between Community Law and the national law of Member States.

Community Law - V - National Law

The Treaties are silent on the question of the relative priorities of Community Law and the national law of the Member States. Whether this was by diplomatic omission or because it was not considered a problem at the time is a matter for speculation.

The question of priorities between directly effective international and domestic law is normally a matter of national law, to be determined according to the constitutional rules of the state concerned. This will depend on a number of factors, but primarily on the terms on which international law is incorporated into the domestic law of the state concerned, which in turn will depend on whether the state is monoist or dualist in its approach to international law. If it is monoist, the relevant international law will form part of the national law from the moment of ratification without the necessity of any further measures being taken. If dualist, the international law does not become binding as part of the domestic law until it is incorporated by the measures required under the domestic law.

The UK and other common law jurisdictions adopt a dualist approach and must provide for priorities in the statute of incorporation, as was done in the European Communities Act 1972. Such statutes are subject to the principle "lex posterior derogat priori": a later statute is deemed to have repealed an earlier one. On a strict application of this doctrine, any provision of any domestic statute passed subsequent to the European Communities Act (ECA) which was inconsistent with the ECA would take priority over it.

Article 5 of the Treaty states, "Member States shall take all appropriate measures, whether general or particular, to ensure fulfilment of the obligations arising out of this Treaty or resulting from actions taken by the institutions of the Community. They shall facilitate the achievement of the Community's tasks."

The European Court has in successive cases taken the pragmatic view that the Member States freely signed the Treaty setting up the Community and its institutions including itself and, as far as they are concerned, all EC law, whatever its nature, must take priority over conflicting domestic law whether it be prior or subsequent to the relevant Community Law. Indeed, the Community would not survive if the Member States were free to act unilaterally in breach of their Community obligations and the continued existence of the Community would be threatened.

In Van Gend en Loos (case 26/62, 1963 ECR 1 at 29), they stated that, in relation to national law, Community Law rested on three characteristics: autonomy, direct applicability and supremacy.

"Autonomy" means that it is quite independent of the legislation passed by the Member States; it extends equally and uniformly over the whole Community and has to be applied in its original form by the national courts.

Certain provisions of the Treaties and Community legislation such as Regulations, are directly applicable without having to be implemented by the national legislature and may impose obligations upon Member States and create rights and remedies available to private parties independently of the national legislation. Individuals can therefore assert rights and claim defences not available to them under the national systems.

"Supremacy" does not mean superior but simply reflects a practical device to resolve conflicts between Community Law and national law. Without it, Community Law would be deprived of its character as Community Law and the very legal foundations of the Community endangered. The validity of a Community act and its application within a Member State remains therefore unimpaired, even if it is alleged that this is in direct conflict with the basic tenets of the national constitution.

Although the UK Courts followed the judgements of the ECJ as precedents ab initio, direct confrontation between Community Law and a subsequent inconsistent act of Parliament was avoided until the Factortame case in which, on 25 July 1991, the ECJ answered questions posed by the Divisional Court, and while conceding that a Member State is competent to lay down conditions when implementing Community Law (in this case in the Merchant Shipping Act, concerning the beneficial ownership of fishing vessels using the British flag), stressed that such power must be exercised in conformity with Community Law. This judgement is in direct conflict with the concept of the absolute sovereignty of Parliament as expounded by Dicey, and despite the outcry that followed the judgement in some circles it was generally realised that the conflict between the doctrines of the supremacy of Community Law and the sovereignty of Parliament had been discussed and recognised before the UK signed the EECT.

Chapter 5

The Legislative Process

An essential part of understanding the EC is to come to terms with the legislative process, which is long, tortuous and bears no relationship to the precedents of Westminster or any other Member State. It rests on a division of responsibilities between the Council, the Commission and the Parliament.

Article 189 of the EECT as amended by the Maastricht Treaty states, "In order to carry out their task and in accordance with the provisions of this Treaty, the European Parliament acting jointly with the Council and the Commission shall make regulations, issue directives, take decisions, make recommendations or deliver opinions." It can be summed up by saying that the Commission proposes, the Parliament interposes and the Council disposes. However, even though the Council reaches the final decision, there are various stages to be completed which, depending on the subject of the measure, can involve the Economic and Social Committee and, in future, the Committee of the Regions as well as the Council itself, the Commission and the European Parliament.

The machinery is set in motion by the Commission, which has the sole and exclusive right of initiative, subject to the right given to the Parliament by Article 138b of the Maastricht Treaty to "request the Commission to submit any appropriate proposal on matters on which it considers that a Community act is required for the purpose of implementing this Treaty".

The proposal is prepared on the responsibility of a member of the Commission by the appropriate Directorate-General for the type of issue concerned; the Commission will generally also consult national and independent experts, professional and other special interest groups at this stage, although it is under no obligation to do so. The draft drawn up here, which is a complete text setting out the content and form of the measure right down to very the last detail, goes before the Commission as a whole where a simple majority is enough to have it adopted. It is now a "Commission Proposal" and is sent to the Council with a detailed explanation of the grounds for drawing it up. Unless otherwise provided for in the Treaty, amendments to the Commission Proposal require the unanimous decision of the Council but, as long as the Council has not acted, the Commission may alter its proposal itself. The Council must also at this stage, check which, if any, of the other EC bodies is entitled to be consulted.

The Treaties give the Parliament the right to be consulted on all politically important measures: "compulsory consultation". Parliament here speaks on behalf of the citizens of the EC; its function is to look after their interest in the development of the Community. Failure to consult Parliament in such cases would be a serious irregularity and an infringement of the Treaties, actionable at the European Court of Justice. In practice, Parliament is also consulted on a voluntary basis on all draft legislation, on the basis that it is better to get agreement at an early stage than risk having a confrontation later on.

Article 198 says, "The Economic and Social Committee must be consulted by the Council or by the Commission where this Treaty so provides"; for example -

- Article 54(2): Freedom of establishment;
- Article 75: Transport matters;
- Article 99: Taxation;
- Article 100: The Approximation of Laws;
- Article 126: Educational Vocational Training and Youth;
- Article 129: Public Health;
- Article 129a: Consumer Protection;
- Article 129b: TENs;
- Article 130: Industry; and
- Article 130a: Economic and Social Cohesion.

As well as these compulsory areas of consultation, the Council is free to consult the Committee in other cases, which it does frequently. When the Committee of the Regions has been established, it too will be similarly consulted. The Committees' part in the process ends with the adoption of a formal written opinion, which their Chairman forwards to the Council and the Commission together with a record of their proceedings. Neither is obliged to follow these opinions.

Before the European Parliament had achieved democratic respectability as a directly elected body rather than an appointed one, its role was limited to expressing a formal written opinion which was submitted by its president to the Council and the Commission. They could recommend amendments to the proposal but the Council was under no obligation to accept those amendments; the final decision was theirs alone.

Following the first direct elections in June 1979, it was recognised that the Parliament was entitled to a more important role. The Single European Act, signed in February 1986, introduced the Co-operation Procedure, incorporated into the EECT as Article 149 and subsequently replaced by the Maastricht Treaty with a new Article 189c.

As with the original procedure, the process starts with a Commission Proposal, but the proposal is sent to the Parliament as well as the Council. The Parliament holds a first reading and transmits its opinion to the Council. The Council, acting by a qualified majority, adopts a "Common Position" on the Commission Proposal, the Parliament's opinion and its own deliberations and the Common Position is the subject of a second reading in the Parliament.

The Parliament now has a three-month time-limit during which it may, acting by an absolute majority:

1. adopt the Common Position,
2. allow the time limit to expire without taking any action,
3. reject the Common Position, or
4. propose amendments.

Under options 1 and 2 the Council adopts the measure in accordance with the Common Position.

Under option 3, unanimity is required for the Council to act on a second reading.

Under option 4, the Commission must, within one month, send re-examined proposals to the Council on the basis of which the Common Position is adopted which takes account of Parliament's amendments and makes detailed comments on the amendments which it has rejected. The Council may adopt the proposals as re-examined by qualified majority, but unanimity is required to amend them further.

The Maastricht Treaty introduces a third procedure, known as the "Co-decision Procedure", which has been incorporated into the EECT as Article 189b.

The procedure is the same as the Co-operation Procedure until the second reading in the Parliament, when the Parliament has the same four options within the three month time limit:

For options 1 and 2, the procedures and positions are the same.

For option 3, if Parliament indicates by an absolute majority that it intends to reject the Common Position it must immediately tell the Council, which may then convene a meeting of the Conciliation Committee consisting of equal numbers of members of the Council or their representatives and representatives of the Parliament. The Conciliation Committee's task is to try to reach agreement, acting by a qualified majority of the members of the Council and an absolute majority of the representatives of the Parliament. The Commission takes part with a view to reconciling the opposing positions. If a joint text is agreed within six weeks in the Conciliation Committee, the Parliament, acting by an absolute majority of the votes cast, and the Council, acting by qualified majority, have six weeks in which to adopt the act in accordance with the joint text. If either fails to approve it, it shall be deemed not to have been adopted.

Where the Conciliation Committee cannot agree a joint text, the proposed act shall be deemed not to have been adopted unless the Council, acting by a qualified majority within six weeks of the expiry of the time allowed to the Conciliation Committee, confirms the Common Position to which it had agreed before the Conciliation procedure was initiated "possibly with the amendments proposed by the European Parliament." In this case, the act shall be finally adopted unless the European

Parliament, "within six weeks of the date of confirmation by the Council, rejects the text by an absolute majority of its component members, in which case the proposed act shall be deemed not to have been adopted." The three month and six week time limits can be extended by up to one month and two weeks respectively.

For option 4, the amended text is sent to the Council and the Commission, which delivers an opinion on the amendments.

If, within three months, the Council approves all the amendments by a qualified majority, it amends the Common Position and adopts the act, but must act unanimously on amendments on which the Commission has delivered a negative opinion. If the Council does not approve the act, the Presidents of the Council and European Parliament convene the Conciliation Committee.

According to the EECT, as amended by the Maastricht Treaty, there are some areas of policy which have to be adopted by the Co-operation Procedure and some by the Co-decision Procedure. It is unclear why it was considered necessary to have the two procedures operating in parallel.

When mention is made of the Council in this context, it does not always mean the full Council. Matters will first be discussed by specialised working parties and then by the Permanent Representatives Committee (COREPER). COREPER is very important in the workings of the EC. It co-ordinates the preparatory work for Council meetings and can also reach agreements on technical points, with the Council merely rubber-stamping measures adopted unanimously by COREPER.

Adoption of the proposal by the Council is the final stage in the legislative process. The final text, in all nine official languages of the Community (Danish, Dutch, English, French, German, Greek, Italian, Portuguese and Spanish), is signed by the President of the Council and published in the Official Journal of the European Communities or notified to the person to whom it is addressed.

The procedure is different in the case of the binding instruments of the ECSC - the General Decision and the ECSC Recommendation. The main difference from the EECT procedures lies in the role of the Commission and the Council. The ECSC Treaty gives the power to adopt these instruments not to the Council but to the Commission. In certain specified cases they require the Council's assent, which then enables the Council to block Commission measures. Before the Commission finally adopts a text it must, in certain cases laid down in the Treaty, consult Parliament and the ECSC Consultative Committee.

The Community's International Agreements

As one of the focal points of the world, Europe cannot confine itself to managing its own internal affairs; it has to concern itself with economic, social and political relations with the world outside. The EC therefore concludes agreements in international law with non-member countries and with other international organisations; these range from Treaties providing for extensive co-operation in trade, or in the industrial, technical and social fields, to agreements on trade in particular products. With the EC's economic significance growing and its trading activities expanding, the number of agreements it has concluded with non-member countries has increased substantially in the past few years.

Two kinds of agreement between the EC and non-member countries are particularly worth mentioning. The first group are the co-operation agreements which are aimed solely at intensive economic co-operation. The EC has such agreements with the Maghreb States (Morocco, Algeria and Tunisia), the Mashreq States (Egypt, Jordan, Lebanon and Syria), and Israel, for instance.

The second type of agreement is association agreements. These go beyond the mere regulation of trade, involving close economic co-operation and financial assistance.

A further distinction may be drawn between two types of association agreement. The first are agreements which maintain special links between certain Member States and non-member countries. One particular reason for the creation of the association agreement was the existence of overseas countries and territories with which Belgium, France, Italy and the Netherlands maintained particularly close ties as a legacy of their colonial empires. The introduction of a common external tariff in the EC would have seriously disrupted trade with these countries, so special arrangements had to be made so that the system of unrestricted Community trade could be extended to them. At the same time, tariffs on goods originating in these countries were progressively dismantled. Financial and technical assistance from the EC was channelled through the European Development Fund.

Agreements of the second type are agreements in preparation for accession to the EC or for the establishment of a customs union. Such agreements serve as a preliminary stage towards accession, during which the applicant country can work on converging its economy with that of the EC. This proved successful in the case of Greece, whose association with the EC started in 1962. Another association agreement with a view to future accession to the EC was concluded with Turkey in 1964. Two other association agreements, whose eventual purpose was the establishment of a customs union, were concluded with Malta in 1971 and Cyprus in 1973.

The association agreements with the Central and Eastern European countries are dealt with in greater detail in Chapter 30.

Chapter 6

The Single Market

The Single Market is the aspect of the EC which has the greatest relevance to the lives of most of the citizens of the EC. The four fundamental freedoms providing for the free movement of persons, goods, services and capital throughout the EC were enshrined in the Treaty of Rome in 1957. They are only now being fully realised, as progress towards them has not made spread evenly during the 36 years of the Community's existence. Progress was rapid in the first ten years and the six original Member States - Germany, France, Italy, the Netherlands, Belgium and Luxembourg - removed all tariffs and quotas on their internal trade in July 1968, 18 months ahead of schedule. By that time they had also finalised their customs union by creating a single set of tariffs on imports from outside the Community.

Progress towards further integration slowed down however during the 1970s and early 1980s. There were various reasons for this. One was the need to absorb three newcomers - the UK, Ireland and Denmark - who joined the EC in 1973. The second more important reason was the economic recessions which followed the international oil crises in 1973 and 1979. Some of the Member States, which had been particularly badly hit by these recessions, took steps to protect their markets from growing international competition. Thirdly, these protectionist attitudes were reinforced by a proliferation of contradictory technical regulations and standards in the different Member States which further served to divide up their historically fragmented markets. It is, after all, much easier to harmonise customs duties than technical regulations or even indirect taxes. A fourth reason was the amount of Community time and energy taken up by the row, which lasted from 1979 to 1984, between the UK and its partners over contributions to the EC budget.

The first half of the 1980s was a gloomy period for the EC. The largest economies, Germany and France, were growing at barely 2% a year, and in some years even less. This was less than half the rate recorded over the EC's first quarter-century to 1973, and no better than the period 1973-79. Although the Member States were starting to have some success in reducing inflation, this was achieved at the cost of spiralling unemployment, which more than doubled in the EC between 1980 and 1985. The problem was made all the more galling to the EC because this economic gloom was not world-wide. Japan was continuing to grow at around 4% each year and the US was bouncing back strongly from its 1981-82 recession, cutting both inflation and unemployment.

The EC scene was no more comforting in other respects. The European Coal and Steel Community (ECSC) was beset by the need to stem massive losses and cut capacity by nearly half. The Regional Fund was failing to contain rapid increases in unemployment in the EC's poorest areas, such as Ireland and Italy's Mezzogiorno. EURATOM's role was dwindling as the nuclear power programme slowed to a trickle, except in France. Apart from Greece, internal tariffs on trade between the other nine Member States had long since gone and the rapid expansion of intra-EC trade that had followed was now grinding to a halt. The CAP was fighting a losing battle against exploding surpluses in a number of commodities and an ever-widening gap between EC and world foodstuff prices. There were huge losses on agricultural intervention and support, taking up over two-thirds of the EC's financial outgoings. Despite this, France and Germany would veto any plan that resulted in politically unacceptable cuts in their farmers' incomes.

There seemed few EC achievements to offset this bleak picture. Although Greece had joined the EC in 1982 and the accession of Spain and Portugal was imminent, they were all poorer countries with large agricultural sectors which would place further strain on the CAP and on the Regional Development Fund. Although the European Monetary System (EMS) had begun to operate in 1979, critics argued that this miniature version of the Bretton Woods system had been devised partly to avoid difficulties in implementing the CAP and that, in any case, it was really just a Deutsche Mark currency bloc. Neither was it functioning totally smoothly, since exchange rate fluctuations were still occurring. The UK was refusing to participate in the system: France and Italy, by holding their currencies close to the Deutsche Mark, were displaying much less financial stability than, for example, Austria and Switzerland which lay outside the system.

In searching for the reasons for its malaise, the EC could not use the excuse of differing budgetary policy to explain the contrast between the state of its affairs and the US's. Contrary to popular public myth, general government budget deficits in the EC were on average no smaller a percentage of GDP than in the US. To add insult to injury, the unemployment-inflation trade-off looked much healthier in the rich European countries like Austria, Finland, Norway, Sweden and Switzerland which were outside the EC.

The EC was therefore looking for a new policy initiative that would return it to the fast track towards economic growth. Such a policy would have to appeal particularly to Germany, the EC's main paymaster, and therefore could not involve financial outlays. It would have to appeal to the UK and therefore work within the ambit of market forces. France would also favour this: although it was the last major country to base its macroeconomic policy on Keynesian principles, Mitterand had done a U-turn on its monetary and fiscal policy formulation in 1983. Above all, the policy would have to restore the momentum towards economic integration without undue infringements of the rights of Member States.

The policy decided upon was the Single European Market programme, subsequently known loosely as "the 1992 programme", which is something of a misnomer since the operative date was 1 January 1993. This single market initiative was launched by Jacques Delors when he became President of the European Commission in January 1985. It was supported by his colleague, Lord Cockfield, who drew up a landmark White Paper setting out the 270-odd measures that would be needed to create a single market and fixing a timetable, running until the end of 1992, for completing it. The White Paper was immediately endorsed by the Member States in the European Council at the Milan Summit in June 1985, and instructions were given to the Commission to draft the enabling legislation without delay. Negotiations were completed in a record six months, and the Single European Act (SEA) was approved by the following European Council at the Luxembourg Summit in December 1985. It was signed in February 1986 and came into force after ratification by the Member States - which by then included Spain and Portugal - in July 1987. The SEA contained a series of amendments to the Treaty of Rome including Article 18 which became Article 100a of the EECT, providing for majority voting instead of unanimity in the EC's main decision-making body, the Council of Ministers, for measures required for establishing the internal market. It has proved to be one of the most far-reaching innovations of the SEA and was reluctantly agreed to by Mrs Thatcher as a trade-off to secure the support of some of the more protectionist Member States for the concept of the single internal market. Without majority voting, it would have been impossible to have the single market ready by the end of 1992, but it set a precedent which has been extended by the Maastricht Treaty and is likely to be further extended in the future.

The 1992 Programme

In its historical context, the 1992 programme seeks to re-establish a 21st century version of ancient freedoms of movement. Passports are an invention of the 19th century "sovereign nation states". Formerly, scholars had moved freely between Europe's great universities and seats of learning, with Latin as their lingua franca. Craftsmen and soldiers offered their skills and services throughout the continent. Merchants traded freely and gold and silver coins - whether sovereigns, marks, shillings, florins, francs, ducats, crowns or even ecus - had been used as forerunners of a universally accepted common currency.

The goals of the 1992 programme were stated as the removal of physical frontiers, of technical barriers and of fiscal barriers, thereby creating equality of choice among buyers and sellers, companies and individuals whilst providing reasonable protection for consumers. There are five practical elements in the single market programme:

1. the simplification and eventual abolition of internal borders;
2. the free movement of capital and labour throughout the EC;
3. the removal of all non-tariff barriers to intra-Community trade;
4. the opening of public procurement contracts to all EC firms; and
5. the approximation of national indirect tax schemes.

These elements are examined in more detail below.

1. SIMPLIFICATION AND EVENTUAL ABOLITION OF INTERNAL BORDERS

The simplification of internal borders has largely already happened. The frontiers between the Benelux countries, France and Germany resemble those separating Canadian provinces, particularly since the signing of the Schengen Agreement in June 1990. The plethora of customs documentation for goods crossing internal borders has been reduced to a single form, the Single Administrative Document, known by its acronym SAD, which is acceptable to all national authorities. It contains eight copies:

- Copy 1 Copy for the office of departure;
- Copy 2 Statistical copy for the country of export;
- Copy 3 Exporter's or consignor's copy;
- Copy 4 Copy for the office of destination;
- Copy 5 Community transit return copy;
- Copy 6 Customs import declaration;
- Copy 7 Statistical copy for the country of destination;
- Copy 8 Copy for the consignee.

The Community Transit (CT) procedure has also been in force for some time, simplifying the formalities carried out when crossing internal frontiers in the EC. It is used for all movement of goods within the customs territory of the EC and also for movements to and from Austria and Sweden.

2. FREE MOVEMENT OF CAPITAL AND LABOUR THROUGHOUT THE EC

Freedom of movement of capital and labour had been in the Treaty of Rome. In this respect, therefore, the 1992 Programme was just reiterating that existing obligations should be honoured.

The intention of the SEA was to establish a true common market in employment as soon as possible. The EC institutions and Member States are gradually making headway through the complex measures required to place every citizen on an equal footing in terms of access to employment, social security benefits and vocational training, which of necessity involve harmonising the relevant national legislation. All EC countries now give automatic rights of residence and employment to citizens of the EC and the concept of citizenship of the Union was included in the Maastricht Treaty. The new provisions on justice and home affairs in the Maastricht Treaty are intended to deal with the remaining obstacles which prevent people moving freely. The Copenhagen Summit in June 1993 stressed that the Single Market could not be brought about without the full implementation of free movement of persons, and that this required, in particular, measures with regard to co-operation in combating organised crime and drug trafficking and in ensuring effective control of the external borders. The European Council invited the ministers responsible to give urgent attention to these matters.

Freedom of capital movements throughout the EC is part of the drive towards a single market in financial services. Such an integrated market also calls for the freedom of establishment for financial institutions within the EC and the freedom for them to offer their products across national frontiers to other Member States without having to set up offices there. The freedom of capital movements was, in fact, the backcloth against which the EC's whole approach to the liberalisation of financial services was set. As far back as the early 1960s, direct investment and portfolio investment in quoted shares and bonds were liberalised. In 1986 the Council adopted a Directive extending the list of liberalised transactions to include long-term loans, unquoted securities and the issuing of foreign securities on domestic markets. In 1988, the Council adopted a Directive to liberalise all other transactions: short-term monetary instruments, current and deposit account operations, financial loans and credits. These Directives are now in force, with some minor derogations for Spain, Portugal, Greece and Ireland.

3. REMOVAL OF NON-TARIFF BARRIERS TO INTRA-COMMUNITY TRADE

The removal of non-tariff barriers to intra-EC trade consists mainly of agreeing upon common technical regulations and standards for goods. Trying to create some semblance of order amongst the regulations that already existed in the 12 Member States has caused outrage at various times on three different fronts. Firstly, over-regulation, when, for example, Regulations were introduced concerning the necessity of putting meat into sausages, contrary to established and accepted practices in the UK; secondly, under-regulation when products with inferior specifications which are allowed under the national laws of one Member State can then be sold under the same description in another Member State which imposes higher standards on national producers - such as weak beer into Germany; and, thirdly, general misunderstandings, for want of a better term. A good example of the latter concerned the story that "Brussels" was trying to standardise the size of condoms throughout the EC. Commissioner Bangemann's spokesman explained that they were in fact trying to produce a quality standard in the interests of Aids-prevention, and then joked to an Italian journalist that if they wanted to standardise the size they would have to make allowances for especially large ones for Italians. This was immediately reported as fact throughout the Community, causing outrage in all Member States except Italy. Perhaps it might have been better if the popular conception that Germans have no sense of humour had been true!

The "New Approach to the Harmonisation of Technical Regulations" adopted on 7 May 1985 relies on the mutual recognition of those prevailing in the various Member States wherever possible, and harmonisation only when necessary in the legitimate interests of all Member States. This has cut the flow of new harmonisation measures, and the Directive 83/189 procedures for the notification of new technical regulations have considerably improved mutual recognition.

The latest report on the detailed measures required for implementing the programme show that over 300 Regulations and Directives have been adopted, and that most of the latter have been incorporated into the domestic law of the Member States.

4. OPENING OF PUBLIC PROCUREMENT CONTRACTS TO ALL EC FIRMS

The opening up of public procurement contracts to all EC firms is a significant aspect of the 1992 Programme. In general, national and local authorities have been found to be seven times less likely to buy imports than the private sector, and this applies as much to the rest of the world as to EC countries. Only 2% of public supply and public construction contracts within the EC have been awarded to firms in other EC countries. EC law has long sought to deal with the problems of public procurement tendering by making the tendering procedures more transparent. In particular, two Directives, the Works Directive 71/305/EEC and the Supplies Directive 77/62/EEC as amended, contain detailed rules on the tendering procedures. They are based on three main principles:

i Community-wide advertising of contracts, so that firms in all Member States have an opportunity of bidding for them;

ii the banning of technical specifications liable to discriminate against foreign bidders; and

iii the application of objective criteria in tendering and award procedures.

In recognition of the fact that only about 25% of public contracts are advertised in accordance with the Directives, the Commission proposed amendments to make them more effective, and to widen their scope to include transport, water, energy and telecommunications. The 1992 Programme, therefore, specifies that a British company, for example should be given the same access to tendering opportunities for a Spanish government or public utility contract as a Spanish company, and vice versa. This provision is particularly important in construction, telephone and electricity generating equipment and public transport rolling stock.

5. APPROXIMATION OF NATIONAL INDIRECT TAX SCHEMES

The fifth element of the 1992 Programme is the plan to approximate the rates of indirect taxation in the EC Member States: this is one of the most significant factors behind the removal of the physical barriers represented by customs checks on the frontiers between Member States. The exporter and importer of any given item just file a declaration with their local VAT authorities in their home country and the national authorities co-operate closely to prevent VAT fraud in such transactions.

The approximation of the rates of indirect taxes is far from complete. A standard rate of VAT of at least 15% has been agreed, subject to a range of exceptions for essential goods like food, medicine, books, and transport which would qualify for a lower VAT rate. The main thrust of these proposals is not to achieve an optimum tax system for the EC, but to achieve a level of approximation sufficient to facilitate the abolition of barriers to intra-Community trade. Indirect tax differentials between adjacent Member States need to be sufficiently small to prevent large-scale cross-border shopping for taxation benefits. An overall difference of up to 5 to 6% is calculated by economists as not significant, which would mean that the temporary agreement would allow for a standard rate within the range of 15 to 21% in any EC country, but there are also substantially different levels of excise duty on such items as alcohol and tobacco, which further distort the picture. The system is due to remain in force for four years, until the end of 1996, when it will be revised. To get a fair overall picture, the review beginning in 1995 will have to look at VAT and other forms of indirect taxation as one.

In 1995, the Council is also due to review the collection system. At present, payment of VAT is made in the country where goods or services are finally sold. The idea is to make it payable after 1996 in the country of origin, which corresponds to the normal application of VAT.

The effects of the 1992 programme, which was heralded as a cure for the "Eurosclerosis" that had afflicted the EC in the first half of the 1980s, are only starting to be recognised. This malady, peculiar to Europe, involved a combination of high unemployment and/or inflation with sluggish economic growth. The only full study on the subject was the 16 volume Cecchini Report, published in 1988, which predicted that the implementation of the 1992 Programme would increase the total national incomes of the twelve Member States by 2.5% as a direct result of removing internal barriers to trade. In addition, it predicted that the indirect effects of the programme would increase the EC's GDP by anything from 4.25 to 6.5%. This once and for all change, resulting from a "more competitive and integrated" European economy, would be spread over a period of about five years.

The aggregate real income gains were quantified by a painstaking microeconomic study of each industrial and service sector where effects could be expected. They were augmented by the application of macroeconomic models such as the OECD "interlink". This indicated a real income gain of some 4.5%, consistent with the microeconomic study. The price level was expected to fall by 6% and unemployment, by some two million, about 1.9% of the labour force. The fall in unemployment would be due to the phenomenon of real wage resistance - which is well attested to in Europe. The idea is that anything which tends to lower a worker's expenditure price index exerts a downward pressure on money wages, with resulting increases in employment and output.

The forecast of the aggregate gain in real income was broken down as follows:

- frontier control removal : 0.4%
- public procurement : 0.6%
- financial services liberalisation : 1.5%
- supply effects: 2.1%

As the report was funded by the EC, sceptics might say that it is not surprising that its findings were so positive. A business survey carried out in Germany on the advantages of the single market also, however yielded the following positive conclusions:

- falling unit costs and lower R&D costs as production runs are lengthened;
- community-wide registration and protection of trade marks;
- better patent exploitation: EC-wide protection enables innovations to be marketed more easily, more quickly and more cheaply;
- removals of distortions to competition in the form of divergent tax rates and types;

- opportunity for longer product life-spans;
- simplified inventory management as special products meeting separate national standards are no longer necessary;
- risks cut with less dependence on the specific German situation;
- shorter border waiting times;
- simplification of formalities through mutual recognition of type-approval procedures;
- falling costs through freedom to choose insurers; and
- the assumption that costs will fall with freedom of capital movements.

The best proof that the single market is benefiting the EC is given by the Community's EFTA neighbours: Austria, Sweden, Finland, Norway, Iceland, Switzerland and Liechtenstein. As a group, they have concluded an agreement with the EC to extend most of the benefits of the single market to them as well. This agreement, the Treaty on the European Economic Area (EEA), was signed in May 1992 and, upon ratification by all parties, was due to take effect by the end of 1993. Switzerland subsequently dropped out when the proposal was defeated by a small majority in a referendum in November 1992. After some uncertainty, it is now clear that the EEA will proceed without Switzerland.

The objectives of the EEA are:

- to involve the EFTA countries in the creation of a single European market with some 380 million inhabitants;
- to broaden the scope of Community policies on research and technological development, transport, agriculture and fisheries, energy, environment, training and education and intellectual property to include the EFTA countries;
- to enable the two organisations to work together to support and consolidate economic recovery and reduce the abnormally high rate of unemployment;
- to step up consultations between the two organisations on multilateral trade.

Although the combined population of the EFTA countries is only one-tenth that of the EC, EFTA and the EC are each other's most important trading partners. The EC takes 58% of EFTA exports while EFTA represents 26% of Community exports, compared with only 17% sold to the US.

The EEA covers most of the four freedoms with some temporary exceptions: freedom of movement for persons is delayed in Switzerland, while Norway and Sweden retain residual controls on the import and export of capital. The EEA gives EFTA countries the right to be consulted, but not to vote, on new EC legislation affecting the single market. Frontier controls between the EC and EFTA countries will remain for goods traffic. These are necessary because the EFTA countries, while removing the main obstacles to trade with the EC, apply a different set of tariffs for imports from outside the EEA.

The EEA is seen by a number of EFTA countries as a first step towards full EC membership. There have already been applications to join from Austria (1989), Sweden (1991), Finland, Norway and Switzerland (1992). The Copenhagen Summit (June 1993) noted that the initial difficulties encountered in launching the negotiations had been overcome and that the pace of the negotiations was speeding up. The European Council is determined that the objective of the first enlargement of the European Union, in accordance with the guidelines laid down by the Lisbon and Edinburgh Summits, would become a reality by 1 January 1995. Thus the EEA looks increasingly like a transitional arrangement, serving as an ante-room for countries economically but not yet politically integrated into the EC and for other European states seeking closer ties. This desire to be part of the EC has led many to believe that the single market must be beneficial. The truth of this statement is difficult to gauge however due to a lack of hard evidence and the problem that what is good for one country may be bad for another.

Critique of the 1992 Programme

The German business survey quoted above predicted certain disadvantages, as well as the advantages of the 1992 Programme. These were:

- that rapidly expanding demand might generate bottlenecks in capital supply;
- that there may be shortfalls in qualified staff available for international business;
- difficulties in operating EC-wide after-sales service;
- language barriers;
- the need to take account of different cultures;
- the higher cost of providing information throughout the EC;
- the distance barrier and the expansion of travel costs;
- the higher costs of managing and controlling international business, especially foreign branches; and
- heavier capital needs in creating and expanding new markets and establishing foreign branches.

These criticisms all deal with matters arising out of the creation of the single market, without questioning the rationale for establishing it in the first place. This can be done under the following headings.

1. UNIFORM PRICES

The Commission's economists predictions were based on the assumption that disparity of prices within the EC was the result of hidden trade barriers and that uniform prices are more beneficial than disparate prices. Much of the income gained following the implementation of the 1992 Programme, with its removal of trade barriers, depends on this assumption.

It is true that some price discrepancies in the EC could be explained by hidden trade barriers. Operating quota systems or hiding behind national technical regulations or standards would generally raise the prices of the relevant goods in the country applying them. This would be particularly true if there are few domestic producers, as those producers will be able to take advantage of their monopoly market power.

However, artificial trade barriers do not alone explain price disparities. For example, there are two possible reasons why a public service agency like the Post Office sets flat rate charges for services that ignore transport costs, so that it costs the consumer the same to send a package two miles or two hundred. The first is that the administration of multiple pricing mechanisms can soon outweigh any extra revenue. The second reason is political. Using the median voter principle, decision-makers may well opt for uniform pricing because it is what the median voter or average consumer prefers. Thus, the Commission's strong penchant for uniform pricing may be have a political rather than an economic basis.

Another aspect of the drive towards uniform prices is that getting rid of international price disparities is not necessarily beneficial to the whole Community. It is obviously not true to say that integration which harmonises prices throughout the EC will be beneficial to each Member State individually, just because it is beneficial to the group as a whole. One Member State's loss will not necessarily be balanced by another's gain and the price advantage enjoyed in the Member State with the originally lower price could in the long term cause that state to be hit twice. Harmonisation will immediately cause its consumers to pay higher prices, while the supplier who also sells the same products in the higher price countries has to drop his price in the latter, which squeezes his profits and then causes him to raise his prices throughout the harmonised market. What benefit is the Member State with the previously lower prices going to get from price harmonisation? It is no good just reminding him of the Monnet principle of finding the national advantage in the advantage of all.

Another important rider to the goal of uniform prices is that the optimal inflation - tax in Germany, for instance, will not be the same as in Italy. This is because Italy has a large black economy which cannot be taxed directly, so that the government has to rely on inflation to tax the black economy indirectly in order to raise its revenue. Germany, on the other hand, has no appreciable black economy and virtually all German output is therefore directly taxable, so the government can afford to opt for a low inflation policy.

The Cecchini Report did not pursue the type of evidence which would be necessary to clarify the reasons for price discrepancies such as international differences in demand elasticities and transport costs, in order to decide whether or not they were beneficial or harmful, nor the extent to which firms in the different economies penetrate each other's markets. We do not therefore know for certain if intra-EC price discrepancies are due to features which place local firms at an advantage compared with rivals in other EC countries, rather than indicating trade barriers. If this were the case, harmonising prices would be inefficient in the short term and harmful to the whole Community in the long term.

2. HARMONISATION OF TAXATION AND BENEFITS

The economists of the EC considered the approximation of indirect taxation to be a necessary precursor to the elimination of intra-EC frontiers. Although the 1992 programme does not specifically insist on it, there is little doubt that this is the direction in which the EC will move. There are however a myriad of differing tax structures among the Member States, which would require careful examination before it can be ascertained whether fiscal harmonisation would be beneficial to each individual country. For instance, they differ in their ratios of public debt to income, in their attitudes towards inequality and income redistribution and in measures of productivity. Hence the convergence criteria in Protocol 6 of the Maastricht Treaty for Member States wishing to proceed to the ultimate goal of Stage 3 of EMU.

In the case of direct taxes and state benefits, there is the problem of determining the appropriate degree of divergence in income tax thresholds and eligibility for benefits. In Greece, for example, the average income per head is less than one-quarter of the Luxembourg levels. If tax and benefit thresholds were set at the same levels in Greece and Luxembourg it would be very likely that Greek unemployment would shoot up as perhaps only one Greek worker in ten would earn more when in work than when claiming benefits on the Luxembourg level. If direct tax and benefit thresholds were determined centrally, disposable income and benefits would rise in Greece and fall in Luxembourg. Taken to its logical conclusion, this could very quickly lead to the disintegrating of the Community.

3. IMPLEMENTABILITY

In the final analysis, implementing any legislative programme in a free society depends on the willingness of the people to accept the legislation, as was clearly demonstrated by the debacle of the Poll Tax.

Contrary to fears expressed before the adoption of the SEA, it has been shown that the Member States, each of which is affected in different ways by the single market, have expressed their willingness to implement the programme and the citizens of the EC have by and large accepted the challenges and restraints which it has imposed. The UK, for instance, remains fearful about a possible increase in terrorism and the arrival of rabid animals as a result of the abolition of frontier controls, and has striven to maintain them in so far as they are consistent with their obligations under the treaties. The results at Heathrow are rather Kafkaesque, which emphasises the need to make the Provisions on Co-operation in the Fields of Justice and Home Affairs in Title VI of the Maastricht Treaty, work as a matter of urgency.

Of course it will be difficult to enforce EC-wide access to public procurement contracts: links between national public bodies and their local suppliers are very close and bias is not easy to prove. The other policy areas complementing the single market are dealt with in later chapters.

Towards a New Model For EC Development

The Copenhagen Summit proposed a number of steps supplementing the 1992 Programme to help lift the EC out of its economic depression. These include:

- tackling environmental issues to create new jobs;
- taxing the consumption of scarce natural resources in order to reduce excessive taxes on the working population, thus enhancing Europe's economic competitiveness; and
- using increases in productivity to improve the quality of life and create new jobs; this is the dynamic view of work-sharing.

The Summit declared that more active policies towards the labour market were needed, with priority being given to providing everyone on the labour market with a job, activity or useful training. Both the quality and number of job agencies should be increased so as to provide effective help to every person out of work and relevant expenditure should rise from 0.1% of Community GDP to 0.5%. In addition, rather than trying to hold back technological and economic change, it must be anticipated and dealt with in good time.

1992 and World Trade

The effects of the 1992 Programme on world trade are still unclear. Some outside observers are still worried about "Fortress Europe" with barriers unbreachable to their exporters. The car industry provides an interesting example. The Danes and Dutch have no quotas against Japanese car imports and the Japanese share of these markets is about 18%. Japanese access to the German market is also relatively free. The UK has a voluntary restraint agreement concerning exports of finished Japanese cars, which currently account for 11% of domestic sales. It has no limits however on the import of car parts. France, on the other hand, restricts the Japanese share to 3% of her domestic car market, while Italy keeps Japanese car imports to under 1%.

Under the single market rules, any car legally imported into Denmark or the Netherlands must be allowed access to any other part of the EC. The French and Italians are therefore pressing for tighter, EC-wide limits on the imports of Japanese cars, fearing for the jobs in Fiat and Renault that might be lost. On the other hand the Danes and the Dutch, who have no domestic motor manufacturers, are pressing for minimal restrictions so that their consumers can benefit from lower prices available from the Japanese manufacturers having equal access to the whole of the single market. The UK is anxious that the part-Japanese cars assembled in the UK are classified as British from the standpoint of any EC-wide common external quotas, or duties agreed upon. Taking such contradictory considerations into account, it is still impossible to quantify with any degree of certainty the overall benefits accruing to the Community as a whole from the single market programme. More worrying is the prospect that, in the long term, it could actually exacerbate the disparity between the richer and the poorer areas, thereby placing an even greater strain on the Regional Funds if any sort of balance is to be preserved.

Chapter 7

Economic and Monetary Union (EMU)

The reason for including this chapter on Economic and Monetary Union in a book on EC Grants and Other Assistance is that, as the year 2000 approaches those contemplating long term funding will, to an increasing extent, have to calculate what effects EMU is going to have on them, if and when it happens.

Monetary union means that, in effect, the currencies of the Member States will be locked irrevocably to one another at the same exchange rate. The Member States' currencies will at all times be fully convertible with the currencies of the other Member States and no national restrictions may be imposed. There can be no more devaluations or revaluations of individual currencies, but the common or combined currency of the Community will still be free to devalue or revalue against other currencies like the US Dollar or the Yen.

Economic union is a necessary counterpart of monetary union: one cannot successfully exist without the other. Monetary union requires the co-ordination of Member States' economic policies because different developments in different places, particularly in relation to inflation and national debt, could jeopardise the fixed exchange rates and, hence, the stability of the common currency. Economic union requires monetary union, because differing exchange rates affect the countries' competitiveness in the world market for goods and capital, with its repercussions on the balance of payments and subsequent government policy.

Although the Treaty of Rome does not specifically state that a European monetary union should be established, its architects foresaw the Community evolving into a fully fledged common market with the complete economic and monetary integration of the Member States, as the recitals to the Treaty very plainly show. EMU has been Community policy since as long ago as the Hague Summit in December 1969, and the Werner Plan of 1971 was the first attempt to bring it about by stages. Before the Werner Plan could get off the ground however, the world currency markets were thrown into turmoil by traders dumping US dollars ahead of its anticipated devaluation as a result of the unprecedented US balance of payments deficit. This caused a rapid, uncontrolled floating of the European currencies, until the formal realignment of the currencies under the Smithsonian Accord in December 1971, which reintroduced a form of fixed exchange rates.

The currency "snake" was set up on 24 April 1972 with the six original Member States agreeing to limit the margin of fluctuation between their currencies to 2.5%. The new Member States, Denmark, Ireland and the UK which had only joined the Community in 1970 were not ready to participate. The constitution of the European Monetary Co-operation Fund (EMCF) was agreed in April 1973.

The idea of monetary union was again proposed in 1977 by the then President of the Commission, Roy Jenkins (now Lord Jenkins of Hillhead). His initial plan was for a quick push towards a single currency and monetary authority. The plan was scaled down at the Bremen Summit in July 1978, to a more modest plan for the creation of a zone of monetary stability in Europe, in the spirit of the Chinese proverb, "may you not live in exciting times". This resulted in the European Monetary System (EMS), which is a compromise mechanism based on parallelism between two linked factors: the maintenance of parity between currencies and the attainment of economic convergence. The main motivation was to minimise the movements of currencies in the foreign exchange markets and it came into being on 13 March 1979.

It has three main components.

The first of these is the ECU, devised as a common currency to replace the old European Units of Account (EUA). Opinion seems to be divided as to whether the ECU is called after a mediaeval French coin embossed with three fleurs-de-lis in the shape of a shield (from the Latin scutum) or, more prosaically, that it is just an acronym for European Currency Unit, reflecting the acronym based Community into which it was born. It consists of a basket of Member States' currencies - as set out in Appendix 6 - and has four basic functions:

i it acts as the unit of account for all Community Transactions: e.g. the EC budget, grants and other assistance and fines are all calculated in ECUs;

ii it is the denominator in the exchange-rate mechanism and provides the basis for divergence calculations and a base for determining divergence indicators;

iii it is used as a unit of account for operations under the intervention and credit mechanisms; and

iv it is used as a means of settlement between the monetary authorities of the Member States.

It is also increasingly used in private transactions particularly for long term financing, because of its stability.

The second component of the EMS is the exchange-rate and intervention mechanism (ERM).

In the ERM, each currency has a central exchange rate, linked to the ECU, which is then used to determine the central rates for calculating the movement between any pair of currencies. Bilateral exchange rates are allowed to fluctuate around the central rate within a band of 2.25% in the narrow band or up to 6% in the wide band. A divergence threshold for each currency is set at 75% of the maximum permissible divergence. As soon as a currency crosses this threshold, the authorities are required to intervene to remedy the situation. The ERM was planned as the first step towards the ultimate goal of fixed exchange rates between the currencies of the Member States in the final stage of EMU. Maintaining exchange rate fluctuations at the tightest possible margins can only be achieved if Member States apply sound and stable economic policies. This is why Member States participating fully in the EMS have increasingly had to strive for price stability.

The third component of the EMS is comprised of the credit mechanisms. The existing credit mechanisms were retained, but the amounts involved were increased. In the final stage of the EMS the credit mechanisms will be consolidated into a single fund.

Having reviewed the workings of the EMS over a nine-year period, the Hanover Summit in June 1988, attended by Mrs Thatcher for the UK, instructed the President of the Commission, Jacques Delors, to set up a committee to prepare a report indicating concrete and immediate steps to be taken towards economic and monetary union. This committee was established at this time because the Single European Act (SEA), signed on 17 February 1986, had come into force with the ultimate aim of completing the frontier-free internal market. The full economic and social benefits of the single market would only be realised if business, industry and ordinary citizens were able to use a common currency - the principle of "one market, one currency". Twelve independent currencies existing side by side in a frontier-free internal market would not be compatible with internal freedom of movement unless the exchange rates between them were maintained at fixed parities. A return to fluctuating exchange rates, opening the door to competitive devaluations, would have the effect of re-compartmentalising markets on the basis of separate currency zones.

The committee's report, subsequently known as the Delors Report, was published in April 1989 and approved by the Madrid Summit despite some handbag swinging from Mrs Thatcher. It proposed that EMU should be completed in three stages.

Stage One began on 1 July 1990 as proposed in the Delors Report, and, in the economic field consisted principally of:

- the removal of physical, technical and fiscal barriers within the Community as part of completing the Single Market;
- increasing the resources and the functioning of the Structural Funds, in order to promote regional development and to correct regional imbalances as part of the reform of the Structural Funds agreed in 1988; and
- strengthening economic and fiscal policy co-ordination;

and, in the monetary field of:

- complete freedom of movement of capital between all Member States;
- the elimination of all obstacles to financial integration in the Community, including the freedom to provide intra-Community financial, banking, and insurance services;
- the flexibility for the currencies of all Member States to participate in the ERM;
- the removal to all obstacles to the private use of the ECU; and

- the strengthening of co-ordination procedures on monetary and exchange rate policy.

Stage Two was scheduled to begin on 1 January 1994, according to the agreement reached at the Rome Summit in December 1990 as modified in the Maastricht Treaty. It was viewed at all times as an irrevocable, intermediate step towards Stage Three, during which the Member States would make intensive preparations for Stage Three. It involves technical measures dealing with the criteria required for participating in Stage Three and the setting up of the European System of Central Banks (ECSB), as the forerunner of the European Central Bank (ECB) and the European Monetary Institute (EMI). The EMI, which will take over the functions of the former European Monetary Co-operation Fund (EMCF), will attempt to co-ordinate policies with a view to achieving price stability and have the job of completing the technical preparations for EMU.

Stage Three is scheduled to start at the very latest on 1 January 1999.

There are four criteria laid down in the Maastricht Treaty which Member States must meet to participate in Stage Three. They must:

- have low inflation, meaning that a Member State must not, for a period of one year before the relevant date, have inflation which exceeds that of the three best performing Member States by more than 1.5%;
- not have an excessive budget deficit, currently defined as under 3% of national GDP, and a public debt ratio of less than 60% of GDP;
- participate for two years within the narrow bands of the ERM without "severe tensions" and, in particular, without having devalued its currency against that of any other Member States on its own initiative; and
- achieve convergence of interest rates, which is defined as not having an average nominal long term interest rate which exceeds that of the three best performing states by 2 %.

The Commission and the EMI will report to the Council on progress made by the Member States regarding these criteria. The Heads of State or Government will decide before the end of 1996, by a qualified majority, whether it is appropriate for a majority of the Member States to move to the final stage of EMU. If, by the end of 1997, no date has been set for the beginning of Stage Three, this stage will automatically begin on 1 January 1999. The number of Member States launching the final stage of EMU would not then have to constitute a majority.

On this, or the earlier agreed date, the ECB and the ESCB will start to function fully. The primary objective of the European System of Central Banks (ESCB) will be to obtain price stability. It is also enjoined to pursue other Community objectives, but only in so far as it does not prejudice price stability. There can be no doubt about it, price stability is king.

Whether the final stage of EMU, when exchange rates will be irrevocably linked to each other, will be launched at the start of 1999 or before, depends on whether a majority of Member States is able to meet the necessary conditions laid down in the Maastricht Treaty.

The main features of EMU's economic policy are as follows.

- Member States must regard their economic policies as a matter of common concern.
- EC leaders in the European Council are to recommend EC economic policy guidelines for Member States. Where national economic policies are inconsistent with the guidelines, the Council of Ministers may make recommendations to the Member State concerned on the basis of a qualified majority vote.
- Where a Member State is in "severe difficulties" the Council may agree unanimously on a Commission proposal to grant financial assistance, by qualified majority if it results from a natural disaster.
- The Commission must monitor government debt and see whether budgetary discipline is being respected. If there is a risk of too high a deficit, the Commission should inform the Council which can make recommendations to the Member State and require that action be taken.
- Failure of the Member State to comply could trigger further action, including an invitation to the European Investment Bank to reconsider its lending policy to the country concerned, or an imposition of fines. The Council decisions are to be taken by a two-thirds qualified majority vote on a proposal by the Commission, not including the Member State concerned.

In practice EMU will mean the creation of a single monetary policy governed by the ECB. Member States will lose their ability to resort to devaluation in situations where competitiveness is perceived to have fallen behind that of the State's EC partners and where employment is falling as a consequence, or to raise / lower interest rates at will. It can be seen that EMU reduces the powers of national governments to manage their domestic economies in the same way that the UK Government's policies of rate capping and charge capping have diminished the ability of local government to manage their own areas.

On the other hand, the permanently fixed parity with other Member States was designed:

- to create certainty in dealings between Member States making long-term planning much easier;
- to encourage intra-Community trade by cutting out foreign exchange costs which, for small deals, can be out of proportion to the overall value of a transaction; and
- most importantly, to ensure that the reserves of all participating Member States become common property, so that the single currency would be much more stable than the individual currencies of the Member States, and less prone to fluctuate against other major currencies than the individual currencies are now.

Under Protocol 11 of the Maastricht Treaty, the UK has an "opt out", which provides that the last step in the process of economic union, the single currency, should be subject to the agreement of the British government at that time. As the opt-out relates only to Stage Three however, the UK is still bound to re-enter the ERM in time to participate in Stage Two in accordance with the agreement reached at the Rome Summit, and to take all the other measures towards economic union right up to the point of the single currency. Contrary to what has been said in the British press and in the debates on the Maastricht Bill, the actualité is and always will be that the final stage of EMU will only happen if and when the Member States want it. It is not something that is being imposed on them from outside.

The practical effects of the UK opt-out are as follows.

It admits that there is already a two-speed Europe and that the UK is firmly in the slow lane with a lame duck economy. It further exasperates and lowers the already low esteem in which the UK is held by its Community partners as the "semi-detached member of the Community".

London has for centuries been one of the major financial centres of the world, and the UK government would have been in a strong position to present a good case for it to be the site of the ECB, particularly since the UK hosted no major EEC institution - the EBRD is hardly in the same league as the ECB. The uncertainty about whether the UK was going to be in or out not only ruled out London as the potential site for the ECB, but, by the wording of the Protocol, the UK has opted out of even having a say where it would be. Paragraph 7 spelled out that, "The UK shall also have no right to participate in the appointment of the President, the vice-president and the other members of the Executive Board of the ECB". Who could have been surprised when Frankfurt was chosen instead? The European Agency for the Evaluation of Medicinal Products is a very poor consolation prize.

The opt-out also suspends the voting rights of the UK in the Council in all matters concerning "the irrevocable fixing of exchange rates leading to the introduction of a single currency, the ECU, and the definition and conduct of a single monetary policy". It is excluded from any calculation of a qualified majority, which means it cannot even join with the other weaker economies to bring influence to bear on the fast-track Member States. What John Major described as "Game, set and match to the UK" after the Summit in Maastricht looks more like "Own goal" since it leaves the UK Government without any say in a matter which, when and if it happens, will radically affect not only its own powers but the lives of every citizen of the UK. Other countries are applying to join the Community at this point precisely to have a say in EMU.

The progress towards EMU has been rather more of a roller-coaster ride than the effortless glide anticipated. The question now is whether the historic decision, included in the Maastricht Treaty, to introduce a single European currency before the end of the century as the final stage in the EMU process is really going to happen, or whether this commitment is going to join the dustbin of treaties broken before the ink had time to dry.

What has gone wrong with EMU?

When sterling joined the ERM on 6 October 1990, the central exchange rate link to the ECU was £1=ECU1.44 and the important rate against the Deutsche Mark was DM2.94. It was argued at the time that the entry level was too high and that the rush to join at any cost was prompted by the need to protect sterling against the speculative selling that had been building up for some time.

Base rate in the UK was 15% against the German Discount Rate of 6%.

The problem was that the British economy had not achieved the degree of convergence required with the overall economy of the Community in general, and the economies of the stronger Member States in particular. It was therefore obliged to maintain interest rates at a high level in order to support sterling's unrealistic entry level. This produced severe deflationary pressures in the UK and thereby worsening the recession.

In the euphoria following the dismantling of the Berlin Wall and the subsequent re-unification of Germany, the implications of swapping Oest Marks for Deutsche Marks on a one for one basis, together with the cost of providing unemployment and other benefits for the mass of former employees of run down state owned industries in the east and generally cleaning up the mess left by nearly 50 years of Communism was not fully taken into account. This caused severe pressure on German Government finances, prompting the Bundesbank to keep interest rates at levels above those reasonably needed to get the economies of the various Member States going. The imbalance between German interest rates and those prevailing in other countries was compounded by the lowering of American interest rates in an effort to pull the US economy out of the recession.

The German economy stopped growing in 1992 and was expected to shrink by 2% in 1993. The UK was alone amongst the major Member States in expecting any growth in the economy in 1993.

There appears to be a general lack of overall direction. The political uncertainty about the ratification and implementation of the Maastricht Treaty has been far from helpful. The two referenda in Denmark, the narrow "Oui" vote in France, the referral of the Treaty to the German Constitutional Court in Karlsruhe, the activities of the Tory rebels in the UK culminating in the Government having to do some, as yet undisclosed, back room deal to buy the support of the Ulster Unionists for the vote and the absolute failure of the Community to give any constructive leadership or even assistance in sorting out the problems in Bosnia, have all detracted from its status in the minds or affections of the people of the Community.

The Copenhagen Summit in June 1993 was forced to address the problem that the Community's share of world exports of manufactured goods had fallen by a fifth since 1980. It also has a widening deficit in trade in high-tech products: the Commission's own study showed that between 1982 and 1990 the volume of EC high-tech exports grew by only 2% per year while such imports grew by 7.7%. There was agreement on the overriding importance of creating the budgetary and economic conditions necessary for bringing interest rates in Europe down quickly, so as to narrow the gap between interest rates in Europe and those in other major industrial countries. Movements in this direction were considered essential for economic recovery and in order to promote investment in Europe.

After so much navel-gazing over the past two years, the Summit, after instructing Jacques Delors to prepare a White Paper proposing concrete action to be taken towards creating new jobs in the Community particularly for the long term unemployed, noted that the effect of action by the EC and its Member States would be increased through the international co-ordination of policy, welcomed the outcome of the joint EC-EFTA meeting of Economic and Finance Ministers held in April and invited the Council to continue to maintain close contacts with the EFTA countries. In the global sphere, they looked to the G-7 summit in Tokyo to provide an agreed basis for a determined effort to promote growth in the world economy: a somewhat belated realisation in the truth of the words of John Donne: “No man is an island”.

Article 3a of the Maastricht Treaty spells out that the primary objective of the single currency and its supporting single monetary policy is price stability. It is anticipated that, as intra-Community trade increases, taking all necessary steps to promote price stability throughout the Community will reduce inflation in the Member States with above average inflation and that Member States which already enjoy lower inflation rates will benefit, because the phenomenon of imported inflation will recede as the rise in the prices of import goods and services slows down. This belief is based inter alia on the fact that since 1979 the European Monetary System has had considerable success in reducing both the average level of, and the variance in, Member States' rates of inflation. Most observers attribute this largely to the role of the Deutsche Mark as the anchor currency of the system. Low German inflation has imposed a discipline on other countries participating in its Exchange Rate Mechanism (ERM). They face the threat of downward realignment of their exchange rates if they inflate excessively. All ERM participants have had confidence in the German Bundesbank as a low inflation institution, due to the record it has built up over many years. The question is whether this view still applies in view of the odium heaped on the Governors of the Bundesbank because of their recent refusals to cut interest rates.

Moving to a single currency with a new institutional framework therefore threatens to remove this known anchor against inflation. A period of time would be needed while the new institutions found their feet and built up their own reputations as effective enforcers of a low inflation policy. Such a reputation would be difficult to achieve, since presumably each Member State will have a voice, if not a vote in the central bank's policy making. The inflation outcome would approximate to an average of all the Member States' short term desires, and one can easily imagine the pressure to inflate if, for example, election years coincided.

The pressures that forced the UK and Italy out of the ERM highlight the problems with the whole system, which does not bode well for EMU. The whole fiasco caused the financial markets to lose confidence not only in sterling and the lira but in the political, economic and monetary will of the Member States to make the system work, which in turn casts doubt over the whole future of EMU and the single currency.

EMU requires, moreover, a single set of interest rates over which national governments have no influence and such rates may not be appropriate for each participating country. If a country were to join EMU before its economy was ready, unemployment could rise steeply. This sorry state of affairs would result in pressures for financial transfers from other Member States - a remedy bound to cause resentment from the economically stronger Member States if used too often.

What does the practical businessman do in the light of so much uncertainty?

Since the UK left the ERM, we have seen base rates fall from 10% to 6% although much of this benefit has been retained by the banks who have moved increasingly from base rate related rates to "managed rates", sterling fell from DM2.80 ($1.90) to a low of DM2.32 ($1.41) in February 1993 increasing the competitiveness of UK industry in both the domestic and export markets; manufacturing output rising and unemployment if not exactly starting to fall at least ceasing to rise.

Sterling has however risen inexorably since February and there was speculation that by the anniversary of Black Wednesday it would be back at the old ERM level against the DMARK, even if it remained at a lower level against the US dollar. Community interest rates are converging at the lower UK levels and the scene could now be set for either an era of competitive devaluations, with successive Member States jockeying to pick up the advantages that the UK has recently enjoyed, or an initially informal ERM type of stability at lower levels.

Whether the movements of currencies which occur over the next year are in the form of competitive devaluations or careful steps aligning currencies towards the eventual goal of a single European currency, there will be winners and losers. One can only be careful in such a volatile market, but George Sorros, who made such a spectacular profit from the devaluation of sterling, is on record as saying that, in his opinion, for the good of the European Community as a whole, it needs a single currency. The biggest losers would be the foreign exchange dealers.

Chapter 8

Competition Policy

Article 3(f) of the Treaty of Rome provides for "a system ensuring that competition in the common market is not distorted": free, open and fair competition is considered to be the cornerstone of the market-based economic system. Free-market economists argue that the benefits of competition are obvious, for example providing consumers with a choice of goods and services and obliging manufacturers and suppliers to keep prices competitive or risk losing business to their competitors. A system of free competition makes companies more sensitive to customer requirements and demands, otherwise they will be left behind by competitors who pay more attention to market needs. It stimulates companies to invest and innovate so that they can produce better products at more competitive prices than their rivals and thereby increase their market share and hence their profits. Companies which can compete successfully within a given market are better able to withstand the pressures from rivals from outside the market and can themselves thus compete more successfully on world markets. More generally, competition is a basic mechanism of the market economy which ensures that prices reflect the real relationship between supply and demand. This enables the economy to reallocate resources to the most efficient ends.

One of the prime reasons for the founding of the ECSC was the well-founded suspicion that the fall in coal and more particularly in steel prices in the late 1940s, was likely to lead to the recreation of the old cartels of producers trying to push prices up by limiting supplies and carving up the market as they had done so successfully in the past. The dangers of this happening in other sectors of the market was very much in the minds of the founding fathers of the Economic Community, given the fragile state of the economies of all the European countries at the time. From the start, the prime purpose of the Economic Community, as stated in the Treaty of Rome, was to found a common market which involved eliminating customs duties and quantitative restrictions in trading between the Member States together, with a common customs tariff and a common commercial policy towards third countries. They realised that, as the market grew bigger, the major players in any given field would grow at least proportionately to the growth in the overall market, and any particular sector could be dominated by a small group of large companies, able to squeeze out the smaller ones. To counter the dangers of the creation of new cartels and other anti-competitive practices in so large a market, they inserted fairly draconian powers in the Treaty to prevent this happening, or to punish the operators of cartels and other anti-competitive practices in cases where they had been unable to act in time to prevent them. This policy is to be found in Articles 85 to 99 of the Treaty.

Article 85 spells out the rules in relation to "undertakings" which basically means trading companies or groups of companies by whichever name they are called by, whether incorporated or unincorporated, be they domiciled or resident inside or outside the EC:

"The following shall be prohibited as incompatible with the common market: all agreements between undertakings, decisions by associations of undertakings and concerted practices which may affect trade between Member States and which have as their object or effect the prevention, restriction or distortion of competition within the common market, and particularly those which:

i directly or indirectly fix purchase or selling prices or other trading conditions;

ii limit or control production, markets, technical development or investment;

iii share markets or sources of supply;

iv supply dissimilar conditions to equivalent transactions with other trading parties, thereby placing them at a competitive advantage;

v make the conclusion of contracts subject to acceptance by the other parties of supplementary obligations which by their nature or according to commercial usage, have no connection with the subject of such contracts."

Article 86 states that:

"Any abuse by one or more undertakings of a dominant position within the common market or in any substantial part of it shall be prohibited as incompatible with the common market in so far as it may affect trade between Member States."

Article 86 contains three essential elements:

i there must be a dominant position;

ii this position must be abused; and

iii the abuse of the dominant position must have the potential to affect trade between Member States.

A lacuna in the policy is that, provided it cannot be proved that they are affecting trade between Member States, undertakings with a dominant position in one Member State, for example the UK, are free to abuse that dominant position in the domestic market as much as they like without infringing Articles 85 and 86. The only remedies available, if any, would be those provided by the domestic law of the Member State.

The enforcement of Competition policy has evolved in such a way as to centre on four well defined areas.

The first is cartels. Companies can easily be tempted to co-operate with their potential rivals by creating anti-competitive cartels rather than competing in the open market. The cartels then fix prices and carve up markets amongst themselves for the benefit of their members. This gives them all guaranteed revenues, allows them to plan future production levels with more certainty, and dispenses with the trouble and expense of having to improve the product range or undertake marketing campaigns. Customers, whether they are private and industrial users, have no choice but to pay the prices fixed.

The second area relates to firms in a "dominant position" in the market.. If firms with a large market share use their dominant position so as to make customers pay higher prices or to squeeze smaller companies out of the market, they are in breach of EC competition rules. They can abuse their dominant position by a variety of either long term or short term measures. Examples of long term measures include charging different prices for identical goods in different markets for no good reason, forcing customer "loyalty" through the use of long term exclusive supply contracts, and making either eventual customers or distributors agree to buy further goods or services either at the time of purchase or sometime in the future, as a condition of supplying the goods or services they want. Short term measures include predatory pricing campaigns, cutting off supplies to dealers who market the competitor's goods, and refusals to supply the most up-to-date models in a given market.

The third is selective distribution systems. Agreements between manufacturers and dealers can be justified in the interest of providing an efficient, specialist distribution system or the provision of high quality after-sales service. On the other hand, they can also be used to prevent customers in one EC country from buying a product in another where the price is cheaper. An example of this is the motor trade, where there have been repeated reports and enquiries relating to allegations of differential pricing policies being operated by manufacturers and restrictions being placed on their distributors so as to prevent them from selling vehicles to customers resident in other Member States.

The fourth area is in mergers and take-overs. In anticipation of the single market, the number of trans-frontier mergers shot up by 90% between 1987 and 1988, and among the 100 largest EC Companies, the number of mergers involving a joint turnover of over ECU 1 billion increased by 31% in 1989 compared with the previous year. To control this "merger-mania", in September 1990 the Commission was given the authority to control mergers and take-overs which, by the size and concentrations of economic power they created, could restrict competition within the EC market. For a "concentration of economic power" to have a European dimension, either two or more previously independent undertakings must merge with one another or one undertaking must obtain control over one or more others. Three further conditions must be met: the combined world-wide turnover of all the undertakings involved must be more than ECU 5 billion, the combined Community-wide turnover of at least two of them must exceed ECU 250 million, and finally, each undertaking involved must achieve less than two thirds of its turnover in one Member State. In 1991, the first full year of operation, it investigated more than 60 mergers of which only one was vetoed.

It was also recognised that governments can restrict or distort competition in a number of ways. They may be tempted to subsidise their own national firms to help them face competition from companies in other parts of the Community, or to subsidise state-owned firms to enable them to compete with private sector rivals. As physical barriers come down, governments are no longer able to protect national firms directly from outside competitors by shutting out imported products, which increases the temptation to resort to indirect methods of protection like subsidies instead. Although government aid which distorts competition is prohibited, there are some exceptions to this rule. State aid is allowed and EC aid may be available to promote the economic development of areas where the standard of living is abnormally low or where there is serious underemployment; aid is also allowed to facilitate the development of certain economic activities. The aid programmes available from the EC are discussed in detail in subsequent chapters.

The governments of the Member States also restrict competition by granting either state owned or privately owned monopolies exclusive rights to supply basic services such as electricity, water, transport or telecommunications. In some cases and in some Member States this has resulted in poor quality services, little innovation and high prices. In general, there is very little to chose between state owned and privately owned monopolies, but this is not say that in all cases the monopoly suppliers of these basic services have provided bad services at high prices. In France, for example, there is a tradition of civic pride in the efficiency of the state run services; and they are amongst the best in the whole Community, and French policies of ensuring integrated, subsidised public transport systems are a precedent which should be followed in other Member States. In other cases where state monopolies have been partially or wholly broken down, the effect on price levels has been noticeable: for example, prices have fallen sharply on international airline routes where competition has been introduced like London-Amsterdam or London-New York, whilst remaining high where there is none like the London-Brussels route. In telecommunications, the introduction of competition has stimulated the development of innovative customer-related services and made a greater range of terminal equipment available at lower prices. There are considerable variations among the Member States, but charges for telephone services which are still under virtual monopoly control, whether public, private or recently privatised, have tended to remain high.

The normal procedure for applying EC competition policy rules is as follows.

- Companies considering entering into agreements that could affect free competition should inform the Commission at the earliest date, and give them full details both of the agreements and the reasons for the agreements well before they are due to come into effect. If the approach is made correctly and the undertakings involved can justify the agreement it is possible to get fairly rapid clearance.

- In cases where the Commission feels an investigation is necessary, it can seek additional information either in writing or by meeting representatives from the companies concerned. Following their investigations, the Commission will either authorise the agreement as submitted, require modifications, or forbid it altogether. Both the outcome of the investigation and the length of time taken will depend very largely on the level of co-operation between the undertakings concerned and the Commission.

- When cases of actual anti-competitive behaviour are proven, the Commission has the power to impose fines on guilty companies of up to the equivalent of 10% of total turnover during the currency of the anti-competitive practice. The fines are intended as act both as a punishment and a deterrent.

- Undertakings which disagree with a decision taken by the Commission can appeal against it to the European Court of Justice in Luxembourg.
- Many anti-competitive practices come to light as the result of complaints made to the Commission either by rivals, or increasingly, by the general public as they become more aware of their rights. For example, the Commission acted on a flood of complaints from individuals who claimed that they had been prevented by the motor manufacturers and distributors from buying cars in other Member States. The subsequent Commission investigation indicated that prices for the same model could differ by up to 40% from one Member State to another. Immediate action was taken to establish consumers' rights to buy cars wherever they chose to do so, even if this is outside their country of residence.

In addition to the Commission's powers to enforce these competition rules, national courts also have jurisdiction to declare that an agreement or practice is anti-competitive, or that an abuse of a dominant position has occurred. Any aggrieved party may bring an action and, according to the particular circumstances, the court may grant an injunction, award damages or declare an agreement to be void. A national court has not got the jurisdiction to declare State aid to be compatible with the common market unless the Commission has already taken a decision to that effect. Where state aid has been given without notification to the Commission, an aggrieved party may apply to the national court for an order prohibiting the award of the aid.

Since the completion of the single market based on the abolition of physical barriers, technical barriers and fiscal barriers to intra-Community trade, it has been even more vital for the Community to enforce a single set of rules applying at Community level to prevent undertakings and governments from behaving in ways which restrict competition or distort the market. The rules apply indiscriminately to all undertakings selling goods and services in the Community, whether based inside or outside the Community. The Commission has had no hesitation in fining offenders.

Article 110 of the Treaty says:

"By establishing a customs union between themselves, Member States aim to contribute in the common interest to the harmonious development of world trade, the progressive abolition of restrictions on international trade and the lowering of customs barriers."

This open door policy has to be qualified in that the Community, as the world's largest and richest single market, has from the very beginning, been the target for dumping. Article 113 deals with the Commission's powers to conduct negotiations with third countries under the authority of the Council in relation, inter alia, to "measures to protect trade such as those to be taken in case of dumping or subsidies". There is no definition of dumping in the Treaty and allegations have to be examined on their individual merits. The provisions relating to dumping do however, refer only to goods coming into the Community from non-Member States, and it is no excuse for undertakings based outside the Community, who adopt anti-competitive behaviour inside the Community, to argue that the practices complained of are normal and acceptable within their own domestic jurisdictions or elsewhere. As the initiation of anti-dumping measures is a highly political matter involving, as it does, negotiations with the governments of non-Member States, it has remained the prerogative of the Council acting on a proposal from the Commission. This means that Community industries alleging dumping have to clear two double hurdles to obtain relief: they have to convince first the Commission and then the Council of not only the facts of the case but of the necessity of taking action on their behalf involving the governments of non-Member States. This makes the process long winded, expensive and uncertain of success, since it elevates the problem from the commercial to the political arena.

Ensuring that the freedom to trade promised by the creation of the internal market is not thwarted by anti-competitive practices, whether by governments or by undertakings, is an important element of Community policy. To this end, the Commission will continue to apply the competition rules rigorously and to take action against those who break them. However, the whole process by which competition policy operates is often seen as having been designed specifically to operate in favour of large undertakings and against the interests of SMEs, despite the rhetoric about encouraging them repeated in successive European Summits and other policy statements. Even submitting the evidence required to substantiate complaints about loss-making sales or other anti-competitive practises by a cartel or the holder of a dominant position under Articles 85 and 86, can involve expenditure of both time and money beyond the resources of an SME but insignificant to the cartel. A case of "Unto those that hath shall be given, and he shall have abundance: but from him who hath not shall be taken away even that which he hath"? (Matthew 25:29)

Chapter 9

Consumer Protection

Grant applications are scrutinised and assessed within the overall context of EC policy, which means that compliance with the Community's policies on consumer protection will be considered where appropriate.

This in turn raises questions about the reasons for the existence of a consumer protection policy on a Community-wide basis, how it operates now and, even more importantly, how it is planned that it should operate in the future.

In the days when markets were highly local in character, buyers and sellers knew one another personally. Concern to maintain a good reputation and the constant renewal of personal contact made a legalistic framework for business relations quite superfluous. The advent of mass production dramatically changed this, reducing manufacturers and merchants to anonymous figures unknown or barely known to one another. As economic activity grew more complex, particularly on an international basis, the need also grew for a statutory framework to regulate relations between manufacturers, shippers, wholesalers, retailers and the eventual consumers. The increasing complexity of the supply system has been compounded or even surpassed by the increasing complexity of the products available and, even more importantly, by the wide range of components contained in individual products. For example, no ordinary consumer can reasonably be expected to make informed judgements on such matters as the safety of soft toys bought for small children. The materials used for stuffing such toys can only be inspected by destroying the toy and submitting them to chemical analysis. This is not only beyond the reasonable capabilities of the average consumer, but rather defeats the object of buying the toy in the first place. Even if the case for protecting consumers in circumstances such as those outlined above would appear self evident, both the concept of a Community-wide consumer protection policy and the manner of its operation are controversial: they are welcomed in most Member States but pilloried in the UK, where recent ministerial statements suggest that the government wants to abandon all statutory controls in favour of a system of self regulation.

The first organisations representing consumer interests were set up in the 1950s. Their membership steadily grew and, with it, their importance. In response to pressure from them, Member States adopted progressively more comprehensive legislation to protect consumer interests. In 1962, the Commission set up the Contact Committee for Consumer Questions which had the right to be consulted when EC-wide measures were being considered. In April 1968, the Commission set up a special consumer affairs unit within the Directorate-General for Competition. This laid the foundations for co-ordination among all the Commission departments dealing with various aspects of consumer protection. Their initiatives and proposals were examined by this unit to ensure that consumer interests were properly respected. The consumer affairs unit was subsequently integrated in the Directorate-General for the Environment, Consumer Affairs and Nuclear Safety.

At the beginning of the 1970s the European Parliament repeatedly stressed the need for a common consumer policy and the Paris Summit in October 1972 gave this the go-ahead, declaring that the positive economic development of the Community had to be translated, first and foremost, into an improvement in the quality of life for the people of Europe.

In September 1973, the Contact Committee for Consumer Questions was replaced by the Consumers' Consultative Committee, to which independent experts were also appointed.

The first decisive step towards a European consumer policy was taken in 1975, when the Council of Ministers adopted the "Preliminary programme of the European Economic Community for a consumer protection and information system". In addition to drawing up an action plan, the programme contained a "charter" of consumers' rights. Five basic rights were stated:

i the right to protection and safety: goods and services must not present a risk under normal conditions of use;

ii the right to protection of economic interests: the purchaser or user must be protected against exploitative practices by the seller such as misleading advertising and against defective products and services;

iii the right of redress in the case of defective goods or unsatisfactory services;

iv the right to information and education, to enable consumers to make an informed choice on the market; and

v the right of representation: consumers' organisations should be consulted on all proposed legislation affecting consumer interests.

The lot of all political bodies is to find themselves having to make choices between conflicting but desirable ends. The proliferation of technical regulations and national standards made by the various Member States to protect their own consumers and affecting every type of product, was de facto acting as a barrier to intra-Community trade, contrary to the objectives of the Treaty. There were also suspicions then, as there still are today in all Member States, that other Member States were intentionally drafting standards and technical regulations in such a way as to discriminate in favour of their own domestic industries, to the detriment of competing industries in other Member States. As early as 1979, in the Cassis de Dijon case, the European Court of Justice established a precedent, which has been followed unvaryingly ever since, that any product legally manufactured and sold in one Member State must be allowed onto the market in all the others. This led to the inescapable conclusion that, if goods which complied with the technical regulations permitting their marketing in one Member State could then be marketed in the other Member States, there had to be some sort of consistency in such regulations throughout the Community, since the whole objective of technical regulations and standards is to give consumers confidence that the products they are buying are both safe and conform to the characteristics they might reasonably expect to find in that type of product.

It was also realised that, whereas the commitment to the free movement of goods throughout the Community was enshrined in the Treaty, the legal basis for a consumer protection policy was uncertain; there was no explicit mention of it in the Treaty, only allusions.

A further reason for difficulties in formulating a consumer protection policy at this stage was the need for unanimity in the Council of Ministers prior to the SEA. Thus, the Commission's attempt to create a uniform level of protection at EC level whilst, at the same time, eliminate trade barriers through harmonising standards and technical regulations, was unlikely to be particularly successful. Discussions on individual provisions often dragged on for many years, with individual Member States, fearing disadvantages for their own economy from harmonisation provisions, constantly blocking them with their veto. The frequent consequence was agreement only on the lowest common denominator.

It was not until May 1981 that a second consumer programme for the period up to 1986 was adopted by the Council. It elaborated on the guidelines and objectives of the first programme, but also stressed the importance of the price/quality ratio to consumers and addressed the problems of the service sector. The main thrust of these two programmes still applies today.

At the same time, the problem of conflicting national standards and technical regulations had to be resolved in a way which provided the necessary level of confidence to consumers in the Member States, without conflicting with the principles laid down in Cassis de Dijon. The first solution tried was to produce strings of standardisation Regulations and Directives relating to wide ranges of products. This policy was universally unpopular and upset the National Governments of the Market States, producers and consumer groups because it failed to take regional and cultural differences into account. Consequently, in 1983, procedures were laid down in Council Directive 83/189/EEC that any Member State proposing to adopt a new:

- "standard", defined as "a technical specification approved by a recognised standardisation body for repeated or continuous application, with which compliance is not compulsory";
- "technical specification", defined as "a specification contained in a document which lays down the characteristics required of a product such as levels of quality, performance, safety or dimensions; including the requirements applicable to the product as regards terminology, symbols, testing and test methods, packaging, marking or labelling"; or
- "technical regulation", defined as "technical specifications including the relevant administrative provisions, the observance of which is compulsory, de jure or de facto, in the case of marketing or use (of a product defined as "any industrially manufactured product and any agricultural product") in a Member State or a major

part thereof" must give prior notice of it to the Commission, which will then inform the other Member States. Such standards, technical specifications and regulations must satisfy basic requirements, specifically certain health and safety requirements which are generally set forth in Directives.

The policy was further developed in 1985 when the Commission adopted a radical "new approach to the harmonisation of technical regulations and standards". This provides for the mutual recognition of technical regulations and standards prevailing in the various Member States wherever possible and for harmonisation only when absolutely necessary in the legitimate interests of all Member States, for instance on safety requirements. This has cut the flow of harmonisation measures, and the Commission's stricter enforcement of the 83/189 procedures has considerably improved confidence in mutual recognition.

The task of drawing up technical standards has now fallen to the experts of CEN and CENELEC, the European standardisation bodies. Although compliance with such European Standards is optional, they are popular with both producers, who can be certain that their products meet the general safety standards of the EC when they conform to CEN or CENELEC standards, and with consumers, who know that the products have been subjected to a rigorous approval process.

This new approach has several advantages. Firstly, decisions are transferred from the political level to the expert level of CEN/CENELEC. This transfer has helped avoid unnecessary harmonisation endeavours and considerably speeded up the process in the last few years. Secondly, it provides manufacturers with a solid European regulatory framework for the design, production and marketing of their goods. Producers who apply CEN standards to their products can be sure of free access to the market of all Member States, while Member States may only prohibit the sale of a product imported from another Member State if it has substantiated reservations about its health and safety aspects - the safeguard clause - but this action is subject to review by the Commission. Thirdly, consumers all over Europe can rely on a uniform minimum level of protection when purchasing food and technical goods.

In principle, the individual Member States still have the right to apply more stringent provisions within their own jurisdictions, as long as this does not constitute a barrier to intra-Community trade. It is for the European Court of Justice in Luxembourg to decide any disputes.

In the food sector in particular, the EC now limits its harmonisation activities to those sectors in which the lack of EC arrangements threatens to create trade barriers and where a European initiative is essential in the public interest. This primarily concerns "horizontal" provisions applying to all foodstuffs - particularly on additives and pesticide residues, materials and articles intended to come into contact with food, food production and handling processes, and the labelling, presentation and packaging of food. The specific composition of individual products or groups of products is no longer harmonised. In the event of disputes over admissibility, the principle of "mutual recognition" of traditional national recipes applies. This means, for example, that

British chocolate can be placed on the market in all EC countries, regardless of its composition.

The completion of the internal market on 1 January 1993 ushered in a new phase in the trend towards global markets, and the predicted surge in intra-Community trade gave a completely new impetus to consumer protection in Europe.

Article 100(a)(3) of the SEA, signed in February 1986, provides that, "the Commission in its proposals ... concerning health, safety, environmental and consumer protection, will take as a base a high level of protection". The majority voting provisions applied to it as it was clearly seen as a single market issue.

The SEA having thus provided a concrete legal basis for consumer protection, the Council of Ministers, by a resolution of 9 November 1989, called for increased efforts in the field of consumer policy as being particularly necessary in view of the completion of the single market which was then approaching.

The Consumers' Consultative Council (CCC), set up in April 1990, was composed of delegates from national organisations and representatives of the disabled and senior citizens as well as representatives of the European consumers' organisations.

In March 1990, the Commission adopted a three year action plan (1990-1993) for consumer policy, covering a limited number of legislative measures to harmonise national rules and action to improve representation of consumers' interests and consumer information. All other areas remain the responsibility of the Member States. This amounts to an advanced application of the subsidiarity principle in consumer policy: national responsibility where possible; Community measures where necessary to protect consumers.

The new action plan, "the Third Action Plan", has four main areas of focus: consumer representation, information, safety and cross-border commercial transactions.

i Consumer representation and active participation are seen as vital for achieving the economic and social objectives of the single market - promotion of economic growth, increased competitiveness of industry and enhancement of the general level of prosperity. To this end, the Commission's action plan advocates the creation of a balance between suppliers of goods and services and consumers' representatives. It is hoped that consumer representation will be increased by the CCC, which is to be recruited in future from a much broader spectrum of consumer groups. An important function of this Council will be the systematic exchange of information and experience of consumer policy in the Member States.

ii The importance of comprehensive information for consumers is highlighted by the fact that, by choosing a specific product, the consumer is sending out a signal to the market, establishing criteria and trends. The growing market share of environmentally-friendly products in the last few years provides eloquent confirmation of this theory: sufficient pressure of demand for such products has stimulated a corresponding supply. Such freedom of choice is not only a consumer's legitimate democratic right, but also makes economic sense. In the final analysis, the collective will of consumers helps to prevent the dissipation of expensive and increasingly scarce resources into goods that cannot be sold.

In order to promote the spreading of information, the Commission proposed encouraging co-operation between consumer organisations and schools, in order to prepare children for their role as responsible consumers. Further Directives on product labelling are planned, since uniform labelling regulations are necessary if consumers are to be able to compare the quality and price of competing products and assess new quality concepts, such as organic products. The most important tool to assist consumer choice, in the opinion of many consumers' associations, is the comparative testing of goods and services: the Commission therefore intends to promote co-operation between the various national testing institutes at EC level as an essential element in the action programmes.

iii Although a great deal of harmonised legislation on consumer safety has already been achieved, the Commission lists a series of measures in its third action plan as a "significant step required to build consumer confidence". These measures include specific directives covering product and service sectors not already addressed. Guide values, limit values and other provisions are to be adapted to progress in technology and research. Effective safety measures for coping with emergencies are to be adopted. A number of ground rules will be established stipulating how Member States have to deal with safety problems. A draft directive regulating civil liability throughout the EC for physical damage caused by defective services will round off the Community's safety profile in the single market.

iv The full benefit of the single market will only be realised when consumers feel that they can exercise the option of making cross-border transactions safely. Consumers have, until now, been inhibited from making significant purchases in other EC countries because the general conditions of sale and the notorious sellers' "small print", which varies so widely among the twelve Member States. Uncertainty and reticence are the response to the unfamiliar legal system and foreign language. The Commission therefore feels that the elements in the existing contract laws of Member States likely to inhibit cross-frontier purchasing must be identified and, as far as possible, eliminated. In order to boost consumer confidence, the Commission has already adopted a proposal for a directive on unfair contract terms and is examining the possibility of preparing a set of model contract terms which would provide that matters like conditions of sale, deposits, after-sales service and guarantees would operate uniformly throughout the EC. The road to consensus at the "Brussels negotiating table" is however, often extremely long and hard and normally it is a case of reconciling conflicting groups' interests, opinions and philosophies in all the fields concerned.

The Third Action Plan was geared largely to the completion of the single market and significant measures have already been adopted at EC level. It was inescapable that a high percentage of the Directives, Regulations and Decisions produced to implement the White Paper on the completion of the internal market should have a direct impact on the interests of consumers: for instance, one Directive in ten concerns the composition, labelling or inspection of foodstuffs.

Other obvious examples are to be found in the field of pharmaceutical products, such as 87/189/EEC on the standards and testing of proprietary medicinal products, and the Directives laying down provisions on the advertising of pharmaceuticals and the content and presentation of the package inserts. These Directives are primarily intended to promote Community-wide competition between pharmaceuticals manufacturers and so to boost the undeveloped cross-border trade in this specialist sector, but they are also of interest to consumers for two reasons. Firstly, keener competition is intended to result in lower prices for medicinal products and, secondly, consumers of medicine presumably have something of a vested interest both in informative and comprehensible package inserts and in advertising that does not make exaggerated claims.

However, the overall impact of all Regulations and Directive is not always so obvious. Quite apart from the core legislation for the internal market, virtually every policy has a consumer dimension.

- Agriculture policy was on the spot in the debate on whether artificial hormones (BST) could be used to increase the productivity of dairy cows.
- The use and consumption of environmentally-benign products is the starting point for any environmental policy. For instance, ecological labelling of goods enables environmentally aware consumers to make informed purchase decisions.
- The rate of tax levied on goods not only has a direct impact on the ECU in the consumer's pocket, but VAT harmonisation measures will enable him to make an informed view as to whether the same goods are consistently priced in the various Member States.
- European competition policy has the task of preventing mergers where they would undermine competition at the consumer's expense.

The position until the Maastricht Treaty can be summed up as follows: in the 1970s, radical measures to protect consumers were seen as a luxury which Member States could ill afford, given that their economies were in deep recession. In the 1980s, consumer protection policy remained something of a Cinderella, lagging behind the quest for economic growth in the march towards the single market. One of the reasons given for this was that tackling the issue would have further overloaded the already ambitious single market agenda, and it was felt that dialogue between consumers, producers, importers and distributors coupled with solidarity between Member States with more advanced consumer protection policies and those with some way still to go, could be the guiding principles in the opinion-forming process, culminating in a Community-wide compromise. Such a compromise would be more likely to bring beneficial results than unilateral national action by individual Member States for which, in any case, the scope had become increasingly narrow.

While cyclical problems are overcome or overtaken by superseding events, the structural impediments to an active consumer policy such as the different cultures of the Member States, different traditions and forms of organised representation, and differences in the extent to which consumer interests are taken into account at national level remain unchanged. In the interests of European Union, a formula had to be reached to which all Member States could subscribe.

Article 3 (s) of the EECT inserted by the Maastricht Treaty provides for "a contribution to the strengthening of consumer protection" as an additional activity of the Community and Article 129a provides that "the Community shall contribute to the attainment of a high level of consumer protection ... ".

It is going to be necessary to watch the agenda very closely to see how this is interpreted, bearing in mind that decisions on consumer protection issues will be taken by qualified majority after consultation with the Economic and Social Committee.

Certainly there is no intention of creating a standardised "Euro-consumer". On the contrary, the goal is diversity within Europe. National and regional particularities in the range of goods and services on offer and in consumer behaviour will continue to be both possible and desirable.

It is too early to say what the practical outcome of the new provisions is going to be, but the one thing which is absolutely certain is that any new measures proposed will go much further than ever before in favour of the consumer.

Chapter 10

Development of Grants Programmes

As pointed out in Chapter 1, one of the cardinal principles advocated by Monnet when laying down the foundations of the Community was that it should have control over its own budgets, even though, in the final analysis, Community funds were provided by the collective taxpayers of the Member States. The principle of providing finance from Community funds to help promote economic development within Member States has been present from the very start. Provisions were included in the Treaty of Paris, which set up the European Coal and Steel Community in 1951 for making loans from Community funds to the coal and steel industries and also to provide assistance to encourage new industries to move into areas hit by coal and steel closures. At the same time, grants were to be made available to assist workers forced to seek alternative employment as a result of changes in their industries and to promote research into all matters relating to the coal and steel industries. From the very beginning, the ECSC played a significant role in the post-war restructuring of these sectors.

The Recitals to the Treaty of Rome, establishing the European Economic Community in 1957 state as the reasons for founding the Community:

- " to lay the foundations of an ever closer union among the peoples of Europe, ...
- to ensure the economic and social progress of their countries by common action to eliminate the barriers which divide Europe ...
- to strengthen the unity of their economies and to ensure their harmonious development by reducing the differences existing between the various regions and the backwardness of the less favoured regions...".

The all embracing nature of the recitals meant that "Community" spheres of interest were expanded dramatically, to include a measure of influence over virtually all aspects of the economic life of the Member States. This was qualified however, in practical terms, by listing the "activities of the Community" in Article 3. These include:

- "the adoption of a common policy in the sphere of agriculture;
- the creation of a European Social Fund in order to improve employment opportunities for workers and to contribute to the raising of their standard of living:
- the establishment of a European Investment Bank to facilitate the economic expansion of the Community by opening up fresh resources ...".

The main themes for Community funding that we know today: agriculture, regional development and job creation were all there already, and they have only been widened and deepened to reflect the additional responsibilities taken on by the Community.

The Common Agricultural Policy (CAP) which had been included in the earlier drafts of the Spaak Report on which the Treaty of Rome was based, immediately established programmes to assist with the restructuring of the farming sector, to help farmers in less favoured areas and to improve the processing and marketing of agricultural products, alongside its market management activities. It was originally intended that these two branches of CAP expenditure should be roughly equal, but this has never been the case, and the market management activities have always accounted for over 90% of CAP expenditure. This is dealt with in detail in Chapter 12.

The European Social Fund was set up to assist with vocational training and job creation, and the European Regional Development Fund was created to promote the balanced development of the Community by assisting regions which, for either geographical or historical reasons, had lagged behind economically. Between them they form the foundations on which the later funds were constructed and which are dealt with in later chapters of this book. The European Investment Bank (EIB) was founded to provide finance for a wide range of projects in both the public and private sectors.

The next major expansion of the grants programmes followed the introduction of the Single European Act (SEA) in 1986. The SEA further extended the competence of the Community by including titles on Social Policy, Economic and Social Cohesion, Research and Technical Development and the Environment. The more recent additions to the Community grants portfolio are based on this extension of competence, and cover specialist areas such as, for example, the improvement of telecommunications, the exploitation of indigenous energy potential, the revitalisation of ship building areas and the conversion of naval shipyards.

The Maastricht Treaty, as well as creating the European Union, further widens the objectives of the Community to include:

Article 2 which imposes the obligation on the Community to promote:

- sustainable and non-inflammatory growth respecting the environment;
- a high level of employment and social protection;
- the raising of the standard of living and quality of life; and
- economic and social cohesion.

The Activities added to Article 3 include;

- a policy in the sphere of the environment;
- the strengthening of the competitiveness of Community, presumably vis-à-vis non-Community industry;

- encouragement for the establishment and development of trans-European networks;
- a contribution to the attainment of a high level of health promotion;
- a contribution to education and training quality and to the flowering of culture;
- a contribution to the strengthening of consumer protection; and
- measures in the spheres of energy, civil protection and tourism.

With this further extension of Community competence the overall scope is enormous. Some of these items have been covered to a limited extent by previous provisions in the Treaties, but now that their importance has been so greatly enhanced by their inclusion in the objectives of Community as spelt out in the Treaty, there can be little doubt that their new status will soon be reflected in a whole range of totally new programmes designed specifically to give them real meaning. Special interest groups from all over the Community will be campaigning for new programmes to deal with their specific aims.

Initially, the Community sources of finance tended to operate not only independently but without much noticeable common purpose. Community effort is much better targeted now towards achieving clearly stated, easily identifiable practical objectives, particularly in the Structural Funds, following their recent reform (Chapters 19 and 20). The intention is to target the most disadvantaged areas of the EC; areas hit by industrial decline and rural development areas, creating employment opportunities for young people and coping with the problems of long term unemployment. The Structural Funds in particular are co-ordinated at national level within the Member States by Community Support Framework Plans.

National or local government support from within the Member States for projects is a condition precedent of obtaining EC funding in many programmes. This support is subject to the principle of additionality which means that "new money" has got to be allocated specifically to the project by local or central government. For this reason, some Member States, most noticeably the UK, have been reluctant to take advantage of these programmes. It is estimated that the UK government's refusal to provide local authorities in the poorest areas of the country with the necessary funds to match EC funds available to them from the European Regional Development Fund (ERDF), lost the UK £300 million in 1993 alone. In addition, an unexpected windfall of £100 million could have been claimed from the European Social Fund as a result of the devaluation of sterling against the ECU on Black Wednesday. The latter would have been available for the training and employment of the under-25s.

As a highly legalistic organisation, both the basic policy relating to grants and its operation have to fall within the framework provided by the Treaties establishing the Community. The Commission, as the body responsible for the administration of the grants and other assistance programmes, has the duty to ensure that the funds are used strictly in accordance with the criteria and objectives laid down in the Regulations and Decisions governing them. It also realises that there are a number of lacunae in the existing programmes, and is always prepared to look at ways of plugging obvious gaps.

They are chronically short staffed and depend on the active involvement of interested parties. It is open to any interested party to submit detailed proposals for new programmes to the appropriate Directorate-General, complete with socio-economic and cash based cost/benefit analyses.

This year, the PACE Guide contains some 175 programmes: it is interesting to speculate on the number that will be in the 1995 edition!

Chapter 11

General Application Procedures

Rejected applications not only cause the applicant frustration, but they represent a considerable waste not only of the applicant's time and other resources but of the Commission's. To minimise this, they have had no alternative but to maintain a list of applicants who persistently submit incomplete, non-complying or frivolous applications. Be warned!

From our experience, we have compiled ten basic rules for potential applicants, some of which might appear obvious, but the obvious is so often overlooked.

i Some programmes accept and process applications throughout the year while others call for applications at irregular intervals with very tight application time-limits. It is therefore essential to keep a constant watch on the publications where information about the programmes which might be of interest is published. This point is dealt with in detail in the sections dealing with the individual programmes.

ii It is our experience that the time limits set either for initial applications or for any stage during the evaluation process are absolute. Miss one and the application will automatically be discarded, even if the failure to meet the deadline is the direct result of a delay by the Commission in reviewing documentation already submitted or in providing additional information requested.

iii The Commission staff are, on the whole, very helpful and want to make the various programmes work. Do not be afraid to ask for additional information but, on the other hand, do not rely on its being supplied within the anticipated time frame. Contrary to popular myth, the Commission is very short staffed and often, with the best will in the world, they just cannot help.

iv Make sure that the application meets all the conditions requested. It is a waste of time, for example, making an application in the name of one company in one Member State when the programme calls for an European Economic Interest Grouping (EEIG) as defined in Regulation 2137/85/EEC - no matter how much technical expertise is offered by the applicant. Nor does it help to say that partners will be found in other Member States if the application gets through the first stage. It will not get through the first stage; so it is therefore essential to have all the members of the EEIG on board before the application is made, which in turn means that it is advisable to have discussions with potential partners well before considering becoming involved in EC programmes calling for collaboration between undertakings in more than one Member State.

v Make sure that all the information requested is provided. The officials scrutinising the bundles of applications received for most programmes have not got the time to contact applicants who have omitted information requested; this also applies to basics like numbers of copies. We recommend always sending at least one extra copy, just in case an additional official wants to have a look, or copies are lost.

vi For most programmes, the administrators are inundated with applications, most of which meet the necessary requirements. As well as making their documentation clear and attractively presented, applicants must therefore find a way to make theirs stand out from the bunch. This is not easy, particularly since all the old hands will be looking for ways to do the same.

vii Read the all the Regulations, Directives or Decisions establishing and regulating the programme concerned. They will set out in detail the reasons for establishing the programme and this can be extremely helpful in anticipating the criteria according to which applications will be assessed. The latter are not always absolutely clear from the documentation supplied and it can improve an applicant's chances of success - particularly for considerations like vi above - if he can demonstrate that his proposal furthers the objectives of the programme in ways that are beyond those specifically mentioned in the information pack.

viii Remember that grant applications are scrutinised and assessed within the context of EC policy as a whole. This means that applicants must have a thorough knowledge and understanding of EC policy in the wider context and should make sure that their application conforms not just to the narrower requirements of the specific programme but also complies with the wider context of EC policies on matters like the environment, competition, consumer protection, cultural matters and social policy where appropriate, even if not specifically mentioned in the documentation supplied. To show that it actually promotes such policies would be a great bonus in making an application stand out from the pile.

ix Be prepared to use experts to help with the application, particularly if new to the game. Make sure that any consultants used are of high repute in their own fields and preferably experienced in dealing with the Commission. It also helps if they are known and trusted by the officials concerned. There are an awful lot of "grants brokers" and general charlatans around, some of whom are also well known to the officials.

x Do not despair if you have not heard by the date when successful applicants are due to be notified. Experience shows, for example, that a tender to undertake a study for a programme like PHARE will say that the successful applicant will be notified by 1 March 1994, the study must start on 1 June and be completed by 31 December 1994. In reality, the successful applicant is unlikely to be contacted before the beginning of May and the final details of the contract are unlikely to be agreed before the proposed starting date. The study will however, still have to be completed by the 31 December.

xi If you do not succeed the first time, try again!

General Application and Assessment Procedure

For some on-going programmes, information packs can be obtained from the addresses given in our chapters about the specific programmes. However, particularly for programmes relating to the supply of technical services or the funding of new technologies or other specific projects, calls for tender are published in the journals listed below and information packages sent out to interested parties. The amount and quality of the information in the packages varies considerably not only from programme to programme, but from call to call within the same programme. Some are full, detailed and precise while others give the impression that the administrators of the programme are not absolutely sure what they want. A third category is so general - and this category applies largely to calls for studies - that they give the impression of being little more than fishing expeditions to find out what expertise is available and if a good idea is suggested they will probably run with it. It is one of the strengths of the system that Community officials are prepared to listen to suggestions from outside experts, unlike so many of their omniscient counterparts in the national administrations of the Member States. It is up to the potential applicants in the latter two categories to come up with practical suggestions.

As an illustration of the general application and assessment procedures used for all programmes in one format or another, we are taking, as an example, a straight-forward research and development project. It shows the steps taken at all stages and gives details of the assessment procedures and criteria generally used.

It goes through five phases.

PHASE 1: PREPARATION AND SUBMISSION

This is the phase when project ideas are developed, the consortium formed, the work planned and the proposal document written.

The Commission's collaborative research and development programmes are implemented through shared cost projects. These projects are normally industry led and are formulated in response to a call for proposals. Full details of the technical areas and priority themes identified by the Commission are contained in an information package, along with guidance on how to prepare and deliver the proposal, by the deadline, to the Commission in Brussels. It is important to have the correct information package, as these are updated for each new call for proposals.

It is advisable to liaise closely with the Commission and the DTI Programme Managers at the earliest opportunity. In preparing your proposal - which can take several months - you should note the following points.

- The contents of the information package should be studied carefully because, although it is not conclusive, it serves as an important guide to what the Commission is seeking. Innovative projects consistent with the technical areas and priority themes will have the best chance of success.
- Background research is required to ensure that similar ideas are not being addressed in existing projects.
- Identify complementary projects which might provide useful results.

- The Commission organises a Proposers' Forum in Brussels, normally once a year. This event provides prospective participants with an opportunity to meet the Commission staff who run the programme to make contacts with potential project partners.
- The Commission can help identify potential partners. Expression of Interest forms are provided in the information package and summaries of completed forms are available on request. DTI staff may also be able to direct companies towards potential partners.
- An outline of the proposed project is required for preliminary discussions with the Commission. The Commission and DTI staff can provide guidance on how to prepare a successful proposal.
- Once a consortium has been assembled, each partner should prepare a short document describing the work they want to do. The consortium should also agree at this point which partner will lead the project as the prime proposer.
- One person from the prime proposer should write the draft proposal documents and act as project driver. A consortium meeting should be held to discuss the draft details.
- If time allows, a copy of the draft proposal should be shown to the Commission staff for comment. An independent consultant may also be considered worthwhile.

A project proposal is submitted in three physically separate parts:

i Part I contains administrative and financial data;

ii Part II contains the technical details of the proposal, together with the proposed schedule of work and sections addressing expected industrial benefits, project management techniques, etc.; and

iii Part III gives partnership details and details of intentions and plans concerning the commercial exploitation of the results of the project.

PHASE 2: INDEPENDENT ASSESSMENT

The criteria to be used for the assessment of each part of the proposal are explained in the information package. The Commission will arrange for proposals to be assessed by a team of independent, external evaluators. The evaluators are experts drawn from industry, universities and research institutes. These individuals are appointed on the basis of their expertise and not as representatives of their organisation or country. Commercial confidentiality of the proposals is ensured.

The assessment has two main objectives:

i to carry out a thorough assessment of the proposal and to make recommendations on its merits and on the action that should be taken; and

ii to select projects so as to cover all technical areas and make the best use of available funds.

The assessment of the project is carried out in four stages.

i The Commission's staff verify the eligibility of the proposal, using Part I of the submitted proposal, the administrative and financial data. This part of the proposal is not seen by the independent experts. Assessment of Part I is based upon eligibility criteria for participation in the programme.

ii. Part II, the technical and management details, is assessed by the independent experts. To ensure an unbiased assessment, this part must not identify any of the proposers by name. Each proposal will be assessed by at least three experts, working independently. Part II is evaluated against criteria such as conformity with the programme's technical areas and priority themes, scientific merit, technical innovations and economic importance to the EC.

Only when the experts have assessed Part II will they have access to Part III, the partnership details. Assessment of Part III is based on criteria concerned with the roles and experience of the partners and the exploitation of results.

iii At stage three the overall merit of individual projects is discussed by the expert group. Projects are then given one of the following ratings:

A - strongly recommended for funding without modification to the proposed project;

B - strongly recommended for funding with modifications to the proposed project;

C - recommended for funding without modification to the proposed project;

D - proposed project not recommended for funding because major changes are necessary; or

E - proposal of low quality or not relevant to the programme.

iv Stage four is the selection of projects, based on the recommendations made by the external independent assessors and the programme budget available.

The assessment phase is the only part of the project life-cycle when the consortium has no direct part to play. It is made solely on the basis of the information given in the application and, in practice, the most important parts of the proposal are the summary, the objectives and the economic and technical benefits set out in Part II.

PHASE 3: CONTRACT NEGOTIATION

The partners in a successful proposal will be invited to the Commission to negotiate a contract.

Contract negotiations centre around reaching agreement on responsibilities of the partners, ownership, exploitation and dissemination of results, monitoring and reporting on the project, financial considerations, etc. The Commission may also ask for some changes to the project, based upon the recommendations of the assessors, and these also need to be negotiated with the Commission. The contract that is agreed with the proposers of a selected project will be based on a standard form of contract, which includes a technical annex based on the proposal document and standard conditions.

Negotiations can take months, depending on the difficulties encountered. Work cannot start on the project until the contract has been signed and delays in signing it do not mean that the date for finishing the project will be automatically adjusted to compensate. It is therefore advisable at this stage to make all possible preliminary arrangements, without expending undue time and money, to get the project off to a flying start once the contract has been signed. If however the contract negotiations are not concluded the project will not be funded. As a general rule, any expenses incurred in negotiating a contract have to be met by the consortium and cannot be recovered from the programme.

PHASE 4: PROJECT EXECUTION

Once the contract has been signed, the project enters the start-up stage. It is at this stage that the partners may appreciate for the first time the complexities of working on an international project. During this period a considerable amount of time is usually devoted to participating in project meetings, in order to ensure that the ensuing research is well integrated.

The Commission's arrangements for monitoring the project will be specified in the contract. This may include visits to the partners' premises, in addition to regular progress meetings in Brussels. A brief written progress report is normally required every six months and a full report, every 12 months, with a final report prepared at the end of the project. Cost statements also have to be submitted every 12 months. The Commission also requires non-confidential summary reports on an annual basis for the purposes of disseminating research results more widely.

PHASE 5: INDUSTRIAL EXPLOITATION

This is the ultimate longer-term objective of Community research and development programmes.

The Commission will expect the consortium to pursue the development of the project through to the industrial exploitation stage. Intentions with respect to exploitation are included in Part III of the proposal. The conditions applying to ownership, exploitation and dissemination of project results will be described in the contract. Any new intellectual property rights generated by the project will be owned by the partners, and the Commission will want to satisfy itself that they have reached an agreement among themselves concerning its protection and use. It will also want to satisfy itself that there are no third party claims against any intellectual property rights being licensed to the project by either the partners or third parties, which could affect the eventual exploitation of the end results.

Exploitation of results must commence within a reasonable period of time. This can be agreed with the Commission at the stage when the final report is being drafted.

Although the confidentiality of all commercially sensitive material is guaranteed, the partners in the project must allow the results of the research to be disseminated by the Commission.

The results of invitations to tender are published once a year in a special number of the OJ (see below).

The following publications contain information useful to applicants looking for opportunities to tender for EC contracts:

- "The Official Journal of the European Communities" publishes calls for tender in the "S" series.
- "Tenders Electronic Daily" (TED) is the electronic form of the "S" supplement of the OJ and constitutes one of a series of databases offered by the European Commission Host Organisation (ECHO). It may be interrogated on-line or it is possible to become a subscriber to the TED-telex system which enables relevant notices, in abbreviated, summary or full-text format, corresponding to a company's activity profile, to be sent automatically. Full details are available from the Office for Official Publications (address in Appendix 2).
- "The Courier", produced by the Commission, is published bimonthly in English and French and contains an operational summary which gives progress reports on schemes prior to their implementation. It is available free of charge from the Courier Office (address in Appendix 2). This information is also available on-line via the PABLI system.
- "Industrial Opportunities", published every two months, is available free of charge from the Centre for the Development of Industry (address in Appendix 2).

Loans and Development Aid

The following are useful sources of information about contract opportunities, particularly relating to development aid programmes:

- indicative programmes, which give a general idea of the type of future project, are deposited at the relevant government ministries as they become available;
- project dossiers for the European Development Fund (EDF) and European Investment Bank (EIB) committees, containing details of project requirements, are similarly available;
- advance information can be obtained from Commission's Delegations in targeted ACP countries: the government of the ACP state concerned can also provide valuable information;
- national representatives of the Committee of Permanent Representatives (COREPER); and
- Commission staff in DG VIII (Development) in Brussels: Directorate B is the geographical division covering West and Central Africa and the Caribbean, and Directorate C covers East and Southern Africa, the Indian Ocean and the Pacific.

There is also a Management of Instruments Directorate covering food aid, emergency aid, STABEX and SYSMIN (mining co-operation). One member of the Commission's staff normally covers several countries.

The details of programmes can be inspected free of charge either at Community Information Offices or at the Commission's Delegation or local office in every ACP state, or through the local liaison officer. They can also be purchased directly from the consultancies which draw them up. Detailed information is attached to the invitation to tender documentation, pointing out useful facts about local conditions like weather, price of materials, wages, transport facilities, tax etc. For major works contracts, visits to the site are organised for interested firms and there is an information meeting when the national authorities and the local Delegation can answer the firm's questions. Minutes of these meetings are sent to all firms which purchase the documentation, whether or not they visit the site.

The Centre for the Development of Industry (CDI) was set up under Lomé III to facilitate industrial participation in EDF projects and in establishing joint relations.

The addresses of all the various organisations mentioned in this chapter can be found in Appendix 2.

Chapter 12

The Common Agricultural Policy

The Common Agricultural Policy (CAP) is by far the largest of all the EC programmes, accounting for no less than ECU 31 billion out of a total EC budget of ECU 55 billion in 1991.

When the Treaty of Rome was signed in March 1957, there were some 17.5 million farmers in the six Member States, who had between them some 65 million hectares from which to feed a population of 150 million. At the same time, the United States had over 400 million hectares to feed a population of 200 million. The average farm size of 100 hectares in the USA was almost 20 times that of the average in the newly-formed EEC.

The Community could only produce some 85% of its own food requirements and the severe shortages of the immediate post-war years were still very fresh in the memories of the founding fathers. When drafting the Treaty therefore, they gave special emphasis to what they saw as the vital importance of securing an adequate supply of food at reasonable prices to consumers, together with the need to ensure a fair standard of living for farmers and to stabilise the markets in the interests of both.

CAP came about as a result of, rather than being the reason for, a common desire among a nucleus of Western European countries to establish a political and economic union. Economic union was to be the first step towards achieving political union, and a guarantee of permanent peace following the devastation caused by two world wars, separated by only 21 years. The impetus for union among European statesmen was encouraged by the US, which considered European integration the only way for Europe to recover from the ravages of World War II, and to construct an effective barrier in Europe against the new threat of Communism approaching from the east.

In 1950 the Council of Europe, set up after the Congress of Europe in the Hague in May 1948, established a special committee to examine the prospects for the integration of European agriculture. France was very keen to open up Europe's agricultural markets and proposed the creation of a "High Authority" for agriculture with many supra-national powers. Production was to be controlled, prices were to be fixed and barriers to trade were to be removed. The UK, however, insisted on the High Authority being an inter-governmental body, with its role limited to reconciling differences between national agricultural policies. No agreement was reached. These proposals and the subsequent discussions highlighted the differences between the countries involved. France was very committed to the "European Movement", while the UK was anxious to maintain her links with the Commonwealth and her "sovereignty" over policy formation.

The creation of the European Coal and Steel Community in 1951 was the next significant step towards European unity. Its success in providing some stability in the markets for coal and steel showed that effective solutions to Europe's economic and political problems could be found through the development of the European Movement.

This was followed by the Messina Conference in June 1955, attended by the Foreign Ministers of the Six plus the UK. They established a committee, under the chairmanship of the Belgian statesman Paul-Henri Spaak, to look at the whole question of what steps should be taken towards European integration. The Spaak Report, which was discussed by the Foreign Ministers of the Six in Venice in May 1956 formed the basis on which the Treaty of Rome, establishing the European Economic Community, was built. Although the report initially specified that the Common Market established by the Economic Community must cover agriculture, the final resolution of the Six contained no specific reference to it. This omission may have been to facilitate British participation in the steering committee set up by Spaak. Indeed, the UK participated for a while, but pulled out because it rejected proposals for economic unification. This left the way open for the committee to draw up its proposals for the common market - including agriculture.

The Spaak Report outlined the special circumstances of European agriculture. These included the social structure of the family farm, the need for a stable supply, the problems resulting from climatic conditions and the inelastic demand for food. The report also recognised that the removal of existing tariffs and quotas would not be enough to allow the free movement of commodities between Member States. After all, problems which required market intervention at a national level would not simply disappear with the creation of a common market involving a number of states.

When the heads of government of the Six met in Rome in May 1957 to negotiate the Treaty establishing "a common market and progressively approximating the economic policies of Member States", they were constrained by the complicated mechanisms each of their countries already had for controlling agricultural production within their own jurisdictions. As set out in Article 3, however, the activities of the Community they were creating included:

> 3a “the elimination as between Member States of customs duties and of quantitative restrictions on the import and export of goods, and of all other measures having equivalent effect”.

It was obvious that, unless they were specifically to remove agricultural products from the common market, they would have to devise a common policy for agriculture within the common market. The alternative was to allow potentially competing state aids to agriculture to flourish in the different Member States, which made something of a nonsense of the whole concept of a "common market".

The objectives of the CAP, as laid down in Article 39 of the Treaty, are:

"(a) to increase agricultural productivity by promoting technical progress and by ensuring the rational development of agricultural production and the optimum utilisation of the factors of production, in particular labour;

(b) thus to ensure a fair standard of living for the agricultural community, in particular by increasing the individual earnings of persons engaged in agriculture;

(c) to stabilise markets;

(d) to assure the availability of supplies;

(e) to ensure that supplies reach consumers at reasonable prices."

The central role played by agriculture in the economies of the Member States was recognised in Article 39 2(c) and the need to "develop the common agricultural policy by degrees", by Article 40. That its objectives were laid down in the Treaty at all was no mean feat and was itself the culmination of much disagreement and protracted bargaining. The compromises required to reach an agreement acceptable to the Member States are still visible in the nature and operation of the policy today. The manner in which decisions were reached established that the CAP would have to be more a compromise arrangement for accommodating national interests than a vehicle for introducing radical adjustments. This was due to the realisation that, to avoid distortion, the Six's national agricultural policies would have to be dismantled. This would result in competitive forces redistributing resources and changing the structure of agriculture in Western Europe - an outcome totally unacceptable to the national governments of the Six. Four of the objectives laid down in the Spaak Report were, however, eventually reflected in the Treaty. These were, the gradual adjustment of the structure of the industry, the maintenance of an adequate income for farms, stabilisation of markets, and security of supply.

The imprecise reference to policy instruments, in Article 40, and the outlining of the process by which the CAP was to be established in Article 43, recognised the need to devote time to consider the machinery behind the CAP. This lack of policy detail in the Treaty is due to the fact that the founding fathers did not want the formation of the whole Economic Community to be held up by wrangles over specific sectoral issues. As a workable compromise, the objectives for agricultural policy were set out in detail in the Treaty, but the means by which they were to be achieved were not. There was general agreement that these important details should be worked out at a high level conference as soon as possible after the signing of the Treaty.

In accordance with Article 43, the Stresa Conference was duly held in July 1958. Although the agreement reached here was not legally binding, it offered a more coherent view of the CAP than did the Treaty. Following the lines of the Stresa resolution, the Commission considered the main problem to be the disparity between income levels in agriculture and those in other sectors of the economy. Thus the EC wanted a policy that would safeguard the family farm and support farm incomes, while at the same time, avoiding surpluses and maintaining trade with third countries. This was an extremely difficult task and it was four years before a policy flexible enough to accommodate such diverse constraints could be established.

1962 saw the official birth of the CAP. On 14 January 1962, after over two hundred hours of intensive negotiations, the Council agreed to adopt regulations giving legal effect to the levy system and instituting a common market organisation for each product. The elements of conflict both between Member States and across policy objectives meant that the Council rejected the strict organisation of trade and markets based on quantitative restrictions. They did, however, agree on three principles:

i there should be no barriers on intra-Community trade in farm products;

ii, preference should be accorded to EC supplies in intra-Community trade in agricultural products; and

iii there should be common financial responsibility for CAP policies. Expenses incurred were to be financed by the EC and income generated was to form part of the EC's "Own Resources".

These principles quickly became inviolable as far as some Member States were concerned.

From 1963-1967, two important issues were resolved which allowed the CAP to have a real impact. The first related to the level and seasonal scale of support prices. Cereals were the most important product under consideration. The US and other important grain exporters wanted to maintain trade flows with Europe, so internal price levels could not be set too high. Germany, on the other hand, was against low cereal prices and demanded compensation. Compromises were only reached after long negotiations.

The second major issue was the EC's financial arrangements, and involved both transitional arrangements for the allocation of national contributions to the operation of the CAP during the interim period before it could be financed from the EC's "Own Resources", and long term plans for the operation of its own budget. This issue was even more controversial than levels of support, and was not finally resolved until the Luxembourg Compromise in January 1966.

The fact that the CAP should be the outcome of a series of compromises between the conflicting priorities of the Member States was inescapable, given the extent and nature of these priorities with which the negotiators had to cope.

In the case of France, agriculture was the dominant industry when the CAP was formed. France accounted for 45% of the Six's total agricultural area, for 40% of their total food production having very fertile regions with a good growing climate and it was the biggest exporter of agricultural products - especially cereals. There are three main reasons why agriculture was so important to the French government. Firstly, as manufacturing industry was concentrated mainly in a few regional centres, there were large areas - such as Brittany and the Midi - where agriculture provided virtually the whole economic base. Secondly, farmers by and large were not committed to any particular political party and therefore provided a large, volatile pool of floating voters which had to be wooed by all competing parties, whether in government or in opposition. The third reason was the long tradition of government support for agriculture. France's interests in forming the CAP were therefore to secure export outlets for its agricultural surpluses and to maintain price levels, arguing for minimum prices to be set.

Many see the provisions on agriculture in the Treaty of Rome as the result of a trade-off between Germany and France, with Germany gaining access to an enlarged market for its industrial products and France gaining a market for agricultural products. This argument would suggest that Germany's interest in the CAP and agriculture was negligible, but this is very wide of the mark. Agriculture was extremely important to the German economy in the 1950s and, although making large concessions in the interest of the "European Movement", Germany went out of its way to ensure some continuity in the way it supported its farmers.

Germany's agricultural sector was inefficient because of its tradition of protectionism which dated back to Bismarck's tariffs on cereal imports in the 1870s. This resulted in the continuation of numerous, small, inefficient farms, which pressurised farm incomes; this in turn, required government support, which further inhibited the structural reforms necessary before agriculture could become a modern competitive industry like any other. This was coupled with a rising population, which caused an increase in Germany's food import requirements. As a major food importer, therefore, Germany's interests were at variance with those of France which were shared by Italy and the Netherlands: on the other hand it could not afford to ignore the interests of the 12% of its population directly employed in agriculture. The policy to which Germany finally agreed reflected these conflicting interests.

Another factor affecting Germany's attitude was that the Treaty was signed so soon after the end of the war. In addition to the potential economic advantage to be gained from the Common Market, Germany was seeking political rehabilitation through the establishment of a truly united Europe. It therefore considered any domestic losses arising from the CAP worth bearing in order to further European integration.

The basic policies and overall operational mechanisms of the CAP remain unchanged from its earliest days.

Every year, the Council of Ministers sets a target price for each agricultural commodity produced within the Community, which tries to strike a balance between the stated objectives of the policy, while remaining within a budget that it is felt that the Community can afford. Internal market prices are kept near the target level by a levy on imports, which varies in such a way that imported products cannot undercut the target price. This import levy keeps internal market prices near the target level only so long as the EC is not producing a surplus of the commodity. When EC farmers supply more of the product than can be sold on domestic markets at the target price, internal prices begin to fall below the target levels. To stop this excessive supply from depressing producer prices, an intervention price is set, somewhat below the target price. If the internal market price falls to the intervention level therefore, one of the official intervention agencies buys up the produce at this price. The agency then stores the produce and exports it at a loss which is of course made up from the CAP budget. Alternatively, and this is more usual, private traders receive a subsidy, known as a refund or restitution, equal to the difference between the intervention price and the world price, to enable them to sell the surpluses outside the Community.

There are also other methods of disposing of surpluses for certain products. For instance, wheat and skimmed milk powder are subsidised for use as animal feed-stuffs, surplus wine is distilled into industrial alcohol and, some products which are too difficult or too expensive to store are just destroyed.

The CAP is financed by the European Agricultural Guidance and Guarantee Fund (EAGGF) - often referred to by its French acronym, FEOGA. The original plan was that CAP would consist of two equal sectors, the Guarantee Sector for the operation of the market stabilisation policies and the Guidance Sector, to finance structural reform. In fact, the market stabilisation sector has dominated with the Guarantee Sector taking some 95% of the total CAP expenditure, leaving only 5% for modernisation, structural improvements and rationalisation under the control of the Guidance Section.

The CAP has not only managed to alienate producers, consumers, and environmentalists, without actually pleasing anybody very much, but has also distorted the economy of the whole Community. Aiming to hold European food prices for both consumers and producers to pre-determined levels, calculated to give farmers adequate incomes, necessitates price levels much higher than the corresponding world prices, so consumers lose out.

The guaranteed returns from this secure market have forced up the prices of agricultural land well beyond the rate of inflation. The high prices for cereals in particular make it profitable to grow them on marginal land which is not really suitable for cultivation. The result of this has been that the worse the land is, the more its price has been inflated in real terms: poor quality hill and mountain land has risen in price proportionately more than good land. This is all very well for those who own large acreages, but it has made it almost impossible for the sons and daughters of farmers ever to buy their own holdings, thereby hastening still further the depopulation of rural areas.

In the overall economy of the Community, agricultural subsidies and assured markets have caused a huge misallocation of capital resources. Particularly in the UK and Ireland, banks have lent millions of ECU to farmers, in preference to other businesses in greater need of fresh capital; financial institutions and others have invested heavily in land, in many cases in the hope of quick speculative profits as a result of obtaining planning permission for non-agricultural development, thereby changing the nature of land owning from a long-term commitment and making land just another commodity to be traded. This capital has been diverted from industries and businesses which are efficient in the sense that they can survive and compete in world markets without subsidies to agriculture, which must be an inefficient business since it only survives as a result of subsidies. This has a snowball effect, in that these efficient industries have been deprived of the capital they need to grow and develop, producing a negative feedback into the economy.

As a result of the CAP, internal prices are not only on average higher than world prices, but are consistent from year to year and from Member State to Member State. These high, stable prices under the CAP give farmers an incentive to over-produce, so more and more has to be bought up by intervention agencies each year, thereby further increasing the cost of the CAP which has to be paid for out of the EC budget. This vicious circle is just about unbreakable, since the UK threatens to veto any rise in food prices and France and Germany, any fall. A "Which" report in April 1988 calculated that the CAP was then costing every man, woman and child in the EC £110 per year as a consumer and £59 as a taxpayer. Both figures will have since risen substantially.

Taking a radical view, it is possible to argue that the market management sector of the CAP was not needed to provide security of food supply in the first place. Security of supply was certainly uppermost in the minds of the CAP policy-makers, since the food shortages of the early post-war years were not just fresh in their memories, but still continued in some cases while the increasing tensions of the Cold War made a stable supply base seem all the more desirable. A common market in agricultural products designed to provide farmers with more outlets would have had the effect of encouraging them to increase supplies in their own interests and the problem could have been solved more quickly, more cheaply and without the creation of a mammoth bureaucracy to manage the market. The common market would, furthermore, cover a large geographical area, so that regional fluctuations in supply would tend to balance each other out and food supplies would be less dependent on the vagaries of the world market. Since the formation of the CAP, agricultural production in Western Europe has certainly increased beyond the level necessary to achieve secure supplies of basic foods, but it has also tended to concentrate on types of agriculture not consistent with security, but which are attractive to producers as a direct result of the operations of the CAP. For instance, modern cereals are heavily dependent on imported fertilisers and modern mechanised farms are heavy consumers of imported energy, chemicals and machinery. The benefits of self-sufficiency in the production of a given commodity are not as obvious as might appear at first sight, particularly if it is readily available on world markets at a lower price.

It can arguably be claimed in favour of the CAP that, if the EC were to attempt to buy its food requirements on the world market, the extra demand would force up prices, so that there would be no guarantee that it would be able to buy the food it needed at the prevailing prices. This argument, however, in concentrating on the demand side is ignoring that other, equally important, economic factor - the supply side. Although it is true that an increase in the demand for a limited supply of food would cause its price to rise, it is also true that the world has the resources to increase food production substantially. Richard Body points out in "Agriculture: The Triumph and the Shame", published in 1982, that nearly half the world's arable land is currently uncultivated. Any extra demand from the EC would not be particularly in global terms either, since the EC makes up only 0.8% of the world's population. Even if the world prices were to rise in the short and medium term, they should not rise unduly over the long term because of the potential to increase supply in areas of the world with lower production costs. The EC is rich, in global terms, and well able to pay existing world prices or more. Taking the radical view a step further, it is even conceivable that, if the CAP were to be scrapped, world prices would actually fall in the short term as a result of the immediate disposal of existing surpluses which are being held in intervention. They would have to be sold on the world market at even more subsidised prices, and this dumping would have the immediate effect of depressing world prices. Although a one off event, its effects could extend into the medium term whilst production policies were being adjusted.

After what it is fair to acknowledge as an initial period of success, the CAP has now found itself in a position where it pleases nobody. It has alienated farmers, particularly small farmers, who have come to see it as a threat to their ability to continue in business. It is loathed by non-farming country dwellers and environmentalists, who see it converting a once picturesque countryside into a wasteland of prairies and concrete buildings. It is blamed by consumers and consumer pressure groups for keeping prices artificially high. It is derided by the general public as wasteful, particularly when they hear about set-aside and see the effect of it as large areas of the countryside are overrun by thistles, and it cannot exactly be loved by the Ministers of Finance in the Member States who have to find their annual contributions to the EC budget.

If nobody likes it, why is it not changed?

A substantial element of the problem arises from the very success of the agricultural producers (with or without the support of the CAP is irrelevant) in securing, firstly an adequate supply of food for consumers and then a surplus. Since the date of the introduction of the CAP, productivity has grown at a rate of 2% per annum whereas consumption has only grown at 0.5%. This was obviously going to create ever increasing surpluses once supply had exceeded demand. There are three possible courses of action available to alleviate the problem:

i to curtail supply; or

ii to stimulate demand either within the EC or in export markets; or

iii to store or destroy the surpluses.

Since the CAP is itself the result of each of the Member States trying to secure the best deal for itself, it is not surprising that it has generated so many problems and, for the same reason, reform has been cautious, slow and inclined towards tinkering with the problems rather than addressing the basic causes. The problem is not helped by the fact that the decision-making body of the CAP operates as a "satisfying" rather than an "optimising" organism. In outline, it first decides acceptable aspiration levels, then once this has been achieved, concentrates on one target variable at a time, rather than simultaneously trying to achieve multiple goals. Satisfactory target levels are normally reached by compromise among different components of the decision-making body. The Commission's proposals are themselves a compromise among opposing factions - farmers, consumers and environmentalists. The Council of Ministers' decisions arise from the resolution of conflicts between Member States with opposing interests balancing, for example, France as a net beneficiary with its politically powerful agricultural sector, and the UK as a net contributor to the budget, with its more powerful consumer lobby.

It is therefore evident that protecting national interests has continued to be a factor in the later evolution of the CAP. The growth of this phenomenon during the 1970s was related to the financial implications of the CAP. Pro-CAP Member States - France and the Netherlands, together with Ireland and Denmark, which had joined at the same time as the UK - sought to protect and maximise the benefits they were getting from the CAP. They pushed for higher support prices and the maintenance of the production of surplus commodities. This, in turn, worsened the budgetary problems. Member States wanting CAP reform - Germany and the UK - pushed for a lower pricing policy and direct compensation for what they perceived as the "unfair" distribution of the CAP's costs.

The UK had originally parted company with the Six at the Messina Conference because it was sceptical about the Six ever achieving anything of political or economic note. It believed that it could maintain its own economic strength and industrial competitiveness through its links with the Commonwealth and its special relationship with the US. Besides, as a large importer of food, it felt that it would lose out twice over: once, by having to pay higher prices for food imported from the EC than it was paying under the concessionary agreements it enjoyed with the Commonwealth and secondly, by having to contribute towards the EC budget, of which such a high percentage went to supporting the CAP which maintained the higher prices in the first place. This line of argument overlooked the level of financial support the UK was already giving to its farmers by way of guaranteed prices and other benefits. In the year of the Messina Conference, 1955, this amounted to £206M which represented 58.9% of total farm income. Despite this, ever since its accession, it has been one of the leading advocates of wholesale reform of the CAP and has achieved some limited success: in particular, it negotiated a series of refunds reversing the imbalance between the financial support it received under the CAP and its budgetary contribution.

The Commission's own proposals for reform in the 1970s were ambivalent. It had to recognise the need to reduce market imbalances and agricultural expenditure because there was a real threat of bankruptcy, but it also reiterated the goals of the CAP and its support of guaranteed prices as its central policy. The opposition to CAP reform was further strengthened when Greece joined the EC in 1981 and Spain and Portugal, in 1986 - all countries with large rural populations who stood to gain from the existing system. Overall, the pace of reform was always painfully slow.

However, in the late eighties and early nineties, the appreciation that the policy could not continue unchanged indefinitely was fostered simultaneously by three different crises.

The cost of agricultural support had continued to rise relentlessly towards levels which were becoming politically unacceptable within the Member States. At the same time:

i farm input costs were rising, while output prices were static or falling, causing a squeeze on farm incomes;

ii the high rates of interest being paid by farmers, who had been encouraged to borrow to expand their holdings and production, was not just speeding up the depopulation of rural areas as farmers laid off staff and gave up farming, but causing an embarrassing number of bankruptcies and, in the UK, made farmers the occupational group with the highest incidence of suicides; and

iii the GATT pressures for a reduction in the level of export subsidies and the dismantling of the protectionist measures against competing imports were making the disposal of surpluses more difficult, while at the same time, opening up the Community market to imports, particularly from the US.

There was an additional sociological factor, in that both farming and the public perception of it have changed radically over the years the CAP has been in existence. It is no longer seen just as a food production industry which happens to take place out doors and in the countryside where everybody can watch whatever is happening. It has become a multi-functional industry, producing foodstuffs, providing a force for social stability vital to many regions which would otherwise become depopulated and a positive environmental and ecological force, maintaining the countryside and providing leisure and other services to the whole population. The problem which this change in perception has caused is that these several objectives seem mutually contradictory and go far beyond the scope of the objectives of the policy as originally devised.

The autumn 1990 review under the Agricultural Commissioner, Ray MacSharry, had to face up to all these problems and strike a balance between the conflicting interests involved. The MacSharry Proposals to reform the CAP broke new ground by taking the whole range of social and economic criteria relating to the countryside as a whole into account for the first time. It identified four main features which had to be taken into account in planning an overall strategy for the countryside. The first two were positive: the regular availability of supplies had been assured and the markets had been stabilised for most products. The other two were, however, highly problematic: surplus production had become a constant, in-built feature of the system, while rural employment and farm incomes had fallen behind other industries.

The proposals for dealing with these problems, published in May 1992, have needless to say been the subject of fierce controversy ever since. They include:

- gradual reduction of support prices in sectors producing surpluses;
- production quotas for milk and tighter control on cereals, wine and olive oil;
- a system of guaranteed maximum quantities;
- a timetable for market intervention on a range of products;
- promotion of higher quality rather than quantity;
- premiums to "set aside" land for less intensive use and for more environmentally-friendly forms of agriculture; and
- switching over to alternative products and encouraging the development of forestry.

As far as overproduction is concerned, realistic estimates suggested that 10% of EC arable land would have to be taken out of production. As the land set aside was likely to be the least productive while production on the remaining 90% could be intensified, the change in overall arable output would only be marginal, particularly since there is no change in the operation of the agricultural support system. External protectionist measures have been increased, while intervention and export refunds to support higher internal market prices have been maintained. As the basic support structures were retained - albeit at lower levels - it is difficult to predict the success of these reforms in solving the on-going problem of the surpluses. Critics say that it has just made the administration of the system more complex.

What is much more certain is that these reforms will do little to solve that other bone of contention - the cost of the CAP. In the medium term, the reforms will greatly increase the level of support for agriculture, since direct compensation payments to farmers are to be introduced to offset the 29% cut in cereal support prices.

Another problem which had to be faced by the EC was the damage done to the environment by intensive farming - particularly from the increased use of fertilisers. From the environmentalists' point of view, the EC is to be applauded for any move towards adopting a policy of discouraging intensive farming, even if the main impetus for this policy change is the need to reduce over-production rather than any intrinsic concern for the countryside. Aid programmes are being developed for the promotion of production techniques which encourage the protection of the environment.

It is questionable, however, whether these reforms are sufficient to remedy the cumulative damage done to the environment since the CAP's inception. In the past, farmers have had little incentive and certainly no encouragement to preserve the rural environment. On the contrary, the policy encouraged production at any cost to the environment. Grants were given, for example, for removing hedgerows and creating prairies, cutting down coppices and for destroying ancient farm buildings and replacing them with concrete and asbestos sheds and silos. Increasing productivity by new farming methods on ever larger holdings speeded up the transfer of jobs from the countryside to the cities, further accelerating the process of rural depopulation. Due to the expansion of farming into lower grade farmland, tens of thousands of acres of moorland and downland were lost, while any conservation done by farmers was at their own expense. "Conservationists" were at least considered rather odd - if not actually subversive.

Set-aside, the environmentally-linked policy which has achieved the most media attention, is unlikely to have much effect in reversing the process since such small quantities of land are involved. In order to qualify for compensation payments for the lower cereal prices, farmers only had to set aside 15% of their arable land for the 1993 harvest. Besides, it is a very regressive policy since only large farms actually benefit. They can set aside strips around the headland of big fields and choose their least productive land. There have been plenty of stories about them getting set-aside payments for such things as farm tracks and land intentionally left derelict for the purpose of making it easier to get planning permission for non-agricultural uses. Small farmers have not got the luxury of being able to make such advantageous selections. The National Farmers' Union (NFU) calculates that, if the full 15% set-aside were achieved, output would fall by less than 10% - without even allowing for the predicted increased yields from new crop varieties. The levels of payment will do nothing to reverse the decline in farm incomes for small farmers, nor to improve the possibilities of creating new jobs in rural areas. It could be that the whole of the EC will become a sea of thistles for nothing. The obligation to control noxious weeds, if not actually non-existent, is certainly not policed in any meaningful way. In the end, the main beneficiaries are likely to be the giant agri-chemical companies when the EC is forced to do something about the uncontrolled spread of weeds.

What must be even more galling to the architects of the CAP is that their policy of protecting rural living standards has not been very effective. Since farm income support is proportional to the volume of production, 80% of the total EAGGF goes to the larger farms which form only 20% of the total. This penalises the smaller, more labour-intensive farms and further widens the gulf between the large, rich farms and the small, struggling ones.

The low level of finance allocated to structural reform reflects the paucity of policy initiatives in this area, particularly in the early days. In 1962, its first year of operation, the CAP took its first, faltering steps towards a structural policy which involved little more than the co-ordination and partial financing of the structural measures taken at national level. It was not until the Commission Memorandum of December 1968 that a real impetus for a policy on agricultural structures was forthcoming. Its main aim was to speed up the improvement of productivity in order to raise agricultural incomes and increase aid to the disadvantaged areas of the EC. The breakthrough came in 1970 when the Council agreed that, in future, they would decide jointly on structural measures instead of making a Community contribution towards national programmes.

The EC's first socio-structural Directives date from 1972, when European agriculture still consisted of a large number of uneconomical farms. Farmers either had insufficient land to use modern machinery and production methods, or had not got the funds to make the investments needed. These Directives were designed to encourage farmers willing to leave agriculture to give up their holdings, making more land available for farms that wanted to expand and also to target resources towards such farms. The rationale was that going into farming requires substantial capital investment and is only profitable if a holding is of sufficient size to provide a reliable, long term income.

The EC's structural Directives of the 1970s failed to make any major impact. The general economic recession and rising unemployment figures since the mid-1970s have made farmers less keen to give up their farms. Inflation and high interest rates pushed up investment costs, discouraging many farmers from modernisation schemes. Those who could hang on tended to do so despite incomes which had been much reduced compared with non-agricultural incomes. Even the threshold for income support became unattainable for many farms.

Additional programmes were proposed to address these new social problems including:

- direct aid to small producers, assessed on the basis of livestock numbers and size of farms;

- subsidies for agriculture in mountain areas and less favoured regions and for non-polluting activities;
- early retirement schemes: more than half EC farmers are aged over 55; and
- training and set-up assistance for young farmers.

These programmes are laudable in that they are a genuine attempt to support rural development, while assisting the diversification of rural economies to help stem and eventually reverse the tide of rural depopulation. Since there is no mention of curtailing support for large farmers however, it is unlikely to have any effect on the income gap between large and small farmers.

The problem regarding rural employment and farm incomes is becoming more acute, particularly since the dominant policy consideration of the CAP has been the protection of rural living standards. If support prices for major farm commodities cease to be set at levels above those on the world market, the incentive for over-production will vanish, causing farm incomes to fall even further. The objectives of maintaining rural living standards and reducing surplus production are clearly mutually exclusive, and the political decision about which should take precedence is one which the Council has shown an understandable reluctance to face.

Despite the problems and pressures for reform, the CAP remains the single most important area of common policy, using up over 60% of the EC's budget. It remains sacrosanct as the banner for European unity, despite the completion of the single market, the quest for economic and monetary union and the key role that the reform of agricultural policy in the developed world played in the Uruguay round of the GATT. The future of the November 1992 "Blair House" agreement between the Community and the US on the agricultural aspects of the Uruguay round remains uncertain. It is sometimes forgotten that it is not just the EC which protects its farmers. In 1987, for example, that bastion of free enterprise the United States spent US$11,250 per farmer on farm aid: almost five times the CAP's cost per farmer!

The talk is only of reform: is it time for a more radical approach? In 1846, before the repeal of the Corn Laws, Lord Melbourne summed up the feeling of the landowners of the time, "To leave the whole agricultural interest without protection, I declare before God that I think it the wildest and maddest scheme that has ever entered into the imagination of men to conceive". In 1875, however, the Encyclopaedia Britannica wrote, "In closing this review of British agriculture it is gratifying and cheering to reflect that never was this branch of national industry in a healthier condition and never was there such solid ground for anticipating for it a steady and rapid progress".

Chapter 13

Agricultural Grants

Agricultural Grants are dealt with under the following headings:

1. Improvement of the Processing and Marketing of Agricultural Products
2. Agricultural Structures
3. Forestry Grants
4. Co-operation in Automation of Data and Documentation for Imports/Exports and the Management of Financial Control of the Agricultural Market Programme (CADDIA)
5. The LEADER Programme
6. R&D in Agriculture, Agro-Industry and Fisheries (AIR)

General

Agricultural policy is shifting away from its original objectives of increased productivity, ensuring a fair standard of living for farmers, stabilising markets and ensuring the availability of supplies at reasonable prices, towards considering how to control the overall cost of the CAP and surplus production and the relationship between agriculture and other aspects of the rural environment.

The European Agricultural Guidance and Guarantee Fund (EAGGF), set up in 1962, has two divisions - the Guidance Section and the Guarantee Section.

The Guarantee Section finances expenditure on the common organisation of the agricultural markets, mainly through various intervention measures to stabilise internal markets and to export rebates to bridge the gap between EC and world prices. The Guarantee Section, which takes up about 95% of the total EAGGF budget, is administered by D-G VI Directorate G for the Commission, the Ministry of Agriculture, Fisheries and Food in the UK and the Department of Agriculture in Ireland. The policies and operation of the Guarantee Section are outside the scope of this book.

The Guidance Section is one of the three EC Structural Funds and, as such, it has to be looked at together with the other two Structural Funds, the European Regional Development Fund (ERDF) and the European Social Fund (ESF), as part of an overall package. It is growing in importance with the new broader-based policies and is fighting to increase its share of the EAGGF budget. Currently, it provides financing under Objectives 1, 5(a) and 5(b) of the Structural Funds, the definition and operation of which are dealt with in detail in Chapter 19.

The Guidance Section measures are embodied in a series of Directives. The majority of these are "common measures" which finance measures of a structural nature, particularly concerned with increasing the overall efficiency of the farming industry and the fulfilment of other EC objectives. The other measures, which are tending to decline in relative importance, are individual projects for the improvement of agricultural structures.

Assistance under the Guidance Section comes within the following main categories:

- measures accompanying the market policy which help to re-establish a balance between production and market capacity, such as set-aside schemes, afforestation, abandonment of certain types of production;
- measures to assist the modernisation and adjustment of production structures, such as the reorganisation of holdings, installation of young farmers, early retirement schemes;
- measures to promote the improvement of the structures for processing and marketing agricultural and fishery products e.g. investment projects, producers' associations, etc.;
- protection and preservation of the environment;
- measures to support farm incomes like income aid, compensatory allowances in less-favoured and mountain areas; and
- the development of rural areas for the preservation of the countryside and the environment: rural and tourist infrastructures, development of forestry activities etc.

The continuous reforms of the Structural Funds are resulting in many changes. The current Regulation concerning the Guidance Section is (EEC) No 4256/88 of 19/12/88. The new thrust in policy is to adopt an integrated approach involving all three Structural Funds and to work on the basis of agreed programmes, rather than on individual projects. Hence, although the Guidance Section is the only Structural Fund able to provide Objective 5a support, both the ERDF and the ESF together with the EIB and other financial instruments are able to contribute to Objective 5b. Objective 5a measures concerning the adjustment of agricultural structures to ensure long-tern competitiveness remain subject to Council legislation.

The five groups of programmes are described in more detail below.

1. IMPROVEMENT of the PROCESSING & MARKETING of AGRICULTURAL PRODUCTS

Statutory Basis

The long-standing Council Regulation (EEC) No.355/77 on common measures for the improvement of the conditions of processing and marketing of agricultural and fishery products has been superseded by Regulation EEC 866/90 (OJ L 91, dated 6/4/90). This Regulation was back-dated to enter into force on 1 January 1990, from which time Regulation 355/77 ceased to have any effect.

Aims

The aims of Regulation 866/90 are to improve and rationalise the treatment, processing and marketing of agricultural produce and, in so doing, to guarantee primary producers an adequate and lasting share of any economic benefits.

Programme Content

The EC Decisions approving the Community Support Frameworks in respect of the UK and Ireland are both published in OJ 350, dated 19/12/91. They cover the period 1 January 1991 to 31 December 1993.

To qualify, investments must satisfy at least one of the following criteria:

- helping to guide production in keeping with foreseeable market trends in encouraging the development of new outlets for agricultural products, in particular through facilitating the production and marketing of new products or of high quality products;
- relieving the intervention mechanisms of the market organisations by furthering the long-term structural improvement where this is needed;
- being located in regions which are faced with special problems in adapting to the economic consequences of developments in agricultural markets, or being of benefit to such regions;
- helping to improve or rationalise marketing channels or processing procedures for agricultural products; and
- helping to improve the quality, presentation and preparation of products or encouraging a better use of by-products, particularly by recycling waste.

Under these broad headings, eligible investments are in:

- rationalising or developing the preparation, preservation, treatment, processing or recycling of by-products or manufacturing waste;
- improving marketing channels, including the transparency of price formation;
- applying new processing techniques, including the development of new products and by-products, or opening up new markets and innovative investments; and
- improving product quality.

Special priority may be given to investments to improve marketing structures for agricultural products, particularly if such investments encourage the development of new outlets by facilitating the marketing of new products or of high quality products, including organically grown products.

Ineligible investments include those at the retail level, those relating to products from outside the EC and those where work commenced more than six months before the grant application was made.

Under Council Regulation (EEC) No.867/90 (OJ L 91, dated 6/4/90), Member States may include the marketing and processing of wood in their programmes under Regulation 866/90.

EC Contribution

Grants of up to 50% in Objective 1 regions, which include Ireland, and up to 30% in other regions may be made available for designated investments. The normal rate of EAGGF grants is 25% of the eligible costs of a project. The maximum payment is £900,000 and the total project cost must have a cost of over £70,000 in the UK and IR£77,000 in Ireland.

To obtain EAGGF grants, projects must also have a national grant of at least 5% of the eligible costs of each project. Where this cannot be obtained from sources such as Regional Selective Assistance, the appropriate Agriculture Department is prepared to consider providing a "back-up" grant, but only if the EAGGF grant is awarded and the subsequent claim approved.

Participation

Selection criteria "to guide the negotiation of sectoral Community frameworks" are to be found in Commission Decision 90/342/EEC, published in OJ L 163/71 dated 29/6/90.

The general priority investments in Clause 1(a) are:

- investments having a substantial amount of technological innovation or leading to the creation of new products;
- investments designed to make the production of processed goods less seasonal and less uncertain;
- investments seeking to cut costs of prepared products, either fresh or processed, by reducing the intermediate costs of collection or of commercial preparation, processing, packaging, storage or marketing; and
- investments leading to an improvement of quality or of hygienic conditions.

Excluded investments in Clause 1(b) are:

- investments for the production of processed goods for which the existence of realistic potential outlets has not been demonstrated; and
- investments for general frozen storage facilities, unless required for the normal operation of processing installations.

Priorities and exclusions are then given for cereals, fruit and vegetables, cow's milk and milk products, flax and hemp, oil seeds, protein crops and fodder plants, olives, potatoes, sugar, tobacco, meat and eggs and for wine. Potential applicants are advised to consult the complete sectoral plans which are available from MAFF.

Status Report

As the Structural Fund Agreements expire at the end of 1993, the final date for receipt of applications under Regulation 866/90 was 30 September 1992. The funding for this round was for a 12-month period. Details of replacement arrangements are still awaited from the Commission for the years 1994-1999.

Value of Successful Applications

The latest round of awards provided £7.7 million in grant aid to 31 projects in the UK.

Applications

Applications are made on form MAP/1, available from the appropriate agricultural department at the addresses below.

Member States all submit sectoral plans lasting up to five years which describe the commodity sectors which may benefit from grant aid, analyse any structural deficiencies in the sector and outline how these can be overcome. Applications should therefore be sent to the appropriate Agricultural Departments. Eligible projects conforming most closely to the aims of the Regulation and to sectoral plan priorities will be incorporated into operational programmes by Member States and forwarded to the European Commission for approval.

INFORMATION

England
Ministry of Agriculture, Fisheries & Food
Room 729
Nobel House
17 Smith Square
London SW1P 3JR
Tel: 071 238 6315/6317
Fax: 071 238 6308

Northern Ireland
Department of Agriculture for Northern Ireland
Room 145
Dundonald House
Upper Newtownards Road
Belfast BT4 3SB
Tel: 0232 650111 ext. 799/277
Fax: 0232 659856

Scotland
Department of Agriculture & Fisheries for Scotland
Room 244, Pentland House
47 Robb's Loan
Edinburgh EH14 1TW
Tel: 031 244 6388/6389
Fax: 031 244 6001

Wales
Welsh Office Agricultural Department
Room 2003
New Crown Buildings
Cathays Park
Cardiff CF1 3NQ
Tel: 0222 825130
Fax: 0222 823562

IRELAND
J McMeel
Food Division
Department of Agriculture and Food
Agriculture House
Dublin 2
Tel: 01 78 90 11

2. AGRICULTURAL STRUCTURES

Statutory Basis

The detailed provisions under which grant aid is provided to modernise and diversify rural holdings have been updated several times, most recently in Council Regulation 3808/89 (OJ L 371/1, dated 20/12/89) "with a view to expediting the adjustment of agricultural production structures".

Programme Content

Provision is made for:

- investment to encourage diversification into tourism, craft trades, manufacture and sale of farm products etc.;
- measures to rejuvenate farms by means of installation grants for young farmers, early retirement incentives, compensatory aids for farmers in mountainous and less-favoured areas; and
- aid for the establishment of Environmentally Sensitive Areas.

INFORMATION

Paul Charlton
MAFF
Rural Structures and Grants Division
Room 724
Nobel House
17 Smith Square
London SW1P 3JR
Tel: 071 238 5651

3. FORESTRY GRANTS

Statutory Basis

Council Regulation (EEC) No 867/90 OJ L 91/7 dated 6/4/90 provides that "measures to speed up the adjustment of agricultural structures with a view to the reform of the CAP may concern measures to improve the marketing and processing agricultural and timber products."

Programme Content

Under Article 1, the EC can provide funding:

1. "For the development of the forestry sector to be able to contribute to the improvement of agricultural structures ... for the purposes of developing or rationalising the marketing and processing of forestry products.
2. (The above) shall mean investments relating to the operations of felling, dismembering, stripping, cutting up, storage, protective treatment and drying of indigenous woods and to all operations prior to the industrial sawing of wood at a sawing mill.

The financing of investments shall be directed preferably to those concerning small and medium-sized undertakings (SMEs) the restructuring and rationalisation of which may contribute to the improvement of the agricultural and rural environment"

Applications

This funding is made available in the UK through grant schemes administered by the Forestry Commission and by the agricultural departments.

INFORMATION

Enquiries about the forestry grants available should be addressed to:
Gordon Inglis
Grants and Licenses Division
Forestry Commission
231 Corstorphine Road
Edinburgh EH12 7AT
Tel: 031 334 0303 ext.2334

Enquiries about the EC contribution towards these grants to:
Bruce Eadie
Forestry Commission
International Relations Division
Department of Forestry
231 Corstorphine Road
Edinburgh EH12 7AT
Tel: 031 334 0303

4. CO-OPERATION IN AUTOMATION OF DATA AND DOCUMENTATION FOR IMPORTS/EXPORTS AND THE MANAGEMENT OF FINANCIAL CONTROL OF THE AGRICULTURAL MARKET PROGRAMME (CADDIA)

CADDIA is dealt with in Chapters 24 and 25

5. LEADER

This concerns the development of rural areas and is dealt with in Chapter 19

6. R&D IN AGRICULTURE, AGRO-INDUSTRY AND FISHERIES (AIR)

AIR is dealt with in Chapter 17.4

Chapter 14

The Common Fisheries Policy

Article 38 of the Treaty of Rome, which lays down that "the common market shall extend to agriculture and the trade in agricultural products", defines "agricultural products" as "products of the soil, of stock-farming and of fisheries and products of first stage processing directly related to these products". Notwithstanding this and despite the official birth of the CAP in January 1962, the first proposals for a Common Fisheries Policy (CFP) were not made until 1966, and it was only in 1970 that the six Member States finally committed themselves to considering a policy. The Council of Ministers then adopted a first scheme embodying the principle of free access for all EC fishermen to all EC waters. The scheme was modelled on the principles of the CAP. It envisaged price support mechanisms and protection for the EC market so as to provide adequate incomes to fishermen, together with measures to ensure fair competition within the market, modernisation of the industry and harmonisation, by intervention if necessary, of the various existing national policies.

The proposals were adopted by the Six while the UK, Ireland, Denmark and Norway - all countries with important fishing interests - were negotiating to join the EC. Without exception, this group of countries resented the EC plan, seeing it as a strategy to rush through a common policy which would only benefit the original Six at their expense. The fisheries issue was considered to be an important factor in influencing the Norwegian rejection of the joining terms in the 1972 referendum. The Community eventually negotiated a compromise agreement with the other three applicants whereby each Member State could, for an interim period, restrict entry within a zone of six nautical miles around its shores generally, or 12 miles in certain areas, to fishing vessels which had traditionally operated within those limits. These interim arrangements were scheduled to last until 1982.

Unfortunately, the scheme never worked satisfactorily, either in terms of national interests or in preventing the depletion of stocks of fish which, according to a growing body of scientific evidence, were under threat in many EC waters. The main problem was the adoption in the 1970s by many countries bordering the Atlantic - particularly Iceland - of exclusive fishing zones, 200 nautical miles around their shores. This action was subsequently endorsed by the United Nations Convention on the Law of the Sea. Deep-sea vessels from the EC were therefore excluded from many of their traditional fishing grounds, and were left with the choice of going out of business or concentrating on EC waters. Although the EC also adopted a 200 mile limit in 1977, it did little to offset the fierce competition within the zone between the various national fleets and the inevitable over-fishing that followed.

The Common Fisheries Policy as we know it today was adopted in 1983, after much disagreement, with the strongest resistance coming from Denmark. The two main elements of the CFP related to access to fishing grounds and the preservation of stocks. On the question of access, it endorsed the principle of all EC waters within a 200 mile limit being open to fishermen from all Member States. This limit is inevitably lower in enclosed waters like the Baltic and the Mediterranean. Member States were however permitted to retain an exclusion zone of up to 12 miles, within which fishing rights were restricted to their own vessels, and those from other Member States which already had traditional rights of access.

There were also numerous measures relating to conservation. The central concept was the Total Allowable Catch (TAC) - that is, the total amount of each species that it is permitted to catch in EC waters. Each year the Council of Ministers was to agree TACs for each individual species, especially those endangered by over-fishing. Each Member State was allotted a quota for each species within the overall TAC, normally after long and acrimonious bargaining. There was also a 12 mile area around the Orkney and Shetland islands where fishing for species under threat was to be controlled by a system of EC licences. The policing of the TAC system, by surveillance and inspection policies set up and enforced by the Member States, was monitored by a body of inspectors answerable to the Commission. The original schedule was for the system to last until 2003, with provision for a review in 1993.

The system has not, however, been completely satisfactory due to the problems of verification and enforcement, and to constant allegations of cheating by some Member States.

Other conservation measures within the CFP regulate the size of fish that could be caught, and the type and size of nets and mesh that could be used. Member States remain free to introduce further conservation measures within their own zone, as long as they do not discriminate against other EC vessels.

Most of the CFP operating procedures are modelled on the CAP. The Council of Ministers sets guide prices annually for all categories of fish. The EC provides compensation for all catches that have to be withdrawn from the market, setting a withdrawal price of between 70% and 90% of the guide price. If both guide and withdrawal prices are higher than world prices, as is usually the case, the EC operates a system of refunds to exporters, along the lines of the CAP model, so as to maintain the income of the fishing industry. When EC catches are insufficient to meet market demands, the duties on imports can be suspended; this has happened several times for various species of fish. The Commission has also set common marketing standards and principles on, for example, the size, weight, quality and packaging of fish. The implementation of these standards is the responsibility of the Member States, but they are monitored regularly by the Commission.

The funds available to the CFP make up only some 0.5% of the EC's budget. Out of these funds, the CFP provides some limited financial assistance to the industry to help with the modernisation and restructuring of fishing fleets.

Fishing was a particularly thorny issue in the negotiations when Portugal and Spain applied to join the EC, and constituted a major reason for the delay in their completion. Both countries had important fishing interests, but in the end agreed to accept the CFP on joining in 1986. The agreement with them on mutual access to some specific fishing zones is due to be reviewed in 1995. Their accession had the effect of doubling the tonnage and size of the EC fishing fleet, making it the third largest fishing fleet in the world.

A rider to the CFP is that the EC has signed reciprocal agreements with other European and Atlantic states, allowing some limited access to each other's fishing grounds and markets. As these reciprocal agreements include the countries of the former Soviet Union, in practical terms they constitute something of a one way traffic system because the former Soviet fishing vessels are powered by low cost fuel, crewed by fishermen whose earning expectations are very low, and they are desperate for hard currency. They are therefore willing and able to sell the fish in European markets at prices which EC fishermen cannot match, and the EC fishermen consider that the Community has stood idly by whilst what they see as blatant dumping goes on under their very noses. They also allege that the fishermen from the former Soviet Union are using equipment which is prohibited to them, are catching undersize fish and therefore causing further unacceptable depletion of the fish available to them. The reciprocal rights to fish in former Soviet waters are, for all practical purposes, valueless since they are either inaccessible from most EC ports because of either their distance or weather conditions, and selling EC caught fish for roubles or zlotties has little appeal. Agreements have also been signed with some African and Indian Ocean countries to allow EC vessels access to their waters, in return for technical and financial aid.

The whole concept of the CFP has been unpopular from the start, and its future in its present format must remain uncertain. The operation of the TAC has meant that most fishermen are restricted to de facto part-time fishing and are finding it very difficult to earn a living. Logically, if there are less fish available to be caught, whether as a result of the implementation of conservation measures or because of a shortage of fish, either less fishermen can earn a living or fish prices will have to rise in compensation. The other great problem is that TACs are calculated on a species by species basis. What happens when fishermen have caught their TAC for species A, but not for species B? They have found it very difficult to instruct species A to keep out of their nets, and by the time the nets have been hauled up and catch sorted, it is too late to put the species A back alive: not a problem which lends itself to neat bureaucratic solutions.

Chapter 15

Fisheries Grants

Fisheries Grants are dealt with under the following headings:

1. Fisheries and Aquaculture Structures Regulation
2. Processing and Marketing of Fishery and Aquaculture Produce
3. Research and Development in Agriculture, Agro-Industries and Fisheries (AIR).

General

The Guarantee Section of the EAGGF provides for the following measures for the fishing industry:

- the restructuring, renewal and modernisation of the fishing fleet;
- the development of aquaculture and the establishment of protected marine areas with a view to improved management of inshore fishing grounds, including the rearing of crustaceans and molluscs;
- the reorientation of fishing activities by means of exploratory fishing voyages, redeployment operations, joint ventures and joint enterprises;
- the adjustment of fishing capacity by the temporary or permanent withdrawal of certain vessels from fishing activities;
- the provision of facilities at fishing ports with a view to improving the conditions in which products are obtained and landed; and
- the search for new outlets for products derived from surplus or under-fished species and for certain aquaculture products.

The existing fisheries structures and fish processing provisions will be subsumed into the 1994-99 Structural Fund arrangements.

In accordance with a decision made at the Edinburgh Summit in December 1992, a new fund, the Financial Instrument for Guidance in the Fisheries Sector (FIGF), will be established to supplement the Structural Funds.

1. THE FISHERIES AND AQUACULTURE STRUCTURES REGULATION

Statutory Basis

Regulation (EEC) No 4028/86 (OJ L 376/7, dated 31/12/86), as amended by Regulation (EEC) No 3944/90 (OJ L 380, dated 31/12/90), is concerned with the modernisation of fishing vessels and the development of aquaculture. Commission Regulation 3856/91 of 18/12/91 (OJ L 362, dated 31/12/91) lays down the detailed rules by which Regulation 4028/86 may be carried out. A proposal for an amendment to the annex, laying down limits in the different regions, was published in OJ C 127, dated 19/5/92.

Commission Decision of 23/12/88 (OJ L 296, dated 26/10/91), laid down the Multi-Annual Guidance Programme (MAGP) for the Irish Fishing Fleet for the period 1987-91.

Aims

The aims of the Regulation set out in Article 1 are:

"1. In order to facilitate structural change in the fisheries sector within the guidelines of the CFP, the Commission may ... grant Community financial aid for measures of the following types:

(a) the restructuring, renewal and modernisation of the fishing fleet;
(b) the development of aquaculture and the establishment of protected marine areas with a view to improved management of inshore fishing grounds;
(c) the reorientation of fishing activities by means of exploratory fishing voyages and temporary joint ventures;
(d) the adjustment of fishing capacity by temporary or permanent withdrawal of certain vessels from fishing activities;
(e) the provision of facilities at fishing ports with a view to improving the conditions in which products are obtained and landed;
(f) the search for new outlets for products derived from surplus or under-fished species".

Articles 27 and 28 are directed at the improvement and rationalisation of facilities at fishing ports, and in so doing, aim to guarantee fishermen an adequate and lasting share of the economic benefits.

Background

Each Member State drew up a MAGP covering the period 1987-91. As technical difficulties were encountered in agreeing the MAGPs for 1992-96, the Commission introduced a Transitional Guidance Programme (TGP) for 1992 only. This TGP became the subject of an Irish application for annulment by the European Court of Justice. However the Commission's Decision adopting the MAGP (1992-96) for aquaculture was given on 20/12/91 (OJ L 29, dated 5/2/92).

Programme Content

Under Articles 27 and 28 of Regulation 4028/86, investments to improve ports may include the following:

- auction halls and facilities for first-hand sale;
- supporting facilities attached to, or in close proximity to, the auction hall and/or port for primary processing and packaging of fish for distribution;
- storage facilities, cold storage and deep-freezing activities;
- facilities to improve quality and hygiene for handling and marketing fish;
- ice supplies;
- water supplies;
- fish-landing equipment;
- fuel supplies;
- the improvement of back-up facilities for fishing vessels; and
- alterations to, or the provision of, quays in order to improve safety conditions during embarkation or the landing of products.

Projects must relate to back-up facilities for fishing or for the marketing of fishery products. Investments may be for a single project or a part of an overall harbour development.

EC Contribution

Funding comes from the Guidance Section of the EAGGF. The fund has a budget of 800 MECU for the first five years, and the 1992-96 programme is scheduled to cost 51 MECU.

Member States are expected to make a financial contribution to the projects. For aquaculture products in designated areas of need, EC aid is 40% and national aid between 10% and 30%. In other regions, EC aid is 25% and national aid between 10% and 25%. For protected marine areas, EC aid is 50% and national aid between 10% to 35%.

To qualify, the total project cost must not be less than £25,000, nor more than £6 million.

Participation

Applications may be submitted by public, semi-public or private bodies and must be aimed at benefiting the fishing industry rather than other harbour users. At least 50% of the vessels affected by a project must be EC registered.

Status Report

The first tranche of funding for 1992 resulted in 463 acceptances, involving grants of 23.8 MECU for the whole of the EC. Of these, 398 were for vessel modernisation. Due to over-capacity of the fishing fleet, there was no approval of grants for construction projects. The second tranche of funding covers 409 projects to a total of 35.73 MECU.

For the UK, the October 1991 awards amounted to 702,088 ECU for 24 projects. All except three of the projects were for the modernisation of fishing vessels, the others being for aquaculture projects.

Under Regulation (EEC) 4028/86, a concerted measure for the implementation of a socio-economic pilot scheme has been approved for the area of Macduff (OJ L 231, dated 20/8/91). The grant amounts to 50,000 ECU (50% of the total) to be spent on creating alternative employment and accompanying social measures.

For Ireland, the 1992 round of applications resulted in approvals for 33 projects totalling IR£1.13M, and comprising of one aquaculture project and 32 vessel modernisations.

Applications

Potential applicants should contact the appropriate agriculture department, requesting copies of EC Regulation No 2515/85 and Annex C and D of Regulation 2321/88.

Two copies of the Commission's application form must be submitted to the agriculture department, which assesses them and sends summaries to the Commission. Work may begin on projects when the Commission has acknowledged the application.

Applications must be received by the Agriculture Department at least two months before the Commission's deadline for receipt. The Commission has two deadlines per year: 31 March and 31 October. The scheme is scheduled to continue until 31 December 1996.

INFORMATION

For further information on any aspect of the grant scheme, contact:

England
Paul Charlton
Ministry of Agriculture, Fisheries and Food
Rural Structures and Grants Division
Room 729, Nobel House
17 Smith Square
London SW1P 3HX
Tel: 071 238 5651

Scotland
Scottish Office Agriculture & Fisheries Dept
Room 259
Pentland House
47 Robb's Lane
Edinburgh EH14 1TW
Tel: 031 244 6387/6388
Fax: 031 244 6001

Wales
Welsh Office Agriculture Department
Room 2003
New Crown Buildings
Cathays Park
Cardiff CF1 3NQ
Tel: 0222 823835
Fax: 0222 823036/3204

Northern Ireland
Department of Agriculture for Northern Ireland
Room 145
Dundonald House
Upper Newtownards Road
Belfast BT4 3SB
Tel: 0232 650111 ext. 799
Fax: 0232 659856

IRELAND
Department of the Marine
Leeson Lane
Dublin 2
Tel: 01 678 54 44
Fax: 01 661 82 14

2 THE PROCESSING AND MARKETING OF FISHERY AND AQUACULTURE PRODUCTS

Statutory Basis

Council Regulation (EEC) No 4042/89 (OJ L 388, dated 30/12/89) lays down guidelines for the Member States' sectoral plans and indicates the types of investment that may be supported. Commission Regulation (EEC) No 650/91 (OJ L 72, dated 19/3/91) lays down the procedure for individual applications. This Regulation, separate from that for agricultural products, was necessary following the adoption of the Common Fisheries Policy.

The Commission Decisions concerning the Community Support Frameworks (CSFs) under Regulation (EEC) No 4042/89 for the period 1991-93 were made on 11/3/91 (OJ L 99, dated 19/4/91).

Aims

The aim is to improve the conditions under which fisheries' and aquaculture produce is processed and marketed in the EC, and thereby help to guarantee fishermen an adequate and lasting share of the economic benefits.

Background

Regulation 4042/89 came into force on 1/1/90. In order to target the aid from the EAGGF more effectively, Member States compile sectoral plans lasting up to five years. The UK sectoral plan is scheduled to run for three years from 1991-93.

Programme Content

Priority is given to:

- the modernisation of auction markets for the first-hand sale of products landed by vessels flying the flag of a Member State;

- facilities for preparation for of first-hand sale and filleting of fresh fish;
- the preparation of finished products from fish which have been caught and deep-frozen on board vessels flying the flag of a Member State;
- undertakings producing preserved products, provided that they are technically advanced, viable and capable of withstanding free international competition;
- the development of new products and new technologies;
- the improvement of the quality and hygiene of production processes; and
- the enhancement of the added value of products.

EC Contribution

The Regulation provides grant aid to be paid from the EAGGF.

Although the Regulation applies to all regions, the level of assistance is not uniform throughout the EC. Community support may take the following forms, of which the first two are the most common:

- part-financing of operational programmes;
- provision of global grants;
- part-financing of suitable projects; and
- support for pilot projects and for technical assistance and studies in preparation for operations.

Assistance is normally in the form of capital grants, with a maximum of 50% in Objective 1 regions (see Chapter 19) and 30% in others. The Member State concerned is required to finance at least 5% of the eligible costs. The beneficiaries' contributions are at least 25% in Objective 1 regions and 45% in others.

The UK's CSF for 1991-93 made provision for 1.6 MECU for processing and 0.4 MECU for marketing in Northern Ireland, and a further 14 MECU for processing and 3.5 MECU for marketing in the rest of the UK.

Ireland's CSF for 1991-93 made provision for 8 MECU for processing and 2 MECU for marketing.

Applications

National or delegated regional authorities administer the applications. Outline projects are examined and detailed information is then requested from those of interest.

Irish applications are submitted to the appropriate state agency, namely the Industrial Development Authority, Udaras Na Gaeltachta, Shannon Free Airport Development Company, or the Irish Fishing Board. These Agencies agree the applications and forward them to the Department of the Marine.

The current scheme is closed in both the UK and Ireland, and no precise information is available as to when it may reopen.

INFORMATION

UK
Paul Kilner
MAFF
Food and Marketing Policy Division
Room 325b, Nobel House
17 Smith Square
London SW1P 3HX
Tel: 071 238 6315

IRELAND
Department of the Marine
Leeson Lane
Dublin 2.
Tel: 01 678 54 54
Fax: 01 661 82 14

3. R&D IN AGRICULTURE, AGRO-INDUSTRIES AND FISHERIES (AIR)

AIR is dealt with in Chapter 17.4

Chapter 16

Research and Development Policy

Background

In 1870 the UK had 2% of the world's population, but accounted for a third of the world's total production of manufactured goods, and two fifths of their export. At the time of Queen Victoria's Diamond Jubilee in 1897, the British Empire covered an area of about 11 million square miles with a total population of some 372 million people: nearly a quarter of the world's land mass, and one person in four in the world lived under the British flag.

These spectacular achievements were brought about not by British military might but primarily through its dominance in world trade. This dominance in world trade was achieved because the UK was the first country in the world to industrialise, which gave it an enormous advantage over its competitors. Throughout the 18th and 19th centuries there was a flood of revolutionary new British inventions, and the entrepreneurs of the time were quick to exploit them commercially, not just in the small domestic market but in the ever-growing captive market provided by the expanding British Empire. In achieving this position of world dominance it was almost incidental that they also produced the most lethal armaments yet seen; as Belloc put it:

> " Whatever happens, we have got
> the Maxim Gun, and they have not."

Far more important were the cargoes of both capital equipment and consumer goods, carried by British ships as described by John Masefield,

> " Dirty British coaster with a salt-caked smoke stack,
> Butting up the channel in the mad March days,
> With a cargo of Tyne coal
> Road-rail, pig lead,
> Firewood, iron-ware, and cheap tin trays"

which made the UK the richest, and hence the most powerful, country in the world. The Navy was there to protect the British merchant fleet - by far the biggest in the world - and other British commercial interests.

Decline came very swiftly when resources were no longer reinvested in research and development, so that the flow of new products dried up and British industry allowed competitors to overtake it. By 1938, the British share of the world production of manufactured goods had fallen to one tenth and of their exports to one fifth; the latter figure fell to 17% by 1960, 11% by 1970 and 9% by 1980. The moral is very clear.

This is not just a British problem, although the scale of the British decline is the most dramatic. The Member States of the EC, en bloc, now feel themselves threatened with being edged out of the front rank of world industrial powers by competition from the commercial giants of the US and Japan: countries which have built their prosperity and hence world influence on the development and exploitation of the most up-to-date technological expertise available at any given time - rather as the UK itself had done two centuries earlier. Besides which, the immense financial resources that they have built up, and the unitary domestic markets in which they can sell their products before they have to think of export markets, make them daunting rivals in the area of technology and industry. The US has played a leading role in the international scientific scene, and Japan now dominates an increasing number of economically crucial technological sectors. Although Europe is well placed in some of the new industries such as software, computer services, industrial automation and telecommunications, Japan's aggressive marketing strategy in computer hardware and peripherals and mass market electronics, has not just left Europe behind but has threatened the very continuance of some of these vital industries. European production in these sectors covers a mere 75% of domestic demand, compared with 140% in Japan. This imbalance has led to a deficit in the balance of payments which, in 1989, came to ECU 31 billion in this sector alone.

This imbalance is not due to any lack of potential in Europe, but rather to a failure to make effective use of the rich mine of European brain power. The thousands of European laboratories, research centres and universities still, to a large extent, carry on their work in a fragmented, uncoordinated way 15 years after that problem was identified and analysed in the Cecchini Report, published in March 1978. This fragmentation has led to dispersed funding, isolated research programmes and the duplication of effort under national programmes.

The Cecchini Report recognised that the institutions of the EC would have to play a pivotal role in integrating research if the Community were ever to break out of this mould. Indeed, ever since its earliest days the EC has had some success in mobilising joint research projects, and exploiting their value as investments for the future. EURATOM, launched at the same time as the Economic Community in 1958, was dedicated to harnessing atomic energy for non-military purposes Community-wide, and the EURATOM Community has its own research organisation, the Joint Research Centre (JRC), set up under the Treaty. The JRC consists of nine institutes spread over four sites in four Member States; Ispra in Italy, Karlsruhe in Germany, Petten in the Netherlands and Geel in Belgium. Each institute specialises in one particular area: the environment, remote sensing, nuclear safety, new materials etc.

Despite these achievements and the emphasis given to the need for co-operation in R&D by the Cecchini Report, it was not until 1984 that the Community produced its first R&D Framework Programme, which covered the period up to 1987. This Programme attempted to promote a fairly even coverage of R&D into energy, the environment, industry, agriculture, raw materials and other areas judged to be important to the Community as a whole.

The rationale for these R&D programmes was that Community-wide technological co-operation was necessary if the Member States were to compete with the US and Japan. European collaborative research encourages industry to develop innovative products; also, by raising standards such research increases competition in Europe and therefore industry's own competitiveness. Individual firms were encouraged to take part so that they could:

i share the costs and risks of R&D, making use of complementary skills and common facilities, in order to participate in projects where the scale of investment would otherwise be beyond their resources;

ii gain commercial advantage from tapping into the technological expertise of firms in other European countries;

iii achieve a more significant role in the development of new international standards for their industry, helping to ensure that a world standard is generated by Europe; and

iv establish broader business contacts with their overseas counterparts, so that they are well placed to take advantage of the single market.

The legal basis enabling the Community to utilise its funds for the promotion of R&D programmes was not spelt out clearly in the Treaty of Rome, but this defect was rectified by Article 24 of the SEA, which introduced new Articles 130f-q into the Treaty. The importance of these Articles was emphasised in Jacques Delors "complete package" speech in Lourdes on 27 October 1988, when he included 'co-operation on research and technology' as one of the six objectives of the SEA.

The Second Framework Programme extended the objectives of the first and covered the period from 1987 to 1991, without any significant changes. The third, covering the period 1990-1994, was much more far-reaching.

The Third Framework Programme 1990 - 1994

The race for innovation gathered speed with the completion of the single market, and the EC has had to broaden the programmes to encourage more mingling between researchers, the breaking down of barriers between disciplines, the increasing of opportunities for commercial exploitation of the fruits of research programmes and the overcoming of administrative red tape and financial obstacles to new technologies.

The Third Framework Programme was agreed at the December 1989 Research Council in Brussels, and formally adopted in April 1990. Its overall level of funding is 5.7 billion ECU, with a supplementary budget of 900 MECU. At the Copenhagen Summit in June 1993, the European Council declared the objective of increasing its present 2% of GNP to research, development and innovation to 3%. The European Council expressed its wish to concentrate EC action on programmes which would complement and enhance the policies of Member States, rather than ones replacing existing national policies.

Like the earlier Framework Programmes, the Third Framework Programme is not just a research programme, but a five year strategy which lays down objectives, devises priorities and fixes the overall level of funding deemed necessary to undertake the specific R&D programmes designed to implement it. The programme will extend the concept of overlapping "rolling" R&D programmes in order to provide the flexibility needed to respond to the dynamic nature of technological development today. It is built around three major themes:

i enabling technologies;

ii management of natural resources; and

iii utilisation of intellectual resources.

Enabling technologies for industry will still receive the majority of resources, but significant new priorities are reflected in the resources devoted to environmental research, biotechnology and agro-industrial research. All these EC activities will continue to focus primarily on priority areas of pre-competitive R&D, and will complement other forms of European collaboration, such as EUREKA and COST, as well as specialised activities like those undertaken by the European Space Agency and other commercial product-targeted schemes. In all areas particular emphasis is placed on "pre-normative" or "pre-legislative" research - that is, research providing the scientific and technological basis for the adoption of common legislative provisions.

The Framework Programme contained fifteen specific R&D programmes in the following areas:

i information technologies;

ii communications technologies;

iii development of telematics systems in areas of general interest;

iv industrial and materials technologies;

v measurement and testing;

vi environment;

vii marine science and technology;

viii biotechnology;

ix agricultural and agro-industrial research;

x biomedical and health research;

xi life sciences and technologies for developing countries;

xii non-nuclear energies;

xiii the safety of nuclear fission;

xiv controlled thermonuclear fusion, and;

xv human capital and mobility.

The programme favours joint projects involving several Member States. It provides incentives for pure research, like the Joint European Torus (JET) programme, which covers the field of controlled nuclear fusion as a potentially inexhaustible source of energy for the 21st century. Many cross-border networks, bringing together engineers and scientists from all over Europe, have been set up in fields such as biotechnology, renewable energy and the environment. In the medical field, university laboratories and hospital units throughout Europe are joining forces to tackle major health care problems such as cancer and AIDS.

The state of the European information technology industry was already causing particular concern ten years ago. To combat this the EC launched the ESPRIT programme in the early 1980s. ESPRIT taught large firms which had traditionally competed with one another, to pool some of their research work and share the risks and results. Esprit can, for example, take the credit for the development in the Supernode project of a completely new, parallel computer architecture which led to substantial improvements in computer graphics and picture synthesis techniques.

The EC has also been running the BRITE/EURAM programme for many years. This deals with the application of new technologies to traditional industries, such as motor vehicles and textiles. For instance, a very promising car engine containing several plastic components and with improved fuel consumption, was developed and tested under BRITE/EURAM.

Another key element of the EC's research effort is interconnection of the various telematics networks in the Member States. This is essential to the completion of the single market, since only a genuinely European "nervous system" will effectively manage the flow of information in areas such as customs, transport and social security. It also intends to take its share of responsibility for resolving global problems such as the greenhouse effect and the climatic changes associated with it.

International co-operation is increasingly important, and the EC's research and technological development programme is not limited to activities within the Member States. It is also involved in a number of scientific and technological co-operation activities, compatible with international trade law and competition rules. The countries most directly concerned are the EC's immediate neighbours: various agreements authorise the EFTA countries - Sweden, Austria, Switzerland, Finland, Norway, Liechtenstein and Iceland - to participate in various ways in EC programmes. The EC is also involved in the EUREKA technological co-operation initiative, focusing on research immediately preceding the marketing of technological products, which supplements and extends certain aspects of EC programmes. The EC also plans to set up specific instruments for co-operation with the countries of Central and Eastern Europe. In certain selected fields it co-operates with major industrial powers such as the US and Japan. For years it has helped many less-developed countries to apply science and technology to development problems.

The Fourth Framework Programme 1994 - 1998

The Maastricht Treaty further elevated the importance of co-operation in R&D by including it in the activities of the Community as a new Article 3(m) of the EECT. It also redrafted Articles 130f-q, laying down the rules for the operation of the policy and re-stating the obligation of the Community to prepare several framework programmes annually. This implemented the policy of "strengthening the scientific and technological bases of Community industry and encouraging it to become more competitive at international level, while promoting all the research activities deemed necessary by virtue of other chapters of this Treaty".

The Commission prepared its proposals for the Fourth Framework Programme in anticipation of the Maastricht policy. These were discussed by the Research Council in October 1992, and it was agreed that the programme would be supported by a total budget of 13,100 MECU (COM (92) 406 final).

The new programme will be similar to the Third Framework Programme, except for a particular emphasis on supporting a small number of generic technologies considered essential to Europe's competitiveness: "big science".

It proposes to reinforce co-operation with third countries and international organisations. Special measures will be introduced to provide financial support to SMEs in their efforts to exploit the results of EC funded projects. Increased emphasis will be placed on the human capital and mobility activities.

The proposed programmes cover four broad areas.

1 Information and Communication Technologies (ICT), including:
- key elements for ICT systems;
- software engineering and best practice;
- high performance computing and networking;
- image technologies;
- electronic networks and linguistics;
- ICT support for function integration in manufacturing;
- advanced communications;
- information exchange between administrations; and
- technologies for integrated and optimised transport systems.

2 Industrial Technologies, covering:
- ICT manufacturers and industrial users: co-operative approaches and opportunities;
- advanced manufacturing technologies;
- human centred manufacturing;
- materials and their processing;
- measurement and testing;
- technology for means of transport;
- science and technology for a new urban habitat;

- science and technology for the preservation of European cultural heritage; and
- science and technology for the struggle against social exclusion.

3 The Environment:
- global change;
- environmental quality and human health;
- natural hazards; and
- innovative technologies and infrastructure for marine and polar research.

4 Life Sciences and Technologies:
- genomes;
- molecular genetics of plants and bio-diversity;
- the cell factory;
- agriculture, forestry and rural development;
- monitoring of agricultural production;
- industrial non-food uses for agricultural products;
- fisheries and aquaculture;
- development of harmonised protocols for clinical and pharmaceutical purposes; and
- addressing Europe's major health problems.

Member States' Role in EC Research and Development Programmes

Commission proposals for a specific R&D programme require approval by the Member States at ministerial level as well as approval by the European Parliament. The Ministers generally consider such proposals at meetings of the specialist research council. National governments thus have a substantial voice in the content, direction and operation of these programmes.

Member States also play an active role in the more day-to-day administration of the programme through a series of official committees. In 1984, 12 Management and Co-ordination Advisory Committees (CGCs) were set up, each with an interest in a particular sector of R&D, to advise the Commission on all aspects of the activities within that sector. These committees are made up of representatives of the Member States and of the Commission, and meet regularly in Brussels, Luxembourg or the Joint Research Centre (JRC) laboratories to discuss, amongst other things, the specific R&D programme within their area. The Member States' representatives are usually government officials or nominated experts of interested bodies, who influence the running of various programmes by making their views known to the national delegates.

For the large information technology and telecommunication programmes, management committees have been set up consisting of representatives of Member States, chaired by the Commission. These implementing committees have considerably more power than CGCs, and are responsible for matters such as approving budgets and annual work programmes. In future, other programmes will also have similar committees, so that Member States continue to have a strong voice in the direction of the programmes.

Types of Support Available

1 Contract Research with Cost-Sharing

The industrial programmes primarily operate as shared-cost activities, this means that the Commission provides up to half the funding, with participating organisations providing the balance. Such generous terms are justified on the grounds that the risks involved are high, with a relatively protracted time-lag before benefits are reaped, especially in the case of basic research. About 80% of the funds available under the Framework Programme fall into this category, and all large scale programmes are carried out in this form.

It is possible for non-industrial participants in some programmes to have the option of obtaining all their marginal costs. This applies to universities, higher education establishments and similar non-commercial bodies, whose primary activities are not related to research and who do not have an adequate costing system for determining the full research costs of a project. All such requests would be considered on a case by case basis.

For small projects involving relatively low costs, the Commission's contribution can be paid in a lump sum.

As the proportional reimbursement of the project costs is always limited to the cost limit stipulated in the contract, subsequent cost increases caused by altered prices or charges, cannot be approved.

2 Co-ordination

This form of support is aimed mainly at co-ordinating national research initiatives and programmes. Accordingly, the EC does not contribute to the costs of the research itself, but reimburses only the administrative costs incurred on meetings, travel expenses etc. This puts much less strain on the EC budget and can therefore cover correspondingly larger areas.

A typical example is medical research where there are numerous, widespread research activities involving a substantial need for information and co-ordination. By far the most widespread and best known of the Community's concerted action activities has been the COST programme, in which non-Community members may participate on an equal basis with the EC Member States.

In contrast to cost-sharing in contract research-sharing, the parties involved in co-ordination are not usually tied to definite tendering deadlines, and can make proposals at any time.

3 The Community's Own Research

The EC carries out its own research in the Joint Research Centres (JRCs). For many years the emphasis was on nuclear research under the EURATOM Treaty, but, in recent years, there has been a shift towards other areas such as research into safety, environmental protection and satellite remote sensing. As a result of reforms carried out in 1988 the JRCs are now divided into eight institutes comprising

- the Central Bureau for Nuclear Measurements,

and Institutes for:

- Prospective Technological Studies;
- Advanced Materials;
- Systems Engineering and Informatics;
- Transuranium Elements;
- Remote Sensing Application;
- Environment; and
- Safety Technology.

In future, the JRC will concentrate on the main priority areas of the Framework Programme, such as industrial technologies, environmental protection, energy and standardisation, and will systematically develop co-operation with industry. In these areas the JRC can certainly be considered a partner in contract research. The doors of the JRC are also open to research groups, guest scientists and holders of scholarships.

Application and Assessment Procedures

The application and assessment procedures have been discussed in detail in Chapter 11 as a general guide to EC grant procedures, as they are not only typical EC procedures but the most clearly defined and documented in any group of EC programmes. The programmes themselves are discussed in Chapter 17.

Chapter 17

Research and Development Grants

Research and development grants have been split into ten separate sub-chapters:

17.1 ENABLING TECHNOLOGIES: COMMUNICATIONS

1. Information and Communication Technologies ESPRIT
   (European Strategic Programme for Research in Information)
2. Communications Technologies RACE II
   (Research in Advanced Communications in Europe)
3. Telematics
   ENS (European Nervous Systems)
   DRIVE II (Dedicated Road Infrastructure for Vehicle Safety in Europe)
   AIM (Advanced Information in Medicine)
   DELTA (Developing European Learning through Technological Advance)
   Libraries Programme
   Linguistic Research and Engineering
   ORA (Opportunities for Rural Areas)
4. DOSES (Research & Development of Statistical Expert Systems)
5. PRISMA (Preparing Regional Industry for the Single Market)

17.2 ENABLING TECHNOLOGIES: INDUSTRIAL AND MATERIALS TECHNOLOGIES

1. Industrial and Materials Technologies Programme
   - BRITE/EURAM II
   - CRAFT
2. Measurements and Testing: Bureau Communataire de Reference (BCR)

17.3 MANAGEMENT OF NATURAL RESOURCES

1. The Environment Programmes
2. MAST II : Marine Science and Technology

17.4 LIFE SCIENCES AND TECHNOLOGIES

1. BIOTECH
2. AIR: Agriculture, Agro-Industry and Fisheries

3. BIOMED I: Biomedical and Health Research Programme
4. STD 3: Life Sciences for Developing Countries

17.5 ENERGY

1. JOULE II: Non-Nuclear Energies
2. Nuclear Fission Safety Programme
3. Management and Storage of Radioactive Waste
4. Controlled Thermonuclear Fusion
5. Decommissioning of Nuclear Installations
6. TELEMAN: Remote Handling in Nuclear Hazardous and Other Hazardous Environments
7. THERMIE: Promotion of Energy Technology

17.6 HUMAN CAPITAL AND MOBILITY

1. MONITOR
2. Human Capital and Mobility Programme
3. European Communities Science and Technology Fellowship Programme in Japan
4. STA : Science and Technology Agency Fellowship Programme in Japan
5. Co-operation in Science and Technology : Asian and Latin American Countries (ALA)
6. Co-operation in Science and Technology : Central and Eastern Europe Countries (CEEC)

17.7 TRANSPORT

1. TELEMATICS : DRIVE II (Dedicated Road Infrastructure for Vehicle Safety in Europe)
2. EURET: Research on Transport Systems

17.8 THE ENVIRONMENT

1. The Environment Programme
2. LIFE : Financial Instrument for the Environment
3. PSEP : The Physical and Social Environment Programme

17.9 COMPLEMENTARY ACTION

1. VALUE II : Valorisation and Utilisation for Europe (and CORDIS)
2. SPRINT : Strategic Programme for Innovation and Technology Transfer
3. Venture Consort Innovation Finance Scheme
4. EUROTECH Capital
5. ESCF : European Seed Capital Funds
6. TPF : Technology Performance Financing
7. MONITOR: Strategic Analysis, Forecasting and Assessment in Research and Technology
8. COST: European Co-operation in the Field of Scientific and Technical Research
9. EUREKA
10. EUROMANAGEMENT
11. STRIDE : (Science and Technology for Regional Innovation and Development in Europe)
12. The Council of Europe
13. ESF : The European Science Foundation
14. ESA : The European Space Agency

17.10 EUROPEAN COAL AND STEEL COMMUNITY SPONSORED RESEARCH GRANTS

1. Steel Research
2. Pilot and/or Demonstration Projects in the Iron and Steel Industry
3. Coal Research
4. ECSC Social Research Programmes
   - Sixth ECSC Programme of Ergonomics for the Steel and Coal Industry
   - Technical Control of Nuisance and Pollution from Iron and Steel Works
   - Research on Safety in the European Coal and Steel Community Industries
   - Industrial Hygiene in Mines
   - Fifth ECSC Medical Research Programme

Chapter 17.1

Enabling Technologies, Communications

This group of programmes includes:

1. Information and Communication Technologies
   ESPRIT (European Strategic Programme for Research in Information)

2. Communications Technologies
   RACE II (Research in Advanced Communications in Europe)

3. Telematics
   ENS (European Nervous Systems)
   DRIVE II (Dedicated Road Infrastructure for Vehicle Safety in Europe)
   AIM (Advanced Information in Medicine)
   DELTA (Developing European Learning through Technological Advance)
   Libraries Programme
   Linguistic Research and Engineering
   ORA (Opportunities for Rural Areas)

4. DOSES (Research & Development of Statistical Expert Systems)

5. PRISMA (Preparing Regional Industry for the Single Market).

1. INFORMATION TECHNOLOGY : ESPRIT

Statutory Basis

Council Decision 91/394/EEC: OJ L 218/22 dated 6/8/91.

Objectives

ESPRIT is a specific research and technological development programme in the field of information technologies within the Third Framework Programme, with a view to accelerating the spread of information technology in the business world, manufacturing and private use.

Background

Over the past two decades, the IT industry has enormously increased its influence on the development of our industrial, economic and social fabric, and the rate at which the technology itself has been advancing over the past 20 years is forecast to continue, or even to increase until at least the first decade of the next century. Despite this, the industry has experienced unprecedented turmoil world-wide, and its growth rate has slackened. This is the background to the current considerations affecting future EC strategy in the industry.

ESPRIT is a shared-cost programme launched initially in February 1984, in response to growing concern at the European IT industry's poor competitiveness in world markets. It was the result of initiatives taken jointly by the Commission and the "Round Table" of leading European IT firms - GEC, ICL and Plessy (UK), Bull, CGE and Thompson (France), AEG, Nixdorf and Siemens (Germany), Olivetti and Stet (Italy) and Philips (Netherlands). It is designed to help the European IT industry with the key components of technology which it needs to be competitive in world markets. The aim is to foster collaboration and pave the way for global standards of European origin, while boosting pre-competitive research and development in the key areas of IT. The programme was based on the perception that no single IT company could succeed on its own, given the soaring costs and inescapable uncertainties of investing in IT, together with the increasing globalisation of the market.

It was originally planned as a ten year programme: ESPRIT I (1984-88), followed by ESPRIT II (1988-92), and has proved highly successful in promoting industrial co-operation. The programme has not only led to many outstanding technological results but has also acted as a catalyst in bringing about collaboration among large, medium-sized and small companies and between industry, universities and research centres. Its catalytic effects often extend beyond the R&D phase: co-operation in R&D has led to a marked change in the attitude of companies and has fostered the necessary, if sometimes painful, process of industrial restructuring.

ESPRIT III was launched in July 1992, and work on projects began in late 1992, but the whole programme is now approaching completion, and is due to be followed by new initiatives under the Fourth Framework Programme for research and technological development (R&TD). Scheduled to start in 1994, this is now undergoing examination by the Council of Ministers and the European Parliament. The proposed initiatives are based on a consensus of the views of many hundreds of IT producers and users of all sizes, and research centres throughout the EC. Intensive independent assessments of EC R&D programmes, including ESPRIT, have contributed to this forward planning exercise.

Programme Content

ESPRIT covers five related areas.

AREA 1: MICROELECTRONICS
The goal of the work in this area is to strengthen the European IT users' capabilities to develop advanced and innovative electronic systems for a broad range of applications, by providing them with a competitive European source of the necessary technologies and tools. The work on the development of CMOS technologies and relevant design, manufacturing and packaging techniques is carried out in conjunction with the Joint European Submicron Silicon (JESSI) programme. Specific actions are run by SMEs to

establish favourable conditions for the use of microelectronics. This covers training and demonstration of the capabilities of integrated circuits and other services.

AREA 2: INFORMATION PROCESSING SYSTEMS AND SOFTWARE
This aims at exploiting the potential for technological developments in concurrent architectures, at providing better interfaces to satisfy the needs of end-users, and at promoting the take-up of new software production technologies.

AREA 3: ADVANCED BUSINESS AND HOME SYSTEMS - PERIPHERALS
Work in this area promotes the development of open, integrated solutions, focused on specific applications and the use and vertical integration of multimedia and related display and memory technologies. Applications lie in three distinct but inter-related fields: professional applications, business applications and personal, high-volume electronics applications.

AREA 4: COMPUTER - INTEGRATED MANUFACTURING AND ENGINEERING
This work contributes to the improvement of the competitive position of European manufacturing and engineering industries, by encouraging the development of advanced IT solutions for cleaner and highly efficient industrial operations and processes. It supports an integrated approach embracing engineering, logistics and operations, process automation and business functions, in a way which takes account of social, organisational, economic and environmental issues.

AREA 5: BASIC RESEARCH
The aim here is to enhance the potential for future technological developments in information technologies, to contribute to the programme's main objectives from upstream, and to reinforce inter-disciplinary links. Apart from projects in this area, there will be additional activities such as working groups, helping to add value to research through co-operation at European level. Planned research includes such areas as, developing low noise, high-speed systems through the use of low temperatures and by incorporating new superconductivity into materials, logical and algebraic foundations, the development of concurrent systems, artificial intelligence and commercial uses for these technologies and training in their applications.

EC Contribution

Funding for ESPRIT I (1984-88) and ESPRIT II (1988-92) was fully committed. ESPRIT III has an overall financial envelope of 2,676 MECU for 1990 to 1994, but the majority of the money will have been allocated by autumn 1993, following the second call for proposals in January. ESPRIT received a top-up of 180 MECU in early 1993. The basic level of EC support is half of all allowable costs, although universities and research institutions can opt to have all additional expenditure met as an alternative.

The Commission was scheduled to launch a technology transfer initiative in the field of software engineering, valued at around £15 million. The initiative was called the European Systems and Software Initiative (ESSI) and was scheduled to commence at the end of 1993.

Participation

ESPRIT is open to companies, academic institutions and research bodies, irrespective of size or whether they are public or private. As a rule, each project must include industrial companies from at least two Member States.

Applications

ESPRIT is organised on a regular cycle. Submissions are invited through calls for proposals which are published in the OJ and advertised by the DTI through the ESPRIT unit. These calls are based on a work programme, published in advance, which sets out the detailed project requirements. The application period for calls is relatively short, about three months from official notification. This is not a long time to put together a collaborative project of the quality necessary to succeed in what is a very competitive process. The DTI can help find partners for such projects and is able to provide other advice required by applicants because of the international nature of the projects.

The 1993 preliminary call for proposals was announced in the OJ of 20 January, with a deadline for applications of 22 April. There may be a further call in 1994.

INFORMATION

UK
For General Enquiries About ESPRIT Contact DTI's ESPRIT Unit:
Julian Thompson
ESPRIT Unit
Department of Trade & Industry
Information & Manufacturing Technologies Division
4th Floor Grey
151 Buckingham Palace Road
London SW1W 9SS
Tel: 071 215 1381

For Enquiries From Universities or Academic Organisations Contact:
The Science & Engineering Research Council
Central Office
Polaris House
North Star Avenue
Swindon SN2 1ET
Tel: 0793 411104
Fax: 0793 411088

Ireland
EOLAS
The Irish Science and Technology Agency
Glasnevin
Dublin 9
Tel: 01 37 01 01
Fax: 01 37 96 20

Commission
Commission of the European Communities
DG XIII
Telecommunications, Information Industries & Innovation
ESPRIT Information Desk
Ave de Beaulieu 29
B-1049 Brussels
Tel: INT+ 322 296 8596
Fax: INT+ 322 296 8597

For ESSI contact:
Commission of the European Communities
DG XIII
ESSI Information Desk
Ave de Beaulieu 29
B-1049 Brussels
Tel: INT+ 322 296 8110
Fax: INT+ 322 296 8364

2. COMMUNICATIONS TECHNOLOGIES (RACE II)

Statutory Basis

Council Decision: 91/352/EEC OJ L 192/8 dated 16/7/91.

Objectives

The main objectives are to continue the development of the Integrated Broadband Communication (IBC), and of the Integrated Services Digital Network (ISDN).

Background

The RACE programme began in July 1985 with a decision of the Council of Ministers to proceed with a "Definition Phase" for EC action in the field of telecommunications technologies. This led to the adoption of RACE I (Main Phase) by the Council in December 1987. A further programme in the field of Communication Technologies, RACE II, under the Third Framework Programme (1990-94), was adopted at the 7 June 1991 Council meeting.

RACE aims to establish a strong EC manufacturing industry in IBC, and to accelerate the emergence of a competitive EC market for telecommunications equipment and services, while working towards uniform standards throughout Europe.

RACE I developed IBC demonstration equipment and industry standards, and created a technological base for advanced IBC equipment and services. RACE II will build upon the work of RACE I and will focus on eight priority areas, as detailed below.

Programme Contents

The eight work areas in RACE II, and the money to be spent on them (in MECU) are listed below. This breakdown does not exclude the possibility that projects could fall within several areas. The programme also provides funds for EC staff and administration.

AREA 1: (111 MECU)
IBCs. This covers systems design, architecture and operation, transition strategies, common operational environment, techniques for basic system functions integration of demonstrators and verification tools.

AREA 2: (43 MECU)
Intelligence in networks/flexible communications resource management.

AREA 3: (53 MECU)
Mobile and personal communications.

AREA 4: (68 MECU)
Image and data communications

AREA 5: (39 MECU)
Integrated services technologies. This covers IBC modular standardisation, integrated services technologies and service technology verification.

AREA 6: (29 MECU)
Information security technologies. This covers service quality, security and reliability, information security technologies and information security verification.

AREA 7: (121 MECU)
Advanced communications experiments. This covers the study of generic functions, technology for advanced communication experiments and application experiments.

AREA 8: (20 MECU)
Test infrastructures and interworking. This is a horizontal R&D area supporting the other priority areas.

EC Contribution

The overall size of the RACE II programme is 489 MECU. The end of RACE I overlapped with the start of RACE II, which ends in 1994. RACE received a top-up of 73 MECU in early 1993, which gave rise to a further call for applications in 1993. Announcements concerning future communications research programmes (CRPs) are expected shortly.

The EC may contribute up to half the project funds

Participation

Work under the RACE II programme is carried out by collaboration among industry, academic institutions and telecommunications operators.

Management

The management of the programme is ultimately the responsibility of DG XIII, which undertakes the day-to-day organisation of the programme. In addition, the RACE Management Committee (RMC), consisting of representatives of the governments of the Member States, acts as an independent advisory body and approves the Commission's proposals on issues such as the programme's Annual Work Plan (AWP), evaluation, the participation of third world countries, departures from the programme's general provisions and major contracts. Contractors working in the RACE programme are required to attend periodic progress meetings, termed "concentration meetings", where mutually dependent deliverables and milestones are examined, necessitating a continuous self-audit by contractors. Each project is audited annually by independent technical auditors.

Status Report

In the two calls for RACE I some 90 contracts were awarded, of which the UK was involved in 76. Projects are audited annually with termination or extension of project times depending on the success of the project. UK companies have received 23% of RACE I funds, and have had the highest success rate in Europe (30%), of converting proposals into contracts. All RACE I projects ended by 1992.

Under RACE II, UK organisations have been involved in 75% of the projects approved so far. The enthusiasm of British organisations, often small in size, for working with European partners has been particularly encouraging.

No new CRPs are expected until Fourth Framework funds are available, which will probably be in late 1994 at the earliest.

The work programme for Communications Technologies was updated early in 1993, and will in general cover the period to December 1995. Recent calls for proposals invited eligible organisations to submit proposals for the extension of ongoing projects, and for new projects to address the following tasks:

- integrated networks, verification of network interoperation and interworking among IBC islands;
- implementation of services for personal communication space, integration of satellites in future mobile networks and components for mobile telecommunications systems;
- Integrated Service Engineering (ISE) demonstrations and architectures;
- digital image communications;
- open network security; and

- advanced communications application experiments in the automotive industry and in rural areas.

Applications

There was an initial call for proposals on 12 June 1991, which closed on 16 September 1991. The call was briefly re-opened until 10 February 1992, to enable more complete coverage of the tasks. Proposals for the updated work programme should have arrived at Commission offices by 3 September 1993.

All documents relating to the RACE programme, such as the workplan, should be obtained directly from the Commission. It is advisable for new potential applicants to register this in time in advance of publication of the details of any new CRPs.

INFORMATION

UK
RMC Member
Mr P McDonald
Telecommunications & Posts Division
Department of Trade & Industry
2/131 Red Zone
151 Buckingham Palace Road
London SW1W 9SS
Tel: 071 215 1795
Fax: 071 215 2909

Ireland
EOLAS
Irish Science and Technology Agency
Glasnevin
Dublin 9
Tel: 01 37 01 01
Fax: 01 37 96 20

Commission
RACE Central Office
Commission of the European Communities
Information Technologies & Telecommunication
DG XIII B
Bu9 4/4b
Rue de la Loi 200
B-1049 Brussels
Tel: INT+ 322 296 3417
Fax: INT+ 322 295 0654

3. THE TELEMATICS PROGRAMME

Statutory Basis

Council Decision 91/353/EEC OJ L 192/18, dated 16/7/91.

Objectives

To facilitate the management and transmission of electronic data as a result of completion of the single market.

Background

The deregulatory legislation leading to the free flow of persons and goods throughout the single market in 1992 has increased the necessity to transfer information throughout the EC. For instance, with the elimination of internal frontiers, it is no longer possible to monitor goods in transit at national frontier posts, so information has to be exchanged between the country in which the goods enter or leave EC territory and the country of destination or origin of the goods.

The telematics programme is looking ahead to electronic information storage, exchange and interpretation in the post-1993 Europe.

Programme Content

The telematics programme comprises seven distinct work areas which are set out below, but it emphasises co-ordination and transfer of results across the whole programme. The results of the former DRIVE, AIM, DELTA and EUROTRA programmes will be used and built on within their respective area in the telematics programme.

The seven areas are:

1. Support for the establishment of trans-European networks between Public Administrations : ENS (European Nervous Systems);
2. Transport Services : DRIVE II (Dedicated Road Infrastructure for Vehicle Safety in Europe);
3. Health Care : AIM (Advanced Information in Medicine);
4. DELTA (Developing European Learning through Technological Advance);
5. The Libraries Programme;
6. Linguistic Research and Engineering, and
7. Telematic Systems for Rural Areas : ORA (Opportunities for Rural Areas).

EC Contribution

The Third Framework Programme includes provision for 380 MECU of EC aid for "the development of telematics systems in areas of general interest". These funds are available for the period up to the end of 1994 for R&D projects designed to stimulate the development of a trans-European electronic information exchange system. The programme was to receive a top-up of 51 MECU during 1993.

Participation in research projects is through shared-cost contracts with the Commission. The EC financial contribution will not normally be more than 50%.

Participation

Organisations established in the EC or EFTA countries are eligible to participate in the programme. EFTA countries must however cover their own costs and contribute to general administrative costs. Public and private sector administrations, industrial firms including SMEs, telecommunication network operators, organisations of users of administrative telematic systems, universities and other research organisations may be involved.

To encourage collaboration between different types of organisations and between different EC countries, each project must involve at least two partners, who must be unconnected and established in different Member States.

These participation guidelines apply to all areas of the Telematics Programme, except where stated in the relevant area.

Applications

Calls for proposals relating to all areas within the Telematics Programme were issued in 1991. In some areas further limited calls were planned for 1993. Calls for proposals are published in the OJ. All contracts are normally let under an open tendering procedure and after independent evaluation of proposals.

INFORMATION

The workplan and information related to calls for proposals is available from:
Commission of the European Communities
DG XIII, Directorate F
Ref: Telematic Systems for Administrations (ENS)
200 Rue de la Loi, B-1049 Brussels
Tel (exchange): INT+ 322 299 1111

AREA 1 : SUPPORT FOR THE ESTABLISHMENT OF TRANS-EUROPEAN NETWORKS BETWEEN PUBLIC ADMINISTRATIONS : ENS (EUROPEAN NERVOUS SYSTEMS).

Objectives

This programme has two objectives:

- i to define common requirements for information exchange and examine the need for interoperability between electronic information networks within Member States; and
- ii to carry out studies and prenormative research for the definition and subsequent establishment of the trans-European telematic services networks essential to national administrations for the completion of the single market, the provision of the services necessary to the free movement of persons, goods, services and capital, and for increasing economic and social cohesion in the EC.

Background

If administrative services throughout the EC are to proceed in achieving the "four freedoms" of the single market, the free movement of goods, persons, services and capital, it will be necessary for them all to function together as though managing one single community. This European administration must be built substantially on the electronic exchange of information between the national administrations in different Member States. Thus there is a growing need for IT/telecommunications networks which will be able to interoperate across the EC.

Programme Content

Priority sub-areas are those most closely linked to the completion of the internal market; customs, social services, emergency services, statistics, etc.

Rather than researching new technology, the work is directed to applying existing technology. All work will be "user-driven" and concentrate on the need for exchange of information between Member States within a particular sector. Projects comprise of a definition phase to model the user requirement, an engineering phase and a verification phase, where results will be tested on data within that sector. Each project involves representatives of the relevant parts of Member States' administrations, to ensure that the end users' needs are being adequately addressed.

Emphasis is on the development of standards, functional specifications and architectures common to both the EC and across many application sectors, which contribute to a broader and more relevant platform for interoperable systems. It is important to note that application sectors were not specified in the work programme, but determined by those specified in successful proposals.

EC Contribution

Area 1 was allocated 41.3 MECU out of the 380 MECU allocated to the Telematics Programme.

Participation

Projects involve the participation of at least two independent partners in the EC, not all from the same Member State.

Applications

A call for proposals was published on 15 June 1991. Following evaluation and negotiation of proposals, 13 contracts were awarded in late 1991 and early 1992, fully committing the current budget. Information is currently awaited concerning future phases.

The programme is managed by a team of officials within the Commission, operating under the control of the Telematics management committee which is composed of representatives of Member States.

INFORMATION

UK
Dr Martin Ridge
Information & Manufacturing Technologies Division
DTI
4th Floor Grey
151 Buckingham Palace Road
London SW1W 9SS
Tel: 071 215 1226

Commission
Commission of the European Communities
DG XIII-C1
BU29 01/68
200 Rue de la Loi
B-1049 Brussels
Tel: INT+ 322 296 3552
Fax: INT+ 322 296 4260

AREA 2: TRANSPORT SERVICES - DRIVE II
(Dedicated Road Infrastructure for Vehicle Safety in Europe)

Objectives

The objectives of DRIVE are:

i to use advanced IT and communications to improve the performance, including security and efficiency, of passenger and goods transport services; and
ii to reduce the impact of transport on the environment.

Background

Under the Third Framework Programme, DRIVE II continues under the heading of Telematics Area 2, Transport Services.

Its activities will contribute to the development of integrated trans-European services, using advanced IT and telecommunications (Telematics) to improve the safety and efficiency of passenger and freight transport services, and to reduce the impact of transport on the environment. The work includes inter-modal links between road, rail and sea transport. DRIVE II is particularly concerned with the needs of users, and is responsible for the safety, provision and maintenance of infrastructure and of transport services.

Programme Content

The activities are divided into three interactive parts as follows.

i Strategies for the use of technologies, telematic services and systems and contribution to the definition of common functional specifications.

The results of the work carried out so far under DRIVE and relevant EUREKA projects have been directed towards the specific needs of road transport, as well as the technologies and systems available for communications and traffic control. Based on these results, strategies for using the technologies and systems will be sought in co-operation with transport users, businesses, providers of transport-related services and the national administrations concerned. Systems engineering work continues on an integrated transport environment, assessing developments and implementing strategies. It will contribute to the development of common functional specifications in terms of equipment, services and operational procedures, and will make recommendations to standard-setting authorities such as CEN/CENELEC and ETSI for traffic control, freight transport management, driver support and road safety.

ii Technologies and experimental development of systems.

This work takes account of the technologies emerging from the information and communications initiatives, and the results of research carried out under DRIVE and in other activities, both in the EC and in the individual Member States.

Technologies and experimental systems for managing transport and controlling road traffic will be developed and evaluated for both passenger and freight transport.

Safety and communications systems concentrate on helping drivers on long journeys. The research takes into account man-machine interactions, so that on-board systems and equipment will increase safety and ensure their effectiveness in communications with fixed infrastructure equipment.

Research and technological development work specific to freight transport, involving the transport of dangerous goods, is included. It covers the software, hardware and communication links necessary to assist in the management of freight traffic. This work involves real-time monitoring of the various transactions, the freight itself and the vehicles. Tracking and management systems for all kinds of vehicle fleets will also be developed.

In the public transport area, work on monitoring and control continues to evaluate the cost-effectiveness of systems for on-line monitoring, scheduling and control, and to establish the necessary functional specifications for both users and providers of services,

The technological solutions will have to ensure that the telecommunications equipment to be applied matches, in terms of size, cost and performance, the intended applications and markets identified. Special attention will be given to existing and emerging systems linked with satellite and digital cellular communication networks. Of particular importance is the assessment of systems able to provide incident detection, and information that is usable by network managers and those using road-vehicle communication links.

iii Validation work through pilot projects.

For the new systems to be accepted by the general public and the relevant authorities, they must be of proven performance and cost-effective, while their potential impact on the environment must be assessed. This requires full-scale pilot projects, oriented towards the integration of multiple sub-systems, functions and services which require strong pre-standardisation efforts.

These experiments cover areas including integrated urban traffic management, monitoring of air pollution, integrated motorway traffic management, vehicle roadside communications, driver information, transport demand management, public transport, freight transport and trip planning.

The potential for rigorous evaluation was a prime requirement in selecting and designing the pilot projects. Projects will also evaluate technologies and systems covering a wide range of applications.

EC Contribution

Area 2 of the Telematics Programme has been allocated 124.4 MECU from a total budget of 380 MECU.

Applications

The European Commission, DG XIII C4, is responsible for the management of the programme.

INFORMATION

UK

Mr A E Waddams
Department of Transport
Chief Scientist's Unit
Room P2/032A
2 Marsham Street
London SW1P 3EB
Tel: 071 276 5878

Mr D Mason
Department of Trade and Industry
IMT
4th Floor
151 Buckingham Palace Road
London SW1W 9SS
Tel: 071 215 1233

Ireland
EOLAS
The Irish Science and Technology Agency
Glasnevin
Dublin 9
Tel: 01 37 01 01
Fax: 01 37 96 20

Commission
Commission of the European Communities
DG XIII Directorate C-4,
BU 29 02/67
DRIVE Central Office
200 Rue de la Loi
B-1049 Brussels
Tel: INT+ 322 296 3449
Fax: INT+ 322 296 2391

AREA 3: HEALTH CARE - AIM (ADVANCED INFORMATION IN MEDICINE)

Objectives

The healthcare section of the Telematics Programme is usually referred to as AIM. This is an R&D programme with the objective of applying information and communication technologies to health care. It aims to increase harmony and cohesion in this area across Europe, to improve the quality and cost-effectiveness of medicine, and to strengthen the competitiveness of the European telematics industry by stimulating the demand for new services.

Background

During an initial exploratory phase in 1989 and 1990, 42 projects were funded from a budget of 20 MECU. This was a precompetitive, shared-cost programme completed in December 1990. It was always intended that, provided the Exploratory Phase was successful, there would be an AIM Main Phase, which would form part of the Telematics grouping within the Third Framework Programme.

Programme Content

While building on the work of the Exploratory Phase, the new AIM programme sets out to develop tools, techniques and practices supporting a common European approach to healthcare, informatics and telecommunications, and to guarantee their acceptance by promoting close collaboration between all those involved - academics, industry and the whole spectrum of health care users. This involves work in three main directions:

i Definition of strategies for the use of telematics technologies, systems and services, with contributions to the definition of common functional specifications:
   a. identification of user needs, regulatory tools, incentives and criteria for the appropriate use of technology in health care; and
   b. harmonisation of medical and health care management data and technology, common functional specifications, standards and communications protocols.

ii Development of telematics technology applied to medicine:
   a. alphanumeric data and coding standards;
   b. images and biosignals;
   c. integrated instrumentation and devices;
   d. knowledge based and decision support systems;
   e. medical use of multimedia workstations;
   f. health care communication systems;
   g. telecommunications systems for medicine;
   h. modularity and integration of medical information and archiving systems; and
   i. technologies and services for the handicapped and elderly.

iii Validation and integration:
   a. Pilot schemes for integrating medical equipment and information systems, which include:
   - computer-aided therapeutic systems;
   - architecture in an integrated biomedical laboratory;
   - use of mobile telematics in emergency health care;
   - telematic and information systems in a departmental environment;
   - development of a pilot scheme for a decentralised hospital information system;

- development of a pilot scheme for machine-readable cards; and
- development of medical software engineering techniques and tools.

b. Validation applications.

EC Contribution

As part of the telematics line of Framework III, the health care programme was allocated a budget of 97 MECU for the period 1991-94. This has recently been topped up with about 11 MECU, which is likely to be used to enhance the existing programme.

The programme normally operates on a shared-cost basis, with the Commission contributing up to half the project costs, but there is provision for 100% funding of marginal costs in some cases.

Approved projects can be for a duration of up to three years, but there is an annual audit and review. The programme also provides for some supporting measures (Accompanying Measures and Concerted Actions), and work is being carried out in the areas of nursing, primary care, medical records, teaching and learning and casemix resource management; there is also likely to be some other work.

Status Report

The call for proposals was published in June 1991, with a deadline of 16 September 1991, by which time 193 project proposals had been received. Following evaluation and negotiation, 37 projects were awarded contracts, with work scheduled to begin in January 1992: work is now in progress on 36 projects. Information is awaited concerning future calls.

Applications

Programme management is carried out by a team within the Commission, operating under the general control of the Telematics Management Committee, which is composed of representatives and experts from each Member State. Proposals are delivered to the Commission.

INFORMATION

UK

Mr D Preston
NHS Management Executive
5th Floor
Quarry House
Quarry Hill
Leeds LS2 7UE
Tel: 0532 546003

Mr Brian Jones
DTI
5th Floor, Green Core
151 Buckingham Palace Road
Tel: 071 215 1224
Fax: 071 215 1966

Ireland
EOLAS
The Irish Science & Technology Agency
Glasnevin
Dublin 9
Tel: 01 37 01 01
Fax: 01 37 96 20

Commission
Commission of the European Communities
DG XIII C3
BU29 03/65
200 Rue de la Loi
B-1049 Brussels
Tel: INT+ 322 296 3512
Fax: INT+ 322 296 0181

AREA 4: DELTA

(Developing European Languages Through Technological Advance)

Objectives

The programme aims to meet the needs of users of electronic distance learning services, including their need for interoperability of services throughout the EC.

Background

DELTA was a two year Exploratory Action programme, adopted in June 1988 as part of the Second Framework Programme (1987-1991). It sought to examine expected technological advances and harness them to European learning needs, and to provide tools to help training throughout Europe, particularly the understanding and use of new technologies.

The specified areas of research involved learning systems research, development of advanced learning technology, testing and validation, compatibility between different learning systems and obstacles to the take-up of new learning methods.

Research was carried out by collaborative projects each of which had to include an industrial partner, a learning interest and representation from more than one Member State. The projects proceeded on a shared-cost basis and research was at the pre-competitive and pre-normative level.

A new phase of DELTA, DELTA 91, follows on from the Exploratory Action within the Telematics Programme.

Programme Content

Activities concentrate on harmonising and adapting the existing technologies, and on testing the performance of the various possible distance learning systems and technologies. The work is carried out in three independent areas of research:

i implementation strategies and scenarios concerned with the use of technologies and telematics systems, including the definition of common functional specifications for the optimal implementation of distance learning services;

ii technology and systems development, concerned with refining the technology to achieve the appropriate telematic facilities for distance learning services; and ii pilot testing and validation, concerned with setting up experiments to integrate facilities to serve real needs, so that the performance of different technological configurations can be assessed.

EC Contribution

The Telematics Programme has an overall budget of 380 MECU for the period 1990-94, of which 54.4 MECU is allocated to DELTA.

The Commission has now announced funding for a series of Concerted Actions, which aim to relate national initiatives to DELTA projects. Funding is available to cover travel to, and attendance at, various workshops and meetings.

Participation

Organisations eligible to participate in the flexible and distance learning line of the new Telematics Programme include: telecommunications network operators, research establishments, universities and production and services undertakings, including small and medium-sized enterprises.

Projects involve the participation of at least two independent partners in the EC, not all from the same Member State. Within each project at least one partner must be an industrial undertaking, and another partner must have education and training interests. Links with other EC projects such as COMETT, RACE, ESPRIT etc. are important.

Status Report

Following technical evaluation in October 1991 and consideration by the Telematics Management Committee, 22 projects were selected for the DELTA programme. Five of the 22 successful programmes are UK-led, with the UK being involved in all but five of the projects.

Applications

Management of the programme is the responsibility of the Commission, assisted by a committee composed of two representatives from each Member State.

Contracts were awarded under an open tendering procedure, by means of a call for proposals published in the OJ. An announcement is awaited from the Commission concerning further calls for proposals.

INFORMATION

Flexible and Distance Learning areas of the Telematics Programme:

UK
Miss J Soloman
Department of Employment
TSIDI, Room 513
Steel House
Tothill Street
London SW1H 9NF
Tel: 071 273 5406

Ireland
EOLAS
The Irish Science and Technology Agency
Glasnevin
Dublin 9
Tel: 01 37 01 01
Fax: 01 37 96 20

Commission
Commission of the European Communities
DG XIII-C2
BU29 04/05
200 Rue de la Loi
B-1049 Brussels
Tel: INT+ 322 296 3416
Fax: INT+ 322 296 2392

AREA 5: LIBRARIES PROGRAMME

The Libraries Programme has four principal objectives:

i to promote the availability and accessibility of modern library services throughout the EC;

ii to introduce new information technologies into libraries in a cost-effective way;

iii to encourage standardisation; and

iv to facilitate the harmonisation and convergence of national policies.

Background

In 1985, the Council passed a Resolution to support the development of library systems and services in the EC. This Resolution led to various meetings and discussion papers, the main one being the "Plan of Action for Libraries in the EC", which was published in draft form in the summer of 1988 and revised in February 1989. This Plan was distributed widely throughout the 12 Member States. It was welcomed by the EC as the first action proposed at Community level dedicated to library co-operation.

Preliminary studies have shown that the development of libraries and of library automation in the Member States is uneven, with different types of libraries having differing objectives, priorities and user populations.

Initial EC activity in the libraries area cannot attempt to resolve all the long-term issues. It can only hope to initiate a process which will ultimately modernise library services to users. The Programme will therefore be selective, concentrating on urgent problems which can stimulate change in a concrete and practical way.

Several projects were supported through the IMPACT Programme to set the scene for the Libraries Programme. The principal projects were for developing compatible CD-ROM products containing national bibliographies for seven European national libraries, and investigating and implementing the Open Systems Interconnection protocol for interlending between France, the Netherlands and the UK. Various smaller projects were also supported.

Programme Content

The Plan of Action is structured into four action lines within which a range of individual, shared-cost, co-operative European projects, can be launched in conjunction with national and regional policies for libraries.

ACTION LINE I
Computerised bibliographies to create, enhance and harmonise machine readable bibliographies and union catalogues, and to develop the necessary tools and methods for the retrospective conversion of catalogues of internationally important collections.

ACTION LINE II
International linking of systems to provide a co-ordinated incentive to test and apply new telecommunication services, analyse their cost-effectiveness and ensure compatibility through appropriate standards, so that libraries will be able to set up networked services.

ACTION LINE III
Provision of new library services that will enable libraries to exploit existing resources in libraries to satisfy user needs more effectively.

ACTION LINE IV
Stimulation of a European market in telematic services and products specific to libraries, to encourage the private sector to investigate the library market and to implement new products which will have cost benefits for the library community.

A checklist for the negotiation and drafting of agreements prepared for the EUREKA programme is also relevant to the Libraries Programme.

EC Contribution

The Libraries Programme falls within the Telematics Chapter of the Third Community Framework Programme, which has a total budget of 380 MECU. Approximately 22.5 MECU will be allocated to libraries over a four year period, from 1992-1996.

There will be two funding mechanisms - up to half of total costs, and up to 100% of marginal costs. Contracts will be modelled on existing contracts for ESPRIT projects.

Applications

Management of the Programme is the responsibility of the Commission, assisted by a committee composed of two representatives from each Member State.

At the Commission's request, each Member State has set up a national focal point to ensure that each country participates effectively in the Programme. In the UK, the Advisory Committee on the European Library Plan (ACELP) was set up in 1990; membership is by personal invitation from the Secretary of State for National Heritage.

INFORMATION

UK
Mr P Bolt, Chairman, ACELP
Department of National Heritage
Libraries Division, Horse Guards Road
London SW1P 3AL
Tel: 071 210 3939

Ireland
T Armitage
An Chomhairle Leabharlanna
53 Upper Mount Street, Dublin 2
Tel: 01 76 11 67
Fax: 01 76 67 21

Commission
Commission of the European Communities
DG XIII-E3
Batiment Jean Monnet
Office C5/63
L-2920 Luxembourg
Tel: INT+ 352 4301 32126
Fax: INT+ 352 4301 33530

AREA 6: LINGUISTIC RESEARCH AND ENGINEERING

Objectives

The aim is to develop a basic linguistic technology which can be incorporated into a large number of computer applications where natural language is an essential ingredient, with a view to accommodating or overcoming limitations and inefficiencies within the EC which are due to its different natural languages.

Programme Content

The area is divided into three parts:

i research aimed at the improvement of the scientific basis of linguistic technologies, the themes open for proposals are -

- improvement of the interlinguality of the linguistic representation of text/discourse;
- use of domain-specific knowledge to constrain linguistic interpretation of text/discourse;
- interfacing with speech technology;

- use of advanced computational technologies; and
- economic and social impact of new linguistic technologies;

ii creation of common methods, tools and linguistic resources; the themes open for proposals are -

- software tools;
- grammars for the EC languages;
- general dictionaries (mono- and multilingual) covering the EC languages;
- terminology collections; and
- textual and phonetic corpus and prenormative research for linguistic tools and resources;

iii applications based on the common linguistic tools and resources; the themes open for proposals are -

- multilingual machine translation (EUROTRA);
- multilingual abstracting and indexing;
- aids for mono and multilingual document generation;
- integration with speech analysis and synthesis;
- multilingual interface to information systems;
- content analysis for building knowledge bases from natural language text; and
- computer aided instruction, especially in the context of language teaching.

Pilot applications and demonstration projects will help to test the progress of research work, and to demonstrate the technical and economic feasibility of tools, methods and resources in an operational environment.

EC Contribution

Linguistics has been allocated 22.5 MECU.

Status Report

The first call for proposals has resulted in awards totalling 7 MECU, and a second call was expected in October 1993.

Applications

Management of the Linguistics Programme is the responsibility of the Commission.

INFORMATION

UK
Gerry Gavigan
DTI
IMT
4th Floor (Green)
151 Buckingham Palace Road
London, SW1W 9SS
Tel: 071 215 1283

Commission
Commission of the European Communities
DG XIII-E4
Jean Monnet Building
Office B4-29
L-2920 Luxembourg
Tel: INT+ 352 4301 32886
Fax: INT+ 352 4301 32355

AREA 7: TELEMATIC SYSTEMS FOR RURAL AREAS (ORA)

Objectives

The objectives of the programme are:

i to create suitable conditions for geographically dispersed small businesses to provide more diverse employment opportunities, and a more balanced economic activity in rural areas;

ii to establish a basis for provision of improved services to dispersed and isolated populations;

iii to raise the level of awareness of the potential for information and communication technologies in rural areas;

iv to encourage manufacturers and service providers to make it easier for rural communities to use equipment and services; and

v to ensure that the applications of telematic systems in rural areas do not contribute to further centralisation of business and administrative activities, or a loss of the cultural and economic diversity of rural areas in Europe.

Background

As part of the "Programme of Research and Technology Development in the field of Telematics Systems of General Interest", the Commission took the decision to undertake a programme of research on telematic systems for rural areas.

This decision was taken in the light of the threat to the economic and social fabric of rural life from the decline in agricultural employment. Services have become less accessible because of rationalisation and centralisation, with the new services in urban areas only slowly penetrating into rural areas. The Commission's report “Europe 2000” in 1991 made it clear that poor services are now a major factor in the spiral of rural decline, as they affect the ability of rural areas to attract and retain employment

The combination of new information and communication technologies in "telematic systems" offers an opportunity to break the spiral by allowing a much greater diversity of employment in rural areas, and providing easier access to a wide range of services.

The importance of the decision is highlighted by the fact that the service sector was often the only source of job growth in rural areas in the 1980s.

Programme Content

The ORA Programme actions are structured as follows:

Part I Co-ordination and consensus development with industry and rural development agencies;

Part II identification of needs and opportunities for telematic services, and assessment of their impact;

Part III specification of applications and technology requirements;

Part IV research and development on telematic systems and conduct of pilot applications; and

Part V research on infrastructure planning and implementation strategies.

There have been 16 projects so far in the context of rural areas, covering:

- delivery of information and organisation;
- market implementation and psychological aspects of teleworking;
- technology strategy for the provision of infrastructure to support advanced telematic services;
- telematics applications for tourism and leisure;
- topological mapping of Mediterranean rural areas;
- distributed, inter-regional, agri-tourism, multimedia management systems;
- telematic systems database and management;
- services and applications for rural business activities;
- professional and financial services;
- analysis of on-going development projects involving telematic systems use; and
- evaluation of telematic applications.

EC Contribution

Approximately 14 MECU was allocated to ORA to cover the period up to the end of 1994.

Status Report

A call for proposals was made on 15 June 1991 and closed on 16 September 1991. The call was reopened until 30 April 1992 so that tasks could be more adequately addressed.

In response to the 1991 call for proposals, 11 projects were selected from 50 proposals submitted. As some tasks were inadequately addressed the call was extended: this attracted a further 48 proposals from which an additional five projects were selected. Information on new calls is awaited.

Work is progressing towards the programme objectives in the 16 projects under contract. UK organisations lead five out of the 13 projects in which they participate.

Applications

Management of the Programme is the responsibility of the Commission, assisted by a Management Committee of Member States' representatives which is chaired by a representative of the Commission. Operational management of the actions is conducted by Directorate III-C of the Commission.

INFORMATION

UK

Ms C Myers
Directorate of Rural Affairs
Dept. of the Environment
Room N19/13A
2 Marsham Street
London SW1P 3EB
Tel: 071 276 3700

Mr K Miltiadou
Department of Trade and Industry
2nd Floor Red
151 Buckingham Palace Road
London SW1W 9SS
Tel: 071 215 1809

Commission

Commission of the European Communities
DG XIII-C1
BU29 01/68
200 Rue de la Loi
B-1049 Brussels
Tel: INT+ 322 296 3552
Fax: INT+ 322 296 4260

4. RESEARCH AND DEVELOPMENT OF STATISTICAL EXPERT SYSTEMS (DOSES)

Statutory Basis

Council Decision 89/415/EEC OJ L 200/46, dated 13/7/89).

Objectives

The main aim is to apply contemporary computer techniques, with emphasis on artificial intelligence technology, to the field of statistics, with a special interest in the needs of the national statistical offices and of EUROSTAT.

Background

The single market is producing an ever growing demand for statistics from many sectors of the economies of the Member States, and to be of any value they must be comparable, trustworthy and timely. Thus Europe naturally plays a role in developing the new statistical tools required.

DOSES is a research programme managed by EUROSTAT which forms part of the Second Framework Programme.

Programme Content

The programme consists of two parts.

Part I Co-ordinated Projects
These are projects of general interest to the Member States. Financial assistance is made available for the organisation of agreed projects, but the participants fund their own share of the work.

Part II Jointly Funded R&D Projects
Work is undertaken in four areas:

i vertical study: preparation of a complete system for automated information processing in a specific field, to act as a prototype for other fields;

ii documentation of data and statistical methods;

iii access to statistical information; and

iv forecasting.

Status Report

The programme is now closed for applications, and information about future calls is awaited.

INFORMATION

Commission of the European Communities
EUROSTAT, D.3
Batiment Jean Monnet, bureau C5/096
L-2920 Luxembourg
Tel: INT+ 352 4301 32052
Fax: INT+ 352 4301 34771

5. PREPARING REGIONAL INDUSTRY FOR THE SINGLE MARKET (PRISMA)

See Chapter 19

Chapter 17.2

Enabling Technologies - Industrial & Materials Technologies

This group of programmes includes:

1. Industrial and Materials Technologies Programme
   a) BRITE/EURAM II
   b) CRAFT;
2. Measurements and Testing: Bureau Communataire de Reference (BCR).

1a. INDUSTRIAL & MATERIALS TECHNOLOGIES PROGRAMME - BRITE/EURAM II

Statutory Basis

Council Decision 91/506/EEC: OJ L 269/30, dated 25/9/91.

Objectives

The principal objective of BRITE/EURAM II is to help the regeneration of European manufacturing industry by using R&D work to reinforce its scientific and technological base.

The programme's main objectives are:

- to increase the competitiveness of European producer and user industries;
- to strengthen European economic and social cohesion; and
- to promote the scientific, technological and economic integration of European industry.

Background

BRITE/EURAM II continues the work of BRITE/EURAM, and will be part of the Raw Materials and Recycling Programme under the Third Framework Programme for a further four years.

The planned rejuvenation of European manufacturing industry will be achieved by advancing the technologies which address the whole life-cycle of materials, so as to reduce the design-to-product lead time and improve the manufacturing process. The activities pursued in the programme are designed to promote the general development of economic and social cohesion in the EC, and to reduce the adverse environmental impact of the manufacturing process.

Programme Content

The programme is divided into three technical areas, the scope of which reflects the multisectoral approach of the programme. It also emphasises the need to combine, in research and development, partnerships of suppliers, producers and end-users, as well as basic research institutes and industrial enterprises.

AREA 1: MATERIALS - RAW MATERIALS

The aim is to improve the performance of both advanced and traditional materials, at a cost which permits competitive industrial exploitation over a broad range of applications. This involves improving technologies to ensure the supply of raw material resources for recycling, so promoting an integrated approach to the whole life-cycle of materials. It also includes the cost-effective use of new materials in a broad range of products and applications and their diffusion to new fields of application. The sub-areas are:

1.1 Raw Materials;
- Exploration Technology,
- Mining Technology,
- Mineral Processing,

1.2 Recycling;
- Recycling and Recovery of Non-Ferrous Metals,
- Recycling, Recovery and Reuse of Advanced Materials,

1.3 Structural Materials;
- Metals and Metal Matrix Composites,
- Ceramics, Ceramic Matrix Composites and Advanced Glasses,
- Polymers and Polymer Matrix Composites,

1.4 Functional Materials for Magnetic, Superconducting, Optical, Electrical and Biomaterial Applications;
- Magnetic Materials,
- High Temperature Superconducting Materials,
- Electrical and Ionic Conducting Materials,
- Optical Materials,
- Biomaterials,

1.5 Mass Commodity Materials;
- Packaging Materials,
- New Construction Industry Materials.

AREA 2: DESIGN AND MANUFACTURING

The aim is to improve the capability of industry to design and manufacture products which are functional, cost-effective, of good quality, reliable, maintainable, and environmentally and socially acceptable. The sub-areas are:

2.1 Design of Products and Processes;
- Innovative Design Tools and Techniques,
- Design Methodologies for Complex Components,
- Design for Reliability,

2.2 Manufacturing;
- Tools, Techniques and Systems for High Quality Manufacturing,
- Manufacturing Techniques for Industrial Use of Advanced Materials,
- Integrated Approach to Chemical Engineering,

2.3 Engineering and Management Strategies for the Whole Product Life-Cycle;
- Design Integrating Strategies,
- Engineering,
- Human Factors in Engineering and Manufacturing Management.

AREA 3: AERONAUTICS RESEARCH

The objective is to strengthen the technology base of the European aeronautical industry, and to contribute to the knowledge base which supports actions to minimise environmental impact and enhance the safety and efficiency of aircraft operations. The sub-areas are:

3.1 Activity in Aeronautical Technology;
- Environment Related Technologies,
- Technologies of Aircraft Operation,
- Aerodynamics and Aerothermodynamics,
- Aeronautical Structures and Manufacturing Technologies,
- Avionic System Technologies
- Mechanical, Utility and Actuation Technologies.

EC Contribution

The programme was launched in December 1991 with a budget of 663 MECU over four years. The indicated allocation of funds is as follows:

AREA		MECU	%
1	Raw Materials and Recycling	80.0	12
	Materials	28.8	35
2	Design and Manufacturing	301.5	45
3	Aeronautics Research	53.0	8

BRITE/EURAM II was due to receive a top-up of 99 MECU in 1993.

The total indicative funding which, it has been indicated, will be devoted to research is:

	MECU	%
Industrial Research	483.8	77
Focused Fundamental Research	62.8	10
Co-operative Research	56.5	9
Concerted Actions	6.3	1
Feasibility Awards	6.3	1
Specific Training	12.6	2

Participation

All industrial companies, universities, other higher education institutes and research organisations from Member States are eligible to take part in the programme, except under the Feasibility Awards scheme, which is for SMEs only. The conditions for participation vary according to the form of support.

If a non-Member State has signed an agreement with the EC for full association with the programme, organisations from that country can "fully participate" in the programme, under the same conditions as organisations from Member States. If a non-Member State does not have a full association agreement, but does have an agreement with the EC for co-operation in science and technology, organisations from that country can participate on a project by project basis. These organisations will not however, receive any funding from the EC.

Industrial Applied Research

The principal form of support is through shared-cost action. Each project requires the participation of at least two legally independent enterprises based in at least two Member States, with the industrial organisations providing at least half their own costs. Universities, higher education institutes and similar organisations may receive up to 100% of their additional costs from the Commission. The total cost of each project will normally fall into the range of 1 to 5 MECU and involve at least ten man-years of activity.

Focused Fundamental Research (FFR)

In some technological areas, industrial progress may seem to be hindered by weakness in basic materials science. So few projects of this type will be sought. Up to 10% of the budget is available for this type of activity. Trans-frontier co-operation is still required, but an independent industrial enterprise need not be involved. However to ensure that there is an industrial focus, there must be a degree of industrial endorsement of the proposed research. Non-industrial participants in FFR projects may receive 100% of their additional expenditure from EC funds. The total cost of projects in this category will normally be in the range of 0.4 to 1 MECU total cost, and will involve at least ten man-years of activity.

Feasibility Awards for SMEs

This scheme enables SMEs to apply for EC support to establish the feasibility of a device, process or concept, as a means of enhancing their status before seeking partners for a proposal under the shared-cost action. The Commission will support up to 75% of the cost of research lasting up to nine months, with a ceiling of 30,000 ECU.

1b. CRAFT: CO-OPERATIVE RESEARCH ACTION FOR TECHNOLOGY

CRAFT is mainly aimed at SMEs who do not have their own research installations but need to solve common technical problems. Co-operative research enables these SMEs to join in assigning outside organisations (research associations, universities or commercial firms) to carry out research on their behalf. Projects in this category will normally cost in the range of 0.4 to 1 MECU, with a duration of one to two years. The EC funds up to 50% of full costs

The proposed R&D should conform with the objectives and contents of the BRITE/EURAM II programme. Research proposals must be:

- the result of a "bottom-up" approach, i.e. projects should be proposed by SMEs and reflect their current industrial problems or technological challenges;
- a response to common problems or R&D opportunities affecting a number of companies within one or more industrial sectors, rather than specific problems occurring in individual companies; and
- submitted by undertakings which are to take part in planning and piloting the research and implementing the results.

CRAFT operates in a simple and straightforward manner which is particularly suited to the needs of SMEs. It is implemented through an open call for proposals and, subject to the availability of funds, applicants are free to present their projects at any time within the two years following the publication of the call for proposals in the OJ.

The proposals are received in two steps.

In step one, outline proposals of three to four pages can be submitted at any time. At this stage the consortium must consist of at least two SMEs from different Member States. Then follows a definition and expansion period for selected proposals, lasting from three to four months. During this time proposer SMEs will have time to develop a larger consortium, define the detailed work programme and identify the organisation, or organisations who will carry out the work. This definition and expansion phase can be funded by the Commission through an expansion award of up to 15,000 ECU.

In step two final proposals of ten to twelve pages are submitted. The consortium must now consist of at least four SMEs from at least two Member States.

The scheme is open to all organisations in the EC. The prime proposer should be a SME, and research should be carried out in Europe. Organisations from non-member states who are members of COST (2), and organisations from Central and Eastern

European countries, are allowed to participate on a project by project basis. They cannot act as prime proposer nor receive any funding from the Commission, but they should contribute to the general administration of the programme.

Information and assistance can be found in the Supportive Network implemented through National Focal Points. The Expression of Interest (EOI) system can be used to look for partners before submitting an outline proposal. For selected outline proposals, the abstract, partners' names, estimated costs and proposers' contributions will be made public immediately after step one. Companies interested in joining the consortium, and R&D organisations willing to carry out the research, are invited to contact the prime proposers as soon as possible during the definition and expansion phase to discuss participation possibilities and conditions. Any organisation interested in the results of step one may consult:

- the Supportive Network of Focal Points,
- EUROKOM electronic mail,
- the Euro-Info Centres, or
- the Commission.

Targeted Research

This aims to co-ordinate a group of individual research projects whose specific objectives, arising from technical areas 1 and 2, converge in a common goal. This will require participation in concentration activities.

Concerted Actions

These are EC actions which co-ordinate individual research actions carried out by Member States. The EC may provide up to 100% of the co-ordination costs (maximum 400,000 ECU), but makes no contribution to the research costs.

Specific Training

Three types of specific training actions are covered:

i research fellowships in selected and ongoing projects, with subsidies paid to the host organisation to cover training expenses within the BRITE/EURAM project;

ii specific grants to enable existing project consortia to engage temporary research scientists, for better promotion of the results of the work; and

iii support for courses and training conferences for European technologists, in specific tasks related to the BRITE/EURAM programme.

Status Report

The first call for submissions of Industrial Research, FFR and Concerted Actions proposals (Areas 1, 2 and 3) was announced in December 1991 and closed on 3 April 1992. This call was allocated a budget of 302.5 MECU. The second call for proposals (Areas 1 and 2 only) was announced in October 1992, with a closing date of 26 February 1993: this was allocated 252.5 MECU. No further call is foreseen for BRITE/EURAM II for the time being.

The CRAFT and Feasibility Awards programmes were open until 31 December 1993.

More than 15% of submissions made following the 1991 call for proposals were ineligible for a variety of reasons, amongst which the most common were project size, unclear industrial relevance and non-compliance with international balance. The Commission has since put forward guidelines to clarify its criteria for eligibility. As far as project size is concerned, the total project cost is defined as the sum of all the partners' costs, which consist of full economic costs for industrial partners and research organisations, and marginal costs or full economic costs for universities and similar establishments. The total project cost must on no account exceed 5 MECU for an Industrial Research Project, nor 1 MECU for a FFP.

Applications

Proposals for research projects are invited in a formal call for proposals published in the OJ.

Management of the Programme is the responsibility of the Commission, assisted by a regulatory committee which is made up of representatives of the Member States and chaired by a representative of the Commission.

INFORMATION

UK

Mr G A Gadge
Department of Trade and Industry
Manufacturing Technologies Division 5B
151 Buckingham Palace Road
London SW1 9SS
Tel: 071 215 1555
Fax: 071 215 2909

For Aeronautics Only:
Dr R Kingcombe
Department of Trade and Industry
Aerospace Division
1/168 Yellow Zone
151 Buckingham Palace Road
London SW1 9SS
Fax: 071 215 2909

The UK CRAFT National Focal Point is:
Dr B Keown
Beta Technology Ltd
Riverside House
Weedon Street
Sheffield S9 2FT
Tel: 0272 422004
Fax: 0272 560950

Ireland

The Irish CRAFT National Focal Point and the contact for the Aeronautics Programme is:

EOLAS
The Irish Science and Technology Agency
Glasnevin
Dublin 9
Tel: 01 37 01 01
Fax: 01 37 96 20

EUROKOM
Computer Conferencing Service Centre
Belfield
Dublin 4
Tel: 01 697890
Fax: 01 838605

Commission

BRITE/EURAM
Commission of the European Communities
DG XII Directorate for Science Research and Development
Directorate for Technological Research
200 Rue de la Loi
B-1049 Brussels
Tel: INT+ 322 295 2345
Fax: INT+ 322 295 8046/296 5987
Tlx: 21877 COMEU B

CRAFT
Commission of the European Communities
DG XII for Science Research and Development
Directorate for Technological Research
BRITE/EURAM Programme (CRAFT)
Rue Montoyer 75
B-1040 Brussels
Tel: INT+ 322 299 11 11

EUROKOM
Avenue de la Joyeuse Entrée 1
B-1040 Brussels
Tel: INT+ 322-230 36 47
Fax: INT+ 322-280 01 32

2. MEASUREMENTS & TESTING: BUREAU COMMUNAUTAIRE DE REFERENCE (BCR)

Statutory Basis

Proposal from the Commission: OJ C 174, dated 16/7/90; amended COM (91) 503: OJ C 4/8, dated 8/1/92.

Objectives

The aim of this programme is to improve techniques of measurement, testing and chemical analysis, where they are not sufficiently accurate for different laboratories to agree their results; and where the techniques are inadequate to satisfy the new requirements of industry, or for monitoring the environment, or food quality and health matters.

Background

The Measurement and Testing Programme, forming part of the Third Framework Programme, is scheduled to run from late 1992 until 1994, and to follow on from the earlier BCR programmes.

Sound, accurate and reliable measurements, be they physical, chemical or biological in nature, are essential to the functioning of modern society. Without them industries, particularly high-technology ones, cannot operate; trade is impaired by disputes, health care becomes empirical and legislation cannot be implemented successfully. Measurements and technical specifications are being harmonised, by means of EC Directives or by the establishment of European norms as part of the process of completing the single market, but this alone does not solve all the problems. The measurements and analyses required to implement these Directives and norms are sometimes so difficult that, even when they apply the same methods, different laboratories may still achieve very different results. If laboratories disagree over results, Directives and norms cannot result in harmonisation.

The Measurements and Testing Programme aims to improve and harmonise techniques of measurement and analysis carried out in the Member States, so as to eliminate discrepancies which could be the source of disputes and which would hinder the operation of the single market. Through such harmonisation and improvement in methods, the programme aims to contribute to:

- the ease of circulation of agricultural and industrial products in the EC;
- improvements in the means of monitoring environment and health; and
- the resolution of the new challenges faced by industry.

Programme Content

The technical content of the Programme covers a wide variety of topics relating to the measurement of physical quantities (applied metrology) and chemical analysis. It will be directed towards four main areas:

i Support Regulations and Directives

These will develop, improve or harmonise the test methods required for the preparation of new Regulations and Directives concerning agriculture, environment, health and industrial products;

ii Sectoral Problems

The work here will include collaborative projects to solve problems of measurements and testing arising in the course of the preparation of new European standards, collaborative projects to solve measurement problems arising in industry in the application of standards and the organisation of inter-laboratory comparisons to facilitate mutual recognition agreements between testing laboratories;

iii Common Means of Calibration for the EC

For fields such as agriculture, food, environment and bio-medical analyses, reference materials will be developed so that laboratories can measure their analyses or tests with a common standard of reference. Similarly, transfer standards will be developed for the smaller national meteorological laboratories so that they can measure their results against primary standards held by larger organisations;

iv Development of New Methods of Measurement

This may include techniques for calibration in automated manufacturing systems, methods of measurement in micro-metrology, food control, the chemical form of pollutants, and for certifying reference materials; as well as R&D into principles of measurement leading to new instrumentation.

Implementation

The projects are implemented largely by shared-cost actions, but also by concerted actions and accompanying measures. To help disseminate the results of the projects, and to ensure the effectiveness of the programme in improving the quality of test laboratories, the following measures are used:

- training of specialists in EC laboratories;
- collaboration among national quality assurance schemes;
- storage and distribution of reference materials certified at EC level;
- workshops and seminars; and
- publicity for the application of results.

By the nature of the Programme, results are widely disseminated through reports and similar mechanisms. In the field of analytical chemistry, most projects so far have produced results in the form of certified reference materials which are then sold by the Commission, although the range of activities in this field is now being broadened.

EC Contribution

The Measurement and Testing Programme has a budget of about 53 MECU, allocated approximately as follows:

Area 1:	Support for Regulations and Directives	13.4 MECU
Area 2:	Sectoral testing problems	12.8 MECU
Area 3:	Support for means of calibration	13.4 MECU
Area 4:	Developments of new methods of measurement	13.4 MECU

Measurements and Testing was due to receive a top-up of 19 MECU during 1993.

Participation

The Programme is open to all persons and organisations established in the Member States. Industrial firms including SMEs, universities, academic institutions and research associations are participating in activities.

If a non-Member State has signed an agreement with the EC for full association with the Programme, organisations from that country can "fully participate" in the Programme under the same conditions as organisations from Member States. If a non-Member State does not have a full association agreement, but does have some agreement on Science & Technology co-operation with the EC, organisations from that country can participate in the programme on a project-by-project basis, but they will not receive any funding from the EC.

The choice of projects is guided by criteria which include the economic importance of the problem to be addressed, its role in intra-Community trade and its relevance to EC policies.

Status Report

Following discussions between the Commission and the Member States on the technical nature of the Measurement and Testing Programme, and consultations with the European Parliament, funding was approved by the Council of Ministers in April 1992.

In July 1992, the Commission issued a call for project proposals in all four areas of the programme, with a deadline of September 1992. Proposals were evaluated by the Commission's panel of independent expert advisers in October-December 1992, and projects for support were chosen on the basis of this evaluation.

Sufficient proposals of quality were identified to commit all the available funds. In Areas 1, 2 and 3,368 proposals were received, requesting a total funding of 110 MECUs. Of these proposals, 350 were eligible and of this number 100 were classified by the experts as A1 (outstanding), and 75 as A2 (excellent, but requiring minor modifications). However, owing to the small budget, only some of the A1 proposals could be funded. Two hundred and three proposals were received for Area 4, requesting a total funding of 114 MECUs. Of these 191 were eligible; 27 were classified as A1, and 30 as A2. Funding was available for only 12 of the A1 proposals.

The first contracts for Areas 1,2 and 3 started in January 1993, and the first for Area 4 started in March 1993.

A series of additional projects from Areas 1, 2, 3 and 4 was to have been funded by the end of 1993. The selection of these projects was discussed with representatives of the Member States in the CEN Advisory Committee on 11 May 1993, and contract negotiations were scheduled to take place between June and September. Moreover, an additional funding has been made available which will allow all the remaining A1 proposals to be funded in 1994, as well as some of the A2 proposals after the necessary re-evaluation.

It is not currently anticipated that there will be a further call for proposals within the Third Framework Programme. On the other hand it is never certain when more funds will be made available. Notice of any future calls will be made through CORDIS (the R&D database), and specifically through TEDIS, the on-line version of the OJ.

A successor Measurement and Testing Programme is expected to start in 1995 under the Fourth Framework Programme, with details available in the second half of 1994.

Applications

The Measurements and Testing Programme is implemented through calls for proposals published in the OJ.

Management of the Programme is the responsibility of the Commission assisted by a Programme Management Committee. This is composed of representatives of each Member State and provides advice to the Commission regularly on priorities, the implementation of the programme and the selection of projects.

INFORMATION

UK

Policy & Programme Co-ordination:
Matthew Clark
Department of Trade and Industry
Research & Technology Policy Division 1
3rd Floor 151 Buckingham Palace Road
London SW1 9SS
Tel: 071 215 1424

Physical Measurements & Applied Metrology:
Dr Jim Bell
Department of Trade and Industry
International Liaison Office
National Physical Laboratory
Teddington
Middlesex TW11 OLW
Tel: 081 943 7120

Chemical Measurements:
Dr R Walker
Department of Trade and Industry
Laboratory of the Government Chemist
Queens Road, Teddington
Middlesex TW11 OLY
Tel: 081 943 7612
Fax: 081 943 2767
Tlx: 9312132476 GC G

IRELAND

Mr C O'Toole
EOLAS
The Irish Science and Technology Agency
Ballymun Road, Glasnevin
Dublin 9
Tel: 01 37 01 01
Fax: 01 37 01 72

Dr M Walsh
State Laboratory
Abbotstown
Dublin 15
Tel: 01 8217700

COMMISSION

Commission of the European Communities
DG XII-C
200 Rue de la Loi
B-1040 Brussels
Fax: INT+ 322 295 8072

Physical Measurements
Group leader: Dr D Gould
Tel: INT+ 322 295 9313

Acoustics, Temperature, Construction Products
Dr T Fairly
Tel: INT+ 322 296 5197

Electricity, Magnetism and Optics
Dr P Salieri
Tel: INT+ 322 296 2951

Mechanical Metrology
Mr C Helmarth
Tel: INT+ 322 296 2720

Surface/Interface Analysis, Flow Measurements:
Dr R Campano
Tel: INT+ 322 295 9580

Chemical and Biomedical Measurements
Clinical and Biological Analysis
Dr C Dirscherl
Tel: INT+ 322 296 4928

Environment - Inorganic Analysis
Dr P Quevauviller
Tel: INT+ 322 296 3351

Environment - Organic Analysis, Microbiology
Dr E A Maier
Tel: INT+ 322 295 6138

Environment - Workplace Hygiene
Dr S Vandendriessche
Tel: INT+ 322 295 9312

Food/Agriculture - Organic Analysis
Dr A Boenke,
Tel: INT+ 322 296 0756

Food/Agriculture - Toxicity Testing
Mrs U Faure
Tel: INT+ 322 296 3334

Medical Devices/Instrumentation
Mr C Profilis
Tel: INT+ 322 295 9735

Medical Industrial Products
Mr C Profilis
Tel: INT+ 322 295 9735

Chapter 17.3

Management of Natural Resources

This group of programmes covers:

1. The Environment Programme and
2. MAST II: Marine Science and Technology.

1. THE ENVIRONMENT PROGRAMME

Statutory Basis

Council Decision 91/354/EEC: OJ L 192/29, dated 16/7/91.

The present work programme is prepared in compliance with Article 5, paragraph 3, of the Council Decision adopting the Programme, and may be updated where and when necessary.

Objectives

The aim of the Environment Programme is to develop the scientific knowledge, and technical know-how, the Community needs to carry out its role concerning the environment.

Background

The specific programme of environmental research under the Third Framework Programme (1990-94) continues the work of the two environment-related Programmes, "Science and Technology for Environmental Protection" (STEP) and "European Programme on Climatology and Natural Hazards" (EPOCH), under the Second Framework Programme 1987-91. Under the new Environment Programme, greater emphasis is placed on problems of a global nature, while the economic and social aspects of environmental issues are addressed for the first time.

Programme Content

The Programme is dived into four areas.

AREA 1. PARTICIPATION IN GLOBAL CHANGE PROGRAMMES
This provides a basis for contribution to global programmes with a focus on topics more specifically of European interest.

Research areas include climatic change (natural and anthropogenic), climatic change impacts, global changes in atmospheric chemistry (stratospheric ozone, tropospheric physics and chemistry), bio-geo-chemical cycles and ecosystem dynamics.

AREA 2: TECHNOLOGIES & ENGINEERING FOR THE ENVIRONMENT
This includes assessments of environmental quality and monitoring, technologies for protecting and rehabilitating the environment (including recycling, with the exception of non-ferrous metals recycling, which is handled within the Industrial and Materials Technologies Programme), major industrial hazards, environmental protection and conservation of Europe's cultural heritage.

AREA 3: ECONOMIC & SOCIAL ASPECTS OF ENVIRONMENTAL ISSUES
This research Area aims to increase understanding of the social and economic causes and impacts of environmental change, and to provide a basis for the formulation of environmental strategies to help achieve sustainable development. Particular attention is devoted to the study of EC and Member States' policies, activities, research and development and other programmes in this field, in order to provide effective co-ordination where appropriate.

The key elements in this Area include the human being, nature and society (perception, knowledge and behaviour, cultural, ethical, religious, philosophical and historical aspects); environmental policy; and international aspects.

AREA 4: TECHNOLOGICAL & NATURAL RISKS
This involves researching possible opportunities for risk reduction in Europe, through a Community-wide vulnerability assessment and development of protection strategies. Included are the study of risks from agricultural technologies and land-use practices to soil, surface and groundwater quality, regional aspects of ecosystem protection, environment and human health, risks to health and the environment from chemicals, seismic hazard and volcanic risk, wildfire prevention and desertification.

EC Contribution

The total funding for the Programme is 414 MECU. Of this 150 MECU is reserved for "direct action" at the European Commission's Joint Research Centre (JRC), while 261.4 MECU is to be used for 'indirect action', comprising shared-cost contracts and concerted action. The remaining 2.6 MECU is for disseminating and exploiting results. Although the official decision is pending, it is likely that a further top-up of 55 MECU will be made available for expenditure under the direct action category of this programme.

The following breakdown shows the expenditure relating to the indirect action component:

Area 1 : Participation in Global Change Programmes	40%
Area 2 : Technologies & Engineering for the Environment	25%
Area 3 : Economic and Social Impacts	6%
Area 4 : Technological and Natural Risks	29%.

Participation

Industrial firms, SMEs, universities, academic institutions and research organisations are eligible to participate in shared-cost projects, which must involve at least two mutually independent partners established in different Member States. Concerted actions and accompanying measures will also be used to implement this programme. Organisations in certain non-EC countries which have Science & Technology agreements with the EC will be able to participate in the programme, but not to receive any EC funding.

In order to ensure effective and realistic project management, the number of partners should not normally exceed five.

Status Report

The first call for proposals, published in July 1991, covered all areas of the Programme except that dealing with technologies for the protection and rehabilitation of the environment. This Area was subject to a separate call for proposals in April 1992. A second call for proposals was published in early 1993, with a deadline of 19 July 1993.

Applications

Proposals should be sent to the Commission.

INFORMATION

UK

Dr A Davies
Department of the Environment,
A3.19 Romney House
43 Marsham Street
London SW1P 3PY
Tel: 071 276 8365
Fax: 071 276 8355
Tlx: 22221 DOEMAR G

D J Carson
Hadley Centre for Climate Prediction & Research Meteorological Office
London Road
Bracknell
Berks RG12 2SZ
Tel: 0344 856611
Fax: 0344 854898

IRELAND

Grainne Ni Uid
EOLAS
The Irish Science and Technology Agency
Glasnevin
Dublin 9
Tel: 01 37 01 01
Fax: 01 37 01 72/37 96 20
Tlx: 32501 OLAS EI

COMMISSION
Commission of the European Communities
DG XII-E (ref.: Environment Call for Proposals)
Rue Montoyer 75
B-1040 Brussels
Tel: INT +322 299 1111 (exchange)
Fax: INT+ 322 296 3024

Dr A Sors (Socio-economic Aspects)
Tel: INT+ 322-295 7659
Fax: INT+ 322-296 3024

Dr S Cole (Major Industrial Hazards)
Tel: INT+ 322 295 0347
Fax: INT+ 322 296 3024

Dr R Fantechi (Climatology and Natural Hazards)
Tel: INT+ 322 295 5735
Fax: INT+ 322 296 3024

2. MARINE SCIENCE AND TECHNOLOGY (MAST II)

Statutory Background

Council Decision 91/351/EEC: OJ L 192/1, dated 16/7/91.

The present work programme is prepared in compliance with Article 5, paragraph 3, of the Council Decision adopting the MAST II programme, and may be updated where and when necessary.

Objectives

This Programme aims to contribute to the establishment of a scientific and technological basis for the exploration, exploitation, management and protection of European coastal waters and the seas surrounding EC Member States. Its specific objectives are:

- to contribute to a better knowledge of the marine environment and its variability, in order to improve its management and protection and to predict change;
- to encourage the development of new technologies for the exploration, protection and exploitation of marine resources;
- to improve transnational co-ordination and co-operation amongst marine R&D programmes in the Member States, to help increase the effectiveness of these programmes through better use of research facilities, and to promote the transfer of expertise and knowledge;
- to provide the technical basis for, and encourage the development of, common norms, standards and design guidelines;
- to facilitate training and exchange of personnel; and
- to assist (as far as possible) EC participation in international ocean programmes.

Background

The sea plays a vital role in the EC's culture and economics. Eleven of the Member States have coastlines, and 90% of the EC's external commerce is accounted for by maritime trade. The sea is essential to food production, transport, resource exploitation, local climate, recreation and tourism, but is the victim of increasing levels of waste disposal. All this means that the oceans and seas around Europe are being used intensively and at an ever-increasing rate. Policy-makers therefore need detailed knowledge of basic marine processes in order to safeguard marine ecosystems from damage. Since those ecosystems know no national boundaries, international co-operation in the field of marine processes is paramount

Accordingly, the EC's Marine Science and Technology Programme aims to introduce the necessary Community dimension to the various on-going research activities. MAST II is a direct development of MAST I (1989-92) which was a pilot programme on marine science and technology. MAST II runs from 1991 to 1994.

Programme Content

MAST II is divided into five Areas.

AREA 1: MARINE SCIENCE

The objective is to study marine processes and fluxes in European coastal waters, in the seas surrounding the EC, in the North Atlantic Ocean and in sub-polar Arctic seas. Topics include the circulation and exchange of water masses, bio-geo-chemical cycles and fluxes, interface and boundary processes, biological processes and marine geosciences.

AREA 2: COASTAL ZONE SCIENCE & ENGINEERING

The aim here is to gain a better understanding of coastal physical processes and morphodynamics, and to promote the application of modern principles in coastal engineering and management.

AREA 3: MARINE TECHNOLOGY

This aims to encourage the development of existing and new instruments required by marine science, and to promote enabling technologies necessary for the advancement of marine science and related future industrial developments. Topics include scientific instrumentation for underwater acoustics, the exploitation of marine biological resources and enabling technologies required for such areas as underwater signal transmission and imaging, marine applications of modern robotics, and testing advanced materials or components for use in marine instrumentation.

AREA 4: SUPPORTING INITIATIVES

These include the exchange of European ocean data and information on the preparation of norms and standards for marine science and technology, modelling co-ordination, co-ordination of research vessels and equipment, the design of large scale facilities, advanced training and new approaches to surveying and mapping.

AREA 5: LARGE TARGETED PROJECTS
This aims to address problems requiring large-scale multi-disciplinary co-ordinated research efforts. At present two projects are planned: topic 5.1 focuses on the Mediterranean and topic 5.2 on the North Atlantic.

Since oceans and seas cross national frontiers, MAST must have a strong international dimension to be effective. It therefore aims to co-ordinate the participation of European marine laboratories and research centres in the large international programmes such as the Joint Global Flux Study, the International Geosphere Biosphere Programme and the World Ocean Circulation Experiment.

Under the European Economic Area (EEA) agreement, bilateral agreements concluded between the EC and EFTA under the Second Framework Programme are set to be replaced by the EEA, which will increase co-operation between the EC and EFTA in several areas, including R&D. From the date when the EEA comes into operation, companies and institutions in EFTA countries can participate fully in the EC's MAST Programme, sharing the rights and obligations of Community partners.

EC Contribution

The budget forecast for the duration of the Programme is:

Area 1	Marine Science	33.0 MECU
Area 2	Coastal Zone Science & Engineering	13.0 MECU
Area 3	Marine Technology	27.0 MECU
Area 4	Supporting Initiatives	4.5 MECU
Area 5	Large Targeted Projects	14.0 MECU

MAST II was scheduled to receive a top-up of 14 MECU during 1993.

Participation

The programme is open to all persons and organisations established in the EC, including industrial firms, universities, higher education institutes and research organisations. Non-member States can also participate if they have an agreement on Science & Technology co-operation with the EC and will receive EC funding only if specified under the agreement.

Research in areas 1, 2, 3 and 5 will be implemented by means of shared-cost contracts and concerted actions. Most of the supporting initiatives described in Area 4 will be carried out by a variety of accompanying measures.

Status Report

Calls for proposals in areas 1, 2, 3, 5.1 and 5.2 are currently closed and projects have been selected. Information is awaited concerning new calls. Area 4 is not open to a call for proposals as the process of adopting ideas in this Area is meant to be continuous over the duration of the programme.

INFORMATION

UK

Mr R Laverick
Technology Programmes and Services 4E
Department of Trade and Industry
Room 1049
151 Buckingham Palace Road
London SW1 9SS
Tel: 071 215 1402
Fax: 071 215 2909

Technology & Engineering Enquiries

J Grant
Marine Technology Directorate Ltd
19 Buckingham Street
London WC2N 6EF
Tel: 071 321 0674
Fax: 071 930 4323

General Enquiries and Marine Science

Dr R Paul
Natural Environment Research Council
Marine and Atmospheric Sciences Directorate
Polaris House,
North Star Avenue
Swindon SN2 1EU
Tel: 0793 411 616

Office Science & Technology Room 1/6

Mr C de Grouchy
Albany House
84/86 Petty France
London SW1H 9ST
Tel: 071 276 2077

IRELAND

L Fegan
EOLAS
Irish Science and Technology Agency
Ocean Services Division
Glasnevin
Dublin 9
Tel: 01 37 01 01

COMMISSION

Commission of the European Communities
DG XII/E (MAST)
SDME 3/48
75 Rue Montoyer,
B-1040 Brussels
Tel: INT+ 322 295 6787
Fax: INT+ 322 296 3024

Chapter 17.4

Life Sciences and Technologies

This group of programmes covers:

1. BIOTECH
2. AIR: Agriculture, Agro-Industry and Fisheries
3. BIOMED I: Biomedical and Health Research Programme and
4. STD 3: Life Sciences for Developing Countries.

1. BIOTECH

Statutory Basis

Council Decision 92/218/EEC: OJ L 107, dated 24/4/92.

Objectives

This Programme aims to reinforce basic biological knowledge as the common and integrated foundation needed for applications in agriculture, industry, health, nutrition and the environment.

Background

The BIOTECH Programme for research in the field of biotechnology, covers the period 1992-94. It complements the BRIDGE Programme which was launched in January 1990 to end in December 1993.

BIOTECH is oriented more towards basic biology than BRIDGE was and is a programme of prenormative research, emphasising the safety assessment of new techniques and novel products. It aims to foster transnational research, to add to basic biological knowledge and to develop application technologies for agriculture, industry, health, nutrition and the environment.

Programme Content

The Programme supports research in the three main areas:

i approaches at the Molecular Level, including the structure and function of proteins involved in the essential functions of living cells, studies of gene structure and function and the expression of genes.

ii approaches at the Cell and Organism Level, including cell regeneration mechanisms, knowledge and control of cell development, methods of in vitro testing of the toxicity of new molecules and improvement of knowledge of the metabolism of plants, micro-organisms and animal livestock and of intercellular communication systems; and

iii the Ecology and Biology of Populations, including the impact of biotechnology on the environment and problems of conservation of genetic resources.

Provision will be made for applications of information technology to these areas.

EC Contribution

The Programme was originally allocated 162.36 MECU, but a further 22 MECU was added at a later date.

Participation

The programme is open to all persons and organisations established in the Member States including SMEs, large industrial firms, universities, higher education institutions and research organisations. Proposals must involve at least two independent partners established in different Member States.

Status Report

The first call for proposals was made in July 1992 for research contracts due to start in February 1993. Two final calls were then made, with respective deadlines of 31 August and 15 December 1993. These calls cover only a restricted number of scientific areas, as follows.

The 15 December deadline covers the following topics:

Area 1: Molecular Approaches
Protein structure and function; and expression of genes;

Area 2: Cellular and Organism Approaches
Metabolism of microbes: essential physiological traits; and cellular regeneration, reproduction and development in farm animals; and

Area 3: Ecology and Population Biology
Ecological implications of biotechnology.

Applications

Proposals should be sent to the Commission.

Management of the Programme is the responsibility of the Commission, assisted by a Regulatory Committee composed of representatives of each Member State, which gives regular advice to the Commission on the Programme, including the final selection of projects.

The Office of Science & Technology has led the UK's participation in the programme.

INFORMATION

UK

Academic Institutions
Mr N Ashcroft
Agricultural and Food Research Council
Central Office
Polaris House
North Star Avenue
Swindon SN2 1UH
Tel: 0793 413027

Industry
Dr I Lawrence
DTI Biotechnology Unit
Laboratory of the Government Chemist
Queens Road, Teddington
Middlesex TW11 0LY
Tel: 081 943 7591
Fax: 081 943 7304
Tlx: 931 213 2476 GC G

Ireland

J Ryan
BioResearch Ireland
EOLAS
Glasnevin
Dublin 9
Tel: 01 370177/370101
Fax: 01 370176

L. Donnelly
Teagasc
National Dairy Products Research Centre
Moorepark
Fermoy
Co. Cork
Tel: 025 31 422
Fax: 025 32 563

Commission

Mr E Magnien
Commission of the European Communities
DG XII F-2
Genetics and Biotechnology Division
200 Rue de la Loi
B-1049 Brussels
Tel: 010 322 295 9347
Fax: 010 322 295 5365
E-Mail : Etienne_Magnien_CEC-BRIDGE @ eurokom,ie

2. AGRICULTURE, AGRO-INDUSTRY AND FISHERIES (AIR)

Statutory Basis

Council Decision 91/504/EEC: OJ L 265/33 dated 21/9/91.

Objectives

The main objective is to provide a better concordance between the production of land and water-based biological resources and their use by consumers and industry. The Programme aims to upgrade and diversify agricultural and silvicultural products, to enhance the competitiveness of agricultural and agri-food undertakings, to contribute to better rural and forestry management and to ensure proper protection for the environment. It also promotes pre-normative research to establish a sound scientific basis for setting standards, particularly for food.

Background

The Programme, which runs until 31 December 1994, forms part of the Third Framework Programme (1990-94). It continues and supplements the activities formerly supported by the separate Competitiveness of Agriculture and Management of Agricultural Resources Programme (CAMAR), the European Collaborative Linkage of Agriculture and Industry through Research Programme (ECLAIR), the Food Science and Technology Programme (FLAIR), the biomass section of the programme for Non-Nuclear Energies and Rational Use of Energies (JOULE) and the renewable raw materials, forestry and wood products (FOREST) section of the Raw Materials and Recycling Programme.

Programme Content

The Programme identifies four areas of interest.

AREA 1: PRIMARY PRODUCTION IN AGRICULTURE, HORTICULTURE, FORESTRY, FISHERIES & AQUACULTURE
This includes: improvements to help achieve high quality, commercially viable products for both food and non-food purposes; improved management, particularly in animal health and welfare and in remedies for over-fishing and work on soil erosion, loss of fertility and deforestation for underdeveloped areas.

AREA 2: INPUTS TO AGRICULTURE, HORTICULTURE, FORESTRY, FISHERIES AND AQUACULTURE
This includes: more profitable but environmentally-friendly inputs; improved strains of animals, plants and fish (for better pest resistance, yield and quality); integrated and biological pest control systems and new systems for monitoring and control.

AREA 3: PROCESSING OF BIOLOGICAL RAW MATERIALS FROM AGRICULTURE, HORTICULTURE, FORESTRY, FISHERIES AND AQUACULTURE
This includes new separation, extraction and processing methods for raw materials, giving more useful products and less waste, particularly where they improve safety and maintain or increase the nutritional value of processed food.

AREA 4: END USE AND PRODUCTS

This includes: work to give a better understanding of the characteristics required in end-use products; more reliable manufacturing processes (particularly in toxicological and quality control of foodstuffs); new processing technologies and biologically based chemical substances, with particular emphasis on biodegradable materials.

EC Contribution

The original budget was 333 MECU, but a top-up of 44 MECU was scheduled for 1993.

Participation

Participants must be bodies such as universities, research organisations and industrial firms, including SMEs. In most cases participants must be established within the EC, but other members of COST may be permitted to participate. In all cases at least two independent partners established in different Member States are required.

Status Report

A second call for proposals was published in the OJ on 2 July 1992, with a closing date of 30 October 1992. A third call was due to be published during 1993. No further calls are anticipated until a new programme is announced, probably in 1995.

Applications

The Commission is responsible for the management of the Programme and is assisted by a committee of representatives of the Member States.

INFORMATION

UK
Mr D Woodward
MAFF
Room 107, Nobel House
17 Smith Square
London SW1P 3JR
Tel: 071 238 5599
Fax: 071 238 6591

Commission
Commission of the European Communities
200 Rue de la Loi
B-1049 Brussels
Tel: INT +322 299 1111 (exchange)

3. BIOMEDICAL AND HEALTH RESEARCH PROGRAMME: BIOMED I

Statutory Basis

Council Decision 91/505/EEC: OJ L 267/25, dated 24/9/91.

Objectives

This aims to improve the efficacy of medical and health research and technology (R&D) in the Member States, particularly by better co-ordination of the Member States' R&D activities and the application of the results through EC co-operation and a pooling of resources.

Background

BIOMED I follows on from and builds upon the fourth Medical and Health Research Programme, MHR 4 (1987-91).

Programme Content

AREA 1: DEVELOPMENT OF CO-ORDINATED RESEARCH ON PREVENTION, CARE & HEALTH SYSTEMS.

This covers harmonisation of methodologies and protocols in epidemiological, biological, clinical and technological research, including drugs and the administration of medicines, occupational medicine, biomedical technology and health services research.

AREA 2: MAJOR HEALTH PROBLEMS AND DISEASES OF GREAT SOCIO-ECONOMIC IMPACT

Major health problems and economically and socially significant disease groupings will be considered, particularly the following:

- AIDS;
- cancer;
- cardiovascular disease;
- mental illness and neurological disease and
- the ageing process and age-related health problems and handicaps.

AREA 3: HUMAN GENOME ANALYSIS

This area subsumed the Human Genome Analysis Programme (1990-92) in June 1992. Research will be aimed at completing and integrating the genetic and physical maps. The genetic basis for biological functions will be also be studied, and a co-ordinating mechanism to sequence portions of the genome of major biological interest is to be established.

AREA 4: RESEARCH ON BIOMEDICAL ETHICS

This area involves the study of problems affecting research carried out in areas 1 to 3 of the Programme and the possible applications of the results of that research. Work will be done to evaluate questions of biomedical ethics linked to the present research programme on biomedicine and health, and to evaluate the social impact of the Programme and the risks, including the technological risks, which might be associated with it.

Support in areas 1, 2 and 4 will be by concerted action only. Shared-cost contracts will be available under area 3. Accompanying measures include seminars, workshops, conferences, studies and training fellowships.

EC Contribution

The total budget available for the BIOMED I Programme is 133 MECU, divided between the four research areas as follows:

Area 1:	Development of Co-ordinated Research on Prevention, Care & Health Systems	27.5 MECU
Area 2:	Major Health Problems and Diseases of Great Socio-Economic Impact (with 25 MECU for AIDS research)	72.0 MECU
Area 3:	Human Genome Analysis	27.5 MECU
Area 4:	Research on Biomedical Ethics	4.6 MECU

BIOMED was scheduled to receive a top-up of 18 MECU during 1993.

Participation

The programme is open to all persons and organisations established in the EC. Projects must involve at least two independent partners, established in different Member States. Non-member States which have signed an agreement with the EC for full association with the programme are Austria, Finland, Norway, Sweden, Switzerland and Turkey.

Status Report

The first call for declarations of intent to participate in the Programme (areas 1, 2 and 4 only) was announced during October 1991, with a deadline of 31 January 1992. Following the submission of full proposals and evaluation by peer review during the summer, 114 projects were awarded funding.

The second and final call for full proposals was published in two parts:

i Area 3: Human Genome Analysis
the only call for proposals in this area was published during December 1992 with a deadline of 29 January 1993;

ii Areas 1, 2 and 4:
the second and final call for proposals in these areas was published during December 1992 with a deadline of 26 February 1993.

Evaluation of the proposals received under calls (i) and (ii) above was scheduled to be completed in time for successful projects to start in October 1993.

There is an open call for fellowships; the selection committee will meet three times a year in March, June and November, with submission deadlines of 15 January, 15 April and 15 August respectively.

Applications

The management of the Programme is the responsibility of DG XII. In addition, the Committee of an Advisory Nature (CAN), consisting of government representatives and experts from each Member State, acts as an independent advisory body and approves the Commission's proposals on issues such as evaluation and participation of third countries. The UK is represented by the Medical Research Council (MRC) and by the Department of Health, MRC having the lead responsibility.

INFORMATION

UK
Mrs G Breen
International Section
Medical Research Council
20 Park Crescent
London W1N 4AL
Tel: 071 636 5422
Fax: 071 436 6179

The MRC operates the UK mailing list for the Biomedical and Health Research Newsletter which is published by the EC. Requests to be added to the list should be made to the International Section at the address above.

Ireland
J V O'Gorman
The Health Research Board
73 Lower Baggot Street
Dublin 2
Tel: 01 76 11 76
Fax: 01 61 18 65

Commission
The Head of the Medical Research Division
DG XII-E-4
Commission of the European Communities
200 Rue de la Loi
B-1049 Brussels
Tel: INT+ 322 295 4041
Fax: INT+ 322 295 5365

4. LIFE SCIENCES FOR DEVELOPING COUNTRIES: STD 3

Statutory Basis

Council Decision 91/366/EEC: OJ L 196/38, dated 19/7/91.

Objectives

The objective is to increase research capacity in both the developing countries and the Member States, in areas defined as having priority for Third World Development, and to improve co-ordination with the EC.

Background

STD forms part of the Framework Programmes. The main objective of STD 1 (1982-86) was to support Europe's strong tropical research potential. In addition STD 2 (1987-91) sought to build up the R&D capacities of developing countries. The current programme (1991-94) seeks more specifically to boost the input of R&D in development. It is not linked to a specific Community co-operation policy (such as ACP, Mediterranean countries, or ALA), but seeks to stimulate simultaneous study in various parts of the world of specific scientific issues, which can contribute to progress in all developing countries.

The general objectives are:

- to raise the scientific community's awareness of the scale of problems in the developing world;
- to improve the co-ordination of Member States' R&D initiatives for development, and set up consultation between scientists;
- to ease the introduction of scientific and technical considerations in the development of co-operation activities supported by the EC and its Member States;
- to contribute to steering the research of European institutions specialising in the study of the tropics and to ensure their adherence to EC development and technological research strategies;
- to raise the level of excellence of institutions and scientific teams in developing countries, enabling them to be full partners in research and thus reducing North-South disparities in science and technology; and
- to contribute to the emergence of a "critical mass" of national researchers able to carry out original research in areas useful for the development process.

Programme Content

In order to ensure maximum efficiency, the STD Programme has focused on major development problems, and since 1982 has covered two main areas:

AREA 1: IMPROVEMENT OF LIVING CONDITIONS

This covers:

i the reduction of food shortages by improving agricultural production, both plant and animal;

ii the protection of natural environments; and

iii the development of agricultural products with high economic value both locally and for export; forests and forestry; and production of bioenergy.

AREA 2: IMPROVEMENTS IN HEALTH

This covers:

i the prevention and treatment of the predominant diseases in developing countries including perfection of new methods of diagnosis, development of new medicines, development and adaptation of existing vaccines and the study of parasitology, haemoglobinoses, diarrhoea, AIDS etc.;

ii developing health care systems appropriate to the rural and urban environment of the developing countries, including the selection, evaluation and validation of health strategies, management and financing of health services etc.; and

iii nutritional matters, including research to develop the scientific basis necessary for improving the nutritional condition of underprivileged populations by means of a multi-disciplinary approach between medicine, agronomy, economics and the social sciences.

Projects undertaken in both areas will take full account of the systems under which they operate and will be compatible with sustainable development. In this context, fundamental research projects in Area 1 which allow an improvement in knowledge and methods could also be eligible. In Area 2 no proposals involving human beings will be considered unless provided with the ethical clearance required by the Helsinki Declaration.

EC Contribution

A fund of 111 MECU is available for 1991-94 allocated as follows: research and accompanying measures, 71.43 MECU for agriculture and 38.46 MECU for medicine, health and nutrition. The remaining 1.11 MECU represent STD 3's contribution to the centralised scheme for the dissemination and exploitation of the results of EC research.

Life sciences were scheduled to receive a top-up of 15 MECU in late 1993.

Participation

From the outset, STD was open only to research projects which involved at least two teams, one belonging to the EC and the other from a developing country. Under the Third Framework Programme (1991-94), each project is obliged to pool the potential of at least two EC teams and at least one from a developing country. Scientists in the developing countries have direct access to STD programme funds from the EC budget, and can thus define their research priorities and choose their partners themselves.

Status Report

For STD 3 there were three calls for proposals, in 1991, 1992 and 1993 respectively. The third call for proposals came out in June 1993, with a deadline for receipt of proposals of 30 November 1993. The scientific and technical areas on which this third call focused are:

- sustainable use and management of natural resources;
- farming systems and their relation to the socio-economic environment;
- improvement of perennial crops, including trees;

- storage and processing of food;
- vaccine research; and
- research on intervention and implementation of disease control strategies.

Priority is given to projects which concern problems common to several developing countries and, in consequence, allow a broader approach to tackling those problems. This includes topics of regional significance, particularly those which have been identified by regional organisations (or other bodies with regional influence), as being of primary importance for the region's socio-economic development.

Special attention is given to selecting projects involving institutions which appear able and willing to maintain research momentum when the programme support from the EC ceases.

Applications

Joint Research Projects are selected on the basis of replies to calls published in the OJ. Project proposals are to be sent to the Commission.

INFORMATION

UK
Overseas Development Administration
Eland House
Stag Place
London SW1E 5DH
Tel: 071 273 0090

Ireland
Dr V O'Gorman
Chief Executive
Health Research Board
73 Lower Baggot Street
Dublin 2
Tel: 01 761 176
Fax: 01 611 865

Dr A Cole
Teagasc EC Unit
19 Sandymount Avenue
Ballsbridge
Dublin 4
Tel: 01 688 188
Fax: 01 688 023
Tlx: 30459 EI

Commission
For general administrative questions contact

The Secretariat
Commission of the European Communities
DG XII/B-4
SDME R2/132
Rue Montoyer 75
B-1040 Brussels
Tel: INT+ 322 295 1731
Fax: INT+ 322 296 3308/6252

For the following specific subjects, please contact the appropriate scientific officials

Agriculture
T J Hall
Tel: INT+ 322 295 2808
Fax: INT+ 322 296 6252

Medicine, Health and Nutrition
M de Bruycker
Tel: INT+ 322 295 9172
Fax: INT+ 322 296 6252

Contact Persons in the Third Countries
Delegations of the European Commission, see Appendix 2 for details.

Chapter 17.5

Energy

This group of programmes covers:

1. JOULE II: Non-Nuclear Energies
2. Nuclear Fission Safety Programme
3. Management and Storage of Radioactive Waste
4. Controlled Thermonuclear Fusion
5. Decommissioning of Nuclear Installations
6. TELEMAN: Remote Handling in Nuclear Hazardous and other Hazardous Environments
7. THERMIE: Promotion of Energy Technology.

1. NON-NUCLEAR ENERGIES (JOULE II)

Statutory Basis

Council Decision 91/484/EEC: OJ L 257/47, dated 14/9/91.

Objectives

This programme aims to contribute to the development of new energy options that are both economically viable and environmentally safe, including energy-saving technologies.

Background

The Third Framework Programme aims to give an innovatory thrust to research and technological development (RTD) action throughout its five year duration (1990-94). One field of RTD activity to be implemented within the energy sector will be the non-nuclear energy programme. JOULE II (1991-94) is a development and extension of the JOULE I Programme on Non-Nuclear Energies and Rational Use of Energy (1989-92).

The specific objectives of JOULE II are as follows.

i To guarantee the supply of energy and to improve quality of life, taking account of energy-environment interactions. Success is dependent upon:
   - the availability and flexibility of conventional energy sources;

- the development of new energy sources;
- the wise management of these resources; and
- the control of efficient and clean energy technologies.

ii To adapt and modernise sectors such as industry, transport, housing, tertiary and agriculture, by offering them products, processes and technologies which in energy terms are cleaner, more efficient, safer and cheaper.

iii To further the development of the technical ability and adaptability of EC industries in the field of energy technologies by stimulating innovation; and to ensure a high level of competitiveness for these industries in the internal market through research which leads to the definition of norms and standards.

iv To take account, in the development of energy technologies, of the needs of less favoured regions and of developing countries. The aim is to contribute to their economic and social development while protecting their environment. Special attention will be paid to the innovative exploitation and rational management of their energy resources as well as technology benefits as appropriate.

These objectives and their priorities will be adapted as the situation evolves to introduce the strategic adjustments necessitated by action taken under the objectives.

Programme Content

There are four areas covered by the programme.

AREA 1: ANALYSIS OF STRATEGY AND MODELLING

This will focus on using Community-wide models to analyse different energy, environmental and related economic policies. It also aims to develop new tools to evaluate energy R&D strategies incorporating environmental, social, internal market and global dimensions. The existing research network supporting these studies and models will be reinforced to ensure the coherence and comparability of results obtained in different EC countries.

AREA 2: MINIMUM EMISSION POWER PRODUCTION FROM FOSSIL FUELS

At present fossil fuels account for some 84% of EC energy consumption, and projections indicate that they will remain on the market because of their abundance, price, ease of global distribution and security of supply. However, when they are not used under optimal environmental conditions fossil fuels contribute substantially to global emissions of nitrogen oxides, sulphur oxides, carbon dioxide and particulated matters.

Activities in Area 2 will mainly address the environmental aspects of fossil fuel conversion and combustion, specifically in relation to greenhouse gas emissions. Area 2 will also cover basic research to improve the exploration and exploitation of fossil fuel resources.

AREA 3a: RENEWABLE ENERGY SOURCES

Renewable energy sources are potentially an important domestic energy resource in the EC. In spite of their great potential advantages for improving the security of Europe's energy supply and alleviating environmental problems, particularly global warming, these technologies are only at an early stage of development. JOULE II, through Area 3A, aims to accelerate this development.

The main emphasis will be on solar photovoltaics, wind energy and biomass, in co-ordination with the Agriculture and Agro-Industry Programme. The programme will also take a new interest in potential applications in rural areas and developing countries for the local production of electricity, water and biomass derived fuels.

AREA 3b: GEOTHERMAL ENERGY AND DEEP RESERVOIR GEOLOGY

The emphasis in geothermal energy will be put on hot dry rock research. Some generic research will also be carried out in the field of high and low enthalpy. Deep reservoir geology will be extend in scope and will use more geophysical and geochemical techniques, in addition to deep reflection seismics.

AREA 4: ENERGY UTILISATION AND CONSERVATION

Combustion systems, which account for 84% of primary energy conversion, are often inefficient at converting energy resulting in high levels of emissions of unburnt fuel. The research in Area 4 aims to achieve energy conservation, a reduction in pollution levels and a lower carbon dioxide discharge, and will involve three types of activity:

- improvement of combustion processes;
- replacement of combustion systems by more efficient and cleaner electrochemical systems, such as fuel cells; and
- more efficient use of energy.

EC Contribution

The Non-Nuclear Energy Programme was scheduled to receive a top-up of 60 MECU in 1993 to enable it to fund projects from the call for proposals which closed on 25 June 1993. It was estimated that the following funds would be available:

Area 2:	Minimum Emission Power from Fossil Sources	15 MECU
Area 3a:	Renewable Energies	30 MECU
Area 4:	Energy Utilisation and Conservation	15 MECU

Out of an additional allocation of 50 MECU to be shared amongst the energy programmes - non-nuclear, fission safety and nuclear fission, priority will be given to non-nuclear energies.

Participation

Individual projects must be multi-partner and transnational in nature, providing for participation from at least two independent partners, established in different Member States. Enterprises established in non-Member States may be allowed to become partners in a project undertaken within the programme. Such bodies will not be eligible for financial support from the EC, but must contribute to the general administrative costs.

Contracts will be implemented on a shared-cost basis.

Only those proposals which respond precisely to the specific call and are submitted within the appropriate deadline will be evaluated. In order to avoid overlapping with other existing EC programmes, applicants should pay particular attention to borderline areas of research, and in particular to the following:

- projects for the promotion of energy technologies situated downstream of the R&D projects are not eligible under this programme, but should be submitted to the THERMIE Programme of DG XVII (Regulation (EEC) No. 2008/90);
- proposals concerned with energy-related environmental issues come under the Environment R&D programme of DG XII/F;
- for materials research topics, contact the BRITE/EURAM Programme; and
- in the area of biomass, projects related to thermochemical conversion should be submitted to the JOULE II programme, whereas projects relating to the production of biomass feedstock and its biological or biochemical conversion should be submitted to the Agriculture and Agro-Industry Programme of DGXII/E.

Status Report

JOULE II was launched in the autumn of 1991; proposals were submitted and assessed during the first half of 1992 and virtually all the resulting contracts were signed by the end of the year.

Budgetary restrictions meant that very rigorous selection criteria had to be applied. Many good proposals had to be rejected, while most of those that were accepted had to be scaled down in scope and duration. The Council recognised that these inadequate financial arrangements could lead to a loss of momentum in the research before new activities can be initiated under the Fourth Framework Programme. To ensure both continuity and the natural evolution of the research, they therefore decided to make supplementary funding available for the years 1993 and 1994 (Council Decision: OJ L No. 69, dated 20/3/93).

An open call for proposals has been issued for topics listed in the Supplementary Work Programme as follows:

AREA 2 - energy production from fossil fuels using advanced technologies;
- security of Supply of Hydrocarbons; and

- more effective and cleaner utilisation of hydrocarbons;

AREA 3a - the solar house;
- renewable power plants;
- biomass; and
- renewable energies for rural electricity, local fuel and water; and

AREA 4 - energy saving in industry;
- energy saving in buildings;
- combustion; and
- electric vehicles.

INFORMATION

UK

Information packs together with application forms can be requested from

The International Liaison Officer
ETSU
B153
Harwell
Oxfordshire OX11 ORA
Tel: 0235 821111
Fax: 0235 432050

For more general enquiries, contact

Mr D Irving
DTI
Energy Technology Division
Room 349, 1 Palace Street
London SW1E 5HE
Tel: 071 238 3318
Fax: 071 828 7969

Mr David Wallace
Department of Energy
Energy Technology Division
1 Palace Street
London SW1E 5HE
Tel: 071 238 3643
Fax: 071 918 777

IRELAND

Mr Pat Bell or Mr David Taylor
EOLAS
The Irish Science and Technology Agency
Glasnevin
Dublin 9
Tel: 01 37 01 01
Fax: 01 37 28 48

COMMISSION

Commission of the European Communities
DG XII Directorate F
Non-Nuclear Energy Programme
(JOULE II)
75 Rue Montoyer
B-1040 Brussels
Tel: INT +322 299 1111 (exchange)

2. NUCLEAR FISSION SAFETY PROGRAMME

Statutory Basis

Council Decision 91/626/EEC: OJ L 336/42, dated 7/12/91.

Objectives

This programme aims to make the use of nuclear energy safer, taking into consideration all aspects of nuclear power plants and the full cycle, including problems of waste management, radioactive and fissile materials. Other objectives are safety in the decommissioning of nuclear installations and the development of new technologies to manage the risk of accidents releasing radioactivity.

Background

The Nuclear Fission Safety Programme is operated on behalf of EURATOM but forms part of the Third Framework Programme. It supersedes the earlier Radiation Protection Programme, which has been in operation since 1980 and was given added impetus by the Chernobyl disaster .

Programme Content

This is a composite programme with a reactor safety element overseen in the UK by the DTI, and a radiation protection element for which the Department of Health is responsible.

The aim of the reactor safety research is to consider how to ensure the safety of future reactor types and to improve public confidence in safety assessments reckoned as probabilities. Studies will consider accident progression analysis (in-vessel phenomena related to containment loading and ex-vessel phenomena and hydrogen-related phenomena; as well as fission product behaviour), containment of radioactivity under severe accident conditions, integrity of containment systems and the management of human behaviour.

Research into radiation protection will cover human exposure to radiation and radioactivity, such as reliable means of measuring radiation, strategies to impede the transfer of radionucleides to man etc., the consequences of radiation exposure to man together with its prevention and treatment, the risk and management of radiation exposure, including overall risks of human exposure to radiation and methods for optimising and managing radiation protection.

Much of the work will be performed by the Community's Joint Research Centres and the balance will be done by means of shared-cost projects and concerted actions.

EC Contribution

The funding originally set aside in the Third Framework Programme for the Nuclear Fission Safety Programme was 199 MECU. Of this, 163.36 MECU was for activity undertaken by the EC's Joint Research Centres, and of the balance 28.64 MECU was allocated to Radiation Protection and 7 MECU to Reactor Safety. Of those 7 MECU, about 1.6 MECU cover staff and administration costs, with the balance of 5.4 MECU, available to finance selected shared-cost projects.

This energy programme was scheduled to receive a top-up of 29 MECU during 1993, when a further 50 MECU was to be allocated among the various energy programmes, although priority was given to non-nuclear energies.

Status Report

A call for proposals for shared-cost projects to be considered for inclusion in the Reactor Safety element of the Third Framework Programme was made in the OJ in December 1991. The closing date was 14 February 1992.

Commission services received and evaluated 107 proposals, assisted by independent experts who considered 46 of them suitable for inclusion in the programme.

Applications

Proposals are sent to the Commission.

No more calls for proposals are expected under the Third Framework Programme. Discussion is continuing on the timing, content and funding of the Fourth Framework Programme, which is provisionally intended to cover the period 1994-97. Present indications are that funding for activity in the area of Reactor Safety will be at a level similar to that of the Third Framework Programme.

INFORMATION

UK

Radiation Protection
Dr H Walker
Dept of Health
Room 917a
Hannibal House
Elephant & Castle
London SE1 6TE
Tel: 071 972 2157

Reactor Safety
Dr Storey
Nuclear Safety Research Management Unit
Health & Safety Executive
Broad Lane
Sheffield S3 7HQ
Tel: 0742 892000
Fax: 0742 892500
Tlx: 54556 HSE RLS G

IRELAND

J D Cunningham
Nuclear Energy Board
3 Clonskeagh Square
Clonskeagh Road
Dublin 14
Tel: 01 283 83 56
Fax: 01 269 74 37

C P O'Toole
EOLAS
The Irish Science & Technology Agency
Glasnevin
Dublin 9
Tel: 01 37 01 01

COMMISSION

DGXII/D/2
Commission of the European Communities
200 Rue de la Loi
B-1049 Brussels
Tel: INT +322 299 1111 (exchange)

3. MANAGEMENT AND STORAGE OF RADIOACTIVE WASTE

Statutory Basis

Council Decision 89/665/EEC: OJ L 395/28, dated 30/12/89.

Objectives

This programme aims to perfect and demonstrate a system for managing the radioactive waste produced by the nuclear industry, ensuring the best protection for people and the environment that is possible at each stage of production.

Background

Three previous research programmes in this field have been undertaken, the most recent of which finished in 1989. A new five year programme (1990-94) has now been agreed under the umbrella of the Commission's Nuclear Fission Safety Programme.

Programme Content

The programme is divided into two parts.

Part A Waste Management and Associated R&D actions.

Part B Construction and/or Operation of Underground Facilities open to EC Joint Activities.

PART A WASTE MANAGEMENT AND ASSOCIATED R&D ACTIONS.
This consists of five tasks:

Task 1: system studies and harmonisation of waste management practices and policies;

Task 2: treatment of radioactive waste;

Task 3: characterisation and certification of waste forms, packages and their environment;

Task 4: radioactive waste disposal, research in support of the development of underground repositories; and

Task 5: safety assessment.

PART B CONSTRUCTION AND/OR OPERATION OF UNDERGROUND FACILITIES OPEN TO EC JOINT ACTIVITIES.
This consists of four projects:

Project 1: pilot underground facility in the Asse salt mine in Germany;

Project 2: pilot underground facility in the argillaceous layer under the Mol nuclear site in Belgium;

Project 3: underground validation facility in France; and

Project 4: underground validation facility in the UK.

Other projects could be added in the course of the programme.
The programme will be implemented mainly through shared-cost research contracts with appropriate organisations and companies, public or private, established in the Member States. In addition to such contracts, the programme may also be carried out by means of study contracts, co-ordinated projects and awards of training and mobility grants.

EC Contribution

Funding of 79.6 MECU was agreed for the 1990-94 programme, of which approximately 70% is intended to be allocated to Part A and 30% to Part B.

Participation

Proposals may be introduced from all sectors engaged in research: universities, public and private research organisations and industry, including SMEs. One-body proposals may be introduced, but the Commission favours joint proposals from individuals or bodies from different Member States. Co-operation between partners can also take the form of a European Economic Interest Grouping (EEIG) constituted according to Council Regulation No. 2137/85(1).

Status Report

The last call for proposals was published in OJ C 55, dated 7 March 1990, with a deadline of 30 May 1990. It is unlikely that there will be any further calls in the foreseeable future, as current funds are virtually exhausted.

INFORMATION

Commission
DG XII D-2
Commission of the European Communities
200 Rue de la Loi
B-1049 Brussels
Tel: INT+ 322 295 6997
Fax: INT+ 322 296 4252

CORDIS
CORDIS, the EC's computer-based R&D information service, gives access to a large number of Community documents, including detailed information on current research contracts in the field of radioactive waste management and decommissioning. Information packages are available from:

ECHO/CORDIS
PO Box 2373
L-1023 Luxembourg
Tel: INT+ 352 349 811
Fax: INT+ 352 981 234

4. CONTROLLED THERMONUCLEAR FUSION

Statutory Basis

Council Decision 91/678/EURATOM: OJ L 375/11 dated 31/12/91.

Objectives

The objectives of this programme are the joint creation of safe, environmentally sound prototype reactors, the preparation of industry for the construction of a "Next Step" device, by continuing the activities of the Second Framework programme and the achievement of self-sustained thermonuclear burn, of a deuterium-tritium plasma and its control during long-pulse operation.

Background

Research in the field of controlled thermonuclear fusion falls within the scope of Article 7 of the EURATOM Treaty. Initially a small group was established in Brussels, and charged with defining the role of EURATOM in European fusion research. It was then decided that fusion activities in Europe should be progressively co-ordinated. The programme subsequently developed into a single programme covering all European activities in the field of magnetic confinement.

The European approach to fusion research has been to concentrate efforts on magnetic toroidal confinement, mainly along the so-called Tokomak line, while maintaining a watching brief on other approaches to controlled fusion. The Joint European Torus (JET) at Culham in Oxfordshire is the largest and most powerful experiment ever attempted in developing nuclear fusion as a raw energy source. This topic is now included in the Third Framework Programme.

Programme Content

There are four areas.

AREA 1 NEXT STEP DESIGN

This will involve activities at European level developing the Next European Torus (NET), and at international level, through the International Thermonuclear Experimental Reactor (ITER) Programme which involves the EC, Japan, the USA and Russia.

Activities in fusion technology will involve superconducting magnets, plasma-facing components, safety, fuel cycle, remote handling maintenance and decommissioning. This work could be undertaken by the Joint Research Centre, or by industry on a shared-cost basis.

AREA 2 LONGER-TERM TECHNICAL DEVELOPMENTS
Work will include the development of low activation materials, reactor blanket modules and a reference design for an electricity-producing fusion reactor.

AREA 3 JET
Full exploitation of JET will be achieved by establishing reliable methods of controlling plasma purity and by preparing for the final phase of JET, which will use deuterium-tritium plasmas.

AREA 4 SUPPORT PROGRAMME
This will involve scientific support for the Next Step device and JET, studies on alternative lines in toroidal magnetic confinement and support for other approaches to controlled fusion.

EC Contribution

This energy programme was allocated 458 MECU. In addition, some 50 MECU will be allocated among the various energy programmes, although priority will be given to non-nuclear energies.

Participation

Participation is only generally possible within the framework of association contracts between the Commission and certain national research institutes in the EC Member States, Sweden and Switzerland. Member States with whom no association agreements have been concluded can make specific applications on a project by project basis.

Research Fellowships

In addition to this programme, there are EC individual research training fellowships in the field of controlled thermonuclear fusion by magnetic confinement. Between 1992 and 1994, the EC Fusion Programme may award some 25 fellowships a year. There will be approximately ten in the General Fusion Programme and between ten and fifteen in JET.

The host laboratory must be either an EC national research laboratory or an institution associated with or participating in the Community Fusion Programme, or the JET Joint Undertaking, or the NET Team. Nationals of Sweden and Switzerland are also eligible for fellowships awarded by this programme.

The fellowship scheme runs continuously and applications can be submitted at any time during the year throughout the period 1992-94. Selection rounds will take place twice a year:

- for the General Fusion Programme: in March and July, with deadlines for receiving applications of 28 February and 30 June respectively; and
- for JET: in April and October, with deadlines for receiving applications of 15 March and 15 September respectively.

INFORMATION

UK

Mr B Freeman
Department of Energy
Room 428
1 Palace Street
London SW1E 5HE
Tel: 071 238 3771

Association EURATOM research unit
AEA Fusion
Culham Laboratory
Abingdon OX14 3DB
Tel: 0235-463231

IRELAND

Ireland participates in the EC fusion programme by co-ordinating relevant fusion research at the following Irish universities

- University College, Cork;
- Dublin City University, Dublin and
- Trinity College, Dublin.

Co-ordinator of research
F J Turvey
Radiological Protection Institute of Ireland
3 Clonskeagh Square
Clonskeagh Road
Dublin 14
Tel: 01 269 77 66

COMMISSION

C Maisonnier
Commission of the European Communities
DG XII Fusion Programme
200 Rue de la Loi
B-1049 Brussels
Tel: INT+ 322 295 4062
Fax: INT+ 322 296 4252

RESEARCH UNITS

JET Joint Undertaking
Abingdon
Oxfordshire OX14 3EA

The NET Team
Max-Planck-Institut fur Plasmaphysik
D-8046 Garching bei Munchen
Germany

EC individual research training fellowships in Controlled Thermonuclear Fusion

Dr K Steinmetz
Commission of the European Communities
DG XII-Fusion Programme
200 Rue de la Loi (SDME 1/126)
B-1049 Brussels
Tel: INT+ 322 295 6651
Fax: INT+ 322 296 4252

Mrs J Waghorn
JET Joint Undertaking
JET Personnel Service
Abingdon
Oxfordshire OX14 3EA.
Tel: 0235 46 47 93
Fax: 0235 46 45 04

5. DECOMMISSIONING OF NUCLEAR INSTALLATIONS

Statutory Basis

Council Decision 89/239/EURATOM: OJ L 98, dated 11/4/89.

Objectives

The programme's objectives are the joint development of management systems for the parts of nuclear installations which are to be permanently shut down, and the treatment of radioactive wastes produced in their dismantling, so as to provide the best possible safeguards.

Background

The Commission has supported research on the decommissioning of nuclear installations since 1979. During the 1980s the technological basis of decommissioning was strengthened, and the number of major nuclear installations being shut down accelerated, as nuclear power plants and fuel cycle facilities built in the fifties and sixties came to the end of their useful lives. These two factors led to a Council agreement for a new and upgraded programme in which the topics will be largely the same as for the previous 1984-88 programme, but with greater emphasis on the testing of new techniques. The current programme runs until 1994.

Programme Content

The programme can be divided into three sections.

SECTION A: TECHNICAL ASSESSMENT AND DEVELOPMENT STUDIES
These activities, which have already been extensively covered in 1979 - '88 by the two preceding research programmes (with the exception of subject (v)), are intended to absorb about one quarter of the programme funds. This section is comprised of the following subjects:

- long-term integrity of buildings and systems;
- decontamination for decommissioning purposes;
- dismantling techniques;
- treatment of specific waste materials: steel, concrete and graphite;
- qualification and adaptation of remote-controlled semi-autonomous manipulator systems; and
- estimation of the quantities of radioactive wastes arising from the decommissioning of nuclear installations in the EC.

SECTION B: THE IDENTIFICATION OF GUIDING PRINCIPLES
This section of the programme aims to identify guiding principles relating to :

- the design and operation of nuclear installations, with a view to simplifying their subsequent decommissioning;

- the decommissioning operations, with a view to making occupational radiation exposures as low as reasonably achievable; and
- the technical elements of an EC policy in this field.

Although by their very nature, these studies do not require a large share of the budget, the Commission is making a substantial effort in this important task.

SECTION C: THE FIELD TESTING OF NEW TECHNIQUES
The programme aims to test new techniques in practice, within the framework of large-scale decommissioning operations undertaken in Member States. The tests will be focused mainly on a few selected pilot dismantling projects, namely:

- the Windscale Advanced Gas-Cooled Reactor (WAGR);
- the Gundremmingen Boiling Water Reactor (KRB-A);
- the BR-3 Pressurised Water Reactor; and
- the AT-1 fuel reprocessing pilot plant.

There will also be complementary tests performed in other nuclear installations and secondment of research staff from other Member States to the pilot dismantling projects will be promoted.

EC Contribution

A budget of 39.1 MECU has been approved for this programme.

Participation

The programme is implemented mainly by means of shared-cost contracts with research organisations and firms in Member States.

Status Report

Section A:
A call for proposals under of section A was published in OJ C 196, dated 13/6/89. Research work is proceeding in all of the chosen projects.

Section B:
A group of experts is assisting the Commission in drafting a report in which principles, regulations and policies for decommissioning will be assembled and discussed. Recommendations will be made for EC actions in this field.

Section C:
A call for proposals under section C was published in OJ C 196, dated 13/6/89. A new call concerning Area C was published in OJ C 24, dated 31/1/91, with a deadline of 31/3/91.

Pilot Dismantling Projects:
Work on the first phase of the four major dismantling projects began between autumn 1989 and spring 1990, and was concluded in 1991. The second phase of the projects has started: this includes the dismantling of further highly activated core internals and large heat exchangers in the reactors, as well as the complete conditioning of the waste resulting from the decommissioning of the fuel reprocessing plant AT-1.

Alternative Tests:
On the basis of two calls for proposals, 19 research and development projects are now being pursued in this part of the programme.

Secondment of Scientific Staff to the Pilot Dismantling Projects:
Contracts for four assignments have been included.

Future support for decommissioning is expected to be provided in the Fourth Framework Programme of RTD and Demonstration Activities (1994-98).

Status Report

As a result of the 1989 call for proposals in Section A, 94 proposals were submitted, of which 44 were selected.

Applications

No further calls for proposals are expected to be made under this programme in the foreseeable future.

INFORMATION

UK
Mr P Hubbard
Department of Energy
Room 4.2.10
1 Palace Street
London SW1E 5HE
Tel: 071 238 3654

Commission
R Simon
Commission of the European Communities
R&D Programme on the Decommissioning of Nuclear Installations
Directorate-General XII/D/2 (Arts 2/37)
200 Rue de la Loi
B-1049 Brussels
Tel: INT +322 299 1111 (exchange)

6. REMOTE HANDLING IN NUCLEAR HAZARDOUS AND OTHER HAZARDOUS ENVIRONMENTS (TELEMAN)

Statutory Basis

Council Decision 89/464/EURATOM: OJ L 226, dated 3/8/89.

Objectives

TELEMAN'S objective is to reinforce the scientific and technological design base of nuclear remote handling equipment. Tele-operators contribute to the safety and productivity of human and plant resources employed in all parts of the nuclear industry, from mining through reactor operation, to reprocessing and decommissioning. The tele-operators concerned are mechanical arms to which a variety of tools and sensors can be attached, manipulators attached to moveable gantries and partially autonomous vehicles equipped for specialised jobs. In particular, TELEMAN will help the nuclear industry to meet the necessity of workers being exposed to the minimum amount of radiation, which must in all cases be kept within stipulated limits, while at the same time enabling personnel to carry out inspection, maintenance and repair operations.

EC Contribution

A budget of 19 MECU for the five year programme has been approved by the Council.

Background

The use of remote handling techniques to separate workers and radioactive equipment enhances safety, and should result in increased efficiency in plant repair and maintenance operations. A new five year sub-programme (TELEMAN), has been approved to encourage the development of equipment for use at all stages of the nuclear fuel cycle.

Programme Content

The programme consists of four areas:

AREA 1: TELE-OPERATOR COMPONENT AND SUB-SYSTEM DEVELOPMENT
Research and development will be carried out to aid the utilisation, modification and where necessary, the development of sensors, perception and decision-making systems, information transmission and engineering, for tele-operator mobility and dexterity in nuclear environments.

AREA 2: ENVIRONMENTAL TOLERANCE
Research will be carried out throughout the life of the programme on the adaptation of sensors and electronic hardware to nuclear environments, the development of machine monitoring systems and design strategies that permit easy repair or recovery of stranded machines.

AREA 3: RESEARCH MACHINE PROJECTS
Products of research on components and sub-systems will be demonstrated by incorporating them into research machines which already exist, or into new machines. Development will focus on tele-operators which typify nuclear industry requirements, such as intelligent manipulators and cranes for use in high radiation fields, and a mobile platform for information gathering in both normal circumstances and emergencies.

AREA 4: PRODUCT EVALUATION AND STUDIES

End-users of TELEMAN technology will be encouraged to test and evaluate the practicality and reliability of the products of the programme in realistic environments, to guide the subsequent commercialisation of successful products. The application of new technologies, new uses for computer-assisted tele-operators, the evolution of guidelines and standards and programme development will be studied.

Status Report

Calls for proposals were first published in September 1989. A second call was published in OJ C 255, dated 1/10/91, with a deadline of 14/2/92. No further calls are anticipated under this programme in the foreseeable future.

INFORMATION

UK
Mr T Hayward
Department of Energy
Room 4.2.7
1 Palace Street
London SW1E 5HE
Tel: 071 238 3798

Commission
Commission of the European Communities
DG XII Science, Research and Development
Directorate D
200 Rue de la Loi
B-1049 Brussels
Tel: INT +322 299 1111 (exchange)

7. PROMOTION OF ENERGY TECHNOLOGY (THERMIE)

Statutory Basis

Council Regulation (EEC) No 2008/90: OJ L 185, dated 17/7/90.

Objectives

THERMIE supports projects for the application of new technologies whose realisation is associated with a considerable degree of risk.

Background

Since 1986 the EC has supported a demonstration scheme to encourage the spread of new technologies which could be used to save energy, increase the use of renewable energy resources and find substitutes for oil-based fuels. A parallel scheme was also launched to help ensure the long-term security of Member States' oil and gas supplies. The total budgets for these programmes were 360 MECU and 140 MECU respectively. Both of these schemes are now fully subscribed and have been replaced by THERMIE.

One outcome of THERMIE activity has been the opening of nine Energy Centres in Central and Eastern Europe which act as focal points for information on EC energy policy.

Programme Content

The programme is aimed at the following areas.

- Rational Use of Energy:
  more effective methods of saving energy in buildings and industry, in heat and electricity generation and distribution, and in transport and urban infrastructure.

- Renewable Energy Sources :
  solar energy, energy from biomass and waste, geothermal energy, hydroelectric energy and wind energy.

- Solid Fuels:
  environmentally benign techniques for exploiting coal and other solid fuels, covering the processes of combustion, conversion of solid fuel into gaseous or liquid products, waste production and gasification integrated with a combined gas and steam cycle.

- Hydrocarbons:
  exploration and exploitation of oil and gas fields, and transport and storage of oil and gas.

Projects are eligible if they are designed to develop and promote innovative technologies in the field of energy, for which implementation involves a large degree of risk. Support may be granted for:

- innovatory projects, implementing techniques where R&D has been completed, or new applications of established techniques. Such projects should aim to prove the viability of new technologies by applying them on a sufficiently large scale;
- dissemination projects designed to encourage preliminary applications of tested technologies under different economic or geographical conditions which entail some risk.

In 1993, the Commission placed a special emphasis on Targeted Projects. These are specific projects set up either to meet a particular need that is being neglected elsewhere, or to realise significant technological advances which can only be achieved by co-operation between undertakings in at least two Member States. For 1993, priority was to be given to targeted projects which met the following conditions:

- large projects which could have a substantial European impact: in practice this meant projects with a total cost greater than 6 MECU; and
- collaborative projects involving substantial co-operation between companies, or other appropriate bodies, from at least three different Member States.

EC Contribution

The allocation for THERMIE is 350 MECU for the three year period 1990 to 1992. A top-up of approximately 150 MECU was scheduled to be made available during 1993 for THERMIE projects. Maximum financial support is 40% of eligible costs for innovatory projects, and 35% of eligible costs for dissemination projects.

Status Report

The Commission issued a call for proposals seeking financial support under the fifth round of THERMIE, which had to be submitted to the Commission by 1 December 1993. Projects eligible for support in the hydrocarbon sector were those dealing with:

- safety and environmental protection, the objectives of which are to reduce risks and reduce the environmental impact of oil and gas production and transport;
- exploration, which includes increased knowledge of the reservoir and reduction in drilling costs;
- new or improved production technologies;
- transport and storage, which includes pipelines and associated facilities.

Preference was to be given to projects aimed at high-pressure, high-temperature reservoirs and operations in deep water. Projects with safety and environmental benefits would also be preferred.

INFORMATION

UK

Application information is contained in "Thermie 1993 - Background Information and Procedures for Submitting Projects", available from:

Mrs A Corral or Mrs D Dodds
Department of Trade and Industry
Offshore Supplies Office
Alhambra House
45 Waterloo Street
Glasgow G2 6AS
Tel: 041 242 5775
Fax: 041 221 1718

COMMISSION

Mr W Folkertsma
Commission of the European Communities
Directorate-General for Energy
THERMIE 1994
200 rue de la Loi
B-1049 Brussels
Tel: INT +322 299 1111 (exchange)
Fax: INT+ 322 295 0577

Chapter 17.6

Research & Development Grants: Human Capital & Mobility

1. MONITOR
2. Human Capital and Mobility Programme
3. European Communities Science and Technology Fellowship Programme in Japan
4. STA: Science and Technology Agency Fellowship Programme in Japan
5. Co-operation in Science and Technology: Asian and Latin American Countries (ALA)
6. Co-operation in Science and Technology: Central & Eastern European Countries (CEEC)

1. MONITOR

See Chapter 17.9

2. HUMAN CAPITAL AND MOBILITY PROGRAMME

Statutory Basis

Council Decision 92/217/EEC: OJ L 107/1 24/4/92.

Aims

This programme aims to increase the human resources available for research and development (R&D) which will be needed by the Member States in the coming years. The main aim is the training of research scientists by encouraging mobility and the formation of networks. In this way, the competitiveness and the economic and social cohesion of the EC will be strengthened, while pursuing scientific and technical excellence.

Background

The Human Capital & Mobility Programme (1991-94) differs from all others in the Third Framework Programme in that it is not subject specific. It aims to develop the

SCIENCE, SPES and Large Facilities Programmes started under the Second Framework Programme.

Programme Content

The programme covers all scientific and technological sectors and areas of the social and human sciences that are able to improve European competitiveness, such as economic and management science, environmental economics and the interconnections of science, technology and society.

For basic research in the natural sciences, there is no a priori definition of the subjects to be covered.

The activities carried out by the programme are as follows:

ACTIVITY 1: FELLOWSHIPS
This involves the development of a system of research fellowships, particularly for young researchers at post-doctoral level, but also at doctoral level in emerging disciplines where there is a shortage of post-doctoral scientists, as well as established researchers who need retraining in a field other than their own, or who want to apply their knowledge in new areas.

There are two types of grant, generally lasting for up to two years: individual fellowships, given on the basis of joint institute-researcher proposals, and those allocated by pre-selected host institutions to groups of fellows. The programme allows for up to 15% of funds to go to host institutions and to the Commission, to pay for associated research expenses and administration costs.

ACTIVITY 2: NETWORKS
This aims to create and develop scientific and technical co-operation networks across all the regions of the EC, with particular regard to the special needs of less favoured regions.

As a general rule, proposals should consist of five or more centres in at least three EC countries, although twinnings or networks of fewer than five centres in different Member States may be supported in exceptional circumstances provided that they assist in the creation of a genuinely European scientific and technical community. Grants will normally cover 100% of the marginal costs of each project, (60% for the subsistence and mobility costs of researchers themselves; 40% for certain expenses related to research and administration).

ACTIVITY 3: LARGE-SCALE FACILITIES
This concerns measures to promote researchers' access to large-scale scientific and technical facilities, and particularly to improve their accessibility to young post-doctoral researchers from other Member States. Of the total amount granted, 40% covers the researchers own expenses (subsistence, mobility, publication of results), while the remaining 60% is for the use of equipment, its adaptation or improvement and for management costs.

ACTIVITY 4: R&D EUROCONFERENCES

This involves organising high level meetings at the cutting edge of scientific and technical knowledge. EC grants cover expenses such as registration, travel and subsistence to enable young researchers to attend and participate in the conferences.

EC Contribution

A budget of 518 MECU has been agreed for the period 1992-1994, of which 25 MECU is reserved for direct action by the EC's Joint Research Centre, while 4.93 MECU is earmarked for centralised dissemination and exploitation of results. The remaining 488.07 MECU is distributed among the different activities as follows:

Training	220.00 MECU
Networks	200.00 MECU
Access to major installations	55.00 MECU
EUROCONFERENCES	13.07 MECU

The programme was scheduled to receive a 69 MECU top-up during 1993.

This complements, rather than replaces funding or training under the other specific R&D Programmes.

Participation

Eligible proposals must involve participants from at least two Member States. Organisations or individuals from non-Member States which have signed a full association agreement with the EC, can participate in the programme on the same terms and conditions as Member State participants. Other European countries, which do not have full association status but do have agreements on science and technology co-operation with the EC, may participate in the programme on a project-by-project basis but will not, however, receive any EC funding.

Applications

Calls for individual fellowships under Activity 1, and for Activities 2 and 4 are always open, so applications may be sent to the Commission at any time. Calls for grouped fellowships (Activity 1) are held once a year, the most recent was at the end of 1993. At present no further calls are planned for Activity 3.

INFORMATION

UK

Edward Bethell
Office of Science & Technology
Cabinet Office
Room 1/1Albany House
84-86 Petty France
London SW1H 9ST
Tel: 071 271 2112

Mr J Walsh
Science and Engineering Research Council
Polaris House
North Star Avenue
Swindon SN2 1ET
Tel: 0793 411 269

COMMISSION
DG XII-G
Commission of the European Communities
200 Rue de la Loi
B-1049 Brussels
Tel: INT +322 299 1111 (exchange)

General Information:
Jean Ferron
Tel: INT+ 322 295 4250
Fax: INT+ 322 295 6995

Networks:
Manuela Soares
Tel: INT+ 322 296 2148
Fax: INT+ 322 296 3307

Fellowships:
Irmela Brach
Tel: INT+ 322 296 0254
Fax: INT+ 322 296 3307

Large-scale Facilities:
Marco Malacarne,
Tel: INT+ 322 295 5277
Fax: INT+ 322 295 6995

Euroconferences:
Jane Shiel
Tel: INT+ 322 296 2984
Fax: INT+ 322 236 3307

Information packs containing application forms and procedural guidance can be obtained from the Commission by telephoning or faxing the following numbers:

Tel: INT+ 322 296 0254 (answering machine)
Fax: INT+ 322 296 3307

3. EUROPEAN COMMUNITIES SCIENCE AND TECHNOLOGY FELLOWSHIP PROGRAMME IN JAPAN

Aims

The main objective is to enable European scientists to interact fruitfully with the Japanese research system early in their research careers.

Background

The Commission and the Government of Japan agreed to establish a pilot exchange scheme to enable young researchers to explore ways in which to interact with Japanese research. In 1986 the Commission established the European Communities Scientific Training Programme in Japan, recently renamed the European Communities S&T Fellowship Programme in Japan.

Programme Content

Participants spend 15-21 months in Japan, taking a language course in the first three months and spending the remainder in a host laboratory.

In Japan, participants may be hosted by any national research laboratory supervised by the Science and Technology Agency, the Ministry for International Trade and Industry, the Ministry for Agriculture, Forestry and Fisheries or other ministries. University laboratories and research institutes attached to national, public and private universities are also included. Private sector research institutes may be considered on an individual case basis.

EC Contribution

The Commission pays travel expenses between Europe and Japan, an installation allowance, language tuition and a fixed monthly allowance of 435,000 yen.

Participation

The STP is open to nationals of the Member States who have completed their doctoral degree or have equivalent professional experience. The usual age range is 25-35.

Applications

Each candidate must complete the standard application form available from the address below, and should also provide a work programme and give evidence of having initiated contact with a potential Japanese host institute. Applications should reach the Commission by 30 June in any year, for fellowships commencing within the following 12 months.

INFORMATION

M Merla
Commission of the European Communities
DG for Science Research & Development
S&T Co-operation with Non-Member Countries
200 Rue de la Loi
B-1049 Brussels
Tel: INT+ 322 295 3990/6509
Fax: INT+ 322 296 3308

4. SCIENCE & TECHNOLOGY AGENCY (STA) FELLOWSHIP PROGRAMME IN JAPAN

Aims

The aim is to offer promising young European scientists the opportunity to carry out research in Japan's national laboratories and non-profit institutions, but not in Japanese universities.

Background

The Science and Technology Agency (STA), an administrative organ of the Government of Japan, established the STA Fellowship Programme in 1988. To promote it and to organise the selection of potential candidates, STA established contacts with several agencies in industrialised countries, including five Member States of the EC and the Commission. The Commission therefore has the opportunity to nominate a limited number of candidates for STA fellowships.

Programme Content

Tenure is for a period of between six months and two years, to be negotiated by the candidate with the host institute: they must also agree on the field of research.

EC Contribution

The benefits granted to recipients of STA Fellowship awards are a round trip airline ticket, language tuition costs for those living in the Tsukuba area, a living allowance of 270,000 yen per month, a family allowance of 50,000 yen per month, a single international relocation allowance of 200,000 yen, a travel allowance within Japan for research activities (up to a maximum of 115,000 yen per year) and a housing allowance.

Participation

Applicants must have a scientific doctoral degree, or the equivalent, and be aged under 35.

Applications

The applicant must arrange for an official invitation letter from the host institution before submitting an application to the Commission.

Applications should reach the Commission by 30 June in any year, for fellowships commencing within the following 12 months. However in exceptional cases, ad hoc interviews can be arranged outside the framework of the general selection process.

INFORMATION

M Merla
Commission of the European Communities
DG for Science Research & Development
S & T Co-operation with Non-Member Countries
200 Rue de la Loi
B-1049 Brussels
Tel: INT+ 322 295 3990/6509
Fax: INT+ 322 296 3308

5. ASIAN AND LATIN AMERICAN COUNTRIES (ALA) see Chapter 31
6. CO-OPERATION IN SCIENCE & TECHNOLOGY WITH CENTRAL & EASTERN EUROPEAN COUNTRIES (CEEC) see Chapter 31

Chapter 17.7

Research & Development Grants: Transport

This group of programmes covers:

1. TELEMATICS: DRIVE II (Dedicated Road Infrastructure for Vehicle Safety in Europe)
2. EURET: Research on Transport Systems

1. TELEMATICS: DRIVE II (Dedicated Road Infrastructure for Vehicle Safety in Europe)

See Chapter 17.1

2. RESEARCH ON TRANSPORT SYSTEMS: EURET

Statutory Basis

Council Decision 91/11/EEC: OJ L 8/16, dated 11/1/91.

Objectives

The broad aims of the programme are to improve the effectiveness, competitiveness and safety of European transport systems, and to reduce their harmful effects on the environment.

Background

The EURET Programme was approved by the Council of Ministers in December 1990 as part of the Second Framework Programme. It is the first research programme to be managed by DG VII (Transport).

Programme Content

The sub-programmes are grouped in three Objectives :

OBJECTIVE 1: OPTIMUM TRANSPORT NETWORK EXPLOITATION

1.1 Cost-benefit and Multi-Criteria Analysis for New Road Construction aims to assess the feasibility of establishing Europe-wide systems and standards for project analysis, and creating a co-ordinated method of evaluating road construction projects.

1.2 European Rail Traffic Management aims to design a control system for rail traffic carrying both passengers and goods, to evaluate location and transmission equipment and develop the main software components of the system.

1.3 Vessel Traffic Services (VTS) Systems aims to assess the benefits and feasibility of measures to make the best use of existing or new investment in VTS.

1.4 Air Traffic Management aims to:

- define, develop and evaluate the applications, requirements and methods of data exchange between ground and airborne systems and between pilot and controller, as a means of backing up voice communications; and
- improve automated support for air traffic controllers resulting from the development of new controller work-stations.

OBJECTIVE 2: LOGISTICS

2.1 Economic Scenario and Demand Projections for Freight Transport in the EC aims to evaluate the extent to which the transport system can be adapted to meet the developing demand for freight transport, so that the necessary innovations can be introduced.

2.2 Intermodal Freight aims to design and implement an innovative and efficient system of rapid transfer of goods between different modes of transport.

2.3 Manning of Ships aims to:

- determine the optimum crew composition for different types of ship according to different circumstances, taking into account increased use of advanced technology; and
- achieve a better interaction between the ship and its equipment, and human behaviour, by assessing the tasks assigned to crew members and their behaviour in various operational situations. It also aims to develop measures to reduce human error.

OBJECTIVE 3: REDUCTION OF HARMFUL EXTERNAL EFFECTS

3.1 Improved Methods of Evaluating the Road Safety of car and Trailer Trains, will assess the significance at European level of accidents involving cars towing trailers, and will make recommendations to improve their safety.

3.2 Assessment of the Driving Safety of possible Truck and Trailer Combinations will consider the present arrangements for truck/trailer combinations, and carry out a technical analysis of a number of different types of road train with a view to drafting new safety regulations.

EC Contribution

EURET had a budget of 26.8 MECU for the period 1990-93.

Status Report

The first call for proposals was published on 15 January 1991. All the resulting shared-cost contracts were signed early in 1992 and most will run into 1994. No further calls for proposals are expected under the existing programme and information about the new EURET II programme is awaited.

Following the first call for proposals, 42 valid proposals were received involving 300 organisations; of these proposals, nine were selected for Community support.

DG VII is preparing the outlines for EURET II, a new transport research programme which should provide new tools for developing sustainable mobility and efficient, safe transport, under the best possible environmental and social conditions.

Applications

Management of the programme is the responsibility of the Commission, assisted by a committee composed of two representatives from each Member State.

INFORMATION

UK
M J Dudding
Department of Transport
P2/032
2 Marsham Street
London SW1P 3EB
Tel: 071 276 5869
Fax: 071 276 0818

COMMISSION
Commission of the EC
DG VII-A4
200 Rue de la Loi
B-1049 Brussels
Tel: INT+ 322 296 8836
Fax: INT+ 322 296 8350

Chapter 17.8

Research & Development Grants: The Environment

This group of programmes includes:

1. The Environment Programme
2. LIFE: Financial Instrument for the Environment
3. PSEP: The Physical and Social Environment Programme

1. THE ENVIRONMENT PROGRAMME

See Chapter 17.3

2. FINANCIAL INSTRUMENT FOR THE ENVIRONMENT (LIFE)

Statutory Basis

Council Regulation (EEC) No 1973/92: OJ L 206, dated 22/7/92

Objectives

The general objective is to contribute to the development and implementation of EC environmental policy by financing:

- priority environmental actions in the EC;
- technical assistance to third countries from the Mediterranean region or bordering the Baltic Sea; and
- exceptionally, actions concerning regional or global environmental problems provided for in international agreements.

Background

The Council Regulation governing the LIFE Programme at the same time repeals Action by the Community for Nature Conservation (ACNAT), MEDSPA and NORSPA.

For many years, the EC has been financing Research and Development programmes, the results of which can be exploited by demonstration and pilot projects. Under LIFE, demonstration schemes, awareness campaigns and actions providing incentives or technical help will be eligible for assistance, but scientific and technical research is not included.

Programme Content

The LIFE Regulation lists actions under five areas which define the scope of the programme.

AREA 1: PROMOTION OF SUSTAINABLE DEVELOPMENT AND THE QUALITY OF THE ENVIRONMENT.

The objectives are:

- to establish and develop new techniques and methods of measuring and monitoring the quality of the environment;
- to establish and develop new, clean technologies - that is, those which create little or no pollution and make fewer demands on resources. The Commission has targeted five industrial sectors in calling for demonstration projects, which are:

  i surface treatments, e.g. metal plating, ceramics;

  ii textiles;

  iii tanneries;

  iv the paper industry; and

  v the agri-food industry, e.g. dairies;
- to establish and develop techniques for the collection, storage, recycling and disposal of waste, particularly toxic and dangerous waste and waste water;
- to establish and develop techniques for locating and restoring sites contaminated by hazardous substances;
- to establish and develop models integrating environmental factors into land use planning and management and socio-economic activities;
- to reduce the discharge into the aquatic environment of nutritive substances and potentially bio-accumulative, toxic, persistent pollutants; and
- to improve the quality of the urban environment in both central and peripheral areas.

AREA 2: PROTECTION OF HABITATS AND OF NATURE

The objectives are:

- to maintain or re-establish biotopes which are the habitat of endangered species, or seriously threatened habitats, or to implement measures to conserve or re-establish endangered species, pursuant to Directive 79/409/EEC;

- to maintain or re-establish types of natural habitats of EC interest;
- to protect soil threatened or damaged by fire, desertification, coastal erosion or the disappearance of the dune belt;
- to promote the conservation of marine life; and
- to protect and conserve areas of fresh groundwater and fresh surface water.

AREA 3: ADMINISTRATIVE STRUCTURES AND ENVIRONMENTAL SERVICES.

The objectives are:

- to foster greater co-operation between the authorities of the Member States, with particular regard to the control of trans-boundary and global environmental problems; and
- to equip, modernise or develop monitoring networks in the context of strengthening environmental legislation.

AREA 4: EDUCATION, TRAINING AND INFORMATION.

The objectives are:

- to promote environmental training in administrative and professional circles;
- to promote environmental education, particularly by providing information and exchanges of experience, training and educational research;
- to foster better understanding of problems and hence encourage models of behaviour consistent with environmental objectives; and
- to disseminate knowledge about sound management of the environment.

AREA 5: ACTIONS OUTSIDE COMMUNITY TERRITORY

The objectives are:

- to promote the establishment of the necessary administrative structures in the environmental field;
- to provide the technical assistance needed for the establishment of environment policies and action programmes;

- to promote the transfer of appropriate, environmentally-friendly technologies and to foster sustainable development; and
- to promote assistance for third countries faced with ecological emergencies.

EC Contribution

A budgetary allocation of 400 MECU has been agreed for the first phase, which ends on 31 December 1995. The budget for 1993 was 65.33 MECU for actions within the EC and 3.5 MECU for actions outside EC territory. The 1994 budget is likely to be slightly larger than that for 1993.

Except for priority biotopes or habitats, EC financial support for operations is subject to the following limits:

- a maximum of 30% of the cost of actions which involve the financing of income-generating investments;
- 50% of the cost of other actions but exceptionally, 75% of the cost of actions relating to nature protection, species, habitats, biotopes; and
- 100% of the cost of measures designed to provide the information necessary for the execution of an action and of technical assistance measures implemented on the Commission's initiative.

Participation

LIFE is open to both EC Member States and third countries. Persons from third countries are eligible for technical assistance in the fields of action listed in the Annex to the LIFE Regulation under the heading "B. Actions Outside Community Territory".

Status Report

The Commission issued a call for tenders for new, clean technology projects on 19 December 1992, with a deadline of 31 March 1993. Decisions on selection were scheduled for the late summer.

Priorities for the Programme are to be appraised annually. Further calls for proposals are expected at the end of 1993 or early in 1994.

INFORMATION

UK

Central Contact: Richard Longman
DOE/EPC, Room A132
Romney House, 43 Marsham Street
London SW1P 3PY
Tel: 071 276 8146
Fax: 071 276 8626

Nature Conservation: Northern Ireland
Mr G. Seymour : Environment Service
Calvert House, 23 Castle Place
Belfast BT1 1FY
Tel: 0232 230560
Fax: 0232 243939

European & International Habitat
Protection Branch:
R.A. Vagg
Department of the Environment
Room 901
Tollgate House
Houlton Street
Bristol BS2 9DJ
Tel: 0272 218570

IRELAND
For general environmental areas, contact:
Mr Ray Dollard
Environmental Control Section
Dept. of the Environment
Custom House
Dublin 1
Tel: 01 6793377

For conservation measures, contact:
Wildlife Service
Leeson Lane
Dublin 2
Tel: 01 613111

For the industries sector, demonstration programmes
and tenders, contact:
EOLAS
Glasnevin
Dublin 9
Tel: 01 370101

COMMISSION
Brian M. Ross
DG X1-C2
Commission of the EC
200 Rue de la Loi
B-1049 Brussels
Tel: INT+ 322 296 3423
Fax: INT+ 322 296 9561

3. THE PHYSICAL AND SOCIAL ENVIRONMENT PROGRAMME (PSEP)

Objectives

This aims to support the preservation of the countryside and wildlife through the funding of interpretative centres, information centres and projects which will open up access to the countryside generally as well as suitable designated areas.

Background

This is an operational programme of the Community Support Framework: Northern Ireland, under Measure 1 of Sub-Programme 2. The Programme was scheduled to cover the years from 1989 to 1993.

Programme Content

Projects must:

- assist the safeguarding or enhancement of outstanding scenic areas;
- protect and conserve nationally important and rare habitats and wildlife;
- promote enjoyment and understanding of the countryside;
- contribute to the development of tourism in Northern Ireland; and
- provide value for money.

EC Contribution

The overall budget for this programme is 1.33 MECU from EC funds with a further 1.33 MECU from UK sources of which 0.9 MECU was assistance from the ERDF. They jointly provided 68% of the funding required for the projects chosen.

Participation

Enterprises in Northern Ireland, comprising district councils, nature preservation societies and the Department of the Environment, may participate.

Status Report

From 1994, nature conservation will cease to be included in the PSEP Programme and will instead form part of a new Environment Programme within the Community Support Framework: Northern Ireland. This new Programme is only at the consultation stage at present.

INFORMATION

Mr G Seymour
Environment Service - Countryside and Wildlife
Calvert House
23 Castle Place
Belfast BT1 1FY
Tel: 0232 230560
Fax: 0232 243939

Chapter 17.9

Research & Development Grants & Loans: Complementary Action

This group of programmes covers:

1. VALUE II: Valorisation and Utilisation for Europe (and CORDIS)
2. SPRINT: Strategic Programme for Innovation and Technology Transfer
3. Venture Consort Innovation Finance Scheme
4. EUROTECH Capital
5. ESCF: European Seed Capital Funds
6. TPF: Technology Performance Financing
7. MONITOR: Strategic Analysis, Forecasting and Assessment in Research and Technology
8. COST: European Co-operation in the Field of Scientific and Technical Research
9. EUREKA
10. EUROMANAGEMENT
11. STRIDE: Science and Technology for Regional Innovation and Development in Europe
12. The Council of Europe
13. ESF: The European Science Foundation
14. ESA: The European Space Agency

1. VALORISATION AND UTILISATION FOR EUROPE (VALUE II) (and CORDIS)

Statutory Basis

VALUE was approved by Council Decision 89/412/EEC: OJ L 200/23, dated 13/7/89. VALUE II arose from a proposal from the Commission: OJ C 53, dated 28/2/91.

Objectives

This Programme aims to give specific added value to the Research and Development activities which are the subject of the Third Framework Programme.

Background

The VALUE II Programme (1992-94) forms part of the Third Framework Programme, following on from the VALUE Programme in the Second Framework Programme. VALUE II is concerned with the dissemination and exploitation of the results of EC scientific and technological research, obtained under programmes such as ESPRIT, RACE, BRITE-EURAM and JOULE. It provides a range of services to contractors involved in EC R&D projects helping them protect, exploit and disseminate the results of their work. It also provides information and advice on the whole range of EC R&D programmes and encourages industrial and research organisations to participate in these programmes.

Programme Content

The VALUE II Programme is composed of three elements:

i Interface between Research and Industry

ii Interface between Research and the Scientific Community

iii Interface between Research and Society.

i INTERFACE BETWEEN RESEARCH AND INDUSTRY

This is the largest of the three elements and covers the following five activities:

a Relay Centres

A network of Relay Centres has been set up throughout the EC to promote the Community's R&D programmes, to help organisations participate in these programmes and to ensure that results arising from projects are disseminated and exploited. The Centres were set up in January 1993. There are four Relay Centres in the UK, each primarily serving one region of the UK:

- the Welsh Development Agency, serving Wales;
- LEDU (Local Enterprise Development Unit), in collaboration with IRTU (Industrial Research and Technology Unit), serving Northern Ireland;
- EuroInfo Centre Ltd in Glasgow, in collaboration with RTC North Ltd, Technology Transfer Centre and Business Info Source, serving Scotland and northern England (including Teesside, Durham, Tyne & Wear, Northumberland and Cumbria); and
- The Technology Broker, serving southern and central England.

b CORDIS and Publications Dissemination Service

These dissemination activities aim to promote access to and exploitation of non-confidential information generated by EC R&D projects. Information is disseminated via books, reports, articles, conference proceedings and CORDIS - the EC's R&D Information Service, based on electronically-accessible databases.

At present, the CORDIS databases are available on-line in English on the ECHO Host in Luxembourg. They can be accessed from the UK in a number of ways:

- using the national PSDN network, the most popular way to connect from the UK;
- direct dialling, via the international telephone network; and
- via the academic network JANET.

The databases can be searched using a menu system or with an interrogation language, the Common Command Language (CCL). All registered users are provided with a full set of user manuals, complemented by a Help Desk service available during office hours via ECHO's freephone number. The on-line service is presently available free of charge to individuals or organisations based in EC or EFTA countries, but users must register in order to obtain a personal password. To register as a CORDIS user, contact the CORDIS Help Desk at the address given below.

A CD-ROM containing complete CORDIS data was due to be launched during 1993; it is designed as an alternative to the on-line service.

Appendix 7 lists the CORDIS databases available at time of publication.

The publication dissemination service includes:

- Research and Technical Development (RTD) Programmes which gives details of the Programmes through which the Commission pursues and finances EC policy on research and technological development.
- RTD Projects contains more detailed information of activities within EC RTD Programmes.
- RTD Publications (EABS) contains bibliographic details of over 50,000 publications, documents and reports arising from the above projects, as well as references to scientific and technical documents published by the Commission but which are not necessarily related to an RTD programme.
- RTD Com-documents contains information on Commission communications to the Council and Parliament on RTD activities.
- RTD Acronyms explains the multitude of acronyms and abbreviations arising from EC RTD activities. Technical abbreviations are excluded.
- RTD News provides the latest news on all aspects of EC RTD activities.
- RTD Results provides information on results and prototypes arising from EC and other RTD research.
- RTD Partners contains profiles of organisations seeking partners for EC or other RTD programmes or projects, including the type of research proposed and the type of partner sought.

c Utilisation of Results

This activity provides finance for projects aiming to exploit results from EC R&D programmes. Exploitation projects can include obtaining advice on intellectual property issues, assessing exploitation potential, carrying out market studies, searching for industrial/financial partners, carrying out feasibility studies, tests and experimental developments and obtaining assistance to identify licensees and negotiate licences.

d Protection of Results

This activity aims to protect the intellectual property belonging to the EC, which is mainly the output of the Joint Research Centre, and to provide aid and advice to organisations which have been involved in EC R&D projects but do not have access to expertise in obtaining patents.

e Promotion of Results

This activity promotes the results of the EC's R&D Programmes by supporting Programmes which disseminate information on EC R&D, organising seminars and conferences and participating in technology and events both inside and outside the EC.

ii INTERFACE BETWEEN RESEARCH AND THE SCIENTIFIC COMMUNITY

This element aims to study the research environment and its impact and has four themes:

a analysing and studying the EC's R&D environment;

b improving communication of research;

c understanding the effectiveness and efficiency of R&D, using a macro-economic approach; and

d studying the management of R&D.

iii INTERFACE BETWEEN RESEARCH AND SOCIETY

This element aims to measure and analyse the impact on society of the scientific and technical knowledge resulting from the EC's R&D activities and comprises three parts:

a evaluation of social impact;

b communication with the public; and

c analysis of public demand and new requirements.

EC Contribution

The Programme originally had a total budget of 57 MECU, divided into:

Research-Industry interface:	50 MECU
Research-Scientific Community interface:	4 MECU
Research-Society interface:	3 MECU

That amount has now been supplemented by an additional 9 MECU from the top-up to the Third Framework Programme which was recently agreed.

Participation

The services of the Relay Centres and the information held in the CORDIS databases and published documents are available to everyone.

Help to utilise, protect and promote results is available only to contractors who are or have been participants in EC R&D projects, their licensees or exploitation partners, including those of the EC Joint Research Centre. Participants can be industrial companies, particularly SMEs, universities and public or private research centres in any of the Member States.

The Commission also uses contractors to assist it in various ways, such as designing and producing promotional literature and publications on EC R&D activities, carrying out surveys and studies in the European R&D community and organising events and workshops on the themes of dissemination and exploitation.

A proposal usually starts informally with a simple letter or telephone call to a VALUE official in the Commission, (all matters discussed are treated as confidential at all stages). After further discussion, ideas may evolve into proposals for action which the Commission then formally evaluates and from which it makes selections.

Action follows in the form of study and services contracts carried out on behalf of the Commission and shared-cost contracts.

Status Report

The Programme was formally adopted by the Council in April 1992 and the Relay Centres were set up in January 1993.

In September 1992, there was a call for proposals under the Utilisation of Results line of action, aimed at exploiting results from EC R&D projects. This call was open-ended, so proposals can be submitted at any time.

There was a simultaneous announcement, specifically for SMEs, of opportunities to facilitate access by them to the results of EC R&D projects. This announcement was also open-ended.

Applications

Management of the Programme is the responsibility of the Commission and a Management Committee composed of representatives from each Member State.

INFORMATION

UK
Carolyn Abel
Department of Trade and Industry
151 Buckingham Palace Road
London SW1W 9SS
Tel: 071 215 1614

RELAY CENTRES

Wales
Welsh Development Agency (WDA)
QED Centre
Main Avenue
Treforest Industrial Estate
Pontypridd CF37 5YR
Tel: 0443 841345
Fax: 0443 841393

Northern England
Regional Technology Centre North
Unit 3D
Hylton Park
Wessington Way
Sunderland
SR5 3NR
Tel: 091 549 8299

Northern Ireland
LEDU Small Business Agency
LEDU House
Upper Galway
Belfast BT8 4TB
Tel: 0232 491031
Fax: 0232 691432

Northern Ireland
Dept. of Economic Development
Industrial Research and Technology Unit
Netherleigh
Massey Avenue
Belfast BT4 2JP
Tel: 0232 764244

Southern and Central England
The Technology Broker
Station Road
Longstanton
Cambridgeshire
CB4 5DU
Tel: 0954 61199
Fax: 0954 60291

Scotland and Northern England
The Co-ordinating Partner
EuroInfo Centre Ltd (EIC)
Atrium Court
50 Waterloo Street
Glasgow G2 6HQ
Tel: 041 221 0999
Fax: 041 221 6539

The Highlands and Islands of Scotland
Business Information Source Ltd
Bridge House
20 Bridge Street
Inverness IV1 1QR
Tel: 0463 715 400

Southern Central and North-East Scotland
Technology Transfer Centre Ltd
43 Falkland Street
Glasgow G12 9QZ
Tel: 041 339 5010

CORDIS - UK
For further information contact the CORDIS Help Desk - UK Freephone 0800 899 256

IRELAND
O. McBreen
EOLAS
The Irish Science and Technology Agency
Glasnevin, Dublin 9
Tel: 01 370101
Fax: 01 379620

Small Firms Association
Confederation House
Kildare Street
Dublin 2
Tel: 01 6779801

COMMISSION
Mr M. Dragoni
Commission of the European Communities
Directorate-General XIII, Directorate C
Batiment Jean Monnet B4/107
Plateau du Kirchberg
L-2920 Luxembourg
Tel: INT+ 352 4301 34194
Fax: INT+ 352 4301 34129

CORDIS
ECHO/CORDIS Customer Service
BP 262
L 2012 Luxembourg
Tel: INT+ 352 34981 240
Fax: INT+ 352 34981 248

E-Mailx400
C=DE
ADMD=DBP
PRMD=GEONET
S=CORDIS-HELPDESK

2. STRATEGIC PROGRAMME FOR INNOVATION AND TECHNOLOGY TRANSFER (SPRINT)

Statutory Basis

Council Decision 89/286/EEC: OJ L 112/12, dated 25/4/89

Objectives

The objective is to improve the competitiveness of industry, particularly SMEs, within the EC by ensuring that technology and aids to innovation can be shared across national boundaries.

Background

SPRINT was launched in 1983 as a three-year experimental programme and was extended in 1986 for a further two years, at a further cost of 8.6 MECU. The main phase of SPRINT consisted of a five-year (1989-93) programme administered by DG XIII, to promote innovation and the transfer of technology. It is primarily aimed at stimulating intermediaries (such as international licensing consultants and technical institutes) to co-operate in transnational networks, which facilitate licensing deals between SMEs or carry out joint projects to disseminate information more widely. SPRINT is not part of the EC R&D Framework Programme, however.

Programme Content

There are three main lines of action within the Programme.

- ACTION LINE A: Strengthening the European infrastructure for innovation services by consolidating or forming EC networks of agents for technology transfer and innovation support.

- ACTION LINE B: Supporting "specific projects" which demonstrate by practical example the intra-Community spread of innovation. Projects are particularly concerned with transferring new technologies, already applied in one sector or region of the EC, to another sector or region which had not previously had the use of such technologies.

- ACTION LINE C: Improving the environment for innovation through a better knowledge of its workings and increased "concentration", i.e. collaboration and exchange of experiences - in areas such as the use of research results, design, patents and innovation - between the Member States and the Commission.

A series of 12 forums covering a wide range of European cities was organised during 1993. The organisation of these forums was entrusted to various organisations, notably the European Venture Capital Association (EVCA) in Belgium, the Agence Nationale de Valorisation de la Recherche (ANVAR) in France and the Technology International Exchange (TIE), also based in France. The investors - averaging between 40 and 60 per forum - were mostly venture capitalists, investment companies and long-term credit institutions, but also included industrial firms interested in joint ventures. The scheme is for forums to be held over two days, beginning with presentations by the firms and followed by confidential face-to-face discussions between the innovating companies and investors.

SPRINT is also launching an experimental scheme called "Managing the Integration of New Technology" (MINT), aimed at promoting the absorption of new technologies by SMEs through the use of consultants experienced in managing innovation. MINT assesses firms' use of technology and assesses their potential for integrating relevant new technology and management techniques as a part of an overall business strategy. MINT is targeted at SMEs in the manufacturing sector which could potentially benefit from the acquisition of a technology or technique from another Member State, or expand rapidly from national to European markets with the assistance of a MINT project.

EC Contribution

SPRINT has a total funding of 90 MECU, broken down as follows:

-	Action line A	50 MECU
-	Action line B	30 MECU
-	Action line C	10 MECU

Participation

SPRINT is open to all organisations, both public and private, whose activities include helping business - particularly SMEs - to exchange technology and to innovate, e.g. regional or local development agencies, innovation centres, technology transfer or licensing consultants, research and technology organisations and Chambers of Commerce.

Project proposals selected by the Commission can receive financial support of up to half eligible costs but, in practice, each partner could expect to receive only about as much as 15,000 - 20,000 ECU per annum.

Status Report

It is anticipated that further calls will be made under all Action Lines during 1994.

Applications

Interested parties can only apply for support when a Commission call for proposals has been published in the OJ. There is usually a three-month period after publication of a call for return of proposals to the Commission.

Companies wanting to participate in Action Line C forums should contact the organisers and/or their corresponding national venture capital association. The selection of the companies for presentation at a forum is the sole responsibility of the organisers and the national venture capital organisations. Financiers interested in participating in these fora should contact the organisers.

Management of the Programme is the responsibility of DG XIII, assisted by the Consultative Committee for Innovation and Technology Transfer (CIT), which is made up of government officials nominated by Member States.

INFORMATION

UK

The DTI contact on CIT is as follows. Organisations wishing to be included on a DTI SPRINT mailing list, which gives early warning of SPRINT initiatives, should notify Linda O'Connor, giving written details of their organisations, at

DTI
3rd Floor Green
151 Buckingham Palace Road
London SW1W 9SS
Tel: 071 215 1656

MINT
Mr Philippe Sowdon
PERA International
Melton Mowbray
Leicestershire LE13 0PB
Tel: 0664 501501

IRELAND
EOLAS
The Irish Science and Technology Agency
Glasnevin
Dublin 9
Tel: 01 370101
Fax: 01 379620

MINT
Mr Owen McBreen
EOLAS
The Irish Science and Technology Agency
Glasnevin
Dublin 9
Tel: 01 370101

COMMISSION
SPRINT
D. Janssens
Commission of the EC
DG XIII
Batiment Jean Monnet
Plateau de Kirchberg
L-2920 Luxembourg
Tel: INT+ 352 4301 34180
Fax: INT+ 352 4301 34544

MINT
Mr R. Miege
Commission of the EC
DG XIII-D
Batiment Jean Monnet
Rue Alcide de Gasperi
L-2920 Luxembourg
Tel: INT+ 352 4301 34180
Fax: INT+ 352 4301 34544

SPRINT Technical Assistance Unit
119 avenue de la Faiencerie
L-1511 Luxembourg
Tel: INT+ 352 46 55 88
Fax: INT+ 352 46 55 50

3. VENTURE CONSORT INNOVATION FINANCE SCHEME

Objectives

The Venture Consort scheme is intended to encourage the growth of SMEs through the formation of cross-border syndicates of venture capitalists. Its three main objectives are:

i to demonstrate that, despite legislative, financial and fiscal differences between Member States, it is possible to finance cross-border innovative projects;

ii to encourage cross-border development and co-operation between SMEs at a European level; and

iii to stimulate systematic use of syndication and the creation of syndicates between venture capital companies established in several countries of the EC.

Background

The scheme was launched in March 1985.

The venture capital sector is made up of financial entities with their own particular characteristics, which often specialise in a particular sector. They do not confine their activities to established companies and may become involved at various stages in the development of a business, from seed capital, start-up and early stage to expansion finance. A venture capitalist is not a lender but a shareholder who provides support for the rapid development of a business. Venture capital institutions actively monitor the businesses in which they have invested their own or other funds. They do not interfere with the management of the company, but maintain a close interest in the implementation of the company strategy. The venture capitalist's profit comes from capital gains made when recouping the investment and he accepts a higher level of risk than bankers or traditional investors, in expectation of a high ultimate return.

Programme Content

The main criteria for project approval are that:

- the proposal concerns SMEs;
- the project is innovative;
- the project is located within the EC;
- more than one Member State is involved;
- it is financed by a transnational venture capital syndicate; and
- it is consistent with other EC policies and programmes.

EC Contribution

Up to 3,000 ECU may be granted to help search for partners in a new venture capital syndicate, in addition to set-up costs of 5,000 - 10,000 ECU. The maximum contribution to the investment is the lesser of 30% of the total input or 300,000 ECU.

If a project is successful and the investment is realised within seven years, the Commission will reap financial benefits like any other investor, but the Commission has agreed to return half its gains to the investing syndicate, as a further incentive to boost innovation in Europe. If the net sale proceeds are higher than the amount initially invested, the lead investor in the cross-border syndicate will refund to the Commission the amount initially invested by it, plus half its share of the increment value (to which it is entitled as a result of its participation in the project), on a pro rata basis.

Participation

Essentially by SMEs involved in innovative work.

Status Report

Since the launch of the scheme, the Commission has contributed 6.2 MECU to support 35 Venture Consort projects.

INFORMATION

European Venture Consort Association
Keibergpark
Minervastraat 6
Box 6
B-1930 Zaventem
Belgium
Tel: INT+ 322 720 6010
Fax: INT+ 322 725 3036

Commission
Philippe Poggioli
Commission of the European Communities
DG XXIII B.3
Rue d'Arlon 80
B-1040 Brussels
Tel: 322 296 5233
Fax: 322 295 2154

4. EUROTECH CAPITAL

Objectives

EUROTECH Capital aims to stimulate private capital funding of transnational high-technology projects (THTPs).

Programme Content

The scheme involves the grant of a EUROTECH Capital label, giving the right to a financial contribution and other benefits, to any financial entity which meets the criteria required and undertakes to acquire holdings in THTPs.

The projects being supported must be transnational in nature, have a high technology aspect and last at least five years. Those forming part of the EEC Framework Programme or having EUREKA project status would automatically be regarded as transnational, while EUREKA or EC R&D projects would be recognised as meeting the high technology criterion.

As part of this initiative, the Commission sponsors INVEST, a confidential database providing technical and commercial information on high-tech projects to EUROTECH Capital members.

EC Contribution

The Commission offers finance companies joining the EUROTECH Capital pilot project a financial contribution equal to 4% of the fund reserved by the company for financing THTPs, but this contribution may not exceed 1 MECU. The EC contribution may be used in two ways:

i the contribution is used, together with the reserved funds, for all investments in THTPs, or

ii the contribution is used exclusively to co-finance the seed-corn phases of THTPs, with the EC contribution and the reserved funds being used in equal shares.

The EC contribution must be reimbursed within three months after approval by the Commission of the final valuation of all holdings in companies promoting THTPs ("final valuation"). This valuation must be supplied by the financial entity within three months of approval of its balance sheet for the tenth year following the granting of the EUROTECH Capital label, or of its final balance sheet, if the entity is wound up before expiry of the ten year period.

Participation

To obtain the Eurotech Capital label, a financial entity must meet the following criteria:

- it must be a company or other legal entity (investment fund, investment company, network of companies etc.), which has as its main objective the acquisition of holdings in non-quoted companies in order to finance their development and subsequently sell the holding, or it must be a financial intermediary whose principal activity is brokerage operations;
- its registered office must be in one of the Member States;
- it must have an investment capacity of at least 50 MECU;
- it must provide a contractual undertaking to earmark at least a fifth of its investment capacity as new risk capital to finance companies involved in THTPs; and
- it must be managed by directors with specific experience in the relevant field and have a management team appropriate to the type and size of the scheme.

To qualify for finance, companies must:

- promote THTPs,
- have their registered office and main seat of activity in a Member State;
- have a majority of their shares held by individuals resident in the EC or companies whose registered offices are situated in the EC.

Priority will be given to:

- businesses employing fewer than 500 persons, whose net fixed assets do not exceed 75 MECU and not more than a third of whose shares are held by large companies; and
- seed capital and start-up phases of companies promoting their THTPs.

Status Report

Under the EUROTECH Capital label, nine European venture capital companies have undertaken to invest about 150 MECU in trans-national high-tech projects.

A IR£1 million fund for young Irish enterprises with growth potential was established in January 1992. It is managed by the Dublin Business Innovation Centre in conjunction with the Cork, Limerick and Galway BICs with the support of the ECSF and twelve Irish investors.

Applications

Financial entities should apply for a EUROTECH Capital label from the Commission.

INFORMATION

UK
Ailie Menzies
Project Manager
Longman Cartermill Ltd
The Technology Centre
St Andrews
Fife KY16 9EA
Tel: 0334 77660

COMMISSION
Philippe Poggioli
DG XXIII B.3
Commission of the EC
Rue d'Arlon 80
B-1040 Brussels
Tel: INT+ 322 296 5233
Fax: INT+ 322 295 2154

5. EUROPEAN SEED CAPITAL FUNDS (ESCF)

Statutory Basis

Commission Decision: 88/1496/EEC of 19/10/88 on a Community pilot scheme to stimulate seed capital.

Objectives

The overall objective is to foster enterprise creation in the EC by strengthening the financing opportunities available to new enterprises.

Background

Seed capital is defined as investment in new or embryonic companies which is required to permit them to develop product prototypes up to a point where venture capital or more traditional sources become available. Projects typically in need of seed capital are those with a long development phase or which involve new technology.

The European Venture Capital Organisation has established that, in 1987, less than 1% of new venture capital investments went into seed projects.

The Commission has adopted a five-year (1989-94) pilot scheme within the framework of its SME policies, under which it will provide financial support to 24 seed funds throughout the EC. The objective is to improve the initial viability of seed funds while the organisations gain the experience and recognition necessary for the funds to become self sustaining.

Programme Content

The seed capital funds should be able to provide, directly or indirectly, a range of support services including:

- financial planning and advice on sources of finance for projects once they are beyond the seed stage;
- market analysis;
- competitive positioning and business strategies; and
- other types of specialist advice.

The 25 seed capital funds selected by the Commission and 25 associated members form a European network - the European Seed Capital Fund Network (ESCFN). It provides counselling, training and information services, either directly or indirectly, via sub-contractors. The EVCA (European Venture Capital Association) is the Unit's host organisation.

To be eligible, projects must meet these criteria:

- the external seed capital required may not exceed 350,000 ECU
- In the case of an existing business, it must be a separate entity, whose maximum size is defined as follows,
  - existing risk capital investment of no more than 50,000 ECU;
  - annual sales of no more than 100,000 ECU;
  - less than 10 employees;
  - total value of share capital at seed funding share price must not exceed 1.5 MECU.

EC Contribution

There are upper limits to the funds which can be made available and the typical seed investment is likely to be between 25,000 and 100,000 ECU.

Status Report

By 1 January 1993, the funds participating in the pilot scheme had raised 38 MECU in capital and had made 131 investments in new enterprises, totalling some 15 MECU. Of these 131 enterprises, the 126 still operating had created 1,219 full-time jobs.

The Network has brought together 24 funds supported by the Commission and seven others which responded to the call in December 1988 for proposals to become full members of the Network. Eleven further seed capital funds and institutions investing in seed stage projects were granted associate membership status, following a call for expressions of interest.

Applications

Firms wishing to obtain seed capital should contact one of the designated seed capital funds, which alone have the power to decide disbursement of funds.
The Network is still open to other seed capital funds for associate membership.

INFORMATION

UK

Welsh Development Agency
Pearl House
Greyfriars Road
Cardiff CF1 3XX
Tel: 0222 222 666
Fax: 0222 390 752

Oxford Seedcorn Capital Ltd
213 Woodstock Road
Oxford OX2 7AD
Tel: 0865 53535
Fax: 0865 512976

Prelude Technology Investments
280 Science Park
Milton Road
Cambridge CB4 4WE
Tel: 0223 423132
Fax: 0223 420869

Strathclyde Innovation
Business Centre
62 Templeton Street
Glasgow G40 1DA
Tel: 041 554 5995
Fax: 041 556 6320

ESCF Network Co-ordinating Unit
Michael Russell
Co-ordination Unit
European Seed Capital Network
EVCA
Keibergpark
Minervastraat 6
Box 6
B-1930 Zaventem
Belgium
Tel: INT+ 322 720 6010
Fax: INT+ 322 725 3036

COMMISSION
Philippe Poggioli / Megan Richards
Commission of the European Communities
DG XXIII, B3
80 rue d'Arlon
B-1049 Brussels
Tel: INT+ 322 296 5233/2443
Fax: INT+ 322 295 2154

6. TECHNOLOGY PERFORMANCE FINANCING (TPF)

Objectives

TPF has the prime objectives of facilitating the uptake of new technology by manufacturing firms and of increasing the interaction between suppliers and users of technology and sources of finance. The ultimate aim is to establish TPF as an accepted market mechanism.

Background

TPF is an initiative suggested by the managers of SPRINT which aims principally to strengthen the innovative capacity of Europe, especially among SMEs.

TPF is based on the system known as "performance contracting" which is widely used in the USA, particularly by firms buying energy-saving technology. EC support makes the financial institutions its direct beneficiaries.

Programme Content

The basis of the scheme is that payment for new technology is at least partly contingent on the technology producing the benefits claimed for it.

The funds are provided by selected banks and other financial institutions. Typically, the bank will advance up to 80% of the cost of the project and will be paid back in several instalments over two to three years. Payment schedules are negotiated on the basis of predetermined targets proving the performance of the technology or services provided. If the product does not work as well as stipulated, the user need not pay the full price.

In addition to the obvious advantage to the user, the supplier will also benefit by being able to penetrate new markets which previously resisted change.

The financing procedure is as follows. The banks charge an agreed premium over the value of the project to cover their interest charges and administration costs plus a small additional premium if agreed targets are achieved, after all money owed to the bank has been repaid. Funds advanced will typically be in the range of 40,000 - 200,000 ECU per project.

EC Contribution

The Commission will provide financial support to the financial institutions, consisting of grants to cover part of the costs of obtaining a technical appraisal of projects and administering the scheme and of a "safety-net", which guarantees part of the losses resulting from underperformance of the new technology or default of the purchaser.

The Commission will sponsor an arbitration scheme to resolve disputes between the parties.

Participation

Any firm is eligible to apply to the nominated financial institution for TPF.

Status Report

The Commission has launched two calls, one for proposals and one for expressions of interest. The call for proposals was addressed to the financial institutions, which were required to participate in the scheme with SPRINT support for two or three years and to continue thereafter on a commercial basis. The institutions could be expected to:

- make advances to support at least ten innovative projects over the pilot two or three-year period;
- manage TPF on behalf of the Commission through its branch network; and

- share experience etc., within a working group.

The deadline for the last batch of applications was 30 June 1991. It is not certain whether any further calls for applications are expected in the foreseeable future.

Applications

The call for expressions of interest is addressed to non-participating financial institutions, inviting them to submit projects eligible for TPF. About 60 are being selected on a first come, first served basis. The level of support to these institutions will be less than those selected under the call for proposals. There are no deadlines for this call.

INFORMATION

UK

Designated financial institutions include:

3i plc
Waterloo Road
London SE1 8XP
Tel: 071 928 3131

National Westminster Bank plc
Commercial Banking Services
London EC3M 4PB
Tel: 071 374 3707

COMMISSION

Robin Miege
Commission of the European Communities
DG XIII C/4
L-2920 Luxembourg
Tel: INT+ 352 43011 (exchange):

7 STRATEGIC ANALYSIS, FORECASTING AND ASSESSMENT IN RESEARCH AND TECHNOLOGY (MONITOR)

Statutory Basis

Council Decision 89/414/EEC: OJ L 200/38, dated 13/7/89

Objectives

MONITOR aims to identify new directions and priorities for EC research and technological development (RTD) policy and to help show more clearly the relationship between R&D and other common policies.

Background

A research programme on Forecasting and Assessment in Science and Technology (FAST) has operated since 1978. The results from the first FAST programme included guidelines for a new EC policy on biotechnology and the conceptual framework for a number of other EC research programmes, including ESPRIT. FAST II (1983-87), with a budget of 8.5 MECU, focused on five areas of research:

i technology, work and employment;

ii transformation of services and new technologies;

iii the communication function;

iv the future of the food system; and

v renewable natural resources.

A proposal for a new FAST programme was published in OJ C 39, dated 11/2/88 but, after further consideration, this was withdrawn and replaced by the broader MONITOR Programme.

Programme Content

The programme has three specific and complementary activities: SAST, FAST and SPEAR.

1. SAST: STRATEGIC ANALYSIS IN SCIENCE AND TECHNOLOGY

The aim of SAST is to identify the options available to solve a given problem and provide precise recommendations for action. SAST research actions can take up to eighteen months and typically include:

- assessment of the strengths and weaknesses of the EC in a specific sector;
- assessment of the state of development of a technology and its future evolution; and
- determination of the likely social, economic and, where appropriate, environmental impact of a selected scientific or technological development.

Current SAST projects include studies on:

- the potential for co-operation in Science and Technology (S&T) between selected advanced developing countries and the EC;
- the role of S&T policy in setting standards;
- a research and technology strategy to help overcome environmental problems in relation to transport;
- a strategy for biotechnology research directed towards farming, forestry and the agro-industry;
- the identification of technology priorities for European RTD;
- S&T policy on use of, and quality problems with, water resources;
- environmental problems associated with the recycling and disposal of plastics; and
- the impact of the service sector on technological innovation.

2. FAST: FORECASTING AND ASSESSMENT OF SCIENCE AND TECHNOLOGY

The FAST activity is a specifically-oriented successor to the previous FAST programmes. It studies scientific and technological developments, and their interactions with economic and social changes in the EC, in the light of world-wide developments.

Research actions last up to two years and include:

- prospective dossiers on major topics or phenomena of a global character that may extend beyond the strictly European framework, such as the long-term development of major world regions, the future of urban societies etc.;
- applied technology assessments on the implications and consequences of selected scientific and technical developments, such as the development of anthropocentric technologies and production systems and of technologies related to health treatment; and
- syntheses giving a critical analysis of the main forecasting studies published world-wide in specific fields, e.g. the biosphere.

3. SPEAR: SUPPORT STUDIES FOR THE EVALUATION OF COMMUNITY R&D

SPEAR aims to provide the Commission with improved theoretical and methodological tools to evaluate the social and economic impact of its RTD programmes. Research actions include:

- methodological studies to improve the methods used to evaluate and measure the impacts of the R&D programmes, to develop indicators and to draft guidelines for evaluations;
- horizontal evaluations, which cover particular activities or mechanisms common to several RTD programmes, such as the effects of EC RTD programmes on social and economic cohesion; and
- "12+1" networks to enable exchange and diffusion of ideas in the field of evaluation

EC Contribution

The Programme has a total budget of 22 MECU for the period 1989-93. The Commission pays 100% of the cost of the research undertaken.

Participation

The SAST, FAST and SPEAR activities are to be undertaken through cross-national and multi-partner projects, carried out by experts and organisations on contract, or through scientific and professional networks. Projects are initiated by the Commission and contracts awarded as a result of a closed call for tender; they are executed in collaboration with, and supervised by Commission services.

Status Report

There was a call for proposals in OJ C 144, dated 10/6/89; the funds available for contracts have now been committed. Reports from the MONITOR Programme are becoming available and details are given in a regular newsletter produced by the Programme of Policy Research in Engineering Science & Technology (PREST). Both the UK and the EC held a number of conferences during 1993.

MONITOR was scheduled to finish in June 1993; the nature of any continuation activities has yet to be decided.

Applications

Applications are made to the Commission, following a call for proposals published in the OJ.

The Commission is responsible for the management of the Programme, aided by a Committee of an Advisory Nature (CAN). CAN-MONITOR consists of representatives of Member States and meets regularly to advise on the structure and implementation of the Programme. UK representatives are provided by the DTI.

INFORMATION

Mrs Janet Evans
UK Monitor National Network Node
PREST
The University of Manchester
Oxford Road
Manchester M13 9PL
Tel: 061 275 5921
Fax: 061 273 1123

Mrs Maureen Reeves
UK MONITOR Co-ordinator
DTI,
Research and Technology Division 2a
3/181 Green
151 Buckingham Palace Road
London SW1W 9SS
Tel: 071 215 1632
Fax: 071 215 2909

IRELAND
EOLAS
The Irish Science and Technology Agency
Glasnevin
Dublin 9
Tel: 01 370101
Fax: 01 379620

Commission
Mrs Clara de la Torre
Commission of the EC
DGXII-A
200 Rue de la Loi
B-1049 Brussels
Tel: INT+ 322 296 4915
Fax: INT+ 322 295 6995

8 EUROPEAN CO-OPERATION IN THE FIELD OF SCIENTIFIC AND TECHNICAL RESEARCH (COST)

Statutory Basis

There is no one statute regulating COST, so it works within flexible, pragmatic operating rules agreed by the Member States. The form of co-operation for each COST project is therefore defined by simple, purpose-built agreements.

Objectives

COST provides a mechanism for European scientific and technological collaboration which complements the Framework Programmes.

Background

COST was established by a European Ministerial Conference in 1971. Membership comprises the EC Member States, Austria, Finland, Norway, Sweden, Switzerland, Turkey, Yugoslavia, Iceland, Hungary, Poland and Czechoslovakia.

COST operates through a series of co-operative projects which enable variable numbers of participants to undertake research in areas of common interest and exchange the results among themselves and other COST members as appropriate.

Programme Content

COST co-operation covers the following areas:

- informatics,
- telecommunications,
- transport,
- oceanography,
- metallurgy and materials science,
- environment,
- meteorology,
- agriculture and biotechnology,
- food technology,
- socio-technologies,
- health and medical research and
- civil engineering.

The COST mechanism has proved suitable for several types of problem including:

- those of an intrinsically international nature e.g. oceanography and the environment;
- problems which are common to many COST member states and which can benefit from joint actions, e.g. data processing, materials; and
- problems which by their nature require harmonisation of international standards, e.g. telecommunications and transport.

COST has established groups to examine the possibility of further activity in a number of fields, including social sciences and chemistry.

EC Contribution

COST activities operate without any central funding towards research expenditure. Additional expenditure is often minimal, as research relating to a particular project is generally already underway. In most cases, the Commission does, however, provide a secretariat.

Non-EC COST states taking part in those projects which have been incorporated into EC programmes contribute towards co-ordination costs. The Commission pays the co-ordination costs of EC countries in such projects. Participants are responsible for all costs in COST projects outside the EC programmes once the projects are underway.

Participation

Any COST member state may propose a new research topic. If any other COST member states are interested in collaboration, this may lead them to set up an agreement among themselves known as a Memorandum of Understanding. This has no binding effect in international law and is merely a declaration of intent, indicating the willingness of the signatory member states to participate in the COST activity. Countries normally choose to participate in a particular project if they are already involved at national level in research in the field under consideration, or intend to initiate a national project.

Because of the nature of COST research activities, participants have been primarily administrations, research institutes and research centres from the public sector, but an increasing number of projects involve participants from industry.

Potential participants would normally be sought during the formative stage of a COST proposal, to establish the level of interest before a Memorandum of Understanding and Implementation is signed. A project management committee is then set up to implement the new COST activity.

Organisations from non-COST countries can participate in COST projects with the approval of the appropriate management committee and the COST Senior Officials Committee.

Status Report

The UK is a signatory to most of the projects of industrial interest on the COST project list. Information on specific projects can be obtained by contacting the individual concerned. The UK is also involved in other projects, which come under the remit of government departments other than the DTI. Details of these can be obtained from the COST Secretariat at the Cabinet Office.

COST is an on-going collaborative mechanism with no set end date. The extent and duration of each project is recommended in the relevant Memorandum of Understanding.

Applications

Decisions on whether proposed COST projects should be undertaken and on participation are taken by the Committee of COST Senior Officials. This committee, which meets four times a year, is composed of representatives of the nineteen COST member states and the European Commission.

INFORMATION

Further general information about COST can be obtained from the COST Secretariat:

COST Secretariat
Cabinet Office
Room 421
70 Whitehall
London SW1A 2AS
Tel: 071 270 0081

Enquiries about specific COST activities should be made to the individual concerned. A list is available from the DTI:

DTI
Research & Technology Policy Division
151 Buckingham Palace Road
London SW1W 9SS
Tel: 071 215 1687
Fax: 071 215 2909

9. EUREKA

Objectives

EUREKA is a European initiative aimed at facilitating industry-led, market-driven, collaborative projects in all sectors of technology with the aim of introducing new products, processes and services relevant to world markets.

Background

EUREKA is not an EC programme, but a framework for industry-led projects aimed at producing high-technology goods and services to compete in world markets against the US and Japan. EUREKA complements the EC R&D programmes, in that it is generally concerned principally with the commercial exploitation of research.

EUREKA members are EC Member States, EFTA countries, Hungary, and Turkey; the European Commission also participates in EUREKA as an equal member.

Programme Content

EUREKA projects can be in any technological area, provided that the simple EUREKA criteria are met, i.e.:

- the project must comprise at least two organisations from at least two EUREKA countries; and
- it must involve technical innovation.

Current projects mostly fall into one of the following nine categories, but these should not be seen as programmes because there are no priority areas where governments are seeking project proposals:

- communication,
- energy,
- environment,
- information technology,
- laser,
- medical/biotechnology,
- new materials,
- robotics and production automation and
- transport.

Projects should, furthermore, be both innovative and technically realistic, with reasonable prospects of eventual commercial exploitation. Both the managerial and technical resources devoted to the project should at the outset be shown to be sufficient to ensure effective completion of the project.

The National Project Co-ordinator network can help find partners by bringing project proposals to the attention of organisations in other member countries. (The UK EUREKA Unit is situated in the Research and Technology Policy Division of the DTI). There are also specialist technology umbrellas which promote loosely structured packages of R&D in given fields, which are:

- FAMOS - flexible automation;
- EUROENVIRON - terrestrial environment;
- EUROLASER - laser technology;
- EUROMAR - marine environment;
- EUROCARE - preservation of the physical heritage;
- MAINE - maintenance of capital equipment;
- EUROVOLTAIC - solar power;
- EUROAGRI - food industry;

- EUROSURF - surface engineering;
- EUROBOND - adhesives; and
- DIAGNOSTICS - all areas involving diagnostic processes

EC Contribution

Since its launch in 1985, EUREKA has embraced 8.8 BECU of agreed projects. Participants in EUREKA can obtain funding from their own national governments; government support must be shown to have a significant influence on the scope or scale of the project.

Participation

In order to keep bureaucracy to a minimum, projects are proposed and run by firms and research institutes from any of the EUREKA member countries.

Status Report

There are now 623 EUREKA projects. Six hundred and two UK organisations are currently involved in 174 EUREKA projects, in 56 of which UK companies take the lead.

Applications

Because of its wide and collaborative nature, applications here are welcome from research institutes, manufacturers of high tech equipment and marketing organisations specialising in technology.

INFORMATION

Further information about EUREKA is available from:

The EUREKA Enquiry Point
Tel: 071 333 5161

DTI Contact:
David Saunders
National Project Co-ordinator
EUREKA Office
Department of Trade & Industry
3rd Floor
151 Buckingham Palace Road
London SW1W 9SS
Tel: 071 215 1621
Fax: 071 215 2909

10. EUROMANAGEMENT

Objectives

The Programme was set up to help SMEs prepare themselves to compete in the Single European Market.

Background

EUROMANAGEMENT is a pilot action of DG XXIII of the Commission. It was launched in 1991 to counterbalance the common belief that SMEs have very little interest in research activities, and demonstrated that SMEs have the potential to introduce dynamism into EC research and the utilisation of its results.

Programme Content

There are two aspects to the Programme:

1. R&TD AUDITS

In launching EUROMANAGEMENT, DG XIII wanted to encourage industrial SMEs which were willing to join forces with research centres, universities or other industrial companies located in other EC Member States. Forty seven selected consultants therefore carried out EUROMANAGEMENT audits "in-house" for 650 SMEs, making them aware of the opportunities offered by EC research and transnational technological co-operation and diagnosing their technological, strategic and managerial potential.

The consultants were selected from both the public and privaté-sectors, under a call for tender procedure. The Commission provided half the consultants' costs, the balance having to be provided by national or regional authorities or from the SMEs' private funds.

2. STANDARDISATION, CERTIFICATION, QUALITY AND SAFETY

Completion of the single market requires European standardisation bodies to adopt a large number of EC-mandated standards which, with associated certification procedures, involves rapid adjustment by EC enterprises on an on going basis. This places particular burdens on SMEs with limited human and financial resources who find it difficult to adjust to new standards. Quality assurance is also increasingly required by principals and contractors, and is placing additional demands on SMEs struggling to maintain competitiveness.

Support for SMEs in the sphere of quality, which covers standardisation, certification and health and safety in the workplace, is therefore essential if they are to be helped to adjust to, and participate fully in, the single market.

The pilot scheme was announced in June 1992 and ran throughout 1993, supporting the services of 40 technical advisers selected by tender from the 12 Member States. Each adviser had to assess the problems and requirements of 10 to 15 SMEs in accordance with a common methodology and to make recommendations in the fields covered by the scheme. A co-ordinator, selected by tender, was responsible for developing the methodology, producing a training seminar and manual for the advisers and co-ordinating and managing the pilot scheme.

EC Contribution

The funding operated similarly to the R&TD audits scheme.

Participation

SMEs throughout the EC with special reference follow in Objective 1 and Objective 2 Areas (see chapter 18 for definition).

Status Report

The call for the R&TD audit scheme was published in OJ C 4, dated 8 January 1991, with a deadline of 14 February 1991 and the pilot action audits ended in January 1992. EUROMANAGEMENT consultants identified some 1000 potential R&TD projects among the SMEs audited. About 100 research proposals were submitted to the Commission in response to the calls for tender under the Third Framework Programme.

DG XIII plans, after consultation with the Member States, to propose an extension of the action in order to benefit other technology-oriented, industrial SMEs. Prolonging the EUROMANAGEMENT Programme will be considered after evaluating the 1991 EUROMANAGEMENT audit campaign.

The call for the standardisation scheme was published in OJ C 146, dated 10 June 1992, with a deadline of 17 July 1992. It is not known whether any further calls are going to be made.

Applications

Direct to the Commission.

INFORMATION

R&TD Audits
Philippe Poggioli
Commission of the European Communities
DG XIII B.3
80 Rue d'Arlon
B-1040 Brussels,
Tel: INT+ 322 296 5233
Fax: INT+ 322 295 2154

Standardisation, Certification, Quality & Safety:
Megan Richards
Commission of the European Communities
Directorate-General XXIII B.3
80 Rue d'Arlon
B-1049 Brussels
Tel: INT+ 322 296 2443
Fax: INT+ 322 295 2154

11. SCIENCE & TECHNOLOGY FOR REGIONAL INNOVATION & DEVELOPMENT IN EUROPE (STRIDE)

See Chapter 19

12. THE COUNCIL OF EUROPE SCIENTIFIC AND TECHNOLOGICAL PROGRAMME

Objectives

The Council of Europe was founded in 1949 to achieve greater unity between its members and foster economic and social progress.

Background

The Council of Europe brings together 25 European democracies, including the EC Member States and EFTA countries. Scientific and technological activities are run by its Parliamentary Assembly, which now includes "special guest" delegations from five Central and Eastern European countries.

Programme Content

Co-operation presently focuses on:

- renewable energy sources,
- North-South technology transfers,
- climate change and
- bioethics.

Status Report

Information is a bit scarce at the moment and it is understood that the programmes are in the course of reorganisation.

INFORMATION

Pat Ashworth
WED
Room W118
Foreign & Commonwealth Office
London SW1A 2AH
Tel: 071 210 3000

13. THE EUROPEAN SCIENCE FOUNDATION (ESF)

Objectives

The ESF is designed to identify areas where international co-operation would bring the most benefit to European research and to provide the initial stimulus for establishing collaborative programmes.

Background

The ESF is an international, non-governmental agency founded in 1974 and based in Strasbourg. It is made up of academics and research councils responsible for supporting scientific research. The ESF currently has 48 member organisations from eighteen European countries, including the EC Member States, and focuses on basic activities in all fields including the humanities and social sciences.

UK members include the Agriculture and Food Research Council, the British Academy, the Economic and Social Research Council, the Medical Research Council, the Royal Society and the Science and Engineering Research Council.

EC Contribution

ESF funding is based on a general budget, to which member organisations contribute, with options to "buy into" certain activities.

INFORMATION

The ESF covers many areas of interest, but contact should be made in the first instance with the local research council.

UK
DTI Innovation Enquiry line
0800 442001
Ashdown House
Victoria Street
London SW1

IRELAND
Dept of Industry and Commerce
Kildare Street
Dublin 2
Tel: 01 6614444

14. THE EUROPEAN SPACE AGENCY (ESA)

Objectives

The European Space Agency was set up to promote co-operation among European states in civil space research, technology and space applications.

Background

The ESA is not a Community institution. It has 13 member states: the EC countries, except Greece, Luxembourg and Portugal, together with Austria, Norway, Sweden and Switzerland. Involvement in the ESA gives members the opportunity to take part in projects that would otherwise be beyond the resources of their national civil space programmes.

Programme Content

The work carried out by the ESA is divided into six main programme areas. These are:

- space science;
- microgravity;
- Earth observation;
- satellite telecommunications;
- space transportation systems; and
- the Columbus space station.

ESA operates a system of "juste retour" which awards industrial contracts to Member States in proportion to their funding of ESA programmes. The UK's main funding goes to the ESA programmes on Earth observation, space science and satellite telecommunications.

INFORMATION

The British National Space Centre represents the UK on the ESA Council and other delegate bodies.

British National Space Centre
Dean Bradley House
52 Horseferry Road
London SW1P 2AG
Tel: 071 276 2688

Chapter 17.10

European Coal & Steel Community Sponsored Research Grants

Article 55 (1) of the European Coal and Steel Community Treaty states,

> "The High Authority shall promote technical and economic research relating to the production and increased use of coal and steel and to occupational safety in the coal and steel industries. To this end it shall organise all appropriate contacts among existing research bodies."

Under Article 55, the ECSC supports a range of research programmes, which fall outside the General Framework Programme and its 1992 budget made provision for 170 MECU for research in the following areas -

1. Steel Research
2. Pilot and/or Demonstration Projects in the Iron & Steel Industry
3. Coal Research
4. ECSC Social Research Programmes:
   - sixth ECSC programme of ergonomics for the steel and coal industry
   - technical control of nuisance and pollution from iron and steel works
   - research on safety in the European coal and steel community industries
   - industrial hygiene in mines
   - fifth ECSC medical research programme

1. STEEL RESEARCH

Statutory Basis

Until 1990, separate guidelines were established for research and for pilot/demonstration projects, but these were then combined to apply to both programmes for the period to 1995 (OJ C 252/3, dated 6/10/90). These guidelines are therefore an extension of those for steel research, 1986-90 (OJ C 294, dated 16/11/85), and supersede those for pilot and demonstration projects (OJ C 317, dated 28/11/87).

Objectives

The main aim is the promotion of technical and economic research relating to the production of steel and the increase in its consumption.

Programme Content

The medium-term guidelines for technical steel research in the period 1991-95 provide for activities in three main sectors:

i Production Processes

Research efforts will try to improve existing production methods and develop new techniques to produce steel faster, better and at less cost by:

- reducing the processing time, improving the technical reliability of the plant, improving quality at the various stages and improving the flexibility of the processing line;
- gaining a more detailed knowledge of the physical and chemical phenomena of multiphase systems; and
- continuing to seek economies in the consumption of raw materials, in manpower and in energy.

ii Steel Products

Research will aim to optimise the properties of existing products and bring to the markets products which are at present being developed, by:

- reducing the production time for the products demanded by clients;
- supplying products of consistent quality and reliability; and
- developing of new uses for steel and the use of new steel grades.

iii Environmental Protection

This focuses on minimising pollution, notably by:

- improving environmental control techniques for existing products;
- developing new, clean technologies for the production and processing of steel; and
- upgrading the value of by-products, to reduce steel plant wastes.

EC Contribution

Financing is by financial aid granted to firms, research institutes or individuals intending to conduct research in accordance with Article 55 of the ECSC Treaty.

In the case of steel undertakings the total amount of grant may not exceed 35% of project costs for basic industrial research and 25% for applied R&D. (These limits do not generally apply to independent research institutes).

The total amount of aid is determined annually. The Commission normally provides 60% of the estimated total cost of the research projects for which it provides aid.

Participation

Any undertaking, research institute or individual, who wishes to carry out research within the meaning of Article 55 of the ECSC Treaty and is established in the territory of the Member States, is entitled to apply for financial aid. The applicant need not necessarily be directly connected with the iron and steel industry, but the project for which support is requested must be within the scope of the Programme and of interest to the iron and steel sector in general.

Priority is given to proposals aimed at improving the industry's international competitiveness through reducing costs and improving productivity and through utilisation and application of steel in products. Preference will also be given to large projects involving cross-border collaboration. Projects involving only one organisation should not cost more than 1 MECU.

Status Report

One hundred and one projects were selected for the 1990 programme, with a provisional funding of 28 MECU.

There are no published calls for projects. Requests for aid should be submitted to the Commission in Brussels by 1 September each year for the following calendar year.

INFORMATION

P. F. Sens
Commission of the European Communities
Directorate-General XII
Unit C-4: Steel
200 Rue de la Loi
B-1049 Brussels
Tel: INT+ 322 295 7700
Fax: INT+ 322 296 5987

2. PILOT AND/OR DEMONSTRATION PROJECTS IN THE IRON & STEEL INDUSTRY

Statutory Basis

Until 1990, separate guidelines were established for research and for pilot/demonstration projects, but these were combined to apply to both programmes for the period up to 1995 (OJ C 252/3, dated 6/10/90). These guidelines are therefore an extension of those for steel research, 1986-90 (OJ C 294, dated 16/11/85) and supersede those for pilot and demonstration projects (OJ C 317, dated 28/11/87). (See 1 above).

Objectives

Financial support is given to pilot and demonstration projects in the iron and steel industry that will assist the transition to industrial and commercial exploitation of production techniques, processes and plant and products, which are innovatory in themselves or in their applications, and for which major capital expenditure is required to establish technical and/or commercial feasibility. Projects must offer prospects of economic viability, demonstrated by previous studies and research.

Programme Content/Participation

The medium-term guidelines for pilot/demonstration projects are now common to steel research and are summarised above under the Steel Research Programme in the sections on programme content and participation.

The pilot stage is characterised by the construction, operation and development of an installation of adequate capacity and using suitably large components, in order to verify the practicability of theoretical or laboratory concepts and/or increase the reliability of the technical and economic data needed to progress to the demonstration stage and, in certain cases, to the industrial and/or commercial stage.

The demonstration stage is characterised by the construction and/or operation of an industrial-scale installation, which should make it possible to bring together all the technical and economic data in order to proceed at the least possible risk to commercial and/or industrial exploitation of the technology.

EC Contribution

Usually, up to half of total project costs is provided for.

Applications

No calls for proposals are published. Applications for aid must be submitted before 1 October of each year for the forthcoming calendar year.

INFORMATION

P. F. Sens
Commission of the European Communities
DG XII C-4
Iron & Steel Demonstration Projects
200 Rue de la Loi
B-1049 Brussels
Tel: INT+ 322 295 7700
Fax: INT+ 322 296 5987

3. COAL RESEARCH

Statutory Basis

Under Article 55 of the ECSC Treaty, the Commission is required to promote technical and economic research relating to the production and increased use of coal and steel and to occupational safety in those industries.

The Commission has adopted new guidelines to cover the years 1990-95: OJ C 52, dated 1/3/89.

Objectives

Support for R&D is considered essential, to enable the industry to:

- remain competitive;
- cope with more stringent legislation on environmental protection;
- offer better working conditions;
- face new problems caused by the increased depth of mines; and
- deal with specific problems of open-cast mining.

Programme Content

The medium-term guidelines for the period 1990-95 are as follows:

i MINING ENGINEERING

Development work:

- shotfiring and related problems;
- mechanised headings;
- modern technologies;
- support systems; and
- shaft sinking and large hole boring.

Mine gases, ventilation, climate:

- gas emission;
- ventilation; and
- mine climate.

Strata Control

Methods of working and techniques of coal-winning:

- coal-winning techniques in particular conditions;
- coal-face equipment;
- modern technologies; and
- face ends.

Mine infrastructures:

- conveying of products;
- material transport;
- man-riding;
- supply and disposal; and
- modern technologies.

Modern Management:

- reconnaissance of deposits;
- planning of operations;
- control of operations;
- mine management; and
- architecture of information systems.

ii PRODUCT UPGRADING

Preparation and transport of products:

- coal preparation;
- handling of coal; and
- residues.

Metallurgical uses of coal:

- basic studies;
- conditioning of the coal blends;
- development of coke ovens;
- by-products;
- new techniques for production of cokes and briquettes from hard coal and lignite; and
- direct use of coal in metallurgy.

Combustion of coal:

- basic studies;
- environmental aspects;
- general amenity; and
- development of new and improved combustion systems.

Coal upgrading and conversion:

- physical and chemical fundamentals;
- gasification and liquefaction;
- new processes and products; and
- environmental protection.

The criteria for the selection of research projects are:

- the objectives of the common energy policy and of the common general research policy, with particular reference to energy research;
- the interest of the research for the EC;
- the value of the research, i.e. the extent to which it lowers costs and its effect on safety, the working environment and environmental protection;
- the repercussions on the environment; and
- the lead time between the completion of the research and its practical application.

EC Contribution

Funds to support coal research are drawn from the ECSC budget, which is itself largely funded from production levies on coal and steel industries in the EC. Community contributions are normally up to 60% of eligible project costs. By Council Assent No 16/92, 50 MECU has been earmarked for the current phase (OJ C 152, dated 17/6/92).

Applications

There are no calls for projects as such. Applications must be submitted on special forms before 1 September each year in order to be effective in the following calendar year.

INFORMATION

Commission of the European Communities
Coal Directorate,Technology Division
DG XVII B-3
200 Rue de la Loi
B-1049 Brussels
Tel: INT +322 299 1111 (exchange)

4. ECSC SOCIAL RESEARCH PROGRAMMES

Statutory Basis

Under Article 55 of the ECSC Treaty, aid for social and medical research can be given in the form of a contribution to the costs of staff or research equipment in the steel and coal industries. In particular the Commission provides financial assistance to social projects through pluri-annual programmes on ergonomics, control of nuisances and pollution at the place of work and in the environment of iron and steel works, safety in the ECSC industries, industrial hygiene in mines and a medical research programme.

In a recent Resolution, the ECSC Consultative Committee called for a strengthening of the social research programmes, making at least 13.5 MECU available from the ECSC budget to continue funding for those programmes. It also requested that means be found to increase the sum of 9.5 MECU set aside for social research in the 1986 budget.

Programme Content

There are currently six individual Programmes under the overall heading of the ECSC Research Programmes:

1 THE SIXTH ECSC PROGRAMME OF ERGONOMICS FOR THE STEEL & COAL INDUSTRY

Statutory Basis

Under Article 55 of the ECSC Treaty, the Commission has approved a Sixth Programme of ergonomics for the steel and coal industries: OJ C 66, dated 14/3/91.

Objectives

The objectives of the Sixth Programme are:

- to respond to the special needs of the ECSC industries in maintaining and improving the conditions affecting workers' health, safety and well-being in these industries;

- to assist the ECSC to undertake the work necessitated by the unique environmental conditions of their industries to comply with the proposed Community Directives and meet EC standards; and
- to ensure the incorporation of the results of previous programmes in the long-term activities of the ECSC industries.

Programme Content

The specific measures to be undertaken in the Programme are set out in detail in OJ C 66 of 14/3/91. In summary, these comprise:

- assessment of cognitive performance;
- the improvement of human reliability;
- the study of biomechanical limitations; and
- means of protection from noxious environments and substances.

EC Contribution

The Commission committed a sum of 15 MECU for the five year period 1990 - 1994.

Participation

The work will be carried out through a series of projects to be undertaken by the ergonomics groups and services established in the industries during the previous programmes.

INFORMATION

Commission of the European Communities
D-G V E3
Batiment Jean Monnet
Rue Alcide de Gasperi
2920 Luxembourg
Tel: INT+ 352 43011 (exchange)

2 TECHNICAL CONTROL OF NUISANCE & POLLUTION FROM IRON & STEEL WORKS

Statutory Basis

The Fifth Research Programme relating to the control of nuisance and pollution was set up under Article 55 of the ECSC Treaty (OJ C 338, dated 31/12/85).

Objectives

The Programme covers control at the place of work and in the environment around iron and steel works and particularly concerns measures to combat air pollution at the workplace, polluting fresh-water and sea-water and waste.

EC Contribution

A budget of 20 MECU was allocated for the period to the end of 1992.

Participation

The work financed by the Commission is to be carried out by firms in the industry and research institutes.

Status Report

The Fifth Research Programme began in 1985 and continued until 1992. It was superseded during 1993 by the First Joint Programme covering the coal and steel industries.

INFORMATION

Commission of the European Communities
DG V Directorate D
Employment, Industrial Relations and Social Affairs
Bâtiment Jean Monnet
Rue Alcide de Gasperi
L-2920 Luxembourg
Tel: INT+ 352 43011 (exchange)

3 RESEARCH ON SAFETY IN THE EUROPEAN COAL & STEEL COMMUNITY INDUSTRIES

Statutory Basis

Commission Decision to implement the Programme: OJ C 325, dated 20/12/89

Background

Under the terms of Article 55 of the ECSC Treaty, the High Authority is required to promote research on safety in the coal and steel industries. Although there have in the past been several programmes dealing with safety in mines, there has been very little work on occupational safety in the steel industry. The First Joint Research Programme, which started in 1989, will probably cover a five-year period and will integrate earlier separate programmes.

Programme Content

The Programme will include the following sectors.

1. General Safety Requirements
2. Specific Requirements of the Steel Industry:
   - blast furnaces and upstream installations such as coking, ore preparation and sinter plants;
   - melting shops;
   - rolling mills;
   - finishing shops; and
   - maintenance.
3. Specific Requirements of Mines:
   - mine fires and spontaneous combustion;
   - explosives;
   - rescue arrangements;
   - monitoring, telemetry, data presentation, remote control, automation and communication;
   - transport and handling;
   - electricity and energy;
   - materials technology;
   - winning methods;
   - rock bursts, associated phenomena and gas outbursts; and
   - surface activities.

The research is on a shared-cost basis, and should, as far as possible, be of a cross-border collaborative nature.

EC Contribution

About 26 MECU, subject to budget availability.

Participation

Projects may be undertaken by firms and research institutes.

Applications

Research applications must reach the Commission by 1 October of each year to be considered for financing for the following calendar year.

The Commission will implement the recommendation of specific research programmes which have been agreed by the ECSC Consultative Committee and received Council approval.

INFORMATION

Commission of the European Communities
D-G V E-3
Bâtiment Jean Monnet
Rue Alcide de Gasperi
L-2920 Luxembourg
Tel: INT+ 352 43011 (exchange)

4 INDUSTRIAL HYGIENE IN MINES

Statutory Basis

Assent No 35/90 by the Council under Article 55 (2) of the ECSC Treaty, provided for a sixth research programme - into industrial hygiene in mines (OJ C 290, dated 20/11/90); a Commission Memorandum (OJ C 14, dated 22/1/91) was subsequently prepared.

Objectives

The main objective is to improve the health of miners.

Background

Since 1957, 30.9 MECU has been spent, spread over five multi annual programmes, in support of projects relating to health in mines. The Fifth Programme had committed all of its budget of 11 MECU by 1988. The Sixth Programme, which began in 1990, will last for at least four years and will build on the knowledge acquired during earlier programmes, as it is recognised that increased competition and the introduction of new technologies can pose additional safety and health problems.

Programme Content

The Programme is sufficiently flexible to accommodate unforeseen industrial hygiene problems. The main headings of the Sixth Programme are:

- control of pollutants;
- dust measurement and determination of dust properties;
- environmental factors and occupation-related diseases; and
- noise and vibration.

Joint research will be encouraged but is not a prerequisite. The maximum level of support will be 60% of eligible project costs.

EC Contribution

A budget of 9 MECU has been agreed for the Programme.

Participation

The work financed by the Commission will be carried out by mining companies and research institutes.

Applications

Applications should be submitted to the Commission before 1 October each year for projects commencing in the forthcoming calendar year.

INFORMATION

Commission of the European Communities
DG V Health and Safety Directorate
Bâtiment Jean Monnet
Rue Alcide de Gasperi
2920 Luxembourg
Tel: INT+ 352 43011 (exchange)

5 FIFTH ECSC MEDICAL RESEARCH PROGRAMME

Statutory Basis

Under Article 55 of the ECSC Treaty, the Commission put forward a proposal for a Fifth Programme (OJ C 47, dated 19/2/88) which was approved by the Council of Ministers on 24/2/88.

Objectives

The objectives of the Programme are:

- to respond to workers' needs by improving the physical and psychological conditions in which they work;
- to help protect the health of workers, including preventing all types of occupational disease;
- to help ECSC industries to implement preventive measures and, in particular, to comply with EC objectives, including EC Directives, relating to health at the workplace; and
- to promote projects using the results of earlier Programmes to fulfil the objectives described above.

Programme Content

The particular subjects selected for the Programme are:

- occupational cancers;
- occupational hypacusis;
- occupational respiratory diseases;
- occupational muscular-skeletal complaints;
- diseases linked to exposure to certain chemicals;
- methods for measuring workers' exposure; and
- training and information of those involved in the industries.

EC Contribution

The Commission will grant aid not exceeding 60% of the total cost of successful projects. 12 MECU was provided for the five-year period from 1988.

Status Report

A sixth five-year programme is planned.

INFORMATION

Commission of the European Communities
DG V
Bâtiment Jean Monnet
Rue Alcide de Gasperi
L-2920 Luxembourg
Tel: INT+ 352 43011 (exchange)

Chapter 18

Economic and Social Cohesion

Article 2 of the EEC Treaty, as amended by the Maastricht Treaty, states,

> "The Community shall have as its task ... to promote throughout the Community a harmonious and balanced development of economic activities, sustainable and non-inflationary growth respecting the environment, a high degree of convergence of economic performance, a high level of employment and of social protection, the raising of the standard of living and quality of life and economic and social cohesion and solidarity between Member States."

Article 130a states,

> "In order to promote its overall harmonious development, the Community shall develop and pursue its actions in leading to the strengthening of its economic and social cohesion.
>
> "In particular, the Community shall aim at reducing the disparities between the levels of development of the various regions and the backwardness of the least-favoured regions, including rural areas."

Article 130c states,

> "The European Regional Development Fund is intended to help redress the principal regional imbalances in the Community through participating in the development and structural adjustment of regions whose development is lagging behind and in the conversion of declining industrial regions."

To see why the Community has given such a high level of priority to this area of policy, it has to be considered under two main headings:

1. Regional Policy and the Structural Funds; and
2. Social Policy and the European Social Fund.

1. REGIONAL POLICY AND THE STRUCTURAL FUNDS

It is argued that, if the Community is to become a true union, which was the motivation behind the Maastricht Treaty, the richer and more developed regions have no alternative but to shoulder a substantial part of the burden of structural adjustment required to enable the less advantaged regions to catch up.

On the economic front, if the poorer regions fail to make progress towards narrowing the gap between themselves and the richer regions, the freedom of movement of workers, goods, capital and persons within the single market programme is likely, in practice, to precipitate a forced, mass exodus from the poorer regions to the more prosperous ones. This would endanger the environment of both rich and poor regions, since the richer ones are already over-populated, while the poorer regions would lose their most highly-trained workers and would further risk being starved of the capital needed to create local jobs. With the advent of economic and monetary union, provided for in the Maastricht Treaty, economic and social cohesion is even more important because only economies at the same level of development will, in the long term, be able to hold together in the common monetary zone.

On the political front, if the EC neglects its less-favoured regions, the whole structure is likely to become unstable, with whole groups of people being relegated to the status of second-class citizens - in sharp contrast to the democratic ideals set out in the Treaties.

From its very foundation in 1957, the Community set itself the targets of ensuring uniform economic development and gradually eliminating differences in levels of prosperity between the regions. In 1987, Article 23 of the SEA incorporated a new Title V in the Treaty of Rome, dealing specifically with the objective of economic and social cohesion. Decisions on how to achieve this goal were taken by the Heads of State or Government in February 1988, based on proposals from the Commission. The resources of the EC's Structural Funds were to be doubled between 1988 and 1992, meaning that approximately ECU 18 billion was available for 1992. The total amount for the entire five-year period exceeded 60 BECU.

As well as being included by the Maastricht Treaty in the tasks of the Community, the importance of economic and social cohesion was reiterated in Protocol 15. Cohesion must be taken into account in the formulation of all EC policies and the Commission must report every three years on the progress that has been made. A new Cohesion Fund was, moreover, to be established "before 31 December 1993" to "provide Community financial contributions to projects in the fields of environment and trans-European networks in Member States with a per capita GNP of less than 90% of the Community average, which have a programme leading to the fulfilment of the conditions of economic convergence as set out in Article 104c."

Ireland provides a useful case study for demonstrating the aims and applications of the Structural Funds. The main features of the Irish economy which are relevant to the Community's aim of furthering economic and social cohesion are identified as follows in the National Development Plan presented to the Commission in March 1989,

> " Low income and output levels; a population structure resulting in rapid growth in labour supply and a high dependency ratio; persistently weak labour demand leading to unemployment and emigration; constraints imposed by budgetary imbalances and public sector indebtedness; high access costs resulting from the nation's peripheral location; poorly developed infrastructure hindering development and adding to costs; a heavy dependence on agriculture

both for employment and output; weaknesses in the industrial structure; low investment by Community standards and dependence on capital imports."

Over the last two decades, European funding has become an increasingly large component of the Irish economy, permeating the economic and social fabric of its society and laying the foundations for its future growth and development. In the last set of Structural Funds, Ireland received 3 billion IR£, representing almost 3.8% of its GDP; this will increase dramatically with the virtual doubling of funding contained in the Delors II package.

In a first report on the effects of the Structural Funds, the Commission concluded that operations undertaken since 1988 had been a considerable success. In the poorest regions of the EC, some 500,000 jobs have been created. They have helped GNP to grow by 4% in Portugal and by 2.6% in Greece. The contribution of the Funds to national investment amounted to between 5% and 7%.

Although the Commission's surveys reveal a reduction in the differences in regional development, there is still a long way to go. The per capita GDP of Ireland, Portugal and Greece is still less than 75% of the EC average. The main causes of backwardness - outdated structures, a lack of skilled labour and insufficient training opportunities - are all still present. The Commission's figures show, for instance, that the percentage of people between the ages of 15 and 19 undergoing some sort of training in the three least developed Member States is barely half that for the three most developed ones. The modernisation of the older industrial areas is also far from complete.

Rural areas - which account for some 80% of the EC's total area and are home to more than half its population - stand in particular need of Community solidarity. The term "rural area" denotes more than simply a geographical area; it specifically implies an entire economic and social structure which, quite apart from its function of providing people there with a living, plays a vital role in preserving the ecological balance and offering scope for recreation for those outside the region.

The 1990s are a crucial period for rural areas. The decline in agricultural employment, the drift of population from many rural areas to towns, environmental problems resulting from diversification and abandonment of land and the fragmentation of rural economies all contribute to major problems for them - not just within the Community but on a world-wide scale. The current programme of reforms to the CAP is intended to help place agriculture on a new footing, but will not alone be sufficient to restore prosperity and vitality to rural areas without a wider rural development effort. The EC's main objectives in this respect are therefore to preserve the traditional, family-run farm, to create permanent and economically viable jobs outside agriculture, through diversification and to ensure greater protection of the rural environment.

Protocol 15, annexed to the Maastricht Treaty, reaffirms, "that the promotion of economic and social cohesion is vital to the full development and enduring success of the Community ... and (the European Council's) conviction that the Structural Funds should continue to play a considerable part in the achievement of Community objectives in the field of cohesion... ."

The Funds

The Structural Funds comprise:

- the European Regional Development Fund (ERDF), which was set up in 1975 to help reduce imbalances in the Community (Regulation EEC 724/75);
- the European Social Fund (ESF), which has the task of promoting job opportunities for workers; and
- the Guidance Section of the European Agricultural Guidance and Guarantee Fund (EAGGF) which, as part of the reform of the Common Agricultural Policy, aims to accelerate the rationalisation of agricultural structures and to contribute to the development of rural areas.

Article 1 of Council Regulation (EEC) No.2052/88 "on the tasks of the Structural Funds and their effectiveness and on the co-ordination of their activities between themselves and with the operations of the European Investment Bank and other existing financial instruments," states,

"Community action through the Structural Funds, the EIB and other existing financial instruments shall support the achievement of the general objectives set out in Articles 130a and 130c of the Treaty by contributing to the attainment of the following five priority objectives:

1. promoting the development and structural adjustment of the regions whose development is lagging behind (Objective 1);
2. converting the regions, frontier regions or parts of regions (including employment areas and urban communities) seriously affected by industrial decline (Objective 2);
3. combating long-term unemployment (Objective 3);
4. facilitating the occupational integration of young people (Objective 4); and
5. with a view to the reform of the common agricultural policy:

   (a) speeding up the adjustment of agricultural structures (Objective 5a) and

   (b) promoting the development of rural areas (Objective 5b)."

Article 2 Provides,

"The Structural Funds - the EAGGF Guidance Section, the ESF and the ERDF shall contribute, each according to the specific provisions governing its operations, to the attainment of Objectives 1 to 5 on the basis of the breakdown given below:

- Objective 1: ERDF, ESF, EAGGF
- Objective 2: ERDF, ESF
- Objective 3: ESF

- Objective 4: ESF
- Objective 5 (a) EAGGF

  (b) EAGGF, ESF, ERDF."

(The meanings of these Objective Areas are covered in more detail further on in this chapter).

It is recognised that the Structural Funds cannot alone cure the EC's regional imbalances, but they can help. The money available from the Structural Funds has grown over the years in both relative and real terms. In 1988, at 7.6 BECU it represented 17% of the EC's budget at 45 BECU. By 1992, this had grown to 17.6 BECU, accounting for 27% of the budget of 66 BECU. The funding for the EC's structural policy programme for the period 1994 -1999 amounts to 160 BECU and is, in real terms, worth three times the total Marshall Aid programme. In 1992 alone, the Structural Funds contributed 11% of the total investment in Greece, 8% in Portugal and 7% in Ireland.

In order to promote the investment projects under the Structural Funds, ahead of funding schedules, the Copenhagen Summit agreed in June 1993 that the Council would examine a Commission proposal which would enable Member States to draw on an EC "bridging facility" of up to a maximum of 5 BECU, available at market interest rates until the end of 1995. Repayment of this Community loan would be drawn from Structural Fund appropriations for subsequent years. Similar arrangements could be made for the Cohesion Fund.

EC structural policy is increasingly supported by Community loans, particularly from the EIB, which has been raising funds on the capital markets for many years and lending them on to the least developed Member States for investment projects. Loans for structural policy are also available from the European Coal and Steel Community. A new fund, the Financial Instrument for Guidance in the Fisheries Sector (FIGF) is being set up to supplement the Structural Funds.

The Maastricht Treaty created the Committee of the Regions to assist the Council and the Commission. The Committee plays a purely advisory role in the legislative process, but it is expected to play an important role in the future construction and policies of the Structural Funds.

The Cohesion Fund which, according to the Maastricht Treaty, was due to be set up "before the 31 December 1993", has the task of financing environmental projects and trans-European networks in the less wealthy Member States to help them introduce programmes to adapt their economies to meet the convergence criteria for joining the single currency laid down in Article 109(j) and Protocol 6. It has a proposed initial annual budget of 1.5 BECU, rising to 2.5 BECU by 1997.

The Reform of the Structural Funds: 1989-93

A RATIONALE

In 1988, a major expansion and reform of the Structural Funds agreed for the period 1989-93, was necessitated by three imperatives - political, economic and legal.

The political imperative arose from the SEA, which clearly establishes the principle of solidarity between Member States, which it is assumed was implicit in the EEC Treaty. Jacques Delors emphasised the high priority to be given to structural policies in his "complete package" speech on the objectives of the SEA in Lourdes on 27 October 1989 when he said,

> "First, the completion of a large market without frontiers, allowing the free movement of people, goods, services and capital. Second, structural policies pursued at Community level, providing opportunities for all regions, particularly those which are lagging behind. To illustrate this point: if the average standard of living in the Community is taken as 100, then it is between 63 and 55 in Greece and Portugal and around 140 in Denmark and Germany. Hence the need for structural policies to enable backward regions to join in the construction of Europe and to allow industrial regions which were once prosperous but have been badly hit by technological and economic changes to redevelop. Another aim is to develop rural areas."

The implementation of such a policy, reinforced by the problems of adapting to the single market by 1993, required not only increasing convergence of Member States' economic policies, but also a reduction in regional disparities. This made it essential to reform the Funds so that they could become true instruments for promoting economic and social development.

The economic imperative was two-fold.

The first part concerned the widening regional disparities brought about by the accession of Spain and Portugal to the EC, which doubled the population of the least favoured regions, which at that time was defined as those with a per capita GDP of less than 50% of the Community average. Regional disparities had to be reduced: this objective was supported both by less-developed regions, who saw the immediate benefits, and by the more prosperous regions, which regarded regional convergence as containing the seeds of further growth in their own economies.

Secondly, steps had to be taken to improve the complex and unwieldy administration of EC funds, which are in the final analysis provided by all the people of the Community.

The legal imperative came from Article 130d of the EEC Treaty, as amended by the Single European Act. This stated that,

> "... the Commission shall submit a comprehensive proposal to the Council, the purpose of which will be to make such amendments to the structure and operational rules of the existing Structural Funds (EAGGF Guidance Section,

(ESF, ERDF) as are necessary to clarify and rationalise their tasks in order to contribute to the achievement of the objectives set out ..., to increase their efficiency and to co-ordinate their activities between themselves and with the operations of the existing financial instruments."

B CONTENT

The basic principles of this reform were:

- to concentrate assistance on five priority objectives (see below);
- to involve local, national and EC authorities, working in partnership in the decision- making process;
- to ensure that structural activities are applied consistently throughout the EC;
- to improve administrative procedures and to move towards a programme-based approach rather than the project-by-project system used previously; and
- to introduce effective monitoring within partnership agreements.

As part of the 1988 reform, five priority categories have been identified throughout the EC, three of which are purely regional (Objectives 1, 2 and 5b below); Objectives 3, 4 and 5a are "horizontal", in that they apply throughout the Community.

Objective 1 regions are underdeveloped areas which have missed out on the progress of other regions and are at the heart of the EC's efforts to bridge the economic divide. Their per capita GDP is less than 75% of the EC average. More than a fifth of the EC's population lives in such areas, which cover the whole of Greece, Portugal, Ireland and Northern Ireland, large parts of Spain, Italy, Corsica and France's overseas departments of Guadeloupe, Guyana, Martinique and Reunion. In Objective 1 regions, the emphasis is on making up lost ground by creating sound infrastructure: modernising transport and communication links, improving energy and water supplies, encouraging research and development, providing training and helping small businesses.

Objective 2 regions are those suffering from the decline of traditional industries like coal and steel, which need help in adjusting their economies to new industrial activities. Their unemployment rates and percentage share of industrial activity are worse than the EC average. Over 50 million people live in these regions, 20 million of them in the UK alone. In these regions, priority is given to creating jobs and improving the environment by encouraging new businesses, renovating land and buildings, developing R&D and fostering links between universities and industry.

Objective 3 is to combat long-term unemployment, defined as those over 25 and unemployed for more than 12 months.

Objective 4 is facilitating the occupational integration of young people: job-seekers below the age of 25.

Objective 5 concerns reform of the Common Agricultural Policy. Objective 5a is to adapt production, processing and marketing structures in agriculture and forestry. Objective 5b regions are rural areas like the Highlands and Islands of Scotland; this area is the least populated part of the EC, where economic development badly needs encouraging. Today, farms provide a living for less than 7% of the EC's workforce, compared to 21% thirty years ago. In such regions, efforts focus on developing new jobs outside farming - in small businesses and tourism. Improvements to transport and basic services are promoted to prevent rural depopulation and ensure better harmony between the EC's urban and rural areas.

3 LEGISLATIVE BASIS

The basic Regulations are as follows:

- Regulation (EEC) No 2052/88 of 24/6/88 on the tasks of the Structural Funds and their effectiveness and on co-ordination of their activities between themselves and with the operations of the EIB and the other existing financial instruments (OJ L 185, dated 15/7/88). This "Framework Regulation" lays down the basic rules, objectives and tasks of the Funds, the method of structural assistance, identification of the five priority Objectives, financial provision, etc.;
- Regulation (EEC) No 4253/88 of 19/12/88, concerning co-ordination of the activities of the different Structural Funds between themselves and with the operations of the EIB and other existing financial instruments, the so-called "Co-ordination Regulation" (OJ L 374, dated 31/12/88);
- Regulation (EEC) No 4254/88 of 19/12/88, laying down provisions for implementing Regulation (EEC) No 2052/88 as regards the ERDF (OJ L 374, dated 31/12/88);
- Regulation (EEC) No 4255/88 of 19/12/88, laying down provisions for implementing Regulation (EEC) No 2052/88 as regards the ESF (OJ L 374, dated 31/12/88); and
- Regulation (EEC) No 4256/88 of 19/12/88, laying down provisions for implementing Regulation (EEC) No 2052/88 as regards the EAGGF Guidance Section (OJ L 374, dated 31/12/88).

D DECISION-MAKING

EC action plans are generated by three basic principles to ensure that aid to the regions is as efficient as possible.

The first is the concept of partnership - that is, the active involvement of everyone with a contribution to make at the regional, national and Community level.

The second principle is that of subsidiarity: this comprises the clear delegation of decision-making to the local, regional, national or Community level, ensuring maximum efficiency and responsibility.

The third principle is of additionality, meaning an unambiguous commitment to EC money being used in addition to, not instead of national funds.

EC assistance is specifically provided in three phases, in which the Community collaborates with the Member States and the regions, as follows,

1. Development plans identifying the main priorities of the regions are prepared by the competent authorities at national, regional or local level. These are submitted to the Commission by the Member States.

2. Next, the Commission draws up the Community support frameworks (CSFs) on the basis of the development plans, in agreement with the national or regional authorities concerned, within the framework of a real partnership. The CSFs are agreements in the true sense of the word, defining priorities, the forms of assistance and the multi-annual financial support provided by the EC.

3. Lastly, the Member State concerned submits operational programmes for each of the priorities in the CSFs or, in certain cases, for individual projects. Once the decisions have been adopted by the Commission, the national and regional authorities are responsible for their implementation. Monitoring is carried out by all parties. Financial aid from the EC is global and coherent, combining the resources of the three Structural Funds. The Funds act together, each in accordance with its means and with the characteristics of the development programmes, so that maximum benefit can be drawn from the synergy between them. In some cases, additional funds are provided by the ECSC or the EIB. As for the Member States, not only do they have an important part to play, but they must also shoulder a large part of the financial cost.

Without neglecting one-off development projects, the EC gives preference to multi-annual programmes of a certain scale, so that EC assistance is planned and targeted over a period of several years.

5 COMMISSION INITIATIVES

As part of the reform of the Structural Funds, the Commission may undertake initiatives of its own to supplement Member States' actions in areas which it considers to have priority or to be essential to the completion of the single market, and which enhance economic and social cohesion. Commission initiatives are intended to accompany other European policies, to act as a catalyst for their application in the regions, or to contribute to the solution of problems common to regions in different categories.

Four of these initiatives STAR, VALOREN, RESIDER and RECHAR - predate the reform of the Structural Funds and were implemented under Article 7 of the old ERDF Regulation.

About 5,500 MECU were made available to finance 12 Community initiatives between 1989-93, of which 1,700 MECU were required under the old rules for programmes such as STAR and VALOREN.

One of the most effective programmes to emerge from the Commission is INTERREG, which encourages cross-border links. The EC has 6000 kilometres of internal borders between the Member States and these border areas, where 10% of the population live, are the most affected by the removal of the old frontiers as the single market is implemented. Schemes being supported range from a Spanish/Portuguese national park, to opening canal links between Ireland and Northern Ireland, creating one of the largest navigable waterways in Western Europe. The programme extends to the EC's neighbours: a business and exhibition centre in Salonika, northern Greece, will also be used by Bulgaria.

There have been various initiatives taken by European regions to increase economic and social cohesion. A new development is the creation of Euroregions, straddling traditional national frontiers. Four million people living along the Meuse and Rhine rivers in Germany, the Netherlands and Belgium now share the use of town halls, schools and conference centres. Franco-Belgian frontier regions are trying to create a special status easing the fiscal and administrative difficulties of local businesses. French and Spanish businesses either side of the Pyrenees now collaborate to maximise the benefits of the single market for their inhabitants.

The Commission actively helps regions in different parts of the EC to cooperate and establish self-help networks. These increasingly involve Eastern Europe, enabling the new authorities there to benefit from the experience of their EC counterparts. Research institutes are encouraged to analyse trans-European trends, rather than national ones. The Commission also ensures that Community policies in areas ranging from R&D to energy take fully into account their impact on the regions. The European Parliament is an equally keen supporter of measures to help the regions: among the several initiatives it has taken was the allocation in 1989 of EC funds to preserve historically important parts of Lisbon and Palermo.

6 FORMS OF ASSISTANCE

Operational Programmes (OPs)

Operational Programmes are the predominant form of assistance: this is reinforced by the Commission's power to take the initiative by proposing schemes to the Member States. OPs can be described as a series of consistent multi-annual measures lasting two to five years. It is possible that within a region, several types of OP could co-exist; they will generally be integrated programmes.

Global Grants

This is a method derived from the principle applied by the EIB and the ECSC: global loans for financial intermediaries.

National authorities entrust an authorised intermediary with the task of administering global grants for operations to be carried out by a number of small or medium-sized promoters. This system was introduced to speed up the processing of applications.

In the case of the ERDF, the Regulation stipulates that intermediaries must satisfy three conditions,

i having a presence in the region concerned;

ii operating in the public sector; and

iii involving the socio-economic interests concerned by implementing the measures planned.

The role of intermediaries is not confined to straightforward management of the funds, but entails involvement in local business promotion.

Support for Technical Assistance and Preparatory Studies

This is a major source of added value, especially as it is combined with other sources of technical assistance. The Funds' total allocation of 0.3% is earmarked for studies and technical assistance linked to joint or co-ordinated deployment of the structural instruments; there is also a special budget heading for the preparation of plans, CSFs and operational programmes, while 0.5% is constituted by the ERDF, 5% by the ESF and 1% by the EAGGF Guidance Section.

Pilot Projects

Demonstration projects have always received encouragement from EC institutions and include:

- in the case of the ERDF: transfrontier projects, co-operation among regions, agencies and local authorities, and network organisation projects;
- in the case of the ESF: measures involving two or more Member States and innovative projects aimed at promoting training and occupational integration; and
- in the case of fisheries and aquaculture: demonstration projects and preparatory studies.

Structural Fund Operations 1994-99

When the future of the Structural Funds was discussed at the Edinburgh Summit in December 1992, it was agreed that the next phase should run from 1994-99. The European Council agreed that whilst some changes were necessary, no far-reaching reforms were required in the foreseeable future.

It was also agreed that the level of funding should be substantially increased. It is predicted that, in order to close the gap between the EC's regions, the overall wealth of the EC must rise and, to rise sufficiently, the EC's economy must grow 2% above the Community average every year for 20 years. In order to meet this challenge, the

Commission has proposed that funds for the EC's weaker regions and countries should rise to 29.3 BECU by 1997. This would allow overall Structural Funds for Greece, Ireland, Portugal and Spain and for the EC's most remote regions (Madeira, the Azores, Canary Islands and French overseas departments), to double their 1992 levels. Money for the Objective 1 areas of Italy, France and the UK would rise by two-thirds. For all other regions eligible for aid, the increase would be 50%.

The Commission has agreed proposed amendments (COM (93) 67 final, dated 10/2/93) to the Framework and Co-ordination Regulations. Negotiations in the Council Structural Funds Working Group on revisions to the Regulations, proposed by the Commission, began in March and finished at the end of June 1993; they were followed by readings in the European Parliament and discussions at Foreign Affairs Council. The revised Regulations were expected to come into force in early 1994 at the latest.

The revised Regulations have redefined the Objective 1 area list which, for the UK, now comprises Northern Ireland, the Highlands and Islands and Merseyside. It is for Member States to propose to the Commission which areas they consider should be made eligible under Objectives 2 and 5b. There are then bilateral discussions between Member States and the Commission on these proposals, with the Commission making its decision on area eligibility towards the end of the year.

The proposed new system has the overall aims of achieving greater transparency, simpler and more flexible procedures and more rigorous financial control. Compared with the 1989-93 operations, the major changes are that:

- Objective 1 will be broadened in scope to include health and education;
- Objective 2 will be treated with more flexibility, allowing additional action to be taken to assist specific zones hit by industrial decline;
- Objective 3 will amalgamate the former Objectives 3 and 4;
- the new Objective 4 makes provision for employing the ESF to facilitate the retraining of workers in employment to help them adapt to new production systems and opportunities etc.;
- Objective 5a will be modified to take into account the fact that measures such as the agri-environment, afforestation of agricultural land and early retirement now form part of the new Common Agricultural Policy; and
- Objective 5b will be broadened to include areas hit by the decline of the fishing sector, resulting in the creation of a new Financial Instrument for Guidance in the Fisheries Sector (FIGF).

New Decision-Making Procedures

It is proposed that the previous three phases of decision-making be reduced to two and that there should be more decentralisation in the detailed definition of projects and the implementation of programmes.

It is proposed that simpler draft plans and programmes be submitted simultaneously, possibly in the form of a single document. Increased flexibility will also permit programmes to be agreed subsequent to the adoption of the CSF. The Commission will be pressing for fewer, larger programmes under the new scheme. Increased measures will also be taken to ensure that the principle of additionality is verified in respect of every CSF.

2. SOCIAL POLICY AND THE EUROPEAN SOCIAL FUND

As well as the various regional initiatives to promote economic and social cohesion, the EC has an active social policy to correct the most glaring imbalances. The European Social Fund (ESF) was set up in 1961 to help create jobs and promote vocational and geographical mobility in industries not covered by the ECSC. The ECSC itself took similar action, mainly in the 1960s, to help redeploy the thousands of miners affected by pit closures: one million jobs were lost, representing 62% of the workforce. Between 1954 and 1988, the EC spent 3 BECU, enabling tens of thousands of miners to take early retirement and creating 180,000 new jobs.

The Community does not merely provide financial assistance, since this alone would not solve the problems caused by recession and underdevelopment. The dynamism generated by economic growth, encouraged by appropriate policies at national and Community level, must be harnessed to social progress, which is stimulated by legislation guaranteeing Community-wide rights.

Being a European means more than being a consumer in Europe or contributing to Europe's economy. Since the Treaties came into force in 1958, the EC has been legislating to flesh out the provisions on freedom of movement for the workers, freedom to provide services and the right of establishment for members of the professions. The EC does not tolerate any discrimination based on nationality against Community citizens seeking employment outside their own Member State. Migrant workers and their dependants are, moreover, entitled to welfare benefits, vocational training and equal treatment in the matter of taxation and social rights under Article 51 of the EEC Treaty. This equality of all citizens of the European Union was clearly spelt out in the Maastricht Treaty.

There have been a number of Directives harmonising the rules on access to regulated professions. Each Member State now recognises the diplomas issued by the others to medical practitioners, nurses, veterinarians, pharmacists, architects and many others. Since so many occupations were still covered by national rules, the Twelve on 21 December 1988 adopted a comprehensive Directive, which established a system of mutual recognition for higher education diplomas. This covers all diplomas issued by a university after a course lasting three years or more and is based on the Member States' mutual trust in each other's educational systems.

In all Member States, the relationship between unions and employers' associations is particularly important. Since 1985, the Commission has therefore sought to promote dialogue between the two at Community level. Between 1985 and 1991 the European Trade Union Confederation (ETUC), the Union of Industries of the European

Community (UNICE), and the European Centre of Public Enterprises (CEEP) have as a result adopted a number of joint opinions on matters such as vocational training, the new technologies, labour market adjustment problems and "European" collective agreements.

Article 21 of the SEA, signed in February 1986, introduced a new chapter on Social Policy into the Treaty of Rome.

Article 117 of the amended Treaty states:

> "Member States agree upon the need to promote improved working conditions and an improved standard of living for workers so as to make possible their harmonisation while the improvement is being maintained......
>
> "They believe that such a development will ensure not only from the functioning of the common market, which will also favour the harmonisation of social systems, but also from the procedures provided for in this Treaty and from the approximation of provisions laid down by law, regulation or administrative action."

Article 118 states:

"... the Commission shall have the task of promoting close co-operation between Member States in the social field, particularly in matters relating to:

- employment;
- labour law and working conditions;
- basic and advanced vocational training;
- social security;
- prevention of occupational accidents and diseases;
- occupational hygiene;
- the right of association, and collective bargaining between employers and workers ..."

The importance of this aspect of the SEA was emphasised in Jacques Delors' “complete package” speech at Lourdes on 27 October 1989: "Fifth, the social dimension. There can be no disputing that the social dimension forms part of the Single Act, it is in the Treaty. It is our duty to apply it along with the rest."

In December 1989, all Member States except the UK adopted the Charter of the Fundamental Social Rights of Workers, otherwise known as the Social Charter. This was a solemn declaration committing them to a series of social policy objectives as part of the single market. They were concerned to add a substantial social dimension to a project that was being viewed in some quarters as too pro-business. The Social Charter sets out twelve basic principles as follows,

1. The right to work in the EC country of one's choice.
2. The right to a fair wage.
3. The right to improved living and working conditions.
4. The right to social protection under prevailing national systems.
5. The right to freedom of association and collective bargaining.
6. The right to vocational training.
7. The right of men and women to equal treatment.
8. The right of workers to information, consultation and participation.
9. The right to health protection and safety at work.
10. The protection of children and adolescents.
11. The guarantee of minimum living standards for the elderly.
12. Improved social and professional integration for the disabled.

The first principle of the Social Charter allows EC citizens to choose where they work in the Community. This is unlikely to lead to a large movement of people from any one Member State to another, since that did not occur in the past, as individual restrictions on residence and working rights were lifted. Most workers and their families have been able, for some time, to move to another EC Member State, provided that work was available. This right has been extended to others as EC governments have recognised the academic diplomas and other professional qualifications obtained in other EC countries. Problems in extending the right of mobility to people not in work, such as pensioners and students, were overcome in 1990. They too can move to another Community country, provided that they show they have sufficient income to ensure that they do not become a financial burden on their host country. In a broader context, the EC encourages student mobility and the study of foreign languages through programmes such ERASMUS for student mobility, COMETT for education and technology and LINGUA for the promotion of foreign languages.

Health and safety in the workplace is the area in which the social aspects of the post-1992 single market have made most progress. Under a general Directive adopted in 1989, a set of principles concerning worker safety and protection had to be implemented by the end of 1992. More specific Directives have been adopted, regulating matters such as the use of equipment and the wearing of protective gear and clothing.

Notwithstanding all these measures, the Commission felt that the social dimension of the internal market was being neglected, as a great many of the proposals made under its social action programme were not enacted by the Council. This is why almost every Member State wanted to progress with the Treaty on European Union.

At Maastricht in December 1991, the Member States - with the exception of the UK - adopted what became Protocol 14 of the Maastricht Treaty, known as the Social Chapter, which follows on from the Social Charter.

The three main changes it made were as follows.

i It expanded the legal basis for Community-led action on social policy.

ii Decisions on some areas of policy, including the improvement of working conditions to protect workers' health and safety, the information and consultation of workers, equality of treatment between men and women with regard to labour market opportunities and treatment at work - which includes equal pay for equal work and the integration of persons excluded from the labour market, will be taken by qualified majority, excluding the UK's vote.

iii Article 3 provides that the Commission shall have the task of promoting consultation between management and labour at Community level and shall take any relevant measure to facilitate their dialogue by ensuring balanced support for the parties.

If and when the Social Chapter is implemented, workers throughout the Community, except (in theory) the UK as a result of the opt-out, could potentially enjoy a considerable degree of social protection. Under the terms of the opt-out written into Protocol 14, the UK is not only not obliged to introduce measures implementing any Community legislation introduced under the Social Chapter - although it remains obliged to implement any social legislation introduced under the Treaty of Rome as amended by the Single European Act - it "shall not take part in the deliberations on the adoption by the Council of Commission proposals made on the basis of the Protocol and the above-mentioned agreement". Strictly interpreted, it would appear that, when participating Member States make claims for contributions from the European Social Fund towards their costs of implementing Social Chapter legislation, the UK will be excluded from participating in the discussions.

The provisions introduced by the Maastricht Treaty which allows all citizens of the Union residing in a Member State other than their own to vote and stand in municipal and European elections marks the beginning of a new phase in the construction of a people's Europe. The details have yet to be worked out, but the principle has sparked a debate on the meaning of national identity and national sovereignty. The concept of European citizenship complementing and enhancing national citizenship is a novel one and raises questions that politicians will have to address particularly in regards to what is meant by "European political union" and what further legally enforceable rights should be attached to "citizenship of the Union".

In spite of these achievements, the EC has admittedly made slower progress on the social aspects of the single market than on the economic ones. This is partly because the SEA introduced majority voting for most economic and technical harmonisation directives, but retained the principle of unanimity for new social legislation.

The main problem with integration is that the Community, as it stands, still lacks a degree of legitimacy. It is not linked directly enough to the will of the people. Although the introduction of direct elections to the European Parliament in 1979, and the increases in the Parliament's powers under both the SEA and the Maastricht Treaty, have helped to legitimise the integration process, the Parliament still does not have a large enough role to play in the decision-making processes of the EC.

European citizenship is still in its infancy: it will need time to develop and flourish. We have had a European passport since 1985, a European anthem in Beethoven's "Ode to Joy" and a flag, but these alone are not enough. The sense of belonging to a single entity cannot be created artificially. The introduction, in accordance with the Maastricht Treaty, of a single currency by 1999 at the latest could have a major psychological impact. Its physical effect would be to introduce bank-notes denominated in ECUs on one side and national currencies on the other. The abolition of border checks under the Schengen Agreement which should eventually include all 12 Member States, should also strengthen the feeling among Europeans that they share a common home as the concept of crossing internal frontiers vanishes. EC encouragement of education and training programmes is partly aimed at helping the emergence of this shared consciousness.

European Social Fund

The ESF was originally established under Article 123 of the EECT which, as amended by the Maastricht Treaty states,

> "In order to improve employment opportunities for workers in the internal market and to contribute thereby to raising the standard of living, a European Social Fund is hereby established ... it shall aim to render the employment of workers easier and to increase their geographical and occupational mobility within the Community and to facilitate their adaptation to industrial changes and to changes in production systems, in particular through vocational training and retraining."

In its early days the ESF was used very much as an economic measure, to facilitate the mobility of labour. As the Community developed, it became apparent that different measures were required to cope with unforeseen, disadvantaged groups, such as the handicapped and migrant workers. More flexibility was required, as well as an extension of the ESF's criteria to allow it to intervene in the private sector. The ESF was accordingly revised in 1971 under Council Decision 71/66/EEC.

The economic situation in the Community subsequently deteriorated and the ESF became considerably over-subscribed. It was therefore again revised in 1977 under Council Decision 77/801/EEC.

A third revision to the ESF, embodied in Council Decision 83/516/EEC (OJ L 289, dated 22/10/83), applied to relevant activities from January 1984. The intention was to simplify the ESF's operations, making it more responsive to changing needs and enabling decisions to be made more speedily. The operations of the ESF were also arranged to reinforce other instruments and priorities of the Commission. The Integrated Development Operations (IDOs) aimed to bring together ERDF, ESF and other EC funds in an integrated manner.

Although it was intended to support all operations relevant to the old rules, the ESF had a distinct bias toward the public sector and SMEs. It dealt with applications under one of two main headings: the "Main Scheme", to which 95% of the money was allocated, and "Innovation", which received 5%.

The ESF was revised again in the 1988 reform of the Structural Funds which established new operating rules from January 1990 and will be further amended for the 1994-99 round.

The ESF had exclusive responsibility for implementing the old Objectives 3 and 4 - the long-term unemployed and young people. One assumes that it will also be responsible for the new Objective 4 under the latest revision of the Structural Funds. It also contributes to the achievement of the remaining three Objectives.

Economic and social cohesion has to be looked at as a whole. It is likely to become not only an increasingly important area of Community policy as rural depopulation continues and the recession drags on, but also an increasingly controversial one, as costs continue to escalate.

Chapter 19

Economic and Social Cohesion Grants

Economic and Social Cohesion Grants have been split into three separate sub-chapters, as follows:

CHAPTER 19.1: GRANTS UNDER THE STRUCTURAL FUNDS

1 ERDF: European Regional Development Fund

2 ERDF Article 10 Programmes - Exchanges Of Experience

- a The Exchange Programme
- b Urban Pilot Projects
- c RECITE Programme
- d ECOS: Eastern Europe City Co-operation Scheme

3. Studies & Technical Assistance

4. Commission Initiatives:

- i ENVIREG: European Regional Fund for Border Areas
- i. STAR: Special Telecommunications Action For Regional Development
- iii VALOREN: Exploiting Indigenous Energy Potential
- iv RENEVAL: Programme for Shipbuilding Areas
- v STRIDE: Science & Technology for Regional Innovation and Development in Europe
- vi INTERREG
- vii REGIS: Programme for Ultra-Peripheral Areas
- viii REGEN: Programme for Energy Networks
- ix TELEMATIQUE: Promoting Advanced Telecommunication Services for SMES
- x PRISMA: Preparing Regional Industry for the Single Market
- xi LEADER: Links between Actions for the Development of the Rural Economy
- xii RESIDER: Programme for the Coal Mining Areas
- xiii RECHAR: Programme for Re-structuring Coal Mining Areas
- xiv RETEX: Programme for Areas Dependent on Textile Industries.

xv PERIFRA: A Special Action for Peripheral Regions and Destabilised Activities - A Measure of Regional Character

xvi KONVER (CONVER): Programme for Areas Affiliated by Reduction in Military Expenditure

CHAPTER 19.2: GRANTS UNDER THE EUROPEAN SOCIAL FUNDS

1 European Social Fund

2 Studies and Technical Assistance

3 Commission Initiatives:

i EUROFORM, HORIZON, NOW

ii Subsidy for Transnational Meetings between Employees' Representatives

iii LEDA: To Promote an Innovative Approach to Job Creation at Local Levels

iv CHILDCARE

v TIDE: Technology for the Socio-economic Integration of Disabled & Elderly People

vi ERGO: Programme for Economic and Social Integration of Long-term Unemployed

vii HANDYNET: Mobility Programme for Disabled

viii HELIOS II; Rehabilitation of Disabled

CHAPTER 19.3: ECONOMIC AND SOCIAL COHESION GRANTS

1 Cohesion fund

2 SPEC: Support Programme For Employment Creation

3 POVERTY 3: The Third Poverty Programme

4 Town-twinning

Chapter 19.1

Grants Under the Structural Funds

Grants under the Structural Funds are grouped as follows:

1 ERDF: European Regional Development Fund

2 ERDF Article 10 Programmes - Exchanges Of Experience

a The Exchange Programme

b Urban Pilot Projects

c RECITE Programme

d ECOS: Eastern Europe City Co-operation Scheme

3. Studies & Technical Assistance

4. Commission Initiatives:

i ENVIREG: European Regional Fund for Border Areas

i. STAR: Special Telecommunications Action For Regional Development

iii VALOREN: Exploiting Indigenous Energy Potential

iv RENEVAL: Programme for Shipbuilding Areas

v STRIDE: Science & Technology for Regional Innovation and Development in Europe

vi INTERREG

vii REGIS: Programme for Ultra-Peripheral Areas

viii REGEN: Programme for Energy Networks

ix TELEMATIQUE: Promoting Advanced Telecommunication Services for SMES

x PRISMA: Preparing Regional Industry for the Single Market

xi LEADER: Links between Actions for the Development of the Rural Economy

xii RESIDER: Programme for the Coal Mining Areas

xiii RECHAR: Programme for Re-structuring Coal Mining Areas

xiv RETEX: Programme for Areas Dependent on Textile Industries.

xv PERIFRA: A Special Action for Peripheral Regions and Destabilised Activities - A Measure of Regional Character

xvi KONVER (CONVER): Programme for Areas Affiliated by Reduction in Military Expenditure

1. ERDF: EUROPEAN REGIONAL DEVELOPMENT FUND

Statutory Basis

The Regulation setting up the ERDF is (EEC) No 724/75.

The ERDF is currently regulated by Council Regulation (EEC) No 2052/88 of 24/6/88 and Nos. 4253/88 and 4254/88 of 19/12/88 (OJ L 374, 31/12/88). It is directed almost exclusively at the public sector, particularly local authorities and regional development organisations.

Objectives

The ERDF was set up in 1975 to reduce regional imbalances in the EC.

Programme Content

ERDF assistance concentrates upon measures which accommodate the differing needs of each of the three types of region identified in Objectives 1, 2 and 5b, defined in Council Regulation (EEC) No. 2052/88: OJ 1 185/9. Generally speaking, the ERDF supports the following types of actions:

a. investment in projects which are likely to encourage the creation or maintenance of permanent jobs in regions which have high rates of unemployment;

b. infrastructure projects which help the economic development of the least favoured regions, promote the regeneration of areas suffering from industrial decline - including inner city areas, or which encourage the creation of non-agricultural jobs in rural areas;

c. local initiatives to promote regional development, including measures to assist the growth of local business and industry - particularly SMEs - e.g. by providing business advisory services or promoting technology transfer and innovation - also, in Northern Ireland, community reconciliation;

d. studies, technical assistance and pilot schemes concerned with the development and application of regional policy, particularly where they concern cross-border regions; measures to provide information for local and regional development agents may also be financed; and

e. investment projects aimed at environmental protection, if they are linked to regional development.

Objective 1 Support

UK

Northern Ireland is the only UK region eligible for Objective 1 support. Details are provided in the Commission Decision of 31 October 1989 on the establishment of a Community Support Framework (CSF) for EC assistance in Northern Ireland (OJ L 370, dated 19/12 89). The full CSF is published as a document by the Office of Official Publications.

The ERDF funding anticipated for the period 1/1/90 to 31/12/93 was 348 MECU, at 1989 prices.

The CSF covered the period 1/1/90 to 31/12/93 and comprised the following operational programmes:

- the improvement of the physical and social environment;
- the improvement of transport to reduce the effects of peripherality;
- the diversification and strengthening of the industrial and tradable sectors of the economy;
- the improvement of tourism;
- the development of agriculture; and
- human resource development.

IRELAND

The whole of Ireland is designated as an Objective 1 area. The Commission Decision adopting the CSF was made on 31/10/89 and the CSF is published as a Commission Document (ISBN 92-826-0171-4).

The ERDF funding anticipated for the period 1989-93 was 1,646 MECU, at 1989 prices.

The initiative has produced the following operational programmes.

i Agriculture, Fisheries, Forestry and Rural Development (704 MECU).

The general aim is to enhance Ireland's comparative advantages of natural endowment and clean environment. The particular objectives for agriculture and rural development are improvement of quality and marketing of agricultural produce in line with market requirements, reorientation and improvement in the efficiency of production, to improve competitiveness, encouragement of environmentally-friendly farming and promotion of rural development farm enterprises and off-farm enterprises and employment.

Fishing facilities also need to be modernised.

Programmes will seek and support new ideas to stimulate enterprise, to improve infrastructure and to provide appropriate training and other ways of optimising the human resources available.

Tourism is being supported principally by matching private sector investment in a wide range of facilities, including infrastructures for sport and leisure.

ii Industry, Services and Supporting Infrastructure (1,019 MECU).

This aims to continue shifting resources to support items of non-capital expenditure, including marketing, technology and training. The focus of support is on the traded goods and services sectors, which are subject to international competition. Special attention is also being given to improving the climate for existing industries and stimulating indigenous enterprises, with the support of initiatives to upgrade management, to foster better links between overseas and local firms and to improve the marketing capability of Irish firms.

iii Offsetting Peripherality (694 MECU).

This concentrates on measures to improve Ireland's major arterial roads, airports, ports and railways.

iv Human Resources (1441 MECU).

The main target is to boost job creation from the 29,000 recorded in 1988 to 35,000 per year, chiefly by modernising the economy and stimulating the employment potential of traditional sectors.

Objective 2 Support

The Objective 2 regions for the UK were listed by the Commission in March 1989.

The CSFs for Objective 2 regions for 1992-93 were decided on 19/12/91. Nine CSFs had already been agreed for the period 1989-91. Development priorities are grouped into the following six categories:

i improving facilities for the development of productive activities, mainly emphasising the provision of industrial and business sites and premises;

ii improvements in the road, rail and inland water networks and public transport facilities, in order to facilitate business development and tourism;

iii measures which facilitate the development of new businesses, particularly SMEs, including the provision of business advice centres, measures to improve the take-up of new technology and the provision of common services;

iv improving the image and environment of regions, e.g. by reclaiming derelict land;

v the development of tourism, including sites of cultural and historical interest; and

vi support for research and development and training facilities designed to overcome shortages of skills and manpower.

Operational programmes based on each category are compiled at a regional level under the supervision of the representatives of the Commission, central government and local authorities. Regional programme committees are established to oversee their implementation and to consider grant applications for specific projects.

Objective 5b Support

UK

The Objective 5b CSFs are summarised in Commission Decisions 90/577-580/EEC of 6/6/90: OJ L 322/41, dated 21/11/90. The four UK regions eligible are the assisted areas of Devon and Cornwall, the assisted areas of Dumfries and Galloway, the Highlands and Islands Development Board area and rural Wales.

EC Contribution

Generally, ERDF rates of assistance will be:

- for regions covered by Objective 1, a maximum of 75% of the total cost and a minimum of half the total public expenditure;
- for other regions, a maximum of half the total cost and a minimum of 25% of the total public expenditure.

ERDF funding is almost invariably conditional on co-financing by national authorities.

Participation

The vast majority of funds are disbursed by the Commission for operational programmes, which are constructed within Member States by the relevant government departments in association with interested third parties. As projects must be part-financed by public authorities, this effectively means that the ERDF is aimed primarily at the public sector, financing projects administered by central and local government and regional development organisations.

Status Report

Negotiations on revisions to the Regulations proposed by the Commission in the Council Structural Funds Working Group began in March and finished at the end of June 1993, and were followed by readings in the European Parliament and discussions at Foreign Affairs Council. The revised Regulations, which were scheduled to come into force at the end of 1993, have determined the Objective 1 area list which, for the UK, now comprises Northern Ireland, the Highlands and Islands and Merseyside. It is for Member States to propose to the Commission which areas they consider should be made eligible under Objectives 2 and 5b.

Applications

In the UK, co-ordinating committees were set up by the regional directors of the Departments of Trade & Industry and Environment to implement each CSF, with representation from central government, the Commission and local authorities. A programme committee was also established for each operational programme to give detailed consideration to applications for funding.

UK applicants for support from the Structural Funds should initially contact the regional office of the Department of the Environment or the Department of Trade & Industry, depending on the nature of the project for which financial aid is being sought.

In Ireland, the Department of Finance is both the co-ordinator of the CSF and the designated authority for the ERDF. Responsibility for running the Operational Programmes is delegated to the appropriate Government departments.

INFORMATION

UK

Contacts for all regional development topics:

Chris North
Department of Trade & Industry
Regional Policy Division
Room 232, Kingsgate House
66-74 Victoria Street
London SW1E 6SW
Tel: 071 215 2556

Eileen McMordie
EC Branch
Department of Finance and Personnel
Room 277, Parliament Buildings
Belfast BT4 3SW
Tel: 0232 521360

Barbara Culrey
Department of Employment
Regional Policy Division
2 Marsham Street
London SW1P 3EB
Tel: 071 276 3798

For Regional Offices of the Department of the Environment, see Appendix 2
For Regional Offices of Department of Trade & Industry, see Appendix 2

IRELAND

Bus & Rail Division: R Byrne
Tourism Division: Sean Goram
Telecommunications Division: P Ryan

Department of Tourism, Transport & Communications
Kildare Street
Dublin 2
Tel: 01 6621444
Fax: 01 6766154

L. Johnston or M. Tobin
Department of the Environment
O'Connell Bridge House
Dublin 1
Tel: 01 6793377

Mary McLoughlin
Department of Energy
Clare Street
Dublin 2
Tel: 01 715233

Mr. Hayden
Department of Enterprise and Employment
Davitt House, Adelaide Road
Dublin 2
Tel: 01 765861

S. O'Flaherty
Department of Industry & Commerce
Kildare Street
Dublin 2
Tel: 01 614444

G. O'Driscoll
Department of Agriculture & Food
Kildare Street
Dublin 2
Tel: 01 789011

CSF Monitoring Committee Secretariat
Department of Finance
Government Buildings
Lower Merrion Street
Dublin 2
Tel: 01 767571

2. ERDF ARTICLE 10 PROGRAMMES

2a. The Exchange Programme

Objectives

Article 10 of the Structural Fund Regulation (EEC) 2052/88 provides for the funding of measures to stimulate the exchange of experience, and co-operation on development between Community regions. The objectives of the experience exchanges are:

- to encourage local and regional authorities to adopt a Europe wide outlook and to take a more active part in the implementation of EC policies; and
- to foster the dissemination of ideas and know-how among decentralised authorities.

Programme Content

The types of exchanges consist of meetings, conferences, seminars, exhibitions, joint publications and expert evaluation visits, and the subjects they cover are:

- government services,
- transport,
- research and technology,
- the environment,
- tourism,
- assistance for SMEs and
- energy and local resources.

EC Contribution

Total commitments from Article 10 for the period 1989-91 were 186 MECU of which 61 MECU, related to Urban Pilot Projects.

Projects can be granted EC co-financing up to a maximum of 75% of the eligible expenditure for authorities in Objective 1 regions and half eligible expenditure for other authorities. An EC contribution to a network will generally range from 1 to 3 MECU.

Participation

Priority is given to projects which involve at least three Member States:

- in which local or regional authorities eligible under Objectives 1, 2 and 5b and decentralised, non-eligible authorities are participating; special encouragement is given to the participation of localities or regions eligible for funding under Objective 1;
- which are related to the implementation of an EC policy;
- which have a highly innovative theme; and
- which represent the first contact among the partners involved.

Areas falling outside Objectives 1,2 or 5b regions may be eligible for funding, provided that other partners are in such regions.

Status Report:

Twelve pilot projects for networks between local authorities were initially established, one of which was "Quartiers en Crise" - for the revitalisation of urban areas in decline.

The UK neighbourhoods taking part in Quartiers en Crise were:

- Manchester, Hulme;
- Paisley, Ferguslie Park; and
- Belfast, New Lodge/Duncairn.

In Ireland, Cork and Dublin were involved in the programme.

Irish involvement in the inter-regional exchange programme is considerable: in 1991, six projects were under Irish leadership. Four further projects are currently under way, namely:

- Inner City Market Development, Dublin Corporation;
- Rural Development, Mayo County Council;
- Small Island Development, Gaelic Regional Development Agency; and
- Reduction of Peripherality, Connacht/Ulster Enterprises.

2b. Urban Pilot Projects

The success of the Quartiers en Crise Programme led to additional funding for Urban Pilot Projects, which involves 21 towns and cities under the broad categories of:

- economic developments in areas with social problems;
- environmental actions linked to economic goals; and
- revitalisation of historic centres.

The Urban Pilot Projects in UK regions and British OCT are as follows:

- London is making available about £4 million for actions geared to fostering economic development in housing areas, by converting garages to workshops and developing training opportunities. The total cost is 10.2 MECU, of which the ERDF is contributing 5.1 MECU and the ESF, 2.9 MECU.
- Belfast is endeavouring to reconcile economic development of the harbour area with environmental protection of the site, which is considered one of the most important bird sanctuaries in Europe. The total cost is 6.7 MECU, of which the ERDF is contributing 3.4 MECU.
- Paisley proposes to create a high-quality multi-functional community centre as a nucleus for reintegrating the Ferguslie Park estate into the economic mainstream of the region. The total cost is 3.9 MECU, of which the ERDF is contributing 1.9 MECU.
- Stoke aims to rejuvenate the Gladstone St James quarter, a run-down former pottery centre in the city centre. The total cost is 4 MECU, of which the ERDF is contributing 2 MECU.
- Gibraltar has been hit by a run-down of ship-repairing activity. A redundant warehouse is being converted into several multi-occupancy manufacturing units. The total cost is 5.6 MECU, of which the ERDF is contributing 2.8 MECU.

In Ireland, an Urban Pilot Project is being undertaken by Dublin Corporation, which involves creating an urban tourist route in the Temple Bar area of the city. The total budget is 9.4 MECU, including 50% co-financing from the EC.

2c. Recite Programme

The success of the pilot projects also resulted in the creation of the RECITE Programme (Regions and Cities for Europe).

Its general aim is to contribute towards economic and social cohesion by supporting co-operation networks.

The total amount of ERDF support for the RECITE Programme was 34.8 MECU, funding 75% of eligible costs for authorities in Objective 1 areas and 50% elsewhere. Projects are expected to last 2-3 years, after which they should be self-financing.

All local and regional authorities representing at least 50,000 inhabitants are eligible. At least two and up to ten authorities from different Member States must be involved.

A call for proposals was published in OJ C 198, dated 27/7/91 with a deadline of 15/10/91. It is not known whether any further calls will be made.

Staffordshire is involved in a grouping of ceramic industry regions within the RECITE Programme.

2d. Eastern Europe City Co-operation Scheme (ECOS)

ECOS is designed to establish co-operative links between regions and cities in the EC, particularly those in disadvantaged areas, and their counterparts in Central and Eastern Europe. Its purpose is to provide financial assistance for projects which encourage regional development and the transfer of expertise, to promote business and trade and to undertake activities geared towards intensifying co-operation, the exchange of experience and organising seminars.

Projects must involve at least two local or regional authorities from different EC countries, one of which must be in an ERDF Objective 1 area, and one local or regional authority from Hungary, the Czech Republic, the Slovak Republic, Albania, Poland, Bulgaria, Romania, Estonia, Latvia, Lithuania or Slovenia.

Applications

The management of projects is entrusted to organisations representing the local and regional authorities. For each set of exchange projects, the Commission concludes a contract with the intermediary which defines the terms of the projects, the obligations of the organisation and its responsibilities as regards funding.

Project selection takes place twice a year in June and October. Approved projects cover the period until the end of the following year.

INFORMATION

UK
Local Government International Bureau
35 Great Smith Street
London SW1P 3BJ
Tel: 071 222 1636

IRELAND
S. O'Riordain
Council of Irish Local Authorities
Institute of Public Administration
57-61 Lansdowne Road
Dublin 4
Tel: 01 686233
Fax: 01 689135

COMMISSION
Commission of the European Communities
DG XVI A.1
200 rue de la Loi
B-1049 Brussels
Tel: INT+ 322 299 1111 (exchange).

Applications should be made to one of the organisations representing local and regional authorities:

Assembly of the European Regions (AER)
Immeuble Europe
Place des Halles 20
F-6700 Strasbourg

Council of the European Municipalities and Regions CCRE
Quai d'Orsay 41
F-75007 Paris
Tel: INT+ 1-45 51 40 01

International Union of Local Authorities (IULA-CEMR)
23 Boulevard Charlemagne
B-1040 Brussels
Tel: INT+ 322 230 4775
Fax: INT+ 322 230 7456

Miss Catherine Stevens
Eurocities Officer
9 rue de Moniteur
B-1000 Brussels

3. STUDIES & TECHNICAL ASSISTANCE

Statutory Basis

Article 5 of the Structural Fund Regulation (EEC) 2052/88 provides for the funding of technical assistance measures which are carried out either at the request of national or regional authorities or on the Commission's own initiative.

Programme Content

There are two separate frameworks:

i Technical Assistance at the Request of the Member States:

- the preparation of development plans and/or the review of the CSFs;
- the preparation of EC assistance according to the CSFs, and the drawing up of OPs; and
- the implementation, follow-up, assessment and dissemination of the results of assistance.

ii Technical Assistance on the Commission's Initiative:

- the analysis of regional development in the EC;
- the preparation, follow-up and assessment of EC assistance; and

- direct provision of expertise to the Commission, notably information, data processing and publicity.

EC Contribution

Finance for measures requested by Member States comes from the budget earmarked for their CSFs. Measures agreed on the initiative of the Commission are funded on the basis of a contract between the Commission and the consultancy.

Applications

Selection procedures vary according to the nature and amount of the assistance given. Commission contracts worth more than 35,000 ECU must follow standard procurement procedures. Calls for expressions of interest and, for larger projects, invitations to tender are published in the OJ C Series.

INFORMATION

Commission of the European Communities
DG XVI 1.A
200 rue de la Loi
B-1049 Brussels
Tel: INT+ 322 299 1111 (exchange).

4. COMMISSION INITIATIVES

i ENVIREG

- see Chapter 23

ii STAR: Special Telecommunications Action for Regional Development

Statutory Basis

Council Regulation (EEC) No 3300/86: OJ L 305, dated 31/10/86

Objectives

Its principal aim was to give improved access to advanced telecommunications systems in less-favoured regions of the EC.

Programme Content

The Programme ran from 1987 to 1991. It appears that the Programme is unlikely to be repeated; as its objectives are being absorbed into other programmes.

The main lines of action of STAR were:

- the co-ordinated development of telecommunications infrastructure;

- the creation of a single internal market in terminals and equipment, presupposing mutual acceptance of type-approvals in order to achieve compatibility between systems;
- the implementation of a pre-normative and pre-competitive R&D programme in the field of integrated broad-band communications technologies;
- the improvement of the way in which these services and advanced networks are introduced in the least-developed peripheral regions of the EC; and
- the development of common European positions in international negotiations.

EC Contribution

STAR was financed jointly by the ERDF and public and private investors. The ERDF contributed 55% for infrastructure projects, 50% for services and 50-70% for studies and consultancy services.

The total ERDF allocation for the Programme was 788 MECU, of which 20% was for promoting the supply and use of new services and 80%, for infrastructures.

Status Report

An allocation of £15.35 million was made towards developing advanced telecommunications services under the STAR Programme in Northern Ireland.

In Ireland an allocation of 50 MECU helped in the introduction of the EIRCELL Mobile Telephone Network, the Eutelstat Earth Station and the digitalisation of the main trunk routes. It also led to the MINITEL tourism information project.

INFORMATION

Commission of the European Communities
DG XVI 1.A
200 rue de la Loi
B-1049 Brussels
Tel: INT +322 299 1111 (exchange)

(iii).VALOREN

Statutory Basis

The legislative basis for VALOREN is Council Regulation (EEC) No 3301/86: OJ L 305, dated 31/10/86.

Objectives

The principal objective of VALOREN, which ran from 1987 to 1991, was to improve the economic base of disadvantaged regions in the EC by encouraging the exploitation of the Member States' indigenous energy potential. This applies particularly to resources which are of little international significance, but important to a particular region. It appears that the Programme is unlikely to be repeated; as its objectives are being absorbed into other programmes.

EC Contribution

The budgetary allocation for the Programme was 400 MECU.

Status Report

The stimulation of Northern Ireland's own energy potential from renewable resources was supported under the VALOREN Programme, as was the electrification of Rathven Island by a wind-powered generator.

Between 1987 and 1991, IR£22.6 million was employed to develop Ireland's peat resources, of which 55% came from the EC and the remainder, from Bord na Mona.

INFORMATION

Commission of the European Communities
DG XVI A.1
200 rue de la Loi
B-1049 Brussels
Tel: INT+ 322 299 1111(exchange).

iv RENEVAL

Statutory Basis

In July 1988, the Council adopted Regulation (EEC) No 2506/88: OJ L 225, dated 15/8/88.

Objectives

The aim of this three-year programme was to improve the infrastructure and the physical and social environment of shipbuilding areas.

Programme Content

The types of operation which may be financed under the ERDF programme were mostly the same as those specified in the non-quota shipbuilding areas (Regulation (EEC) No 2617/80, as amended by Regulation (EEC) No 217/84), namely:

- the improvement of run-down industrial areas;

- the creation or development of business consultancy firms and economic promotion agencies;
- the establishment or development of common services for a number of undertakings;
- the promotion of innovation in industry and services; and
- better access for SMEs to risk capital.

EC Contribution

A budget of 200 MECU was agreed.

The Programme was financed jointly by the Member States concerned and the EC, the rates of whose assistance were laid down in Article 5.1 of Regulation 2617/80. Aid under the EC programme might not be combined with aid granted for the same project under non-quota measures.

Participation

The Commission decided on the areas eligible for support, based on the submissions of the Member States. To be eligible, areas had to have experienced substantial job losses in shipbuilding in the previous three years, or to be threatened with such losses.

Bodies eligible for assistance included local and regional authorities, businesses, co-operatives and self-employed persons.

INFORMATION

Commission of the European Communities
DG XVI 1.A
200 rue de la Loi
B-1049 Brussels
Tel: INT+ 322 299 1111 (exchange).

v STRIDE: SCIENCE & TECHNOLOGY FOR REGIONAL INNOVATION AND DEVELOPMENT IN EUROPE.

Statutory Basis

Notice to the Member States: OJ C 196, dated 4/8/90

Objectives

The aim is to strengthen the research, technological and innovatory capacity of the regions whose development is lagging behind, so that they are better placed to attract or retain both technologically advanced activities in the productive sectors of the regions and highly-qualified staff.

Programme Content

The STRIDE initiative is directed mainly at Objective 1 regions, although some funding is also available for Objective 2 but not for Objective 5b areas.

The priority sectors include agro-food production, biotechnology, soil, timber and water quality.

STRIDE concentrates on three categories of measures.

i Strengthening Research Facilities

Research activities which are particularly relevant to the region are emphasised, e.g. aid may be given to increase facilities in universities and research centres. Assistance is given to help regions assess their RTD capabilities and requirements and may also be available for the improvement of RTD infrastructure, such as science parks. The additional costs of transferring public RTD activities from the more prosperous areas to Objective 1 regions are also eligible.

ii Promoting Increased Participation in EC Research Programmes and Networks

STRIDE may finance the dissemination of information about existing EC schemes and support preparatory work for participating in cross-border, collaborative ventures. Assistance may also be given for the hardware necessary to gain access to networks. Demonstration and pilot projects may also be assisted, following participation in EC R&D programmes.

iii Encouraging Co-operation Between Research Centres and Firms

This measure aims to make research more relevant to local needs and to stimulate SMEs to use local research facilities. Funding may be awarded to set up bodies to encourage the co-operation desired. Various vocational training measures are also eligible.

EC Contribution

STRIDE is financed jointly by the Member State and the EC. The total contribution from the ERDF and the ESF for the period 1990-93 was 460 MECU.

Participation

Measures (i) and (ii) apply to Objective 1 regions only, while measure (iii) applies to both Objective 1 and 2 regions.

Status Report

Of the £11.5 million designated for the UK, £4.4 million is being used to provide additional support for the DTI's SPUR Programme for SMEs' R&D projects. In July 1992, the DTI called for applications for participation in the "STRIDE Programme for Great Britain", which comprises five measures for grant support:

i access to research centres for SMEs;

ii regional innovation and technology transfer centres;

iii strengthening regional R&D capacity;

iv education and training in measures I to III; and

v the SPUR Scheme.

Grant levels are up to half total eligible costs, the minimum grant being £50,000. SMEs benefiting from the project must be in Objective 2 areas. Applications should be made to the regional Department of Trade and Industry Office, the Scottish or Welsh offices.

Northern Ireland has been granted £10 million under STRIDE. As it is an Objective 1 Region, most of this is being employed to strengthen research facilities.

The 1991-93 Operational Programme (OP) for Ireland has an allocation of 13 MECU. It is directed at:

- marine resources (8 MECU);
- environmental research (3 MECU);
- forestry (1 MECU); and
- food, particularly upgrading the National Food Centre (0.7 MECU).

INFORMATION

UK
Objective 2 areas:

England
Ms S. Platteuw
STRIDE Programme Secretariat
Department of Trade and Industry
Bay 317
Kingsgate House
66-74 Victoria Street
London SW1E 6SW
Tel: 071 215 2555

IRELAND
Department of the Marine
Leeson Lane
Dublin 3
Tel: 01 6785444
Fax: 01 6618214

Northern Ireland
Dr T. Courtney
Department of Economic Development
Netherleigh
Massey Avenue
Belfast BT4 2JS
Tel: 0232 529 409

COMMISSION
Commission of the European Communities
DG XV1 A/1
200 rue de la Loi
B-1049 Brussels,
Tel: INT +322 299 1111 (exchange)

vi INTERREG

Statutory Basis

The INTERREG initiative was introduced under Article 11 of Regulation 4253/88: OJ L 374, dated 31/12/88.

Objectives

Its objectives are:

- to assist both internal and external border areas of the EC to overcome the special development problems arising from their relative isolation;
- to promote the creation and development of networks of co-operation across internal borders;-
- to assist the adjustment of external border areas to their new role as border areas of a single integrated market; and
- to respond to the new opportunities for co-operation with third countries in external border areas of the EC.

Background

The INTERREG initiative was initially called FRONTIERS.

Programme Content

Guidelines appeared in OJ C 215, dated 30/8/90.

Eligible activities which promote co-operation across internal borders include:

- studies related to development plans treating border areas as an integrated geographical unit;
- joint development and management of services and facilities for SMEs;
- the development of tourism, agritourism and natural parks through which a border runs;
- the provision of local water, gas and electricity supplies and local telecommunications and the development of renewable energy resources;
- pollution control, waste disposal or environmental conservation programmes;
- measures to improve agricultural processes;
- the establishment of trade and professional organisations;
- improved communications; and
- training and employment measures.

A specific initiative has been established to retrain customs agents, which must not be confused with the MATTHAEUS Programme for Customs Officers (see Chapter 23). This scheme for agents will be funded largely from INTERREG and the ESF Objective 3.

A complementary pilot scheme called "Observatory for Cross-Border Co-operation" with a budget of 1 MECU was launched for the three years from July/August 1990. Its main objectives were to provide support for border regions and enable them to exploit opportunities created by the single market. Most of its services relate to the provision of information by various means.

EC Contribution

The programme was jointly financed by the individual Member States concerned and the EC.

914 MECU was provided from all three Structural Funds for the period 1990-93, together with 100 MECU from the ERDF under Article 10.

Participation

Eligible areas included all Objective 1, 2 and 5b areas along the internal and external land borders of the EC delineated by NUTS III. Certain other areas, such as islands in close proximity to other countries, were also eligible. Priority was given to Objective 1 areas. Frontier regions, which were not eligible for regional funding, might benefit from Article 10 support.

In the UK, INTERREG applied to Northern Ireland, other than the City of Belfast, and to Kent.

Status Report

A joint Belfast-Dublin three-year programme allocated 76 MECU to Northern Ireland.

A joint Kent-Nord-Pas de Calais programme allocated 22 MECU to support actions for transport/telecommunications, environment, economic development, education and training and tourism.

It is thought unlikely that the programme will be extended as its objectives are being incorporated into other programmes.

Applications

Member States were required to submit Operational Programmes (OPs) within the scope of the CSFs. The guidelines for OPs which Member States are invited to establish are published in OJ C 215, dated 30/8/90, which also lists the areas eligible.

INFORMATION

UK

Daniela Druce
Kent County Council
Economic Development Department
Springfield
Maidstone
Kent ME14 2LL
Tel: 0622 694066

Catherine Cavanagh
EC Branch
Room 278
Department of Finance and Personnel
Parliament Buildings
Belfast BT4 3SW
Tel: 0232 521509

IRELAND

Department of Finance
Structural Fund Section
Merrion Street
Dublin 2
Tel: 01 767571

COMMISSION

DG XVI A/I
Commission of the European Communities
200 rue de la Loi
B-1049 Brussels
Tel: INT+ 322 299 1111 (exchange)

Observatory for Cross-Border Co-operation:

EC Pilot Project LACE
Association of European Border Regions
c/o EUREGIO
Enscheder Strasse 362
D-4432 Gronau

vii COMMISSION INITIATIVES : REGIS

Statutory Basis

The REGIS initiative was introduced under Article 10 of Council Regulation No. 4253/88 of 19 December 1988: OJ L 374/1.

Objectives

Its objectives are:

- to promote economic diversification in the ultra-peripheral regions;
- to consolidate the links between these regions and the rest of the EC;
- to stimulate co-operation between neighbouring remote regions and between them and nearby non-Member countries, particularly those enjoying preferential arrangements with the EC; and
- to increase where appropriate their capacity to cope with natural disasters.

Programme Content

The Guidelines to Member States for Operational Programmes are set out in Notice C (90) 1562: OJ C 196, dated 4/8/90.

EC Contribution

The total contribution from all three Structural Funds for the period 1990-93 was 234 MECU.

Participation

The regions eligible for REGIS funding are Guadeloupe, French Guyana, Martinique, Reunion, the Canary Islands, the Azores and Madeira.

INFORMATION

Commission of the European Communities
DG XVI A.1
200 rue de la Loi
B-1049 Brussels
Tel: INT +322 299 1111 (exchange)

viii REGEN

Statutory Basis

REGEN was established as a Commission Initiative within the meaning of Article 11 of Council Regulation (EEC) No 4253/88.

Objectives

REGEN aims to accelerate:

- the creation of infrastructures for the reception and transmission of natural gas in peripheral regions; and
- the completion of EC-wide networks for the transmission and distribution of gas and, in exceptional cases, electricity.

Programme Content

The guidelines for Operational Programmes are published in OJ C 326, dated 28/12/90.

EC Contribution

Three Hundred and forty seven MECU was made available by the ERDF for the period 1990-93.

Status Report

A grant of 108 MECU was agreed to support the construction of a gas pipeline between Ireland and the UK, linking the British distribution network at Moffat to Brighthouse Bay, from where it will run to Loughshinney, north of Dublin.

INFORMATION

Commission of the European Communities
DG XVI A.1
200 rue de la Loi
B-1049 Brussels
Tel: INT+ 322 299 1111 (exchange)

ix TELEMATIQUE

Statutory Basis

TELEMATIQUE was established as a Commission Initiative within the meaning of Article 11 of Council Regulation (EEC) No 4253/88.

Objectives

Its main aim is to promote the use of advanced telecommunications services in Objective 1 regions and to improve access to such services in other regions. By contrast with STAR, the emphasis is on investment in services rather than infrastructure. This fund is intended to help implement systems developed under the RACE, DRIVE, DELTA and AIM Programmes.

Programme Content

The guidelines for Operational Programmes are set out in a Notice to the Member States (OJ C 33, dated 8/2/91).

The following measures are eligible under the TELEMATIQUE Programme:

a. promotion of the use of advanced telecommunications services by SMEs and of the provision of such services by them:
   - promotion of advanced services by agencies, chambers of commerce etc.;
   - feasibility studies and demonstration projects relevant to SME requirements; and
   - aid to SMEs for the purchase of software and hardware;
b. promotion of services offered by SMEs, including aid to develop such activities;
c. development of services in the public sector for data transmission services likely to contribute to regional development; and
d. development of networks within Objective 1 regions and linking them with those in the rest of the EC.

EC Contribution

A budget of 233 MECU was allocated for the period 1991-93.

Status Report

By virtue of its Objective 1 status, Northern Ireland is the only UK region to qualify for assistance. The ERDF allocation is 5.4 MECU and President Computer Consultants are acting as the managing agents for this programme.

The 1991-93 ERDF funding for TELEMATIQUE in Ireland amounts to 11 MECU, which is essentially being used for the supply and use of Advanced Telecommunication Services (ATS).

Applications

The Programme is scheduled to end on 31/12/93. In Northern Ireland it is run by the Industrial Development Board and LEDU, the Small Business Agency. It is not yet certain whether it will be repeated or the objectives incorporated into other programmes.

INFORMATION

UK
Industrial Development Board for Northern Ireland:
A. Kingston, Programme Manager
Department of Economic Development
Room 324
IDB House
64 Chichester Street
Belfast BT1 4JX
Tel: 0232 233233
Fax: 0232 231328

IRELAND
T. Burke
Department of Tourism, Transport and Communications
Scotch House
Hawkins Street
Dublin 2
Tel: 01 718211

COMMISSION
DG XVI A/2
Commission of the European Communities
200 rue de la Loi
B-1049 Brussels
Tel: INT+ 322 299 1111 (exchange)

x PRISMA

Statutory Basis

PRISMA was established under Article 11 of Council Regulation (EEC) No 4253/88: OJ L 374, dated 31/12/88.

Objectives

Its main aim is to help SMEs in Objective 1 regions adapt to the completion of the internal market and, specifically:

- to support efforts to develop certification and testing infrastructures, particularly calibration and metrology services; and
- to prepare SMEs for the opening up of public procurement and related developments.

Programme Content

The guidelines for Operational Programmes are set out in a Notice to the Member States: OJ C 33, dated 8/2/91.

The following measures are eligible:

- the creation or modernisation of testing laboratories;
- expenditure related to the control of testing equipment; and
- consultation fees incurred by SMEs to assist them in developing appropriate production methods to comply with EC policy or certification and quality assurance.

Assistance may also be given to make the Tenders Electronic Daily (TED) and related systems more freely available to SMEs. Support for improved information systems on quality control requirements, standards and other related activities is also eligible, as is assistance to encourage co-operation with other firms.

EC Contribution

A budgetary allocation of 114 MECU from the ERDF was made for the period 1991-93.

Status Report

In the UK, PRISMA applies to Northern Ireland only.

In Ireland, the ERDF funding for PRISMA amounts to 9.4 MECU, most of which is being used to improve information services to SMEs and to improve competitiveness in the textile, shoe and clothing industries.

Five measures are proposed in Ireland's Operational Programme:

- Measure 1 concerns calibration/metrology;
- Measure 2 concerns the setting up and expansion of testing facilities;
- Measure 3 concerns assistance to SMEs by providing SMEs with information on public procurement;
- Measure 4 concerns assistance to companies protected under Article 115 of the EC Treaty (concerning deflection of trade); and
- Measure 5 concerns the provision of technical assistance for monitoring the OP.

Following advertisements in the daily newspapers, 36 projects were submitted, 17 of these were offered contracts and are now working towards completion of their agreement. Several unsolicited proposals have been received and two further contracts have been signed, with a third under consideration by the Technical Committee.

Applications

An advertisement requesting submissions was placed in the daily newspapers, but no further advertisements are expected in the immediate future.

The OP is operated under the aegis of the Department of Industry and Commerce. There is provision for EC Commission involvement in the selection of projects. Each project is independently rated and examined for fitness for support under the PRISMA OP by evaluators, with the final selection being made by the Technical Committee.

INFORMATION

UK
Leslie Woods
Department of Economic Development
Industrial Science Centre
17 Antrim Road
Lisburn BT28 3AL
Tel: 0846 665161

IRELAND
Liam Ryan
Department of Enterprise and Employment
Frederick Building
Setanta Centre
South Frederick Street
Dublin 2
Tel: 01 6614333 ext. 270
Fax: 01 6795710

COMMISSION
DG XVI A/2
Commission of the European Communities
200 rue de la Loi
B-1049 Brussels
Tel: INT+ 322 299 1111 (exchange)

xi COMMISSION INITIATIVES : LEADER - LINKS BETWEEN ACTIONS FOR THE DEVELOPMENT OF THE RURAL ECONOMY

Statutory Basis
LEADER was established by the Commission on 15/3/91, under Article 11 of Council Regulation (EEC) No 4253/88.

Objectives

The aim is to demonstrate the potential for local initiatives in the development of rural areas.

Programme Content

The guidelines to Member States are published in OJ C 73, dated 19/3/91.

The measures eligible are:

a. measures benefiting the inhabitants of the rural areas concerned:

   - technical support to aid rural development for local authorities, project promoters and initiatives already running;
   - vocational training and recruitment aid;
   - rural tourism and farm tourism;
   - SMEs, craft enterprises and local services;
   - local value enhancement and marketing of agricultural products; and
   - other rural development measures;

b. managing and equipping local rural development groups, particularly with computer and telecommunications equipment; and

c. networking local groups across the EC - promotion, assessment and dissemination.

A LEADER Co-ordination Unit has been set up to provide an information exchange between the partners and external parties.

EC Contribution

The budgetary allocation for the three-year programme in 1991-93 was 450 MECU. Member States are required to contribute to the operation of the local groups.

Participation

A network of 213 local groups has been set up, all of them located either in Objective 1 rural areas or in Objective 5b regions.

The body submitting the plan may be public. private or a mixture of the two. It is essential that it should have a real local presence, that it should be representative of the community, and able to demonstrate its solvency, that it should have administrative expertise and the ability to carry out the plan.

Status Report

The UK allocation is :

- Northern Ireland: 2.167 MECU from the ERDF, 0.676 MECU from the ESF and 0.958 MECU from the Guidance Section of the EAGGF; and
- Objective 5b areas: 6.81 MECU from the ERDF, 1.497 MECU from the ESF and 3.298 MECU from the Guidance Section of the EAGGF.

This funding has led to the creation of 13 local groups in the UK.

The EC allocation for Ireland is IR£21 million, which is being used to support 16 Irish Rural Development Groups over the period 1991-93.

The two characteristics common to all successful applicants were:

i an approach closely adapted to local requirements and resources; and

ii optimum use of local expertise and know-how.

Applications

The scheme is administered by DG VI (Agriculture) through designated national bodies.

In Ireland, the Department of Agriculture and Food is the authority designated to administer LEADER. The deadline for submitting plans to the Department was 15/7/91 and it is unlikely that any further calls will be made, as its objectives have largely been incorporated into subsequent programmes.

INFORMATION

UK

Wales
Mr A. Lansdown
Section ERP 2A
Welsh Office
New Crown Building
Cathays Park
Cardiff CF1 3NQ
Tel: 0222 823127

England
Mr C. Rice
Department of the Environment
South West Regional Office
Room 202, Tollgate House
Houlton Street
Bristol BS2 9DJ
Tel: 0272 218172

Scotland
Mr P. Smith
Industry Department
Room 5/88, Scottish Office
New St Andrew's House
St James Centre
Edinburgh EH1 3TA
Tel: 031 244 5283

Northern Ireland
Murdo Murray
Rural Development Council
Loughry College
Cookstown BT80 9AA
Tel: 06487 66980

IRELAND

Mary Cullinan
The Rural Development Division
Department of Agriculture Food and Forestry
Agriculture House
Dublin 2
Tel: 01 6789011
Fax: 01 6616263

Secretary of the Irish LEADER Network
Ms M. Walsh
IRD Duhallow/West Cork LEADER Group
James O'Keeffe Institute
Newmarket
Co Cork

COMMISSION
Directorate-General for Agriculture (DG VI)
Commission of the European Communities
200 rue de la Loi
B-1049 Brussels
Tel: INT+ 322 299 1111 (exchange)

The LEADER Co-ordinating Unit facilitates communication and exchanges between participants in the Programme and provides documentation, databases and technical expertise.

LEADER Co-ordinating Unit
AEIDL, Chaussée St Pierre 260
B-1040 Brussels
Tel: INT+ 322 736 4960
Fax: INT+ 322 736 0434

xii COMMISSION INITIATIVES : RESIDER

Statutory Basis

Council Regulation (EEC) No 328/88: OJ L 33, dated 5/2/88

Objectives

It aims to help convert declining industrial regions in the EC which are affected by the restructuring of the steel industry.

Programme Content

The Programme consists of a series of multi-annual measures aimed at improving the infrastructure and the physical and social environment of the areas concerned, as well as the establishment of new activities, the growth of SMEs and the development of innovation.

EC Contribution

The budget for the Programme's first year was 300 MECU, but the Commission stressed that this sum was provisional and could be increased.

The Programme is financed jointly by the Member States and the EC. Assistance from EC funds, which may not as a rule exceed 55% of the total public expenditure taken into account in the Programme, is provided from the European Regional Development Fund.

Participation

RESIDER applies to areas which meet the following criteria:

- there are at least some 3,500 jobs in the steel industry;

- industrial employment is dependent in large measure, in principle at least 10%, on the steel industry;
- major job losses, in principle at least 1,500, occur in the steel sector; and
- there are major employment problems in the general region where the area concerned is located.

Status Report

The only UK programme to be announced covered the steel areas of South Yorkshire and Scunthorpe, with a grant of £3.6 million to improve employment prospects. A major consequence of this was that Regional Enterprise Grants were available not only to firms in Development Areas, but also to the Barnsley, Sheffield and Doncaster Travel-to-Work Areas, to support capital expenditure and R&D by small firms. The UK programme for South Yorkshire has now ended.

Applications

National governments have to make submissions to the Commission for areas to be given RESIDER status.

INFORMATION

UK
Department of Trade & Industry
Room 317
Kingsgate House
66-74 Victoria Street
London SW1E 6SW
Tel: 071 215 5000

COMMISSION
R. Shotton
Commission of the European Communities
DG XVI A-2 (Regional Policy) -
200 rue de la Loi
B-1049 Brussels
Tel: INT+ 322 295 6965
Fax: INT+ 322 296 2568

xiii RECHAR

Statutory Basis

The Commission approved this programme: see OJ C 20, dated 27/1/90.

Objectives

The objectives are:

- to improve the physical and social environment in coal-mining areas, thus contributing to their economic regeneration;
- to promote alternative economic activities, particularly through the creation and development of SMEs; and
- to develop human resources, particularly by vocational training.

Programme Content

Grants and loans may be provided for the following purposes:

- environmental improvements, including reclamation of coal-tips, cleaning up and conversion of disused coal-mining buildings and their surroundings, landscaping, road improvements, subsidence correction etc.;
- improvement of community facilities, roads, water and electricity supplies in mining villages;
- provision of factory premises;
- promotion of SMEs;
- promotion of tourism, particularly activities based on industrial heritage;
- vocational training and employment measures;
- early retirement assistance; and
- redeployment aids under Article 56 of the ECSC Treaty.

EC Contribution

This programme is jointly financed by the individual Member States and the EC. The total contributed by the ERDF and the ESF during the period 1989-93 was 369 MECU and the ECSC contributed 120 MECU in the form of interest subsidies. The ECSC could provide up to 120 MECU more in interest rebates on loans and 40 MECU, in supplementary redeployment aids.

Loans may also be available from the EIB.

Participation

RECHAR applies to coal-mining areas in regions which are already eligible for ERDF assistance under Objectives 1, 2 and 5b and which meet the following criteria:

- heavy economic dependence of the area on coal-mining activity; and
- significant job losses in the coal-mining industry in the recent past and/or expected job losses likely to bring about a worsening of the regional unemployment situation.

Areas outside these regions with particularly severe problems related to coal-mining may also be considered, but assistance is directed specifically at coal-mining areas and not at the wider regions in which they are located.

Status Report

The UK's allocation is £124 million, of which £105.5 million is from the ERDF and the remainder from the ESF. Access to the funding was blocked by the Commission for some time because of disagreements with the UK government over whether the re-allocation of existing UK funding to particular projects constituted "additionality" within the terms of the Regulations. These problems were eventually resolved in February 1992 and the list of localities eligible for assistance under RECHAR was published in OJ C 177 on 18/7/92.

The following activities are being supported:

- regenerating areas left derelict by coal-mining and setting up new facilities to help generate economic activity;
- supporting the development of small businesses;
- improving the environment and the quality of life in the mining communities;
- helping set up and develop local and community initiatives which create jobs; and
- providing training in new skills for all members of the mining communities.

Applications

Member States are required to submit detailed proposals for Operational Programmes to the Commission. Further information on the application of the scheme in the UK may be obtained from the DTI or from its regional offices.

INFORMATION

UK
Carlton Evans
Department of Trade and Industry
Kingsgate House
66-74 Victoria Street
London SW1E 6SW
Tel: 071 215 2557

Commission
Directorate-General XVI A/1
Commission of the European Communities
200 rue de la Loi
B-1049 Brussels
Tel: INT+ 322 299 1111 (exchange)

xiv. RETEX

Statutory Basis

RETEX was established by the Commission on 13/5/92, within the terms of Article 11 of Council Regulation (EEC) No 4253/88.

Objectives

It aims to accelerate diversification of economic activities in those regions which are heavily dependent on the textiles and clothing sector.

Programme Content

The guidelines for Operational Programmes are included in a Notice to the Member States: OJ C 142, dated 4/6/92.

Specific measures may include:

- improving know-how for businesses, including aid for advisory services;
- financial support for the temporary employment of engineers and other specialists to implement modernisation and diversification within SMEs;
- vocational training for the various teams and groupings and for the staff or former staff of textile and clothing firms;
- the rehabilitation of industrial wasteland and aid to reduce pollution and facilitate recycling; and
- improved access to venture capital and loans.

The Programme will not generally be used to support capital projects.

EC Contribution

The contribution from the Structural Funds was 100 MECU for the period up to the end of 1993. A contribution of 400 MECU is anticipated for the period 1994-97.

The level of support for these measures ranges from 20% to 80%, depending on the appropriate Structural Fund Objective and the importance of the textile industry to the area.

Participation

Only regions in Objective 1, 2 or 5b areas are eligible.

Status Report

Member States have already submitted their nominated regions and programmes. In June 1993, the Commission announced that Ireland and Northern Ireland were to receive 11.5 MECU and 2.6 MECU respectively.

INFORMATION

UK
Contact the regional offices of the DTI.

COMMISSION
Commission of the European Community
DG XVI A/2
200 rue de la Loi
B-1049 Brussels
Tel: INT+ 322 299 1111 (exchange)

xv PERIFRA - A SPECIAL ACTION FOR PERIPHERAL REGIONS AND DESTABILISED ACTIVITIES, A MEASURE OF REGIONAL CHARACTER

Statutory Basis

PERIFRA was initiated by the European Parliament.

Objectives

The 1992 programme was intended to alleviate the problems caused by the negative impact on:

- peripheral regions, of the trade concessions to Central and Eastern Europe e.g. the PHARE Programme; and
- any regions affected by the cut-back in arms production or closures of military installations.

Programme Content

PERIFRA is aimed particularly at small-scale projects, defined as those within the 0.5 to 0.4 MECU range.

EC Contribution

PERIFRA differs from the other EC regional initiatives in that it is independent of the Structural Funds.

PERIFRA is a modest pilot project, initially intended only for 1991, with a budget of 40 MECU, but then extended for a further year, with a budget of 50 MECU.

The level of financing for projects is 50% throughout the Community.

Participation

PERIFRA is not restricted to Objective 1, 2 or 5b areas.

Status Report

More funding has been requested for a continuation of this initiative as PERIFRA II.

The 1992 allocations for the UK were 5.7 MECU for five defence-related projects and 2.4 MECU for three projects in the textile industry.

The 1992 allocation for Ireland was 1.5 MECU.

Applications

Applications are submitted by the Member States to the Commission.

INFORMATION

UK
Carlton Evans
DTI
Kingsgate House
66-74 Victoria Street
London SW1E 6SW
Tel: 071 215 2557

COMMISSION
Commission of the EC
DG XVI A/2
200 rue de la Loi
B-1049 Brussels
Tel: INT+ 322 299 1111 (exchange)

xvi KONVER (CONVER)

Statutory Basis

Proposed Commission Initiative

Objectives

KONVER aims to assist regions affected by reductions in military expenditure and military forces.

Its main objectives are:

- to improve the material and socio-economic situation in regions with high concentrations of the armaments industry and military establishments;
- to support the conversion of armaments industries and military bases to civilian output and activities of general interest; and
- to support new economic activities of public interest, especially the establishment, setting up, conversion and development of SMEs.

Programme Content

The following measures will be supported:

a. new economic activities of public interest, particularly the establishment, setting-up, conversion and development of SMEs;

b. drawing up integrated conversion programmes and studies, development and planning frameworks and proposals for conversion schemes;

c. the conversion of military establishments:

   - the release, conversion and restoration of buildings, workshops and military establishments;
   - conversion of military air bases into civil airports; and
   - support for trading estates and technology parks in previously military establishments;

d. environmental rehabilitation of areas affected by military use and manoeuvres.

e. supporting the conversion of bases:

- drawing up conversion programmes at local authority and regional levels, feasibility studies and pilot projects;
- promoting cultural assets and tourism; and
- conversion and expansion of public transport infrastructures and social infrastructure measures, where they are related to the conversion of military establishments; and

f. training for new job opportunities.

EC Contribution

Funding of 130 MECU from the ERDF and ESF was agreed for 1993. Funding for research will also be available from the third and fourth Framework Programmes.

Participation

The Programme applies not only to those areas supported under Objectives 1, 2 and 5b of the Structural Funds, but also to areas fulfilling the following conditions:

- heavy dependence of the regional economy on the arms industry and military establishments; and
- substantial job losses in the arms industry or military establishments in the recent past or foreseeable future, leading to a deterioration in the regional employment situation; areas must also identify high unemployment statistics as caused by disarmament or troop withdrawals.

A list of eligible regions will be published in the OJ.

INFORMATION

Commission of the European Communities
DG XVI 1.A
200 rue de la Loi
B-1049 Brussels
Tel: INT+ 322 299 1111 (exchange)

Chapter 19.2

Grants Under the European Social Funds

Grants under the European Social Funds are grouped as follows:
CHAPTER 19.2: GRANTS UNDER THE EUROPEAN SOCIAL FUNDS

1 European Social Fund

2 Studies and Technical Assistance

3 Commission Initiatives:

  i EUROFORM, HORIZON, NOW

  ii Subsidy for Transnational Meetings between Employees' Representatives

  iii LEDA: To Promote an Innovative to Job Creation at Local Levels

  iv CHILDCARE

  v TIDE: Technology for the Socio-economic Integration of Disabled & Elderly People

  vi ERGO: Programme for Economic and Social Integration of Long-term Unemployed

  vii HANDYNET: Mobility Programme for Disabled

  viii HELIOS II; Rehabilitation of Disabled

1. EUROPEAN SOCIAL FUND

Statutory Basis

The European Social Fund was established under Article 123 of the Treaty of Rome. It is governed by Regulation (EEC) No 4255/88: OJ L 374, dated 31/12/88.

Objectives

In order to ensure that measures make an effective contribution to both EC and national employment policies, the distribution of funds is now determined by medium-term development plans, which establish priorities and provide a coherent policy framework within which individual proposals can be judged.

The Community Support Framework (CSF) for ESF assistance in the UK identifies six priorities, three for each of the two Structural Fund Objectives with which the ESF is principally concerned (OJ L 64, dated 13/3/90). These are:

Objective 3 - to combat long-term unemployment:

- training and retraining of the long-term unemployed;
- creation of stable jobs and self-employed activities for the long-term unemployed; and
- training, retraining and the creation of stable jobs for long-term unemployed women, migrants and the disabled;

Objective 4 - to integrate young people into the job market:

- basic vocational training for young people;
- higher skills training for young people; and
- training, retraining and the creation of stable jobs for young women, migrants and the disabled.

The CSF for ESF assistance to Ireland identifies seven priorities under Objectives 3 and 4. Under Objective 3 these are:

i alternate training for older persons who generally have work experience;

ii vocational training measures and recruitment subsidies which facilitate the training and occupational integration of women;

iii special courses in skills training for marginalised people, including ex-offenders; and

iv basic training for disabled adults;

and, under Objective 4:

v training for school leavers with no or poor qualifications;

vi basic training for the young disabled; and

vii vocational training measures and recruitment subsidies for young women.

The ESF also assists measures under Objectives 1, 2 and 5b which are designed to promote stable employment and to develop new employment opportunities for the unemployed, persons threatened with unemployment and persons employed in SMEs. These would include the human resources elements of the Industry and Services, Tourism and Rural Development OPs.

In Objective 1 regions the ESF also assists:

- apprenticeship training outside the firm;
- part of secondary level education specifically devoted to vocational training; and
- recruitment subsidies for non-productive projects which fulfil a public need, involving the creation of jobs of at least six months' duration. (This was a transitional provision which expired at the end of 1991 and has not been renewed, although the objective is partially covered in subsequent programmes).

Programme Content

UK

The ESF complements national employment policies by providing finance for schemes to improve the employment prospects of the long-term unemployed and of young people, by providing them with training opportunities and by stimulating the job market to help them find work. There are various types of scheme available, as follows:

i Vocational Training and Guidance

Cash is provided for training to provide the new or improved skills demanded by a labour market which is undergoing rapid technological and economic change. Support is also provided for vocational advice. In areas seriously affected by industrial decline, schemes concerned with the introduction of new production and/or management techniques in SMEs are also eligible for support.

ii Job Creation
Subsidies are provided for recruitment into newly-created, stable jobs and there are start-up aids for the self-employed. In Northern Ireland, recruitment subsidies are extended, for a period of three years from 1 January 1989, to schemes which create additional jobs of at least six months' duration.

iii Support Measures
A relatively small amount of ESF aid is reserved for a range of back-up measures including studies, technical assistance, exchanges of experience and knowledge and other innovatory schemes concerned with the development of training and employment initiatives.

iv Apprenticeship Schemes
These apply to Northern Ireland, where support may be given to the theoretical portion of apprenticeship training given outside the firm. In specific cases, that part of national secondary education systems specifically devoted to vocational training after compulsory schooling may qualify, where it meets the challenges posed by economic and technological change.

To ensure that money is channelled into key areas, the Commission has established guidelines for the allocation of funds for the three years from 1 January 1990 (OJ C 45, 24/2/89). Priority will be give to measures which, for the long-term unemployed:

- combine several types of intervention to give training a key role in promoting occupational and social integration;
- make the most of local employment development potential;
- provide incentives for recruitment to newly-created jobs of a stable nature;
- expand opportunities for self-employment; and
- provide for the training and occupational integration of women who wish to return to work after a long break.

For unemployed school leavers, priority is given to measures which:

- provide young people with work experience and theoretical training to develop the skills required by the labour market;
- provide basic vocational training linked to work experience, particularly where it leads to a recognised qualification;
- provide training leading to high-level qualifications requiring substantial use of new technologies;
- provide recruitment aids for newly-created jobs of a stable nature; and
- expand opportunities for self-employment.

For all projects, priority is given to:

- measures in the less prosperous regions and areas;
- training schemes operating in two or more Member States;
- training in advanced technology;
- innovation in the content, methods or organisation of training;
- training and recruitment incentives to modernisation, particularly in SMEs and sectors sensitive to the effects of the single market;
- programmes leading to more effective training systems; and
- training for people encountering special difficulties in the labour market, particularly the disabled, women and migrant workers.

IRELAND

There are eight human resources programmes either totally or partially funded by the ESF, as detailed below.

The Operational Programme targeted at the long-term unemployed is designed to give an average of 2.5 days work per week for up to a year in newly-created jobs. The Programme costs £42 million and receives ESF aid of IR£27 million for the 1990-93 period.

The Vocational Integration of Young People Operational Programme is designed to assist the transition of young persons from full-time education to the labour market. It targets people who have completed junior and/or senior education but have inadequate skills to secure employment. The scheme will provide training in a broad range of skills in various sectors such as industry, services, rural development, agriculture and tourism. The programme costs IR£209 million and receives ESF aid of IR£136 million for the 1990-93 period.

The Operational Programme under Articles 1(5) and 1(6) of Regulation 4255/88 now involves two measures - apprenticeship and secondary level vocational training:

- the apprenticeship measure is designed to provide comprehensive off-the-job vocational training for apprentices; and

- the secondary level vocational training measures aim to provide secondary vocational training to prepare young people for direct entry to the labour market or to middle-level technical training. Expenditure on this programme is IR£452 million supported by IR£238 million of ESF aid.

The Operational Programme for the Occupational Integration of the Disabled aims to provide training for the disabled leading to placements in the open job market. Projects for the disabled are based at three levels:

Level 1 is targeted at disabled people who are in need of low-level training in order to enter the job market;

Level 2 training is for disabled people who have been assessed as able to take up employment in medium-level skills in industrial sectors such as horticulture, services and manufacturing; and

The Level 3 target group includes those who have been assessed as capable of highly skilled jobs.

ESF aid of IR£102 million supports expenditure of IR£157 million over the four years.

The Vocational Training Infrastructure Operational Programme is largely funded by the ERDF and aims to meet the most urgent needs for the development of training infrastructure in Ireland. The ESF funds the Training of Trainers sub-programme, designed to improve the quality of trainers who are involved in the delivery of training measures under the CSF. This sub-programme involves expenditure of £5 million and aid of IR£3 million over the years 1990-93.

The Human Resources for Agriculture and Rural Development sub-programme aims to provide an advisory, training and education service to farmers to help them adjust to changes arising under the Common Agricultural Policy, to address viability problems, improve existing standards and acquire the new skills necessary to adapt their enterprises to the diversified approach to rural development envisaged under the Rural Development Operational Programme. The sub-programme will also provide continuing, in-service training to facilitate restructuring in the fishing industry by meeting technological and skills needs for the transfer from the catching industry to aquaculture. This sub-programme attracts about £30 million of ESF aid, taking the total expenditure to £47 million for the period 1990-93.

The aim of the Human Resources for Industry sub-programme is to ensure that the workforce has the skills which are required in a developing economy. Almost £450 million of ESF aid will be spent on training and employment schemes between 1990 and 1993 at a total cost of about £712 million.

The Human Resources for Tourism sub-programme aims to extend training provision to produce enough trained personnel with the necessary range of skills, to match new employment opportunities, arising in the expanded tourism sector during the period of the CSF. About £33 million of ESF aid will be spent in the 1990-93 period, involving a total cost of £51 million.

EC Contribution

ESF funding is now programme, rather than project-based, in the sense that cash is distributed to the Member States on the basis of development plans and Operational Programmes prepared by governmental departments in conjunction with competent authorities at national, regional and local level.

UK

The UK received a total of approximately 1,025 MECU for ESF expenditure under Objectives 3 and 4 during the period 1 January 1990 to 31 December 19292. Of this, 514 MECU was set aside for actions to combat long-term unemployment, 470 MECU to combat youth unemployment and 41 MECU, for other measures.

ESF support normally takes the form of part-financing agreed Operational Programmes and public funds from either central or local government are expected to be available to supplement it, under the principle of additionality.

The exact amount of the ESF contribution depends on a number of factors, but a maximum of 50% of total costs and at least 25% of public expenditure is the norm in all parts of the UK except Northern Ireland, where a maximum of 75% of total costs and at least 50 % of public expenditure is the general rule.

Preparatory studies and technical assistance measures may be financed in full, in exceptional circumstances.

Financial assistance may only be granted for the following:

- general running costs of vocational training and guidance schemes, including operational costs, administrative costs and the income, subsistence and travel costs of both trainees and staff;
- wage subsidies for job-creation schemes; and
- the costs of ESF support and development measures.

IRELAND

The total EC allocation for human resources is 1441.5 MECU, at 1989 prices, for the period 1989-93. The Irish national financing required to supplement this objective is 1394.4 MECU. Included within this total are two OPs concerning training and recruitment measures for young people, the long-term unemployed and the handicapped, which will receive 366.2 MECU.

Participation

UK

All parts of the UK qualify for funding for measures under Objectives 3 and 4. The ESF may also contribute to measures taken in the areas designated under Objectives 1, 2 and 5b to promote stable employment and to develop new employment opportunities for the unemployed, people threatened with unemployment and those employed in SMEs.

Applications for funding from the ESF must be presented not by individuals, but by organisations which are financially supported by a public authority, such as: central government, local authorities as represented by the European Liaison Officers, the voluntary sector, the Industrial Common Ownership Movement, Women's Training Network, industry training boards and institutions of higher education.

IRELAND

The ESF is not generally available to individual firms in Ireland. There are some minor exceptions to this but manufacturing firms, for example, would have no direct access to the Fund.

The Irish Development Agency makes training grants available to companies for operative training and management development.

Applications

UK

Individual organisations wishing to apply for ESF support under Objectives 3 and 4 are expected to do so through the Operational Programme co-ordinators appointed to deal with each of the sectors listed above. Application forms are available from, and must be returned to them; eligible projects may then be recommended to the Department of Employment for formal approval and funding.

In the regions covered by Objective 2, selection of projects is the responsibility of Operational Programme committees, which then submit projects to the Department of Employment for formal approval and funding. Enquiries should normally be directed to the appropriate regional or sectoral co-ordinator.

The deadline for UK submissions for 1993 programmes was September 1992; information is still awaited about future programmes.

IRELAND

The principal agent through which the ESF operates is the Department of Enterprise and Employment, which deals with the agencies that are engaged in ESF-related activities. These agencies are almost invariably public bodies and include the Department of Education, the Training Authority, the National Rehabilitation Board and the development organisations, such as the Irish Development Agency (IDA) and the Shannon Development Company.

INFORMATION

UK

A list of regional and sectoral co-ordinators, general information on the operation of the ESF and other technical assistance and advice may be obtained from the following contact points:

England
Department of Employment
European Communities Branch
236 Gray's Inn Road
London WC1X 8HL
Tel: 071 211 4740/4741
Fax: 071 211 4749

Northern Ireland
European Community Branch
Department of Economic Development
Netherleigh
Massey Avenue
Belfast BT4 2JP
Tel: 0232 529900
Fax: 0232 768990

If assistance towards training of particular racial groups is being claimed, contact should be made with:
Equal Opportunities Branch
Department of Employment
Steel House
Tothill Street
London SW1H 9NF
Tel: 071 273 4856

IRELAND

P. Leonard
Department of Enterprise and Employment
65a Adelaide Road
Dublin 2
Tel: 01 765861

Institute of Public Administration
57-61 Lansdowne Road
Dublin 4
Tel: 01 686233
Fax: 01 689135

COMMISSION

Commission of the European Communities
DG V Directorate D
European Social Fund - Technical Assistance Section
200 rue de la Loi
B-1049 Brussels
Tel INT+ 322 299 1111 (exchange)

2. STUDIES AND TECHNICAL ASSISTANCE

Objectives

Funding is available direct from the Commission for studies and other technical assistance which help the Directorate-General for Employment, Industrial Relations and Social Affairs (D-G V) to prepare, carry out and adapt the various activities of the ESF.

Programme Content

The Programme covers the following topics:

- technical assistance and studies of a general nature, including socio-economic statistics, the analysis of labour market structures, training infrastructure and the effects of new qualifications and methods of training; and
- employment and training strategies aimed at improving convergence and consistency in the EC.

Participation and Applications

The OJ is used to invite firms, research institutions and other organisations to express interest in and tender for contracts of this kind.

By way of example, a call for expressions of interest was published in June 1990, which included a comprehensive list of topics on which external assistance would be sought during the period from 1990-93 (OJ C 134, dated 1/6/90). Information about future calls is awaited.

INFORMATION

Commission of the European Communities
DG V Directorate D
European Social Fund - Technical Assistance Section
200 rue de la Loi
B-1049 Brussels
Tel: INT+ 322 299 1111 (exchange)

3. COMMISSION INITIATIVES

i EUROFORM, HORIZON, NOW

The Commission has initiated a number of programmes designed to provide a European dimension to vocational training in specific areas. These programmes are EUROFORM, HORIZON and NOW, and can be found in Chapter 23 on education grants.

ii Subsidy for Transnational Meetings Between Employees' Representatives

Objectives

The objectives of the Programme are:

- establishing relations between the representatives of employees of undertakings on a transnational basis;
- developing a strategy which paves the way towards setting up structures for consultations;

- training employees' representatives so that they may benefit from using their places in such structures; and
- improving and propagating codes of practice, especially for those European works councils already in existence.

Background

This programme is intended to support structured exchanges for the information and consultation of workers, pending the adoption of the Commission proposal to set up a European works council in undertakings, or groups of enterprises, of a Community-wide dimension.

Programme Content

A certain number of operations are eligible, which may take the form of:

- collective visits;
- seminars on the general aims, promoting the training of employees' representatives;
- regular meetings, enabling representatives of employees to familiarise themselves with and jointly define the work procedures, so as to accomplish the set objectives: certain such meetings may serve the additional purpose of improving codes of practice; and
- relevant study projects, expert meetings and publications.

Projects may not consist of one-off, unlinked operations. Isolated projects must have links with the national and European organisations representing employees. Projects should make allowance for developments in EC policy in the area and sector concerned and for subsequent action planned by the state.

EC Contribution

A budget of 17 MECU was agreed for 1993.

Own contributions must be at least 10% of project costs. EC contributions are made towards travel costs and personnel expenses.

Participation

The projects must benefit representatives of company employees, who may be members of Works Councils or similar bodies, company or workshop trade union representatives, or members of health and safety committees. They must have their origins within the EC. The project should concern at least two Member States.

Applications

Project applications must be submitted directly by the employees' representatives of the undertakings concerned.

INFORMATION

Commission of the European Communities
DG V Directorate A
Social Dialogue and Industrial Relations Directorate
Rond Point Schuman 11
B-1049 Brussels
Fax: INT+ 322 295 1744
Tel: INT +322 299 1111 (exchange)

iii LEDA

Objectives

The objectives of this programme are to identify, evaluate and promote successful, innovatory approaches to employment creation at the local level, especially those which involve partnerships between potential employees and development agencies.

Programme Content

The second phase of LEDA runs from 1990-1993.

The following activities are supported:

- a European network of local areas where local people are actively engaged in the promotion and development of employment;
- exchange of experience between areas - rural, urban and mixed; and
- practical and technical assistance, including guides and training.

EC Contribution

The budget is 1 MECU per year.

Participation

Eligible persons are those unemployed or facing employment difficulties because of economic underdevelopment or structural change.

Status Report

Information is awaited about future extensions of the programme.

INFORMATION

IRELAND
FAS
27-33 Upper Baggot Street
Dublin 4
Tel: 01 685777

COMMISSION
Commission of the European Communities
D-G V
200 rue de la Loi
B-1049
Brussels
Tel: INT+ 322 299 1111 (exchange)

iv CHILDCARE

Objectives

This programme aims to reconcile work and family responsibilities by ensuring an increase in the provision of child-care for parents in employment and training.

Background

CHILDCARE was set up under the second Action Programme for equal opportunities, and will continue during the third Action Programme, 1991-95.

Programme Content

The Programme's activities are as follows:

- the collection and dissemination of information, the analysis of data and the formulation of policy options; and
- the stimulation of pilot projects in rural areas.

INFORMATION

Commission of the European Communities
D-G V Directorate B
Equal Opportunities Unit
200 rue de la Loi
B-1049 Brussels
Tel: INT+ 322 299 1111 (exchange)

v TIDE - TECHNOLOGY FOR THE SOCIO-ECONOMIC INTEGRATION OF DISABLED AND ELDERLY PEOPLE

Background

The Commission believes that a programme to develop telecommunications applications for the benefit of the disabled and elderly must continue. In this context, it launched the TIDE Programme in 1991, on the basis of preparatory work carried out under the framework of COST action 219. The objective of the exploratory programme was to evaluate the reaction of the EC market to the launch of development activities in this area. The response was excellent: following the 1991 call for proposals, 70 tenders were received and, of these, 21 were selected and financed.

EC Contribution

Of the 10 MECU budget available in 1992, the Commission allocated 3 MECU to finance extensions to the contracts which were awarded in 1991 and which had not been fully provided for in the budget for that year. The remaining 7 MECU was reserved for the continuation of the 21 projects from the first phase of TIDE, together with additional preparatory work. These measures will enable the TIDE activities in industry to be maintained during 1992-93.

Status Report

Difficulties posed by the lack of a strictly legal basis prevent a corresponding budget heading from being continued through 1993-94. Instead, the Commission intends from 1993 onwards to initiate measures for disabled and elderly people under the Third Framework Programme, within the specific programme "Telematics systems in areas of general interest". This would give TIDE a legal basis and secure adequate funding. These measures will then find their natural extension in the Fourth Framework Programme, 1994-98, under the heading "Science & Technology against the struggle for exclusion" (OJ C 95, dated 5/4/93).

INFORMATION

A work plan and information package can be obtained from:

Commission of the European Communities
TIDE Office
DG XIII Directorate C3
Avenue de Beaulieu 29
Room 3/13
B-1160 Brussels
Tel: INT+ 322 2990204
Fax: INT+ 322 2990248

vi ERGO

Objectives

The objectives are to identify, evaluate and promote successful innovatory approaches for the economic and social integration of the long-term unemployed.

Programme Content

The first phase of ERGO ran from 1989-91.

ERGO covers the following activities:

- a European network of innovative programmes and projects;
- exchanges of experience regarding different categories of long-term unemployed; and
- co-operation in research and evaluation.

EC Contribution

ERGO's budget was 1.5 MECU per annum.

Status Report

It is believed unlikely that ERGO will be revised in its original format as its objectives have been carried on by other programmes.

INFORMATION

Commission of the European Communities
D-G V
200 rue de la Loi
B-1049 Brussels
Tel: INT +322 299 1111 (exchange)

vii HANDYNET

Programme Content

HANDYNET is a complementary programme, whose purpose is to allow the disabled to achieve the maximum possible mobility within our society.

INFORMATION

Glynis Phillips
Department of Health
Wellington House
Room 3B2
133-135 Waterloo Road
London SE1 8UG
Tel: 071 972 4125

viii HELIOS II

See Chapter 23 on Education grants.

Chapter 19.3

Economic and Social Cohesion Grants

Economic and Social Cohesion Grants are grouped as follows:

1. Cohesion Fund
2. SPEC: Support Programme for Employment Creation
3. POVERTY 3: the Third Poverty Programme
4. Town-twinning

1. COHESION FUND

Statutory Basis

Article 130d of the EECT, introduced by the Maastricht Treaty, provided for the establishment of a Cohesion Fund before 31 December 1993. A proposal for a Council Regulation establishing the fund (COM (92) 339 07) was published in OJ C 248/14, dated 25/9/92, and amended by COM (92) 599, published in OJ C 38/21, dated 12/2/93.

Objectives

Article 1 of COM 92 599 states:

> "2. The Fund shall contribute to the strengthening of the economic and social cohesion of the Community ..."

It will support projects in the field of the environment and trans-European network infrastructure in those Member States whose per capita GNP is less than 90% of the Community average and which have a programme for the fulfilment of the conditions of economic convergence set out in Article 104c of the Maastricht Treaty.

Background

This initiative is independent of the Structural Funds. The Fund will only be introduced after the ratification of the Treaty, so some slippage is anticipated in the starting date.

Programme Content

Article 3 provides:

> "The Fund may provide support for:

- environmental projects contributing to the achievement of the objectives of Article 130r (action to preserve, protect and improve the environment, to contribute towards human health and to ensure a prudent and rational utilisation of natural resources);
- transport infrastructure projects of common interest financed by Member States (Trans-European Networks); and
- preparatory studies and technical support measures related to eligible projects."

By contrast with the Structural Funds, applications by Member States will be for projects or groups of projects - not for programmes.

EC Contribution

Article 4 provides for a total commitment of BECU 15 (at 1992 prices) for the period 1993-99, with annual commitments rising from BECU 1.5 in 1993 to BECU 2.6 in 1999.

Article 7 provides for a rate of assistance of 80% or 85% "of public or similar expenditure as defined for the purposes of the Structural Funds."

Preparatory studies and technical support measures may be fully financed.

Participation

The Fund is directed to Member States, not regions.

Article 10 provides that "The projects to be financed ... shall be decided upon by the Commission in agreement with the Member State concerned."

Status Report

To enable Cohesion Fund assistance to be given to eligible Member States before the ratification of the Maastricht Treaty, the Commission has proposed an Interim Cohesion Financial Instrument (OJ C 38/18, dated 12/2/93). This instrument will last for a maximum of two years and be replaced as soon as possible by the final instrument. Funding available is (as proposed under the Cohesion Fund proper) 1,500 MECU for 1993 and 1,750 MECU for 1994, at 1992 prices.

INFORMATION

Commission of the European Communities
DG XVI Directorate D
Office of the Cohesion Fund
200 rue de la Loi
B-1049 Brussels
Tel: INT+ 322 299 1111 (exchange)

2. SPEC: SUPPORT PROGRAMME FOR EMPLOYMENT CREATION

See Chapter 23 on Educational Grants.

3. POVERTY 3: THE THIRD POVERTY PROGRAMME

See Chapter 23 on Educational Grants.

4. TOWN-TWINNING

See Chapter 27 on Cultural Grants.

Chapter 20

Environmental Policy

Evolution of Environmental Policy

The prime aim of the single market was to promote economic growth in the Member States and economic growth cannot be achieved without incurring costs. Historically, the costs of economic growth have usually been paid by the environment, social progress and economic expansion being dependent on activities which exploit the Earth's resources. Materials drawn from the earth are used to produce goods and energy, which at the same time generate waste and pollution. The planet's capacity to deal with such pollution is increasingly being stretched to the limit. Over the past few years there has been a long succession of ecological disasters: radioactive pollution caused by accidents at nuclear power stations, pollution of the sea by wrecked tankers or the dumping of waste, pollution of the atmosphere, lakes, rivers and ground water, acid rain and industrial and chemical pollution of all kinds.

The single market, promoting a faster-growing Europe could easily lead to dirtier rivers, smokier air, ever more car-clogged cities and, worst of all, increasing quantities of toxic and other waste. Furthermore environmental considerations are generally played down, especially when economic conditions are hard, as being an expensive luxury.

Since it is now almost universally recognised that the issue of environmental protection is closely linked to that of economic growth, the EC's recent actions have been aimed at devising and implementing policies that take both priorities into account in a more balanced manner. This was not always the case, however. The initial Treaties had little to say about the protection of the environment. Only the EURATOM Treaty refers to it and then only under the heading "Health and Safety". It imposes basic standards on Member States, provides for inspections and, in the event of infringements, allows for actions to be brought before the European Court of Justice. Given the recognition in EURATOM of the environmental threat from ionising radiation, it is unfortunate that similar provisions were not included in the other Treaties, the economic objectives of which had an obvious and predictable impact on the environment.

This initial lacuna was first addressed at the Paris Summit in 1972, and in early 1973 the Commission put forward an initial action programme. This first programme however, was mainly an attempt to harmonise national legislation on the environment, chiefly to ensure that the national rules of the individual Member States, introduced as a result of the 1972 Paris Summit, did not distort the policy of fair competition in the common market. In particular, it was felt necessary to prevent certain more ecologically-minded members from taking unilateral measures that their partners could interpret as constructing barriers to intra-Community trade. Neither this first action programme, nor the second in 1977, was wholly effective since they merely listed remedial measures to combat pollution rather than considering preventative measures.

The awakening of public awareness in Northern Europe, particularly in Germany, where public concern was, however, aroused by the extent of the damage done by acid rain to conifer forests, was a determining factor in persuading first national and then Community authorities to take action to reduce air pollution. The rising strength of the ecologists in national parliaments and the European Parliament, together with the headway made by the Green movement's agenda in most of the major political parties, gave environmental protection a higher priority. This "greening" of public opinion - most notably among consumers - gave an economic impetus to environmental protection: it was felt that EC industry not only had an obligation to tackle the problem of an increasingly polluted society, but would actually benefit by controlling waste and creating new markets overseas for the techniques and equipment developed for dealing with the problem at home. Despite this, it was not until 1983 that the central philosophies which now govern policy formulation emerged: that prevention is better than cure and that polluters should pay for clearing up operations.

Environmental protection was given official status as a major plank of Community policy in the SEA, adopted in 1986. Its importance was emphasised by its inclusion in Jacques Delors' "complete package" speech which he gave at Lourdes on 27 October 1989. Explaining the six items which constituted the total package of the SEA he said: "And finally, sixth, environmental policy".

Article 25 of the SEA was incorporated into the EECT as Title VII Articles 130r-t. Article 130r, as subsequently amended by the Maastricht Treaty, states:

1. Community policy on the environment shall contribute to the pursuit of the following objectives:
   - preserving, protecting and improving the quality of the environment;
   - protecting human health;
   - prudent and rational utilisation of natural resources;
   - promoting measures at international level to deal with regional or world-wide environmental problems.
2. Community policy on the environment shall aim at a high level of protection taking into account the diversity of situations in the various regions of the Community. It shall be based on the precautionary principle and on the principles that preventative action should be taken, that environmental damage should as a priority be rectified at source and that the polluter should pay. Environmental protection requirements must be integrated into the definition and implementation of other Community policies. ..
3. In preparing its policy on the environment, the Community shall take account of:
   - available scientific and technical data;

- environmental conditions in the various regions of the Community;
- the potential benefits and costs of action or lack of action;
- the economic and social development of the Community as a whole and the balanced development of its regions. .."

To interpret the Community's determination to use the EC-wide dimension to achieve progress in this area of policy, which is seen as directly affecting the lives of Community citizens, Article 130 should be read within the context of Article 100a(3) on the approximation of laws, which says:

> "The Commission, in its proposals...concerning health, safety, environmental protection and consumer protection, will take as a base a high level of protection."

This quality requirement is a guarantee that the basis for common action will not be the lowest common denominator in the Member States; rather, it will encourage governments with backward policies in this area to align themselves with the highest standards. If the Council adopts such a measure, a Member State may feel it necessary to provide national provisions, but only on the grounds of important national requirements such as public order, public safety or protection at the workplace.

Environmental protection has now clearly become a priority concern of the EC: it is in the Treaty so the institutions are obliged to implement and enforce it. Pressure groups both for citizens concerned that the measures might not go far enough and corporations who fear that they will have to meet the costs involved are eagerly presenting their cases in the appropriate places.

In the Maastricht Treaty, apart from various aspects of EMU and the social chapter, environmental policy is the only substantial area for which qualified majority voting has been substituted for unanimous voting, thus preventing one or two Member States from blocking a decision agreed on by a majority of others.

There are however exceptions to the majority voting rules. Two key exceptions are fiscal and energy policy. This is disappointing for the environmentalists, since energy use is the main source of atmospheric pollution and of global warming gases, while taxing energy use is one of the simplest ways of encouraging energy saving or the use of substitute resources. Other exceptions to majority voting are measures concerning town and country planning, land use (with the exception of waste management) and measures of a general nature. These exceptions were designed to take account of national sensitivities.

As usual, the EC's power to legislate via Directives is not effective unless firstly, such Directives are transposed into national law in full and by the specified deadlines and secondly, their implementation is adequately policed in the field. According to Article 189, "a Directive is binding as to the result to be achieved ... but shall leave to the national authorities the choice of form and methods." In an area of policy as cost-sensitive as the environment, there is a suspicion that this could lead to misinterpretation or distortion of a Directive, thereby reducing its effectiveness. The present resources for ensuring the proper application of EC standards are far from adequate. It is largely left to environmental protection associations, non-governmental organisations and European citizens to exercise this control. The Commission has also devoted considerable time to identifying and rectifying the many deviations and omissions in national law, notably by starting infringement proceedings in the European Court of Justice.

A significant limitation of EC environmental policy to date has been the somewhat narrow emphasis on administrative instruments, such as licensing standards, emission limits, bans and restrictions. While a few EC Directives expressly permit economic incentives, such as the Directives on waste oils and on large combustion plants, the effectiveness of this policy has progressed little beyond declarations of intent in successive environmental programmes.

The basic principle that "the polluter pays" has faced differences of interpretation and practise as to the extent of the polluter's responsibility. While there is broad agreement that such responsibility covers the costs of compliance with pollution control standards, there has been uncertainty about the extent to which polluters should pay for resultant damage, particularly in cases where it may be remote in either time or distance from the source of the pollution, or the damage could not reasonably have been foreseen by the polluter. However, recent draft Directives introduced following the Fifth Environmental Action Programme adopted in April 1992, suggesting establishing the civil liability of those responsible for creating waste, which would indicate a much tougher new approach.

Costs of Pollution

Such evidence as there is suggests that the financial costs of environmental policies at the moment are relatively slight - at most a few hundred ECUS per head. An analysis in the independent report "1992 and the Environment" concluded that the macroeconomic impact of additional investments in environmental protection equivalent to 1% of Community GDP would be minor and would in no way affect the benefits of the single market.

One of the key justifications of environmental action is the high cost to future generations of doing nothing. Inevitably, the relative costs are difficult to quantify, precisely because the exercise often involves comparing the situation before a policy was introduced with what happened afterwards.

Many of the costs of pollution are also borne by the present generation. One study in Germany estimated that the effects on health by air pollution - including lost working hours, medical costs and the cost in human life - amounted to between 1.1 and 2.7 MECU per year. Water purification is a major cost in all Member States: in France the total estimated cost of water purification, excluding investment, was 1.4 BECU in 1982. The damage caused to buildings in the EC by acid deposits was variously estimated in the early 1980s at between 540 MECU and 2.7 BECU per year.

It is arguable that the greatest benefit could result from reducing the knock-on effects of industrial pollution on other economic activities. Tentative estimates in the state of the environment report of 1986 suggested that the cost of the damage to forests caused by acid deposits was around 300 MECU per year, while agricultural production lost for the same reason was valued at almost 1 BECU.

Pollution - Its Causes and Remedies

Pollution is often a trans-frontier phenomenon, and its control and elimination clearly have to be dealt with on a Community-wide basis. Fall-out from the Chernobyl nuclear disaster affected large parts of Western Europe, and spread as far westward as Scotland and North Wales. Sulphur emissions from one country produce the forest-killing acid rain in another, as was forcefully pointed out by Thorbjorn Berntsen, the Norwegian Minister for the Environment, in his description of John Gummer the UK Environment Secretary - in which he taught the whole world a useful Norwegian word. The quality of the drinking water the Dutch draw from the Rhine depends on the substances that find their way into the river long before it enters Dutch territory.

Although the threat from air pollution was vividly illustrated in the early 1980s by the damage caused to forests by acid rain, it is the output from car exhausts, accounting for 90% of air contamination in some areas, which is forcing home the lessons of individual responsibility for pollution. EC policy has sought to set general air quality standards for dangerous substances such as sulphur dioxide, lead and nitrogen dioxide, and product standards for gas, oil and petrol. Due in part to pressure from the EC and particularly the European Parliament, all Member States have now introduced lead-free petrol. Legislation has been passed which is expected to cut car exhaust gases such as carbon monoxides and nitrogen oxide by 60-70% after 1992. The EC has joined international agreements to eliminate the use of chlorofluorocarbons (CFCs) which deplete the earth's vital protective ozone layer; this ban on ozone-depleting gases is due to come into effect in 1995, ahead of the date set by the Montreal Protocol. The EC also gave a moral commitment at the Rio Earth Summit in June 1992 to stabilise emissions of carbon dioxide, which is presumed to be the main cause of global warming, at their 1990 levels by the year 2000.

EC policy has been concerned to prevent the discharge of dangerous substances into water and to set minimum standards for certain types of water. More than 25 Directives concerning the purification of both fresh and sea water have been issued since the early 1970s, adding up to one of the most comprehensive bodies of EC legislation on the environment. One of the Directives that was recently adopted, 91/271/EEC (OJ L 135/40 dated 30 May 1991) makes the treatment of urban waste water mandatory. All towns and cities will have to install purification plants, a measure that will benefit an urban population of between 160 and 200 million. A priority target of the EC has been the titanium dioxide industry, which has a history of dumping its waste at sea or into river estuaries. Three Directives have now been adopted, limiting discharges from this source. However, despite the investments made over the last 20 odd years, there has been little general improvement in the state of the EC's water resources. Unfortunately there have been more cases of deterioration in quality than of improvement. If demand for water continues to rise even at the present rate, the impending depletion of freshwater resources in certain regions may create major problems in the future, particularly in the Mediterranean countries.

Public opinion surveys confirm that noise is an environmental problem which EC citizens consider to be of the utmost importance. All measures so far have been concerned with limiting noise emissions from specific products, notably cars, aircraft, tractors, plant and machinery, lawnmowers and household appliances. Action is also being taken within the framework of the EC's 1986 social action programme, aimed at protecting workers from occupational noise and requiring employers to take the necessary protective measures. In future, the Commission is likely to move beyond its traditional product-based approach to deal with overall noise quality, so that, for example, other noises would have to be taken into account when a machine is operating.

Many chemicals are hazardous and toxic, highly mobile once released, and are long lasting and pervasive, in that small quantities can do considerable damage to the environment and human health. EC rules put the onus on manufacturers and importers to supply information, on, among other things, the quantity of the chemicals being produced, the uses which they are being put to, and ways of rendering the substance harmless. Existing chemicals have been put on a special EC inventory, and those that are dangerous are gradually being classified and labelled as such. Attention has been focused on the biotechnology industry as one that holds the promise of economic benefits in the 21st century but which could pose environmental problems if not carefully controlled. Directives have been adopted on the contained use of genetically modified micro-organisms.

The EC has policies in the field of nature conservation and the protection of natural resources. The growing pace of industrial and agricultural development increases the risk of serious soil and coastal erosion, and the EC has made efforts to make soil degradation and coastal decline a particular priority - for instance, in its policies for combating forest fires and acid rain. The protection of flora and fauna is clearly of public concern. Europe displays a great variety of climates, soil conditions and landscapes. It harbours more than 6,000 plant species, about 100,000 species of invertebrates and nearly 600 varieties of birds. By the end of the century, the Commission intends to establish a comprehensive network of protected natural and semi-natural habitats in the EC. Other EC actions include the prohibition of whale imports for commercial purposes, successive bans on the import of seal-pup skins and regulations for the protection and well-being of bred animals.

Each year the EC produces 2 billion tonnes of waste, of which around 30 million tonnes are classified as dangerous. The volume of waste generated is increasing considerably faster than the capacity necessary for its treatment and disposal. The EC's strategy to combat this has three clear strands: waste prevention, waste recycling and safe disposal. The Commission proposed a "green" labelling scheme to help consumers identify environmentally-friendly products and packaging. It has developed special rules for the recycling of waste oils, waste paper, drink containers, used batteries and plastic waste. National regulations governing the dumping of waste vary significantly, but the EC is determined to harmonise the rules and introduce measures that encourage the disposal of waste as near as possible to the place where it was generated. However, despite the growth in processes such as composting and recycling, landfill remains the most common method of waste disposal.

Environmental protection is not just a matter of negative constraints: the EC has also allocated funds to encourage environmentally beneficial projects. About 1.2 BECU was allocated to environmental improvement programmes in underdeveloped regions for the period from 1989 to 1993. In particular the Commission has released an appropriation of 500 MECU for the ENVIREG Programme to combat pollution in Mediterranean coastal regions.

In 1990 the EC decided to set up a European Environment Agency (EEA). This decision has yet to be implemented, as there has been some difficulty in reaching an agreement as to where it should be located. The task of this agency will be to provide objective and comparable data on the state of the environment in Member States, thereby producing a sound scientific basis for newly drafted Commission initiatives and enhanced authority of those trying to enforce existing ones.

Recognising that measures to protect the environment will never work if they are considered in isolation, the EC has recently adopted an integrated approach. This important principle has been given force by the EC's environmental impact assessment programme, which came into force in mid-1988. This integrates ecological awareness into the wider planning and decision-making process in all sectors, but notably in agriculture, the oil industry, energy, transport, tourism and regional development.

Agriculture and the Environment

The position of agriculture is of particular concern. In the recent review of the CAP, besides the price cuts and market adjustments which received most of the public attention, a forum was provided for reflection on the role of agriculture in the economy and in society as a whole. In the past 40 years agriculture has undergone a technological revolution which has led to widespread mechanisation, the growing use of agrochemicals and vastly improved cultivation techniques. Such intensification of farming not only produced increased yields thereby creating great wealth for large producers and the notorious food mountains, but also disrupted country life and left the countryside changed beyond recognition. in some Member States.

Among the resulting specific environmental problems are the deterioration of animal habitats and the extinction of some species due to disturbance, pollution and wetland drainage; low water quality arising from the misuse of chemicals, animal manners and other organic material; soil degradation or erosion, caused as much by the abandonment of farming in uneconomic hilly or mountainous regions as by the direct application of intensive farming techniques and declining air quality, due to ammonia evaporation from fertilisers and manure.

The EC has finally adopted agricultural measures directly or indirectly aimed at promoting environmental objectives and reducing the impact of modern farming. These include aid payments for farmers who comply with certain practices in environmentally sensitive zones, subsidies to help maintain farming in mountainous or other less-favoured areas, the prohibition of harmful pesticides and incentives for less intensive farming, such as the setting aside of surplus arable land.

The newly enlarged Structural Funds are an important instrument for the integration of the EC's environmental and agricultural objectives. Applications for aid for large-scale agricultural projects such as the restructuring of holdings, or changes in the water regime, are now subject to environmental impact assessments to make sure they conform to the EC's environmental policies.

Energy and the Environment

The EC views nuclear energy as an essential resource for industrial development, and a means of limiting environmentally destructive carbon emissions from all oil and coal-fired power stations. However, in recognition of the grave risks of nuclear power, priority has been given to ensuring that it is produced in the safest conditions possible. EC research into radiation has long been used as the basis for fixing permissible national levels for workers and the general public. Member States, meanwhile, are legally bound to monitor radiation and report the results to the Commission, notably where new installations are concerned. In the wake of the Chernobyl disaster maximum contamination levels for foodstuffs were established, and a rapid response system for radiological emergencies was introduced.

Renewable energy sources in general, not just the major initiatives such as the EC funded JET project, offer undoubted benefits in terms of protection of the environment. Admittedly, fierce local opposition to the establishment of hydro-electric power stations, even small-scale ones, has been encountered, as has often been the case with municipal waste incineration plants; noise and visual intrusiveness have sometimes hampered the development of wind power. When used instead of fossil fuels they make a considerable contribution towards reducing emissions of greenhouse gases. The environmental impact of renewable energy sources is however generally slight, although this is small consolation to the people who find a new installation planned in their areas; the NIMBY (not in my back yard) philosophy takes over.

Certain technologies for exploiting renewable energy sources are already competitive today, while others could become competitive within five to ten years. True economic comparisons between renewable energy sources and fossil fuels are extremely complex and are generally biased towards the fossil fuels, since they take only direct costs into account. If all the external costs that society has to bear, such as social charges and damage to the environment and public health, were taken into consideration, the economic assessment might be substantially different, making it easier for alternative energy sources to increase their share of the market.

Of all the renewables, the use of biomass in particular is likely to expand considerably, since this source of energy has many advantages. There is a great variety in its end-uses, it encourages the development of new and sustainable technologies and it offers the possibility of reducing emissions of carbon dioxide into the atmosphere and establishing synergy with agriculture in the EC.

Very large areas are needed in order to obtain significant quantities of energy from the sun, the wind and biomass. However, land-use intensity should not be an argument against using renewable energy sources when it is clear that with solar energy, for example, the main obstacle is not the amount of land involved but the intermittent nature of production and the difficulties of economic storage.

The Commission has put forward the essential elements of a Community policy for renewable energy resources (COM 92 180 final, dated 29/6/92). It includes proposals for:

- implementation of legislation and administrative procedures for removing obstacles to the development of renewable energy sources;
- promoting the completion of national inventories of potential renewable energy resources and the widest possible dissemination of these inventories, to inform the public about the practical possibilities of exploiting these resources;
- preparation and start-up of a statistical recording system for renewable energy sources, in conjunction with the Statistical Office of the European Communities;
- preparation of uniform standards for products and equipment in the field of renewable energy sources;
- promotion of opportunity and feasibility studies concerning projects to exploit renewable energy, especially to benefit local authorities and SMEs;
- promotion of co-operation between the industries manufacturing equipment for the exploitation of renewable energy sources and promoting the transfer of technologies;
- promoting exchanges of information about the development of renewable energy sources between Member States; and
- taking account in public investments of the possibility of using renewable energy sources in conjunction with energy-saving measures.

The International Dimension

The cross-border and even global nature of certain environmental challenges requires the EC to intensify its regional and international co-operation. Global issues have become so important, that in the run up to the year 2000, they could become an important factor in determining the ways in which international relations develop - economically, politically and in terms of security.

Over the next 50 years, the world's population may double. Even with a very modest rise in living standards, there could be a fivefold increase in economic activity, touching all the key sectors such as energy, transport, industry and agriculture. Even if most of these changes occur outside Europe, the EC will not escape their impact. Environmental problems differ throughout the world. In the EC and other industrially advanced countries, the essential aim is to modify consumption patterns. In Central and Eastern Europe, years of neglect and under-investment in pollution control including, most worryingly, in the safety of nuclear reactors, have left a heritage of environmental degradation which has to be considered a priority target for action. In the developing countries, population pressure and poverty have been key factors in allowing unsustainable development patterns to emerge.

The internal and external dimensions of EC policy are therefore inextricably linked; for in terms of thermodynamics the world is one closed system. No material either enters it or leaves it except for the sun's radiant energy. The only processes that occur within the closed system are those which change material from one form to another. It follows that the developed world has to take the lead in measures that ensure that these processes are not permitted to run in a manner which is harmful to us all. A coherent and effective response to the complex problems must be made as a matter of urgency; some effort was made in the 21st Agenda, adopted at the United Nations Conference on Environment and Development (UNCED) in June 1992, but more will have to be done and at an increasing pace.

Chapter 21

Environmental Grants

Environmental Grants are grouped as follows:

1. Environment Programme: Management of Natural Resources
2. ENVIREG: European Regional Fund for the Environment
3. LIFE: Financial Instrument for the Environment
4. PSEP: The Physical and Social Environment Programme
5. NETT: Network For Environmental Technology Transfer
6. JOULE II: Joint Opportunities for Unconventional or Long-term Energy Supply
7. SAVE: Specific Actions for Vigorous Energy Efficiency
8. ALTENER: Promotion of Renewable Energy Resources
9. Cohesion Fund

1. ENVIRONMENT PROGRAMME: MANAGEMENT OF NATURAL RESOURCES

See Chapter 17.3 on R&D grants for the management of natural resources.

2. ENVIREG

Statutory Basis

Commission Decision 90/C 115/03 (OJ C 115/03, dated 9/5/90), made on 2 May 1990 "within the meaning of Article 11 of Council Regulation (EEC) No 4253/88."

Objectives

The objectives are to help the least favoured regions to tackle some of their environmental problems and thereby help put their economic and social development on a firmer footing.

Background

ENVIREG covered the period from 8 November 1990 to 31 December 1993 and complemented LIFE, the non-regional environmental programme.

ENVIREG was launched in recognition of the fact that environmental difficulties may hinder socio-economic development in the least favoured regions. They detract from the inhabitants' quality of life and make these areas less attractive to tourists and to those wishing to set up modern industrial, commercial or leisure enterprises requiring a high quality environment.

Programme Content

ENVIREG is restricted to coastal areas covered by Objective 1 and the Mediterranean coastal areas covered by Objectives 2 and 5b. A coastal area is generally defined as a zone up to 10 km from the coastline.

Eligible measures include the following.

i Reduction of Pollution in Coastal Areas:

- development of infrastructure and equipment for the treatment of waste water, initially in urban areas with fewer than 100,000 inhabitants;
- development in urban areas of infrastructure for the collection, recycling and disposal of solid waste;
- studies, technical assistance and demonstration projects relating to the agricultural use of compost and sewage sludge; and
- port installations for the treatment of ballast and bilge water, and small-scale equipment to avert accidental discharges of pollutants.

ii Land Use Planning for Coastal Areas:

- costs of studies for regional land use planning; and
- protection of flora and fauna and their enhancement within tourism.

iii Control of Industrial Waste:

- infrastructure and productive investments related to the collection and treatment of solid waste and sewage sludge; and
- studies to identify industries causing pollution.

iv Strengthening of Know-how:

- studies on treatment processes;
- assisting local authorities by establishing service centres for the installation and maintenance of equipment;
- transfer of know-how between regional experts;
- training, particularly for personnel responsible for the maintenance of the equipment.

EC Contribution

ENVIREG was allocated a budget of 500 MECU for the period 1990-93.
The ERDF funding amounts to £11.3 million for Northern Ireland and 28 MECU for Ireland.

The sub-programmes and measures in the ENVIREG Operational Programme for Ireland are financed jointly by Ireland and the EC. The level of EC aid is 75%.

Status Report

The Operational Programmes have now been finalised. Within the present programme no new projects are expected in the immediate future.

In Northern Ireland, ENVIREG is financing new sewage works in areas important to tourism and shellfish industries such as the Foyle Estuary, Larne and Carlingford Lough. Studies are being carried out to assess the environmental risks of landfill disposal sites.

In Ireland, the ENVIREG programme provided funding in 1993 for the treatment and recycling of waste water and sewerage at Killorglin and Dingle in County Kerry, Bantry in County Cork, Tramore in County Waterford, the Greystones Treatment Works in County Wicklow and the Sligo Main Drainage, stage IV.

INFORMATION

IRELAND
John Harte
Department of the Environment
O'Connell Bridge House
Dublin 2
Tel: 01 6793377 ext. 2156

COMMISSION
DG XV1/A.1
Commission of the European Communities
200 rue de la Loi
B-1049 Brussels
Tel: INT+ 322 299 1111 (exchange)

3. LIFE: FINANCIAL INSTRUMENT FOR THE ENVIRONMENT

Statutory Basis

Council Regulation (EEC) No 1973/92: OJ L 206, dated 22/7/92.

Objectives

The general objective is to contribute to the development and implementation of EC environmental policy by financing:

- priority environmental actions in the EC;
- technical assistance to third countries from the Mediterranean region, or to those bordering on the Baltic Sea; and
- exceptionally, actions concerning regional or global environmental problems provided for in international agreements.

Background

The Council Regulation initiating the LIFE Programme also repealed Action by the Community for Nature Conservation (ACNAT), MEDSPA and NORSPA.

For many years the EC has been financing R&D programmes, the results of which can be exploited by demonstration and pilot projects. Under LIFE demonstration schemes, awareness campaigns and actions providing incentives or technical help will be eligible for assistance. Scientific and technical research is not included.

Programme Content

The LIFE Regulation lists actions under five fields which define the scope of the programme.

i Promotion of Sustainable Development and the Quality of the Environment:

- to establish and develop new techniques and methods of measuring and monitoring the quality of the environment;
- to establish and develop new clean technologies - that is, those which create little or no pollution and make fewer demands on resources. The Commission has targeted five industrial sectors in calling for demonstration projects. These are surface treatments (e.g. metal plating, ceramics), textiles, tanneries, paper industry and the agri-food industry (e.g. dairies);
- to establish and develop techniques for the collection, storage, recycling and disposal of waste, particularly toxic and dangerous waste and waste water;
- to establish and develop techniques for locating and restoring sites contaminated by hazardous substances;
- to establish and develop models to integrate environmental factors into the planning and management of land use and socio-economic activities;
- to reduce the discharge into the aquatic environment of nutritive substances and potentially bio-accumulative toxic, persistent pollutants; and
- to improve the quality of the urban environment in both central and peripheral areas.

ii Protection of Habitats and of Nature:

- to maintain or re-establish biotopes which are the habitat of endangered species or seriously threatened habitats, pursuant to Directive 79/409/EEC, or to implement measures to conserve or re-establish endangered species;
- to maintain or re-establish types of natural habitats of EC interest;
- to protect soil threatened or damaged by fire, desertification, coastal erosion or the disappearance of the dune belt;
- to promote the conservation of marine life; and
- to protect and conserve areas of fresh groundwater and fresh surface water.

iii Administrative Structures and Environmental Services:

- to foster greater co-operation between the authorities of the Member States, particularly in controlling trans-boundary and global environmental problems; and
- to equip, modernise or develop monitoring networks in order to strengthen environmental legislation.

iv Education, training and information:

- to promote environmental training in administrative and professional circles;
- to promote environmental education, particularly by providing information, exchanges of experience, training and educational research;
- to foster better understanding of problems and encourage models of behaviour consistent with environmental objectives;
- to disseminate information about sound management of the environment.

v Actions outside Community territory:

- to promote the establishment of the necessary administrative structures in the environmental field;
- to provide the technical assistance needed for the establishment of environment policies and action programmes;
- to promote the transfer of appropriate environmentally-friendly technologies and to foster sustainable development; and
- to promote assistance for third countries faced with ecological emergencies.

EC Contribution

A budget of 400 MECU has been agreed for the first phase which ends on 31 December 1995. The budget for 1993 was 65.333 MECU for actions within the EC and 3.5 MECU for actions outside EC territory. The 1994 budget is likely to be slightly larger than in 1993.

EC financial support for operations, with the exceptions of priority biotopes or habitats, is subject to the following limits:

- a maximum of 30% of the cost of actions involving the financing of income-generating investments;
- half of the cost of other actions, but exceptionally 75% of the cost of actions relating to nature protection - species, habitats, biotopes; and
- the whole cost of measures designed to provide the information necessary to execute an action implemented on the Commission's initiative or to provide relevant technical assistance measures.

Participation

LIFE is open to both EC Member States and to third countries. Persons from third countries are eligible for technical assistance in the fields of action listed in the Annex to the LIFE Regulation under the heading "B. Actions Outside Community Territory".

Status Report

The Commission issued a call for tenders for new, clean technology projects on 19/12/92, with a deadline of 31/3/93. Final details on selection were due to be taken in mid-July.

Priorities for the programme are appraised annually. A further call for proposals was expected in autumn 1993.

INFORMATION

UK

England
Central Contact:
Richard Longman
DOE/EPC Room A132
Romney House
43 Marsham Street
London SW1P 3PY
Tel: 071 276 8146
Fax: 071 276 8626

Northern Ireland
Nature Conservation: Northern Ireland
Mr G Seymour
Environment Service (Countryside & Wildlife)
Calvert House
23 Castle Place
Belfast BT1 1FY
Tel: 0232 230560
Fax: 0232 243939

IRELAND
Mr Ray Dollard
Environmental Control Section
Dept. of the Environment
Custom House
Dublin 1
Tel: 01 6793377

Mr Tom Wright
National Parks and Wildlife Service
Office of Public Works
51 St Stephen's Green
Dublin 2
Tel: 01 613111

Deirdre O'Connor
Marine Environment Section
Department of the Marine
Leeson Lane
Dublin 2
Tel: 01 6785444

COMMISSION
DG X1 Directorate C2
Commission of the EC
200 Rue de la Loi
B-1049 Brussels
Tel: INT+ 322 296 3423/9561

4. PSEP: THE PHYSICAL AND SOCIAL ENVIRONMENT PROGRAMME

Objectives

This programme aims to support the preservation of the countryside and wildlife through the funding of interpretative centres, information centres and projects which will open up access to the countryside in general and to suitable designated areas.

Background

This is an operational programme of the Community Support Framework: Northern Ireland, the relevant section of which is Measure 1 of Sub-Programme 2. The programme lasted from 1990 to 1993.

Programme Content

Projects must:

- assist the safeguarding or enhancement of outstanding scenic areas;
- protect and conserve nationally important and rare habitats and wildlife;
- promote enjoyment and understanding of the countryside;
- contribute to the development of tourism in Northern Ireland; and
- provide value for money.

EC Contribution

The overall cost of this programme is 1.33 MECU, with an EC aid rate of 68%. Public sector participation contributes 1.33 MECU, of which 0.9 MECU is assistance from the ERDF.

Participation

Enterprises in Northern Ireland, comprising of district councils, nature preservation societies and the Department of the Environment may participate.

Status Report

From 1994 nature conservation will cease to be included in the PSEP Programme, and will instead form part of a new Environment Programme within the Community Support Framework: Northern Ireland. The latter programme is only at the consultation stage at present.

INFORMATION

Mr G Seymour
Environment Service - Countryside and Wildlife
Calvert House
23 Castle Place
Belfast BT1 1FY
Tel: 0232 230560
Fax: 0232 243939

5. NETT: NETWORK FOR ENVIRONMENTAL TECHNOLOGY TRANSFER

Objectives

NETT aims to promote co-operation between industrial enterprises and users in the field of new technologies.

Background

Consultancy services such as specialists, representatives of trade and industry, university research services etc., are associated with the network, which was established in 1988 as an independent association, with the backing of the EC Commission .

Programme Content

NETT concentrates on providing the following three services:

- DATANETT: specialised information from on-line data banks on environmental standards and regulations, markets for environmental technologies, potential technical options, programmes of support and financial and technical support by the EC and national institutions;
- Research and Development Service: individual advice for NETT members, for example, in the search for partners or with regard to financial support; and
- Meeting Service: organisation of meetings, seminars, lectures, workshops, attendance at trade fairs etc.

INFORMATION

NETT
207 Avenue Louise
BUS 10
B-1050 Brussels
Fax: INT+ 322 646 4266

6. JOULE II

See Chapter 17.5 on Energy Research Grants.

7. SAVE: SPECIFIC ACTIONS FOR VIGOROUS ENERGY EFFICIENCY

See Chapter 25 on Trans-European Networks.

8. ALTENER: PROMOTION OF RENEWABLE ENERGY RESOURCES

See Chapter 25 on Trans-European Networks

9. COHESION FUND

See Chapter 19.3 on Economic and Social Cohesion Grants.

Chapter 22

Education Policy

The accelerating pace of change in industry and the completion of the single market have created a demand both for greater adaptability and greater mobility in the work force. These two requirements must be satisfied if the Community is ever to bring down the persistently high levels of unemployment throughout the EC, particularly amongst young people, and also to safeguard the competitive position of European industry in world markets. Education and training also prepare people for responsible citizenship by fostering a free interchange of ideas and the acceptance of common values which transcend purely sectoral, regional and national interests.

Of the Community's 346 million citizens, over 130 million are under 25; it is this age group that the EC is mainly targeting, since they are perceived as being the most susceptible to new ideas. The young are generally more mobile, being prepared to move around and learn about other peoples' ways of life and languages, so they should be more able to take advantage of the opportunities that an integrated Europe has to offer. Unemployment statistics show, however, that the young are in great need of assistance to enter in the labour market; despite longer training periods, 40% of the unemployed across the Community are under the age of 25, although this age group accounts for only 20% of the working population.

To encourage young Europeans further along the path of geographical and occupational mobility, the EC has been trying to meet young people's needs in the areas of education, training, employment and culture.

There was no mention of education and training in the founding treaties, but the Community recognised their importance as early as the mid-1970s. Even without a clearly defined legal basis in the treaties, a number of initiatives were developed on the basis of Resolutions, Conclusions and Declarations. In 1976, in response to the evident need for information on a Community-wide basis and increased mutual co-operation, the Council and appropriate ministers of the Member States adopted a first resolution on education. They set up the EURYDICE network, to collect and disseminate information on national education policies and systems in the Member States and then to make sure that details of EC initiatives were available throughout the Community. The aims of this network are pursued by the ARION programme, which promotes the mobility of education experts and persons in positions of responsibility in this field.

The Commission entrusted MIDA, the technical assistance bureau for Community Human Resources initiatives, with the task of compiling and managing a database listing all trans-national actions and detailing the partners involved in each action and the various stages of its development.

The EC also launched measures targeting specific groups, such as children of migrant workers and the handicapped. Other measures were concerned with equal opportunities for girls and boys and with, for example, encouraging new ways of thinking on environmental issues or health and the introduction of new technologies at school.

Since 1985 the EUROTECNET programme has encouraged innovation in initial and ongoing vocational training to take account of technological change. A network of pilot projects is encouraging the proliferation of innovative activities by creating cross-border partnerships aided by the European Social Fund. The programme also funds co-operation in the area of research and the dissemination of research findings.

The IRIS programme is concerned with devising training methods especially geared to women's needs and with increasing the commitment to meeting these needs.

The EC receives help in devising and implementing its vocational training initiatives from the European Centre for the Development of Vocational Training (CEDEFOP), whose mission is to inform, conduct research and consult. CEDEFOP was set up by the EC in 1975 and is based in Berlin. It is administered with assistance from governments, employers and trade unions.

Despite the fact that the opportunity to include a legal basis for education and training programmes in the SEA in 1986 was missed, the initiatives continued on a piecemeal basis.

The COMETT programme, which began in 1986, is designed to give young people help in entering the labour market, which is seldom easy with or without qualifications. COMETT promotes cross-border co-operation between higher education establishments, business and industry, and aims to develop training in the new technologies. The intention was to help business and industry, particularly SMEs, to recruit young people with expertise in these important, developing skills. The second five year phase of COMETT was launched in 1990, when the programme had already set up 125 partnerships between universities and industry, with 232 grants being awarded for staff exchanges between universities and industry. Some 329 joint training programmes have also been funded.

In 1988 the EC launched the ERASMUS programme, which aimed at promoting greater mobility of young people throughout the Community. It was decided to name the programme after Desiderius Erasmus (c. 1466 - 1536), the Dutch born humanist and scholar He was one of the most influential figures of the Northern Renaissance because he was the archetypal European scholar, studying and teaching in most of the cultural centres of Europe including Paris, Oxford and Cambridge and travelling throughout Europe to meet the foremost intellectuals of his time. It is a fitting tribute to him that to date one hundred and fifty thousand young people have benefited by spending a period of time studying in another Member State. This mobility of young people is assisted not only by grants, but also by a network of inter-university co-operation programmes (ICPs). In March 1991 nearly 73,000 students were involved in these ICPs, 33% more than in the previous year. The operation of this system has caused universities and professional bodies to change established procedures so as to recognise studies completed in another Member State. Since 1989-90 the EC Course Credit Transfer Scheme (ECTS), an experimental system which allows credits to be accrued and transferred anywhere within the EC, has been in operation. In tandem with this system, the National Academic Recognition Centre (NARIC), a network of national centres for information on recognised degrees, has been set up.

In 1988, the EC launched the "Youth for Europe" programme, to encourage young people to meet in joint projects of a cultural, social or other nature. The emphasis is on the cross-border character of these projects, which are intended to create European awareness and solidarity among young people aged 15 to 25.

The objectives of vocational training are:

- to facilitate adaptation to industrial changes, in particular through vocational training and retraining;
- to improve initial and continuing vocational training, in order to facilitate vocational integration and reintegration into the labour market;
- to facilitate access to vocational training and encourage mobility of instructors, trainees and, particularly, young people;
- to stimulate co-operation on training between educational or training establishments and firms; and
- to exchange information on and experience of issues common to the training systems of the Member States.

To help combat unemployment amongst the young, the European Social Fund is now devoting more than three-quarters of its budget to vocational training and recruitment subsidies for the under 25s, mainly in less-favoured regions.

"PETRA" is a vocational training programme which aims to train and prepare young people for the world of work. It enables them to receive one or two years of vocational training, over and above their compulsory schooling, and thus a chance to obtain recognised qualifications. It also provides easier initial training for the teaching staff of technical and vocational networks. The programme is targeted at young people under the age of 28 who do not have a university education, the idea being to give all categories of young people a chance to prepare themselves for a Europe-wide labour market. The PETRA programme has given rise to a European network of partnerships which are already engaged in over 240 cross-border joint training projects.

The Young Worker Exchange Programme also provides young workers, or young unemployed people between 18 and 28, with the chance to obtain work experience or training in another Member State. This programme, which was started in 1963, is due to merge with the PETRA programme.

In order to fulfil the EC's intention to provide ongoing vocational training, the FORCE programme has been launched. This will encourage investment in ongoing training, dissemination of the best training practices, innovative developments in management, methods and equipment and measures to cope with the consequences of the single market, notably measures which will cater for changing requirements in respect of qualifications.

The concept of a Europe without national frontiers makes language learning more necessary than ever as any deficiencies in this essential skill will seriously hamper the mobility of Europeans. The LINGUA programme, which began in 1990, helps to fund scholarships, exchanges and teaching aids aimed at improving the quantity and quality of the language training available to EC citizens.

In 1990 the Commission also launched the Jean Monnet action programme, designed to assist universities in the speedy development of training courses on European studies. Under this programme subsidies will be granted to universities for the joint funding of chairs in Community Studies, of which there are 91 to date, for graduate and post-graduate courses, study modules and research programmes on all aspects of European integration.

On matters of education and training, as in many other areas, the Community co-operates with its neighbours. The EFTA countries are already involved in the COMETT programme and will also shortly be taking part in the ERASMUS programme. Contacts were also developed with the countries of Central and Eastern Europe as they moved towards democracy. TEMPUS, launched for the benefit of these countries, aids both youth exchanges and the mobility of students in higher education, in order to promote the development of education and training systems.

Training and education are central and crucial to the EC's employment and research policies, so there are many links between the various programmes and other EC policies. ERASMUS, for instance, complements the R&D programme Science, which encourages mobility among research workers. COMETT and EUROTECNET interface with regional policy and the R&D programme DELTA, which funds the development of computer-based educational aids.

The European Social Fund, which is primarily concerned to create and safeguard jobs, especially in regions facing difficulties, helps with vocational training initiatives by funding a large number of national programmes with structural objectives, as well as EC initiatives of a cross-border nature. The latter are concerned with training for new qualifications (EUROFORM), equal opportunities for women (NOW), and access to the labour market for handicapped people (HORIZON).

It is astonishing how much has already been achieved without any firm legal basis in the treaties, and it is hoped that the Maastricht Treaty will open a whole new horizon on youth and training. Amongst the new tasks of the Community is Article 3(p): "a contribution to education and training of quality and the flowering of the cultures of the Member States". It is augmented by a whole new chapter inserted into the EECT entitled "Education, Vocational Training and Youth".

On education, Article 126 states:

"1. The Community shall contribute to the development of quality education by encouraging co-operation between Member States and, if necessary, by supporting and supplementing their action, while fully respecting the responsibility of the Member States for the content of teaching and the organisation of education systems and their cultural and linguistic diversity.

2. Community action shall be aimed at:

- developing the European dimension in education, particularly through the teaching and dissemination of the languages of the Member States;
- encouraging mobility of students and teachers, inter alia by encouraging the academic recognition of diplomas and periods of study;
- promoting co-operation between educational establishments;
- developing exchanges of information and experience on issues common to the education systems of the Member States;
- encouraging the development of youth exchanges and of exchanges of socio-educational instructors; and
- encouraging the development of distance education.

3. The Community and the Member States shall foster co-operation with third countries and competent international organisations in the field of education, in particular the Council of Europe."

On vocational training, Article 127 states:

"1. The Community shall implement a vocational training policy which shall support and supplement the action of the Member States for the content and organisation of vocational training.

2. Community action shall aim to:

- facilitate adaptation to industrial changes, in particular through vocational training and retraining;
- improve initial and continuing vocational training in order to facilitate vocational integration and reintegration into the labour market;
- facilitate access to vocational training and encourage mobility of instructors and trainees, particularly young people;
- stimulate co-operation on training between educational or training establishments and firms; and
- develop exchanges of information and experience on issues common to the training systems of the Member States.

3. The Community and the Member States shall foster co-operation with third countries and the competent international organisations in the sphere of vocational training."

It is too early to say exactly what new policies and programmes will be developed as a result of these new articles in the Treaty, but the priorities expressed at the Copenhagen Summit in June 1993 are as follows:

- learning how to keep on learning throughout our lives;
- combining knowledge with practical know-how;
- developing each individual's creativity and initiative; and
- establishing the right of each individual to lifelong training: all young people should be given vouchers entitling them to initial education and/or training later on.

White papers on the European dimensions in education and vocational training were published late in 1993. It is safe to predict however, that the new provisions will make it possible to increase both the scope of the measures already undertaken by the EC and the numbers able to participate, in particular through increasing the funding available for vocational training measures from the European Social Fund. All new measures will be introduced by qualified majority voting, except in cases where they affect the harmonisation of laws in the Member States.

We may anticipate increasing emphasis on improving the quality and mutual recognition of training systems, particularly by increasing exchanges of information and experience and promoting the mobility of both students and knowledge, whilst at the same time respecting the rich diversity of national traditions in education. This would suggest either new programmes, aimed at mobility of both students and teachers at all levels, or substantial widening of the existing ones. It is also expected that the new initiatives will place high emphasis on cross-border operations and the need for networks, within which partners can work together on joint projects. Programmes will be implemented via a process of consultation and co-operation in which the Commission is assisted by governments, employers, trade unions, voluntary bodies, youth organisations, universities and other centres of education.

Now is the time for interested parties to put forward their own proposals for new programmes. It can be expected that the Commission will welcome well researched proposals in the correct format, with the appropriate cost/benefit analysis.

Chapter 23

Education Grants

Education grants have been split into three sub-chapters as follows:

Chapter 23.1 NON-VOCATIONAL TRAINING PROGRAMMES:

1.1 Jean Monnet Project

1.2 Jean Monnet Fellowships

1.3 ARION: Programme of study visits for education specialists

1.4 ERASMUS: Programme for exchange visits for students in higher education

1.5 LINGUA: Programme for improving the teaching of foreign languages

1.6 College of Europe Scholarships

1.7 EC Student Grants to permit students to study in other Member States on an equal footing

1.8 STOA: European Parliament Scientific and Technological Options Assessment

1.9 TEMPUS: Training for Central and Eastern European Countries

1.10 Research Fellowships in Controlled Thermonuclear Fusion

1.11 Research Fellowships in Human Capital Mobility

1.12 ACE: Action for Co-operation in the Field of Economics

1.13 Co-operation in Science & Technology in Central & Eastern Europe

Chapter 23.2 VOCATIONAL OR NON-VOCATIONAL TRAINING PROGRAMMES:

2.1 Robert Schuman Scholarships

2.2 Paul Finet Foundation

2.3 EUROQUALIFICATION

2.4 HELIOS II: Community Action Programme to Assist Disabled People

2.5 COMETT II: Community Programme for Education and Training in Technology

Chapter 23.3 VOCATIONAL TRAINING PROGRAMMES:

Chapter 23.1

Non-Vocational Training Programmes

This group of programmes includes:

1.1 Jean Monnet Project

1.2 Jean Monnet Fellowships

1.3 ARION: Programme of study visits for education specialists

1.4 ERASMUS: Programme for exchange visits for students in higher education

1.5 LINGUA: Programme for improving the teaching of foreign languages

1.6 College of Europe Scholarships

1.7 EC Student Grants to permit students to study in other Member States on an equal footing

1.8 STOA: European Parliament Scientific and Technological Options Assessment

1.9 TEMPUS: Training for Central and Eastern European Countries

1.10 Research Fellowships in Controlled Thermonuclear Fusion

1.11 Research Fellowships in Human Capital Mobility

1.12 ACE: Action for Co-operation in the Field of Economics

1.13 Co-operation in Science & Technology in Central & Eastern Europe

1.1 JEAN MONNET PROJECT

Statutory Basis

"Invitation to demonstrate interest" issued by the Commission: Notice 89/C 308/12 (OJ C 308/13 dated 7/12/89)Objectives

The Project's objectives are to:

- encourage universities to adapt the content of their courses, particularly law, economics, political and social science and history, to take account of EC developments, notably by creating teaching posts and establishing obligatory study courses; and

- develop the research capacity of universities in the sphere of European integration, by strengthening research facilities.

Background

With the completion of the internal market, there is an ever increasing need for a wider knowledge of EC affairs; especially of the process of European integration at all levels. It is important, therefore, that students at higher educational institutes are given appropriate teaching.

EC Contribution

About 6 MECU has been made available since the first pilot project in 1990.

The Project provides funds on a co-financing basis at a level of assistance calculated on the basis of the actual costs in each country. Funds are granted for three years, after which the university is expected to support the activities for a further four years.

Status Report

In the 1992 round, nine chairs, 18 courses - both graduate and post graduate, nine modules and two research projects were awarded to the UK, whilst three chairs, one module and one research project were awarded to Ireland. At the request of the European University Council, it is likely that a Jean Monnet Project II will carry on from 1994-96.

Applications

There will be no more calls under the first programme; information is awaited on the second.

INFORMATION

UK
Economic and Social Research Council
160 Great Portland Street
London W1N 6DT
Tel: 071 637 1499

COMMISSION
Commission of the European Communities
DG X Directorate C/6
University Information (Jean Monnet Project)
75 Rue de la Loi
B-1049 Brussels
Tel: INT+ 322 299 1111 (exchange)

IRELAND
Irish Association for European Studies (IAES)
CEEPA - University College Dublin
Belfield
Dublin 4
Tel: 01 263244
Fax: 01 2694409

Irish Office of the Commission of the EC
39 Molesworth Street
Dublin 2
Tel: 01 712244

1.2 JEAN MONNETT FELLOWSHIPS

Programme Content

Each year the European University Institute offers 30 Jean Monnet Fellowships of one year's duration to academics who wish to undertake full-time research in Florence on topics which contribute to the work of the University Institute.

Applications

Further particulars and application forms for these and other bursaries are available from the addresses below.

INFORMATION

UK
Department of Education and Science
Sanctuary Buildings
Great Smith St
London SW1P 3BT
Tel: 071 925 5000

IRELAND
Department of Education
General Section 1
Irish Life Centre
Lower Abbey Street
Dublin 1
Tel: 01 734700

COMMISSION
The Academic Service
European University Institute
Via Dei Roccettini, 5
San Domenico di Fiesole
Provincia di Firenze 50016
Italy

1.3 ARION: PROGRAMME OF STUDY VISITS FOR EDUCATION SPECIALISTS

Statutory Basis

Resolution of the Council and of Ministers of Education meeting within the Council on 9/2/76 (OJ C 381, dated 19/2/76), containing an action programme in the field of education.

Objectives

The main objectives are:

- to enable those exercising important educational responsibilities at local or regional, and in some cases, national levels, to review and modify their work in the light of direct experience of developments in other Member States; and
- to increase the amount of high-quality, selected and up-to-date information about education developments throughout the EC that is available to policy-makers.

Programme Content

For 1992-93 the study visits were organised within the following framework.

a. The education systems and their values:

- general study of education systems at primary and secondary level, including structure and methods as well as the evaluation of education systems, including certification and assessment of pupils; and
- measures to prevent school failure.

b. The users of education, the pupils, their teachers and parents:

- integration of handicapped children into ordinary schools;
- equal opportunities for boys and girls in education;
- education of migrants' children;
- initial and in-service training of teachers; and
- the role of parents and their participation in school life.

c. Education and its tools:

- introduction of new technologies into education.

d. The school and its environment:

- introduction of the European dimension;
- health education; and
- environmental education.

Participation

Participants should represent all aspects of the education system at local, regional and national level. It is for the Member States to ensure that all branches of education are represented and that applicants are able to communicate in at least one EC language in addition to their own. There is a numerical allocation of places by country.

Status Report

Within the 1992-93 programme, 120 grants were awarded to UK applicants and 30 to applicants from Ireland, out of the total 850 grants available.

Applications

Member States are required to submit global applications by 31 May each year for the subsequent academic year.

INFORMATION

UK
Sue Ling/Kay Tallamy
Central Bureau for Educational Visits and Exchanges
Seymour Mews House
Seymour Mews
London W1H 9FE
Tel: 071 486 5101
Fax: 071 935 5741

IRELAND
Department of Education
EEC Section, Room 210
Marlborough Street
Dublin 1
Tel: 01 734700

COMMISSION
Commission of the European Communities
Task Force "Human Resources, Education Training & Youth"
200 rue de la Loi
B-1049 Brussels
Tel: INT+ 322 299 1111 (exchange)

1.4 ERASMUS: PROGRAMME FOR EXCHANGE VISITS FOR STUDENTS IN HIGHER EDUCATION

Statutory Basis

Council Decision 89/663/EEC of 14/12/89, amending Decision 87/327/EEC adopting the EC action scheme for the mobility of university students (ERASMUS) (OJ L 395/23 dated 30/12/89)

Objectives

The key objectives of the ERASMUS Programme are to:

- achieve a significant increase in student and staff mobility among European higher education institutions;
- promote broad and lasting inter-institutional co-operation;
- contribute to the concept of one single united "people's Europe"; and
- contribute to the economic and social development of Europe by providing a significant number of graduates and post graduates with direct personal experience of co-operation between the Member States.

Background Information

ERASMUS was adopted as an action plan in June 1987, in order to promote student mobility and co-operation between eligible institutions of higher education within the Member States. Participation in ERASMUS was extended to the EFTA countries through a series of agreements which came into force in the academic year 1992-93.

Programme Content

i Inter-University Co-operation Programmes
Some activities in the area of modern European languages are managed jointly with Action II of the LINGUA Programme.

Financial support to institutions of higher education encourages those of different eligible States to establish Inter-University Co-operation Programmes (ICPs), through one or more of the following activities.

a. Student Mobility Programmes:

This support is intended for institutions which organise programmes enabling students of partner institutions to undertake fully recognised periods of study, lasting from three months to one academic year, in another eligible State as an integral part of their studies towards their degree or diploma.

Student mobility programmes involving students in any field of study at any level up to and including Ph.D. or the equivalent, are eligible under ERASMUS.

Priority is given to programmes where:

- the study abroad forms a significant and integrated component of the students' overall higher education;
- there is thorough provision for the academic preparation, monitoring, assessment, linguistic preparation, social integration and good quality accommodation of the students; and
- the general organisation and management demonstrate full commitment by the participating institutions.

Financial support awarded by the Commission may be used to help cover:

- the costs of setting up and operating the programme;
- students' linguistic preparation expenses;
- costs relating to the orientation, reception, monitoring and academic assessment of students and assistance in obtaining student accommodation;
- preparation and translation of relevant teaching material; and
- the expenditure directly related to implementing the student mobility programme.

b. Teaching Staff Mobility Programmes:

This support is intended for institutions which organise regular programmes enabling the teaching staff of one institution to teach in a partner institution in another eligible State, for periods of at least a week and up to a year. Periods of less than a month must be sufficiently intensive to make a real impact.

Priority is given to reciprocal programmes in which teachers make a substantial contribution to the regular teaching programme at the host institution.

Financial support may be used for:

- travel and subsistence expenses;
- costs of preparing and translating teaching material; and
- in certain cases, the cost of temporary replacements for teachers who go abroad.

c. Joint Development of New Curricula (This type of support is not available under LINGUA II).

Special preference is accorded to projects which:

- incorporate the modular approach to curriculum design;
- incorporate into existing curricula, European components or modules which are designed to contribute in some way to the development of the European internal market and the further political and economic integration of Europe;
- assist one or more partners in the development of new curricula for partner institutions which do not have significant experience in teaching the subject area concerned; and
- develop or adapt curricula for use in open learning or distance teaching systems.

Financial support may be used for:

- travel and subsistence expenses for planning meetings; and
- the costs of producing, translating and circulating necessary documents.

d. Intensive Programmes (NB. Not available under LINGUA II)

Financial support is for short, full-time programmes, up to one month long which focus on a specific theme and bring together students and teachers from each partner institution.

Financial support may be used for:

- travel and subsistence costs of preparatory meetings;
- the costs of travelling and staying abroad for teaching staff and students; and
- the costs of producing, translating and circulating information documents and teaching material.

ii Mobility Grants for Students

Under the terms of ERASMUS and LINGUA (Action II), student mobility grants of up to 5,000 ECU per person per year may be awarded to students who carry out a recognised part of their higher education in another eligible State, for a minimum of three months. The home university must undertake formally and in advance to grant full recognition of the study abroad period towards the home degree/diploma, provided that the student reaches the level of attainment required in the agreed selection of courses. The student shall not be required to pay tuition fees at the host institution; the student may, however, be required to pay normal tuition fees to the home institution during the study period abroad.

Student mobility grants are intended to contribute to the "mobility costs" of study abroad, i.e.:

- cost of travelling between the home and host countries;
- if the need arises, linguistic preparation costs directly incurred by the students;
- extra living expenses arising from the higher general costs of living in the host country; and
- additional costs relating to change in the individual material circumstances of the student.

Preferential treatment is generally given to student mobility which is organised within the European University Network, comprised of ICPs approved in the current year. Students who are free movers i.e. those who do not form part of an ICP of the European University Network, may also apply for student mobility grants, provided that they satisfy all the conditions of eligibility for such grants. The overall number of "free mover" grants is very limited.

Grants for UK-based students are confined exclusively to those participating in approved ICPs. It is an absolute disgrace that so many of the UK universities give no publicity whatsoever to the student mobility programme or any advice to potential applicants, with the result that the total number of places available to UK-based students is seldom filled.

iii Visit Grants for Higher Education Staff

Visit grants for higher education staff enable teaching or administrative staff members in higher education institutions in the eligible States to undertake information, preparatory and teaching visits, to eligible institutions of higher education in one or several other eligible States. These grants may also be awarded to staff members of non-profit-making organisations or associations in the field of higher education.

Visit grants are intended to cover travel and subsistence costs for a period of between one and four weeks. Visits may be undertaken by individuals or small groups. The grants are not available to students, nor are they available to cover the costs of research activities or the planning of or participation in symposia, seminars or conferences.

Grants for study and preparatory visits are intended for applicants who wish to:

- study the possibility of setting up or extending an ICP;

- improve the content of their lectures by liaising with colleagues from other countries;
- increase their understanding of certain specific aspects of the higher education system, of one or several eligible States.

Grants for teaching visits are intended for teaching staff who apply on an individual basis. The aim of such grants is to facilitate teaching periods spent abroad in one or several eligible institutions

Grants for preparatory meetings may be used to assist potential ICP partners in attending a meeting at one location.

iv Other Financial Support Under ERASMUS

a. Associations or Consortia of Higher Education Institutions:

Financial support may be awarded to associations or consortia of higher education institutions working on a European basis, particularly with a view to making initiatives in specific fields concerning higher education better known throughout Europe, Such financial support may be up to an annual maximum of 20,000 ECU per project.

b. Publications Related to Mobility:

The ERASMUS Programme may support all forms of publications designed to enhance awareness of study and teaching opportunities in the other eligible States, to draw attention to the important developments and innovative models for university co-operation throughout Europe, or to contribute in other ways to enhancing co-operation and exchange in the field of higher education

c. NARIC and ECTS:

These aim to promote mobility through the academic recognition of periods of study and qualifications. The ERASMUS Programme provides annual grants to facilitate the exchange of information between the eligible States' network of National Academic Recognition Information Centres (NARICs), as well as to institutions participating in the pilot phase of the European Community Course Credit Transfer System (ECTS). The aim of ECTS is to develop credit transfer as an effective means of academic recognition. The six-year pilot phase for the academic years 1989/90 to 1994/95 covers business administration, chemistry, history, mechanical engineering and medicine.

d. ERASMUS Prizes

Prizes are awarded by the Commission to ERASMUS networks, to staff members and to students who have made a particularly outstanding contribution to promoting co-operation in higher education.

Participation

All types of higher education institutions in the EC or in EFTA may participate. EFTA countries may participate as long as all applications involving an EFTA institute of higher education also include eligible institutes of higher education from at least two Member States. This requirement will no longer apply when the European Economic Area comes into force, except with regard to ICPs from Switzerland as the only EFTA partner.

Applications

UK universities and other HEIs and post-graduate students making direct applications, should apply to the UK ERASMUS bureau.

Deadlines for the mailing of applications or update forms:

- application forms and update forms for ICPs which cover the period 1 July 1994 to 30 September 1995: 31 October 1993 (as per postmark);
- applications for grants in the 1994/95 academic year to students not participating in an ICP ("free movers"): 1 January 1994 (as per postmark). Free mover grants are not available in all eligible States;
- applications for grants for visits and other financial support: five months before the visit/project is due to take place. Applications may be sent at any time, but the closing dates for the next three selection rounds are:

i 1 January 94 for a decision by March 1994

ii 1 April 94 for a decision by June 1994.

iii 1 July 94 for a decision by September 1994.

Students interested in applying for a student mobility grant should refer in the first instance to:

The UK Guide to ERASMUS
ISCO Publications, 12a-18a Princess Way, Camberley, Surrey GU15 3SP
This should also be available from bookshops and gives information about the institutions which offer ERASMUS and/or LINGUA Programmes and the subjects in which the Programmes operate. Students should then contact the higher education institution to which they intend to apply, to ask about their involvement in either ERASMUS or LINGUA. This enquiry is normally best directed to the Admissions Officer who may, if appropriate, refer it to the institution's European Office.

INFORMATION

National Grant-Awarding Authorities: UK
UK ERASMUS Student Grants Council
The University of Kent
Research and Development Building
Canterbury
Kent CT2 7PD
Tel: 0227 762712
Fax: 0227 762711

National Grant-Awarding Authorities: IRELAND
NGAA (Ireland)
Higher Education Authority
21 Fitzwilliam Square
Dublin 2
Tel: 01 612748
Fax: 01 610492

NARIC Network: UK
NARIC
The British Council
Medlock Street
Manchester M15 4AA
Tel: 061 957 7063
Fax: 061 957 7561

NARIC Network: IRELAND
Higher Education Authority
21 Fitzwilliam Square
Dublin 2
Tel: 01 612748
Fax: 01 610492

COMMISSION
ERASMUS Bureau
Rue Montoyer 70
B-1040 Brussels
Tel: INT+ 322 233 0111
Fax: INT+ 322 233 0150

1.5 LINGUA: Programme for improving the teaching of foreign languages

Statutory Basis

The LINGUA Action Programme was adopted by Council Decision 89/489/EEC of 28/7/89 (OJ L 239, dated 16/8/89).

Objectives

The LINGUA Programme promotes the teaching and learning of EC languages, i.e. the nine working languages of the EC plus Irish and Letzeburgesch. Its principal aim is to assist Member States with the qualitative and quantitative improvement of foreign language teaching and training.

The specific function of LINGUA Action II is promoting the learning of foreign languages in institutions of higher education, by means of grants for Inter-University Co-operation Programmes (ICPs) and visiting grants for teachers and administrators in higher education.

Background

The LINGUA Programme was adopted in July 1989, as the EC's main initiative to promote a qualitative and quantitative improvement in the knowledge of foreign languages within the Member States. Action II of LINGUA is modelled on ERASMUS and is run closely in conjunction with it, although it maintains separate aims and a separate identity.

Programme Content

LINGUA ACTION I: measures to promote the in-service training of foreign language teachers and trainers.

The following aid will be provided:

Part A: - grants to enable foreign language teachers and trainers to take part in in-service training courses and activities, particularly in a country where the language they are teaching is spoken.

Grants of up to a maximum of 1,500 ECU per beneficiary will be allocated to contribute towards the costs of travel, subsistence, fees and other expenditure incurred in attending the course or other in-service training activity.

Part B: - assistance in setting up European Co-operation Programmes (ECPs) between establishments for in-service training in different Member States; the maximum financial support will be 25,000 ECU annually to each participating establishment, although this support will not exceed 50% of project costs; and

- preparatory visits to explore the possibility of a ECP; the maximum grant is 1,500 ECU per visit per person.

LINGUA ACTION II: the promotion of foreign language learning in institutions of higher education and support for the initial training of future foreign language teachers.

The following aid will be provided:

- support for ICPs in the teaching of LINGUA Programme languages, when taught as foreign languages, between institutions of higher education;
- grants for individual foreign language students to spend periods of time studying in another Member State, generally within the ICP mentioned above;
- grants to mobilise teachers and administrators to assist in setting up and carrying out these programmes, or to increase their experience of foreign language teaching in other Member States.

LINGUA (Action II) is run by the ERASMUS Bureau on a similar basis to ERASMUS (for which see the section on ICPs and student grants).

Funding for ICPs under LINGUA (Action II) is only available for the mobility of students and teaching staff. Curriculum development projects and intensive programmes cannot be funded under LINGUA (Action II), although proposals of these two types may, under certain circumstances, be eligible for funding under other Actions of LINGUA and are eligible under ERASMUS.

LINGUA ACTION III: measures to promote knowledge and use of foreign languages in work relations and in economic life.

Grants will be provided for transnational projects in the following fields:

- the development and dissemination of techniques used in the diagnosis and analysis of language learning needs in different sectors of economic life;
- the development of curricula and certification arrangements for foreign language training;
- the design of language teaching materials for specific purposes, particularly using self-learning methods;
- preparatory visits to explore the possibility of a project; and
- study visits for representatives of SMEs, professional and workers' organisations and for foreign language trainers working in this field, to explore co-operation in foreign language training.

Applications from institutes of higher education are eligible under this Action if they involve the active participation of commercial enterprises and/or enterprise organisations.

LINGUA ACTION IV: measures to promote the development of exchanges for young people.

The following support will be provided:

- grants for young people carrying out an exchange, within the framework of Joint Educational Projects, set up by education establishments in different Member States in order to support foreign language learning; and
- grants for preparatory visits by those responsible for setting up Joint Educational Projects and arranging exchanges for the young people concerned.

LINGUA ACTION V: complementary measures.
The following aid will be provided:

Part A: - support for the creation and/or activities of organisations and bodies at European level which further the objectives of the LINGUA Programme. Grants will not normally exceed 20,000 ECU per project or half the project costs.

Part B: - support on an experimental basis, for the development and exchange of teaching materials for the least widely used and least taught languages of the EC. Financial support will be in the form of annual block grants over a period of up to three years, with an annual maximum not normally exceeding 200,000 ECU or half the total costs.

Participation

Action I, part A: grants can be made to individual foreign language teachers and trainers, to establishments of in-service training, to teachers' associations or to national agencies themselves, on behalf of groups of foreign language teachers and trainers.

Action I, part B: ECPs must be based on active co-operation between in-service training establishments in at least two Member States. In the UK, eligible establishments are:

- local education authorities;
- higher education institutions, universities and polytechnics;
- voluntary and charitable organisations;
- teachers' centres and associations;
- establishments teaching English as a foreign language on the approved British Council list;
- The British Council;
- The Bell School and
- The International House.

In Ireland, eligible establishments are:

- the Department of Education, ITE/The Linguistics Institute of Ireland;
- universities and other institutes of further and higher education;
- voluntary, state-supported organisations, national or local, teaching English or Irish as a foreign language;
- teacher centres and associations;
- the Franco-Irish Pedagogical Committee;
- the German-Irish Advisory Committee; and
- English language schools providing approved EFL teacher training courses.

Action I, part B: the application for preparatory visits must be made by the establishment which employs the individual.

Action II: this is open to the same participants as ERASMUS, except that EFTA countries are not eligible.

Action III: applications can be made, among others, by:

- SMEs, employers' or employees' organisations, professional organisations, chambers of commerce and industrial, vocational training or similar organisations, provided relevant foreign language expertise is clearly involved in the partnership;
- universities and language research centres, provided that SMEs and economic institutions are clearly represented in the partnership.

Action IV: when a Joint Educational Project has been agreed between the partner establishments, each partner should apply to the National Agency in their Member State, for a grant to finance an exchange of the young people working on the project.

In the case of preparatory visits, establishments for professional, vocational, technical and general education are eligible, as follows:
UK:

- all state-funded institutions providing vocational education and training programmes for students within the 16-25 age range; and
- courses in which language skills are offered as a component, but not as the main component.

Ireland:

- post primary schools;
- ESF Section, Department of Education Vocational Preparation and Training Programmes;
- non-degree courses at colleges and universities;
- industry-sponsored training courses with part-time release;
- CERT-sponsored courses;
- FAS-sponsored courses;
- Dublin Institutes of Technology;
- all state-funded colleges providing professional or technical courses with language as a component;
- approved private schools.

Status Report

The first round of LINGUA resulted in 35 Action IV grants to UK colleges and six Action I awards. The amounts available for the second round are ten times larger and there is a risk that not all the funds allocated will be utilised.

Applications

Different application procedures apply to different Actions of the Programme. Application forms are available from the National Agencies and from Bureau LINGUA. The procedures and annual deadlines are as follows.

Under Action I, applications for part A are available from, and should be sent to, the National Agency in the Member State. Applications for part B should be sent to Bureau LINGUA in Brussels: the closing dates are 1 February, 1 May, 1 August and 1 November. Applications for European Co-operation Programmes should be sent to Bureau LINGUA in Brussels: the closing date is 15 January each year.

Under Action II (all sections), application forms are available from, and should be sent to, the ERASMUS Bureau in Brussels. The ERASMUS Bureau processes them in parallel with applications for ERASMUS, Inter-University Co-operation Programmes and visit grants. The closing date is 31 October each year.

Under Action III, applications for preparatory and study visits should be sent to Bureau LINGUA in Brussels, in time for the closing dates of 1 February, 1 May, 1 August and 1 November. For all other sections, applications should be sent to Bureau LINGUA in Brussels, where the closing dates are 15 March and 15 September each year.

Under Action IV, applications for preparatory visits and Joint Educational Projects are available from, and should be sent to, the National Agency in the Member State.

Under Action V, part A, applications for support for organisations and bodies should be sent to Bureau LINGUA in Brussels, to meet the closing dates of 1 February, 1 May, 1 August and 1 November. Under part B, applications for the development and exchange of teaching materials should be sent to Bureau LINGUA in Brussels, in time for the closing dates of 15 March and 15 September each year.

INFORMATION

UK

LINGUA Action II student grants are administered by the UK ERASMUS Unit

England
LINGUA National Agencies:
Rosemary Martin
UK LINGUA Unit
Seymour Mews House
Seymour Mews
London W1H 9PE
Tel: 071 725 9493

Northern Ireland
Northern Ireland LINGUA Office
Central Bureau
16 Malone Road
Belfast BT9 5BN
Tel: 0232 664418
Fax: 0232 661275

Scotland
Scottish LINGUA Office
Central Bureau
3 Bruntsfield Crescent
Edinburgh, EH10 4HD
Tel: 031 447 8024
Fax: 031 452 8569

COMMISSION
The LINGUA Bureau
Rue du Commerce, 10
B-1040 Brussels
Tel: INT+ 322 511 4218
Fax: INT+ 322 511 4376

IRELAND

Actions I, III and V
ITE/The Linguistics Institute of Ireland
31 Fitzwilliam Place
Dublin 2
Tel: 01 6620446
Fax: 01 610004

Action IV
The Youth Exchange Bureau
Avoca House
189-193 Parnell Street
Dublin 1
Tel: 01 731411
Fax: 01 731316

LINGUA National Agencies:
Co-ordinating Agency
Department of Education
Marlborough Street
Dublin 1
Tel: 01 734700
Fax: 01 6791315

1.6 COLLEGE OF EUROPE SCHOLARSHIPS

Background

The College of Europe in Bruges, Belgium, was founded in 1949 following the European Congress of the Hague in 1948, which stressed the need to promote an awareness of European unity through educational institutions.

Programme Content

The College of Europe offers university graduates a one-year graduate programme on matters relating to the European progress of integration and to the further development of the EC.

The programme of specialised European studies includes three departments:

- European studies in Politics and Administration;
- European studies in Economics; and
- European studies in Law.

All students admitted to this programme choose the area of studies which corresponds to their previous university education. In addition to the course run by their department, students must choose two courses from the pluri-disciplinary part of the programme.

The Central and Eastern European Programme (CEEP) is a branch of the College of Europe located in Warsaw. Its pluri-disciplinary programme is designed for students who hold a degree in Law, Economics, History, Political or Administrative Sciences or International Relations. It forms a coherent body of courses which focus principally on the EC and Central and Eastern Europe.

EC Contribution

Most of the students at the College of Europe are granted scholarships by their government, or by another public or private institution.

A number of places are reserved for students who intend to study at their own expense. The fees for the year are 490,000 Belgian Francs (ECU 11,800) - or 310,000 BFs (ECU 7,500) for students from the Member States. Financial support is provided by the EC and it covers tuition and board and lodging in a student hostel.

Participation

A good knowledge of French and English is an essential condition for admission to the College.

Candidates for the College of Europe must hold a university degree in:

- Economics, Law, Political and Administrative Sciences or International Relations, for the programme of specialised European studies;
- Economics, History, Law, Political and Administrative Sciences or International Relations, for the Central and Eastern Europe Programme.

Applications

Application forms should be sent to the Selection Board of your country before the closing date set by it, and to the Admissions Office of the College of Europe before 15 March.

INFORMATION

UK
UK Committee for the College of Europe
UACES Secretariat
King's College London
Strand
London WC2R 2LS
Tel: 071 240 0206

IRELAND
Irish Council of the European Movement
32 Nassau Street
Dublin 2
Tel: 01 714300

COLLEGE of EUROPE
Admissions Office of the College of Europe
Dyver 11
B-8000
Brugge

1.7 EC STUDENT GRANTS

Programme Content

This is a programme which aims to set students from every Member State who wish to study in any other Member State, on an equal footing with students resident in that Member State.

UK

Under the mandatory awards scheme, students from other Member States can have their tuition fees paid for them by the UK authorities, provided that they satisfy eligibility conditions similar to those which must be met by UK students while studying on a higher education and designated mandatory course only. They must also have been ordinarily resident in the EC for three years prior to the start of the course and not have received any UK statutory funding for that period of time. If they have been ordinarily resident in the UK during that period of time, they may also apply for a maintenance grant, which will be paid by the Local Education Authority.

Applications

Application forms must be obtained from the Local Education Authority in whose area the student has been resident, or in the area where the higher education establishment is located.

INFORMATION

General enquiries can be addressed to:
Department of Education
Further and Higher Education Branch 3 (EC students fees)
Sanctuary Buildings
Great Smith Street
London SW1P 3BT
Tel: 071 925 6057
It is hoped that equivalent information concerning the other Member States can be included in future editions.

1.8 STOA: EUROPEAN PARLIAMENT SCIENTIFIC AND TECHNOLOGICAL OPTIONS ASSESSMENT

Statutory Basis

Commission call for expressions of interest: OJ C 288/8, dated 6/11/91

Objectives

Set up in 1991, STOA's function is to provide expert scientific and technical advice to MEPs and Parliamentary Committees, in order to help them assess policy options.

Programme Content

STOA organises workshops on scientific and technical issues, and arranges for expert opinions to be given as required.

There are STOA Scholarships for young scientists and engineers, available for those at first degree level. They last for six months, and their terms and conditions are broadly similar to the Robert Schuman Scholarships.

Applications

Applications may be made at any time.

INFORMATION

Directorate General for Research
European Parliament
L-2929 Luxembourg
Tel: INT+ 352 4300-1

1.9 TEMPUS: Training for Central and Eastern European Countries

The programme is to provide assistance with the education of university students in Central and Eastern Europe.

See Chapter 31.

1.10 RESEARCH FELLOWSHIPS IN CONTROLLED THERMONUCLEAR FUSION

See Chapter 17.5 on energy R&D grants.

1.11 RESEARCH FELLOWSHIPS IN HUMAN CAPITAL MOBILITY

See Chapter 17.6 on human capital & mobility R&D grants.

1.12 ACE: ACTION FOR CO-OPERATION IN THE FIELD OF ECONOMICS

See Chapter 31.

1.13 CO-OPERATION IN SCIENCE & TECHNOLOGY IN CENTRAL & EASTERN EUROPE

See Chapter 31.

Chapter 23.2

Vocational or Non-Vocational Training Programmes

This group of programmes includes:

2.1 Robert Schuman Scholarships

2.2 Paul Finet Foundation

2.3 EUROQUALIFICATION

2.4 HELIOS II: Community Action Programme to Assist Disabled People

2.5 COMETT II: Community Programme for Education and Training in Technology

2.1 ROBERT SCHUMAN SCHOLARSHIPS

Objectives

Robert Schuman Scholarships are designed to enable the holders to add to the knowledge they have acquired during their studies and to familiarise themselves with the activities of the European Parliament.

Background

Robert Schuman Scholarships were established by the European Parliament to honour the memory of one of its most distinguished Presidents, who was also one of the founding fathers of European integration.

Programme Content

Robert Schuman Scholarships are offered for research into subjects relating to the EC and particularly to the European Parliament.

Scholarship holders are based at the Secretariat of the European Parliament in Luxembourg, under the supervision of a senior official of the Directorate-General for Research. They are expected to assist with the research projects of the Directorate-General and have free access to the facilities of the Parliament, such as the library.

Although the work of the Parliament has absolute priority, the Directorate-General's staff can usually also provide assistance or advice to scholarship holders who have research work of their own to do during their stay.

It is normally possible for a student to attend a session of the European Parliament in Strasbourg and a meeting of one of the Parliament's Committees in Brussels. Visits to other EC institutions may occasionally be arranged.

The duration of the scholarship is two or three months within specific periods: mid-January to mid-April, mid-April to mid-July and mid-September to mid-December. Dates can sometimes be arranged to meet a student's requirements. Scholarships are renewable, no more than once for a further period of one to three months.

The number of Robert Schuman Scholarships is currently limited to about 57 per year.

EC Contribution

The amount of each scholarship is at present 45,000 Belgian francs (1,100 ECU) per month.

Participation

The scholarships are awarded to post-graduate students, normally nationals of an EC Member State. They cannot normally be awarded to anyone who has already had a similar award, traineeship or stage at one of the other EC institutions.

Applicants whose speciality is languages are not normally accepted for Robert Schuman scholarships, but can apply to the Director of Translation and Terminology, European Parliament.

Applications

Application forms are available from the European Parliament. Applications may be submitted at any time during the year, preferably at least four months before the desired starting date. Awards are made about three times a year.

INFORMATION

UK
European Parliament
2 Queen Anne's Gate
London SW1H 9AA
Tel: 071 222 0411

IRELAND
European Parliament
43 Molesworth Street
Dublin 2
Tel: 01 71 91 00

COMMISSION
European Parliament
Directorate-General for Research
(Robert Schuman Scholarships)
Office 6/20 Schuman Building
L-2929 Luxembourg
Tel: INT+ 352 4300 3697

2.2 PAUL FINET FOUNDATION

Objectives

The Paul Finet Foundation operates a scheme giving financial support to the children of workers employed in the coal and steel industries who had died after 30 June 1965 as a result of an industrial accident or from an occupational disease.

Programme Content

The conditions are:

- the child must be at least 14 years old;
- he/she must be attending a course of vocational training, general secondary education or higher education; and
- he/she must have good school reports.

EC Contribution

The amount of the grant is settled on an individual basis, taking into account each applicant's economic circumstances.

Applications

Applications are reviewed by the Paul Finet Foundation each year. The grants are made annually and can be renewed.

INFORMATION

UK
Vos Jones
Chief Executive
Coal Industry Social Welfare Organisation
27 Huddersfield Road
Barnsley
South Yorkshire S7O 2LX
Tel: 0226 294 139

COMMISSION
Secretary General
Foundation Paul Finet
JMO/C4/26A
Jean Monnet Building
Plateau du Kirchberg
Luxembourg
Tel: INT+ 352 43011

2.3 EUROQUALIFICATION

Objectives

There are five key objectives:

i to train people to carry out their occupation in partnership and/or in occupational mobility situations;

ii to lend a European, vocational and linguistic dimension to the training of 6,000 people in some forty selected occupations in twelve occupational fields - hotel trade and tourism, transport, electricity, electronics and telecommunications, office automation, environment and local development, commerce, the food processing industry, mechanics, construction and public works, car repair and vehicle maintenance, the graphics industry, and textiles;

iii to ensure greater coherence and convergence of EC vocational training programmes;

iv to ensure joint and/or mutual recognition of the newly attained qualifications, vocational, linguistic and transnational; and

v to make this joint approach an original and transferable experience for national and EC organisations and to make sure that it has good prospects for expansion.

Background

With the creation of the single market, businesses are having to adjust to the increasingly international requirements of their customers; others, seeking cost-effective economic partnerships, will have to overcome the culture-bound differences between occupations. They will all have to find the new qualifications and skills which increased mobility and new forms of co-operation will demand.

The thirteen organisations participating in the EUROQUALIFICATION initiative have decided to collaborate in seeking the most effective training strategies to prepare target groups to meet these challenges. This is the first programme created on the joint initiative of thirteen national organisations active in the area of training and vocational qualifications for adults. All EC Member States are involved.

Programme Content

The vocational qualification attained in the country of origin is maintained and guaranteed. A strengthening of this qualification and an opening towards Europe will be offered to selected groups, using a system developed specifically to be compatible with individual national situations. This system of 600 or 1000 teaching hours comprises a coherent set of training actions whose vocational basis will cover three aspects:

i the essential skills and knowledge required for the occupation concerned, which will be generally recognised and accepted;

ii particular national or regional training contents that will constitute an occupational added value to be offered to the target groups by all organisations; and

iii imparting new skills and capacities for adaptation necessary for further evolution in the occupation.

This system prepares the participants for integration, mobility and transnational partnership.

There is a language component of 120 or 240 hours which prepares candidates for the contacts which will be made in carrying out their occupation and a further training course of 120 or 240 hours at a training centre or company in another EC country.

For the target groups, access to the training programmes is free of charge.

Both national and transnational assistance are involved in implementing EUROQUALIFICATIONS. There is a permanent team in Brussels, one correspondent for each organisation, one project leader for each occupational field and specialists in training in each organisation. There is a network and permanent partnership among all the participants in the Programme. There is a joint, integrated translation network and a computerised communications network among all partners.

EC Contribution

The programme is scheduled to last for three years with a total budget of 101.7 MECU, 68% of which is financed by the ESF and the remainder by Member States.

Participation

As of 1993, target groups are:

- young people and the long-term unemployed, prepared to be mobile in the framework of their training; and
- people employed in insecure work situations in the countries or regions for which particular conditions are or will be applicable.

INFORMATION

UK
The Partner Organisation is:
DALI Ltd - The London Institute
388-396 Oxford Street
London W1R 1FE
Fax: 071 499 5789

IRELAND
The Partner Organisation is:
FAS
27-33 Upper Baggot Street
PO Box 456
Dublin 4
Tel: 01 68 57 77
Fax: 01 68 13 73

COMMISSION
Mrs V Kolotourou
Commission of the European Communities
DG V Technical Assistance
Avenue de Nerviens 9
B-1049 Brussels
Tel: INT+ 322 295 5090
Fax: INT+ 322 295 9022

Permanent Transnational Technical Assistance Team:
EUROQUALIFICATION Office
Rue Duquesnoy 38
Box 13
B-1000 Brussels

2.4 HELIOS II: COMMUNITY ACTION PROGRAMME TO ASSIST DISABLED PEOPLE

Statutory Basis

Council Decision 93/136/EEC: OJ L 56, dated 9/3/93

Objectives

The main objectives of HELIOS II are :

- to develop an EC disability policy improving access to education and work, promoting socio-economic adaptation and participation by the disabled and supporting social integration;
- co-ordinating EC measures to assist the disabled;
- supporting Member States in developing and implementing programmes to assist the disabled;
- improving exchange and information activities at European level; and
- strengthening co-operation with non-government organisations and national disability councils.

Background

A programme to promote educational, occupational, economic and social integration and an independent way of life for the disabled was established in 1988 under Council Decision 88/231/EEC, published in OJ L 104, dated 23/4/88. The programme HELIOS II was subsequently proposed for the period 1/1/92 to 31/12/96 (OJ C 293, dated 12/11/91). Amendments to HELIOS II have now been adopted and the programme is to run from 1993-96.

Programme Content

Support will be made at the following levels for the following activities:

- up to half of the cost of conferences;
- up to the whole cost of projects aimed at the development of an EC disability policy;
- up to the whole cost of projects to raise public awareness of the integration of the disabled;
- up to half the costs of co-operation with non-government organisations and national disability councils;
- up to the whole costs incurred by external experts supporting the Commission in the implementation of the programme; and
- up to the whole of the costs of meetings of a European Forum for the disabled.

EC Contribution

The programme has a budget of 37 MECU.

INFORMATION

UK
Glynis Phillips
Department of Health
Wellington House
Room 3B2
133-135 Waterloo Road
London SE1 8UG
Tel: 071 972 4125

COMMISSION
DG V Directorate B 1
Commission of the European Communities
200 rue de la Loi
B-1049 Brussels
Tel: INT+ 322 299 1111 (exchange)

2.5 COMETT II: COMMUNITY PROGRAMME FOR EDUCATION AND TRAINING IN TECHNOLOGY

Statutory Basis

Council Decision of 89/27/EEC of 16/12/88: OJ L 13/28, dated 17/1/89.

Objectives

COMETT II is designed to promote co-operation between universities and industry in the field of training for technology. More specifically, its objectives are:

- to improve the contribution of training to the economic and social development of the EC and, in particular, the contribution that can be made by advanced technology training at the various levels concerned;
- to foster the joint development of training programmes and the exchange of experience, and to optimise the use of training resources at EC level, particularly through the creation of transnational sectoral and regional networks of advanced technology training projects;
- to respond to the specific skill requirements of SMEs, having regard to specified priority measures;
- to promote equal opportunities for men and women in initial and continuing training, particularly in advanced technology; and
- to give a European dimension to co-operation between universities and industry in initial and continuing training relating to technologies with particular reference to their applications and transfer.

Background

COMETT I was introduced in 1986 and its first three-year operational phase ran from 1987 to 1989. The second operational phase for COMETT (COMETT II) is for a five year period beginning on 1/1/90.

Programme Content

In order to meet its general objectives, COMETT focuses on three inter-related areas of action, each of which constitutes a strand within the Programme as a whole.

Strand A: UETPs: University-Enterprise Training Partnerships

UETPs were set up as part of the original COMETT structure and are therefore the backbone of the programme. There are two main types of UETP:

- Regional UETPs which bring together groups from higher education institutions and enterprises within a particular geographical area; and

- Sectoral UETPs: these partnerships, transnational in nature, promote co-operation among higher education institutions and companies within a given technological field or industrial sector.

UETPs seek to:

- identify training needs in the field of technology;
- respond to the training need for highly-skilled human resources;
- provide a support structure for COMETT activities; and
- reinforce inter-regional co-operation and exchange between EC Member States and EFTA countries.

Strand B: Mobility of Training - Transnational Exchanges

Co-operation among higher education institutions and enterprises begins with the exchange of human resources. Strand B of the COMETT Programme was set up to foster mobility in the form of exchanges between companies and universities in different countries. These exchanges aim to give participants - students, recent graduates, university staff and enterprise personnel - first-hand experience of professional training in technology with a European dimension. They also increase participants' awareness of technological change and enhance skills.

More specifically, grants are allocated to:

- students undergoing periods of three to twelve months training in industry in another Member State;
- persons who are between study and first employment and have either completed their initial training and are enrolled at a university or have just graduated, so as to enable them to take up placements of between six months and two years in a business undertaking in another Member State in order to take part in an industrial development project within that undertaking; and
- personnel seconded from universities and industry in one Member State to a comparable industry or university in another Member State, for the purpose of bringing their skills in training activities and professional practices to the host organisation to help them improve their training procedures.

Strand C: Joint Projects for Continuing Training in Technology and for Multimedia Distance Training

Enterprises are gradually realising that continuous training of employees is a key investment for the future. Higher education institutions are being called upon to play a more substantial role in the continuing training of graduates and to adopt a flexible approach to the changing demands of society.

Strand C was conceived as a means of achieving these objectives and responding to present and future challenges. Financial aid is provided for joint university-industry projects for continuing training in technology and multimedia distance learning, as follows:

- advanced training courses in technology aimed at the rapid dissemination of R&D results and the promotion of technological innovation;
- devising and testing European training projects in the field of advanced technology by responding to industrial training needs, particularly by organising courses; and
- joint training projects ("pilot projects") which are more specialised in nature and have a direct impact on the training systems in a given sector. These pilot projects are large-scale training initiatives with funding of 500,000 ECU for an average project period of four years. Within the COMETT Programme, pilot projects are likely to generate the highest volume of courses and training materials.

Strand D: Complementary Promotion and Back-up Measures

This includes support for preparatory activities, notably in the form of visits or meetings aimed at formulating transnational projects.

EC Contribution

The estimated budget for the five-year COMETT II Programme is 230 MECU. EC support is allocated on the principle of cost-sharing between the EC and those undertaking the project, except for:

- actions under Strand D, where the funding may be up to 100%; and
- under Strands A and C, additional costs met by universities in the preparation and implementation of projects may be up to 100%.

Participation

Industrial firms including SMEs, Higher Education Institutes and Research Associations in EC Member States and EFTA countries are eligible to apply.

Status Report

Applications for participation in the 1992 programme were over-subscribed by a factor of ten. The budget allocation for the year was 55 MECU. Approximately 5,200 companies, 1,700 HEIs and 2,000 professional organisations are now involved in COMETT.

Applications

Calls for applications are published in the OJ and are accompanied by the issue of an Application Package. The latest call was in September 1993.

INFORMATION

UK

Department of Trade and Industry
Enterprise Initiative Division
Bay 543
Kingsgate House
66-74 Victoria Street
London SW1E 6SW
Tel: 081 943 7000

For the Information Centre, contact:
Miss Nichol
UK COMETT Liaison Office
Department of Education
Sanctuary Buildings
Great Smith Street
London SW1P 3BT
Tel: 071 925 5254

COMMISSION

Commission of the European Communities
Task Force for Human Resources, Education, Training & Youth,
COMETT Programme
200 rue de la Loi
B-1049 Brussels
Tel: INT+ 322 296 6322
Fax: INT+ 322 295 5719

COMETT Technical Assistance Office
14, Rue Montoyer
B-1040 Brussels
Tel: INT+ 322 513 8959
Fax: INT+ 322 513 9346

IRELAND

Mrs Grainne Ni Uid
EOLAS
The Irish Science and Technology Agency
Glasnevin
Dublin 9
Tel: 01 37 01 01
Fax: 01 37 96 20

Chapter 23.3

Vocational Training Programmes

This group of programmes includes:

3.1 CEDEFOP: European Centre for the Development of Vocational Training

3.2 PETRA: Action Programme on the Training and Preparation of Young People for Adult and Working Life

3.3 EUROLEADERS: a European dimension in the training of entrepreneurs

3.4 EUROTECNET: Development of Training Programmes

3.5 FORCE (Formation Continuée en Europe): Continuing Vocational Training in Europe

3.6 SPEC: Support Programme for Employment Creation

3.7 WNLEI: Local Employment Initiatives for Women

3.8 IRIS: Demonstration Projects on Vocational Training for Women

3.9 EUROFORM: Development of New Qualifications, Skills and Employment Opportunities

3.10 NOW: Training Measures for Women

3.11 HORIZON: Initiative for Training Handicapped and Disadvantaged Persons

3.12 POVERTY 3: The Third Poverty Programme

3.13 Language-Based Traineeships

3.14 EC Commission Traineeships

3.15 Stagiaires: Temporary traineeships with the Institutions of the EC

3.16 MATTHAEUS: Vocational Retraining of Customs Officials

3.17 MATTHAEUS - TAX: Training Officials in the Administration of Indirect Taxation

3.18 KAROLUS: Training Officials in the Enforcement of EC Regulations

3.19 Training in Restoration Techniques

3.1 CEDEFOP: European Centre for the Development of Vocational Training

The European Centre for the Development of Vocational Training promotes a concerted approach to vocational training problems. Funds are available for research and studies concerning vocational training.

INFORMATION

UK
Karen Newham
National Liaison Officer
Employment Department
Room N704
Moorfoot
Sheffield S1 4PQ
Tel: 0742 594 131

3.2 PETRA: Action Programme on the Training and Preparation of Young People for Adult and Working Life

Statutory Basis

Council Decision 91/387/EEC of 22/7/91 (OJ L 214/69, dated 2/8/91) provided approval for the second action programme PETRA II.

Objectives

The objectives of PETRA can be summarised as follows:

- to complement and support Member States' policies aimed at ensuring that all young people who want it receive one, or if possible, two or more years initial vocational training in addition to their full-time compulsory education, leading to a recognised vocational qualification;
- to support and complement Member States' policies designed to raise the standards and quality of initial vocational training, diversify vocational training provision for young people and enhance the capacity of systems of vocational training to adapt to rapid economic, technological and social change;
- to add a Community dimension to vocational qualifications;
- to stimulate and support practical co-operation and the development of training partnerships at a transnational level;
- to develop opportunities for young people to benefit from periods of training or work experience in another Member State; and
- to foster EC co-operation in the sphere of vocational information and guidance through specific actions at EC level.

Background

The PETRA Programme and the Young Workers Exchange Programme are the only major EC initiatives which include the whole range of youth training, covering schools and colleges, apprenticeships and other forms of vocational training. The other schemes such as ERASMUS, LINGUA, COMETT and EUROTECNET are concerned primarily with higher education. The former Exchange of Young Workers scheme was merged into the PETRA Programme at the end of 1991.

The current phase of PETRA was launched in January 1992 and is scheduled to run until 31 December 1994. It builds on the previous stage of the Programme, which ran from January 1988 to December 1991.

Programme Content

The Programme consists of three Actions, together with complementary measures under which EC support is also provided.

Action I

Two kinds of support for placements in another Member State are provided under this Action, on the one hand for young people in initial vocational training and, on the other, for young workers, young unemployed and young people taking part in advanced programmes in order to complete their training.

Action II

This provides support for transnational co-operation in the joint development of training modules and joint training of trainers, through the participation of training institutions and projects in the PETRA European Network of Training Partnerships (ENTP). Action II also includes youth initiative projects (YIPs) set up by young people themselves.

Action III

This supports national systems for the exchange of vocational guidance information, and experience and examples of good practice in vocational guidance, through the establishment of a Community network of national contact points and the training of guidance counsellors/specialists on EC aspects of guidance.

Complementary Measures

These include support for disseminating the results of the Programme and transnational co-operation in research on the vocational training of young people, as well as technical assistance at EC level and in Member States for the implementation, co-ordination and evaluation of the Programme.

EC Contribution

The total budget is 177.4 MECU over three years.

Action I

- for initial training and work experience placements: financial contribution to travel, accommodation, preparatory visits by organisers and language training for young participants. Financial support will vary according to the Member State of the applicant and the nature of the placement. Information will be sent to applicants by the National Co-ordination Units (NCUs) concerning the support available both for individual and group placements.

Action II

- for joint projects in the Network: up to 60,000 ECU over a period of two years;
- for YIPs: non-renewable grant up to 10,000 ECU.

Action III

- Projects are designated by Member States and the EC's financial contribution to designated projects is decided on an annual basis.

Participation

The following may apply for financial support:

- individual young workers, young unemployed and trainees in advanced programmes, for placement grants; training bodies, employers and trade unions, for placement grants on behalf of young people in initial vocational training (Action I);
- training bodies, for participation in the Network; groups of young people, for youth initiative grants (Action II);
- vocational guidance systems, through their Member States (Action III).

Only young people aged 27 and under who are permanently resident in a Member State are eligible to participate.

Applications

Different procedures apply to individual Actions of the Programme. Further information and application forms are available from NCUs explaining the procedures for the Member States concerned.

At Community level, technical assistance and further information on complementary measures, are provided by the PETRA Office in Brussels, which is responsible to the Commission for the implementation of the Programme. In Member States, technical assistance is provided by National Co-ordination Units set up by Member States.

INFORMATION

UK

The NCUs are run by:
ACTION 1:
Ms Jane Owen

ACTION II (European Network of Training Partnerships):
Mr Jason Forsythe - both at
Central Bureau
Seymour Mews House
Seymour Mews
London W1H 9PE
Tel: 071 486 5101
Fax: 071 935 1017

ACTION II (Youth Initiative Projects):
Mr Ian Pawley
Youth Exchange Centre
British Council
10 Spring Gardens
London SW1A 2BN
Tel: 071 389 4030
Fax: 071 389 4033

ACTION III:
David Oatley
European Training
Employment Department
Room 513
Steel House
Tothill Street
London SW1H 9NF
Tel: 071 273 5660

IRELAND

Ms Elizabeth Watters
Youth Exchange Bureau
Avoca House 1st Floor
189/193 Parnell Street
Dublin 1
Tel: 01 73 14 11/73 10 72
Fax: 01 73 13 16

COMMISSION

PETRA Youth Bureau (IFAPLAN)
2-3 Place du Luxembourg
B-1040 Brussels
Tel: INT+ 322 511 1510
Fax: INT+ 322 511 1960

3.3 EUROLEADERS: A European Dimension in the Training of Entrepreneurs

Aim

The objective of the EUROLEADERS Programme is to introduce a European dimension to the training of selected young entrepreneurs, preparing them for the business challenge of the single market.

Background

The EUROLEADERS Programme is developed and managed by one of the largest networks for supporting innovative business in Europe - The European Business and Innovation Centre Network (EBN). The programme is being developed with the support of Directorate-General for Regional Policies (DG XVI).

Programme Content

The course is designed to sharpen analytical skills and decision-making reflexes and is based on a case-study approach. The 1993 programme combined collective training in two separate sessions, one of nine days in Belgium and one of seven days in Sicily, with personalised follow-up. At the end of the course, participants presented their business plans in front of an international jury and had privileged access to venture capital finance from a group of investors.

The programme fee was 5,000 ECU.

Participation

The candidates for EUROLEADERS will have developed a business concept, created a company, or be managing a young enterprise. They will be assessed principally by their managerial capabilities and should be totally committed to taking a full part in the scheme. The business projects will be judged on the innovative nature of the product or service involved and by the growth potential of the business in the single market. Twenty five candidates will be selected by a panel of proven professionals who will operate in strict confidence.

Applications

The last closing date for submitting applications was 12 March 1993. It is expected that there will be further calls at the same time in subsequent years.

INFORMATION

European Business and Innovation Centre Network,
Avenue de Tervueren 188a
B-1150 Brussels
Tel: INT+ 322 772 8900
Fax: INT+ 322 772 9574

3.4 EUROTECNET: Development of Training Programmes

Statutory Basis

Council Decision 89/657/EEC of 18/12/89 (OJ L 393, dated 30/12/89)

Objectives

The main objectives of EUROTECNET II are:

- to improve the capacity for basic and continuing education in the EC to take account of technological changes and their impact on employment, work and qualifications; and

- to assist in the design and development of future training provision, in order to take account of the implications of future technological developments for new and existing occupations and to provide the necessary new skills and qualifications required.

Background

EUROTECNET II is an action programme to promote innovation in the field of vocational training resulting from technological change. Its predecessor, EUROTECNET I, ran from 1985 to 1988 and led to many cross-border co-operative training ventures among private companies, public bodies and other organisations.

Programme Content

Member States are expected to:

- strengthen co-operation at all levels between vocational training systems, including public and private sectors, employers and employees and all sections of the economy;
- raise the level of vocational training for the employed and unemployed workforce to take account of the impact of technological change, with particular regard to SMEs;
- stimulate innovation in experimental or demonstration training actions, with wide dissemination of information;
- enable unemployed young people to enter the workforce providing training;
- promote equal opportunities for men and women, particularly by retraining women; and
- promote the training and retraining of trainers in order to upgrade social and technical skills, including the use of multi-media techniques.

EC measures include:

- promoting the use of innovative approaches in adapting training to technological change, including the core activity - an EC-wide network of demonstration projects;
- strengthening the links between Member States, including encouraging links between projects and setting up a clearing-house for exchange of learning materials and transnational study visits;
- improving the capacity of Member States to obtain the greatest possible benefit from EUROTECNET II, including setting up a mechanism in each Member State for the dissemination of information on the impact of the programme, advice and constancy services to Member States in order to identify training needs, a model scheme for the trainers, and a series of publications;

- provision for the adaptation of future training systems, including research and analysis, giving priority to developing new models for curriculum development, easier access to training for disadvantaged groups and developing training approaches which are designed to anticipate future needs and multiply the effects of investment in technology;
- information activities, including high-level demonstration conferences, training seminars, colloquia, workshops and round tables, and the use of new technologies in the provision of information.

EC Contribution

A budget of 7.5 MECU was agreed for the first three years. The basic funding of the projects is the responsibility of the Member States, but projects considered eligible under national programmes may qualify for extra funding under the ESF.

Applications

Applications should be submitted to the Member State representative who will transmit approved projects to the Task Force. Final selection is made on their model value and the contribution they can make to the EC network.

INFORMATION

UK

Karen Newnham
National Liaison Officer
Employment Dept, Room N704
Moorfoot
Sheffield S1 4PQ
Tel: 0742 594 131

National Animation & Dissemination Unit
Mr C. Leonard
Coventry University Enterprises Ltd
Priory Street
Coventry CV1 5FB
Tel: 0203 838 727

IRELAND

National Animation & Dissemination Unit:
Irish EUROTECNET Unit
FAS
Training and Employment Authority
PO Box 465
27-33 Upper Baggot Street
Dublin 4
Tel: 01 68 57 77

COMMISSION

Commission of the EC
Task Force Human Resources, Education, Training & Youth,
200 rue de la Loi
B-1049 Brussels
Tel: INT+ 322 299 1111 (exchange)
EUROTECNET

Technical Assistance Office
Rue des Deux Eglises 37
B-1040 Brussels
Tel: INT+ 322 230 5378
Fax: INT+ 322 230 0254

3.5 FORCE: Formation Continuée en Europe - Continuing Vocational Training in Europe

Statutory Basis

Council Decision 90/267/EEC of 29/5/90 (OJ L 156, dated 21/6/90) established an action programme for the four-year period 1990-94.

Objectives

The objectives of the FORCE Programme are:

- to encourage a greater and more effective investment effort in continuing vocational training and an improved return from it, in particular by developing partnerships designed to encourage greater awareness on the part of the public authorities, undertakings, especially SMEs, and individual workers of the benefits accruing from investment in continuing vocational training;
- to encourage continual vocational training measures by, for instance, demonstrating and disseminating examples of good practice in continuing vocational education to those economic sectors or regions of the EC where access to, or investment in, such training is currently inadequate;
- to encourage innovations in the management of continuing vocational training, methodology and equipment;
- to take better account of the consequences of the completion of the internal market, in particular by supporting trans-national and trans-frontier continuing vocational training projects and the exchange of information and experience; and
- to help increase the effectiveness of continuing vocational training mechanisms and their capacity to respond to changes in the European labour market by promoting measures at all levels, particularly monitoring and analysing the development of continuing vocational training and identifying better ways of forecasting requirements in terms of qualifications and occupations.

Background

FORCE is scheduled to run from July 1991 to December 1994.

The philosophy behind FORCE is that continuing training in industry and commerce represents an investment by firms: the inclusion of continuing training in the firm's overall strategy or business planning will reinforce its competitive edge, increase profitability and help to protect jobs. Improved access to, and wider participation in, continuing training will facilitate the acquisition of new skills and broader, skill-based knowledge for a large part of the working population. In this way continuing training serves the interests of employers and employees alike and so, the interests of the EC as a whole.

Programme Content

In order to supplement and support the activities developed by Member States to promote the development of continuing vocational training, the Commission will implement transnational measures, which are aimed at workers in undertakings. These measures are as follows.

a. Support for Innovation:

- supporting the activities of a European network of trans- national operations with a view to improving the design, organisation and assessment of continuing vocational training operations and encouraging the transfer of knowledge and know-how in the EC;
- setting up an exchange scheme to encourage the dissemination of innovations to full-time instructors, staff in human resources departments, staff representatives in undertakings and training specialists in regional consortia;
- assistance with the design and development of transnational or trans-frontier continuing vocational training pilot projects by undertakings or training bodies in Member States, taking into account the consequences of the completion of the internal market; and
- carrying out sectoral surveys of continuing vocational training plans at the level of undertakings.

b. Convergence of Initiatives:

- setting up a system for the exchange of comparable data, using a common methodological framework, and launching a specific statistical survey of the subject;
- analysis of contractual policy on continuing vocational training in the various countries, in order to stimulate the dissemination of innovatory contract terms;
- development of an exchange scheme for those involved in the social process: employers' organisations and trade unions; and
- analysis of trends in the demand for qualifications and occupations in undertakings and sectors, with a view to improved forecasting of requirements.

c. Accompanying Measures:

- technical assistance, National Co-ordination Units to implement the programme, evaluation and information.

Participation

Those eligible are large, medium-sized or small companies, training bodies working with industry or commerce, employer organisations or trade unions and training or human resource experts or managers.

Status Report

Of the 263 projects approved in the 1992 call, 31 were led by UK organisations. Overall, 291 UK partners are involved in the new projects.

Applications

Invitations for the selection of exchanges, pilot projects and qualification projects are published in the OJ C Series.

There are two strands within the 1993/94 open call for applications:

Strand I: "Response to Change" - e.g. training issues that arise from new work organisation or skill requirements resulting from new technology. Closing date: 9 September 1993.

Strand II: "Training issues arising from the results of FORCE Sectoral and Collective Bargaining Surveys" Closing date: 31 October 1993.

INFORMATION

UK
National Co-ordination Unit:
Will Thompson
FORCE UK Co-ordination Unit
Employment Department TSID3
Room N704
Moorfoot
Sheffield S1 4PQ
Tel: 0742 594 819
Fax: 0742 594 103

IRELAND
National Co-ordination Unit:
Mr Jim Keogh
FAS - Training and Employment Authority
27-33 Upper Baggot Street
Dublin 4
Tel: 01 68 57 77
Fax: 01 68 24 80

COMMISSION
Commission of the European Communities
Task Force Human Resources, Education, Training & Youth,
200 rue de la Loi
B-1049 Brussels
Tel: INT+ 322 299 1111 (exchange)

FORCE Technical Office
34 rue du Nord
B-1000 Brussels
Tel: INT+ 322 209 1311
Fax: INT+ 322 209 1320

Institute of European Trade & Technology (IETT)
29 Throgmorton Street
London EC2N 2AT
Tel: 071 628 1647
Fax: 071 628 7692

3.6 SPEC: SUPPORT PROGRAMME FOR EMPLOYMENT CREATION

Statutory Basis

SPEC is the result of an initiative of the European Parliament.

Objectives

SPEC aims to provide financial and technical support to employment creation projects, in particular, those linked with the impact of the completion of the internal market and other processes of economic and social integration in Europe.

Background

The European Commission has been active for several years in the field of developing local employment initiatives aimed at tackling the persistently high level of unemployment. SPEC is not intended to solve the unemployment problem, but to stimulate employment initiatives at grass-roots level.

Programme Content

The project should be in the field of local employment development. Priority is given to:

- projects aimed at tackling the challenges of European economic and social integration;
- projects emanating from priority areas designated under Objective 1 of the Structural Funds;
- transnational co-operation involving at least two identified actors located in different Member States of the EC; and
- small, local initiatives which involve innovative actions or which are expected to have demonstrable effects.

EC Contribution

The budget for 1992 was 920,000 ECU.

Projects are co-financed by the Commission, with the grant normally ranging between 5,000 and 20,000 ECU. For projects mainly involving information and advice, such as seminars or research studies, an upper limit of 10,000 ECU is applicable. Within these limits, the co-financing will not exceed:

- a maximum of 70% of the total costs for projects emanating from Objective 1 areas or the new German Länder; and
- a maximum of 50% for projects from other areas.

Selected projects also benefit from technical assistance, including documentation, guidelines and workshops.

Participation

Projects eligible for support are those submitted by a local organisation which can give a clear commitment to complete the project. Submission is open to local government, enterprises, chambers of commerce, trade unions, development agencies, training institutions, non-profit organisations or any other local organisation which can give the guarantee requested.

Applications

The programme is administered by the Council of European Municipalities and Regions (CEMR) on behalf of the Commission.

The deadline for submission was 19 October 1992. It is not yet known whether the programme will be renewed.

INFORMATION

IRELAND
IPA
57-61 Lansdowne Road
Dublin 4
Tel: 01 68 62 33

COMMISSION
Commission of the European Communities
Directorate-General for Employment, Industrial Relations & Social Affairs
Unit V B.1
200 rue de la Loi
B-1049 Brussels
Tel: INT+ 322 299 1111 (exchange)

Commission Technical Assistance Unit:
Local and Regional Development Planning (LRDP)
106 Rue Franklin
B-1040 Brussels
Tel: INT+ 322 732 4250
Fax: INT+ 322 732 4973

Commission Programme Secretariat:
Council of European Municipalities and Regions (CEMR)
23 Boulevard Charlemagne
B-1040 Brussels
Tel: INT+ 322 230 4927
Fax: INT+ 322 230 7456

IRELAND
IPA
57-61 Lansdowne Road
Dublin 4
Tel: 01 68 62 33

3.7 WNLEI: Local Employment Initiatives for Women

Statutory Basis

The Women's LEI Programme originates from Council Resolution 84/C 161/02 of 7/6/84 (OJ C 161/4 dated 26/6/84) on actions to be taken to combat unemployment among women.

Objectives

The Programme's main objective is to help women to create their own businesses which must, in turn, create paid jobs for women.

Programme Content

The Third Action Programme continues the programme for the years 1991 to 1995.

Priority is given to projects which:

- create jobs for categories of women with special problems; and
- create "non-traditional" jobs for women.

Projects of an innovative character will be given preference.

EC Contribution

A total of 1.5 MECU is made available each year.

The funding, which is in the form of start-up aid and is non-renewable, is paid at the level of 1,500 ECU per permanent full-time job created, with a maximum of 7,500 ECU and a minimum of 3,000 ECU per project.

Participation

Any woman, or group of women, who plan to start new businesses, co-operatives and LEIs may apply.

Applications

Applications should be addressed to Women's LEI Grant Management in Brussels, with a copy to the national contact. Applications should be made at the start-up of the business, or not more than two months beforehand.

There are three deadlines per year: 1 February, 1 June and 1 October.

INFORMATION

UK
Business Training Co-ordinator
Birmingham Women's Enterprise Development Agency Ltd
22 Augusta Street
Hockley
Birmingham B18 6JA

IRELAND
Patricia Brand
Contact International
1 Westland Square
Dublin 2
Tel: 01 677 91 99
Fax: 01 677 93 55

COMMISSION
Equal Opportunities Office
Service V A.4
Commission of the European Communities
200 rue de la Loi
B-1049 Brussels
Tel: INT +322 299 1111 (exchange)

Women's LEI Grant Management
Gerda Van Biervliet - Simonetta Riasaio
Comitato Impressa Donna-CNA
1 Avenue de la Joyeuse Entrée
B-1040 Brussels
Tel: INT+ 322 280 0054

3.8 IRIS: Demonstration Projects on Vocational Training for Women

Background

The IRIS Network was launched in 1988 on the initiative of the Commission, at a time when the growing European skills shortage and the need for higher participation by women, especially qualified women, in the labour market was becoming evident.

Programme Content

IRIS offers a wide variety of services and activities, aimed at promoting women's training and building links between the women's training programmes, social partners and government authorities. These activities include:

- contacts with other training programmes for women throughout the EC;
- information distribution;
- possibilities for transnational partnerships and co-operation through its partnerships grant scheme;
- publicity grants for model programmes;
- the IRIS database of women's training programmes;
- national technical evaluation meetings;
- publications, including the IRIS bulletin with up-to-date news on training and on the network; and
- a computerised electronic mail and bulletin board.

Participation

IRIS members represent a wide spectrum of organisations, from small women's workshops to large government-run programmes. The biggest target is the 25 to 40 age group, followed by the 18 to 25 year olds.

Training programmes applying for admission to the IRIS network should fulfil the following criteria:

- the training must help women to gain access to paid employment;
- it must be targeted at women and/or contain various specific measures for women;
- the training programmes must respond to the needs of the regional and local labour markets;
- the training offered under the programme should be recognised by at least one of the parties concerned: trade unions, employment agencies, training bodies and public authorities;
- it must use innovatory training techniques; and

- it must provide an assessment of the training methods and the results obtained by the trainees.

Status Report

There are now over 500 member training programmes throughout the EC.

Applications

CREW, an independent organisation, is responsible for the general co-ordination and running of IRIS.

Any vocational training programme for women which satisfies the IRIS selection criteria can become a member. Applications should be sent to the IRIS Unit/CREW.

INFORMATION

UK
John Sharman
Equal Opportunities Commission
Overseas House
Quay Street
Manchester M3 3HN
Tel: 061 833 9244
Fax: 061 835 1657

IRELAND
FAS
Training & Employment Authority
PO Box 456
27-33 Upper Baggot Street
Dublin 4
Tel: 01 68 57 77
Fax: 01 68 26 91

COMMISSION
The IRIS Office
CREW s.c
21 rue de la Tourelle
B-1040 Brussels
Tel: INT+ 322 230 5158
Fax: INT+ 322 230 6230

3.9 EUROFORM: Development of New qualifications, Skills and Employment Opportunities

Statutory Basis

This initiative was drawn up by the Commission under Article II of Regulation (EEC) No 4253/88. The guidelines are published in OJ C 327, dated 29/12/90.

Objectives

The objectives are:

- to provide a Community dimension for vocational training and employment promotion projects; and

- to foster the convergence of occupational skills, particularly between regions whose development is lagging behind, and the occupational and geographical mobility of workers.

Background

On 18 July 1990, the Commission decided to create three new EC Initiatives in the field of human resources - EUROFORM, NOW and HORIZON. For a project to be eligible under one of these three initiatives, it must meet:

- general criteria, i.e. criteria derived from the regulations of the EC's Structural Funds, particularly the ESF;

- specific criteria, i.e. criteria applying to EC initiatives.

Operators in regions other than Objective 1 regions who apply for the three new EC initiatives will be concerned only with the ESF, while those in Objective 1 regions may be concerned with both the ESF and the ERDF.

Descriptions of activities and persons eligible for ESF and ERDF assistance can be found in Chapter 19.3 on the sources of Economic and Social Cohesion grants.

Programme Content

The programme operates through the preparation, implementation, assessment and dissemination of joint training and employment promotion projects.

Preparation consists of studies and activities concerned with training methodology and products etc. Such preparation must take into consideration the Community dimension of the training and labour markets.

Implementation focuses on joint vocational training projects which aim to develop the new skills needed in order to take advantage of the new opportunities offered by technological changes associated with the single market.

The projects must be transnational in character.

The programme operators encompass public and private bodies or organisations concerned with vocational training and employment promotion. In order to realise the transnational dimension of EUROFORM projects, operators may rely on regional, local, sectoral or technological consortia set up by all those responsible for vocational training and employment policy. The operations of such consortia must be designed to lead to the establishment of transnational partnerships.The ERDF provides assistance with facilities, amenities and investment in Objective 1 regions.

Priority is given to transnational partnerships which integrate at least one partner from an Objective 1 region. This priority results in the promotion of activities by regional or local consortia located in Objective 1 regions. Priority is also given to actions linked with EUROTECNET, FORCE, ERGO and LEDA.

EC Contribution

300 MECU was made available from the Structural Funds for EUROFORM over the period 1990-93. Although most of the funding is from the ESF, 8.4 MECU from the ERDF was also approved. The initiatives are to be jointly financed by the Member States and the EC.

Participation

The following are eligible for financial assistance:

- long-term unemployed and young people throughout the EC (Objectives 3 and 4);
- persons employed in SMEs, unemployed or threatened by unemployment (in Objective 1, 2 and 5b regions only);
- persons under apprenticeship contracts, the apprenticeship being confined to theoretical aspects of the craft, and those undergoing training in national secondary vocational education systems in Objective 1 regions; and
- the entire working population, to the extent that they are affected by an integrated programme in Objective 1 regions (ESF & ERDF).

Applications

Member States submit their applications for aid in the form of operational programmes rather than individual projects.

Applications for aid should be addressed to the ministries for labour and employment in the individual Member States.

Since all current funding has been committed, no further calls for applications can be anticipated for the time being.

INFORMATION

UK
Ms L Huggins
European Social Fund Unit
236 Grays Inn Road
London WC1X 8HL
Tel: 071 211 4710
Fax: 071 211 4749

IRELAND
Youth Exchange Bureau
Avoca House, 1st Floor
189/193 Parnell Street
Dublin 1
Tel: 01 73 14 11

COMMISSION
Rapporteur:
Barbara Nolan
DG V D. 1 ESF Unit
200 rue de la Loi
B-1049 Brussels
Tel: INT+ 322 296 0755

Co-ordinator of EUROFORM, NOW and HORIZON:
Mr G Katzourakis
DG V Directorate D1
200 rue de la Loi
B-1049 Brussels
Tel: INT+ 322 295 9044

3.10 NOW: Training Measures for Women

Statutory Basis

The initiative was drawn up by the Commission under Article 11 of Regulation (EEC) No 4253/88. The guidelines are published in OJ C 327, dated 29/12/90.

Objectives

The objectives are to contribute to:

a. the upgrading and development of women's qualifications, as well as changing the business environment to help them establish their own enterprises or co-operatives; and

b. the re-entry of women into the regular labour market, in an effort to avoid worsening the incidences of exclusion from that market and undermining the stability of women's employment.

Background

Women's opportunities for employment are much scarcer than those for men. Throughout the EC, the level of female unemployment is 12% compared with 7% for men. The 30% participation of Irish women in the labour market is the second lowest in the EC. In combating this, NOW also reinforces programmes like IRIS, WNLEI and Childcare Network and forms part of the implementation of the third medium-term programme on equal opportunities (1992-95).

For a project to be eligible under NOW it must meet:

- general criteria, i.e. criteria derived from the regulations of the EC's Structural Funds, in particular the European Social Fund (ESF); and
- specific criteria, i.e. criteria applying to EC Initiatives.

Operators in regions other than Objective 1 regions who apply for the three new EC initiatives will be concerned only with the ESF, while those in Objective 1 regions may be concerned with both the ESF and the ERDF.

Descriptions of activities and persons eligible for ESF and ERDF assistance can be found in Chapter 19.3 on the sources of Economic and Social Cohesion grants.

Programme Content

Measures to achieve objective (a) are as follows:

- vocational training measures, including preparation measures, adapted to the operating needs of such enterprises and co-operatives;
- helping to create self-employed activities and employee recruitment; and

- start-up assistance for services designed to help women gain access to existing structures, facilitating the setting up of craft businesses or of SMEs. This measure is limited to Objective 1 regions.

Measures to achieve objective (b) are as follows:

- guidance and advisory measures; and
- vocational training measures including vocational preparation and employment assistance.

Supplementary measures, for which eligibility depends on their being linked directly to the preceding measures, have also been planned as follows:

- measures concerning the setting up of day nurseries for women working in enterprises, enterprise groups or vocational training centres in Objective 1 regions only but including construction costs and the purchase of equipment;
- measures concerning the operating costs of day nurseries attached to vocational training centres; and
- measures concerning vocational training for persons working professionally with young children.

Technical assistance measures are also being planned, including assistance with establishing or extending networks, awareness projects, transfers of experience etc.

Under the NOW Programme, in Objective 1 regions the ERDF supports:

- start-up assistance for services designed to help women gain access to existing structures, facilitating the setting-up of craft businesses or SMEs; and
- the establishment of day nurseries: both construction and equipment.

The operators of NOW are national, regional and local authorities, public and private vocational training agents, socio-economic partners, and public and private research and information centres for women.

The projects must be transnational in character and targeted solely at women.

Priority will be given to those measures which combine the establishment of day nurseries with the vocational training of the staff working in such nurseries.

Priority is also given to projects implemented in Objective 1 regions and to those agreed upon between workers and employers in an undertaking, on the one hand, and vocational training organisations, on the other, and actions linked with IRIS, WNLEI, and CHILDCARE.

EC Contribution

NOW received 153 MECU from the Structural Funds for the 1990-93 period. The major part of these resources is controlled by the ESF and, in a complementary manner, by the ERDF. The initiatives are to be jointly financed by the individual Member States and the EC. The contribution covers, on average, approximately 65% of total public expenditure on action programmes presented by the Member States in the Objective 1 regions and 45% of expenditure in other regions.

Participation

The following are eligible for support:

- long-term unemployed women, defined as those unemployed for more than 12 months, regardless of their age (Objectives 3 and 4) throughout the EC;
- women seeking to re-enter the labour market after a long interruption, who are treated in the same way as long-term unemployed women;
- women employed in SMEs, unemployed or threatened by unemployment in Objective 1, 2 and 5b regions; and
- the entire female working population in Objective 1 regions, where the action concerned forms part of an integrated operation (ESF & ERDF).

Applications

Member States submit their applications for aid in the form of operational programmes rather than individual projects. Since all current funding has been committed, no further calls for applications can be expected for the time being.

INFORMATION

UK

Ms L Huggins
European Social Fund Unit
236 Grays Inn Road
London WC1X 8HL
Tel: 071 211 4710
Fax: 071 211 4749

National Co-ordinator:
Mr Pat Pinkerton, EC Unit
Training and Employment Agency
Clarendon House, Adelaide Street
Belfast BT2
Tel: 0232 23 99 44
Fax: 0232 89 56 75

IRELAND

Ms C Tiernan
Administrative Officer
Dept. of Enterprise & Employment
Davitt House
65a Adelaide Road
Dublin 2
Tel: 01 76 58 61 ext. 3202
Fax: 01 76 48 52

National Co-ordinator:
Ms M Donnelly
Council for the Status of Women
32 Upper Fitzwilliam Street
Dublin 2
Tel: 01 61 52 68/611791
Fax: 01 76 08 60

COMMISSION
Ms C Alexopoulu
DG V Directorate D.1
200 rue de la Loi
B-1049 Brussels
Tel: INT+ 322 295 4295
Fax: INT+ 322 295 6506

Co-ordinator of EUROFORM, NOW and HORIZON:
Mr G Katzourakis
DG V Directorate D 1
200 rue de la Loi
B-1049 Brussels
Tel: INT+ 322 295 9044

CHILDCARE Network:
Ms J Hemsley
Directorate-General for Employment
Action Unit for Employment and Equality for Women
200 rue de la Loi
B-1049 Brussels
Tel: INT+ 322 296 0656
Fax: INT+ 322 295 0125

3.11 HORIZON: Initiative for Training Handicapped and Disadvantaged Persons

Statutory Basis

The initiative has been drawn up by the Commission under Article 11 of Regulation (EEC) No 4253/88. The guidelines are published in OJ C 327, dated 29/12/90.

Objectives

The objectives are as follows:

- for the disabled: to improve access conditions to the labour market and the ability of the disabled to compete; and
- for the disadvantaged: to reinforce capacities for local action and to establish a network for the exchange of experience at EC level, to help confront situations specific to the various categories of disabled persons and promote the integration of disadvantaged groups into the labour market and society. The aim is also to foster the rapid socio-economic integration of those confronted with a socio-economic context new to them.

Background

According to the World Health Organisation (WHO), there are around 30 million disabled people in the EC. The HORIZON Programme recognises that such persons and other disadvantaged groups face serious problems in obtaining employment and aims to help overcome those problems.

For a project to be eligible under HORIZON it must meet:

- general criteria, i.e. criteria derived from the regulations of the EC's Structural Funds, in particular the ESF; and
- specific criteria, i.e. criteria applying to EC Initiatives.

Operators in regions other than Objective 1 regions who apply for the three new EC initiatives, will be concerned only with the ESF, while those in Objective 1 regions may be concerned with both the ESF and the ERDF.

Descriptions of activities and persons eligible for ESF and ERDF assistance can be found in Chapter 19.3 on the sources of Economic and Social Cohesion grants.

Programme Content

To be eligible, projects must be transnational in character.

The disabled are helped by implementing transnational projects designed to improve access conditions to the labour market, the ability of the disabled to compete and their entry into every-day working life. For a project to help the disabled to be eligible, the transnational partnership must include at least one partner from an Objective 1 region.

The disadvantaged are helped by setting up pilot schemes developed within the framework of transnational partnerships. For those confronted by a socio-economic context new to them, the EC aims to support activities concerned with employment promotion, vocational training, guidance and advice on socio-economic integration, combined with a command of the language and measures designed to facilitate their reception. All EC regions are eligible for the "disadvantaged" strand of the initiative.

Under the HORIZON Programme, in Objective 1 regions, the ERDF supports:

- start-up assistance for services designed to help the disabled gain access to existing structures, facilitating the setting up of craft businesses or SMEs;
- assistance in adapting facilities and amenities of community interest for the disabled;
- disseminating information concerning existing technology and problem solving experience relating to the special needs and problems of the disabled among commercial and technical enterprises;
- equipping vocational training centres with physiotherapy and occupational therapy facilities for the disabled;
- start-up services designed to help the disadvantaged to gain access to structures, facilitating the creation of SMEs and craft businesses; and
- equipping transition centres for multiple public use for the disadvantaged.

The programme operators will be public and private organisations specifically responsible for the disabled, the disadvantaged and those confronted with a socio-economic context new to them.
Regional priority will be given to projects undertaken in favour of those confronted with a socio-economic context new to them and also to actions linked with HELIOS, HANDYNET and POVERTY III.

EC Contribution

The Commission decided to increase the original funding for the 1990-93 period from 180 MECU to 291.3 MECU. Although most of the EC funding is from the ESF, about 19.4 MECU from the ERDF was also approved. The initiatives are to be jointly financed by the individual Member States and the EC.

Participation

The following are eligible:

- the disabled, defined as individuals subject to severe handicaps as a result of physical and mental disabilities, throughout the EC (Objectives 3 and 4);
- the unemployed disabled, under Objectives 1, 2 and 5b; and
- the disadvantaged, defined as persons subject to specific problems which are hindering or slowing their economic and social integration, e.g. the long-term unemployed, early school-leavers and migrants.

Applications

Member States submit their applications for aid in the form of operational programmes rather than individual projects. All current funding has been committed and there is no information available at present concerning any future calls for applications.

INFORMATION

UK
Ms L Huggins
European Social Fund Unit
236 Grays Inn Road
London WC1X 8HL
Tel: 071 211 4710
Fax: 071 211 4749

IRELAND
National Co-ordinator:
Anthony Tyrrell
Department of Enterprise and Employment
Davitt House
Adelaide Road
Dublin 2
Tel: 01 76 58 61
Fax: 01 76 48 52

Support Structure (Disabled):
National Rehabilitation Board
25 Clyde Road
Dublin 4
Tel: 01 684181
Fax: 01 685029

Support Structure (Disadvantaged):
WRC Social & Economic Consultants Ltd
4 Lower Ormond Quay
Dublin 1
Tel: 01 723100
Fax: 01 723840

COMMISSION
Co-ordinator of EUROFORM, NOW & HORIZON:
Mr G Katzourakis
DG V (see page 412)

Bernard Vanderhaeghen
Tel: INT+ 322 295 3975

3.12 POVERTY 3: THE THIRD POVERTY PROGRAMME

Statutory Basis

Council Decision 89/457/EEC of 18/7/89 (OJ C 244, dated 2/8/89), establishing a medium-term Community action programme to foster the economic and social integration of the least privileged groups.

Objectives

The main objectives of the Programme are:

- support for prototype schemes to combat and prevent poverty; and
- encouragement of integrated actions involving both centralised government and decentralised operations.

Background

The first Programme ran from 1975-1980 and the second, from 1985-89. These Programmes focused on the research and diagnosis of the problems caused by poverty at a social level. Poverty 3 covers the period 1989-94. It has moved on from the action research phase to the selective development phase - in other words, the implementation of a few selected prototype schemes on a larger scale and rooted in the local context.

Programme Content

Poverty 3 identifies the following operational priorities:

- specific job creation and vocational training measures to ensure the integration of the most deprived;
- the necessary development and co-ordination of public and private institutions and services involved in the campaign against poverty;
- support measures for families and local authorities to prevent increased dependence on institutions by persons in insecure situations; and
- anti-poverty measures, taken in conjunction with the economic and social development of the area where the project is located.

The types of action undertaken are pilot schemes, which are selected by the Commission in consultation with national governments. Each scheme is managed by a steering committee composed of representatives of all the bodies involved in carrying out the scheme. The steering committee is assisted and advised on technical matters by Research and Development Units (RDUs) under contract to the Commission, located in each Member State or group of Member States.

EC Contribution

All prototype schemes should have a mixed form of financing, with up to 55% coming from the Commission and the balance, from central and local authorities and private sources. The Commission will finance up to 75% of the cost of some innovative experiments concerning extreme poverty for which it is difficult to obtain national funding.

INFORMATION

UK

The RDU is run by:
Katherine Duffy
The Local Government Centre
Warwick Business School
University of Warwick
Coventry CV4 7AL
Tel: 0203 524 109

IRELAND

Department of Social Welfare
Store Street
Dublin 1
Tel: 01 74 84 44

Combat Poverty Agency
8 Charlemont Street
Dublin 2
Tel: 01 78 33 55

COMMISSION

Odile Quintin
Directorate-General for Employment, Industrial Relations and Social Affairs
Commission of the European Communities
200 rue de la Loi
B-1049 Brussels
Tel: INT+ 322 299 1111 (exchange)

Co-ordination of Poverty 3 has been delegated to:
Animation & Research
Lille
France
Fax: INT+ 33 20 54 35 27

3.13 LANGUAGE-BASED TRAINEESHIPS

Objectives

These traineeships are designed to enable the holders to add to the knowledge they have acquired during their studies, and to familiarise themselves with the activities of the European Parliament.

Programme Content

There are three types of traineeships for conference interpreters.

i Traineeships for young interpreters who have recently qualified

These are designed for candidates with a combination of languages of interest to the Parliament but who have as yet no professional experience. Candidates are admitted after a test involving consecutive and simultaneous interpretation. Traineeships are awarded within the Parliament under the supervision of established interpreters with a view to supplementing the existing complement of freelance interpreters at the end of the traineeship.

ii Traineeships organised in conjunction with university institutes recognised by the Parliament

These are designed as crash courses for applicant interpreters who are already able to interpret into languages, where the market supply of interpreters does not cover the Parliament's requirements, or to broaden the trainee's combination of languages. Training courses may be taken outside the Parliament at the University or institute selected and shall be organised after the candidate's professional aptitude has been tested. The Parliament will bear the cost of enrolment and course fees.

iii Advanced traineeships for freelance interpreters

These are designed for interpreters who wish to learn new languages to cover the requirements of the European Parliament and who have shown, after taking a test, that they have made great personal efforts in this respect. Training courses are normally undertaken in a foreign country at a university institute recognised by the Parliament. A trainee who has already undertaken one of these courses may under no circumstances be admitted to another course involving the same language.

Traineeships are awarded for periods of one to three months and are renewable.

EC Contribution

Trainee linguists shall receive a grant equal to 35% of the basic monthly grade A 8/1 salary.

Participation

Trainee linguists must:

- be nationals of one of the Member States except where the Director-General offering acceptance decides otherwise;
- have been awarded a diploma certifying that the holder has completed a full university course or a course of education at a similar level; and
- have perfect command of one official language of the EC and thorough knowledge of at least two others.

Trainee translators must not have held any scholarship awarded by the EC institutions.

Applications

The above rules cover traineeships for both translators and conference interpreters, although the two categories come under different Directorates-General. Accordingly, if you wish to apply for a traineeship as a conference interpreter, write to the Interpretation Directorate.

INFORMATION

Applications for a traineeship in the Translation Directorate should be sent to:

Directorate for Translation And Terminology
European Parliament
Office 711 - Tower Building
Plateau du Kirchberg
L-2929 Luxembourg
Tel: INT+ 352 4300 1
Fax: INT+ 352 43 70 09

For a traineeships as a conference interpreter write to:
Secretariat of the Interpretation Directorate
European Parliament
Office 5/38
BAK
L-2929 Luxembourg
Tel: INT+ 352 4300-1

3.14 EC COMMISSION TRAINEESHIPS

Programme Content

The Commission organises in-service traineeships lasting from three to five months, part of which may be devoted to preparing a post-graduate thesis or academic paper.

EC Contribution

The grant is currently 22,000 Belgian francs (ECU 530) per month, plus travelling expenses.

Participation

The scheme is open to graduates, students who have successfully completed at least four years of study and public and private sector employees in administrative posts. Applicants must not be more than 30 years old.

Applications

Starting dates are 1 March and 1 October each year, and applications must be received by:

- 31 March for the period beginning on 1 October; and
- 30 September for the period beginning on 1 March.

INFORMATION

Commission of the European Communities
Secretariat-General
Training Office
200 rue de la Loi
B-1049 Brussels
Tel: INT + 322 299 1111 (exchange)

3.15 STAGIAIRES

Objectives

The purpose of in-service training with the European Commission is:

- to give trainees a general idea of the objectives and problems of European integration;
- to provide them with practical knowledge of the working of Commission departments;
- to enable them to acquire personal experience by means of contacts made in the course of their everyday work; and
- to enable them to develop and use the knowledge they have acquired during their studies or professional careers.

Programme Content

The Commission provides the opportunity for a limited number of graduates to follow training courses of three to five months at the Commission.

Part of the period may be devoted to preparing a postgraduate thesis or an academic paper.

Trainees or "stagiaires" are recruited twice a year, with the training periods starting on 1 March and 1 October.

Participation

The following may apply:

- university graduates or equivalent;
- students who have successfully completed at least four years of university study; and
- public or private sector employees, provided they have a university degree or equivalent diploma, or have been engaged for at least three years in advisory duties. For such applicants, the Secretary-General may fix a different date of commencement or length of training period in each individual case.

Trainees must not be more than 30 years old, and must have a thorough knowledge of one EC language and a satisfactory knowledge of at least one other as well as their own. They are mainly selected from among nationals of the Member States, but a limited number of nationals of non-member countries may be accepted.

Applications

Applications must be received by: 31 March for the period beginning on 1 October; and- 30 September for the period beginning on 1 March.

Enquiries should be made to the Bureau de Stage at the address below. Since competition is fierce, potential applicants should also seek advice from local offices of the Commission.

INFORMATION

UK
UK Office of the Commission of the European Communities
Jean Monnet House
8 Storey's Gate
London SW1P 3AT
Tel: 071 973 1992
Fax: 071 973 1900

IRELAND
Irish Office of the Commission of the European Communities
39 Molesworth Street
Dublin 2
Tel: 01 71 22 44
Fax: 01 71 26 57

COMMISSION
Commission of the European Communities
Secretariat-General - Training Office
200 rue de la Loi
B-1049 Brussels
Tel: INT+ 322 299 1111 (exchange)

WARNING

Whilst three years ago all places were not filled, it is now very difficult to get one. The most critical question to be answered is which department of which Community Institution the applicant wants to join and why. A large number of applicants are rejected almost immediately and those who get through the first round are entered into the "Blue Book" which is sent around to the relevant institutions who make selections from it. Under this system applicants only really get one shot so they have to aim it fairly carefully, and chose an institution where their qualifications give them the best chance of success. Some institutions, D-Gs and Commission offices are obviously more popular than others and some qualifications more useful than others. A Russian speaking agronomist willing to travel has a better chance than a law graduate who speaks only Community languages and wants to work in Brussels. The list of D-Gs can be found in Appendix 3 and the other institutions and Community Office in Appendix 4.

The Commission recommend that applicants ask their MEPs to help them find a place. A straw poll amongst recent applicants shows that of 23 English MEPs approached, only one took the trouble to reply and that was to say he could not help. It might however, be different in 1994, being election year!

Potential applicants should also be warned:

- Brussels is very expensive and stagiaire's pay is only just about enough for survival;
- doing a stage - even if the duration is extended beyond the normal six months - does not count as employment for Social Security purposes or as time spent

working in a country for obtaining a carte de sejour. This is particularly relevant in Belgium but also applies in some other countries. Although health care is covered under Form E.111 in other Member States, stagiaires on leaving are not entitled to unemployment benefits.

3.16 MATTHAEUS: VOCATIONAL RETRAINING OF CUSTOMS OFFICIALS

Statutory Basis

Council Decision 91/341/EEC of 20/6/91 adopting the MATTHAEUS Programme (OJ L 187, 13/7/91). Commission Decision 93/23/EEC of 11/12/92 sets out the application arrangements (OJ L 16, dated 25/1/93). Commission Decision 93/15/EEC of 16/12/92 establishes specific training programmes for inward processing, temporary admission and transit (OJ L 10, dated 16/1/93).

Objectives

This programme is a response to the challenges of the single market and the new role customs officials are called upon to play to ensure that the customs union runs smoothly.

Programme Content

The following measures are supported:

- exchanges of officials between national administrations;
- seminars;
- common vocational training programmes in Member States customs schools; and
- language training.

EC Contribution

The budget for MATTHAEUS for 1992 was 2.7 MECU. In 1993 the budgetary allocation was 2.427 MECU, less 600,000 ECU for the MATTHAEUS-TAX Programme. The cost of the Programme is shared between the Commission and the Member States. Travel and subsistence costs incurred in cross border exchanges and seminar participation are borne by the Commission.

INFORMATION

Commission of the European Communities
DG XXI A.4
200 rue de la Loi
B-1049 Brussels
Tel: INT+ 322 295 4913
Fax: INT+ 322 295 6501

3.17 MATTHAEUS-TAX: Training Officials in the Administration of Indirect Taxation

Statutory Basis

The Commission proposal on the MATTHAEUS-TAX Programme COM(92) 550 final (OJ C 15/4 dated 21/1/93) was submitted to the Council on 15 December 1992 and a decision is expected in early 1994.

Objectives

The objectives of the Programme are:

- to prepare the officials in the domestic administrations of Member States, who would be responsible for indirect taxation, to deal with the implications arising from the establishment of the internal market and also to ensure a better and more consistent application of the relevant EC rules;
- to allow the national officials concerned a better understanding of the administrative procedures of other Member States;
- to increase the officials' awareness of the Community dimension of their work; and
- to allow a fruitful exchange of ideas between the officials of the administrations of different Member States on the best way to implement the EC legislation and, at the same time, to facilitate a form of collaboration which will intensify in the context of the internal market.

Background

MATTHAEUS-TAX was originally known as "Interfisc": this was a pilot programme, run during 1991 and 1992, for the exchange of indirect taxation officials between national administrations and for training seminars to collect information to allow the implementation of a more ambitious training programme.

The adoption by the Council of the Directives instituting the transitional VAT regime, the harmonised excise regime, and the Regulation relating to administrative co-operation in dealing with VAT, forms a fundamental aspect of the internal market. To guarantee a proper application of indirect taxation rules to the exchanges between Member States, the removal of fiscal frontiers requires the establishment of in-depth, permanent co-operation procedures between the administrations responsible. The exchange of officials between the relevant administrations in different Member States provides an ideal method of achieving this reciprocal understanding.

Programme Content

MATTHAEUS-TAX comprises the following elements:

- exchanges of officials between national administrations;
- training seminars for officials, particularly trainers in training schools, officials responsible for administrative co-operation and officials responsible for indirect taxation controls and the fight against fraud and tax evasion;

- the co-ordinated implementation of vocational training programmes in the training schools of Member States; and
- the organisation in Member States of language training courses for officials likely to participate in exchanges.

EC Contribution

The budget allocated for 1993 was 600,000 ECU. The EC shall pay the travel and subsistence expenses for exchanges of officials between national administrations, for officials participating in seminars and the costs relating to the organisation of the seminars. Member States shall pay the expenses relating to the language training of their staff.

3.18 KAROLUS: Training Officials in the Enforcement of EC Regulations

Statutory Basis

Council Decision 92/481/EEC (OJ L 286, dated 1/10/92).

Objectives

The objectives of the action plan are as follows:

- to develop a convergent approach to the enforcement of EC legislation throughout the single market;
- to make national officials aware of the European dimension of their work and to build mutual confidence between the national administrations in charge of the enforcement of EC law; and
- to permit cross-fertilisation of ideas between national administrations on the way in which EC legislation can best be enforced.

Background

This action plan is for the exchange, between Member States' administrations, of national officials who are engaged in implementing EC legislation required to achieve the internal market. The action plan, which is scheduled to last for five years starting on 1 January 1993, is planned to encompass some 1,900 participants.

Programme Content

The action plan is made up of the following stages:

- training seminars dealing with the European Communities and their foundations, common policies and recent developments, in order to contribute towards a greater awareness of the EC's activities and relevance to national administrations throughout the Member States;

- language courses, where necessary, to enable participants to gain optimum benefit from the exchange; and
- the exchange of officials, for a minimum period of two months, between the administrations the Member States at both national and local levels, together with a number specifically designated from the private sector by the responsible administrations, .

For the 1993 financial year, the priority areas listed in Commission Decision 93/11/EEC (OJ L 8, dated 14/1/93) were: pharmaceutical products, public procurement, export controls on certain dual-use products and technologies, conformity testing and market supervision, foodstuffs, plant health, banks, insurance companies, stock exchanges and institutions for collective investment in securities and road transport.

EC Contribution

A total of 17.3 MECU is estimated to be necessary. Member States pay half the subsistence allowances for the participants they send, and the Commission covers all other expenses.

Participation

The officials concerned must be engaged in the enforcement of EC legislation in the field of the internal market, be employed at middle management level and be prepared to undertake the maximum possible dissemination of results.

INFORMATION

UK
European Staffing Unit
Cabinet Office (OPSS)
House Guards Road
London SW1P 3AL
Tel: 071 270 6291
Fax: 071 270 6138

IRELAND
Careers and Appointments Section
Department of Finance
Agriculture House
Kildare Street
Dublin 2
Tel: 01 76 75 71
Fax: 01 77 39 49

COMMISSION
Commission of the European Communities
Internal Market and Financial Services
200 rue de la Loi
B-1049 Brussels
Tel: INT+ 322 295 7456/5643
Fax: INT+ 322 296 0950

European Institute of Public Administration
OL Vrouweplein 22
PO Box 1229
NL-6201 BE MAASTRICHT
Tel: INT+ 3143 296 222
Fax: INT+ 3143 296 296

3.19 TRAINING IN RESTORATION TECHNIQUES

See Chapter 27 on Cultural Grants

Chapter 24

Trans-European Networks (TENS)

The Maastricht Treaty introduces a new task to be undertaken by the Community in "the encouragement of the establishment and development of trans-European networks" - new Article 3(n) of the EECT. This is fleshed out by a new Article 129b which states:

"1. To help achieve the objectives ... (of completing the internal market and strengthening economic and social cohesion) and to enable the citizens of the Union, economic operators and regional and local communities to derive the full benefit from the setting up of an area without internal frontiers, the Community shall contribute to the establishment and development of trans-European networks in the areas of transport, telecommunications and energy infrastructures.

2. Within a framework of a system of open and competitive markets, action by the Community shall aim at promoting the interconnection and inter-operability of national networks as well as access to such networks. It shall take account in particular of the need to link island, landlocked and peripheral regions with the central regions of the Community."

This is, as such, a new area of policy for the Community, which has been developed out of established Community policies on creating a large market without frontiers and allowing the free movement of people, goods, services and capital, coupled with policies providing opportunities for all regions, particularly those lagging behind. It would appear that the aim of the policy is not to establish a master plan for Europe, but to encourage more systematic trans-national co-operation in the important fields of transport, telecommunications infrastructure and energy supplies. The Commission has already emphasised that it is not its function to take over functions that already are, or can be, adequately carried out by the individual Member States.

In framing the SEA, it was expected that the internal market would lead to an increase in longer distance economic activities and greater mobility in employment throughout the EC, thereby reducing the economic and geographical imbalances between the prosperous centres and the rest of the EC. There are still, however, well-defined core areas within the EC where economic activity is concentrated. The traditional centre of European development, bounded by the Paris-London-Amsterdam-Ruhr quadrangle, is now being complemented by a second centre covering the wealthy regions of southern Germany and northern Italy, and extending rapidly westwards across increasingly large areas of the French Midi to reach the regions around Barcelona and Valencia.

These core areas exist because the location of economic activities is still largely determined by proximity to suppliers and services. New firms tend to be attracted by clusters of economic, administrative and political decision-making. These core areas have also been the traditional destinations for immigrants seeking work, and the ready supply of cheap labour they provided has always been an additional incentive for locating new firms in these areas.

There are now four increasingly important factors which could stimulate the decentralisation of economic activities to other parts of the Community.

The first is that the costs of congestion in large cities and the age structure of their populations could reduce the dynamism of the traditional commercial areas. The increased centralisation of economic activities in the 1980s has resulted in further pressures on urban space and transport systems. An increase in the overhead costs of running businesses and the general deterioration in urban environments has decreased the attractiveness of the large urban areas as working environments. This is a factor common to both the North and the South and is leading towards more decentralised urban systems as the large metropolitan areas either grow more slowly than the surrounding areas or, in many cases, lose population. This is augmented by the fact that while new immigrants are still settling in the traditional urban industrial areas, they are increasingly drawn to the southern parts of the EC such as Greece, Spain and the south of Italy.

The second factor is that enterprises have gradually acquired a much freer choice of location than they had in the past. At the beginning of the 1960s, there was very limited flexibility over the choice of location for an estimated 70% of the total EC work force. By 1990, this proportion had fallen to 50% due to changes in economic structure and, in particular, the relative decline in the industries dependent on natural resources and on services tied to local markets. For instance, over the past decade, major firms have introduced flexible production systems and, although their scope for economies of scale is diminishing, there have been increasing opportunities for small firms not necessarily tied to mass production methods or a strong local market.

The third stimulus towards decentralisation is that the final choice of location is often more affected by qualitative factors than quantitative factors, such as availability of labour, telecommunications and transport infrastructures, and market-related factors like access and economic climate. Firms are prepared to trade off these cost disadvantages to secure qualitative advantages, such as a pleasant climate and a good general living environment. These factors have contributed to the economic growth of the southern arc stretching from northern Italy through southern France to northern Spain. They have also led to the growth, in the more prosperous regions, of small and medium-sized towns near, or easily assessable to large metropolitan areas.

The fourth factor is the new possibilities provided by modern means of transport, telecommunications and the integration of energy transmission networks, which will help to overcome the disadvantages of the more remote regions. It is with this fourth factor that the new EC policy of TENs is concerned: the others are by and large covered by the Structural Funds. The importance of this factor is evident from the fact that the Copenhagen Summit in June 1993 invited the Commission and the Council to complete the network plans in the transport, telecommunications and energy sectors by early

1994, and the Summit also noted with satisfaction the progress already made on high speed trains, roads, inland waters and combined transport systems.

Transport

Given the problem of congestion at all levels in and around large urban areas, the increased use of distance-shrinking technologies should reduce the pressure on central regions and improve the quality of life. The transport network renders a vital service to many sectors of the EC economy, representing more than 7% of EC GDP. It is easy to see, therefore, that the completion of high-speed transport networks would significantly reduce the regional disparities in economic competitiveness, by making the policy of free movement of goods and labour a reality.

In the original Treaty of Rome, the tasks of the Community included in Article 3(e) "the adoption of a common policy in the sphere of transport", and in Article 74 provided that "The objectives of this Treaty shall, in matters governed by (transport) be pursued by Member States within the framework of a common transport policy." The liberalisation of the transport sector has, however, proved to be an extremely politically sensitive area and the Council has been very slow to adopt the framework of measures necessary for a common transport policy. The necessity for taking more radical measures was highlighted, and given impetus, by the European Court in 1985, when it held that, although the absence of a common transport policy did not in itself constitute a breach of the Treaty, the Council was in breach of its Treaty obligations in failing to introduce measures to ensure the freedom to provide services in the sphere of international travel.

The lack of a common transport policy in the past is obvious from the present state of European transport. Overall, one fifth of the long-distance, international road network is still below motorway standard. In the Iberian peninsula, Ireland, Greece and many parts of the UK, continuous, long-distance, high-quality motorways simply do not exist. Similar inadequacies exist in the EC rail network, where a fifth of the inter-regional passenger network is run at speeds of less than 70 km/hr and only 5% at average speeds above 120 km/hr.

It is the aim of the Community that emphasis should be given, in formulating EC transport policy, not just to the development of high-speed transport which merely strengthens the existing links between the main economic centres. The objective is the development of Community-wide high-speed integrated systems of transport to include maritime connections, so as to reduce disparities between the centre and the peripheral areas, and providing connections between the most isolated areas and the main high-speed network so as to enable these regions to obtain as much benefit as possible from the system.

The Channel Tunnel provides an obvious example of the potential regional effects of a major investment in transport links. It is estimated that passenger traffic across the Channel, including air traffic, will increase over the period between 1991 and 1996 from 84 million to 107 million journeys: a factor of 27%; and by a further 26% to 135 million by 2001. The number of lorry crossings is expected to grow from 3.3 million to 4.4 million between 1991 and 1996: a 35% increase; and by a further 18% to 5.2 million by 2001. The economic gains from the construction of the Tunnel can be expected to be concentrated in the regions around the exits on either side of the Channel and benefiting mainly the economies in the London-Brussels-Paris triangle. Unless they are linked to a new high-speed network, the Tunnel could further marginalise the northern and western regions of England as well as Scotland, Wales and Ireland which are so dependent on transport across England to the mainland of the Community, and further emphasise the peripheral status of areas like Brittany, Zealand, southern Italy, Denmark, Greece and Portugal,

Although the liberalisation of road, rail, air and sea transport has been started, progress to date has been small and uneven. In road transport, the main milestone was the removal on 1 January 1993 of all remaining quota restrictions imposed by national authorities on hauliers from other EC countries. These quotas had limited the number of licences for international traffic which were available for foreign trucks. July 1990 saw the introduction of a limited and temporary provision for cabotage - the right of an operator based in one Member State to carry out transport operations between two points in another Member State - and the removal of technical checks on vehicles from frontiers to within Member States as part of their overall road safety policy. The advent of the Single Administrative Document (SAD) cut down the delays in crossing the internal frontiers considerably, and the removal of the frontier posts on 1 January 1993 has further improved matters, although there can be problems at loading and unloading facilities.

In air transport, several packages of measures have been adopted to liberalise this sector which was previously dominated by cartels and vested interests. The most significant to date has been what is known as the third liberalisation package, which does three things:

i It creates common licensing and safety standards. A carrier licensed in one Member State can operate services all over the EC.

ii Airlines will have the freedom to fly between any two Member States and carry domestic passengers during any leg of such a flight that links two points within one EC country. Full liberalisation of domestic flights allowing foreign firms to fly purely internal routes is not due until 1997.

iii Airlines will be free to set their own fares within the limits of predatory pricing.

The third liberalisation package was agreed in principle in June 1992. Some airlines believe the package could bring down air fares by as much as 25% in the short to medium term.

In sea transport, attention is being given to co-ordinating the expansion of ports on the Mediterranean and Atlantic. The Community gives grants under the Structural Funds to assist such projects, which are financed mainly from national and private resources. The first such grants were made available in 1990, when the amount advanced was ECU 60 million, which was increased to ECU 105 million in 1991.

Telecommunications

Telecommunications and information technology are at the heart of today's post-industrial society. They are vital economic sectors in themselves, with forecasts suggesting that they could make as big a contribution to the EC's economy by the end of the century as the motor industry does now. The past decade has witnessed enormous growth in the field of information technology. There was a five fold increase in international traffic on public networks alone during the 1980s and global traffic is expected to continue to expand at a minimum of 15% to 20% annually, up to and beyond the year 2000. In association with this, there has been a rapid growth in new industries dependent on information services and communications, and more than half of present employment is now directly involved in some aspect of information management. Some 80% of all new jobs are created by small businesses in the service and information sectors.

These new developments in information technology and telecommunications are changing the concept of distance and reducing some of the cost disadvantages associated with the remoteness of certain regions. This is particularly so because SMEs have proved to be the main vehicle for industrial innovation and job creation in the 1980s and small businesses are better placed to benefit from the advantages of operating in areas away from the main concentrations of population. SMEs have always been the mainstay of rural economies, taking advantage of the smaller pool of skilled labour and the lower establishment overheads. Modern industries can only survive, however, if they have access to the professional services and markets essential to their business activities. Peripheral and rural areas will therefore only be able to compete on an equal basis for new employment opportunities if telecommunications services are available and appropriate telematics systems are developed.

The present trend towards greater competition for the provision of telecommunications services in Europe may lead to the concentration of investment in areas and services giving an immediate return for investors thus leaving rural areas increasingly disadvantaged. Market and regulatory mechanisms are having to be found and enforced rigorously to enable SMEs in rural areas to obtain cost-effective access to the advanced services equivalent to those in the major commercial centres: hence the Telematics Programme.

The Copenhagen Summit in June 1993 reiterated the aim of a decentralised economy with a properly trained workforce, encouragement for SMEs and co-operation between them at all levels. It was recognised that, to achieve this, it was necessary to create a "European information infrastructure" to serve as the arterial system of the future economy and to stimulate the information industry. It was decided that, in view of the scale of the problem, an initial investment of 5 BECU would be required, followed by an annual programme worth 5.8 BECU. The need to set up Community wide training courses for the new trades and professions and to encourage distance working through computer networks was recognised as a priority.

A start has been made in opening up the national markets for telecommunications in the Member States in parallel with the main legislative programme required to implement the 1987 White Paper on completing the internal market, although the vital importance of telecommunications had not been appreciated at the time. It hardly features in the Cecchini Report and is not included in Delors' "Complete Package" speech. Previously closed national markets have been opened to competition for all telecommunications services, except for basic voice telephony and telex. Private companies now compete with the national telecommunications organisations to offer services like electronic mail or data transmission. Directives have also been adopted which make way for pan-European services for mobile telephones and radio-paging. The problem of mobile phone systems and radio pagers which work only in one Member State, is an obvious hindrance to the operation of the internal market and is proving difficult to resolve.

Negotiations to start liberalising basic voice telephony, which is by far the biggest telecommunications service sector and which is still under monopoly control in most Member States, got under way in early 1993. The aim here is to introduce competition in the expectation of lowering charges for calls between Member States, which the Commission believes are excessive in many instances. At present, it can cost four times as much to make a call between two places 300 kilometres apart in two different Member States as over the same distance within one Member State.

Recent studies show that peripheral regions in southern Europe in suffer particularly badly from very poor to non-existent telecommunications services. The average number of telephone lines per 100 people in 1989 was 25 in the Structural Funds' Objective 1 regions compared with 46 in France, for example. To bring these regions up to the same standard as the rest of the EC would require expenditure of around ECU 50 billion. Such expenditure is vital, however, in order to reduce both urban and rural problems. Rural areas must be seen increasingly as areas of opportunity for Europe's economic and social development, rather than as areas of declining economic activity, always in need of subsidy and external support.

Energy

A secure supply of energy at competitive prices is a precondition for economic development. To guarantee competitively priced supplies to all regions requires both the development of local or renewable energy resources and the completion of the single market in energy. This, in turn, calls for the strengthening and integration of energy transmission networks on an EC-wide basis. Intra-Community trade in electricity in 1990 represented 8% of total consumption in the EC, compared with 2% in 1950. It has been calculated that the interconnection of national grids would save up to 3% of total costs of supply, equivalent to around 1 BECU per year.

In southern Europe, priority projects for natural gas include increasing the capacity of the trans-Mediterranean pipeline, constructing pipelines between Algeria and Spain and between Spain and France, and new gas distribution infrastructures in both Greece and Portugal.

In northern Europe priority projects are new pipelines between western Germany and the former GDR, between Ireland and the UK, across the North Sea from the Norwegian wells, and between the Dutch and British installations.

In transferring responsibility for trans-European networks to the Community, the Maastricht Treaty is also contributing to economic and social cohesion, since many of these large infrastructure projects will speed up the linking of the outlying regions - and hence their economic development - with the central regions. They can promote the establishment of trans-European networks by way of feasibility studies, loan guarantees and interest-rate subsidies. Transport projects are also eligible to receive financial support from the new Cohesion Fund.

Decisions on TENs are to be taken by qualified majority after consultations with ECOSOC and the Committee of the Regions. This is an area where the Committee of the Regions could be expected to have a valuable input and it will be interesting to see how it performs.

Chapter 25

Trans-European Networks Grants

Trans-European Networks grants are divided among the three areas of the TEN policy: transport, telecommunications and energy infrastructures.

1. Transport Infrastructure

   1.1 Transport Infrastructure Fund

   1.2 EURET: Research on Transport Systems

2. Telecommunications Infrastructure

   2.1 Telematics:

   DRIVE II: Dedicated Road Infrastructure for Vehicle Safety in Europe

   ENS: European Nervous System

   AIM: Advanced Information in Medicine

   DELTA: Developing European Learning through Technological Advance

   Libraries Programme

   Linguistic Research and Engineering

   ORA: Opportunities for Rural Areas

   2.2 The Impact Programme: Action Plan for a European Information Services Market

   2.3 CADDIA: Co-operation in Automation of Data and Documentation for Imports/Exports and the Management of Financial Control of the Agricultural Market

   2.4 INSIS: Inter-Institutional Integrated Services Information System

   2.5 TEDIS II: Trade Electronic Data Interchange System

   2.6 STAR: Special Telecommunications Action for Regional Innovation and Development in Europe

   2.7 TELEMATIQUE: Advanced Telecommunications in the Least Favoured Areas

3. Energy Infrastructure
    3.1 SAVE: Specific Actions for Vigorous Energy Efficiency
    3.2 ALTENER: Promotion of Renewable Energy Resources
    3.3 Energy Technology Transfer with Less-Developed Countries

1. TRANSPORT INFRASTRUCTURE

1.1 Transport Infrastructure Fund

Statutory Basis

Council Regulation (EEC) No 3359/90 of 20/11/90 provided for a three-year action programme in the field of transport infrastructure, with a view to completing an integrated transport market in 1992 (OJ L 326, dated 24/11/90). By COM(92) 231 final of 2/7/92 (OJ C 236/3 dated 15/9/92) the Commission proposed a Council Regulation amending No 3359/90, extending its scope and converting it into a rolling annual programme.

Objectives

The principal objectives of this fund are:

- the elimination of bottlenecks;
- the integration of areas which are either landlocked or geographically on the periphery of the EC;
- the reduction of costs associated with transit traffic in co-operation with any non-member countries concerned;
- the improvement of links on land/sea routes; and
- the provision of high-quality links between the major urban centres, including high-speed rail links.

If COM(92) 231 is accepted, it would include a plan for a trans-European network by the year 2002.

Background

A transport infrastructure fund has been under discussion for several years. In August 1983, the Commission put forward a proposal for a five-year programme of support for transport infrastructure projects (OJ C 36, dated 10/2/84). Since then, various Commission initiatives have been rejected by the Council because some Member States took the view that such infrastructure projects, which were not part of regional policy, should not be funded by the EC. The deadlock was broken largely as a result of initiatives from the European Parliament, and the problem should now have been overcome since, following the Maastricht Treaty, decisions can be taken by a qualified majority.

Programme Content

The Community contribution to carrying out these objectives may take the form of:

- financial support using appropriations earmarked in the general budget; and
- financial support under other relevant financial instruments, such as the Structural Funds and EIB loans.

Funding may be granted for feasibility studies or preparatory work for infrastructure projects, as well as for the projects themselves. Non-repayable support may not exceed 25% of the total project costs except for preparatory studies, for which the limit is 50%.

The Commission must declare a project to be of European interest before it can be considered.

Priority projects are as follows:

i contribution to the high-speed rail network with the following links:

- Paris, London, Brussels, Amsterdam, Cologne and connecting lines to other Member States;
- Seville, Madrid, Barcelona, Lyons, Turin-Milan, Venice and from there to Tarvisio and Trieste; and
- Oporto, Lisbon and Madrid;

ii the Brenner Alpine transit route;

iii contribution to the combined transport network of EC interest;

iv international trans-Pyrenean road links (Somport);

v the road link UK to Ireland: A5/A55 North Wales Coast road; and the improvement of the Dublin-Belfast railway line;

vi the Scanlink; and

vii the strengthening of land communications in Greece.

EC Contribution

The amount earmarked for the Programme was 60 MECU in the 1990 budget, 105 MECU in 1991, 140 MECU in 1992 and 180 MECU in 1993.

Applications

It is for the Member States to submit proposals to the Commission under the terms of this Regulation.

INFORMATION

Commission of the European Communities
DG VII Directorate C. 2
200 rue de la Loi
B-1049 Brussels
Tel: INT+ 322 299 1111 (exchange)

1.2 EURET: Research on Transport Systems

See Chapter 17.8

2. TELECOMMUNICATIONS INFRASTRUCTURE

2.1 Telematics:

DRIVE II: Dedicated Road Infrastructure for Vehicle Safety in Europe

ENS: European Nervous System

AIM: Advanced Information in Medicine

DELTA: Developing European Learning through Technological Advance

Libraries Programme

Linguistic Research & Engineering

ORA: Opportunities for Rural Areas

See Chapter 17.1

2.2 THE IMPACT PROGRAMME: Action Plan for a European Information Services Market

Statutory Basis

Council Decision 91/691/EEC of 12/12/91 adopting a programme for an information services market (OJ L 377, dated 31/12/91).

Objectives

The objectives are as follows:

- to establish an internal market for information services;
- to stimulate and reinforce the competitive capability of European suppliers of information services;
- to promote the use of advanced information services; and
- to reinforce joint efforts to achieve Community cohesion with respect to information service policies.

Background

In order to ensure that information users throughout Europe have access to cheap and reliable sources, the EC has sponsored several initiatives. The First Action Plan, 1975-83, led to the creation of a computer data-network, EURONET. One of the many benefits of this initiative was that it created, for the first time, a unified tariff for telecommunications which applied irrespective of the distances covered.

The Second Action Plan, 1984-88, encouraged the development of new data banks and databases for on-line interrogation and computer hosts. The Direct Information Access Network became known as EURONET DIANE. Parallel action under the DOCDEL programme encouraged such activities as electronic publishing and document delivery.

The next phase was the setting up of an action plan for a European Information Services Market, IMPACT. The initial phase was adopted in July 1988 and ran for two years with a budget of 36 MECU. The successful completion of the pilot phase is being followed by the main phase, IMPACT II, which is scheduled to run from 1992 to 1995.

Programme Content

There are four action lines.

i Improving the Understanding of the Market

The European Information Market Observatory (IMO) will extend its scope to identify the EC's strengths and weaknesses and provide data for policy decisions. There will be an increased emphasis on business and trade publishing markets. The IMO will also encourage the harmonisation of statistical methodologies and stimulate the development of models and forecasting tools. Market survey work by the private sector will be encouraged.

ii Overcoming Legal and Administration Barriers

A number of horizontal legal actions which will encourage the creation and use of European services will be undertaken. These include tackling the problems relating to protection of privacy, responsibility for data accuracy, and the security, proof and authentication of electronic signatures. The Legal Advisory Board (LAB) will be reinforced. Rates will also be developed for the marketing of data held by public and quasi-public bodies. European codes of conduct will be proposed to cover the private sector marketing of mailing lists and credit rating databases.

iii Stimulating the Application of Norms and Standards; and Awareness, User Support and Training

The development and use of Open Systems Interconnection (OSI) and Open Information Interchange (OII) will be encouraged. The development of generic interfaces which provide flexible and economic solutions for accessing a large number of information services, will be encouraged. This will include multimedia services and European-wide access. Multiplier groups such as educational institutions, professional associations, National Focal Points, gateway operators and the specialised press will be encouraged to promote information literacy among professionals. In order to increase awareness and training activities, a network of National Awareness Partners was established in September 1992.

iv Supporting Strategic Information Initiatives

The supply of electronic information services in science and technology will be stimulated and strengthened.

EC Contribution

A budget allocation of 64 MECU has been agreed for the four-year programme .

Status Report

A call for proposals for the development of multimedia information services was published in OJ C 139, dated 2/6/92, with a deadline of 14 August 1992. Information is still awaited concerning future calls.

INFORMATION

UK

The following freephone number for the Impact Central Office is available from Monday to Friday between 0800 and 1800 hours: 0800 899 237

England

A list of National Awareness Partners is available from:
Ms S Jespersen
ASLIB (The Association for Information Management)
Information House
20-24 Old Street
London EC1V 9AP.
Tel: 071 253 4488
Fax: 071 430 0514

Scotland

Mr Jonathan H Cape
Scottish Enterprise Tayside
Enterprise House
45 North Lindsay Street
Dundee DD1 1HT
Tel: 0382 23100
Fax: 0382 305576

Dr Peter Gregor
University of Dundee
Centre for Continuing Education
Dundee DDI 4HN
Tel: 0382 23181 ext. 4914
Fax: 0382 21057

IRELAND

The following freephone number for the Impact Central Office is available from Monday to Friday between 0800 and 1800 hours: 1 800 555 237

A list of National Awareness Partners is available from:
Dr Barry Harrington
EOLAS
The Irish Science and Technology Agency
Glasnevin
Dublin 9.
Tel: 01 37 01 01 ext. 2303
Fax: 01 37 90 82

A list of National Focal Points is available from:
Mr D Toomey
EOLAS
The Irish Science and Technology Agency
Glasnevin
Dublin 9.
Tel: 01 37 01 01
Fax: 01 37 96 20

COMMISSION
The Commission of the European Communities
IMPACT Central Office
D-G XIII. E
Batiment Jean Monnet C4/33
L-2920 Luxembourg.
Tel: INT+ 352 34 981 222
Fax: INT+ 352 4301 32847

2.3 CADDIA: Co-operation in Automation of Data and Documentation for Imports/Exports and the Management of Financial Control of the Agricultural Market

Statutory Basis

Council Decision 85/214/EEC of 26/3/85: OJ L 96/35 dated 3/4/85

Objectives

The aim is to create an efficient electronic system for data exchange.

EC Contribution

The Programme's budget was 22.75 MECU.

Programme Content

The Programme ran from 1987-1992. It is thought unlikely that it will be extended, as its objectives are being absorbed into other programmes.

CADDIA covered three areas:

i automation of information collected in the course of administering the European customs union, the agricultural market organisations and the statistical procedures for trade at the European level;

ii co-ordination of initiatives taken by national administrations; and

iii purposes relating to standardisation, adaptation of industrial and commercial standards and developments of standards and standards programmes within the EC.

INFORMATION

Commission of the European Communities
DG XIII
200 rue de la Loi
B-1049 Brussels
Tel: INT+ 322 299 1111 (exchange)

2.4 INSIS: Inter-Institutional Integrated Services Information System

Statutory Basis

Council Decision 82/869/EEC: OJ L 368/40 dated 28/12/82.

Objectives

The aim was to promote the use of new electronic technologies for exchanging information among Member States and the organs of the EC.

Programme Content

The programme lasted from 1983-1992. It is thought unlikely that it will be extended, as its objectives are being absorbed into other programmes.

INSIS included horizontal programmes to prepare the technical and industrial environment, as well as pilot projects to evaluate the impact of the introduction of new technologies into administrations. The Programme safeguarded the establishment of European standards and provided support for the early stages of development of user-oriented telematics products, as well as for the development of mutually compatible public communications services at a European level.

EC Contribution

INSIS received 6-7 MECU annually.

INFORMATION

Commission of the European Communities
DG XIII
200 rue de la Loi
B-1049 Brussels
Tel: INT +322 299 1111 (exchange)

2.5 TEDIS II: Trade Electronic Data Interchange System

Statutory Basis

Council Decision 91/385/EEC of 22/7/92: OJ L 208/66 dated 30/7/91.

Objectives

The Programme aims to co-ordinate the development of electronic data interchange systems for purposes relating to trade, industry and administration.

Programme Content

The Programme is scheduled to run for three years from 1991.

The specific needs of users, including those in SMEs, are to be taken into account.

The Programme is carried out in co-ordination with other EC policies and initiatives in such areas as information and communications technologies, the information market, security of information systems, standardisation and with the CADDIA Programme.

Phase two of the Programme seeks to ensure that the installation of electronic data interchange systems runs as smoothly as possible.

EC Contribution

25 MECU has been allocated to the Programme.

INFORMATION

Commission of the European Communities
DG XIII
200 rue de la Loi
B-1049 Brussels
Tel: INT +322 299 1111 (exchange)

2.6 STAR: Special Telecommunications Action for Regional Innovation and Development in Europe

See Chapter 19.1

2.7 TELEMATIQUE

See Chapter 19.1

3. ENERGY INFRASTRUCTURE

3.1 SAVE: Specific Actions for Vigorous Energy Efficiency

Statutory Basis

Council Decision 91/565/EEC of 29/10/91 (OJ L 307/34 dated 8/11/91). The specific actions proposed by the Commission are given in 92/C 23/04 (OJ C 23/8 dated 30/1/92).

Objectives

The main aim of SAVE is to establish the mechanisms and infrastructures necessary to achieve the EC's energy efficiency and environmental goals, notably the reduction of carbon dioxide emissions.

Background

The estimated growth rate of carbon dioxide emission in the EC for the period 1990-2000 is about 12%. This estimate is based on an average annual economic growth rate of 2.4% and higher growth rates would lead to a proportionately greater increase in carbon dioxide emissions.

The Council approved SAVE - a five-year EC energy efficiency programme commencing in 1991 - in order to help Member States augment and co-ordinate their own national energy efficiency programmes. It is estimated that timely and full implementation of the SAVE Programme could reduce the projected growth rate of carbon dioxide emissions by about 3% during the period up to the year 2,000.

Programme Content

The main thrust of the Programme is a comprehensive series of legislative measures supported by targeted pilot actions, as well as a significant effort to improve the flow of information between Member States and between the EC and other interested parties.

SAVE is to be implemented via the following measures:

- energy certification of buildings;
- the billing of heating, air-conditioning and hot-water costs on the basis of actual consumption;
- promoting third party financing for energy efficiency investments in the public sector;
- thermal insulation of new buildings;
- regular inspection of boilers;
- regular inspection of vehicles; and
- energy audits of businesses.

This approach will allow action on every energy-related source of carbon dioxide emissions except for power stations, which are dealt with under different programmes.

In view of the different situations and behaviour patterns within the EC, it has been left to the Member States to define the procedures best suited to their individual circumstances.

EC Contribution

A provisional budget of 35 MECU has been set for the five-year programme, of which 14 MECU was earmarked for 1991-92.

INFORMATION

UK
Energy Efficiency Office
Department of Energy
1 Palace Street
London SW1E 5HE
Tel: 071 238 3000

COMMISSION
Commission of the European Communities
DG XVII Directorate-General for Energy
200 rue de la Loi
B-1049 Brussels
Tel: INT+ 322 299 1111

3.2 ALTENER: Promotion of Renewable Energy Resources

Statutory Basis

Commission Proposal: COM(92) 180 (final) of 29/6/92.

Objectives

The purpose of the ALTENER Programme is to develop the growth of renewable energy resources within the EC and to increase trade in products, equipment and services both within and outside the EC.

Background

The Commission's proposals for the ALTENER Programme form part of the package of measures being drawn up to limit carbon dioxide emissions. The overall EC objective is to reduce carbon dioxide emissions by 180 million tonnes by the year 2005. The Programme is scheduled to run from 1993 to 1997.

Programme Content

The ALTENER Programme will comprise actions in the following four areas.

i Promoting the Market for Renewable Energy Sources and Integrating them into the Internal Energy Market

The harmonisation of legislation and the formulation of common technical standards at EC level is part of the process of completing the internal energy market. Incentive measures concerning the production of renewable energy resources, investment in their exploitation and attractive conditions for the purchase of electricity produced from renewable energy resources will provide a powerful impetus for their development.

These measures will cover schemes involved in small-scale hydro-electric generation, wind power, thermal solar energy, photo-voltaic solar energy, biofuels and geothermal energy.

ii Financial and Economic Measures

Tax measures are planned to reinforce certain existing arrangements such as the inclusion of external costs of energy production, especially the environmental costs when pricing energy, the introduction of tax structures promoting energy saving and the imposition of a special tax on sources of energy producing carbon dioxide emissions.

An extension of measures to promote third-party financing of projects exploiting renewable energy resources is anticipated.

The Commission is encouraging the development of integrated resource planning, formerly known as least-cost planning, through a series of pilot schemes.

In the case of major, high-risk operations to exploit renewable energy sources, the EC may contribute towards the financing of guarantee funds.

For local plans to develop renewable energy sources, the EC may provide aid for planning studies and studies into the establishment of renewable energy development programmes.

Member States should ensure that feasibility and pre-feasibility studies are carried out when constructing new buildings, to assess the possible contribution of renewable energy sources to the lighting and heating of buildings and the production of domestic hot water.

The Commission will concentrate its attention on developing biodiesel, short-rotation coppices and biogas installations - three options which appear particularly promising in the specific context of the EC and the reform of the CAP.

iii Training, Information and Outreach Activities

The EC will support training, information and outreach activities concerning renewable energy sources which have been insufficiently developed within the Community, or which have been developed in fragmented ways without any overall strategic plan. Particular attention will be paid to training architects on the use of passive solar energy.

iv Co-operation with Third Countries

Greater use of renewable energy sources in the world as a whole would ensure greater security of energy supply and make a greater contribution to protecting the environment. The EC will therefore encourage the exchange of experience and will continue to co-operate with:

- the developing countries, with a view to exploiting renewable energy sources and slowing down the damaging exploitation of forest resources; and
- the countries of the former Soviet Union and the countries of Central and Eastern Europe, with which co-operation has already begun under the technical assistance programmes and the PHARE Programme, and with which

a specific protocol on renewable energy sources will be drafted under the European Energy Charter.

EC Contribution

A budgetary allocation of 40 MECU is being requested for the five-year programme.

The level of funding recommended for projects is 30-50% or, in exceptional cases, 60%.

Applications

The Commission publishes calls for proposals relating to the market development actions in the OJ and will send the Member States a copy of the proposals received.

The Commission will draw up annual guidelines for support action programmes in the Member States and, each year, the latter will submit their proposals to the Commission for programmes which conform with those guidelines.

INFORMATION

Commission of the European Communities
DG XVII Directorate C. 2
200 rue de la Loi
B-1049 Brussels
Tel: INT+ 322 299 1111.(exchange)

3.3 ENERGY TECHNOLOGY TRANSFER WITH LESS-DEVELOPED COUNTRIES

See Chapter 31

Chapter 26

Cultural Policy and Sport

What does a cultural policy mean and what place does it have in an economic community?

The first task of the European Community laid down in the Treaty of Rome as originally drafted was to promote a harmonious development of economic activities and a continuous and balanced expansion. Article 2 says that "the Community shall have as its task ... to promote ... an accelerated standard of living and closer relations between the States belonging to it". It was pointed out in Chapter One that the Community was founded on a twin track approach of idealism and pragmatism and it was intended that the economic expansion anticipated and the consequent creation of wealth would help to alleviate the drudgery from the lives of the peoples of the Community and increase the leisure time available. An improved standard of living must include more than just the acquisition of more consumer goods: as Disraeli put it, "Increased means and increased leisure are the two civilisers of men."

Josef Pieper points out in "Leisure, the Basis of Culture" that one of the foundations of Western culture is leisure or, as Plato put it, "... the Gods, taking pity on mankind, born to work, laid down the succession of recurring Feasts to restore them from their fatigue, and gave them the Muses, and Apollo their leader, and Dionysus, as companions in their Feasts, so that, nourishing themselves in festive companionship with the Gods, they should again stand upright and erect."

> The word "culture" has moved a long way from the original meaning of "divine worship". In 1873, Matthew Arnold in "Literature and Dogma" defined it as "acquainting ourselves with the best that has been known and said in the world, and thus with the history of the human spirit". Although not recognised by the Oxford English Dictionary, the word seems to be used increasingly in every day speech to cover the whole ambit of how individuals or groups see and organise themselves in relation to one another, including their shared experiences, beliefs, tastes and aspirations.

A common characteristic of the founding fathers was that they were not philistines, as is so obvious from their writings. They would have been very familiar with the Aristotelian distinction between *artes liberales* and *artes serviles* (liberal arts and servile work) and how the two were inextricably interwoven. Although the promotion of a European cultural identity was not spelled out in the Treaty, it would have been considered integral to promoting an accelerated standard of living and, from a very early stage, the Community engaged itself in "cultural matters" - interpreted in the widest possible manner.

Many aspects of culture in this wide sense have been dealt with within other areas of Community policy such as education, since the earliest days of the Community, and it was as long ago as 1974 that the European Parliament became the first Community institution to call for the Community to become an active partner on the cultural stage. Since then the EP has consistently supported and proposed specific measures in this field, and has been a persistent advocate of a separate budget for culture.

This cultural initiative was expanded at the Fontainebleau Summit in June 1984, when the Adonino Committee on "a people's Europe" was set up to give European integration a more human dimension. It was decided that a Community-based policy on sport should be added to the measures being considered in the field of culture and the Adonino Report was unanimously adopted at the Milan Summit in 1985. It was emphasised that sport - which accounts for 1% of Community GDP - could provide a unique method of promoting a sense of Community identity.

The Council really took up the running in 1986, when it expressed interest in measures to promote cultural activities at Community level, and its interest has helped improve follow-up and continuity. The establishment of a Council on Cultural Affairs made it possible to initiate more structured action.

The lacuna of omitting any specific mention of culture in the Treaty of Rome was finally rectified by the Maastricht Treaty. The amended activities of the Community in Article 3 now include the new Article 3(p) which states:

“A contribution to education and training of quality and the flowering of the cultures of the Member States.”

The new Article 128 fleshes this out:

“1. The Community shall contribute to the flowering of the cultures of the Member States, while respecting their national and regional diversity and at the same time bringing the common cultural heritage to the fore.

2. Action by the Community shall be aimed at encouraging co-operation between Member States and, if necessary, supporting and supplementing their action in the following areas;

   - improvement of the knowledge and dissemination of the culture and history of the European peoples:
   - conservation and safeguarding of cultural heritage of European significance;
   - non-commercial cultural exchanges; and
   - artistic and literary creation, including in the audio-visual sector.

3. The Community and the Member States shall foster co-operation with third countries and the competent international organisations in the sphere of culture, in particular the Council of Europe.
4. The Community shall take cultural aspects into account in its actions under other provisions of this Treaty."

As can be seen from the wording of the Maastricht Treaty, the Community's cultural policy is two-fold. Cultural action should contribute to the flowering of national and regional cultural identities whilst at the same time reinforcing the feeling that Europeans share a common cultural heritage and common values. In a way, this returns to the philosophy of the "Grand Tour", when rich and educated young people toured Europe with a view to learning what other countries had to teach them and then implementing what they had learnt when they returned home. A practical application of a common European cultural heritage applied in a particular way so as to suit the different regions of Europe, very much in line with Matthew Arnold's definition of culture.

In the development of Community cultural action programmes, care has to be taken to ensure that the principle of subsidiarity is fully respected. The objective is to produce action of Community interest geared primarily to breaking down barriers, to transparency and to genuine added value throughout the EC.

The EC encourages cultural co-operation only when it complements action taken by the Member States. A number of practical measures have been taken to this end, one of which is increasing the involvement of all those active in the field of culture in formulating policy over a wide range of issues. The cultural sensitivity of the various individual Member States means that a specific style of co-operation must be introduced, with a view to:

- preparing, in conjunction with the professionals and the authorities in the Member States, clear and specific proposals and action programmes for the different priority areas;
- increasing the involvement of the national, regional and local authorities in the cultural life of the Community as a whole.

The EC makes its contribution to the efforts made in the Member States to encourage artistic and cultural creation through a three-pronged approach:

i improved access to EC programmes and funds for culture-related training schemes;

ii stimulating talent, creativity and awareness of other cultures through exchanges between performing and creative artists and others working in the arts and culture; and

iii promoting pilot projects of Community-wide interest.

If cultural activities are to acquire a new status and reach a wider audience in our post-Maastricht society, it will be important to increase people's awareness of the different cultures and their common European heritage from the earliest possible age. It is also important to stimulate and increase the flow of information on subjects of Community-wide interest to those responsible for making and implementing the cultural policies of the individual Member States.

The EC recognises that, given the vast area covered by the general concept of "culture", identifying priorities is essential to avoid dissipating effort and resources. With this in mind, the Commission favours a horizontal approach based primarily on increasing the involvement of all those directly active in the field of culture, while constantly taking account of wider cultural dimensions within the whole range of EC policies and programmes.

Priority is being given to the development of this horizontal and focused approach in the three target areas already approved by the Council:

i our cultural heritage;

ii books and reading; and

iii the audio-visual sector.

At the same time the Commission feels that the Community should turn its attention to other cultural areas. It has already shown on many occasions its commitment to music and the performing and visual arts, but there has as yet been little common action on this front.

The starting point for action in each of these three areas was different:

i for our cultural heritage, a pilot scheme to conserve the architectural heritage;

ii for literature and reading, a general analysis and a pilot project on literary translation; and

iii for the audio-visual media, a three-fold objective: rules of the market, technology required and promotion of the programmes industry.

i Our Cultural Heritage

Visible evidence of Europe's historic and artistic past, our architectural and cultural heritage, is of fundamental importance to European culture. It reflects both the different stages in the development of our civilisation and the various expressions of our identity. It is both irreplaceable and vulnerable and must be preserved for future generations, so as to provide a constant source of inspiration for contemporary creativity.

The policy is not intended to promote an elitist activity: it is an integral part of the objective of making the Community a better place to live in, which includes beautiful surroundings as well as employment and economic sufficiency. Quite apart from its intrinsic cultural value, this aspect of the European heritage is closely bound up with other EC policies relating to economic and social life, aimed at improving the quality of life and the environment, promoting tourism, research and new technology and providing opportunities for training and employment.

ii Literature and Reading

Literature represents one of the main forms of cultural expression being an aid to creativity and to the dissemination of knowledge and ideas, and reading is an essential cultural and educational activity. One of the Community's main objectives is to improve the dissemination of our written heritage and guarantee its preservation.

The EC has already taken account of the culture-related element in literature under its other policies; there is, for example a Commission programme under way in the field of copyright and neighbouring rights (COM(90) 584 final). Books are among the items which can qualify for a lower rate of VAT (COM(87) 324 final, 10/11/87).

The EC has also developed a series of ancillary measures to promote literature and reading:

- a Resolution adopted by the Council and the Ministers responsible for Cultural Affairs on 18/5/89 concerning the promotion of books and reading (OJ C 183/1 dated 20/7/89);
- a pilot scheme to provide financial aid for the translation of contemporary literary works (OJ C 86, dated 3/4/91); and
- grants for the development of a network of translation colleges (Straelen, Arles, Tarazona, Procida, Norwich).

The EC's linguistic diversity represents a cultural treasure which must be safeguarded. It also, however, constitutes a significant obstacle to the circulation of and access to literature. There are therefore two further reasons for the Community to give priority to supporting translation as one of the best ways of promoting cultural exchanges, while preserving the originality of the artistic and literary creativity of our different countries.

Community support for translation takes the following forms:

- support for the translation of a greater number of literary works;
- paying greater attention to minority languages;
- greater focus on the different literary genres, in particular, those which are less widely published (drama and poetry);
- setting up specific operations to increase knowledge and improve dissemination of European culture and history;
- promoting quality, notably through exchanges of experience between translators by means of networking;
- extending the scope of existing schemes to the countries of Central and Eastern Europe, mainly under the cultural clauses in association agreements; and
- helping to increase public awareness of the wealth and cultural value of our various languages; this is essential if translation is to have a real impact in commercial or cultural terms.

iii The Audio-visual Sector

The audio-visual media play a major and increasing role in promoting and disseminating contemporary culture and the development of artistic creativity. There is therefore increasing disquiet throughout the Community about the quantity of low-grade American crud shown on television and at the cinemas, and heavily promoted in all audio-visual formats. This disquiet concerns not only damage that this is causing to the local audio-visual industry but the overall effect this "cultural imperialism" is having on European culture in general. On the purely economic front, Joe Kennedy, the father of President Kennedy, pointed out in the early 1930s the important role American films played in promoting the concept of the desirability of American goods in export markets. That was before the days of "character merchandising" and the flood of products carrying logos and representations of characters associated with films or television series.

The cultural aspects of the audio-visual sector have already been considered within the EC's audio-visual policy - particularly in the MEDIA Programme, which is involved both upstream and downstream of the production process. There is still a very real need for more specific Community action to promote artistic and cultural creativity in the audio-visual sector and for increased support in promoting both the European culture and the cultures of the individual Member States and their various regions, in co-operation with all relevant international organisations.

The audio-visual sector has now been included in the top priority list for attention by the Council and the Ministers for Cultural Affairs.

The Cultural Aspect of Other EC Policies

The Community has already attempted to incorporate the cultural dimension into a growing number of measures as part of other programmes, including the free movement of cultural goods and persons, the environment, research, the new technologies, social and regional policies, tourism, training and external policies. Specific measures include:

- audio-visual policy (COM (90) 78 final, dated 21/2/90); and
- VAT (COM(88) 846 final and COM(87) 324 final, dated 10/11/87).

On the sensitive issue of protecting national treasures, efforts have been made to take account of the cultural dimension at every stage of the discussions (COM(91) 447 final, SYN 382).

The Commission feels that by focusing on economies of scale and the exemplary function of Community action on this front, even with relatively limited financial resources, this could have a significant impact.

The International Role of Culture

The increasing role of culture in international relations involving the EC and its Member States demonstrates that the Community is no longer perceived on the world stage purely as an economic power.

The cultural breakthrough has been demonstrated by the inclusion of cultural co-operation in a number of agreements signed by the EC and its Member States with non-member countries.

The Third Lomé Convention, signed in December 1984 by the EC and the ACP countries, was the first to give culture a new status by including a section largely given over to cultural co-operation. Its successor, Lomé IV, which came into force in 1990, includes a title on culture with two distinct but closely linked chapters: one on the cultural dimension in development projects and programmes (Articles 142 to 144), and the other, on support for cultural action (Articles 145 et seq.). The Lomé Convention and ACP/EC cultural co-operation are aimed at supporting the self-reliant development of the ACP countries and to encourage their participation in the development process and increase their creative capacities.
The relative importance of cultural co-operation in some of the agreements concluded by the EC and individual Member States with non-member countries is particularly noteworthy for those Latin American countries linked to the EC by third-generation agreements. Progress in the cases of Asia, North America and Australia is more modest, however.

Overall cultural co-operation in Europe has changed decisively since the major political events which marked the opening-up of the EC to the countries of Central and Eastern Europe. Existing cultural affinities between the participants have facilitated this dialogue. This co-operation is part of the process of European integration in the broadest sense of the term. On 16 December 1991, association agreements were concluded between the EC and the Member States and Poland, Hungary and Czechoslovakia which include cultural clauses providing for the possible extension of existing EC co-operation programmes to those countries.

The EFTA countries have already shown interest in participating in EC cultural actions and programmes, and are becoming increasingly involved in joint programmes e.g. the joint declaration on co-operation in the field of culture and the joint declaration on unlawful trading in cultural goods.

The EC also aims to develop co-operation with non-member states within the international organisations active in the field of culture. There are three main organisations which are being targeted:

i The Council of Europe, constituting as it does an important forum for dialogue with the other European countries, has a major role to play in cultural co-operation in Europe.

ii UNESCO has been using cultural co-operation in its attempt to help defend the values of humanism and peace in the world for a number of years now; EC cultural action is being integrated into this approach.

iii Finally, specialised non-governmental organisations are being called upon to play a greater part as advisors and mediators in international cultural co-operation. The EC must encourage such organisations to participate more fully in the development of its actions.

Exciting times for cultural activity in the Community should lie ahead once the full implications of the Maastricht Treaty have been absorbed. The new Article 92(3)(d) says, "Aid to promote culture and heritage conservation where such aid does not affect trading conditions and competition in the Community to an extent that is contrary to the common interest ... shall be compatible with the common market." It is to be hoped that the spirit of this ideal will be embraced enthusiastically and that imaginative new programmes designed to involve an ever-increasing number of the citizens of the Union will be developed as a matter of priority.

Chapter 27

Cultural Grants

Cultural grants fall within the following programmes:

1. Pilot Projects to Conserve the EC's Architectural Heritage
2. Training in Restoration Techniques
3. The Media Programme
   - 3.1 EAVE: European Audio-visual Entrepreneurs
   - 3.2 Media Business School
   - 3.3 European Script Fund
   - 3.4 SOURCES: Stimulating Outstanding Resources for Creative European Screen Writing
   - 3.5 Documentary
   - 3.6 Cartoon
   - 3.7 Media Investment Club
   - 3.8 SCALE: Small Countries Improve their Audio-visual Level in Europe
   - 3.9 EFDO: European Film Distribution Office
   - 3.10 EVE: Espace Video Européen
   - 3.11 GRECO: Groupement Européen Pour La Circulation Des Oeuvres
   - 3.12 EURO AIM: European Association for an Audio-Visual Independent Market
   - 3.13 BABEL: Broadcasting Across the Barriers of European Language
   - 3.14 Media Salles
   - 3.15 Europa Cinemas
   - 3.16 EFA: European Film Academy
   - 3.17 MAP-TV: Memory-Archives-Programmes TV
   - 3.18 Lumière Project Association
   - 3.19 Euro Media Guarantees
4. Town Twinning
5. KALEIDOSCOPE: Artistic and Cultural Events

6. European City of Culture
7. European Cultural Month
8. Projects Based on European Parliament Resolutions
9. Translation of Contemporary Literary Works
10. Grants and Travel Allowances for Courses at Literary Translation Colleges, College Networks
11. European Literature Prize and European Translation Prize.
12. The European Prize for Architecture
13. YFE: Youth for Europe: Exchange Activities for 15-25 year olds

1. PILOT PROJECTS TO CONSERVE THE EC'S ARCHITECTURAL HERITAGE

Statutory Basis

The initiative is the result of several European Parliament Resolutions, the most recent of which was published in OJ C 261, dated, 10/10/92. The initiative is based on Council Resolution 86/C 320/01, dated 13/11/86 (OJ C 320/1, dated 13/12/86).

Objectives

The two main objectives are to increase awareness of the importance of the preservation, improvement and promotion of Europe's architectural heritage by creating and publicising exemplary projects and to encourage the development of similar initiatives.

Background

The Commission established a first scheme in 1984 which called for support for pilot projects to conserve European architectural heritage.

Programme Content

In Communication 88/C 308/04 (OJ C 308/3, dated 3/12/88) the Commission presented a four-year plan in which each year is devoted to a particular aspect. The theme for 1992 was the restoration of public spaces in historic centres and their integration into the contemporary life of the area.

The theme for 1993 was the conservation and restoration of historic gardens, which are regarded as having the status of a monument. This applied to landscaped creations considered to be of public interest for either their historical or artistic merit.

Guidelines published in OJ C 284, dated 31/10/91 specify the following conditions:

- all projects must fall within the theme for the year and demonstrate, by the quality of the proposed study and conservation techniques to be used, that they merit the Commission's financial support;
- the monuments and open spaces concerned must be open to the public; and
- financial support is confined to conservation work.

Each year, additional projects on the conservation of architectural and cultural heritage are carried out, depending on the budget available. Since 1991, these initiatives have included emblematic restoration actions, training programmes and scholarships, colloquia, seminars, exhibitions, etc.

Participation

The Programme is open to national, regional and local authorities, private associations and individuals.

Status Report

The notice in respect of 1993 was published in OJ C 261, dated 10/10/92 and is now closed to applications.

The 1994 scheme will focus on the conservation and restoration of historic buildings and/or sites related to theatres, cinemas, opera houses, concert halls etc.

Applications

Owners of relevant sites or their agents should make their applications to the Commission at the end of January each year, sending a copy to their nominated national organisation.

Application forms are available from the organisations listed below and from the Commission's offices.

INFORMATION

UK

England
English Heritage
Fortress House
23-25 Saville Row
London W1X 1AB
Tel: 071 973 3849
Fax: 071 973 3001

Wales
CADW
Brunel House
2 Fitzalan Road
Cardiff CF2 1UY
Tel: 0222 465511
Fax: 0222 450859

Scotland
Historic Scotland
20 Brandon Street
Edinburgh EH3 5RA

Northern Ireland
Historic Monuments and Buildings Branch
5-33 Hill Street
Belfast BT1 2LA

IRELAND
Office of Public Works
Director of National Monuments and Historic Properties
51 St Stephen's Green
Dublin 2
Tel: 01 661 31 11
Fax: 01 661 07 47

COMMISSION
Commission of the European Communities
DG X - Culture
200 rue de la Loi
B-1049 Brussels
Tel: INT+ 322 299 1111 (exchange)
Fax: INT+ 322 299 9283

2. TRAINING IN RESTORATION TECHNIQUES

Background

From the outset, the Commission has recognised the link between the problems of conserving Europe's architectural heritage and the availability of adequate vocational training in conservation and restoration techniques. Although this programme is conducted on a fairly small scale, it generates a considerable ripple effect.

Programme Content

Every year the Commission allocates a lump sum to international institutions specialising in restoration, which then use these funds to award grants to young craftsmen, architects, town planners, archaeologists and art historians undertaking advanced training courses.

Participation

Initially awarded only to EC nationals, these grants are now available to nationals of all European countries.

Applications

Specialist training organisations are required to submit a detailed programme of their courses together with a list of proposed participants, some of which must be from other countries.

INFORMATION

Commission of the European Communities
Cultural Action Division - DG X
200 rue de la Loi
B-1049 Brussels
Tel: INT+ 322 299 1111 (exchange)

3. THE MEDIA PROGRAMME

Statutory Basis

Council Decision 90/685/EEC of 21/12/90 concerning the implementation of the MEDIA Programme (OJ L 380, dated 31/12/90)

Objectives

The MEDIA Programme is scheduled to run for five years from 1 January 1991, and contains five priority areas for the audio-visual industry:

i creating a European audio-visual area;

ii setting up professional synergies;

iii mobilising "seed capital";

iv maintaining a balance between market forces; and

v maintaining a balance between the various media.

EC Contribution

An estimated budget of 200 MECU has been set aside for the five-year programme.

Programme Content

There are six current action lines, as described below:

i Professional training in the industry

ii Improving production opportunities

iii The improvement of distribution mechanisms

iv The promotion of cinema and European films

v Contributions to the Establishment of a "Second Market"

vi The stimulation of investment in the industry

ACTION LINE I: PROFESSIONAL TRAINING IN THE INDUSTRY

3.1 EAVE: European Audio-Visual Entrepreneurs

EAVE's objective is to provide professional training for European cinema and television producers to develop genuine European co-productions, to create a pan-European network for producers and to disseminate its expertise as widely as possible.

The EAVE training cycle entails three intensive eight-day sessions during the course of a year, each session taking place in a different European country. The programme for the sessions is based on the development of some 25 production projects presented by the participants, analysed and followed up at each stage by experts in the field of script, budgeting, marketing, contracts, financing and packaging.

Participation in EAVE is open to independent European producers with projects in the development phase and for candidates without projects who have creative potential and commitment to the audio-visual field.

EAVE requires registration and participation fees for the candidates selected amounting to 1000 ECU for participants without a project and 2000 ECU for participants with a project. Participants also have to pay for their own travel and accommodation expenses during the sessions.

3.2 Media Business School

The aim of the MEDIA Business School is to provide the European audio-visual sector with a formula and strategies designed to help take advantage of the opportunities offered by the single European market.

The MEDIA Business School designs projects "a la carte" on financial, legal, commercial and technical aspects of the audio-visual industry. Projects are designed to target different segments of the profession in the areas of film, television and video. Professionals can submit training projects or can participate in existing activities.

The Business School can contribute up to half the cost of approved projects in training, research and development.

ACTION LINE II: IMPROVING PRODUCTION OPPORTUNITIES

3.3 European Script Fund

The European Script Fund lends money to producers and writers across the EC for the development of fiction on film and television. The European Script Fund is looking for strong stories which can appeal across one or more European borders.

Those eligible to participate are large established production companies, small independent producers, broadcasters and individual writers from the EC Member States, Austria and Switzerland.

SCRIPT loans do not normally exceed 37,500 ECU.

Application forms are available in ten languages. Completed applications accompanied by treatments of draft scripts are welcomed all year round.

3.4 SOURCES: Stimulating Outstanding Resources for Creative European Screen Writing

SOURCES aims to create inspiring and stimulating training workshops for professional screenwriters during the development stage of their scripts for film and television in Europe.

SOURCES offers two series of workshops for different phases within the development of a script:

i treatment phase: workshop for writers; and

ii full draft phase: workshop for writers; producers will be asked to attend a specific part of the workshop.

In addition to the workshops, SOURCES initiates the following activities:

- mediation between individual screenwriters and script analysts;
- establishing a database on schools and courses in the field of screen writing; and
- limited participation in activities that stimulate European screen writing.

The participation fee for the treatment workshop (two sessions) is 1,000 ECU, including accommodation and meals. Participants pay their own travel expenses.

3.5 Documentary

This project aims to promote the status of film and television documentaries as creative works in their own right as distinct from TV-journalism and information films.

Loans are available to stimulate the professional industry in both the development and fund-raising phases and the marketing and exhibition phase.

For project development, loans of up to 15,000 ECU, representing a maximum of half the global development budget can be allocated in order to assist research on projects and increase their opportunities for attracting further national and international funding.

For promotion packaging, loans of up to 5,000 ECU, representing a maximum of half the global promotion budget, can be given to finished films or programmes so as to help establish international promotion packages.

Independent producers and film-makers acting as producers in Member States are eligible to participate.

3.6 Cartoon

CARTOON's activities are directed towards developing cartoon production capacities in Europe.

CARTOON's activities cover all the professionals in the industry: authors, producers, directors, technicians and studio directors, as well as their co-production partners, the television stations.

Various forms of aid are available.

- Pre-Production Aid: there are two sessions per year starting on 31 March and 31 October, accessible to industry professionals who can submit proposals for animation projects lasting at least 50 minutes in order to be eligible for a grant for graphics research, for script writing or for the film plot. Pre-production aid varies from 5,000 to 35,000 ECU.
- Studio Groupings: this is financial aid given over a period of three years to groups of at least three studios which are permanent structures in different European countries so as to enable them to increase their creative potential and their financial and production capacities. Aid varies from 300,000 to 600,000 ECU for three years.
- Training: this is financial aid organised by studios for professional training, and aimed at overcoming the skills shortage in the animation industry in Europe. The level of training aid varies according to the type of training, with a maximum of 35,000 ECU.
- Cartoon Forum: this aims to improve co-productions and speed up financial arrangements for European cartoon productions. Projects, which must have a minimum duration of 26 minutes, can be submitted by European producers who are members of CARTOON, and whose business is established in Europe. The projects must involve co-operation between at least two European countries, and must be accompanied by an expression of interest from a recognised television channel.
- Database: the CARTOON MEDIABASE is free, accessible to all animation industry professionals and provides information on studios, production companies, on-going projects, television channels etc.

3.7 Media Investment Club

The aim of MEDIA Investment Club is to promote audio-visual creation and production by means of advanced technologies. It intervenes in three main areas:

i applications in the audio-visual field of digital and computer techniques;

ii the production of programmes in European standard High Definition video; and

iii the production of interactive multi-media programmes.

The Club is intended for professionals involved in the creation of programmes which use new techniques: audio-visual production companies, publishers, broadcasters and distributors, as well as industrialists and financial partners.

The Club launches priority lines of action:

- it initiates and runs activities in the form of European Calls for Projects;
- COMPUTER CARTOON is a call for European projects for the development of computer animation software, run in collaboration with CARTOON; and

- it develops training courses and circulates information.

Financial investment is negotiated on a case-by-case basis.

3.8 SCALE: Small Countries Improve their Audio-Visual Level in Europe

SCALE provides support to existing European audio-visual programmes, to new initiatives or production companies which propose to introduce programmes of action which will benefit the audio-visual industries of small countries.

SCALE will provide a resource centre for the audio-visual industries of the smaller European countries; its objective is to provide incentives for Development Pools, Co-production Pools, Marketing Pools, Information and Research. The Resource Centre will also run specific actions.

SCALE can provide up to half the costs of supported projects.

Rules and application forms for grant systems implemented by SCALE will be available at MEDIA desks.

ACTION LINE III: THE IMPROVEMENT OF DISTRIBUTION MECHANISMS

3.9 EFDO: European Film Distribution Office

EFDO aims to assist the distribution of European theatrical films from the Member States, Austria, Finland, Iceland, Norway, Sweden and Poland.

EFDO supports the distribution of European films when at least three distributors from three different participating countries agree to exhibit the film. The production budget for these films must not exceed 4.5 MECU.

EFDO's distribution aid is granted directly to the distributors who release the European films to the cinemas in their countries, and covers up to half of the distribution costs. Each distribution company can receive a maximum of 100,000 ECU per film for its distribution territory. These funds are made available in the form of conditionally repayable loans.

Applications must be submitted to the EFDO Office by 1 April and 1 November each year.

3.10 EVE: Espace Video Européen

EVE's aim is to establish and promote systems which encourage the publication and distribution of European audio-visual works in all formats intended primarily for use in the domestic environment, such as video, video disc etc.

This is to be achieved by a number of measures:

i Feature Film Loan Scheme: With three deadlines per year, this scheme provides loans of up to 40% of the publication and distribution costs for contemporary European fiction films. Three countries must apply together and the scheme functions both as a "soft" loan and a guarantee fund. These loans must not exceed 25,000 ECU.

ii Documentary Film Loan Scheme: this scheme functions broadly along the lines of the Feature Film Loan Scheme, but applications can be accepted from only two countries under certain conditions. The loans must not exceed 15,000 ECU for single films but there are special provisions for up to 30,000 ECU to be made available for collections.

iii Classic Film Scheme: this is dedicated to the exploitation of the heritage of European Film. It functions in a manner similar to the other loan schemes with loans up to 15,000 ECU for individual films and 30,000 ECU for collections.

iv Regroupment Scheme: this aims to foster the development of cross-border co-operation between European countries, the strengthening of distribution infrastructure and to promote the reinvestment of the financial and technical expertise of the publication sector into production. It operates through partnership with professionals, MEDIA initiatives and others. The initial grant for cross-border groupings is 7,000 ECU.

v MEDIABASE and Information Services Conferences: through the creation of a computerised database, the publication of industry reviews and the provision of consultancy services, EVE encourages all sectors to exploit the resources of the video market.

vi New Technology & Development: EVE initiates experimental actions and research in the areas of new technology and disseminates the results.

3.11 GRECO: Groupement Européen Pour La Circulation Des Oeuvres

GRECO aims to promote the circulation of high quality television fiction. It is designed for independent producers from the EC, the associated countries which contribute to the fund's finances via the EUREKA audio-visual programme and other associated countries. Those producers must warrant the contribution of at least three broadcasters from three different linguistic zones and must possess the distribution rights to the works supported.

Financial support cannot exceed 12.5% of the total budget with an absolute limit of 2.5 MECU. These amounts are to be reimbursed from the first returns at a rate of at least 25% of the producer's net returns. A 5% success bonus may be charged to top up the fund.

3.12 EURO AIM: European Association for an Audio-Visual Independent Market

EURO AIM is a service and support structure for the promotion and marketing of European independent productions.

Its activities are open to independent European production and distribution companies. It provides them with links to the potential partners necessary for the financing, marketing and distribution of their work.

EURO AIM supports the following markets and events:

- EURO AIM Umbrellas at MIP-TV/MIPCOM: in April and October each year, the EURO AIM Umbrella offers more than a hundred independent European companies access to these markets on reasonable terms through the use of a group stand of more than 600m.sq. Interested participants must make their own applications direct to EURO AIM, and the deadlines are February for MIP-TV, and August for MIPCOM. Companies selected pay 5,000 FF. (750 ECU) for one delegate or 9,000 FF. (1350 ECU) for two, which is the maximum.

- EURO AIM Screenings Donostia: this is an annual showcase screening of recent European independent productions to an invited audience of a hundred international buyers. Companies enter productions by sending EURO AIM an entry form and a viewing cassette. There is no charge for these screenings, but producers or distributors of programmes selected who would like to attend the event pay a registration fee of 290 ECU.

- Rendez-Vous - Finance & Co-production: this international gathering brings together the producers of around a hundred European fiction projects seeking finance and/or co-production partners, and as many as a hundred financial decision-makers. There is no charge for entering a project but any project selected is charged a fee of 1,000 ECU.

- Other Markets: Monte Carlo, Berlin, Cannes, etc.: EURO AIM takes stands at many of the major European film and TV markets, providing a meeting place for independents and promoting its services, especially the databases. There is no charge for using the EURO AIM stand at these markets, but companies must register directly with the organisers.

EURO AIM offers the following services:

- Production Mediabase: this is a database of more than 7,000 European independent productions designed to facilitate buyers' searches for programming within wide ranging parameters. Producers or distributors may enter their productions by completing a questionnaire. This Mediabase can be consulted at all markets attended by EURO AIM or by letter, fax or telephone to the Brussels office.

- Producers' Mediabase: this database offers profiles of more than 1,100 European independent production companies, established to help producers find the most appropriate, potential partners in Europe for their projects. Companies enter their profiles by completing a questionnaire. This Mediabase can be consulted at all markets attended by EURO AIM or by letter, fax or telephone to the Brussels office.

- Marketing Consultancy Service: European independents with specific questions about marketing and distribution may write to EURO AIM (c/o EURO AIM Consultants).

- AD Scheme: this aims to assist European independent companies in advertising their productions and in establishing market presence. The fund reimburses up to half the costs of placing advertisements in trade publications or display advertising at the event itself.
- Rendez-Vous Service: this operates all year round for the producers whose projects have been selected. There is no charge for entering a project but, once selected, there is a fee of 500 ECU per project per year.

3.13 BABEL: Broadcasting Across the Barriers of European Language

The aim of BABEL is to promote the wider distribution of television programmes by providing financial support for dubbing and/or subtitling, by conducting training operations and by collaborating in research into developing techniques associated with multilingual production.

BABEL's support is intended mainly for productions in less widely spoken languages or for transfer from and into these languages. BABEL's activities also include training in the multilingual audio-visual sphere and research into new technologies.

Requests for assistance in the form of returnable advances for dubbing and/or subtitling are granted when production of the programme, or the pilot in the case of a series, has been completed. Reimbursements are made at the rate of 10% of the rights payment for each broadcast until the whole of the advance has been repaid.

The advances granted by BABEL cannot exceed the sum invested by the applicant in dubbing or subtitling, and are subject to a maximum of 30,000 ECU for dubbing and 7,500 ECU for subtitling.

Action Line iv: The promotion of cinema and European films

3.14 Media Salles

MEDIA SALLES reinforces the action of the MEDIA Programme in the field of film distribution. It acts by proposing initiatives within the fields of:

- promotion for the cinema and European films;
- information addressed to cinema exhibitors as well as their professional or political partners; and
- the training of the professionals particularly in marketing skills and introducing initiatives to increase young people's interest in films.

The MEDIA SALLES' budget for 1993 was 600,000 ECU.

3.15 Europa Cinemas

This aims to promote the showing of European films in key EC cities and to increase their audience by improving the way in which they are presented to the public.

The following may apply:

- competitive first-release cinemas situated in capitals and key cities; and
- cinemas which operate policies of actively favouring European films and have included a proportion of at least 40% new European films in their total screenings of new films over the previous twelve months.

This programme provides exhibitors with technical and financial support so that they can develop their programming, promotion and in-house activities.

The exhibitor will have to finance at least half of the cost of these actions. The maximum amount of aid is 30,000 ECU per year, per cinema or group of cinemas.

3.16 EFA: European Film Academy

The European Film Academy was founded in Berlin on 30 November 1991 to promote European cinema world-wide and strengthen its commercial and artistic position, to improve knowledge and awareness of European cinema and to provide a forum for passing on the experience of the Members of the Academy to the younger generation of film professionals.
The EFA is a meeting place for Europe's film makers. It is currently made up of 85 active members, eight honorary members and eight associated members. It promotes meetings between Europe's film professionals, organises Master classes for young professionals, symposia and film screenings for the general public and produces publications. At its foundation, it took over responsibility for the organisation of the European Film Awards.

The EFA carries out its projects in close co-operation with co-production partners at the project location and is able to contribute up to half the costs involved in project financing. The exception to this is the European Film Awards which are financed through a separate budget.

Action Line v: Contribution to the Establishment of a "Second Market"

3.17 MAP-TV: Memory-Archives-Programmes TV

MAP-TV's objective is to enhance the value of the European audio-visual archives, particularly by assisting co-productions of creative programmes using archive-based materials.

Independent producers looking for European partners to co-produce archive-based programmes, broadcasters interested in these programmes and archive holders wishing to publicise their holdings may become members of the Association. It is not necessary to become a member to apply for a development grant, however.

MAP-TV acts like a club, facilitating communication among its members and circulating their programme proposals, thus allowing them to set up co-productions together.

Financial aid can be available, worth up to 7.5% of the estimated programme budget with a maximum of 40,000 ECU, providing that the applicants and their partners undertake to contribute an equal amount to the financing of the development phase.

3.18 Lumière Project Association

The Lumière Project Association is intended to help European film archives whose main goal is the protection and preservation of film heritage.

The project has the following objectives:

- the physical preservation and restoration of European film heritage;
- the research and publication of a European filmography;
- the creation of a database containing the holdings of European film archives;
- the identification of and search for, lost films; and
- the promotion and presentation of restored films, ploughing back any benefits into further preservation work.

The maximum grant for a preservation/restoration/promotion project eligible for financial support from the Lumière Project Association is half the qualifying part of the project's budget. The maximum grant available for a restoration project is 30,000 ECU, but an extra sum may be awarded at the request of the applicant for large or especially complex projects. This applies particularly to projects associated with the Centenary of Cinema celebrations.

Action Line vi: The stimulation of investment in the industry

3.19 Euro Media Guarantees

European film and TV productions require proper finance, particularly for larger budget productions. EURO MEDIA GUARANTEES was founded to provide financial guarantees and to link up the audio-visual production sector with sources of finance right across Europe.

It is aimed at European independent producers and the financial institutions providing loans for audio-visual productions.

Applications for finance are addressed to the co-ordinator and guarantees are given according to the financial and commercial feasibility of the proposed project. Co-producers from at least three European countries must be involved and distribution should already be arranged in at least these three countries.

In principle, up to 70% of the loan finance could be guaranteed depending on the nature of the production and the total guarantee fund available.

INFORMATION

UK

England -Media Desk UK
Mrs Louise Casey
21 Stephen Street
London W1P 1PL
Tel: 071 255 1444
Fax: 071 436 7950

Wales - Media Antenna Cardiff
Mr Robin Hughes
Ty Oldfield
Liantrisant Road
Llandaf
Cardiff CF52 PU
Tel: 0222 57 23 07
Fax: 0222 57 26 01

Scotland - Media Antenna Glasgow
Mrs Margaret O'Connor
74 Victoria Crescent Road
Glasgow G12 9JN
Tel: 041 334 4445
Fax: 041 334 8132

Ireland -Media Desk Ireland
Mrs Siobhan O'Donoghue
6 Eustace Street
Dublin 2
Tel: 01 679 57 44
Fax: 01 679 96 57

IRELAND -Media Antenna Galway
Mrs Dairena Ni Chinneide
4-5 High Street
Galway
Tel: 091 672 62
Fax: 091 667 28

COMMISSION
Commission of the European Communities
Directorate-General Audio-visual, Information, Communication, & Culture
120 Rue de Trèves
B-1040 Brussels
Tel: INT+ 322 299 9436
Fax: INT+ 322 299 9214

EAVE
Mr Raymond Ravar, Managing Director, Head of Programmes,
EAVE
14 rue de la Presse
B-1000 Brussels:
Tel: INT+ 322 219 0920
Fax: INT+ 322 223 0034

Media Business School
Mr Fernando Labrada, General Manager
MEDIA Business School
10 Torre Galindo
E-28016 Madrid
Tel: INT+ 341 359 0247/0036
Fax: INT+ 341 345 7606

European Script Fund
Mr Bo Christensen, Director-General
Mrs Renee Goddard, Secretary General
European Script Fund
39c Highbury Place
London N5 1QP
Tel: 071 226 9903
Fax: 071 354 2706

Sources
Mr Dick Willemsen, Secretary-General
Mrs Margot Knijn, Project Director
MEDIA-SOURCES
92 Jan Luykenstraat
NL-1071 CT Amsterdam
Tel: INT+ 3120 672 08 01
Fax: INT+ 3120 672 0399

Documentary
Mr Thomas Stenderup, Secretary-General
MEDIA-DOCUMENTARY
29a Skindergade
DK-1159 Copenhagen K
Tel: INT+ 4533 15 00 99
Fax: INT+ 4533 15 76 76

Media Investment Club
Mr Patrick Madelin, Secretary General
Media Investment Club
4 avenue de l'Europe
F-94366 Bry-sur-Marne Cedex
Tel: INT+ 331 4983 2863/3272
Fax: INT+ 331 4983 2582

EFDO
Dieter Kosslick, Chairman
Ute Schneider, Secretary-General
Media-EFDO
14-16 Friedensallee
D-2000 Hamburg 50
Tel: INT+ 4940 390 9025
Fax: INT+ 4940 390 6249

MEDIABASE
Bruno Gosse
Mediabase Espace Video Europeen
Mediatheque de la Communauté Francaise de Belgique
18 Place Eugene Flagey
B-1050 Brussels
Tel: INT+ 322 640 3815
Fax: INT+ 322 640 0291

EURO AIM
Mr Nicolas Steil, General Director
Karol Kulik, Market Director
EURO AIM
210 Avenue Winston Churchill
B-1180 Brussels
Tel: INT+ 322 346 1500
Fax: INT+ 322 346 3842

Media Salles
Mrs Elisabetta Brunella
MEDIA SALLES
24 Piazza Luigi di Savoia
I-20124 Milano
Tel: INT+ 392 669 0241
Fax: INT+ 392 669 1574

Cartoon
Mrs Corinne Jenart, Director
MEDIA-CARTOON
Mr Marc Vandeweyer, General Secretary
418 Boulevard Lambermont
B-1030 Brussels
Tel: INT+ 322 245 1200
Fax: INT+ 322 245 4689

SCALE
Mr Artur Castro Neves, General Secretary
Media-SCALE
Rua D Joao V 8-R/C Dto
P-1200 Lisboa
Tel: INT+ 3511 386 06 30/386 09 82
Fax: INT+ 3511 386 06 47

EVE
Espace Video Europeen
The Irish Film Institute
6 Eustace Street
Dublin 2
Tel: 01 679 5744
Fax: 01 679 9657

GRECO
Mr Robert Strasser, Secretary General
Mrs Marietta von Uechtritz, Co-ordinator
Media-GRECO
Bahnhofstrasse 33
D-85774 Unterfoehring bei Muenchen
Tel: INT+ 4989 95 08 32 90
Fax: INT+ 4989 95 08 32 92

BABEL
Mr Frank Naef, Co-ordinator
c/o UER/EBU
17a Ancienne Route
67 Case Postale
Ch-1218 Grand Saconnex (Geneva)
Tel: INT+ 4122 717 2111
Fax: INT+ 4122 798 5897

Europa Cinemas
Mr Claude-Eric Poiroux, Chairman
Sylvie Peyre, Co-ordinator
EUROPA CINEMAS
10 rue Auber
F-75009 Paris
Tel: INT+ 331 40 17 07 74
Fax: INT+ 331 40 17 06 47

European Film Academy (EFA)
Mrs Aina Bellis, Secretary General
EFA
Katharinenstrasse 8
D-1000 Berlin 31
Tel: INT+ 4930 893 4132
Fax: INT+ 4930 893 4134

Memory Archives Programmes TV (MAP-TV)
Mr J J Lemoine/Mrs A J Hindhaugh
c/o France 3
Place de Bordeaux
F-67005 Strasbourg Cedex
Tel: INT+ 3388 56 68 46
Fax: INT+ 3388 56 68 49

Lumière Project Association
Mr Jose Manuel Costa, President
MEDIA-LUMIÈRE
Rua Bernardo Lima, 35-5
P-1000 Lisboa
Tel: INT+ 3511 57 09 65/57
Tel: INT+ 3511 57 08 97/25
Fax: INT+ 3511 57 06 67

Euro Media Guarantees
Mrs Sylvie DuPont, Co-ordinator
EURO MEDIA Guarantees
66 Rue Pierre Charron
F-75008 Paris
Tel: INT+ 331 43 59 88 03
Fax: INT+ 331 45 63 85 58

4. TOWN TWINNING

Background

The Preamble to the Treaty of Rome states that EC Member States are "determined to lay the foundations of an ever closer union among the peoples of Europe". That objective formed the basis of the report adopted by the European Parliament in 1988 (EP document A2-0312/87) which emphasised the need for the Community to expand town twinning, and the EP insisted that funds should be provided in the Community budget for town twinning throughout the EC.

Programme Content

Funding is to be used to help overcome problems impeding the extension of town twinning such as the distances involved, language difficulties and problems arising because of the small size and lack of resources of so many towns.

The support consists of contributions towards travel expenses in attending town twinning meetings, the organisational costs and the costs incurred by the host town in providing subsistence and entertainment for the visitors.

Participation

The following have first call on EC support:

- new twinnings;
- twinned towns which are disadvantaged because of their geographical location, because their languages are not widely used, or because their countries have only recently joined the EC;
- small twinned towns; and

- multilateral exchanges between broadly-based, representative groups from towns in several different Member States.

Five per cent of the total appropriation has been set aside to encourage twinning between towns in the EC and towns in the Central and Eastern European countries participating in the programme: Bulgaria, Hungary, Poland, Romania, the Czech Republic, Slovakia and Slovenia.

Applications

Applications must be made by the host community.

Applications must reach the Commission at least three months before the date on which the event starts. There are two different forms: form 1, for exchanges between towns, and form 2, for conferences and seminars. Both are available from:

- the Secretariat-General of the Commission in Brussels;
- the offices of the European Commission or Parliament in the Member States; and
- national or European twinning organisations such as the Council of European Municipalities and Regions or the United Towns Organisation and their national sections.

Addresses can be found in Appendix 2.

The Commission will only accept one set of grant applications per twinning relationship in each calendar year, allowing one visit each way.

INFORMATION

UK
Local Government International Bureau
35 Great Smith Street
London SW1P 3BJ
Tel: 071 222 1636
Fax: 071 233 2179

COMMISSION
Commission of the European Communities
Secretariat-General - Town-Twinning
200 rue de la Loi
B-1049 Brussels
Tel: INT+ 322 295 2685
Fax: INT+ 322 296 2389

5. KALEIDOSCOPE: Artistic and Cultural Events Programme

Statutory Basis

EC support is based on European Parliament Resolutions of 1982 and 1989 on architectural heritage in the EC.

Objectives

Set up in 1990, the aim of the KALEIDOSCOPE Programme is to promote greater public awareness of the culture and history of the European peoples including easier access to source materials, and to foster artistic and cultural co-operation among professional circles.

Background

Notice of the Kaleidoscope Programme was published in OJ C 205, dated 6/8/91.

Programme Content

The Programme was reorganised in 1993 to hinge on three distinct areas of activity as follows:

i Cultural events and activities with a distinct European dimension, i.e. activities in which partners from at least three Member States are involved as either organisers or participants. In 1993, priority was granted to theatrical events.

ii Encouragement of artistic and cultural creativity: this area concerns projects to increase the mobility and further development of creative artists, performers and other categories operating in the cultural sector.

iii Co-operation through networks: the aim here is to support forms of transnational co-operation between cultural bodies collaborating on an equal footing.

EC Contribution

Under the 1993 KALEIDOSCOPE Programme, a total of just under ECU 4 million has been awarded. Details of the 1994 budget are still awaited.

Applications

Application forms are available from the National Offices of the Commission.

INFORMATION

Commission
Commission of the European Communities
Directorate-General X C.1
200 rue de la Loi
B-1049 Brussels
Tel: INT+ 322 299 1111.(exchange)
Fax: INT+ 322 299 9283

6. EUROPEAN CITY OF CULTURE

Statutory Basis

Resolution 85/C 153/02 of the Culture Ministers meeting within the Council on 13/6/85: OJ C 153/2, dated 22/6/85.

Background

The European City of Culture event was established by the Ministers with responsibility for cultural policy in the various Member States meeting as the Cultural Council. The objective was to "help bring the peoples of the Member States closer together", promote cultural activity, and stimulate cultural exchanges in the countries, regions and cities concerned.

Programme Content

The first cycle of one city from each Member State will be completed by 1996. The following cities have been selected:

1985: Athens

1986: Florence

1987: Amsterdam

1988: Berlin

1989: Paris

1990: Glasgow

1991: Dublin

1992: Madrid

1993: Antwerp

1994: Lisbon

1995: Luxembourg

1996: Copenhagen

1997: Thessaloniki

After 1996, non-EC countries basing themselves on the principles of "democracy, pluralism and the rule of law" will be eligible to host the event.

The Ministers of Culture meeting within the Council on 18 May and 12 November 1992, decided on new criteria for selecting cities after the current round is completed. The new rules ensure that the event moves around not only from one Member State to another but around the regions, so that there is a fair balance between capitals and other cities.

EC Contribution

In 1992 the EC provided 200,000 ECU for the event.

Applications and Information

General enquiries about the eligibility of events for EC support should be made, in the first instance, to the appropriate national office of the Commission. (See Appendix 2)

7. EUROPEAN CULTURAL MONTH

Statutory Basis

Conclusions of the Culture Ministers' meeting within the Council on 18/5/90: OJ C 162, dated 3/7/90.

Objectives

The main aim is to enable cities in Central and Eastern Europe and EFTA to join with the cities in the EC in an event similar to the City of Culture.

Background

On 18 May 1990, at the suggestion of the Commission, the Council agreed to set up a new cultural initiative to be known as the European Cultural Month. It was planned initially to run for a trial period, to be held in a different European city each year, running parallel with the European City of Culture. It has since been extended, and it is hoped that it will become a permanent feature of the European cultural scene.

Programme Content

The first four host cities for the European Cultural Month are:

1992: Cracow

1993: Graz

1994: Budapest

1995: Prague

EC Contribution

In 1992, the EC provided a total of 150,000 ECU for the event in Cracow, which can probably be taken as a benchmark figure for future events.

Applications and Information

General enquiries about the eligibility of events for EC support should be made, in the first instance, to the appropriate national office of the Commission.

8. PROJECTS BASED ON EUROPEAN PARLIAMENT RESOLUTIONS

The EC launched its prestige projects at a time when it was endeavouring to establish its presence in the cultural sector by promoting a cultural programme of which the public was still largely unaware. The European Parliament lent its support to a number of these projects, such as:

- the European Community Youth Orchestra (Parliament Resolution of 28/3/76: OJ C 79, dated 5/4/76); in 1992 it received 420,000 ECU;
- the European Poetry Festival (Parliament Resolution of 16/12/83: OJ C 10, dated 16/1/84): in 1991, it received 25,000 ECU;
- the EC Baroque Orchestra, which was launched in 1985 to mark the European Year of Music; in 1992 it received 210,000 ECU; and
- the EC Youth Opera (Parliament Resolution of 20/5/88: OJ C 167, dated 27/6/88).

9. TRANSLATION OF CONTEMPORARY LITERARY WORKS

Statutory Basis

Commission Notice 93/C 5/08: OJ C 5 dated 9/1/93 gives details of the "pilot scheme to provide financial aid for translation of contemporary literary works".

Objectives

The aim of this pilot scheme is to promote the wider circulation of contemporary literary works representative of European culture.

Background

The scheme was launched in 1989 and is scheduled to run for a trial period of five years.

Programme Content

Assistance is granted for the translation of contemporary literary works, typical of the culture that produced them and likely to be of interest to a wide, European, reading public.

"Contemporary literary works" means literature first published in the twentieth century, preference being given to works first published later than 1945.

Priority will be given in descending order to the translation of:

- works written in one of the EC's minority languages, into the more widely spoken languages;
- works written in one of the EC's minority languages, into other minority languages;

- works written in a widely spoken EC language, into an EC minority language; and
- works written in a widely spoken EC language, into other widely spoken EC languages, the emphasis being on literature which has been less widely translated.

Assistance will be granted for works whose publication on the European market would not be viable without an EC grant.

It may also be granted for the translation of extracts from a literary work written in one of the minority languages so as to enable a publisher considering publishing it in translation but unable to read in the original, to evaluate its literary value and saleability more accurately.

EC Contribution

The grant will cover the full amount of the translator's fees, negotiated in accordance with standard practice in the country concerned. Works translated must be published within the year following the payment of the grant, and all advances must be repaid in the event of non-publication within this time limit.

Applications

The deadline for applications for the 1993 programme was 14 May, and similar dates can be expected in future years.

Application forms can be obtained from the addresses below.

INFORMATION

UK
Director of Literature
The Arts Council of Great Britain
14 Great Peter Street
London SW1P 3NQ
Tel: 071 333 0100
Fax: 071 973 6590

IRELAND
An Chomhairie Ealaion/ The Arts Council
70 Merrion Square
Dublin 2
Tel: 01 661 1840
Fax: 01 676 1302

COMMISSION
Commission of the European Communities
DG X Cultural Activities Division
Room 4/39
120 rue de Trèves
B-1049 Brussels
Tel: INT +322 299 1111 (exchange)

10. GRANTS and TRAVEL ALLOWANCES for COURSES at LITERARY TRANSLATION COLLEGES, COLLEGE NETWORKS

Background

In 1983, the Commission awarded an initial grant to the Europaisches Ubersetzer-Kollegium in Straelen, Germany; this was followed by the College International des Traducteurs Litteraires in Arles, France in 1987, the Collegio Italiano dei Traduttori Letterari in Procida, Italy, and the Casa del Traductor in Tarragona, Spain in 1989. The British Centre for Literary Translation at the University of East Anglia in Norwich was added to the list for annual funding in 1990.

The Commission allocates these colleges a lump sum each year which is then distributed by the institutions themselves in the form of grants for advanced literary translation courses.

EC Contribution

In 1992 the total budget was 180,000 ECU, shared among the five colleges as follows:

- Straelen (Germany) 40,000 ECU
- Arles (France) 40,000 ECU
- Taragona (Spain) 35,000 ECU
- Procida (Italy) 30,000 ECU
- Norwich (UK) 35,000 ECU

INFORMATION

COMMISSION
Commission of the European Communities
DG X Cultural Activities Division
120 rue de Trèves
B-1049 Brussels
Tel: INT +322 299 1111 (exchange)

11. EUROPEAN LITERATURE PRIZE and EUROPEAN TRANSLATION PRIZE

Statutory Basis

These prizes were created by the Council and Culture Ministers in May 1989 (OJ C 183, dated 20/7/89).

Programme Content

The rules and procedures are published in OJ C 35, dated 15/2/90.

These annual prizes are awarded on the recommendations of an independent panel, as part of the European City of Culture Event. Each Member State may nominate up to three translations for consideration by the European jury.

EC Contribution

The Commission's contribution to the organisation of these prizes is 350,000 ECU, which covers the prizes themselves - worth 20,000 ECU each - the prize giving event, administration and publicity costs.

Applications

A call for participation in these initiatives is published in the OJ once a year.

INFORMATION

Commission
Commission of the European Communities
Directorate-General X C.1
200 rue de la Loi
B-1049 Brussels
Tel: INT+ 322 299 1111 (exchange):
Fax: INT+ 322 299 9283

12 THE EUROPEAN PRIZE for ARCHITECTURE

Background

The purpose of this prize is to draw the attention of all those directly responsible for architecture and planning in the public, national and local authorities, to the cultural significance of modern architecture and its impact on the future development of European cities.

This prize, which is organised jointly by the Commission, Parliament and the Mies Van der Rohe Foundation, is awarded every two years.

EC Contribution

The winner receives 50,000 ECU and a trophy representing the Mies Van der Rohe Pavilion.

INFORMATION

COMMISSION
Commission of the European Communities
Directorate-General X C.1
200 rue de la Loi
B-1049 Brussels
Tel: INT +322 299 1111 (exchange)
Fax: INT+ 322 299 9283

13. YFE: YOUTH FOR EUROPE

Statutory Basis

Council Decision 91/395/EEC of 29/7/91: OJ L 217/25, dated 6/8/91.

Objectives

Youth for Europe (YFE) aims to promote exchanges and mobility of young people.

Background

An action programme for the promotion of youth exchanges in the EC began in 1988, under the title "YES for Europe", later changed to "Youth for Europe". The first phase of activity was for three years, ending on 31 December 1992, and the second phase is scheduled to run until 31 December 1994.

Programme Content

The following kinds of activity are supported.

Action I.1: Exchanges of Young People
YFE provides support towards exchange programmes for young people aged 15-25. These exchanges, based around a theme or project organised in young peoples' free time can be bilateral, trilateral or multinational. Each exchange package should involve between 16 and 60 young people, working together on a project lasting at least six full days.

For phase II of YFE, a third of the direct support to youth exchange activity has been reserved for exchanges involving disadvantaged young people.

Action I.2: Voluntary Service Activities
This is a pilot action to begin building a wide-ranging network of voluntary community service opportunities for young people. Although only 40 places will be created in the first year, it is hoped that the scheme will expand into a fuller framework programme by 1994-95. The pilot scheme will be co-ordinated by the Youth Bureau in Brussels.

Action I.3: Short Study Visits for Youth Workers
This offers youth workers, whether full-time, part-time or voluntary, an opportunity to make contacts for organising youth exchanges, and to gain a greater understanding of youth work systems and structures in other Member States. The study involves multi-national groups of up to 15 participants and lasts one week.

The UK has 55 places each year for these outward study visits. Bursaries are given towards the travel costs of each participant, and the costs incurred by the hosts in each Member State are fully covered.

Action I.4: Professional Development for Youth Workers
The National Agencies or European non-governmental youth organisations may organise multilateral training activities designed to develop the skills of youth workers involved in organising exchanges, and to provide them with an inter-cultural learning experience. Priority will be given to youth workers working regularly and directly with young people.

Local, regional or national organisations in the UK or Ireland wishing to organise multinational training activities concerning exchanges should apply to their Youth Exchange Centre (YEC) or Youth Exchange Bureau (YEB).

Action I.5: Pilot Projects
National Agencies or European non-governmental youth organisations may submit proposals for the preparation of activities or materials which promote the exchange and mobility of young people. Key areas which will be considered for funding are:

- the development of information materials, particularly those targeted at disadvantaged young people and those youth workers working with them;
- the development of training materials; and
- the exchange of information between youth worker trainers and training institutions at European level.

Action II
Action II provides support for services at a national level to support the YFE Programme

EC Contribution

The amount estimated to be needed for the three-year programme is 25 MECU.

Applications

Each Member State has nominated a National Agency to run the YFE programme.

The provisional deadlines for submitting grant applications are:

- 1 February 1994, for activities taking place between 1 June and 31 August 1994; and
- 1 May 1994, for activities taking place between 1 September and 31 December 1994.

INFORMATION

UK
National Agency:
Information Officer
Youth Exchange Centre
The British Council
10 Spring Gardens
London SW1A 2BN
Tel: 071 389 4030
Fax: 071 389 4033

IRELAND
National Agency:
Youth Exchange Bureau
Avoca House, 1st Floor
189/193 Parnell Street
Dublin 1
Tel: 01 73 14 11

COMMISSION
Current technical assistance bureau for the programme:
PETRA/Youth Bureau
2/3 Place du Luxembourg
1040 Brussels
Tel: INT+ 322 511 1510
Fax: INT+ 322 511 1960

Chapter 28

External Trade Policy

The EC was set up primarily as a trading bloc, but the founding fathers did not plan a club of inward looking, isolationist Member States, trading with one another to the exclusion of the rest of the world. Article 3(b) of the original Treaty of Rome provides for "the establishment of a common customs tariff and of a common commercial policy towards third countries."

Over the years, the EC has come to mean different things to different countries, depending on whether their links with it are economic, diplomatic, cultural or strategic. It can be viewed as an open trading partner or a protectionist bloc - both are possible interpretations of Article 3(b) - a major political power or a regional economic grouping. The US tends to see it as an ally with which it shares common values but, at the same time, as a rather mysterious commercial, technological and, increasingly, political rival to be treated with suspicion: "Fortress Europe". By contrast, the EC's relationship with Japan is dominated by the necessity to induce Japan to open up its markets to offset the ever increasing flood of Japanese products coming into the open markets of Europe. The Central and Eastern European countries (CEECS), no longer cut off by the Iron Curtain, are very anxious to develop closer links with the EC and want to join as soon as they can comply with the economic and political criteria demanded of potential applicants. The Mediterranean countries have always been extremely important to the EC because of their nearness to the southern Member States, the historical and cultural links between the peoples of the Mediterranean and northern Europe going back thousands of years, and the current and potential migration patterns. The Less-Developed Countries (LDCs) see the EC as their main market, not merely because of its size and wealth but because they have been guaranteed unrestricted rights of access for the majority of their industrial and agricultural products.

The EC is both the world's richest single trading bloc and the biggest market in the world. It has a population of 346 million with a per capita GDP of 15,895 PPS. It is also one of the most open markets. Its external exports, which exclude Member States' trade with one another, amounted to ECU 413 billion in 1989. This represented 15% of total world exports, compared with 12% for the US and 9.1% for Japan. The principal exports are high value manufactured goods - 80% of the total - and processed foodstuffs.

On the other hand, it is a substantial importer of energy and raw materials, and is the world's biggest importer of agricultural products. It therefore needs world markets to be kept as open for its exports as its own market is for imports. This is reflected in Article 110 of the Treaty of Rome which says:

"By establishing a customs union between themselves, Member States aim to contribute, in the common interest, to the harmonious development of world trade, the progressive abolition of restrictions on international trade and the lowering of customs barriers."

This principle forms the basis of the EC's relations with its trading partners throughout the world, and it has built up a complex network of multilateral, regional and bilateral trading relationships.

Specific relationships have developed because of geographic or other proximity: agreements with the EFTA countries, the CEEC and the Mediterranean region, through former colonial ties (the Lomé Convention) or because of similar interests or levels of economic development: the OECD countries.

Its dependence on an open world trading system has made it an enthusiastic supporter of the multilateral trading principles of the GATT. Since coming into force in 1948, the GATT has become the principal instrument governing the conduct of world trade. It is both a code of rules and a forum in which trade negotiations take place. As a result of successive GATT-inspired tariff reductions, the EC's weighted average tariff level for industrial goods is now less than 5%. Once the various tariff preferences which the EC grants to many suppliers have been taken into account, the average industrial tariff applied falls effectively to about 1%. LDCs further benefit from duty-free access to the EC for their manufactured or semi-manufactured goods through either direct agreements with the EC or because of the EC's generalised system of preferences (GSP).

The EC has a special position in the GATT. It is the Member States and not the EC as such which are contracting parties to the GATT agreements. However, the EC is itself a signatory to a number of international agreements concluded under the auspices of the GATT. Articles 113 and 228 of the Treaty of Rome, as amended, give the EC exclusive competence in negotiating the external trade matters of Member States within uniform principles and Article 228.7 provides that "Agreements concluded under the conditions set out in this Article shall be binding on the institutions of the Community and on the Member States." It has therefore established itself as a de facto contracting party, with the Commission as the negotiator and spokesman on behalf of the Member States. The articles of the GATT and the various international agreements drawn up under its aegis form the legal basis for the EC's own trade policy instruments. This covers areas such as tariffs, the application of safeguard measures and anti-dumping actions.

The EC's contribution to the GATT has been substantial. It has been a key player in the successive rounds of negotiations held at regular intervals, attempting to achieve agreement on the liberalisation of world trade. It was a prime mover in the promotion of the Uruguay Round of talks which began in 1986 and brought both agriculture and the provision of services within the scope of the GATT negotiations for the first time.

At the Copenhagen Summit in June 1993, the European Council underlined the need for the EC's maintaining an active role in achieving further progress in the on-going negotiations while preserving the European identity and need for solidarity. It stressed that it was essential to re-launch the multilateral process in Geneva as soon as possible on all topics, including agriculture, in order to complete a comprehensive, durable and balanced agreement before the end of the year deadline. This is urgently needed in order to create a new, rules-based world trading system in which unilateral action by any one country is effectively ruled out. A GATT round concluded on this basis will promote the durable expansion of international trade which is the key to job creation both in Europe and throughout the world. It is to be hoped that the appointment, as Secretary General of GATT, of the former EC Trade Commissioner Peter Sutherland, with his intimate knowledge of the subject and years of experience of difficult international trade agreements, will help to achieve a positive outcome to the negotiations before the expiry of the American-imposed deadline in December.

The EC also has a special status within the OECD. Although it is not actually a member of the organisation, the Commission regularly speaks on behalf of the Community on issues of EC competence or where the Member States have agreed a common position.

The OECD's work covers a wide field of macro- and micro-economic issues, including monetary and financial matters and, since the 1970s, energy questions. It has also increased its involvement in commercial issues, playing a leading role in the fields of the provision of export credits and business ethics in overseas trade. All EC countries now accept the OECD consensus on export credits which, since 1978, has provided the framework for keeping export credit subsidies under control and has been instrumental in bringing interest rates on credits closer to actual market conditions. The OECD has also been instrumental in pushing forward discussions by members on issues such as trade in services and high-technology products.

The EC meets regularly with its principal partners in several other institutions. One is the annual "G7" Economic Summits of the Group of Seven Industrialised Nations, consisting of the USA, Japan, Canada, Germany, the UK, France and Italy, together with representatives from the Commission and the Presidency. It also joins with the trade ministers from the USA, Japan and Canada for periodic meetings as the "Quadrilateral Group".

Special features should be noted concerning some of the EC's main trading partners.

The USA

For historical and strategic reasons as well as shared political values, relations between the US and the EC have always been close, and the US was a committed supporter of European integration even before the foundation of the first Community, the ECSC. It is also linked to various individual Member States through common membership of the Atlantic Alliance and other international organisations. The solidity of this relationship has enabled it to withstand the impact of various transatlantic trade disputes. These started with the "chicken war" of the 1960s which concerned the possible effects of the introduction of variable EC import levies on US poultry exports. They have continued more recently with disputes about US limitations on imports of EC steel, about EC restrictions on imports of American meat containing growth-promoting hormones, about subsidies paid by both sides to their aircraft industries and the American domination of the audio-visual market.

In the wake of changes in East-West relations resulting from the collapse of Communism in the old Soviet Union, the return to democracy in the CEEC and the re-unification of Germany, the then US Secretary of State, James Baker, proposed in December 1989 the establishment of new institutional links between the US and the EC. This took concrete form in the following November with the adoption of a declaration on EC-US relations, the key paragraph of which states that:

> "...to achieve their common goals, the European Community and its Member States and the United States of America will inform and consult each other on important matters of common interest, both political and economic, with a view to bringing their positions as close as possible without prejudice to their respective independence. In appropriate international bodies, in particular, they will seek close co-operation."

The declaration also sets out the framework for these consultations to take place at five levels:

1. twice-yearly meetings between a EC team made up of the head of government of the country holding the Presidency, the Commission President and the President of the United States;
2. twice-yearly consultations between EC foreign ministers, the Commission and the US Secretary of State;
3. ad hoc consultations between the foreign minister of the country holding the EC Presidency and the US Secretary of State;
4. twice yearly consultations between the Commission and the US government, at cabinet level; and
5. briefings to US representatives at ministerial level, by the country holding the EC Presidency on matters concerning European Political Co-operation (EPC).

A similar declaration was agreed between the EC and Canada in November 1990. This builds on their relationship established by the 1976 framework agreement on commercial and economic co-operation and enhances the present structures for consultation.

Japan

The EC's ties with Japan have not developed in the same way as the trans-Atlantic relationship. Japan and the Member States are not linked by any formal security treaty or joint membership of other specific organisations, and it is only in recent years that bilateral economic relationships have acquired their present significance, reflecting Japan's relatively late emergence as one of the world's economic superpowers.

Trade tensions and disputes are a more constant feature of EC-Japanese bilateral relations than of those between the EC and the USA. The EC's trade relations with

Japan have tended to be dominated by the structural consequences of what the Europeans considered as Japan's incomplete integration into the world multilateral trading system. Japan has reaped considerable economic benefit from access to world markets, but its domestic market has not offered comparable access to its trading partners. There are three main reasons for this.

The first is the plethora of technical and administrative barriers to imports which make gaining access slow, difficult and very expensive. The second relates to the tightly-knit structures and entrenched attitudes which prevail in the Japanese economic system: potential exporters to Japan have got to be able to buck the system, which requires a kind of expertise which is often difficult to find and, when found, is very expensive. The third is to be found in Japanese habits and attitudes in general: the traditions of international trading which have always existed in Europe, the Middle East, China, India and other more central countries never developed to the same extent in the more remote Japan. There is no long history of markets full of exciting new goods imported from far-off places, and imported goods can still be viewed with suspicion.

The severe difficulties in gaining access to the Japanese market and the consequent failure of foreign companies to achieve any substantial market shares have helped create Japan's substantial current account surpluses, not only with the EC, but with the US and its Asian and Far Eastern neighbours. The temptation to try to resolve this imbalance by unilateral measures against Japanese exports has posed a serious threat to the wider multilateral trading system.

The EC's policy towards Japan consists of three elements.

1. It has sought a greater opening up of the Japanese market, not only for manufactured goods and processed foodstuffs, but also for banking and financial services. To increase export possibilities, it has encouraged the Japanese authorities to boost internal demand, to carry out the necessary structural reforms and to remove certain identifiable obstacles to market access on a sector by sector basis.

2. The Commission has closely monitored Japanese exports to the EC in certain sensitive areas, so as to be able to respond rapidly in case of market disturbance.

3. The EC has been trying to foster a higher level of co-operation with Japan in areas of science and technology and in the industrial field. It has also welcomed direct, long term investment in Europe, whereby Japanese firms establish local manufacturing plants instead of exporting finished goods from Japan. The aim is to bring about a closer, multilateral integration of Japanese industry into the world trading system and to develop a more broadly-based bilateral relationship. A dialogue on foreign policy matters has also been established.

The CEECS

The Central and Eastern European Countries are, after all, fellow Europeans, with whom the various Member States have had long historical and cultural ties which were only temporarily disrupted by the Cold War and the Iron Curtain. Prague, Budapest and Krakow are just as much European cities as London, Rome or Madrid and the EC had started rebuilding ties with them long before the dramatic events of 1989. Hungary and Czechoslovakia had already approached the EC with requests for wider trade links. The pace of co-operation accelerated with the liberalisation of contacts with the outside world permitted under Mikhail Gorbachev, and culminated in the signing of a Joint Declaration between the EC and the COMECON in June 1988. This set up an official relationship between the EC and COMECON and opened the way for trade and co-operation agreements with each of the central and eastern European countries individually. Agreements with all the CEECs and the old Soviet Union itself were negotiated between 1988 and 1990.

The objectives of the unilateral trade concessions granted to the COMECON countries in these agreements were primarily to help support the transition from command economies to free market economies. The results were dramatic. The EC's imports from the CEECs (Poland, Hungary, Czechoslovakia, Romania and Bulgaria) increased by 24% to reach 16.1 BECU by 1991, and the proportion of their total exports to OECD countries going to the EC rose from 69% in 1989 to 75% in 1991. The proportion going to other major OECD countries like the USA and Japan actually declined during the same period. In the period between January and August 1992, the CEECs' share of the EC's total imports rose to 3.7% and they took 4.6% of the EC's exports.

At the G7 meeting in Paris in July 1989, the leading industrialised nations asked the Commission to co-ordinate the pilot programme being planned to provide economic aid to Poland and Hungary. This eventually developed into the PHARE Programme. Other OECD countries supported this decision and came together to form the "Group of 24": the twelve Community countries, the six EFTA countries, the US, Canada, Japan, New Zealand, Australia and Turkey. In July 1990, the Group of 24 took the decision to extend the Programme to the GDR, Czechoslovakia, Bulgaria and Yugoslavia. The basic philosophy underlying the Programme is that aid should facilitate the process of economic and social change in the countries of Eastern and Central Europe and enable them to participate in the process of European integration.

The EC devised a new type of association agreement for the former Eastern Bloc countries, or "European Agreements" based on Article 238 of the EEC Treaty. As amended by the Maastricht Treaty, this Article says:

> "The Community may conclude with one or more states or international organisations agreements establishing an association involving reciprocal rights and obligations, common action and special procedures."

Agreements of this type are more far-reaching than existing trade and co-operation agreements and are planned for all CEECs to complement EC action under the PHARE programme. In November 1991, the Commission initialled agreements with Poland, Hungary and Czechoslovakia, reflecting a significant rapprochement. Although the Agreements do not commit the Community to admitting these three countries (now known as the Visegrad countries) to the EC, they do, in fact, represent a step on the road to membership. The preamble recognises that membership is the ultimate aim of the countries concerned and that this form of association will help them to achieve it. The Agreements straddle areas of national and Community competence. They are preferential and valid for an indefinite period, and provide not only for free trade, but also economic and technical co-operation, financial assistance and the creation of a political dialogue. The EC has paid particular attention to the "specificity" of its partners in East and Central Europe, which is defined as treating each according to its own particular situation. This is why negotiations on the first European agreements took place with Hungary, Czechoslovakia and Poland - the three countries in the region which have made the most progress in the reform process. The Agreements also incorporate principles of liberalisation; "conditionality" for transition to the second stage, "asymmetry" meaning more generous trade arrangements for the associated countries, and product classification.

The Agreements required ratification by the parliaments of Poland, Hungary and Czechoslovakia and the European Parliament, as well as the approval of the Member States. Provisions were made for interim agreements covering areas of exclusive Community competence while these more complicated procedures were being implemented.

The Copenhagen Summit in June 1993 recognised the crucial importance of trade in the transition to a market economy and agreed to accelerate the Community's efforts to open up its markets. It expected that this step forward will go hand in hand with further developments of trade among those countries themselves, and between them and their traditional trading partners. The European Council underlined the importance of the process of the approximation of laws in the associated countries to those applicable in the EC, particularly in relation to competition policy, company law, and the laws relating to financial services. They would also need to consider other matters including, the protection of workers, environmental policy and consumer protection as a second stage in view of their intentions to join the Community in due course. It was also agreed that officials from the associated countries should be offered training in EC law and practice, and the decision was taken that a task force composed of representatives of the Member States and the Commission should be established to co-ordinate and direct this work.

The Copenhagen Summit also agreed that the associated CEECs which wanted to become members of the European Union should be eligible to do so. Accession would take place as soon as an associated country was able to assume the obligations of membership by satisfying the economic and political conditions required. Membership requires that the applicant country must have achieved sufficient stability in its institutional framework to guarantee reasonable democratic stability under the rule of law, respect for human rights and the protection of minorities, the existence of a functioning market economy, and the capacity to cope with the competitive pressures of market forces within the Union. Membership presupposes the candidate's ability to take on the obligations as well as the benefits of membership, including adherence to the aims of political, economic and monetary union. The European Council agreed that future co-operation with the associated countries should be geared towards their stated objective of Community membership.

The Mediterranean / Middle East

The EC's Mediterranean neighbours were among the first countries to establish special economic and trading relations with the Community. From the outset, the EC accepted that it has an enlightened self-interest in the social and thus, political stability of the Mediterranean region. The Mediterranean countries are of considerable economic significance for the EC, constituting as a group one of its largest trading partners.

Apart from a common civilisation dating from the time of the Roman Empire, close historic and cultural ties bind these countries to certain EC Member States: France with Morocco, Algeria, Tunisia, Lebanon and Syria; Italy with Tunisia; Spain with Spanish North Africa; and the UK with Cyprus, Malta, Egypt and Israel. Since the 1960s and 1970s the EC has been linked with almost all the Mediterranean countries by a network of twelve separate co-operation or association agreements, and only Albania and Libya have no current links with the Community.

The association agreements with Turkey, Cyprus and Malta are designed to lead to the progressive establishment of customs unions with the EC. The agreement with Turkey goes a step further, envisaging Turkey's ultimate full membership of the Community and, in April 1987, Turkey submitted a formal application to join. The Commission must deliver an opinion on each application for membership before entry negotiations can begin, and it took the view at that time that the EC should not consider new membership applications until after the completion of the single market in 1993. This standstill was subsequently further extended so that the sensitive questions of political union and EMU included in the Maastricht Treaty had been implemented by the existing members. Notwithstanding this, Cyprus and Malta submitted formal applications in 1990 to join as soon as possible.

The Maghreb countries (Algeria, Morocco and Tunisia) and the Mashreq countries (Egypt, Jordan, Syria and Lebanon) together with Israel, are linked to the EC through co-operation agreements covering trade, industrial co-operation and technical and financial assistance. The agreement with Israel provides for free trade in industrial products.

Although their wider political provisions vary in scope, there are common elements in all the EC's Mediterranean agreements. Each provides for unlimited, duty-free access to the EC for industrial products originating in the country in question. The agreements also provide individual concessions of various sorts for their major agricultural exports, including fruit and vegetables, wine and olive oil. Turkey, Cyprus, Malta and Israel grant some reciprocal concessions to EC exports. In addition to these trade concessions, the EC provides financial aid to the Mediterranean countries in the form of direct grants and loans from the EIB.

Despite the accession in 1986, of Spain and Portugal, with their large Mediterranean-type agricultural sectors, the EC has committed itself to trying to maintain the traditional policy of permitting the free access of agricultural goods from the Mediterranean countries into the Community.

Africa, Asia and Latin America

The EC Member States are, both individually and collectively, the LDC's most important partners. The EC accounts for 21.5% of their exports and provides 36% of the official aid they receive, of which 63% goes to sub-Saharan Africa, 12% to Asia, and 11% to the Latin American and Caribbean regions. Two thirds of this aid is for development projects and the remaining third for food aid. Details of the EC's aid to the LDCs is detailed in Chapters 30 and 31 on development co-operation.

CAP and World Trade

The EC is the largest importer and second largest exporter of agricultural products in the world. Its actions therefore have a significant effect on world trade.

Many non-member countries accuse the EC of trying to insulate itself from world agricultural markets through its system of levies, designed for the benefit of its domestic producers. There is some truth in this criticism. The EC's imports of cereals and some other products have indeed fallen over the past few years, but it remains the world's biggest importer of farm produce. The US, one of the sharpest critics of the CAP, actually has a surplus in its agricultural trade with the EC, amounting to more than ECU 2.5 billion in 1986. The parable of the mote and the beam appears to be little known in official circles in the US.

Another criticism is that the EC has unwarrantably expanded its share of world trade by paying export refunds to offset its uncompetitive production costs, and it is thereby unfairly denying access to world markets to other countries wanting to export farm produce. Again, there is some truth in this criticism. EC export subsidies artificially boost the EC's exports at the expense of other countries unable to afford competing subsidies. The EC's subsidised exports also put heavy downward pressure on the world price levels for the commodities in question, to the detriment of non-subsidised exporters. This is particularly significant in the cases of products heavily protected by EC subsidies such as wheat, coarse grains, dairy products and ruminant meat.

It must, however, be remembered that export subsidies for agricultural products are also practised by other major producers, particularly the US, and are allowed under the GATT rules provided they do not lead to unfair changes in market share. The EC's share of world farm exports has not increased significantly over the past few years: between 1973 and 1986, it rose from around 10% to 12.3%, which hardly makes it guilty of the cut-throat competition of which it is accused - particularly by the US. Although the US' share of world farm exports has fallen slightly over the past few years from 19% to 17%, the verdict reached by a GATT investigation, following a formal complaint made by the US about the EC's export subsidies on wheat flour, was that this fall could hardly be explained by the increase in the EC's market share alone.

What is of greater concern is whether or not the EC's export subsidies have damaged the LDCs' export prospects. If low world prices and a reduction in export opportunities brought about by the operation of the CAP were to be reflected onto LDC agricultural markets it would act as a disincentive to production in those countries. Since agriculture is not only the biggest sector in the economies of most LDCs but the largest single earner of valuable foreign exchange, any setback in agricultural production would also reduce the pace of overall economic development in those countries.

Various studies show that the LDCs could benefit from the long-term increase in world prices that should result from the abolition of the CAP. The line of reasoning is as follows. The abolition of the CAP would change the terms of trade, thus affecting real incomes. This effect would be positive for net exporters of agricultural products (i.e. the LDCs) and negative for net importers (the more developed countries including the EC). There would then be a gain in efficiency in the LDCs as resources are shifted from the relatively inefficient non-agricultural sectors to the increasingly lucrative agricultural sector. The reallocation of resources in favour of agriculture would result in an increase in taxation revenue for their governments, since many LDCs tax agriculture in order to be able to subsidise their non-agricultural sectors. This higher total tax revenue would permit a fall in the average level of taxation, encouraging both local investment and consumer spending. All sectors of the LDC's economy should therefore benefit.

There would also be positive macro-economic effects arising out of the abolition of the CAP. The very fact that agriculture is protected in the EC means that this sector must be inefficient, otherwise it would not need protection. The EC's inefficient agricultural sector eats up its resources and abolition of the CAP would free these resources for use in other sectors of the economy. This more efficient allocation of resources would increase the EC's economic growth which would, in turn, provide scope for an increase in the European market for the exports of the LDCs. The OECD calculated in 1990 that the loss to the LDCs caused by the protectionism of the CAP could be as much as $26 billion per annum. There is an additional benefit to the developed countries from this scenario in that the increased prosperity in the LDCs would mean that they did not need to supply so much aid.

Although it is undoubtedly true that the CAP has the effect of both lowering world prices and reducing export opportunities, the EC has created some safeguards to protect the LDCs. For one thing, it has considerably improved LDCs' access to its markets. The Generalised System of Preferences (GSP) is considered in more detail in Chapter 30 on Development Co-operation. Under this scheme, nearly 130 LDCs are able to send the EC industrial goods, textiles and farm products on preferential terms. More than 400 agricultural products now qualify for preferences of which about 100 are imported completely free of duty or quotas, and the poorest LDCs have been granted complete freedom of duty on about 700 mostly Mediterranean and tropical agricultural products. In 1985, farm products worth about ECU 2.3 billion were exported to the EC by LDCs taking advantage of these special terms, which provided a welcome boost to their balance of payments positions, but created a new range of problems in the LDCs because they were not necessarily able to expand their agricultural sectors to accommodate both domestic and export demands. Because of changing tastes and eating habits in the richer EC, the demand for these products has soared which has caused prices to rise in the LDCs to levels which the shoppers in their domestic markets cannot afford. The benefits of this export trade are enjoyed by the few - mostly middle-men - and the poorest people in the LDCs have become even poorer.

A further criticism of the CAP is that empirical research has shown that the CAP has a destabilising effect on world commodity prices - particularly on more heavily protected commodities like wheat, coarse grains and dairy products. Price stability is very desirable for LDCs from a welfare point of view since, without the certainty of a guaranteed income, they will be loath to invest their scarce resources in agriculture and, of course, no investment means no returns. To counteract this, in a major innovation to the Lomé Convention, the EC guarantees the ACP contracting states minimum returns on the export of certain raw materials to Europe. This "Stabex system" covers about 50 products, including many agricultural commodities such as coffee, cocoa, tea and sisal. Despite a high degree of self-sufficiency, the EC has also committed itself to taking 1.3 million tonnes of raw sugar each year at the price obtaining on the internal EC market, and this provides considerable benefits to Caribbean countries since even the EC intervention price is likely to be higher than the price they could obtain on the open market. ACP countries are also able to export nearly 40,000 tonnes of beef a year to the EC at a fraction of the import levy. This means that all these exports by ACP countries are largely protected from the speculative ups and downs of world commodity markets, and are thus assured of at least some stable supply of foreign exchange.

In conclusion, it is difficult to classify the CAP categorically as either a positive or negative force on LDCs and some of its most obvious negative effects are balanced by gains from some of the EC's other policies. Due to the operation of the CAP, net exporters of temperate zone products lose and net importers gain. Since most LDCs are net importers of temperate zone products, they would appear to benefit from the CAP in the short term through the improvement in their terms of trade on the import side. If the LDCs were able to take advantage of the long term higher prices for these commodities that would probably prevail in the absence of the CAP, however, they would be able to expand their export markets, everyone would eventually benefit: the LDCs by earning more foreign exchange and the EC by no longer having to support LDCs through measures such as food aid and preferential treatment for LDC farm exports, as well as earning back some of the LDCs increased foreign exchange by supplying them with the goods and services that they would need in their expanding economies. This would, prima facie, appear to be a much more efficient mechanism than the current one of expending resources to mitigate the damage done to LDC agricultural exports by the CAP. It must, however, be recognised that we have not yet attained Utopia and this remains a second-best world, where the CAP is still deemed necessary to protect the interests of European farmers, at least there are policies in place to mitigate its worst effects on the international scene.

As will be seen in Chapter 29, there are a number of EC initiatives designed to promote external trade and more can be expected in the very near future as part of the Delors package for the creation of jobs in the Community. As aid and trade are so closely interlinked, a number of the Development Co-operation programmes described in Chapters 30 and 31 are also combined with trading policies.

Chapter 29

External Trade Grants

External trade grants come within the following groupings:

1. Euromarketing: Marketing Assistance for SMEs
2. Promotion of SME Access to Markets in Third Countries and Export Promotion
3. ETP: Executive Training Programme in Japan
4. EC-Japan Centre for Industrial Co-operation
   - 4.1 Information Service
   - 4.2 Senior Management Training Programmes in Japan

1. EUROMARKETING

Objectives

The objectives of this programme are to provide SMEs with guidelines on marketing strategies and to enable them to maintain a presence in two or more EC markets by using shared facilities.

Programme Content

A study is being undertaken to examine the opportunities which the internal market can provide SMEs in the field of Euromarketing, i.e. for:

- developing European products;
- defining a consistent pricing policy;
- selecting appropriate distribution channels; and
- drawing up a single marketing strategy which takes account of a multi-cultural context.

Based on the results of the study, a guide will focus on case studies including both successes and failures. It will provide SME managers with guidelines on existing opportunities and enable them to carry out a self-diagnosis.

Participation

SME executives and managers may participate.

INFORMATION

COMMISSION
Enrique Buatas
Commission of the European Communities
D-G XIII B.3
Rue d'Arlon 80
B-1040 Brussels
Tel: INT+ 322 295 1557
Fax: INT+ 322 295 2154

2. PROMOTION of SME ACCESS to MARKETS in THIRD COUNTRIES and EXPORT PROMOTION

Objectives

The aim is to facilitate access by SMEs to markets in third countries and to promote exports.

Programme Content

DG XIII has prepared practical guides on doing business in Canada, the USA and Australia and is examining the possibility of extending this series to other countries or regions.

An experimental scheme promoting co-operation between enterprise support organisations in the EC and Poland has been carried out with the assistance of the Association of French Chambers of Commerce and Industry (ACFCI). Under this project, a series of data sheets on 17 Polish regions was drawn up and made available to SMEs throughout the EC by means of the Euro-Info Centre network and the Euro-Info newsletter.

A pilot project was launched during the second half of 1992 to promote the establishment of links between business support organisations like chambers of commerce, craft and industry, regional development agencies, business centres etc. in the EC and their counterparts in Central and Eastern Europe. The aim is to provide SMEs based in the Community with information and contacts so as to foster commerce, investment and co-operation. The project has links with measures being implemented under the PHARE Programme for promoting the development of private enterprise in Central and Eastern Europe. The latter include measures to promote local SMEs and the services they supply, together with assistance in establishing support organisations .

Participation

SME managers may participate.

INFORMATION

COMMISSION
Hella Gerth-Wellman/Veronique Daussy
Commission of the European Communities
D-G XIII B.3
Rue d'Arlon 80
B-1040 Brussels
Tel: INT+ 322 295 4942/9040
Fax: INT+ 322 295 2154

3. ETP: EXECUTIVE TRAINING PROGRAMME in JAPAN

Objectives

The overall objective of the Executive Training Programme is to increase the effectiveness of European industry in the Japanese market by building up a core of young business people with specialised knowledge of the Japanese business environment, language and culture.

Background

The Programme began in 1979.

Programme Content

The ETP aims to equip participants with the linguistic and cultural skills needed to do business in Japan.

The first 12 months of the ETP are spent on an intensive Japanese language course in Tokyo, supplemented by a parallel series of seminars and company visits. While the emphasis is naturally on Japanese business and management techniques, studies also cover many other aspects of Japanese culture so as to enable the participants to understand the complexities of Japanese society.

In the final six months of the Programme, participants receive in-house training and work experience with Japanese companies.

EC Contribution

The Programme receives an annual allocation of 90,000 ECUs.

Participating companies have no direct costs other than the initial costs of travelling to Japan. Thereafter, participants receive a monthly allowance to cover living expenses plus the costs of tuition, seminars, educational visits and the fare home are also reimbursed.

Participation

Participants must be nationals of an EC Member State and must work for an export-oriented, EC-based company. Applications from SMEs are particularly welcome.
Candidates are not required to be marketing specialists or have management experience, but are normally expected to have a university degree or equivalent qualification although, in certain cases, relevant professional experience may be acceptable instead. They should have a minimum of two years' business experience and be able to demonstrate an interest in international business, particularly in dealing with Japan.

Applications

Recruitment for the 1994 ETP started in January 1993 and continued until 1 July. It is anticipated that the same time frame will be followed for future programmes.

The initial recruitment process is handled in the Member States by the local office of the PA Consulting Group. Interviews are arranged and selections made for final consideration by the Commission in Brussels. The time-frame for this is:

- PA forward their recommendations in August of each year;
- interviews are held in Brussels in November and the selected group is notified in December/January; and
- the programme starts in May of each year.

The selection process places heavy emphasis on the degree of commitment to relations with Japan shown by each candidate's European employer. For this reason, the sponsoring company must complete an application form, stating its reasons for wishing to send the candidate on the programme and setting out how it proposes to use the participant's skills after completion of the programme.

INFORMATION

UK
Mr J Patrick
PA Consulting Group
123 Buckingham Palace Road
London SW1W 9SR
Tel: 071 730 9000
Fax: 071 333 5050

IRELAND
Mr R Cunningham
PA Consulting Group
10/12 Lansdowne Road
Ballsbridge
Dublin 4
Tel: 01 68 43 46
Fax: 01 68 17 71

COMMISSION
For general information on ETP, contact:
Leon Midson, DG 1
Commission of the European Communities
200 rue de la Loi
B-1049 Brussels
Tel: INT+ 322 299 0100
Fax: INT+ 322 299 0204

4. EC-JAPAN CENTRE for INDUSTRIAL CO-OPERATION

Statutory Basis

The EC-Japan Centre for Industrial Co-operation was established in Tokyo in 1987 as a joint operation at government level.

Objectives

The Centre is designed to provide European industry with a better knowledge of Japan's industrial structure and the Japanese market. It is considered that better understanding will lead to broader and more balanced trade and to increased stability in the relations between the EC and Japan.

Background

The general policy of the Centre is determined by a Supervisory Board made up of Japanese and European business leaders and government officials. In Tokyo, a Management Committee which groups together prominent members of both the local European business community and leading Japanese companies takes an active part in the operation of the Centre. Daily management is in the hands of a team of Europeans and Japanese drawn from government institutions and private industry, with two general managers, one Japanese and one European. The total staff numbers about 20.

EC Contribution

The Centre is financed jointly by European and Japanese government institutions and private industry.

The budget for the 1991 financial year was set at around 2,600,000 ECU.

Programme Content

The Centre's activities are carried out along two main lines:

i the supply of information to EC companies; and

ii the organisation of training courses in Japan for senior managers from EC companies.

INFORMATION

Dr Malcolm Trevor/Mr Thierry Consigny
EC-Japan Centre for Industrial Co-operation
Ichibancho-Eight-One Bldg.5F
6-4 Ichibancho
Chiyoda-ku
Tokyo 102
Tel: INT+ 81 (3) 3221 6161
Fax: INT+ 81 (3) 3221 6226

4.1 INFORMATION SERVICE

The Centre's Information Service supplies a range of services to European companies interested in the Japanese market or in Japanese industries. It provides:

- a library which can be used by European businessmen;
- an enquiry service to answer enquiries on the Japanese market, products, technologies and the local investment climate in Japan; and
- a database exhibition service, which provides individual exhibitions of Japanese on-line databases free of charge;

It also organises:

- Seminars on various problems that face foreign companies in Japan. Participation in these seminars is free of charge. They are publicised through the Centre's newsletter, "EC-Japan Business" which is published every quarter.
- Access to trade fairs and exhibitions: the Centre can assist European associations exhibiting at the main industrial trade fairs organised in Japan. It also guides European visitors around trade fairs or exhibitions in Japan which would normally only be accessible to a Japanese audience.
- Topical missions: the Centre organises two-week topical missions on topics drawn from the long courses described in the Training Programme section below, or on topics on Japanese management or production techniques which are of interest to European companies. Participation in these topical courses is free of charge, but is restricted for logistical reasons to 15 persons per course. Candidates must be sponsored by a European company, and the level of their qualifications must be commensurate with the content of the programme.
- Industrial tours of Japan: if properly channelled through the Commission, the Centre can help national groups organising industrial tours. This help consists of co-ordination with Japanese companies or organisations and assistance with the design of the programme. The funding of such missions is the responsibility of the European body concerned, although the Centre's assistance is free of charge.
- Publications: the Centre publishes reports on its topical missions, directories of Japanese sources of information and transcripts of lectures which are available free of charge to European companies.

INFORMATION

EC-Japan Centre
(as 4 above)

4.2 SENIOR MANAGEMENT TRAINING PROGRAMMES IN JAPAN

The scheme has two objectives:

i providing the participants with knowledge and information on Japanese life, society and value systems, the structure of Japanese industry and features of business practice; and

ii assisting with the establishment of local operations and improved relations with Japanese companies.

The Commission pays for the training programmes themselves, including lectures and language training, in-house training and field trips and all tuition and teaching materials. The sponsoring company must pay for travel to and from Japan, accommodation and living costs, and travel costs on company assignments.

Participants from SMEs may be eligible for scholarships of roughly 2,250 ECU per month, up to a maximum of 10,000 ECU per programme.

Programmes are run twice yearly, January to March (eleven weeks) and August to November (sixteen weeks). There is a "seminar phase" of nine to twelve weeks and a "company phase" of two to four weeks.

General topic areas dealt with in the course include:

- Japanese industrial structure and policy decision-making;
- basic Japanese language training;
- joint studies with Japanese managers; and
- insights into Japanese history and culture.

Specific topics covered include personnel management, industrial relations, distribution systems, production management, quality control, product development, value engineering, factory automation, sub-contracting, research etc.

Eligible participants must:

- be nationals of an EC Member State and at least 35 years old;
- have a minimum of ten years' professional experience and currently hold a key management or specialist function;
- be sponsored by an employer;
- guarantee attendance throughout the whole programme; and
- have a good command of English.

Applications for places on these courses must be made at least four months before the starting date. KPMG undertake pre-selection on behalf of the Commission in each of the Member States.

INFORMATION

UK
KPMG - Peat Marwick
1 Puddle Dock
London EC4
Tel: 071 236 8000
Fax: 071 248 6552

IRELAND
KPMG
Russell Court
Stokes Place
St Stephen's Green
Dublin 2
Tel: 01 708 1800
Fax: 01 708 1888

COMMISSION
Dr Walther Fleig
Commission of the European Communities
Directorate-General - Internal Market and Industrial Affairs
DG III A1
200 rue de la Loi
B-1049 Brussels
Tel: INT+ 322 295 6411
Fax: INT+ 322 296 6026

JAPAN
Dr Malcolm Trevor/Mr Thierry Consigny
EC-Japan Centre for Industrial Co-operation
Ichibancho-Eight-One Bldg.5F
6-4 Ichibancho
Chiyoda-ku
Tokyo 102
Tel: INT+ 81 (3) 3221 6161
Fax: INT+ 81 (3) 3221 6226

Chapter 30

Development Co-operation Policy and Humanitarian Aid

Distinguishing between development co-operation - which can roughly be defined as helping others to help themselves - and humanitarian aid is not always easy. As this chapter aims to deal more with the practical application of the various policies than with the philosophical reasoning for the EC's involvement in the first place, it therefore treats them as the same in most instances.

Donors usually regard it as a foregone conclusion that aid is both welcomed by and beneficial to the recipients: otherwise they would not give it. This view, however, ignores the important issue of whether the type of aid given is appropriate and the fact that inappropriate aid may do nothing more than exacerbate the downward spiral of economic and political decline faced by some developing countries.

If, for instance, aid is given in monetary form to a country run by a dictatorial regime, it is impossible to say that it will benefit the sections of the population for which it was intended. No matter what safeguards have been attached to the aid by the donors or what assurances have been given by the recipients there is always the possibility that the former will be evaded, the latter broken and the administrators and officials supporting the recipients' regime will use it to line their own or their henchmen's pockets or for undesirable purposes like buying armaments. It may also contribute to the long term survival of undemocratic regimes, by alleviating the worst effects of their harsh or totalitarian policies. If the masses can be bought off by the material benefits provided by the aid received, they are more likely to tolerate the status quo and be less inclined to demand political or economic reform.

Short-term aid designed to meet emergencies may also have harmful effects if it is used in the wrong circumstances. For instance, if a country suffering from repeated droughts receives only short-term emergency food aid rather than long term investment to improve its irrigation and agricultural systems, it is only dealing with the visible effects of the problem and not the under lying causes. People may be kept alive in the short term, but they remain unprepared to cope with the next disaster, and all that is achieved is the creation of a culture of dependency. The donors meanwhile lose interest in the plight of these victims, feeling that, by down-loading their surplus foodstuffs onto the LDCs, they have "done their bit" for humanity. This donor fatigue is exacerbated by the frequency and extent of disasters, particularly in the LDCs.

This is not to say that the combination of development co-operation and humanitarian aid cannot be beneficial to both recipients and donors; it is merely that each situation needs to be assessed on its individual merits to determine what type of aid is appropriate. After all, can it not be argued that the use of resources in the donor states for creating jobs in their own industries which can then in turn be used to assist the LDCs is more beneficial to themselves than either paying unemployment benefits or the manufacture of armaments? The EC, to its great credit, has a wide range of operations and instruments for use both inside and outside the Community for the purpose of stimulating such development and, at the same time, offers many different types of humanitarian aid.

The operations vary quite widely and cover industrial production, transport, education, health and trade. The procedures used are laid down, in some cases in the Co-operation Agreements and others in unilateral EC Decisions include:

- promotion of the LDCs' trade via the EC's Generalised System of Preferences (GSP), the trade provisions of agreements, and trade promotion activities;
- emergency aid, covering all LDCs and other non-member countries;
- food aid for countries other than the LDCs specifically to help them to cope with emergencies and food shortages;
- development finance, including the European Development Fund for ACP countries; financial protocols annexed to the agreements with Mediterranean countries, EIB loans to the ACP and Mediterranean countries and the CEECs and financial aid to Latin America and Asia; and
- rural development, including regional integration and training, support for joint ventures between European firms and firms from Latin America, Asia and the Mediterranean counties, support for non-governmental organisations, research and development programmes in agriculture and health and special budgets for specific operations.

The Community has three principal programmes for aid to developing countries: the Lomé Convention, the Asia/Latin America Programme and the Mediterranean Protocols. There is also the PHARE programme for the CEECs and the Structural Funds for the Member States, which are dealt with in Chapters 19. and 31 respectively.

The Lomé Convention

The EC has already provided a great deal of aid for development. The first European Development Fund was established in 1958 - the very year that the Treaty of Rome came into force - when the process of decolonisation was still going on. The central item of this original policy was co-operation with countries in Africa, the Caribbean and the Pacific (ACP States), which now number 69 in all. Most of these countries have close traditional ties with one or other of the Member States - a fact that is acknowledged in the Community's Treaties and, later, in the Yaoundé and Lomé association agreements.

The Lomé Convention is the largest single aid programme in the world and is one of the principal elements of the EC's policy on overseas development. The signatories include the majority of the world's poorest nations and the terms of the Convention are updated at regular intervals. The first Lomé Convention - itself the successor to a more limited arrangement - came into force in 1975. Since then, successive Lomé Conventions in 1979, 1984 and 1989 have given increasing emphasis to agricultural and rural development, which alone account for almost half the funding.

The current Lomé Convention, Lomé IV, was signed on 15 December 1989 and came into force on 1 September 1991. It is scheduled to run for ten years, twice the duration of any of its three predecessors, which gives greater stability to EC-ACP relations. It provides for 12 BECU of aid in the form of grants, soft loans and interest rate subsidies over the first five year period. Of this, 10.8 BECU will come from the EDF and 1.2 BECU from the EIB's own resources. This level of aid represents an increase in real terms of 20% over Lomé III . The Financial Regulation applicable to Lomé is published in OJ L 266, dated 21/9/91.

A number of major innovations have also been introduced under the Lomé Convention. A special allocation of 150 MECU within the EDF will allow the Community, in liaison with other donors, to work towards a realistic approach to structural adjustment. The Stabex Programme has been expanded, with more funds available and new rules which enable a country in need of assistance to join the system automatically. "Stabex" is the export earning stabilisation scheme, which covers 48 of the most important agricultural products exported by the ACP countries. It provides a vital degree of stability through compensatory transfers designed to offset shortfalls in export earnings. The "Sysmin" system is the equivalent scheme for key mineral exports and has now been extended to cover gold and uranium.

Under the trade provisions of the Lomé Convention, the EC, without requirements for reciprocity, gives preferential access for ACP products to the EC markets, so that 99% of ACP products come in free of customs duty or equivalent taxes. EC exports to ACP markets enjoy "most favoured nation" (MFN) treatment.

Aid terms have been improved in an effort to reduce ACP indebtedness. All EC aid is now non-repayable except for risk capital and EIB loans. A ban on the trade of hazardous and radioactive waste between the EC and ACP countries has been agreed.

In addition to the twin pillars of trade development and humanitarian aid, Lomé relies on a third pillar - political and economic co-operation - which makes it one of the most distinctive contributions to North-South relations. The political neutrality of Lomé enables the EC to co-operate with ACP governments of every political hue. The Convention allows for a considerable degree of power-sharing and joint decision-taking within projects and programmes financed by the EC. It also lays down procedures for a continuous dialogue between the EC and ACP governments, which is designed to render the instruments of co-operation as effective as possible. Under Lomé IV, the areas of EC-ACP co-operation have increased to include new fields and more comprehensive approaches to matters such as the development of services and environmental protection.

In 1993, the EC and Member States took a number of steps towards deeper and wider co-operation with sub-Saharan Africa in particular. The Copenhagen Summit in June stressed the importance of expanding co-operation in democratisation, peaceful development and development assistance for Africa and specifically the importance of support for policies of good governance, sound economic management and respect for human rights. It is the intention that the EC should use its influence to foster the process of democratisation in Africa and it has been active in supporting the democratic process in a number of African countries. The Community has strengthened development co-operation with Africa, partly through the Lomé Convention, and partly through the European Development Fund, the effectiveness of which has been greatly increased. Ministers responsible for development have agreed on a special rehabilitation initiative for Africa. At least 100 MECU will be allocated immediately to fast-track rehabilitation programmes in selected sub-Saharan countries and the Council of Ministers is examining a further special rehabilitation programme for developing countries.

Asia and Latin America

The EC is one of Latin America's main trading partners, accounting for some 20% of its exports and 20% of its imports.

In the 1980s an ACP-type network of agreements was extended to Asia and Latin America. Some of these are bilateral but others are regional like, for instance, the ones with the Asian countries, the countries of the Andean Pact and Central America. This regional approach is highly favoured by the EC as part of its overall philosophy of promoting regional integration, firstly on an economic basis and then on a political basis, rather in its own image. These agreements are neither as varied nor as complete as the Lomé Convention. They do not give preferential access for exports from Asian and Latin American nations to EC markets; nor do they contain provisions for financial aid from the EC to the partner country.

Both Asian and Latin American states are, however, eligible for preferential treatment under the EC's GSP for exports from LDCs, and to financial aid under special provisions in the EC budget. The purpose of the GSP is to assist LDCs in diversifying their economies - notably through industrialisation - and to develop export outlets for their industrialised products. The system, which dates from 1971 now covers nearly 130 independent countries and more than twenty dependent territories. The scheme is aligned with internationally-agreed objectives and allows entry free of duty for all otherwise dutiable manufactured and semi-manufactured goods, including textiles. Import ceilings apply in certain circumstances. Preferences, usually in the form of tariff reductions, are also offered on 360 agricultural products.

Over the years the EC has refined its GSP structure, managing its preferential access concessions so as to prevent more competitive LDC from swamping their rivals. This control of the LDC suppliers is known as the principle of differentiation. The EC has also, through a series of concessions, progressively liberalised access under the GSP for all exports from the world's least developed countries, consisting of about forty of the poorest countries. They now enjoy exemptions from virtually all preferential ceilings.

The LDCs of Asia and Latin America have also benefited from aid direct from the EC budget since 1976. This only goes to the poorest countries, with priority being given to rural development schemes and to the improvement of food supplies. Like the ACP countries, they are all eligible for the EC food aid programme which is worth about 500 MECU per year. Food aid is given either directly by the EC or through non-governmental organisations working with the local populations. The EC has funds available to provide emergency aid in the event of natural disasters or political upheaval and it also finances programmes for refugees.

The EC's relations with Latin America evolved from simple trade co-operation agreements to programmes designed to promote co-operation in fields such as industry, energy, science and technology, the environment, training and the promotion of investments. In line with its policy of supporting organisations committed to regional economic integration, as a first step it signed a non-preferential framework agreement for commercial and economic co-operation with the Andean Pact countries: Bolivia, Colombia, Ecuador, Peru and Venezuela. The aim of this agreement was to stimulate diversity and improve trade, to encourage co-operation between industrialists and to stimulate scientific and technical co-operation.

Similarly an agreement was reached in 1985 with the Signatories of the General Treaty on Central American Economic Integration: Costa Rica, Guatemala, Honduras, Nicaragua and El Salvador, and with Panama.

The accession of Spain and Portugal to the EC in 1986 added a new dimension to its relations with Latin America. In 1987, the Council adopted a declaration calling for the strengthening of relations with Latin America and the establishment of economic and political dialogues.

In Asia, non-preferential co-operation agreements have been signed with the individual countries of the Indian sub-continent: Sri Lanka in 1975, Bangladesh in 1976, India in 1981 (replacing an earlier trade agreement) and Pakistan in 1986 (also replacing an earlier agreement). They are broadly similar to the agreements concluded with the Latin American countries. India, Bangladesh and Sri Lanka also benefit from special concessions under sectoral agreements for a number of their exports such as sugar, jute and cocoa products.

A regional agreement with the member countries of the Association of South-East Asian Nations (Asean) was concluded in 1980, setting out a framework for commercial, economic and development co-operation. A regular political dialogue also takes place with the Asean group. Special emphasis has been placed on the promotion of European investment in the region and joint investment committees have been set up in all Asean countries.

The Mediterranean

The first agreements with the Mediterranean region, signed in the 1960s, were fairly limited in scope but, from 1975 onwards, these agreements were expanded to cover all aspects of mutual co-operation.

The twelve Mediterranean states which have signed financial protocols with the EC - Algeria, Morocco, Tunisia, Egypt, Lebanon, Jordan, Syria, Israel, Cyprus, Malta, Turkey and the former Yugoslavia - are eligible for aid worth 2.9 BECU under the current generation of protocols, which are scheduled to run for five-year periods. Of this amount, 2.25 BECU would come from EIB loans, and 0.65 BECU from the Community budget.

Arab States

A Co-operation Agreement was signed in June 1988 between the EC and the countries of the Gulf Co-operation Council (GCC), with a view to expanding co-operation in fields such as energy, science and technology. At the same time, a political dialogue was established. This agreement is scheduled to be replaced by one which will lead to the creation of a free trade area between the two parties.

Central and Eastern Europe

The EC supports the process of political and economic reforms in Central and Eastern Europe in several complementary ways.

i A first important category of support measures are designed to ease access to the EC market by means of a number of unilateral trade concessions. Trade relations were subsequently formalised in a contractual framework and further developed either in Europe/Interim Agreements or in "second generation" trade and economic co-operation agreements. Since 1 March 1992, trade relations with Poland, Hungary and the Czech and Slovak Republics have thus been governed by Interim Agreements which provide, among other things, for the establishment of free trade areas. The Interim Agreements are mixed agreements, covering areas of the competence of both the EC and the individual Member States. In addition to trade and commercial and economic co-operation, they provide for almost all aspects of economic activity, for political dialogue and for cultural and financial co-operation. The agreements are for unlimited periods, with transitional periods of ten years, and aim at the eventual integration of the Central European countries into the Community.

   Since 1 December 1992, trade relations with Albania have been governed by the Trade and Economic Co-operation Agreements, which provide for the abolition of quantitative restrictions on Albanian exports to the EC, and grant Albania MFN status. The EC also applies the GSP on a unilateral basis. Similar agreements are being negotiated with the Baltic States and in the meantime GSP will also continue to apply to Estonia, Latvia and Lithuania.

ii The PHARE Programme is specifically designed to support the process of economic restructuring and consists of non-repayable grants to the beneficiary governments for the financing of agreed actions.

iii The EC extends loan facilities to Central and Eastern European countries, including EIB loans, ECSC loans and loans in support of macro-economic policies. In addition to these bilateral actions, the G-7 meeting in Paris in June 1989 gave the Commission a mandate to co-ordinate Western economic assistance to Central European countries.

The European Bank of Reconstruction and Development (EBRD) was set up specifically to help these countries change from command economies to market economies. Once it has recovered from its disastrous start, it is hoped that it will complement the EIB.

The Former Soviet Union

The volatility of the political situation in the former Soviet Union and throughout both the CIS and the newly independent republics has created major problems for the EC in drawing up aid programmes. There are currently three forms of initiative:

- emergency aid to the people of Moscow, St Petersburg and other cities;
- technical assistance in the form of the TACIS Programme; and
- credit guarantees and loans.

The Council agreed to make a medium-term loan of 1,250 MECU available specifically for the import of agricultural products, food and medical supplies originating in the EC or the PHARE contracting countries (OJ L 362, dated 31/12/91). The detailed rules for the implementation of this loan are laid down in Commission Regulation (EEC) No 1897/92 (OJ L 191, dated 10/7/92).

The Copenhagen Summit made a number of points about Russia. The European Council expressed its readiness to continue and increase its support for the Russian reform process. The forth-coming G-7 summit was regarded as a timely opportunity to redouble the substantial efforts already made to support the reform measures under way in Russia and other constituent parts of the former Soviet Union. The Summit took stock of the preparations being made for the discussions planned at the G-7 summit on aid to Russia. Particular importance was attached to progress in Tokyo on issues relating to nuclear safety and, in this context, they welcomed the substantial follow-up along the guidelines laid down at the Lisbon Summit, including the agreements reached by the Council on EURATOM loans for improving safety in nuclear power stations in the former Soviet republics, as well as in Central and Eastern European countries. The European Council pledged EC support for all concrete steps which promoted efficiency in the use of the aid provided to Russia, particularly for projects aimed at accelerating the process of privatisation, the training of Russian entrepreneurs and the provision of technical assistance. The European Council emphasised that the effectiveness of such aid initiatives depended on the existence of political stability and the continuation of policies to promote the free market economy in Russia.

The Future

The near future could see some dramatic changes in the Community's role in development co-operation and humanitarian aid. The Maastricht Treaty added to the activities of the Community a new Article 3(q) which provides for "a policy in the sphere of development co-operation", and a new Article 130(u) which spells out what this means:

"1 Community policy in the sphere of development co-operation, which shall be complementary to the policies pursued by the Member States shall foster:

- the sustainable economic and social development of the developing countries, and more particularly, the most disadvantaged among them;

- the smooth and gradual integration of the developing countries into the world economy;

- the campaign against poverty in the developing countries.

2 Community policy in this area shall contribute to the general objective of developing and consolidating democracy and the rule of law, and to that of respecting human rights and fundamental freedoms.

3 The Community and the Member States shall comply with the commitments and take account of the objectives they have approved in the context of the United Nations and other competent international organisations."

A number of new programmes or extensions to the existing programmes can be anticipated within the next year or so.

The current system for implementing existing programmes is that an indicative programme is drawn up for each of the potential recipient states, specifying the amount of money to be allocated and the priority sectors. These may be inspected at the World Aid Section (WAS). Next, the recipient states propose specific projects and programmes together with requests for finance, via the National Authorising Officer (NAO). The Commission publishes a Bi-monthly Operational Summary (BOS) in the Courier of projects which it is considering funding but has not yet approved. There is also an electronic version of BOS, known as PABLI, which is updated twice monthly and is therefore more up-to-date than the Courier.

Each month the Commission considers a number of proposals and submits qualifying ones to the relevant committee for final approval. Finally, international calls for tender for the projects chosen are then advertised in the OJ S Series, leading to the process described in Chapter 11.

It must be stressed that the right to submit programmes rests solely with the recipients, many of whom are not certain exactly what can be done under the various programmes. Potential suppliers of goods and services under the various programmes have considerable scope for advising them what is available and helping with their applications.

Chapter 31

Development Co-operation Grants

Development Co-operation Grants come under the following headings:

1. European Investment Bank (EIB) and Lomé Convention Countries
    - 1.1 EIB Own Resources
    - 1.2 EIB Risk Capital
2. European Development Fund CEDF and Lomé Countries
3. EDF and OCT: Overseas Countries and Territories
4. EDF and Asian and Latin American (ALA) Countries
5. Energy Technology Transfer with LDCS (Lesser Developed Countries)
6. STD3: Life Sciences for Developing Countries
7. Mediterranean Countries and EIB
8. MED-Campus
9. The Avicenne Initiative: Science & Technology Co-operation with MAGHREB and Mediterranean Countries

10 ECIP: European Communities Investment Partners

11. PHARE - The Economic Reconstruction of Eastern Europe
12. PHARE Assistance Programmes
    - 12.1 RIPP: Regional Industrial Property Programme
    - 12.2 Telecommunications Programme
    - 12.3 Environmental Action Plan for Central and Eastern Europe
    - 12.4 Regional Environment Sector Programme
    - 12.5 Regional Quality Assurance Programme
    - 12.6 Regional Energy Sector Programme
    - 12.7 Regional Transport Programme
    - 12.8 Regional Programme for the Fight Against Drugs
    - 12.9 Nuclear Safety Programme in CEEC
    - 12.10 ACE: Action for Co-operation in the Field of Economics

13. Jean Monnet Chairs for PHARE Countries
14. Loans to CEEC: Central & Eastern European Countries
15. EIB and CEEC
16. JOPP: Joint Venture PHARE Programme
17. EBRD: European Bank for Reconstruction and Development
18. Co-operation in Science & Technology in CEEC Countries
19. TACIS: Technical Assistance to the Former Soviet Union: The CIS and Georgia
20. TEMPUS-PHARE: Trans-European Mobility Programme for University Students
21. TEMPUS-TACIS: Trans-European Mobility Programme for University Students
22. ECOS: Eastern Europe City Co-Operation Scheme

1. EUROPEAN INVESTMENT BANK AND LOME CONVENTION COUNTRIES

(See Chapter 30)

Statutory Basis

The European Investment Bank (EIB) was set up in 1958 by the Treaty of Rome.

Background

As a major international borrower, which has always been awarded the highest "AAA" credit rating by the world's leading rating agencies, the Bank is able to borrow large volumes of funds at optimum terms. It then lends on the proceeds on a non-profit making basis: cost plus a small margin to cover administrative expenses.

The volume of the its operations has grown steadily and today the Bank is one of the largest financing institutions of its kind in the world. While the bulk of its lending is within the EC, it has been increasingly called upon to participate in the implementation of the EC's development co-operation policy and to make available expertise in project financing for the benefit of developing countries. Within this framework, the EIB operates under successive conventions with ACP States.

Programme Content

The frameworks for programming EC aid are set out in the Lomé Convention. The programming exercise, in which the EIB participates with the Commission, is designed to establish indicative programmes for each ACP State, specifying the main sectors to be assisted principally by grant aid managed by the Commission, the measures necessary to achieve the development objectives of the sectors agreed upon together with the timetable for their implementation, the proposals for regional projects and, where appropriate, the support to be given for structural adjustment reforms.

For the EIB, the exercise typically leads to the establishment of a list of priority projects or sectors, which the ACP government concerned wishes the EIB to examine without committing either party.

There are two sources of finance available - the EIB's own resources and risk capital resources. Whenever feasible, the funds will be provided from a combination of the EIB's own resources and risk capital.

1.1 EIB Own Resources

Financing from the Bank's own resources is always in the form of loans and is principally used for viable projects in countries whose economic and financial situation is such that they can assume the debt involved and ensure that debt service payments are maintained. The operating forecasts for the project itself should also show sufficient margin to cover both interest payments and the repayment of principal over a reasonable term.

The Bank's interest rates are independent of the type of project financed, its location, the nationality or status of the borrower or the economic sector concerned. They are governed by the rates prevailing on the capital markets, the term of the loan and the currencies in which the loan is made. Loans provided by the EIB's own resources benefit from a 4% interest subsidy from the European Development Fund (EDF). The subsidy is automatically adjusted where necessary, so that the true rate of interest paid by the borrower is neither less than 3% nor more than 6% per annum.

The credits are denominated in ECUs and disbursed in a mixture of currencies or in a single currency, taking into account the preference of the borrower and depending upon availability of currencies. The principal currencies used are the ECU, those of the individual Member States as well as the US dollar, Swiss franc or Japanese Yen.

Like any lender whose resources consist of funds borrowed on the capital markets, the EIB must obtain appropriate security for its loans, in accordance with its Statute. The guarantee of the state in which the project is located is generally required, although other first-class guarantees may also be considered.

Loans from the EIB's own resources must always be accompanied by funds arranged from other sources and its loans may cover up to half the total costs of the project.

1.2 EIB RISK CAPITAL

Risk capital is a financing instrument developed by the EIB in the early 1970s and first used under the Second Yaoundé Convention. It is a form of aid particularly suited to the difficult financial and economic situation prevailing in a large number of ACP states. Drawn from budgetary funds, risk capital resources permit the EIB greater flexibility in setting terms and conditions. It may be provided in two forms:

i Direct equity investments made on behalf of the EC in enterprises or financial intermediaries in the ACP states which are, at the same time, usually combined with a loan from the EIB's own resources or with quasi-capital assistance. Such equity investments are minority holdings of a temporary nature and are intended to be disposed of in due course to the nationals or institutions of the ACP state, or as otherwise agreed.

ii Quasi-capital assistance is mainly in the form of:

- subordinated loans which will only be repaid, and on which interest is only paid, after other agreed prior claims have been met; and
- conditional loans, whose interest and repayment terms are linked to the performance of the project financed, such as, for example, after certain target output levels or profit thresholds have been met. These performance conditions are always specified at the time of signing the contract.

Risk capital assistance may also be used for financing studies to identify projects for assistance at a later date, to provide aid to enterprises during the pre-investment start-up phase or for rehabilitation purposes.

The terms and conditions for quasi-capital assistance depend upon the nature of the project financed. When it is provided in the form of loans, the interest rate will generally be less than 3% and the term anything up to 25 years.

Risk capital assistance is denominated in ECUs and disbursed either in ECUs or the currency of one or more Member States. In the case of risk capital operations designed to strengthen an enterprise's own funding, the exchange rate risk is generally carried by the EC. In the case of risk capital in the form of loans, particularly for SMEs, the exchange rate risk may be shared by the EC and the other parties involved.

No guarantees are required for risk capital financing, but the same appraisal and monitoring procedures are applied as for projects funded by loans from the EIB's own resources.

The proportion of the total costs of a project covered by risk capital financing will be dependent on the nature of the project, its importance to the area concerned and the availability of alternative sources of funding. It is generally quite a small percentage of the total investment, but it can cover the total costs in exceptional cases. Feasibility studies, for instance, are often financed in their entirety.

The Fourth Lomé Convention places even greater emphasis than earlier Conventions on promoting the private sector, notably SMEs. To achieve this objective, the range of financing facilities at the EIB's disposal has been enlarged and the EIB has been authorised to work with new intermediaries. In addition to its traditional operations, the EIB is now authorised to:

- provide partial funding to EC promoters to acquire a stake with an ACP partner in a joint venture with an ACP state;
- make funds available to EC financial intermediaries to help them assist SMEs in the ACP States;

- in certain circumstances, assist long-term lending institutions within the ACP States to restructure or rebuild their capital base; and
- finance certain pre-investment costs.

EC Contribution

Under the Financial Protocol spanning the first five years of the Fourth Lomé Convention (1991-95), 1.2 BECU will be provided in the form of loans from the EIB's own resources and 10.8 BECU will be financed from Member States' contributions to the EDF. Of the EDF resources, 280 MECU have been reserved for interest rate subsidies on loans from the Bank's own resources and 825 MECU, for risk capital operations wholly managed by the EIB under mandate from the EC. The EIB thus manages 2,305 MECU, approximately 20% of the total assistance under the first five-year protocol, and is able to offer financing on attractive terms.

In conjunction with the Lomé Convention and following established practice, a Council Decision makes specific provision for assistance for the Overseas Countries and Territories (OCT) which enjoy special ties with three EC Member States. For the EIB, this involves a maximum of 25 MECU in loans from its own resources and 25 MECU, in the form of risk capital operations, both on the same terms and conditions as in the ACP States.

Applications

In accordance with the division of responsibilities between the Commission and the EIB provided for under the Lomé Convention, financing applications for projects or programmes in industry, including agricultural processing, mining, tourism and energy, should be submitted for appraisal to the EIB. The EIB is also empowered to finance infrastructure projects of benefit to the economy in such sectors as transport, telecommunications, water resources and commercial agriculture.

INFORMATION

European Investment Bank
Operations Outside the Community
100 Boulevard Konrad Adenauer
L-2950 Luxembourg
Tel: INT+ 352 43791
Fax: INT+ 352 437704

London Office
European Investment Bank
68 Pall Mall
London SW1Y 5ES
Tel: 071 839 3351
Fax: 071 930 9929

2. EUROPEAN DEVELOPMENT FUND AND LOME COUNTRIES

Background

The European Development Fund (EDF) is the EC's principal instrument for development co-operation and is directly financed by the Member States. The seventh EDF operates under the Lomé IV Convention, while the sixth EDF will continue under

Lomé III until all the aid has been allocated. The Commission is responsible for the management of the EDF, which is administered by DG VIII: Development.

As a first step in the development of aid programmes, each ACP state is given an indication of the amount of financial assistance from which it can expect to benefit and the terms or conditions attached to the aid. Next, a "country report" is drawn up which sets out the needs and context of aid for each ACP state. Following this, programming missions visit each state concerned, to start drawing up an Indicative Aid Programme (IAP). The IAPs are adopted by agreement between the EC and each ACP state on the basis of proposals made by the state concerned. The proposals set out the guidelines and scope for financial and technical co-operation, the ACP state's objectives and the priorities for which the EC's support is seen as particularly appropriate. Specific projects are sometimes included, and IAPs are open to revision.

Projects are then identified by the ACP states from within the IAP. Details of the projects chosen are then submitted to the Commission which appraises them using the same assessment criteria as for other aid programmes - that is, their economic, social, technical, financial and administrative aspects. This is done in conjunction with the state concerned, and the Commission then draws up a financing proposal, which serves as a basis for a decision on the project.

The results of each project appraisal are summed up in a financing proposal, which is then submitted to the relevant EC decision-making body. Representatives of the EC governments have the opportunity to consider the proposals at a committee stage. If they decide in favour of financing a project, a financing agreement is drawn up, specifying the size of the EDF's commitment and the technical and administrative rules for the implementation of the project, which can then start as soon as the contract has been signed by both parties.

In the spirit of decentralising responsibility for the management of the EDF, projects are executed in accordance with the financing agreement under the supervision of national authorities and are subject to the laws and regulations of the ACP country. The national authorities collaborate on the preparation of invitations to tender, receive and examine tenders, put forward proposals for the placing of contracts, sign contracts, authorise payments and carry out acceptance formalities. All measures which may give rise to expenditure must be preceded by a proposal from the authorising officer, who subsequently sends them to the financial controller in Brussels. The final authorisation of expenditure is effected in Brussels by officers of D-G VIII Directorate E, Finance and Administration.

Programme Content

The EC finances three types of contract:

i works contracts to build roads, ports, airports, railways, telecommunications networks, irrigation and drainage, schools and public health premises;

ii supply contracts for the provision of equipment, vehicles, fertilisers, pesticides, farm tools and furniture; and iii service contracts for feasibility studies, training programmes, technical studies and supervision of works.

The general regulations and procedural rules for works, supply and service contracts for the seventh EDF are given in OJ L 382, dated 31/12/90. The technical provisions on payment procedure mean that firms are, in effect, completely covered against exchange risks.

EC Contribution

The financial resources of the seventh EDF for the period 1990-2000 will be 10.8 BECU.

Status Report

Under the sixth EDF, ACP firms won 54% of the works contracts, 4% of the supply contracts and 76% of the technical assistance contracts. Firms from outside the EC and ACP countries have only managed to obtain 1.4% of all EDF-financed supply contracts and no works contracts at all.

As of 31 December 1990, UK firms had been awarded 11.4% of the total contracts within the 6th EDF, worth a total of 174.3 MECU. Irish firms had 0.7% of the contracts, worth 10.6 MECU.

Applications

The Commission's policy is to launch a public, international invitation to tender which is open, on equal terms, to firms in both the EC and ACP states. It seeks to stimulate as much competition as possible, in the interests of both recipients and donors, and tries to exploit the diversity of technological resources offered by private firms.

Tenders for public works, supply and service contracts to implement the contents of IAPs agreed between the Commission and each ACP state are published in the OJ S-series and through TED (Tenders Electronic Daily). Project information also appears in an "Operational Summary" in each issue of The Courier, published bi-monthly by the Commission. Programme and tender documents may be consulted and information about EDF contacts, obtained from the Commission Office in each Member State.

In urgent cases it is not always possible to have unrestricted invitations to tender so, in such cases, a restricted system is operated through direct contacts with contractors who have previously worked satisfactorily on such projects with the EC or with public works departments elsewhere, or sometimes, through recommendations.

In order to encourage national firms and industries, accelerated invitations to tender are published only in the recipient countries for projects where the estimated cost of the work does not exceed 4 MECU. ACP firms are given preference for work costing less than 4 MECU, provided that their price does not exceed the most competitive non-ACP tender by more than 10%, or 15% when they are providing materials originating in ACP countries.

When two or more equal tenders are received, preference goes to the ACP tender or to the tender involving the greatest use of physical and human resources from the ACP countries. European firms, on the other hand, do not encounter much serious competition from third countries. Exceptions are only made in rare cases, such as those involving co-financing with international organisations or third country donors, when procedures for contract allocation can be extremely complex.

Consultants may register with the Commission to be considered eligible for contracts financed by the EDF. The register is kept by the Finance and Administration Directorate of D-G VIII which is responsible for the technical details of tenders and contracts. To obtain consultancy contracts under the EDF, it is advisable to contact the relevant Geographical Directorate of D-G VIII where shortlists are drawn up for each project. It should be noted that no advance publicity is given for consultancy opportunities so it is up to firms to make themselves known to the Geographical Directorate, and provide evidence of expertise in the relevant fields, the quality of their professional staff and their managerial and financial capabilities to carry out contracts of the relevant size. The shortlist is then sent to the ACP government concerned which makes the final choice, sometimes after calling for proposals or tenders.

The Commission has published a Communication (COM (87) 69 final) in which it puts forward proposals for general conditions to govern contracts for services financed by the EDF. The draft contains three parts: regulations, contractual clauses relating to study contracts and contractual clauses relating to technical assistance contracts.

INFORMATION

The Centre for the Development of Industry
26-28 rue de l'Industrie
B-1040 Brussels
Tel: INT +322 299 1111 (exchange)

The Register of Approved Consultants
D-G VIII
Commission of the European Communities
200 rue de la Loi
B-1049 Brussels
Tel: INT +322 299 1111 (exchange)

UK

The World Aid Section (WAS), part of the DTI's Projects and Export Policy (PEP) Division, acts as the central information and advisory point for projects funded by the EDF and by other multilateral development agencies. WAS holds details of all current projects in various stages of development. Also available are economic reports, sector analyses, tender notices, procedural guidelines and details of contracts awarded. These may be interrogated on-line. Firms may examine documents at WAS or arrange for them to be sent to their local DTI regional office.

World Aid Section (WAS)
DTI
Ashdown House
123 Victoria Street
London SW1E 6RB
Tel: 071 215 6520
Fax: 071 215 6535

The on-line information service is run by Export Opportunities Ltd (EOL). Subscribers may indicate a profile of their interest by country product etc. and they will automatically receive copies of relevant notices of opportunities to tender.

Export Opportunities Ltd
87 Wembley Hill Road
Wembley
Middlesex HA9 8BU
Tel: 081 900 1313
Fax: 081 900 1268

IRELAND

The national contact point for firms interested in tendering opportunities under the EDF is:

Irish Trade Board
Merrion Hall
Strand Road
Sandymount
Dublin 4.
Tel: 01 269 50 11

3. EDF AND OCT: Overseas Countries and Territories

Statutory Basis

The areas of EC-OCT co-operation are set out in full in a Council Decision 86/283/EEC (OJ L 175, dated 1/7/86). The new arrangements are covered by Council Decision of 25 July 1991 (OJ L 263, dated 19/9/91).

Background

Different provisions cover the arrangements for providing financial and technical co-operation to OCTs and Lomé countries.

Programme Content

The general regulations, conditions and procedural rules for works, supply and service contracts are embodied in Council Decision of 16/12/91 (OJ L 40, dated 15/2/92).

The new provisions for OCTs proposed by the Commission include:

- the extension of duration from five to ten years;
- better financing terms;
- emphasis on environmental considerations, a further 24 MECU has been set aside for saving the tropical rain forests;
- provisions on the role of women;
- improvements in STABEX and SYSMIN; and
- greater stress on regional co-operation between ACP countries and OCTs in the same geographical area.

EC Contribution

Under new arrangements which parallel Lomé, 140 MECU of aid will be made available to OCTs under the seventh EDF as follows:

- grants 106.5 MECU
- risk capital 25.0 MECU
- export earnings 6.0 MECU
- aid to mining industries 2.5 MECU.

The EIB will also make 25 MECU available.

Participation

French, Dutch and British OCTs are all eligible to participate.

INFORMATION

See 2 above: the Programme on the EDF and Lomé Countries.

4. ASIAN AND LATIN AMERICAN (ALA) COUNTRIES

Statutory Basis

Financial and technical co-operation between the EC and the Asian and Latin American (ALA) countries began in 1976. The basic policy objectives were laid down in Council Regulation 442/81 but are amplified annually. The latest proposals, which were published in OJ C 284, dated 31/10/91, were adopted in November 1991. This aid includes food aid, emergency and humanitarian aid and a mechanism for stabilising export earnings. The export earnings stabilisation for 1991-2000 is published in COM (91) 169 final of May 1991.

Programme Content

Human rights and the needs of local people are an important factor in determining aid programmes. The main beneficiary of aid should be the local population and special consideration is given to the needs of ethnic groups and of women. Since food security is of great importance, priority is given to the rural sector, particularly the development of fishing and agriculture. As governments may not attach much importance to the environment, at least 10% of funds is set aside for environmental projects. Energy conservation is being increasingly encouraged.

The EC seeks to encourage regional co-operation in the fields of the environment, inter-regional trade, regional institutions and communications. Multilateral initiatives were launched by the Punta del Este Conference in 1986 and the policies then evolved are being further refined and developed in various parts of Asia. The EC is also continuing its efforts to ensure greater access for products from the ALA countries to the Community market, identify areas of mutual interest including arranging contacts with potential partners and assisting in the establishment of joint ventures.

A new priority is the structural dimension. Sectoral problems are being taken into account when development projects are considered. Measures supporting the reform of land tenure are encouraged, especially when it involves helping communities to take charge of the development of their own areas. There should be an element of training in all schemes and special attention is paid to the training of administrators and technicians.

There are also post-doctoral fellowships for scientists of third countries who wish to benefit from a short stay in a research institution in the EC.

All EC schemes must be integrated and adapted to fit the individual needs of the country in question: for instance, over-crowding problems are given attention in appropriate countries. Another area of concern is the tropical rain forests in South-East Asia and the Amazon.

EC Contribution

Financial and technical co-operation totalled 133 MECU in 1991. All aid is in the form of grants because of the huge debts of the ALA countries.

Participation

All developing countries in Asia and Latin America are eligible except the signatories to the Lomé Convention. In practice, aid goes to the least developed countries. This is extended to the richer countries only in response to specific problems such as natural disasters, the environment, the fight against drugs or to assist with regional co-operation.

INFORMATION

See 2 above on the EDF and Lomé Countries.

5. ENERGY TECHNOLOGY TRANSFER WITH LDC: (Less Developed Countries)

Aims

The aim is to encourage the transfer of Community energy technology to LDCS and to develop technological co-operation with them.

Background

The LDCS targeted are those which have already achieved a degree of industrialisation and include those in the Mediterranean region, Latin America, Asia, and Central and Eastern Europe.

Programme Content

The objectives are:

- the rationalisation of energy use in all areas of consumption, energy-saving apparatus and combustion techniques;
- the improvement of industrial processes and efficiency;
- the improvement of electricity supply systems;
- decentralised electricity production; and
- the production and use of solid fuels, and the distribution and use of natural gas.

The ultimate objective is to establish partnerships between firms in LDCS and those in the EC.
Projects must include co-operation in scientific or technical research and must be undertaken by an industrial body or firm, preferably one with previous links with developing countries. The need for co-financing should be demonstrated and the work should be carried out, where possible, with a partner in the developing country.

EC Contribution

The EC may finance up to half of the total cost of each proposal selected up to a maximum of 100,000 ECU for each specific project, for a period of about one year.

Status Report

A call for proposals was published in OJ C 122, dated 8/5/91, with a deadline of 23 August 1991. It is not anticipated that further calls will be made in this specific programme in the foreseeable future, as these objectives are being absorbed into other programmes.

INFORMATION

Commission of the European Communities
Directorate-General for Energy
200 rue de la Loi
B-1049 Brussels
Tel: INT+ 322 295 1485
Fax: INT+ 322 295 0150

6. STD3: Life Sciences for Developing Countries

See Chapter 17.4

7. MEDITERRANEAN COUNTRIES AND EIB

Background

The Community assists a number of Mediterranean countries which are linked with the EC by Association or Co-operation Agreements, although actual financial arrangements are the subject of individual financial protocols. The economies of these countries were badly threatened by the accession of Spain and Portugal to the EC, the creation of the internal market and now by the increased links with Central and Eastern European countries.

The New Mediterranean Policy (NAP) (SEC (90) 812 dated 30 June 1990), introduced originally in 1989 but refined and expanded in 1990 aims to develop co-operation networks between the EC and the Mediterranean area.

The majority of the financial protocols under the Association Agreements came into force in 1991. The finance available for each country is allocated according to the specific national priorities agreed between the EC and the recipient country, and recorded in the Memoranda. These Memoranda are analogous to the national IAPs formulated under the EDF procedure. They are, however, more rigid in that they specify the projects for which allocations are to be made.

Programme Content

The main components of the NMP are:

- back-up for the process of economic adjustment;
- encouragement of private investment;
- increase in bilateral and EC financial assistance;
- maintenance or improvement of arrangements governing access to the EC market;
- close involvement with the progress of the EC towards the single market; and
- strengthening of economic and political dialogue, at the regional level where possible.

The EIB's financing operations in non-EC Mediterranean countries comprise two main facets.

i Bilateral Co-operation and Association Agreements with Mediterranean countries which include financial protocols and run for five years. These protocols detail EC participation in the financing of capital investment intended to foster the economic and social development of signatory countries; they also set out a series of financial support measures, funded from the EC's budgetary resources, and aimed at facilitating implementation of structural adjustment and economic reform programmes undertaken by certain Mediterranean countries. The bilateral agreements also encompass a package of commercial and tariff arrangements.

ii "Horizontal Financial Co-operation" which complements the bilateral financial arrangements referred to above and supports regional projects of relevance to the

EC. This co-operation embraces all those non-EC Mediterranean countries which have links with the EC through co-operation or association agreements.

Within this overall framework, financing provided by the EC normally covers:

- loans from the EIB's own resources, which account for the bulk of financing. The interest rates applied to these loans closely reflect conditions on the capital markets on which the Bank raises its funds. In some cases, loans attract an interest subsidy: for instance, loans granted under horizontal financial co-operation for environmental protection attract a 3% interest subsidy;
- risk capital assistance administered and granted by the EIB from EC budgetary resources under an EC mandate, which is used to assist in establishing or bolstering businesses' equity bases; and
- direct grant aid from the Commission, part of which is earmarked, in some cases, for financial interest subsidies on EIB loans.

The EC uses the "global loan" formula (see Chapter 32) to support the small and medium-scale productive investments which are needed for economic expansion in non-EC Mediterranean countries.

EC Contribution

Unlike the finance provided under the Lomé Conventions, which largely consists of grants, approximately 70% of the assistance provided under the NMP is in the form of loans from the resources of the EIB. It provides for an overall aid package of 4,405 MECU, which is allocated as follows:

- 2,075 MECU for the specific protocols for 1991-96;
- 2,030 MECU for broad based co-operation including the environment; and
- 300 MECU as back-up for economic reform.

Participation

The Mediterranean countries associated with the EC fall into three groups, as follows:

i The Mashreq group: Egypt, Jordan, Lebanon, and Syria;

ii The Maghreb group: Algeria, Morocco, and Tunisia; and

iii Israel, Cyprus, Malta, Turkey.

Applications

Projects eligible for financing by the EIB under the financial protocols or horizontal financial co-operation are submitted to the Bank for appraisal. The initial approach can be made on an informal basis, and it is advisable to enter into consultations with the Bank at the earliest possible stage of preparatory work on a project as these initial contacts can often facilitate subsequent project appraisal and financial negotiations.

In the cases of projects eligible for financing under a global loan, contact should be made with the intermediary banks which deploy such loans.

INFORMATION

European Investment Bank
Operations outside the Community
100 Boulevard Konrad Adenauer
L-2950 Luxembourg.
Tel: INT+ 352 43791
Fax: INT+ 352 437704

London Office
European Investment Bank
68 Pall Mall
London SW1Y 5ES
Tel: 071 839 3351
Fax: 071 930 9929

8. MED-CAMPUS

Statutory Basis

The MED-CAMPUS initiative was approved by the Commission during October 1992 and forms part of the New Mediterranean Policy (30/6/90, SEC (90) 812).

Objectives

The main aim is to encourage the establishment of co-operation networks between Higher Education Institutes (HEIs) in the EC and the non EC Mediterranean countries, and generally to facilitate the mobility of teachers, scientists, civil servants and technicians between these geographical areas, in order to improve the opportunities for institutional, social and economic development in the non-EC Mediterranean countries.

Background

A pilot phase covering 62 projects was operated during the academic year 1992-93 and the full programme is expected to cover the period 1993-96.

Programme Content

Priority fields covered by the MED-CAMPUS Programme are:

- training for regional, social and economic development;
- training for management of public and private enterprises;
- training for environmental management; and
- training for cultural exchanges.

The Commission will also be receptive to proposals which cover other areas, as long as they are faithful to the general objective of the NMP - modernising the societies and economies of the non-EC Mediterranean countries.

The MED-CAMPUS Programme is able to finance teacher training and continuous training projects. Complementary activities may also be financed, including temporary attachments, applied research, equipment and access to the EC's data banks.

The final objective of the Programme is to promote the consolidation of participating networks, widening their contacts with business and public administration and opening them to all potential users in both the EC and the non-EC Mediterranean countries. Networking depends on the establishment of an appropriate flow of information that allows all members of the network to interact efficiently. This interaction should concern not only scientific and technical aspects of co-operation but also defining projects and budgets and taking administrative decisions. Each member among other things must play an active role by acting as a source, as well as a recipient, of information and favouring the circulation of technical papers and publications in the appropriate languages.

EC Contribution

A budget of 6.5 MECU was approved for the 1992-93 pilot phase.

The Commission provides co-financing for selected projects varying between 60% and 80% of the proposed total budget. Each project's total annual budget cannot exceed 200,000 ECU.

Participation

The Mediterranean countries involved are Algeria, Cyprus, Egypt, Israel, Jordan, Lebanon, Malta, Morocco, Syria, Tunisia and Turkey.

Grants are awarded to HEIs and public and private training bodies organised on a network basis. The projects must involve at least one Mediterranean partner and two other partners from Member States.

Applications

The call for proposals for the academic year 1993-94 set a deadline of 28 June 1993 and June deadlines can also be expected in future years. Proposals are to be sent to the Commission.

INFORMATION

The Technical Assistance Office (TAO) facilitates and monitors networks' operations and provides a specific information service covering projects, network experiences and opportunities. The address is:

Technical Assistance Office
Ismeri Europa
Via GG Belli 39
00193 Rome
Tel: INT+ 396 3208 378/ 3212 246
Fax: INT+ 396 3612 249

COMMISSION
Commission of the European Communities
DGI - H/2 (Science 14 - Room 8/9)
200 rue de la Loi
1049 Brussels
Tel: INT +322 299 1111 (exchange)
Fax: INT+ 322 299 0203

9. THE AVICENNE INITIATIVE: SCIENCE & TECHNOLOGY CO-OPERATION WITH MAGHREB AND MEDITERRANEAN COUNTRIES

Objectives

The pilot actions (1992-94) have the objective of exploring the opportunities for co-operation between the EC and the Maghreb and other Mediterranean countries in the fields of:

- science and technology;
- environmental protection (1992);
- the management of health systems and water resources (1993): and
- applied technology (1994).

Background

Co-operation with the non-EC Mediterranean countries in science and technology is a stated aim of the NMP. The intention is to develop co-operation networks in the Mediterranean area which deal specifically with problems of particular significance in the area.

Programme Content

The following sectors are eligible under the 1993 call for proposals.

- Health Systems:

  Ways of organising health care should be studied by taking into account the specific constraints imposed by the prevailing socio-economic and cultural situations of the countries together with the on-going changes taking place in them. The research should promote reforms in the structure and function of the health systems, while guarding against the trend towards providing only technological solutions to solve complex social problems. Research may involve quantitative as well as qualitative elements of health systems, employing a variety of research methods.

  Under this call, health systems research is expected to concentrate on health problems and related diseases whose predominance and burden on the health services is common throughout the region.

- Water Resources Management

  In the context of developing lasting and efficient systems for the management and utilisation of water resources, the research priorities for the Avicenne Initiative 1993 will concentrate on:

  - characterisation, evaluation and classification of water resources including both freshwater and sea water;
  - definition and development of scientific methods for the control and surveillance of water resources;
  - monitoring pollution levels;
  - new techniques to develop greater efficiency in the use and consumption of water, and assessing their qualitative and quantitative needs;
  - treatment processes for waste water and its regeneration after use;
  - water conservation and storage techniques; and
  - protecting underground water supplies from contamination particularly by agrochemicals and industrial wastes.

As a general rule, proposed research may be applied or fundamental. However, applied research should be of a pre-competitive nature. Pilot or demonstration projects are not eligible for financial support.

Joint research and development projects will be funded in a similar manner to those described in Chapter 17, except that partners from the developing countries may be treated more generously.

Participation

The programme is open to partnerships made up of individuals and organisations based in the EC, Algeria, Cyprus, Egypt, Israel, Jordan, Lebanon, Morocco, Malta, the Occupied Territories, Syria, Tunisia and Turkey. Partnerships are generally required to include at least one representative from a Member State and at least one from each of two Mediterranean countries.

Applications

Proposal forms may be obtained from the EC delegations in the non Member States, and from D-G XII at the Commission

The deadline for applications for the 1993 call for proposals was 15 September 1993. September deadlines can also be expected for future calls.

INFORMATION

Commission of the European Communities
DG XII/G-4
Science, Research and Development Co-operation with Developing Countries
Avicenne Initiative
Rue Montoyer 75
B-1040 Brussels
Tel: INT+ 322 295 1618/8389
Fax: INT+ 322 296 3308

10. ECIP: European Communities Investment Partners

Statutory Basis

After a successful pilot phase, the Council approved a further three-year trial period from 1/1/92 (OJ L 35, dated 12/2/92).

Objectives

ECIP is an initiative aimed at promoting joint ventures between firms in the Member States and those in Latin America, Asia or the Mediterranean.

Programme Content

Project proposals are analysed on the basis of their financial viability and their contribution to the development of the country concerned. The EC makes financial assistance available but does not interfere with the projects, so companies retain complete control over their operations.

Financial support is available for four types of operation.

Facility No.1: Identification of Potential Partners and Projects
A grant covering up to half the eligible costs, subject to a maximum grant of 100,000 ECU, is available in the participating countries and sectors to facilitate the identification of EC firms which have the technology and financial resources for involvement in eligible joint ventures, and to identify local firms which would be suitable potential joint venture partners for European investors.

Facility No. 2: Operations Prior to Launching a Joint Venture
An interest-free advance covering up to half the eligible costs, subject to a maximum advance of 250,000 ECU, is available for firms wishing to undertake a joint venture investment project. Eligible operations include the search for partners, marketing and feasibility studies, setting up pilot production units and the manufacture of prototypes.

The advance does not need to be repaid if the sponsor does not proceed with the project. The advance must be repaid, however, if the project does proceed and the financial institution itself decides to fund it based on the conclusions of a study financed under this programme. The sponsoring firm may, alternatively, apply to the EC, via the financial institution, to convert it either into a loan with equity features - referred to as an equity loan - or into an equity holding by the EC in the capital of the joint venture.

Facility No.3: Financing of Capital Requirements
Up to 20% of capital requirements may be available in the form of an equity holding or an equity loan for joint ventures set up between partners from the EC and from one of the eligible countries. The European partner must take up an equity holding of at least 10% in the joint venture's capital. The maximum total support per project is 1 MECU.

Facility No.4: Training and Management Expertise
An interest-free loan of up to 250,000 ECU is available to cover up to half the cost of training local technicians and managers employed in the joint venture, the provision of a suitably qualified national from one of the EC Member States to administer the joint venture on a temporary basis, and the use of consultancy services to provide temporary management or technical assistance.

EC Contribution

The 1992 budget for ECIP was 39.4 MECU.

Participation

Facility No.1 is restricted to financial institutions, chambers of commerce, professional associations and public agencies, to undertake general studies. It is not available to individual firms wishing to undertake a specific investment project.

Facility No.2 is available to local and EC-based firms, acting either individually or jointly, who wish to undertake a joint venture investment project.
Facilities 3 and 4 are available to joint ventures established by partners from the EC and from eligible countries or to local companies making investments under a licensing and technical assistance agreement with an EC company.

The Programme is aimed at the following, medium-income, developing countries:

- South America: Argentina, Brazil, Chile, Paraguay and Uruguay;
- Andean Pact: Bolivia, Colombia, Ecuador, Peru, Venezuela;
- Central America: Costa Rica, El Salvador, Guatemala, Honduras, Mexico, Nicaragua and Panama;
- Asia: Bangladesh, Buthan, Cambodia, China, India, Laos, Macao, Maldives, Mongolia, Nepal, Pakistan, Sri Lanka and Vietnam;
- ASEAN: Brunei, Indonesia, Malaysia, Philippines, Singapore and Thailand; and
- Mediterranean and Middle East: Albania, Algeria, Bosnia Herzegovina, Croatia, Cyprus, Egypt, Gulf Co-operation Council, Iran, Israel, Jordan, Lebanon, Malta, Morocco, Slovenia, Syria, Tunisia, Turkey and Yemen.

Applications

ECIP operates through a network of financial institutions, the names of which are available from the Commission.

Under Facility No.1, eligible bodies may apply directly to the EC or through a financial institution. Bodies applying for the other facilities must apply through a financial institution.

INFORMATION

UK

The UK signatories for the EC International Investment Partners Scheme are:

The Business Development Adviser
Commonwealth Development Corporation
1 Bessborough Gardens
London SW1V 2JQ
Tel: 071 828 4488
Fax: 071 828 6505

Head of Aid & Development Services
Banco del Pacifico
45-47 Cornhill - Ground Floor
London EC3V 3PD
Tel: 071 283 7559
Fax: 071 283 7673

Mr Suratgar, Director
Morgan Grenfell
23 Great Winchester Street
London EC2P 2AX
Tel: 071 588 4545
Fax: 071 826 7130/6535

Head of Aid & Development Services
Standard Chartered Bank
1 Aldermanbury Square
London EC2V 7SB
Tel: 071 280 7399
Fax: 071 280 7875

IRELAND

The Irish Participant in the EC International Investment Partners Scheme is:

B Twomey
Allied Irish Banks
AIB International Centre
PO Box 2748
Dublin 1
Tel: 01 874 02 22
Fax: 01 679 71 27

Most recent list of financial institutions participating in ECIP:

Commission of the European Communities
Directorate-General for External Relations
DG-I-K-3
B-1049 Brussels
Tel: INT +322 299 1111 (exchange)
Fax: INT+ 322 299 0204

COMMISSION

T Roe
EC Investment Partners
GDI Economic Co-operation Sector
Commission of the European Communities
200 rue de la Loi
B-1049 Brussels
Tel: INT+ 322 299 0926
Fax: INT+ 322 299 0203

11. PHARE - The Economic Reconstruction of Eastern Europe

Statutory Basis

Council Regulation (EEC) No 3906/89 of 18 December 1989 (OJ L 375, dated 23/12/89) established the Programme for Poland and Hungary. This was amended by Regulation (EEC) No 2698/90 (OJ L 257, dated 21/9/90) and again by Regulation (EEC) No 3800/91 (OJ L 357, dated 28/12/91) both of which broadened the Programme. Regulation 2334/92 (OJ L 227/1) extended the PHARE Programme to Slovenia.

Objectives

The fundamental objective is to provide financial and technical support for the process of transforming the system of Central and Eastern Europe countries' economies from a centralised command basis to one based on market principles.

Background Information

The PHARE Programme was established in December 1989 as a result of a decision taken at the Paris Summit. At first, only Hungary and Poland were covered but Bulgaria, Czechoslovakia, the former Yugoslavia and the former GDR were subsequently included, as political reforms were introduced in these countries. The former GDR was assisted by the PHARE Programme until the end of 1991, after which it became eligible for assistance under the Structural Funds. It was agreed that Romania should have access to the PHARE Programme in January 1991, the three Baltic States and Albania on 1 January 1992 and Slovenia in August 1992. The remainder of the former Yugoslavia is currently ineligible because of the political situation. The PHARE Programme is scheduled to be replaced by the European Association Agreement in early 1994.

Programme Content

The PHARE Programme is not intended to be either a Community export guarantee scheme or a macro-economic stabilisation fund. Assistance is conditional upon political stability in the country concerned and its continuing commitment to democratic ideals and free market principles.

The EC has decided to concentrate on key sectors of the reform process, in order to avoid dilution of effort and to ensure the maximum efficiency and effectiveness of its contributions to multilateral assistance. In particular, it was agreed that, to enable the countries concerned to operate in a free market environment based on private ownership, the most appropriate use of EC PHARE funds would be in an number of priority areas: agriculture, industry, investment, energy, environmental protection, trade and services, and training to speed up the process of economic reform and structural adjustment, including associated legislative and regulatory programmes.

In practice, this involves transforming the production and distribution system, with an emphasis on private ownership and investment, together with the establishment of a broader regulatory, organisational and commercial infrastructure and environment, without which a competitive market economy cannot function properly. To this end, a number of core areas were identified:

- restructuring of public enterprises, including de-monopolisation of state monopolies and the associated regulatory and legal aspects;
- modernisation of financial services, including the commercial operation of the banking system, development of capital and securities markets, insurance, accounting and tax systems;
- promotion of the private sector, particularly SMEs, together with the appropriate support services including vocational training; and
- development of the labour market and social sectors as part of the restructuring process.

Funding is targeted upon priorities identified by the recipient rather than donor countries. The Commission and the beneficiary country agree an indicative programme of objectives and priorities. This general framework is further broken down into a series of projects and programmes, followed by a financing proposal, a Commission decision made after consultation with the beneficiary countries and then tenders, where appropriate.

EC Contribution

300 MECU was provided for 1990, the first year of the operation of the PHARE Programme for Poland and Hungary, and an additional 200 MECU was added to the fund in late 1990 for the new beneficiary countries. The budget was 785 MECU for 1991, 1.015 BECU for 1992 and 1.04 BECU for 1993.

The overall PHARE budget is broken down as follows:

- national programmes: 75%;
- regional activity: 10% (possibly rising to 15% by 1997); and
- non-programmed PHARE funding, including humanitarian aid: 15% (possibly decreasing to 10% by 1997).

Allocations per country, which take account of their immediate needs and abilities to cope with reforms as well as objective factors such as population, GDP and debt burden, are as follows (1993-97):

Bulgaria	7-9%	Romania	0-13%
Czech Republic	8-10%	Slovenia	1%
Slovak Republics	8-10%	Albania	2-4%
Hungary	8-10%	Baltic States	4-6%
Poland	17-20%	Former Yugoslavia	*12%.

* The Former Yugoslavia allocation will probably be used exclusively for humanitarian aid purposes.

Participation

Countries currently eligible are Albania, Bulgaria, the Czech and Slovak Republics, Estonia, Hungary, Latvia, Lithuania, Poland and Romania. PHARE support for Yugoslavia was suspended by the EC with effect from 11 November 1991. In the meantime, following recognition by the EC of the independence of Slovenia, a decision was taken to include it in PHARE support. The situation regarding the rest of the former Yugoslavia is less clear and companies should keep in touch with the DTI's World Aid Section (WAS) or FSU, Central and Eastern Europe Branch.

Applications

Copies of the IAPs are available from the Department of Trade and Industry's World Aid Section.

As is common with other forms of EC external aid and assistance, PHARE follows established EC procedures and regulations which govern the general EC budget. Open or restricted tendering procedures are always applied for contracts in excess of 50,000 ECU. The Programme therefore follows the open tender procedure for the procurement of goods or supplies whenever possible, and interested parties from the EC and any of the recipient countries can compete on equal terms. The calls for tender are published in each country, according to its normal practices, and in the OJ C series and S supplement. These invitations to tender expressly indicate the national or other authorities from which the detailed tender documents may be obtained and contain the address of the agency responsible, to which tenders should be sent.

Full details of all projects and programmes funded under PHARE are available from the WAS database and/or through Export Intelligence. WAS also either hold or can obtain copies of the tender documents for all calls advertised in the OJ.

A considerable amount of professional and consultancy work is required under the PHARE Programme. The very nature of the technical expertise and level of professional proficiency needed usually makes it more expedient for the administrators of the Programme to restrict contracts and tenders to firms or persons with proven experience in the relevant fields. To gain access to this work, it is essential for consultants to apply to register with the Consultancy Register for Development Projects in the Directorate-General for Development (D-G VIII). It uses the DACON computerised system; copies of the EC's DACON Registration Form and Guidance Notes can be obtained from WAS. Suitable firms will be selected, on the basis of proven experience and capacity, for "long" and "short" lists for any given "restricted" tender procedure for technical assistance.

It is very important to respond to the pre-qualification tenders issued by the PHARE Operational Service in Brussels. This is in order to secure a place on the "long" lists of companies from which the names of companies selected to bid for projects in specific sectors are drawn. The PHARE Operational Service has its own computerised database of consultants with specific expertise relating to Central and Eastern Europe, which it shares with TACIS. Consultants should register on this database: a registration form is available from Ms Sylvie Koch in PHARE Unit 4. Such registration should secure entry on the "long" list.

Consultants wishing to register their interest in specific PHARE consultancy projects should write to the specific PHARE Unit, outlining, in no more than two or three pages, their skills and previous experience in the region, and requesting further information as appropriate.

For areas where the requirements for projects, programmes or studies have not yet been finalised, it is important for UK and Irish companies to make their first point of contact in the relevant beneficiary country rather than in Brussels, since people "on the ground" are better able to influence their national authorities in favour of giving priority to a particular proposal. Prospects of success can be enhanced by suggesting initiatives, making an early input to the project specification and by good first-hand contacts. Initial contact should be made with the appropriate project implementation organisation or other relevant officials in the country concerned: addresses are in the "INFORMATION" section below or Appendix 2.

INFORMATION

UK

Central & Eastern Europe Trade Policy Section
FSU, Central and Eastern European Branch
Department of Trade and Industry
Bay 932
Kingsgate House
London SW1E 6SW
Tel: 071 215 5112/4817
Fax: 071 215 5269

World Aid Section
EC Aid/PHARE:
Room 290
Ashdown House
123 Victoria Street
London SW1H 6RB
Tel: 071 215 6157
Fax: 071 215 6535

Export Intelligence is operated on behalf of the DTI by:
Prelink Limited
Export House
Wembley Hill Road
Wembley
Middlesex HA9 8BU
Tel: 081 900 1313
Fax: 081 900 1268

COMMISSION

An up-to-date PHARE address book is available from the following:
PHARE Advisory Unit
1st Floor, Office 26
Rue d'Arlon 88
B-1049 Brussels
Belgium
Tel: INT+ 322 299 1356/1400/1500/1600
Fax: INT+ 322 999 1777

Commission of the European Communities
Directorate General I (L 86)
PHARE Operational Service
Rue d'Arlon 88
B-1049 Brussels
Tel: INT+ 322 29 + extension as set out below:

Unit 1: Agriculture, Environment, Telecommunications, Energy, Transport
- agricultural projects: ext. 58386/ 52014/ 65678
- transport projects: ext. 50422
- environmental projects: ext. 65679
- energy projects: ext. 51511
- telecommunications projects: ext.99071

Unit 2: Industry, Finance and Enterprises
- industry, SMEs, privatisation, investments etc.: ext.56172
- finance, tax, accounting etc.: ext. 53378

Unit 3: Non-Governmental Organisations (NGOs), social adjustments and programming
- programming, geographical co-ordination, social and institutional aspects: ext. 92333
- customs, statistics: ext. 92017
- science & technology: ext. 92022
- NGOs: ext. 91341
- health and humanitarian aid: ext. 91900

Unit 4: Internal Administration
- general consultancy registrations: Ms Sylvie Koch ext. 58216

Consultancy Register for Development Projects,
Commission of the European Communities
(DG VIII)
Directorate-General for DevelopmentRue de Geneve 12
B-Brussels
Tel: INT+ 322 299 2809
Fax: INT+ 322 299 2875

CONTACTS IN THE EC REPRESENTATIVE OFFICES OF RECIPIENT COUNTRIES IN CENTRAL & EASTERN EUROPE

Albania
Mr Marchini Camia
Delegation of the Commission of the EC
Deshmoret e Kombit
Keshili 1 Ministrave
Tirana

Baltic States
Mr Hans Jorn Hansen
Acting Delegation for Estonia, Latvia, and Lithuania
c/o Delegation in Sweden
PO Box 7323, Hamngatan 6
S-103 90 Stockholm
Sweden
Tel: INT+ 468 611 1172
Fax: INT+ 468 611 4435

Czech & Slovak Republics
Leopold Giunti
Delegation of the Commission of the EC
Pod Hradbami
16000 Prague 6
Tel: INT+ 422 322051-55
Fax: INT+ 422 328617

Hungary
Mr H Beck
Delegation of the Commission of the EC
Berc Utca 23
H 1016 Budapest
Tel: INT+ 361 166 4487/4587
Fax: INT+ 361 166 4221
Tlx: 061 225984

Poland
Mr A Dijckmeester
Delegation of the Commission of the EC
Aleja Ujasdowskie 14
PL-00-567 Warsaw
Tel: INT+ 482 625 0770
Fax: INT+ 482 625 0430
Tlx: 813 802 COMEU PL

Bulgaria
Mr Tom O'Sullivan
Delegation of the Commission of the EC
Suite 557, Sheraton Hotel
5 Sveta Nedelya Square
BG-1000 Sofia
Tel: INT+ 3592 876541
Fax: INT+ 3592 871038

Romania
Mr E A Hap
Informal Representation in Romania
7 Boulevard Magheru
Scara A
Etaj 3, Camera 70
Bucharest
Tel: INT+ 400 415069
Fax: INT+ 400 120074

NATIONAL CO-ORDINATORS OF THE PHARE PROGRAMME

Albania
Mr Gjergj Konda, Minister for the Economy
"Deshmonet et Kombit"
Tirana
Albania
Tel: INT+ 35542 28264
Fax: INT+ 35542 28362

Initial contact:
Mr Dulaku, Ministry of Economy or Director of the Aid Co-ordination Unit

Estonia
Mr Madis Uurike, Minister of Finance
Ministry of Finance
Suur-Ameerika Street 1
EE0100 Tallinn
Republic of Estonia
Tel: INT+ 372 268 3602/3616
Fax: INT+ 4530 310050 (c/o Denmark)

Initial contact:
Mr Rasmussen, Ministry of Finance

Latvia
Mr Uldis Osis, Deputy Minister of Finance
International Collaboration Department
Smilsu Str. 1
226170 Riga
Republic of Latvia
Tel: INT+ 371 221 0352
Fax: INT+ 4530 249841

Initial contact:
Ms Vita Terauds (Director Foreign Aid Co-ordination Division)
Mr Luc Zwaenenpoel,
Ms Rachel Mai Jones

Bulgaria
Mr S Alexandrov, Minister of Finance
Ministry of Finance
102 Rakovski Str.
1040 Sofia, Bulgaria
Tel: 3592 870622
Fax: INT+ 3592 870581/801148
Tlx: 22727 minfin bg

Initial contact:
Mr Plamen Gogov (PHARE Co-ordination Officer)
Tel and Fax: INT+ 3592 869219/870945
Tel and Fax: INT+ 3592 869219/870945

Slovak Republic
Mr Milan Knazko
Ministry of Foreign Affairs
Stromova 1
831 01 Bratislava
Tel: INT+ 427 37 39 56
Fax: INT+ 422 370 4487

Initial contact:
Mr Julius Hauser
Head of Multilateral Affairs
Ministry of Foreign Affairs
Tel: INT+ 422 370 4467/4209
Fax: INT+ 422 370 4487

Lithuania
Mr Povilas Gylys, Minister for Foreign Affairs
Ministry of Foreign Affairs
J Tumo-Vaizganto 2
2000 Vilnius
Republic of Lithuania
Tel: INT+ 370 222 6400/262 4670
Fax: INT+ 370 222 6892/262 5940

Initial contact:
Mr Algivdas Miskinis
Mr Derek Blink
Mr Nicholas Maddock (EC/PHARE Advisors)

Czech Republic
Mr Josef Zieleniec,
Ministry of Foreign Affairs
Loretanske nam 5
125 10 Prague 1
Tel: INT+ 422 2193 25555/2161
Fax: INT+ 422 2193 2041

Initial contact:
Mr Pavel Bratinka, Deputy Minister of Foreign Affairs
Tel: INT+ 422 2193 2525
Fax: INT+ 422 2193 2037

Hungary
Dr Laszlo Bogar, Secretary of State
Ministry of International Economic Relations
Honved Utca 13-15
H-1055 Budapest, Hungary
Tel: INT+ 361 153 0000
Fax: INT+ 361 153 2794

Initial contact:
Mr I Gyurkovics
Director-General OECD Aid
Co-ordination Secretariat
Ministry of International Economic Relations
Tel: INT+ 361 153 2394/131 4735
Fax: INT+ 361 153 0895

Poland

Mr Jan Krzysztof Bielecki
Minister for European Integration and European Assistance
Council of Ministers
Al Ujasdowskie, 9
PL-00-950 Warsaw
Poland
Tel: INT+ 482 628 0315/628 8630
Fax: INT+ 4822 294 888

Initial contact:
Dr Pawel Samecki
Director-General for PHARE office
Council of Ministers
Tel: INT+ 482 628 8630
Fax: INT+ 4822 294 888/216 686

Prof. Jacek Saryusz-wolski
Under-Secretary of State for European Integration and Foreign Assistance
Council of Ministers
Al Ujasdowskie, 9
PL-00-950 Warsaw
Poland
Tel: INT+ 482 628 0315/628 8630
Fax: INT+ 4822 294 888

Initial contact:
Dr Pawel Samecki
Director-General for PHARE office
Council of Ministers
Tel: INT+ 482 628 8630
Fax: INT+ 4822 294 888/216 686

Romania

M Negritoiu
President of Romanian Development Agency
7 Boulevard Magheru
Bucharest - Sector 1
Romania
Tel: INT+ 401 615 6686
Tel: INT+ 401 615 6624
Tel: INT+ 401 615 9367
Tel: INT+ 401 312 2834
Fax: INT+ 401 312 0371

Initial contacts:
Mr N Idu (Director)
Division of International Economic Organisations

PHARE Desk
Ina Iliescu
Catalin Guran
Elena Mocanu
Tel: INT+ 401 615 4698

Slovenia

Prof. Rado Bohinc
Ministry for Science & Technology
Slovenska 50
61000 Lubljana
Tel: INT+ 3861 11 11 07
Fax: INT+ 3861 30 29 51

Initial contact:
Mr Marijan Manfredo
Head of National Bureau for Financing Technical Assistance
Mr Alan Eames, PHOS Representative Office
Fax: INT+ 3861 22 47 32

12. PHARE ASSISTANCE PROGRAMMES

12.1 RIPP: Regional Industrial Property Programme

Statutory Basis

Decision taken on 30 July 1992 at PHARE Management Committee meeting No 18.

Background

In 1990, the Administrative Council of the European Patent Office (EPO) approved proposals for technical co-operation with the CEEC and, as a result, the EPO assisted Bulgaria, Czechoslovakia, Hungary and Poland to draw up five-year modernisation plans linked to detailed investment schedules. The EPO is now helping Romania prepare a similar plan.

Programme Content

The RIPP includes three main project components to be implemented by a programme management unit at the EPO:

i the organisation of training courses and seminars for staff of national authorities and the patent profession (1.42 MECU);

ii the development of common software to administer patent and trademark procedures (0.56 MECU); and

ii the modernisation of documentation procedures component (0.88 MECU);

There is also a project management unit (0.14 MECU).

EC Contribution

3 MECU has been allocated to this programme, as above.

Applications

The Programme will be implemented by a separate management unit within the EPO, which will draw up a six-month work programme in consultation with the beneficiary countries. The EPO will be in charge of measuring the effectiveness of the programme, in collaboration with the recipient institutions, and will report regularly to the Commission.

Services will be sub-contracted by the EPO to bodies such as EC Member State patent offices and suitably qualified private firms. These will be subject to the usual EC tendering procedures of restricted calls for tender, except in the case of small contracts which may be awarded by direct agreement.

INFORMATION

See the information section of the PHARE Programme (above).

12.2 TELECOMMUNICATIONS PROGRAMME

Statutory Basis

Decision taken on 30 July 1992 at PHARE Management Committee meeting No. 18.

Objectives

The Programme's objectives are as follows:

- to assist the CEECs in the process of modernising their telecommunications sectors;
- to promote harmonised regional approaches and co-ordination as well as information exchange;
- to support the identification and preparation of investment-related projects at regional level; and
- to upgrade the existing knowledge base of staff in selected fields of telecommunications regulations and operation.

Programme Content

Assistance will be provided by means of a modular approach to answer the needs of the target groups who will principally benefit from the Programme. The target groups consist primarily of qualified staff actively taking part in activities in the key areas of institutional and legislative reform. Specific actions will be proposed for each defined module, involving theoretical and practical aspects which take into account the varying level of expertise available among national staff. Particular emphasis is to be laid on achieving continuity of impact for the programme after its initial implementation, through on-going training, as well as actions calling for urgent attention in the context of sectoral reforms. Joint teams of foreign and national experts will encourage the involvement of national staff.

EC Contribution

7 MECU has been allocated to the Programme, to be distributed as follows:

- modules (special case studies and training) 5.6 MECU
- management and co-ordination 0.7 MECU
- evaluation and monitoring 0.1 MECU
- contingencies 0.6 MECU

Applications

Contractors for technical assistance will be selected through the normal procedures applicable under the PHARE programme. Procurement of equipment will be made by international tender or by direct agreement.

Contracts will be concluded with independent consultants for the monitoring of the Programme's progress and for a comprehensive ex-post-facto evaluation of the programme after completion.

INFORMATION

See the information section of the PHARE Programme (above).

12.3 ENVIRONMENTAL ACTION PLAN FOR CENTRAL AND EASTERN EUROPE

Statutory Basis

Decision taken on 2 December 1992 at PHARE Management Committee meeting No.20.

Objectives

The overall objective of the Environment Plan is to support and enhance the political and technical process towards closer regional co-operation on environmental protection at a pan-European level.

Background

The Dublin meeting of European Environment Ministers in 1990 concluded that the protection of the environment was one of the most urgent political priorities in the pan-European dialogue. In June 1991 Western European Environment Ministers met the Environment Ministers of Central and Eastern Europe in Dobris and four main initiatives were decided:

- the preparation of a "Pan-European State of the Environment Report", which will map existing environmental damage be used as the basis for the effective implementation of environmental policies and strategies;
- the preparation of a programme on nature conservation, which is being co-ordinated by the Council of Europe and focuses on the problems of preserving the natural heritage of the CEECs, the compatibility of tourism and recreational activities with nature conservation and increasing public awareness of the problems involved in the conservation of nature;
- the preparation of an "Immediate Environmental Action Programme" for the CEECs; and
- the development of an “Environmental Action Programme” for Europe, to be co-ordinated by the Senior Advisers on Environmental and Water Problems from the Economic Council for Europe.

Programme Content

The Programme started in 1992 and is scheduled to last for three years. It will finance the creation of a Project and Investment Preparation Fund, linked to the priority areas and projects identified in the Action Programme. The fund will be used to prepare investment and other projects as well as financing technical assistance and studies. These will be used to support project assessment, pre-investment studies, feasibility studies, detailed design and other technical studies and financial co-ordination and preparation of co-financing arrangements.

Applications

The PHARE Operational Service will be responsible for selecting projects in consultation with the national PHARE Environmental Project Implementation Units (PIUs). The PIUs will be involved in the implementation of the Programme and support may also be channelled through the existing instruments for environmental investments in the country in question, such as the National Fund for Environmental Protection in Poland.

Equipment procurement will be by international tender, or by restricted consultation, if justified by the cost or special technical characteristics of the equipment. Technical assistance will be recruited by either restricted consultation or direct agreement, depending on the cost and special nature of the services. Small expenditure may be subject to direct agreement.

INFORMATION

See the information section of the PHARE Programme (above).

12.4 REGIONAL ENVIRONMENT SECTOR PROGRAMME

Statutory Basis

Decision taken on 30 July 1992 at PHARE Management Committee meeting No. 18.

Objectives

The objective of the Programme is to alleviate some of the most critical, trans-national, environmental problems prevailing in Europe by supporting a number of regional initiatives started as a part of the 1991 Regional Environmental Programme, and by launching two new initiatives. The key objectives are:

- to support two regional and integrated environmental programmes aimed at tackling the critical pollution problems identified in the 1991 Regional Environmental Programme, and by launching two new initiatives concerning regions which have been identified as deserving priority attention - the Danube River Basin and the Black Sea.
- to enhance the availability of reliable and up-to-date data on natural resources and sources of pollution, to be used as a base for longer-term preventative and curative actions; and
- to help develop institutions which can focus, develop and express public opinion on environmental matters as part of the development of a functions of a democratic civic society. This support will be provided through the Regional Environment Centre in Budapest.

Programme Content

This programme started in 1992 and is scheduled to last for three years.

The following areas will be covered:

- integrated environmental programme for the Danube River Basin (3.9 MECU);
- regional environmental programme for the Black Sea (1 MECU);
- Baltic Sea integrated programme (2 MECU);
- environmental rehabilitation of the Black Triangle area (2.9 MECU);
- remote sensing and use of satellite data (4.9 MECU); and
- support for public participation and awareness building - Regional Environmental Centre (REC) in Budapest (1 MECU).

The REC is an independent, non-profit making organisation which was established in 1990 to help develop NGOs and increase public participation in and awareness of environmental issues in the countries of Central and Eastern Europe.

EC Contribution

This Programme has been allocated a budget of up to 16 MECU, disbursed as shown above.

Applications

Equipment procurement will be by international tender or by restricted procedures, while technical assistance will be recruited either by restricted consultation or direct agreement.

The implementing authority will be the Commission and specifically, the PHARE Operational Service under the responsibility of the Directorate-General for External Relations, working closely with the Directorate-General for Environment, Nuclear Safety and Civil Protection and the Directorate-General for Science, Research and Development.

INFORMATION

See the information section of the PHARE Programme (above).

12.5 REGIONAL QUALITY ASSURANCE PROGRAMME

Statutory Basis

Decision taken on 30 July 1992 at PHARE Management Committee Meeting No.18.

Objectives

The objective is to help PHARE countries not covered by the 1991 programme to implement institutional and legislative reform in the field of quality assurance and to make the transition to a voluntary system of standardisation, as well as setting up appropriate institutions to offer guidance.

Background

Quality assurance is the key to economic development, as it creates a favourable environment for growth in the fields of production and services and allows for international competition according to common rules for market quality. Whereas quality assurance is undertaken at a voluntary level in Western Europe, it was enforced by legislative requirements in the Central and Eastern European Countries (CEECs). Standards were thus imposed by the national authorities, in the absence of a private sector, as a direct consequence of the need to trade with Western countries. This resulted in a cumbersome and regressive system, subject to strict administrative controls. Subsequent economic and political changes coupled with the desire of the emerging private sector to opt for a voluntary system based on free market values, have made the need for urgent reform overwhelming.

This programme aims to remedy the lack of technical know-how and insufficiency of financial resources which characterise the transition to the voluntary system.

Programme Content

The Programme started in 1992 and is scheduled to last for three years.

It is made up of four parts:

i technical assistance for reform of legislation and institutions;

ii funds for training by Western institutions;

iii funds for promotion of technical exchanges with Western Europe; and

iv technical and financial assistance to interest designers, manufacturers and distributors in quality assurance.

Projects will be decided on a country-by-country basis, as the Programme is implemented so as to make sure that the programme has the maximum possible impact given the financial resources available.

EC Contribution

The programme has been allocated 2 MECU.

Applications

The Programme will be run by the Centre Européen de Normalisation (CEN).

INFORMATION

See the information section of the PHARE Programme (above).

12.6 REGIONAL ENERGY SECTOR PROGRAMME

Statutory Basis

Decision taken on 30 July 1992 at PHARE Management Committee meeting No.18.

Objectives

The objective of the Programme is to further the restructuring of the energy sectors in the CEECs towards free market criteria, and to seek common solutions to common problems so as to avoid duplication of effort, while giving practical expressions to the ideals embodied in the European Energy Charter.

Programme Content

The Programme started in 1992 and is scheduled to last up to the end of 1994. It comprises the following measures:

- interconnection of Eastern and Western electricity grids (2 MECU);
- natural gas interconnections (2 MECU);
- oil refining and transportation (1 MECU);
- management training and twinning (1 MECU); and
- legislation, regulation and strategy (1 MECU).

Applications

Procurement of equipment will be by international open tender, unless costs or special technical requirements justify a restricted tender process.

Technical equipment will be procured by restricted tender procedures. Direct agreements may be entered into for expenditure of minor significance or when justified by the specific nature of the goods or services.

Overall co-ordination of the project rests with PHARE's Operational Service ,in close co-operation with the Ministries responsible for energy policy.

INFORMATION

See the information section of the PHARE Programme (above).

12.7 REGIONAL TRANSPORT PROGRAMME

Objectives

The objective of the Programme is to assist in the restructuring of the transport sector and in upgrading the transport infrastructure in the CEECs. It will promote the on-going integration of Western and Eastern transport networks and will help co-ordinate the various offers of technical and financial assistance.

Background

Traffic on the main link roads in the region has increased massively since the revolutions of 1989 made the liberalisation of travel possible. The import of Western second-hand cars led to a steep climb in car ownership, thereby further clogging the already inadequate roads. The situation has been further aggravated by the diversion of Greek traffic from Yugoslavia to routes further east. The existing road transport infrastructure is totally unable to deal with the increased volume of traffic, causing slow travel, frequent tailbacks, high accident rates and ever growing pollution. Customs posts are inadequate and waiting periods of several days are not uncommon for commercial vehicles.

The only chance of solving the problems is through a co-ordinated programme supported by all the countries concerned. The present Programme grows out of this common desire and builds on the various 1991 PHARE transport programmes.

Programme Content

The Programme started in 1992 and is scheduled to last for three years. It has four main priorities:

i transit infrastructure and border-crossing project (15 MECU);

ii trans-European north-south motorway and trans-European north-south railway (2 MECU);

iii integrated training and technical assistance programme (2 MECU); and

iv sectoral studies on the potential for future developments (2 MECU).

Applications

Investment projects undertaken under the transit infrastructure component of this programme will be undertaken in close collaboration with the EIB.

Technical assistance will be recruited by restricted tender. Procurement will be by international tender or restricted consultation, if justified by financial or technical considerations. Direct agreements may be entered into for minor expenditures.

INFORMATION

See the information section of the PHARE Programme (above).

12.8 REGIONAL PROGRAMME FOR THE FIGHT AGAINST DRUGS

Statutory Basis

Decision taken on 16 October 1992 at PHARE Management Committee Meeting No.19.

Objectives

The general objective of the Programme is to help the recipient states in their struggle against the drugs problem and enable them to monitor the trends. The programme is also intended to encourage co-operation between the EC Member States and the CEECs.

Programme Content

The Programme started in 1992 and is scheduled to last for two years. It includes a pilot phase proposing a range of measures which provide assistance in drafting legislation, and developing both services and expertise. Specific measures include:

- monitoring precursor chemicals used to manufacture drugs (0.25 MECU);
- measures against money laundering (0.25 MECU);
- development of drug information systems and networking (0.5 MECU); and
- support for demand reduction programmes (0.9 MECU).

EC Contribution

A budget of 2 MECU has been allocated to the programme, as well as a reserve of 100,000 ECU.

Applications

The Commission will arrange for specialised expertise to be recruited from the competent authorities in the Member States for the first two elements of the Programme. For the latter two elements, technical assistance and other staff will be recruited by restricted consultation with specialised institutions or by direct agreement, as appropriate, depending on costs and the specialised nature of the services required.

INFORMATION

See the information section of the PHARE Programme (above).

12.9 NUCLEAR SAFETY PROGRAMME IN CEEC

Statutory Basis

Decision taken on 16 October 1992 at PHARE Management Committee meeting No.19.

Objectives

The general objectives of the programme are:

- the reduction of risk linked to the operation of nuclear power plants in the CEEC;
- optimising the use of resources, through regional co-operation and collaboration with the relevant international institutions; and

- the implementation of the G-7 approach to nuclear safety in the region.

Background

The nuclear installations in Central and Eastern European Countries (CEEC) share similar characteristics. A multinational approach to the regulatory as well as the operational aspects is therefore the most efficient way to tackle the problem of nuclear safety in these countries. For the same reasons, it is necessary to establish links between the nuclear safety interventions funded by the PHARE and TACIS Programmes.

Programme Content

The Programme began in 1992 and is scheduled to last for 18 months. It has five strands:

i Safety Authorities

The programme covers the adoption of safety standards and regulations compatible to those used in Western countries.

ii Fuel Cycle, Waste Management and Decommissioning

Since the CIS does not provide the services on fuel cycle management or waste management provided by the former USSR, a re-definition of the regional approach to these matters is needed.

iii VVER230-Operational Safety and Near-Term Improvements

This component concerns four reactors in Bulgaria and two reactors in the Czech and Slovak Republics. The Programme will take into account similar international programmes, particularly those planned in the former CIS to deal with the same types of reactors. It will support investment-related activities aiming to improve their safety parameters. The Programme also covers the improvement of measures to ensure on-site preparedness to cope with all types of potential emergency.

iv VVER213 and VVER1000 Operational Safety: Near-Term Improvements and Upgrading.

This component concerns two reactors in Bulgaria, four reactors in the Czech and Slovak Republics and two reactors in Hungary. The approach is similar to that outlined above.

v RMBK - Operational Safety and Near-Term Improvements

This type of reactor constitutes perhaps the most serious risk to global nuclear safety in Europe. Some resources are therefore devoted to a housekeeping effort, improving conditions of exploitation in the short-term.

EC Contribution

20 MECU has been allocated to this programme.

Applications

The contract for the implementation of strand (ii) of the programme will be awarded after a tendering process involving the countries directly concerned. In the event of a major investment in safety equipment being required, a restricted tender will be offered and direct contracts concluded, owing to the highly specialised nature of the equipment.

INFORMATION

ESARDA
(the European Safeguards Research & Development Association)
Scientific Secretariat
Joint Research Centre
I-21020 Ispra (Varese)

12.10 ACE: Action for Co-Operation in the Field of Economics

Statutory Basis

Decision taken on 16 October 1992 at PHARE Management Committee meeting No 19.

Objectives

The general objective of the ACE Programme is to help the Eastern European economies to become better equipped to implement the processes of liberalisation and reform. ACE consists of a range of activities which aim to establish co-operation and interchange between economists and managers in EC countries and in Eastern European countries.

Background

After ACE started on an experimental basis for Poland and Hungary in 1990, the Commission decided to extend it to the other eligible Eastern European countries and provided funding of a further 5 MECU. A large number of proposals have since been forthcoming, testifying to the success and popularity of the programme.

Programme Content

The topics to be supported must be related to the process of economic reform and integration. This includes, in particular, projects dealing with operational implementation issues, managerial development analysis systems, the diagnosis and therapy of macro-economic disequilibria, micro-economic liberalisation, reforms in specific sectors such as agriculture, banking, the labour markets and social protection and other reform and integration issues.

Support will take the following forms:

- six-month fellowships and two-year scholarships for CEEC economists and managers to attend universities in the EC;

- six-month fellowships for senior economists and managers from the EC to work at CEEC universities;
- grants for research projects and networks, bringing together managers and economists of the EC and Eastern Europe;
- grants for recognised centres of excellence in the CEECs for the development of international PhD and MBA programmes;
- grants to CEEC economists and managers to attend seminars, conferences and high-level courses; and
- grants for seminars and publications linked to the circulation of research and related documentation in PHARE countries.

EC Contribution

The programme has a budget of 6 MECU for 1992.

Participation

All PHARE countries may participate.

Applications

The latest call provided for a 1 May 1993 deadline for the submission of applications for grants by individuals or institutions. Further calls with similar deadlines are expected in subsequent years.

INFORMATION

Commission of the European Communities
D-G XII H-1 ACE
200 rue de la Loi
B-1049 Brussels
Tel: INT+ 322 295 6876
Fax: INT+ 322 296 3307

13. JEAN MONNET CHAIRS FOR PHARE COUNTRIES

See Chapter 23.1 for the Jean Monnet Project and Fellowships.

Status Report

From autumn 1993, several Polish and Hungarian universities are to participate in the EC's Jean Monnet project, which sponsors university chairs and courses relating to aspects of European integration. In the light of their possible future EC membership and increasing need for knowledge on EC issues, both Poland and Hungary wished to allocate part of their EC PHARE funds to extending the Jean Monnet Project to their countries. A total of 36 projects for Poland and 20 projects for Hungary have been selected.

14. LOANS TO CEEC: CENTRAL & EASTERN EUROPEAN COUNTRIES

See Chapter 33

15. EIB AND CEEC

See also Chapter 33.

Statutory Basis

In spite of the creation of the EBRD, the EIB continues to operate in CEEC, following Council Decision 41/252/EEC (OJ L 123, 1991).

Background

The EIB's actions in the CEECs complement the PHARE Programme. Since 1989, the EIB has made available its resources, know-how and experience to assist CEECs in their transition to market economies.

Programme Content

Unlike EIB loans, most of the aid provided under this technical assistance programme, consisting mainly of technical know-how, is non reimbursable. In line with EIB practice both inside and outside the EC, however, lending in the CEECs is closely tied to specific projects in the public and private sectors. All projects are carefully appraised to ensure their viability and justification from an economic, technical, financial and environmental point of view.

The EIB may finance up to half the project costs but, in most cases, it provides less than half the funding and co finances investments with other banks and specialised financial institutions. The most likely co financing partners in the CEECs are the financing institutions of the EC's Member States, the World Bank Group and the European Bank for Reconstruction and Development (EBRD).

In the CEECs the EIB, in agreement with the government authorities of each country, is giving priority to projects in:

- transport and telecommunications: the EIB supports investments to improve national networks and extend communication links with other countries, particularly the EC;
- the energy sector, where there is a need for restructuring and technological modernisation, the EIB also finances investments aimed at saving energy and improving the environment; and
- industry, with special reference to joint ventures with EC partners and procuring direct investments by EC firms; the EIB is providing global loans, i.e. temporary lines of credit to CEEC banks to be used for financing small and medium sized projects.

EC Contribution

The EIB Board of Governors, in decisions taken at the end of 1989 and in April 1991, authorised lending of up to 1.7 BECU for investment projects in Bulgaria, the Czech Republic, Hungary, Poland, Romania and Slovakia.

INFORMATION

European Investment Bank
Operations Outside the Community
100 Boulevard Konrad Adenauer
L-2950 Luxembourg
Tel: INT+ 352 43791
Fax: INT+ 352 437704

London Office:
European Investment Bank
68 Pall Mall
London SW1Y 5ES
Tel: 071 839 3351
Fax: 071 930 9929

16. JOPP: Joint Venture PHARE Programme

Objectives

JOPP aims to encourage joint ventures between EC companies and those from CEECs, and to encourage foreign investment and the development of the competitive private sector in those countries, thus supporting their efforts to become an integral part of the wider European trading system.

Background

JOPP was launched in 1991 as part of the PHARE Programme.

Programme Content

JOPP offers a number of different types of support for the different stages in the establishment and development of a joint venture, from feasibility studies and pilot projects to training and technology transfer, including financing requirements and management structures in the joint venture.

There are three phases which attract support.

i The Preliminary Phase

This aims to cover part of the pre-feasibility and feasibility studies. This phase can be comprised not only of market analysis, business plans and contract negotiations between the future partners in the joint venture, but also of the production of prototypes and the conduct of pilot projects. The EC may contribute an advance, which may, under certain conditions, be converted into a grant. The maximum amount of the EC contribution is 2,500 ECU for pre-feasibility studies and 150,000 ECU for feasibility studies and pilot projects.

ii The Co-financing Phase

This aims to contribute to the financing requirements of the joint venture being established or expanded. The EC contribution is in the form of finance for a maximum amount of 1 MECU for a term of up to ten years, and is subject to the provision of matching funds from other investors. The Community contribution may not exceed 20% of the total capital requirements of the joint venture.

iii Technical Assistance Phase

This aims to strengthen the human capital base of joint ventures through technology transfer and training. The EC contribution is in the form of an interest-free loan of up to half the eligible costs of the venture, with a ceiling of 150,000 ECU, and is repayable within five years

The total contributions for the three phases must not exceed 1 MECU per joint venture. A network of financial intermediaries forms the link between the Commission and the beneficiaries. Their role is to:

- analyse and forward to the Commission the projects submitted by businesses wishing to benefit from the programme;
- arrange direct or indirect co-financing of the project submitted, if necessary;
- manage the disbursement of the EC contribution to the business whose project has been accepted; and
- monitor the implementation of the project.

Participation

A joint venture can be any business with two or more shareholders. To qualify as a joint venture for JOPP purposes it must meet the following criteria:

- it must be considered a joint venture under the legislation of the relevant CEEC;
- at least one shareholder must be from an EC country;
- at least one shareholder must be based in a CEEC; and
- at least 75% of the share capital must be held by the shareholders in the EC and the CEEC.

EC businesses which can benefit from JOPP are those which intend to create a joint venture in a CEEC or to expand or restructure an existing joint venture in a CEEC. This applies to businesses in all productive sectors, including the service sector, provided they are making a direct investment which is not purely a financial investment. The bank lending sector is excluded.

Priority will be given to joint ventures involving SMEs and joint ventures in CEECs where the net assets do not exceed 10 MECU.

Applications

In order to benefit from the JOPP Programme, the business must adopt the following procedure:

a. identify a potential partner, EC based companies find one in a CEEC and CEEC based ones, a partner in the EC;

b. prepare a plan that will lead to the creation or expansion of a joint venture;

c. present the plan to one of the financial intermediaries that form part of the network, which will assess the plan and, if its assessment is favourable, will submit it to the Commission;

d. once the project has been accepted by the Commission, the business will sign a financial agreement with the financial intermediary who submitted its project; and

e. the EC contribution will be disbursed in accordance with the provisions lain down in the financial agreement.

INFORMATION

UK
Financial intermediaries are:

Andrew Brzozowski
Commonwealth Development Corporation
1 Bessborough Gardens
London SW1V 2JQ
Tel: 071 828 4488
Fax: 071 828 6505

Nicholas Kennedy/Richard MacGeorge
Morgan Grenfell Plc.
23 Great Winchester Street
London EC2P 2AX
Tel: 071 588 4545
Fax: 071 826 7130

IRELAND
Financial Intermediary:
Mr Michael Aherne
Corporate Finance Department
ICC Bank Plc
32-34 Harcourt Street
Dublin 2
Tel: 01 72 00 55
Fax: 01 78 19 02

COMMISSION
Mr J M Magnette (Head of Unit)
Commission of the European Communities
Directorate-General XVIII - Credit and Investments
Batiment Wagner
Rue Alcide de Gasperi
L-2920 Luxembourg
Tel: INT+ 352 4301 36261
Fax: INT+ 352 436322

JOPP Assistance Unit
20 rue Louvigny
L-2920 Luxembourg
Tel: INT+ 352 467096
Fax: INT+ 352 467097

17. EBRD: European Bank for Reconstruction and Development

Statutory Basis

Council Decision 90/674/EEC (OJ L 372, dated 31/12/90).

Objectives

The EBRD's purpose is to foster the transition towards open market-oriented economies and to promote private and entrepreneurial initiative in those countries of Central and Eastern Europe that are members of the Bank. The EBRD will endeavour to help the CEECs to escape from the isolation of the COMECON command economies and integrate their domestic economies into the world economy. Particular emphasis is placed on strengthening their democratic institutions, developing greater respect for human rights and for introducing environmentally-sound policies.

Background

The EBRD was established in May 1990 and inaugurated in April 1991, with it headquarters in London. Its first President, Jacques Attali, was subsequently forced to resign amidst a barrage of recriminations concerning lavish expenditure on the Bank's premises, staff, entertainment and travel arrangements.

The Bank initially had 41 members consisting of 39 countries spanning Europe, the USA, and Japan plus two international institutions. They were all represented on the Board of Governors. By the end of March 1993, as a result of the political changes in Central and Eastern Europe, the number of CEEC members had grown from 8 to 22 and the overall membership had reached 56.

The initial paid up capital is 10 BECU, of which 30% was due to be subscribed in five equal instalments, commencing in 1991. The remaining 7 BECU will be borrowed in the international capital markets. Since the gearing ratio is one-to-one, the Bank can make total commitments of 10 BECU.

The powers of the EBRD are vested in a Board of Governors. Each member appoints one Governor and one Alternate Governor, and this board has delegated powers of management to a Board of Directors which comprises 23 members who hold office for a term of three years. The Board of Directors is responsible for both the general direction of the EBRD, including the approval of its budget and the management of its operations. The President is elected by the Board of Governors for a term of four years, and vice-presidents are appointed by the Board of Directors on the recommendation of the President.

Programme Content

The EBRD performs a wide range of functions designed to help the countries of Central and Eastern Europe to implement structural and sectoral economic reforms, including de-monopolisation, decentralisation and privatisation. The Bank finances projects designed to help:

- create a competitive private sector;
- foster entrepreneurial activity and SMEs;
- privatise state-owned enterprises;

- encourage direct foreign investment;
- create and strengthen financial institutions;
- restructure the industrial sector;
- create a modern infrastructure for private sector development and transition to a market economy; and
- improve the environment.

The EBRD merges the principles and practices of merchant and development banking as follows:

- it carries out its funding of private or privatisable enterprises in the competitive sector through Merchant Banking, which includes the full range of private sector financing skills and experience; and
- it carries out its funding of physical and financial infrastructure projects through Development Banking, which includes the full range of development bank financing, involving economic, country and sectoral expertise;

A full range of financing instruments is offered on a market basis including:

- loans, which can be either secured or unsecured, subordinated, convertible or equity-linked, with a maximum financial maturity of ten years for commercial enterprises and of fifteen years for infrastructure projects;
- equity stakes;
- debt guarantees; and
- debt and equity underwriting.

Loans can be denominated in ECUs or any other major currency. The EBRD does not issue guarantees for export credits, undertake insurance activities, or accept the risks of foreign exchange loss on repayment. Loans to commercial enterprises which are not guaranteed by the host government are typically without recourse to foreign sponsors, if any. Financing to state-owned enterprises under privatisation is on a similar basis.

Advisory services and technical assistance are a major feature of the Bank's activities and, to date, co-operation fund agreements for a total of over 150 MECU have been concluded for this purpose.

Development Banking offers assistance to governments and their agencies in the following areas:

- project identification, preparation and funding in the physical and financial infrastructure sectors;
- mobilisation of additional finance from public and private sources on a co-financing basis; and
- support of project implementation, including procurement.

The terms of the Bank's funding are designed to enable it to co-operate both with international financial institutions and public and private financial institutions through co-financing arrangements. There are benefits to be gained from co-financing with the EBRD as follows:

i. The Agreement establishing the EBRD provides it with adequate protection for its investments. Its member governments have agreed not to impose any restrictions on the payments of principal, interest, dividends and other charges in respect of the Bank's loans and investments or the proceeds of disposal of such investments. Under certain circumstances, international banks participating in EBRD transactions may benefit from this protection.

ii. A number of banking supervisors have recognised that co-financing through the participation technique used by international financial institutions should be given preferential treatment in applying country risks provisioning requirements. As a result, participation by banks regulated in these jurisdictions is exempt from country risk provisioning requirements, thereby substantially improving the returns to the banks. A number of Western European countries accord this favourable regulatory treatment to transactions co-financed with the Bank.

iii. In public sector operations, parallel co-financing of contracts or joint financing under EBRD procurement rules provide opportunities for tied lenders to participate in public sector projects that have been prepared with Bank assistance, have provision for necessary management and operational improvements and where the Bank will remain as the principal lender. The Bank also offers optional cross defaults and co-operation agreements to co-lenders. In some circumstances the Bank accepts a share of tied contract financing.

The simplest form of co-financing is participation by other banks in the EBRD's loans. Through this technique, commercial banks can share the benefit of the Bank's status as an international institution.

The Bank seeks to mobilise capital for Central and Eastern Europe, in addition to using its own capital, and syndication is an important component of its financing arrangements. Currently the most widely-used technique is for the Bank to remain the lender of record, giving participating institutions the benefit of its preferred creditor status.

EC Contribution

The EBRD generally favours projects where one third of the project's or company's capitalisation is covered by the sponsor's equity contribution even when some of the equity participation has been in kind. The Bank can often provide a third of the financing, often in the form of loans, and is prepared to assist in finding the remaining third.

Participation

In general, membership of the EBRD is open to all European countries, International Monetary Fund Members, and the EIB.

As at March 1993, the following countries are members of the EBRD: Albania, Armenia, Australia, Austria, Azerbaijan, Belarus, Belgium, Bulgaria, Canada, Cyprus, Denmark, Egypt, Estonia, Finland, France, Georgia, Germany, Greece, Hungary, Iceland, Ireland, Israel, Italy, Japan, Kazakhstan, the Republic of Korea, Kyrgyzstan, Latvia, Liechtenstein, Lithuania, Luxembourg, Malta, Mexico, Moldova, Morocco, the Netherlands, New Zealand, Norway, Poland, Portugal, Romania, the Russian Federation, Slovenia, Spain, Sweden, Switzerland, Tajikistan, Turkey, Turkmenistan, Ukraine, the United Kingdom, the United States of America and Uzbekistan.

Membership procedures are currently being finalised for Croatia, the Czech Republic, the former Yugoslav Republic of Macedonia and the Slovak Republic.

Applications

Funding proposals should meet the following criteria:

- business plans or feasibility studies must be completed and endorsed by their sponsors and advisers;
- partners must be identified and where appropriate, letters of intent signed;
- the sponsor must have a solid track record and proven expertise;
- the proposal must match the Bank's priorities; and
- the availability of an appropriate level of equity financing in the enterprise or for the project must be demonstrated.

Proposals from commercial enterprises are processed by the Merchant Banking arm. Requests for financing should be submitted directly to the Bank by the commercial enterprises seeking finance, or by intermediaries authorised to act for them.

Proposals from central and local authorities, utilities, financial institutions and other public sector agencies are processed by the Development Banking arm. Requests for financing should normally be submitted directly to the Bank by the government or public authority sponsoring the project, rather than by individual contractors competing for such projects.

From time to time, the EBRD calls on the services of consultants and financial advisers to work on projects or to provide expertise in technical co-operation. Consultants seeking to do business with the Bank should contact the Consulting Services Administrator who maintains a database of approved consultants.

The Bank announces contracts for which external financing is sought through its publication "Procurement Opportunities", and seeks bid offers accompanied by offers of finance for selected contracts. Banks and export credit agencies can subscribe to this publication.

INFORMATION

EBRD
1 Exchange Square
London EC2A 2EH
Tel: 071 338 6000/496 6000
Fax: 071 338 6100/496 6100
Tlx: 8812161 EBRD L G

Proposals for private enterprise or related to privatisation:

Ronald Freeman
First Vice-President, Merchant Banking
Fax: 071 338 6102

Proposals for physical and financial infrastructure projects:

Mario Sarcinelli
Vice-President, Development Banking
Fax: 071 338 6105

Telephone enquiries:

Laura Nicholson/Suzanne Franklin
Project Enquiries Unit
Tel: 071 338 6282/6252
Fax: 071 338 6102

Consultants should contact:

Consulting Services Administrator
Tel: 071 338 6682
Fax: 071 338 6106

18. CO-OPERATION IN SCIENCE & TECHNOLOGY IN CEEC COUNTRIES

Background

This pilot programme is the result of a European Parliament initiative entitled "Let's go East/Let's go West" and of a Research Council proposal under the acronym COPERNICUS.

Programme Content

The sectors covered include all the exact and natural sciences economic and management sciences, and human and social sciences. The specific actions are as follows.

A: The Mobility Scheme

The fellowship scheme for scientists and researchers from Central and Eastern Europe (Go West) is to permit them to practice their skills in Western institutes, laboratories and enterprises. Applicants must hold either a doctorate, or a normal degree plus two years research experience. Stays will normally be up to three months for senior fellows and six months for junior fellows. The stipends will vary but are likely to be between 1,500 and 2,500 ECU per month.

The Go East fellowships are directed at more senior scientists whose stay will normally be for one to three months. The stipend will be negotiable and could amount to a grant of up to 4,000 ECU per month or simply a reimbursement of expenses.

B: Networks, Conferences, Workshops and Seminars

The Pan-European Scientific Networks Scheme has the objective of promoting contacts and of facilitating exchange of information. Support will be given, therefore, for setting-up networks and extending existing ones which interlink research institutions, universities and enterprises across Europe. Financial support will be given to cover secretarial tasks and database creation and networks. Funding will be on the basis of 100% of marginal costs and will also be available for organising conferences, workshops and training seminars where these are considered to be relevant to East/West European co-operation.

C: Joint Research Projects

This part of the Programme will operate in a similar way to the shared-cost research contracts (see Chapter 17). There is a requirement for East-West collaboration and the research should fall within the following priority areas.

- Quality of Life:
    - Environment: pollution of air, water and soils; environment and health; socio-economic factors;
    - Biomedicine and Health: health care systems and management; diseases of major socio-economic importance; bio-technological applications; cell and molecular biology; and
    - Social Sciences: social and economic aspects of technology transfer to Central and Eastern Europe; requirements for scientific training; ways and means for socio-economic progress in these countries.
- Industrial Technologies:
    - Information and Communication Technologies: introduction into the production process; information processing systems; networks for information and data exchange.
    - Materials and Production/Manufacturing: saving energy and raw materials, clean technologies; advanced materials; and
    - Agricultural and food industries: production, storage and distribution; environmentally-friendly processing.

D: Participation in EC R&TD Programmes:

Funding is being made available to permit bodies and enterprises in the East to participate in the following R&TD Programmes:

Environment;

- Non-Nuclear Energy (JOULE);
- Nuclear Fission Safety;

- Biomedical and Health Research (BIOMED); and
- Human Capital and Mobility.

The onus is on the organisations to contact the Commission, expressing their wish to participate in the programmes in selected sectors. The Commission will then discuss the feasibility of collaboration with the existing partners.

E: Participation in COST Projects:

COST is a framework for co-operation in R&D throughout Europe (see chapter 17). This normally takes the form of concerted action (CA) projects. Additional funding is being made available to encourage organisations from CEEC to take part.

Participation

This programme is open to persons in the Member States and in the PHARE beneficiary countries.

Applications

A full information pack and set of application forms is available from the Commission.

The first deadline for proposals for participation in actions A, B and C and for expressions of interest for actions D and E was 7 August 1992. Information is awaited concerning further calls.

INFORMATION

The Central Commission contact is:
Commission of the European Communities
Scientific & Technical Co-operation with Central & Eastern European Countries
75 Rue Montoyer
B-1040 Brussels
Tel: INT+ 322 299 1111 (exchange)
Fax: INT+ 322 296 3308

19. TACIS: Technical Assistance to the Former Soviet Union: The CIS And Georgia

Statutory Basis

Council Regulation (EEC, EURATOM) No 2157/91 of 15/7/91 (OJ L 201, dated 24/7/91).

Objectives

This programme is designed to help the CIS and Georgia bring about economic reform and recovery.

Background

TACIS is administered on the basis of agreed programmes, not individual projects. Only projects which provide a structural contribution to economic development and the setting up of a market economy may be included in programmes supported by TACIS. The promotion of individual or isolated activities does not, therefore, fall within the scope of the programme.

After sectoral programming, the Commission draws up an Action Plan for each state, consisting of individual projects. These projects will be carried out by qualified independent contractors from the CIS and Georgia or the EC selected by the Commission from its register of approved contractors, and invited to tender.

The principal role of the EC economic operators is to assist with the implementation of those programme activities which have been defined and chosen by the Commission in close co-operation with its counterpart in the beneficiary states.

EC economic operators can always submit their specific ideas and proposals for consideration to the Co-ordination Unit or the Commission provided they fall within the agreed sector priorities. Their proposals, however, cannot normally be treated in isolation for financing but, if considered worthy of pursuing, can become the basis for a programme concept or component for future financing.

Programme Content

In contrast to the PHARE Programme, TACIS is essentially about the transfer of know-how, specifically in relation to policy advice, institutional frameworks, design of legal and regulatory frameworks and training. In some cases, funds may be granted for the supply of key equipment such as computers or demonstration equipment which may be essential for carrying out the above activities. The financing of capital goods is not covered by the Programme.

The areas to be covered are:

- management training in both the public and private sectors;
- the modernisation of the financial sector;
- energy;
- the improvement in the transport infrastructure; and
- the improvement of food distribution.

Focal sectors for co-operation in 1992 were human resources, food production and distribution, energy, transport and telecommunications networks, enterprise support services and nuclear safety.

The Programme was originally negotiated with the government of the old Soviet Union and co-ordinated by the Co-ordination Unit in Moscow, which had been established specifically for this purpose. Since the demise of the Soviet Union, each Independent State has nominated its own "National Co-ordinator", who acts as an official national link with the EC for the TACIS Programme.

EC Contribution

A budget of 400 MECU was agreed for 1991. The assistance took the form of grants to be paid in instalments. An allocation of 450 MECU was agreed for 1992 and 510 MECU, for 1993.

In contrast with many other co-operation programmes, the TACIS Programme funds are in the form of grants, i.e. they are not reimbursable.

Participation

All proposals for the financing of projects within the framework of the relevant Programmes must be submitted by applicants from the CIS and Georgia. The Baltic States were originally included within TACIS but are now covered by PHARE.

The applicants from the CIS or Georgia could be:

- government institutions at state or local level;
- co-operative associations;
- private enterprises;
- state enterprises;
- universities, academies or training institutions; or
- any qualified autonomous operator of the civil society.

It should be stressed that TACIS is demand-driven. Project proposals are therefore not submitted by EC economic operators or consultants, but by the potential recipients through the Co-ordination Unit in the recipient state.

Status Report

In September 1992, a tender was issued to select a consortium of major European banks to provide support to the Russian Project Finance Bank (RPFB). In February 1993 a call was issued for expressions of interest from legal experts.
Following the expiry of TACIS on 31 December 1992 the Commission proposed a new draft Regulation, published in OJ C 48, dated 19 February 1993, to establish a

continuation of the Programme, adding the State of Mongolia to the list of beneficiaries.

Applications

EC operators can demonstrate their interest in participating in the implementation of projects by registering with the Central Consultancy Register, which gives them the chance of being considered during the process of awarding direct contracts or launching restricted tenders, whether or not they have been involved in project design.

Depending on the size of the project and other factors, three different procurement procedures are used: open tender, restricted tender and direct agreement with approved contractors. (see PHARE).

INFORMATION

Registration forms for EC economic operators are available from:
Mrs Sylvie Davrou-Koch
Commission of the European Communities
D-GI External Relations
Central Consultancy Register
200 rue de la Loi
B-1049 Brussels
Belgium
Tel: INT+ 322 295 8216
Fax: INT+ 322 296 6012

TACIS Official Address
Commission of the European Communities
D-G 1 - External Relations
GD 1 E-2 TACIS
200 rue de la Loi
B-1049 Brussels
Tel: INT+ 322 295 8216
Fax: INT+ 322 296 6012

TACIS Information Office
Commission of the European Communities
D-G 1 - External Relations
GD 1 PR TACIS
200 rue de la Loi
B-1049 Brussels
Tel: INT+ 322 295 1116/2585

TACIS Operational Units:

E/3: Programming, support to enterprises, privatisation, financial services, SMEs, agriculture, defence, conversion. environment.
Joannes ter Haar: Tel: INT+ 322 295 3544

E/4: Infrastructure - incorporating telecommunications, transport and energy (including nuclear safety).
Rolf Timans: Tel: INT+ 322 295 6963

E/5: Management training, support to government (including legal reform) and social adjustment.
Giorgio Bonnacci: Tel: INT+ 322 299 3271

E/6: Financial resources management and administration.
Jurgen Koppen: Tel: INT+ 322 295 3233

Armenia

National Co-ordinator:
Armen Darbinian
Deputy Minister of Economics
Ministry of the Economy
Dom Pravitelstva
Ploshchad Respubliki, 1
Yerevan 375095
Armenia
Tel: INT+ 7 88 52 85 33
Fax: INT+ 7 88 52 43 32

Co-ordinating Unit Manager:
Korun Edgarovitch Danielyan
Executive Director
Ministry of Economy
(as above)
Tel: INT+ 7 88 52 63 34
Fax: INT+ 7 88 52 43 34

Azerbaijan

National Co-ordinator:
Ziad Aliabbasovitch Samed Zade
Tel: INT+ 7 8922 92 22 57

Co-ordinating Unit Manager:
Jahingir Kasimov
Executive Director
TACIS
Lermontova Street 68
Baku 370066
Local system
Tel: INT+ 7 8922 92 77 71
Fax: INT+ 7 8922 92 73 39/65 10 70
Tlx: 142 107 ALOV SU
Satellite:
Tel: 871 115 1572/1574
Fax: 873 14 46 512

Belarus

National Co-ordinator:
Mikail Demchuk
Deputy Chairman Council of Ministers.
(Contact Mr O T Gavrischuk, Office of Mr Demchuk)
Kirov Street 17
220050 Minsk
Tel: INT+ 7 0172 29 67 30

Co-ordinating Unit Manager:
V M Koleshko
Co-ordination Bureau
(as above)
Tel: INT+ 7 0172 27 32 39
Fax: INT+ 7 0172 27 26 15

Georgia

National Co-ordinator:
Merab Klimiashvili
Deputy Chairman of the State Committee for Foreign Economic Relations.
Tel: INT+ 7 8832 22 13 29

Co-ordinating Unit Manager:
Jemal Akobia
Executive Director
Ministry for Science and Technology
12 Jeorjiashvili Street
Tbilisi 380004
Georgia
Tel: INT+ 7 8832 98 84 36/99 55 04
Fax: INT+ 7 8832 98 84 37
Tlx: 212 148 HALLO SU

Kazakhstan

National Co-ordinator:
Beysenbey Izteleuov
Deputy Chairman
President's High Economic Council
Office of the President
4 Ploschad Respubliki
480091 Almaty
Kazakhstan
Tel: INT+ 7 3272 62 13 91/34 34
Fax: INT+ 7 3272 63 76 33

Co-ordinating Unit Manager:
Kazy-Korpesh Djanburtshin
Member of the President's High Economic Council
(as above)
Tel: INT+ 7 3272 63 68 23
Tel: INT+ 7 3272 62 11 73/63 78 97
Tel: INT+ 7 3272 62 13 91
Tel: INT+ 7 3272 62 76 33
Fax: INT+ 7 3272 62 39 42
Fax: INT+ 7 3272 63 78 97
Fax: INT+ 7 3272 69 59 77

Kyrgyzstan

National Co-ordinator:
Mr K Shakyrov
Erkindik Prospekt, 58
720084 CIS BISHKEK
Kyrgyzstan
Tel: INT+ 7 3312 22 66 04
(after 5 rings it switches to fax automatically)
Fax: INT+ 7 3312 22 66 04
Tlx: 251239 SALAM SU

Co-ordinating Unit Manager:
Mr Amangeldy Davletaliev
Advisor to Prime Minister
Office of the President
Government House - Room 509
720 003 CIS BISHKEK
Tel: INT+ 7 3312 22 57 89/22 55 52
Fax: INT+ 7 3312 22 66 04

Moldova

National Co-ordinator:
Andrei Keptine
Ministry of Foreign Economic Relations
Government House
Piata Marij Adunary, Nationale sg1
277033 Kishinev
Moldova
Tel: INT+ 7 3732 23 33 60/23 27 80
Fax: INT+ 7 3732 23 40 46

Co-ordinating Unit Manager:
Marian Ilych Lupu
Ministry of Foreign Economic Relations
(as above)
Tel: INT+ 7 3732 23 46 28
Fax: INT+ 7 3732 23 41 43
Tlx: 641 63 171 ITOG SU

Russian Federation

National Co-ordinator:
Alexander Shokhin
Deputy Prime Minister
4 Staraya Ploshchad
103132 Moscow
Tel: INT+ 7 095 206 29 46
Fax: INT+ 7 095 206 36 84

Co-ordinating Unit Manager:
I A Markov
Executive Director
Radisson Slavyanskaya
Hotel and Business Centre
Berezhkovskaja Nab.2
121059 Moscow
Tel: INT+ 7 502 224 11 85 (satellite)
Fax: INT+ 7 502 224 11 69 (satellite)

Tajikistan

National Co-ordinator:
Abdurakhman M Mukhtashov
Deputy Chairman of the Council of Ministers.
Rudaki Prospect
Dunshanbe
Tajikistan
Tel: INT+ 7 3772 22 89 06
Tlx: (in Hotel Tajikistan) 201114 SAFAR SU

Co-ordinating Unit Manager:
Mr Machmadamin Oimachmadov
Director
c/o State Committee for External Economic Relations
(as left)

Turkmenistan

National Co-ordinator:
Valery G Otchertsov
Deputy Head of Government
Ulitsa Karla Marksa, 24
Ashkabad
Turkmenistan
Tel: INT+ 7 3632 25 60 46/25 31 14
Fax: INT+ 7 3632 25 51 12

Co-ordinating Unit Manager:
Mr Mukhamedberdy Berdyev
Director
17 Gogol Street
744000 Ashgabat
Turkmenistan
Tel: INT+ 7 3632 25 31 14
Fax: INT+ 7 3632 25 58 74
Tlx: 116201 MECAN SU

Ukraine

National Co-ordinator:
Mr Ihor R Yukhnovsky
First Vice-Prime Minister
12/2 Grushevskogo Street
252 018 Kiev
Ukraine
Tel: INT+ 7 044 226 26 91
Fax: INT+ 7 044 262 26 06

Co-ordinating Unit Manager:
Mr L L Kistersky, Chairman
National Centre for the Implementation of International Assistance to the Ukraine,

Mr Zalko Titarenko, Director
1 Mihailovska Square
252018 Kiev
Ukraine
Tel: INT+ 7 044 212 84 87/212 83 27
Fax: INT+ 7 044 229 60 14/212 81 62

Uzbekistan

National Co-ordinator:
Mr Utkur Sultanov
Deputy Prime Minister
Ministry for Foreign Economic Relations
Dom Pravitelstva
700008 Tashkent
Uzbekistan
Tel: INT+ 7 3712 39 82 62

Co-ordinating Unit Manager:
Mr Alisher A Shaikhov
Head of Department of Foreign Economic Relations
Head of the Co-ordination of International Assistance
Cabinet of Ministers
Dom Pravitelstva
Room 426
700008 Tashkent
Uzbekistan
Tel: INT+ 7 3712 39 80 41/39 86 60
Fax: INT+ 7 3712 39 86 60 .

20. TEMPUS-PHARE: Trans-European Mobility Programme for University Students

Statutory Basis

TEMPUS was adopted by Council Decision 90/223/EEC of 7/5/90 (OJ L 131, dated 23/5/90). The initial pilot phase of three years, began on 1/7/90 and was extended by another year (OJ L 122, dated 7/5/92). The Commission made a proposal for a Council Decision adopting the second phase of the scheme for the period 1994-98 (OJ C 311, dated 27/11/92), and on 29/4/93 TEMPUS was extended for a second four-year phase commencing with the academic year 1994/95 (TEMPUS II).

Objectives

The objectives of TEMPUS-PHARE are:

- to promote the quality and support the development of higher education in the eligible countries; and
- to encourage the growing interaction and co-operation between partners in the PHARE and EC countries through joint activities and relevant mobility;

Background

TEMPUS II forms part of the PHARE programme of EC aid for the economic restructuring of the CEEC and for economic reform and recovery in the newly independent states of the former Soviet Union, as part of the TACIS Programme. The TEMPUS Council Decision provides the legal basis for activities within both programme frameworks.

TEMPUS within the TACIS Programme and TEMPUS within PHARE should be seen as two parallel but separate schemes in administrative and budgetary terms.

Programme Content

TEMPUS-PHARE supports the following types of activities:

- co-operative education/training actions;
- structural development of higher education;
- development of universities' capacities to co-operate with industry;
- regional activities;
- student mobility for first degree level students and for post-graduates and doctoral students undertaking further study abroad for up to a year in a higher education institute, or for a practical placement in an enterprise; and
- teacher mobility.

Throughout the TEMPUS scheme, Joint European Projects (JEPs) have been the main instrument by which co-operation is fostered between higher education institutions. JEPs are typically organised between departments or faculties of institutions of higher education, with the support of the whole institution, in keeping with the "grass roots" approach which characterises the whole TEMPUS scheme. JEPs will be able to run for a three-year period

EC Contribution

TEMPUS is funded from the overall PHARE budget under budget line B7-600. Funding was approximately 107 MECU for the academic year 1993-94.

The financial assistance available for JEPs will be up to a maximum of 200,000 ECU per year for a large-scale JEP, excluding mobility grants.

Participation

Within TEMPUS-PHARE, support is restricted to cross-border projects involving organisations in eligible CEECs: from all PHARE recipient states, i.e. Albania, Bulgaria, Czechoslovakia, Estonia, Hungary, Latvia, Lithuania, Poland, Romania and Slovenia on the one hand, and organisations within the Member States on the other. The EFTA countries, Australia, Canada, Japan, Turkey, New Zealand and the USA may also participate in TEMPUS, but will not receive funding from the TEMPUS Programme.

JEPs must be based on the participation of at least:

- one university per eligible country involved;
- one EC Member State university; and
- one partner organisation (university, enterprise or organisation) from another EC Member State.

Applications

Under TEMPUS-PHARE, application forms for activities for the academic year 1994-95 are available from September 1993 onwards.

INFORMATION

UK
Europe Unit
Education & Science Division
The British Council
Medlock Street
Manchester M15 4PR
Tel: 061 9577074/75/76
Fax: 061 9577561

IRELAND
Higher Education Authority
Fitzwilliam Square
Dublin 2
Tel: 01 61 27 48
Fax: 01 61 04 92

COMMISSION
Application forms and information are available from:

EC TEMPUS Office
14 rue Montoyer
B-1040 Brussels
Tel: INT+ 322 504 0711
Fax: INT+ 322 504 0700

21. TEMPUS-TACIS: Trans-European Mobility Programme for University Students

Statutory Basis

TEMPUS was adopted by Council Decision 90/223/EEC of 7/5/90 (OJ L 131, dated 23/5/90). The initial pilot phase of three years, began on 1/7/90 and was extended for another year (OJ L 122, dated 7/5/92). The Commission made a proposal for a Council Decision adopting the second phase of the scheme for the period 1994-98 (OJ C 311, dated 27/11/92), and on 29/4/93 TEMPUS was extended for a second four-year phase commencing with the academic year 1994/95 (TEMPUS II).

Objectives

The objectives of TEMPUS-TACIS are:

- to promote the quality and support the development of higher education in the eligible TACIS countries;
- to encourage their growing interaction and co-operation with partners in the EC through joint activities and relevant mobility; and
- to reinforce, in the sector of higher education, the assistance provided as part of the TACIS Programme so as to optimise the value added within the scarce resources available.

Background

TEMPUS II forms part of the overall package of PHARE and TACIS Programmes. The TEMPUS Council Decision provides the legal basis for activities within both programme frameworks.

TEMPUS within the TACIS Programme and TEMPUS within PHARE should be seen as two parallel but separate schemes in administrative and budgetary terms.

TEMPUS-TACIS focuses on activities best suited to the different needs and priorities of beneficiary countries within the TACIS Programme. TEMPUS-TACIS begins a new system of financing with the 1994 implementation of the second stage. 1993 is therefore a transition year in which priority will be given to providing funding for the completion of projects which had begun in 1991 and 1992. As a result, the number of new projects which could be accepted for the 1993-94 academic year was severely limited.

Programme Content

In 1993-94, TEMPUS-TACIS is only supporting activities focusing on the following subject areas:

- humanities and social sciences, including history and law;
- political sciences and economics (but not business/management);
- modern European languages (but not literature or linguistics); and
- the improvement of university management.

In order to take into account the overall objectives of the TACIS Scheme, projects in the above-mentioned subject areas which are relevant to the fields of agriculture, energy and transport will receive particular attention.

Many projects with an education/training focus or component, which may be eligible for funding under the general TACIS Programme, will not be so under TEMPUS-TACIS. Only training/continuing education projects targeted at university staff, which are not already eligible for funding under TACIS, are eligible for TEMPUS-TACIS support.

JEPs have been the main instrument by which co-operation between higher education institutions is fostered throughout the TEMPUS Scheme. They are typically organised between departments or faculties of institutions of higher education, with the support of the whole institution, in keeping with the "grass roots" approach which characterises the whole TEMPUS Scheme. JEPs will be able to run for a three-year period

Eligible JEP activities comprise:

- the development of higher education institutions in the eligible countries; and
- promoting teacher and student mobility between the EC and an eligible country.

Under the TEMPUS-TACIS Scheme, pre-JEP grants will be awarded in 1993-94 for preliminary contracts and mobility, aimed at enlarging the basis for a "bottom up" approach in future co-operation. Participation in pre-JEP activities is, however, a compulsory prerequisite for all institutions interested in developing Joint European Projects with TEMPUS-TACIS funding. Eligible pre-JEP activities include:

- short visits for higher education teachers and staff between the EC and the eligible country involved;
- purchase of essential equipment for the partner institution in the eligible country if it is needed to facilitate contacts and prepare JEP activities; and
- administrative activities which are directly linked with the preparation of the JEP application.

For 1994-95, TEMPUS-TACIS is using JEPs as the main instrument to deliver assistance and to organise co-operation with eligible countries. JEP grants will be up to a maximum of 1 MECU for the full three-year period, including the mobility grants.

Only consortia funded under TEMPUS-TACIS during the pre-programme phase in 1993-94 will be eligible to apply for JEPs in 1994-95.

Grants will also be available in 1994-95 for complementary activities including:

- publications and other information activities;
- surveys and studies; and
- youth exchanges, operating in a similar manner to Youth for Europe and Young Workers' Exchange Programmes.

EC Contribution

The budget for TEMPUS-TACIS is drawn from the overall funds made available for the TACIS Programme in a given year. A very limited amount will be available for TEMPUS preparatory activities for 1993-94.

The financial assistance available for JEPs will be up to a maximum of 1 MECU for the full three-year period, including the mobility grants.

Grants averaging 50,000 ECU per consortium of institutions will be available to support pre-JEP activities.

Participation

Not all TACIS countries will enter the TEMPUS-TACIS Scheme at the same time. TEMPUS-TACIS will expand by allowing for their admission in successive steps. For the academic year 1993-94, the eligible countries are Belarus, the Russian Federation and the Ukraine. It is envisaged that the other republics of the former Soviet Union will be included at a later date.

Within TEMPUS-TACIS, the following institutions may participate:

- classical and technical multi-disciplinary universities in Belarus, the Russian Federation and the Ukraine; and
- all types of higher education institutions in the individual Member States of the EC which form part of the state higher education sector, or are recognised or financed by the competent national authorities.

Pre-JEP contracts/mobility must be organised within a framework of stable consortia of eligible institutions of higher education, and comprise:

- on the EC side: two to three institutions of higher education, located in at least two different Member States;
- in the eligible countries: one eligible university from either Belarus, the Russian Federation or the Ukraine; and
- consortia may also include one higher education institution located in a non-EC, G-24 country.

Applications

Individuals cannot apply directly for grants under TEMPUS-TACIS, they may only participate as teachers/staff from an institution participating in a consortium funded under TEMPUS.

For each JEP, a joint application for the global grant must be made by one of the participating organisations, which has been designated as the project co-ordinator. For mobility of all kinds organised as part of a JEP, a block application covering all planned mobility within the project must be an integral part of the application submitted by the consortium of organisations concerned.

Under TEMPUS-TACIS, the final submission date for pre-JEP applications was 20 September 1993 for activities taking place between 1 January 1994 and 31 December 1994. The deadline for applications for a JEP grant for 1994-95 will be 30 June 1994.

There will be a new call for pre-JEP grants for the academic year 1994-95. A number of pre-JEP grants will be awarded to initiate a new two-phase cycle in which some of these pre-JEPs will be developed as new JEPs for the academic year 1995-96. The application packages will normally be published in November each year for the following academic year.

INFORMATION

UK
Europe Unit Education & Science Division
The British Council
Medlock Street
Manchester M15 4PR
Tel: 061 9577074/75/76
Fax: 061 9577561

IRELAND
Higher Education Authority
Fitzwilliam Square
Dublin 2
Tel: 01 61 27 48
Fax: 01 61 04 92

COMMISSION
Application forms and information are available from:
EC TEMPUS Office
14 rue Montoyer
B-1040 Brussels
Tel: INT+ 322 504 0711
Fax: INT+ 322 504 0700

22. ECOS: Eastern Europe City Co-Operation Scheme

See Chapter 19

Chapter 32

Other Assistance

Other assistance has been split into two main categories: financial and non-financial. On the financial side, it consists of loans, guarantees and direct investments by Community institutions. On the non-financial side the most obvious form it takes is the provision of information.

Financial

In order to lend, the Community first has to borrow. Given its political backing and financial stability, the Commission is not restricted to borrowing on the capital markets of the Member States, and is able to operate freely on the international markets. The choice of market is determined firstly by its borrowing requirements at the time and secondly, by the conditions prevailing on the different markets themselves. The two leading American rating agencies, Moody's and Standard & Poor's, have both given EC borrowing "AAA", their top rating. It can therefore not only pick and chose markets and currencies, but also obtain the best possible terms.

EC and EURATOM borrowings are guaranteed by the general budget of the EC. ECSC borrowings are guaranteed by the Community's reserves, the guarantee fund, together with the "fiscal power" represented by the ECSC levy on the value of coal and steel production within the Community.

The EC makes loans under many different programmes, most of which are described individually in other Chapters. In many cases they are made through the European Investment Bank (EIB) which is described in Chapter 33 section 4, but, in some cases, they are made by the Commission itself. The loans, whether through the EIB or direct from the Commission, have the following general characteristics.

- The amount of any structural loan advanced by the Commission cannot exceed 50% of the overall project cost. In the case of EURATOM, loans cannot exceed 20% of the overall cost.

- Loans are in principle granted at the rates of interest prevailing in the market at the time of making the loan, without any additional profit margin or risk premium.

- Most loans are made at fixed rates of interest, but interest rates can be scheduled to take into account the type of funding, together with the requirements of the recipients and their ability to fund the interest payments.

- As well as making loans at the market-based rate of interest, the Community also makes loans at subsidised rates of interest as part of its various aid programmes -

e.g. ECSC redevelopment loans for which an interest subsidy of 3% over a period of 5 years is available.

- Loans can be made in a cocktail of currencies, but exchange risk cover is available in some Member States, including the UK; as far as possible, the Commission encourages the use of the ECU.
- The term of loans and the repayment schedule should ensure that each project is financed in accordance with sound investment practice; every effort is made to take the borrower's wishes into account.
- ECSC and EURATOM loans tend to be long-term whereas other EC loans tend to be medium-term. Short-term loans are only made in exceptional circumstances. As a rough guide, medium-term means up to seven years and long term up to fifteen years but can be even more in special circumstances.
- Rates are agreed with the borrower in accordance with the availability of borrowed funds.
- The Commission may make provision for a certain period of grace on a loan in order to facilitate the launch of a project. The Commission will also entertain "bullet" repayment loans, i.e. loans repaid by a single payment at the end of the term of the loan.
- Loans are secured according to standard banking practice.
- Loans may take the form of direct individual loans advanced by the Commission to any given recipient, or indirect loans advanced by the Commission to a financial intermediary in favour of the recipient.
- Loans may also come in the form of global loans. In this case, the Commission provides a financial intermediary with a sizeable overall budget which the intermediary then uses for funding either SMEs, of for investment projects which do not exceed a total cost of 15 MECU. Any sub-loan granted by an intermediary as part of a global loan cannot exceed an amount of 7.5 MECU.

Non-Financial

As a provider of information, the Commission is thankfully free of the Whitehall culture that all those seeking information must be spies, muck-raking journalists or other undesirables who want it for some nefarious purpose. Provided that the enquirer knows exactly what he wants and is fluent in at least three Community languages, information is given by the Commission freely, willingly and in most cases quickly - once he has identified the correct source which, admittedly, can often be extremely difficult. The number of follow-up calls that have had to be made in obtaining information for this book has been relatively small - even though some of the information supplied was rather out of date. On the other hand, despite "Open Government", "Citizens' Charters" etc. and even after having first had to prove IN WRITING his legitimate reason for wanting it, the writer is, in some cases, still waiting some nine months later, for information from more than one Whitehall department who had PROMISED it "within a week or so"!

The Community has its own Office for Official Publications in Luxembourg and publishes information both on paper and increasingly on CD, on-line and other advanced systems.

The Official Journal (OJ) is published in all Community languages. The L Series, containing Legislation and the C Series - Information and Notices - are both published about six times per week and vary in size from a mere handful of pages to many hundreds - the number containing the budget published in February each year is about the size of the London Business Telephone Directory! The combined annual subscription is £426 for the English language version. The Supplement, which contains information that does not fit neatly into either of the above categories, is published about five times per week for a separate annual subscription of £324.

The printed catalogue of publications, which runs to nearly 150 pages, is available from the Publications Office or the various EC Information Points which can be found not only throughout the Member States but in most other countries as well. They are listed in Appendix 2.

The quality of the publications is variable: some are absolutely excellent but others show all the signs of having been written by committees without any overall editorial policy and are simplistic or lack objectivity. They also tend to deal with very specific subjects and to approach them from an extremely narrow perspective which means that it is often necessary to read through a considerable number of publications to understand the overall picture. Some are issued free but others are fairly expensive.

The Community also maintains a number of on-line databases to which interested parties can subscribe. On the whole, these are extremely good, once the user has worked out the system and learnt the codes. They are listed in Appendix 7.

The normal complaint amongst those dealing with the Community is not that it publishes too little information but, rather that it publishes too much: keeping up with it is more than a full-time job.

Chapter 33

Other Assistance Sources

FINANCIAL

1. European Coal and Steel Community Loans

   1.1 Industrial Loans

      i Loans for Projects which Promote the Consumption of EC Steel

      ii Loans for Investments aimed at Promoting the Consumption of EC Coal

   1.2 Conversion Loans

   1.3 Readaptation Grants

   1.4 Housing Loans

   1.5 Loans to Central and Eastern European Countries (CEEC)

2. EURATOM Loans

3. EC Loans

   3.1 Medium-Term Financial Support Mechanism for Member States

   3.2 Medium-Term Financial Support for Central & Eastern European Countries and Non-member States

4. EIB: European Investment Bank

5. EBRD: European Bank for Reconstruction and Development

6. EIF: European Investment Fund

   i Financial guarantees

   ii Equity

NON-FINANCIAL

1. Publications

2. Data-bases

3. Community Offices and Information Points

1. EUROPEAN COAL AND STEEL COMMUNITY LOANS

The objective of the ECSC is to promote the economic development of Member States through the creation of a common market for coal and steel, as laid down in the Treaty of Paris. Articles 49, 54 and 56 of the Treaty empower the Commission to engage in financing investment in the coal and steel industries by raising the necessary funds and granting loans to undertakings whose operations are governed by the Treaty. The Commission may also help finance investment upstream and downstream of the actual plants - such as port facilities for unloading raw materials used in the iron and steel industry.

The ECSC's principal sources of funds are:

- the borrowing it makes on the financial markets and from banks;
- resources from placement of funds awaiting disbursement; and
- its own resources, raised from the levy it imposes on the production of coal and steel. The levy is calculated on the basis of the average EC values of the various products subject to the levy. Most of the levy proceeds in the early years went to creating a reserve guarantee fund of US$ 100 million, which serves as security enabling the ECSC to establish its credit rating for borrowing on the financial markets. The levy rate for 1993 has been reduced to 0.25%.

Loans or guarantees for investment programmes are available both to those directly involved in coal and steel production in the EC and also for projects which contribute directly towards production, growth or reduced production costs, or which ensure re-employment for those made redundant in these industries.

The operating budget for 1993 was estimated at 548 MECU.

INFORMATION

UK

UK/ECSC Policy:
Department of Trade and Industry
Ashdown House
123 Victoria Street
London SW1E 6RB
Tel: 071 215 5000

DTI
Coal Division
Room 3.2.15
1 Palace Street
London SW1E 5HE
Tel: 071 238 3000

1.1 Industrial Loans

Statutory Basis

Article 54 of the ECSC Treaty authorises the Commission to facilitate the implementation of investment programmes by granting loans to undertakings or by guaranteeing other loans for which they may contract.

Background

Separate provision is made under the provisions of the ECSC Treaty for financial assistance in the form of grants, loans and guarantees to improve economic and social conditions in the coal and steel-producing areas of the EC, which have suffered particular hardship as a result of industrial decline.

Article 54 of the ECSC Treaty provides for loans to be made at attractive interest rates to help carry out projects which increase production, reduce costs and facilitate the marketing or promote the consumption of coal and steel products.

Loans are only available for projects which reflect EC policies for coal and steel. Those for the steel industry must therefore be linked to rationalisation and not increased capacity.

The amount of a loan is decided on a case by case basis by the Commission, but may not exceed half the gross capital costs of the relevant project. Priority projects may, however, receive assisted loans, which are granted at the normal rate of interest but attract an interest rebate of 3 percentage points per year for the first five years of the loan, paid directly by the Commission to the beneficiary.

Programme Content

i LOANS FOR PROJECTS WHICH PROMOTE THE CONSUMPTION OF EC STEEL

The Commission has published special guidelines for loans for projects aimed at promoting the consumption of EC steel (OJ C 121, dated 17/5/85). In this context, the term "steel" refers to any of the following:

- raw materials for iron and steel production;
- pig-iron and ferrous-alloys;
- crude and semi-finished products of iron, ordinary steel or special steel, including products for re-use and re-rolling;
- hot finished products of iron, ordinary steel or special steel; and
- end products of iron, ordinary steel or special steel.

The finance may be in the form of global loans, or direct loans for industrial or infrastructure projects.

GLOBAL LOANS

The total project value for which a loan is sought under a global loan facility via an agency should not exceed 15 MECU, allowing for a maximum loan of 7.5 MECU. The agent or intermediary is responsible for negotiating individual loans with borrowers and for evaluating projects. The Commission gives the final assent.

DIRECT LOANS

The following types of industrial investment project aimed at increasing or, in the case of restructuring, maintaining the level of consumption of EC steel, may qualify for direct loans:

- projects aimed at introducing new applications for steel;
- projects aimed at improving steel's competitiveness in relation to other products;
- projects by undertakings for which the cost of steel purchased, reflected in the price of the finished product, accounts for at least half the total cost of raw materials, including steel; or, if this provision cannot be applied for technical reasons, at least 20% of the total cost of the constituents, including raw materials, of the finished project; or, if this provision cannot be applied for technical reasons, at least 5% of the selling price of the finished product.

Only expenditure on installations directly connected with the continuous use of steel will be considered. The maximum loan is set at 50% for such industrial investment projects.

Major infrastructure projects, as defined in the Commission's proposal dated 23/12/86 (OJ C 80, dated 27/3/87), may also be eligible for direct loans. Qualifying expenditure will be limited to the total actual value of the steel used in the project, up to a maximum of 20% of the investment value of the project.

The Commission will assess the economic aspects of the industrial investment or infrastructure project, principally in terms of the contribution the investment will make to the consumption of EC steel and the technical and financial prospects for its implementation, its viability, the market outlook for the products and the situation in the sector concerned. The Commission will also assess the financial situation of the borrower and of any parent companies - particularly in respect of guarantees. Environmental factors will also be taken into consideration.

ii LOANS FOR INVESTMENTS AIMED AT PROMOTING THE CONSUMPTION OF EC COAL

The Commission has published guidelines for industrial loans under Article 56 (2a) for projects aimed at promoting the consumption of EC coal.

The term "coal" refers to the following:

- hard coal;
- hard coal briquettes;
- coke, excluding electrode and petroleum coke;
- brown coal briquettes; and
- run-of-mine brown coal.

GLOBAL LOANS

The total investment value of projects for which a global loan is sought may not normally exceed 15 MECU. The fundamental objective of the policy for global loans is the same as those for direct loans. The difference lies in the size of the loan and the degree of administrative decentralisation, which occurs at two levels:

i firstly, at EC institution level: once the Council has given its assent to a global loan, each individual loan can be approved by the Commission; and

ii secondly, between the Commission and the national or regional agency. Subject to the final assent of the Commission, the agency is responsible for negotiating individual loans with borrowers and evaluating projects, on the same basis as the Commission uses for evaluating direct loans, and will forward its recommendations to the Commission. The agency also advises the Commission of any national aids granted for the project.

DIRECT LOANS

Projects which may qualify for direct loans are installations and equipment relating to the combustion, handling and preparation of coal and to the treatment and disposal of effluents.

The Commission will assess the economic aspects of the industrial project, principally in terms of the contribution the investment will make to the consumption of EC coal and of the technical and financial prospects for its implementation. The Commission will also assess the financial situation of the borrower and of any parent companies. The value of the guarantees offered will likewise be assessed.

An analysis may be made of any significant effects on the environment from emissions and waste produced by the project. In any case, projects must meet the requirements of EC legislation on the environment.

Participation

Business organisations, public bodies or local authorities may participate.

Finance is not restricted to the coal and steel industries themselves. Any industry or project which assists the use of coal and steel could be eligible; such as shipyards using steel, port installations exporting coal, or power stations burning EC coal. Projects are not restricted to EC countries, provided that the project benefits the Community in some way.

In the case of direct loans, applications should relate to investment projects on which work has not yet started or is still in progress and which can, as a rule, be completed within three years.

Applications

Applications for industrial loans must be made by the companies concerned direct to the Commission. Applications for loans for projects whose total investment value does not exceed 15 MECU may be made direct to financial agents in receipt of global loans from the Commission. The addresses of financial intermediaries are given below.

INFORMATION

UK
The financial intermediaries for global loans are:

England

Mr A Woodward
Barclays Bank PLC
European Loans Unit
PO Box 256
Fleetway House
7th Floor
25 Farringdon Street
London EC4A 4LP.
Tel: 071 832 3081

Richard Watson
Midland Bank PLC
Manager of Loans Schemes Unit
Griffin House
1st Floor
Block 2
2 Silver Street Head
Sheffield S1 3GG
Tel: 0742 529 316

Mr G Cripps
National Westminster Bank
Product Marketing and Sales
3rd Floor
Fenchurch Street
8 Fenchurch Place
London EC3M 4PB
Tel: 071 374 3629

Mr S Saltaire
3i Plc
Trinity park
Bickenhill
Birmingham, B37 7ES
Tel: 021 782 3131

Scotland

Mr R Roger, Assistant Manager
Bank of Scotland
Uberior House
PO Box 12
61 Grassmarket
Edinburgh EH1 2JF.
Tel: 031 243 5764

Mr Bernard, Regional Lending Manager
Clydesdale Bank
30 St Vincent Place
Glasgow, G1 2HL
Tel: 041 248 7070

Mike Rabone
The Royal Bank of Scotland
Commercial Banking Services
PO Box 31
42 St Andrews Square
Edinburgh EH2 2YE
Tel: 031 523 2091

Alan Glass
TSB Scotland
Advances Department
120 George Street
Edinburgh EH2 4TS
Tel: 021 600 5153

Wales
Mary O'Brian
Welsh Development Agency
Finance Department
Pearl House
Greyfriars Road
Cardiff, CF1 3XX
Tel: 0222 222 666 Ext.2330

COMMISSION
Directorate-General XVIII
(Credit & Investments)
Commission of the European Communities
Batiment Wagner
Plateau du Kirchberg
L-2920 Luxembourg
Tel: INT.+ 352 43011
Fax: INT.+ 352 436322

1.2 CONVERSION LOANS

Statutory Basis

Article 56 of the ECSC Treaty.

The latest guidelines and operating rules are published in OJ C 188, dated 28/7/90 and subsequently amended in OJ C 59, dated 6/3/92.

Background

The Commission is pursuing a conversion policy to revitalise the areas affected by the reduction of activity and employment in the coal and steel industries. By granting conversion loans, the ECSC helps to create new and economically healthy activities or to transform existing companies. Its objective is to improve the employment prospects of those who have been made redundant by restructuring and/or the disappearance of the coal and steel industries.

This sectoral conversion policy is concurrent with the more general efforts made by the EC to use the Structural Funds and other existing financial instruments to rejuvenate regions or areas seriously affected by industrial decline.

Programme Content

The ECSC provides fixed interest rate, medium-term loans for projects which create new jobs in areas affected by redundancies in the coal and steel industries. The loans are for up to half the fixed asset costs of the project.

ECSC sterling loans are normally for five years. The interest is payable six-monthly in arrears, with the capital repayment made at the end of the five-year loan period. Foreign currency loans are also available, normally for eight years with a four-year grace period on the repayment of capital. Interest is payable six-monthly in arrears. The interest rate is fixed for the period of the loan shortly before the signing of the contract.

Both global loans and direct loans are available. Direct loans to enterprises and public authorities are arranged when the total amount of the loan exceeds 7.5 MECU. Global loans for smaller amounts are granted to intermediary financial organisations for them to redistribute as subsidiary loans benefiting enterprises and/or public authorities.

Aid may be given for the following purposes.

a. Individual productive investments which help to create new and economically sound activities, expand existing activities or transform enterprises which may be expected to generate additional employment.

b. Multi-annual investment programmes comprising:

   - infrastructure investment for the redevelopment of derelict industrial land arising from the closure of ECSC activities and investment for the installation of large sites, including infrastructure where this contributes to the creation of new activities likely to create jobs;

   - investments involving technology transfer from ECSC industries; and

   - assistance to firms, especially SMEs, which introduce new technology or innovative procedures.

c. Investment in the above activities which are financed by leasing operations.

d. Support for multi-annual investment programmes agreed under the new procedures for the Structural Funds. The new procedures announced in March 1992 introduce a list of excluded categories as follows:

   - the retail trade, except for central productions, storage and distribution services for the products marketed;

   - hospitals and related activities except in Objective 1 regions or where the establishment is reserved for current and former ECSC workers;

   - leisure, sport and cultural centres or activities which are not tourism-oriented;

   - general educational establishments, except in Objective 1 regions;

   - the construction and renovation of housing;

   - the finance sector, except in the development of central services; and

   - agriculture, forestry and fisheries.

A further restriction is that projects which have already started may not be eligible for a Conversion Loan.

Special Provisions

Both direct and global loans exceeding 10 MECU must now be approved by Community Support Framework (CSF) Committees or CSF ECSC Sub-Committees, which will look at the project in relation to the Structural Fund CSFs and advise accordingly.

The project assessment process involves not only the usual appraisal of the economic and environmental aspects of the project, but also an evaluation of the employment situation in the area in which the investment projects are located.

Rebates on loans for productive investments may not exceed 3% per year for five years. The amount of the loan eligible for rebate will be 20,000 ECU per job for two-thirds of the new jobs created. If the project is outside a designated Closure Area, then the rebate is calculated on the basis of the number of jobs actually filled by ECSC workers. The Commission may reduce the level of rebates if the new jobs are not maintained. In some cases, claw-back may operate.

When the investments form part of Operational Programmes involving the Structural Funds, interest rebates may be provided by the ERDF up to a normal maximum of 3%. Rebates of up to 5% may be negotiated in exceptional circumstances but only by countries whose interest rates are at least 25% above the EC average. The rebates may be funded by the ERDF as well as from ECSC funds.

Participation

Conversion loans for co-financing individual, productive projects are available in designated ECSC Closure Areas, lists of which are published by the Commission. There are no eligible Closure Areas in Ireland. The designated employment areas in the UK are as follows:

COUNTY/REGION	ELIGIBLE AREAS
Cleveland	County
Clwyd	Shotton and Wrexham TTWA
Cumbria	Workington, District of Copeland TTWA
Derbyshire	County
Durham	County
Dyfed	Llanelli TTWA
Fife	Local Authority Region
Greater Manchester	County
Gwent	County
Humberside	Scunthorpe TTWA
Kent	Districts of Dover and Thanet
Leicestershire	Coalville TTWA
Lothian	Local Authority Region
Merseyside	County
Mid-Glamorgan	County
Northamptonshire	Corby TTWA
Northumberland	County
Nottinghamshire	County
South Glamorgan	County
South Yorkshire	County
Staffordshire	County
Strathclyde	Local Authority Region
Tyne & Wear	County
Warwickshire	Boroughs of North Warwickshire, Nuneaton & Bedworth
West Glamorgan	County
West Midlands	County
West Yorkshire	Leeds, Wakefield and Castleford TTWA.

Projects outside these areas may be eligible, provided that the jobs created are actually for former ECSC workers. In cases where RECHAR areas fall outside ECSC Closure Areas, these locations are also eligible.

Status Report

As from 1 July 1985, Exchange Risk Cover (ERC) in the UK has been limited to the first £500,000. Application for ERC should be made by the agent to the appropriate DTI regional office, the Welsh Office or the Industry Department for Scotland. Where a project is not in an Assisted Area, applications should be made to the DTI in London.

Applications

Applications for direct loans of £3 million or more should be addressed to the Commission via the competent national authorities. When the project concerns an activity outside the iron and steel industries, the assent of the Council is required.

SMEs with net fixed assets below 75 MECU may apply for loans of between £10,000 and £3 million through the intermediary financial institutions to which global loans have already been granted.

INFORMATION

UK
DTI
Regional Development and Inward Investment Division
Kingsgate House
66-74 Victoria Street
London SW1E 6SW
Tel: 071 215 2605
Fax: 071 931 0397

COMMISSION
Commission of the European Communities
D-G XVIII Division B.2
Batiment Jean Monnet
Kirchberg
L-2920 Luxembourg
Tel: INT.+ 352 43011

The addresses of the UK financial intermediaries can be found in the information section of the Industrial Loans Programme.

1.3 READAPTATION GRANTS

Statutory Basis

Article 56 of the ECSC Treaty.

Objectives

The Commission may award grants to help workers affected by fundamental changes in market conditions in the steel and coal industries. This programme has been included under loans because the grants can be repayable by the recipients.

Programme Content

Grants may be made for the following purposes:

- additional income benefits, often in the form of a guaranteed wage or complement to unemployment benefit, during the transition period from redundancy to new employment or retirement;
- resettlement allowances for workers; and
- vocational training allowances for workers undergoing approved retraining.

EC Contribution

Readaptation schemes are agreed between the Commission and each Member State, with the ECSC contributing up to half the costs within defined limits.

Participation

Companies whose workers are affected by closures or contraction resulting in job losses may apply; applications from private individuals are not eligible.

Applications

In the UK, benefits for steel workers are provided for under the Iron and Steel Employees' Readaptation Benefits Scheme (ISERBS), which is administered by the DTI. In the case of coal workers, applications should be made to the Department of Energy.

INFORMATION

UK

Applications for Steel Workers should be addressed to:
Brian Greenwood
DTI
Steel Metals and Materials Division
151 Buckingham Palace Road
London SW1W 9SS
Tel: 071 215 1087

Applications for Coal Workers should be addressed to:
David Hough
DTI
Coal Division
1 Palace Street
London SW1E 5HG
Tel: 071 215 5000

IRELAND
B Foley
Cork Regional Committee
Irish Steel Company
Haulbowline
Co Cork
Tel: 21 31 17 31
Fax: 21 81 13 47

1.4 HOUSING LOANS

Statutory Basis

Article 54 of the ECSC Treaty.

Objectives

The ECSC runs a low-cost housing programme for the purpose of providing long-term loans, normally at an interest rate of 1%, to build, purchase or improve dwellings. This aims to satisfy the housing needs of a workforce which is growing younger, to ensure an appropriate quality of housing and to ease restructuring without social conflict.

Programme Content

In July 1989, the Commission published guidelines for the implementation of the Eleventh Programme covering the period 1989-92 (OJ C 176, dated 12/7/89).

Housing funds may be provided for:

a. the construction, purchase or improvement of individual houses by owner-occupiers;

b. the construction or improvement of rented accommodation; and

c. the improvement of the housing environment, associated with the construction or modernisation of housing estates benefiting from ECSC loans.

EC Contribution

The exact amount of the loan available for each dwelling and other details, such as income limits and cost ceilings, are determined by the Commission with advice from Housing Committees. Small amounts of money are allocated to local authority schemes.

Participation

Loans to build, purchase or improve homes under (a) above are available only to active workers; loans for collective schemes under (b) and (c) may include dwellings occupied by retired ECSC workers or their widows/widowers, provided these do not account for more than half the dwellings involved.

Applications

Applications should be made through national Housing Committees in each Member State.

INFORMATION

UK

Contact for the Coal Industry:
Vos Jones
Coal Industry Social Welfare Organisation Ltd
25-27 Huddersfield Road
Barnsley
South Yorkshire S70 2LX
Tel: 0226 298 871

Contact for the Steel Industry:
Bruce Howick
British Steel Plc
9 Albert Embankment
London SE1 7SN
Tel: 071 735 7654

Contact for Private Steel:
H Billot,
Personnel Director
Sheerness Steel Company
Sheerness
Kent, ME12 1TH
Tel: 0795 663 333

IRELAND
B Foley
Cork Regional Committee
Irish Steel Company
Haulbowline
Co. Cork
Tel: 21 31 17 31
Fax: 21 81 13 47

COMMISSION
Commission of the European Communities
DG V Directorate-A
Employment, Industrial Relations and Social Affairs
200 rue de la Loi
B-1049 Brussels
Tel: INT.+ 322 299 1111

1.5 LOANS TO CENTRAL AND EASTERN EUROPEAN COUNTRIES (CEEC)

Statutory Basis

Decision of the Council of Ministers, in accordance with Article 95 of the ECSC Treaty: OJ C 122, dated 18/5/90.

Programme Content

The following types of investment may be financed:

- investments promoting the consumption of EC steel including, in particular, infrastructure projects;
- industrial projects in the steel sector, carried out as part of co-operative activities in which at least one EC company is involved; and
- projects in the coal sector, carried out as part of co-operative activities in which at least one EC company is involved and which are aimed at improving the environment, safety at work and working conditions in mines.

EC Contribution

ECSC loans of up to 200 MECU are available to finance industrial developments in the eligible countries.

Loans for investments for infrastructure projects which promote the consumption of EC steel will be limited to the value of the EC steel used in the project and may not exceed half the costs of the fixed investment.

In cases requiring continuous consumption of steel, such as pipe production plants, up to half the fixed investment may be financed from ECSC funds, provided that exclusively EC steel is used.

Loans for co-operative activities or joint ventures in the steel or coal sectors will also be limited to 50% of the fixed investment.

Participation

Initially only Poland and Hungary were eligible, but Bulgaria, the Czech and Slovak Republics and Romania also became eligible in 1991.

INFORMATION

Directorate-General XVIII (Credit & Investments)
Commission of the European Communities
Batiment Wagner
Plateau du Kirchberg
L-2920 Luxembourg
Tel: INT.+ 352 43011
Fax: INT.+ 352 436322

2. EURATOM LOANS

Statutory Basis

Articles 172 and 174 of the EURATOM Treaty.

Objectives

The aim is to reduce the EC's dependence on external energy supplies by promoting the use of nuclear energy.

Background

The Commission is empowered to raise loans on behalf of EURATOM for lending on to finance investment projects involving the industrial generation of nuclear-based electricity and industrial fuel cycle installations.

The borrowing and lending-on machinery set up by EURATOM enables electricity producers, who are faced with a substantial increase in their investment and operating costs, to make more extensive use of credit.

Programme Content

Projects are eligible if they relate to investment in nuclear power stations and industrial fuel installations.

Loans are usually set at not more than 20% of total project cost, with the terms and interest rates reflecting market conditions.

On 23 April 1990, the Council increased the new EURATOM borrowing ceiling from 3 BECU to 4 BECU (OJ L 112, dated 3/5/90).

Status Report

EURATOM loans totalling 2.967 BECU have been made since the programme began in 1977. No loans have been made since 1991 because conditions continue to be unfavourable in the industry,

Applications

Applications should be made to the Commission.

INFORMATION

Commission of the European Communities
Directorate-General for Credit and Investments
Jean Monnet Building
Luxembourg
Tel: INT.+ 352 43011
Fax: INT.+ 352 436322

3. EC LOANS

3.1 MEDIUM-TERM FINANCIAL SUPPORT MECHANISM FOR MEMBER STATES

Statutory Basis

Council Regulation (EEC) No 1969/88 of 24/6/88: OJ L 178/1 dated 8/7/88.

Objectives

The objective is to establish a single facility providing medium-term financial assistance for Member States' balances of payments.

Programme Content

This Regulation makes it possible to grant loans to Member States which are experiencing difficulties in their balance of payments, on either current or capital accounts. This is a vital instrument of support between the Member States which, subject to certain conditions, allows any which are in temporary difficulties to overcome their problems.

Decisions to implement the medium-term financial support mechanism to assist a Member State are adopted by the Council of Ministers, acting by a qualified majority, at the instigation of the Commission and after consultation with the Monetary Committee. The granting of any such loan is usually dependent on the acceptance, by the Member State concerned, of a range of economic policy conditions imposed by the Council of Ministers. Borrowing and lending activities launched in 1978, under the title of the New Community Instrument (NCI), have not been extended by the Council of Ministers.

The Commission is authorised to raise the borrowings required on the capital markets or with financial institutions on behalf of the EC. Member States are entitled to request early repayment of such loans.

EC Contribution

There is a ceiling of 16 BECU for the total principal amount of loans which may be granted to Member States via this mechanism.

3.2 MEDIUM-TERM FINANCIAL SUPPORT FOR CENTRAL & EASTERN EUROPEAN COUNTRIES AND NON-MEMBER STATES

Statutory Basis

Following the impetus generated by the Rome Summit in December 1990, the Commission, as the co-ordinating institution of the Group of 24 industrialised countries, put a series of initiatives to the Council of Ministers for individual approaches towards CEECs, in the form of medium-term financing to supplement what had been made available by the international financial institutions.

Programme Content

This is an EC-to-government programme, restricted in terms of time and other conditions, falling within the context of provisions agreed between the IMF and recipient countries. It is intended to assist the CEECs in their efforts to set up democratic institutions, adopt appropriate macro-economic policies and make structural reforms in accordance with the principles of a market economy.

The loans are administered by the Commission, working hand-in-hand with the EC Monetary Committee, in accordance with arrangements established between the IMF and the recipient country.

EC Contribution

During 1990 and 1991, 1050 MECU was granted to Hungary, 375 MECU to the Czech and Slovak Republics, 375 MECU to Romania, and 290 MECU to Bulgaria.

In 1991 the Council also agreed to provide 160 MECU in financial assistance to Israel and a 400 MECU medium-term loan to Algeria.

4. EIB: European Investment Bank

Statutory Basis

Annex to the Treaty of Rome.

Objectives

The EIB was established by the Treaty of Rome in 1958 to contribute to the EC's balanced development by providing loans or guarantees for capital investment projects, which:

- help economic development in less-favoured areas;
- improve transport and telecommunications between Member States;
- help the EC's energy objectives;
- involve protection of the environment;
- involve the modernisation of industry and the introduction of advanced technologies; and
- support the activities of SMEs.

Background

Article 198e of the Maastricht Treaty, replacing the old Article 129 of the Treaty of Rome, states:

> "The task of the European Investment Bank shall be to contribute, by having recourse to the capital markets and utilising its own resources, to the balanced and steady development of the common market in the interest of the Community. For this purpose the Bank shall, operating on a non-profit-making basis, grant loans and give guarantees which facilitate the financing of the following projects in all sectors of the economy:
>
> (a) projects for developing less-developed regions;
>
> (b) projects for modernising or converting undertakings or for developing fresh activities called for by the progressive establishment of the common market, where these projects are of such a size or nature that they cannot be entirely financed by the various means available in the individual Member States.
>
> (c) projects of common interest to several Member States which are of such a size or nature that they cannot be entirely financed by the various means available in the individual Member States.
>
> In carrying out its task, the bank shall facilitate the financing of investment programmes in conjunction with assistance from the Structural Funds and other Community financial instruments."

The Bank's contribution to promoting economic and social cohesion is spelt out in Protocol 15:

> " ... REAFFIRMING (the Member States') conviction that the EIB should continue to devote the majority of its resources to the promotion of economic and social cohesion, and declare their willingness to review the capital needs of the EIB as soon as this is necessary for the purpose. ..."

Its obligation to contribute towards development co-operation includes fostering:

- the sustainable economic and social development of the developing countries, and more particularly the most disadvantaged of them;
- the smooth and gradual integration of the developing countries into the world economy; and
- the campaign against poverty in the developing countries, as set out in Article 130w.

The EIB is owned by the Member States, who have each subscribed towards its capital. It raises the bulk of its funds on the world's capital markets, where it has an AAA rating, and then lends the proceeds to finance projects on a non-profit basis: cost of funds plus 0.15% to cover operating expenses.

There is no quota system for each country. Lending is concentrated in those areas of the EC where investment needs are greatest. The lending rates are influenced neither by the status nor nationality of the borrower, nor by the type or location of the project. Rates have to be adjusted where appropriate to reflect market trends and are set for each currency, varying with loan maturity and timing of repayment.

The EIB has a three-tier decision-making structure. The top tier consists of a Board of Governors, whose members are government ministers, one from each Member State - generally the Minister for Finance. The Governors lay down general directives on credit policy, approve the annual report and balance sheet, and decide on any necessary increases to the Bank's capital.

The second tier consists of a Board of Directors comprising 22 Directors, 21 of whom are nominated by the Member States and one by the Commission. There are also 12 Alternates, 11 of whom are nominated by the Member States and one by the Commission. The Directors ensure that the Bank is managed in accordance with the provisions of the Treaty, with the Bank's Statute and with the general directives laid down by the Board of Governors. The Directors are also responsible for deciding on the granting of loans, raising funds and fixing interest rates.

There is a full-time Management Committee, which is responsible for day-to-day operations and implementing the decisions made by the Directors. The Committee consists of a President and six Vice-Presidents.

Programme Content

The amount of any structural loans advanced by the Commission cannot exceed half the overall project cost; this also applies to EIB funding.

The EIB makes both individual and global loans.

Individual loans are usually only made available for major projects costing more than about £20 million. Potential borrowers should contact the EIB directly for further information.

Global loan facilities are made available to banks and financial institutions, to help them provide finance to small and medium-sized projects. Under the global loan scheme, projects may range from ECU 20,000 to 10 MECU. Virtually all the EIB's operations under the New Community Instrument (NCI), which has a sectoral focus, take the form of global loans.

In the UK, a global loan facility has been negotiated by Barclays Bank PLC. Under these schemes, the credit risk on loans to customers remains with the bank/financial institution. Thus, in the UK, the availability of EIB funds to Barclays does not in practice have any direct effects on its decision whether to finance a particular small or medium-sized customer. EIB funding can, however, encourage small companies to fund new investment by medium or long-term finance rather than overdrafts.

The EIB is a flexible source of medium and long-term funds: a high percentage of the loans are made at fixed rates of interest although there is a choice between fixed, adjustable-fixed, floating and convertible interest rates. There can be an interest rate advantage, although this is not the main feature of EIB funding. Long-term loans usually have terms of between four and twelve years for industrial projects and twenty years or more for infrastructure and energy schemes. The EIB does not normally charge commitment fees or other expenses.

Loans can be in a single currency or in a mixture of currencies, depending on the borrower's preferences and the Bank's holdings. However the ECU is the preferred currency for the bank, and is becoming increasingly popular with borrowers because of its stability.

Like any long-term lending institution, the EIB requires adequate guarantees or security to ensure repayment of its loans, and is bound, by its Statutes, to make all reasonable efforts to enforce the security in the event of default by the borrower.

The Edinburgh Temporary Lending Facility

Following the Commission's proposals for initiatives to promote economic growth and reduce unemployment in the EC, discussed at the Edinburgh Summit in December 1992, the EIB has established a 5 BECU lending facility for financing infrastructure projects, in particular in the areas of trans-European Networks as defined by Article 129b of the EECT, introduced by the Maastricht Treaty - transport, telecommunications and energy networks - and environmental protection and conservation. The expectation is that this additional support will have a major impact on speeding up economic recovery.

This facility is to be spread over the years 1993-94 and is to be in addition to the EIB's normal financing. The lending ceiling for EIB loans has been raised for projects supported under the facility from 50% to 75% of the eligible costs of qualifying projects. The combined ceiling of EIB loans and EC grants has also been raised from 70% to 90%.

Priority has been given to projects which are already underway in order to allow for the rapid release of the funds, but loans will, in future, also be available on equal terms for new projects.

Participation

From the standpoint of regional development in the UK, Northern Ireland and all Assisted Areas (as defined by the Department of Trade and Industry on 29 December 1984), City Grant Areas and the Scottish Highlands are all eligible. Areas suffering from the decline of the coal, steel and shipbuilding industries are also eligible, even if they are not in Assisted Areas.

There are no geographical restrictions in Ireland, as the whole country is designated as an Objective 1 region.

To qualify for EIB finance, projects are judged not only on their potential profitability, or indirect profitability in the case of infrastructure, but must also meet at least one of the Bank's stated objectives.

Economically and technically viable projects in all productive sectors of the economy may be financed; this includes investment in industry, agriculture, agricultural processing, energy, tourism, infrastructure and services of direct benefit to industry. Social investment such as health, general education and welfare cannot be financed by the Bank.

Loans are made irrespective of a borrower's legal status or nationality, to private, public or semi-public bodies, local or regional authorities, companies, co-operatives etc., or to the State itself. The EIB may also guarantee loans from other sources where the projects being financed meet its financing criteria. Financial beneficiaries of global loans are usually SMEs.

Once initial discussions show a project to be eligible, meeting an EIB aim and being consistent with EC policy guidelines, the Bank will appraise the investment and discuss the most suitable form of financing with the borrower. The appraisal covers the project's technical viability and economic benefits, its purpose, costings, financial requirements, timetable and forecast returns. It also covers the promoter's financial position, cash-flow projections, compliance with regulations, repayment terms and guarantees. During the appraisal, the EIB seeks confirmation from both the Member

State in which the project is located and the Commission that the investment complies with national economic policy and EC objectives.

Works and supply contracts for projects financed by the EIB must be open, as far as possible, to competitive tendering, and where appropriate, comply with the public works and supply policies of the Community. The EIB discusses with borrowers steps to be taken to meet this aim, encouraging the use of international competitive bidding where appropriate.

International Commitments

The Bank's activities were initially confined to the Member States themselves but have since been extended under various agreements and conventions to a number of overseas countries. It supports the economic development of the 69 ACP states which are signatories to the Lomé Convention, 12 Mediterranean countries and several Central and Eastern European countries. Information on the Bank's activities in these countries can be found in the section on Development Co-operation Grants Sources in Chapter 31.

In June 1992 a co-operation agreement was signed by the EIB and representatives of EFTA giving the EIB responsibility for the management of the financial mechanism set up within the framework of the European Economic Area (EEA) Agreement. This has the objective of supplementing EC aid to Portugal, Greece, parts of Spain, Ireland and Northern Ireland. It will cover the period 1993-97 and comprises 1.5 BECU in EIB loans attracting 3% interest rebates financed by the seven EFTA states, which will also provide grants totalling 500 MECU.

Applications

Enquiries about loans may be made directly to the EIB on an informal basis, by telephone or in writing. Contact can be made either with the EIB's headquarters in Luxembourg or one of its other offices. For small and medium-sized ventures, enquiries should be made to the intermediaries for EIB global loans.

INFORMATION

UK

For borrowings of less than £1 million: applicants should contact their local Barclays office;

Contact point for projects of £1-20 million:
Barclays Bank PLC
European Loans Unit
PO Box 256
Fleetway House
7th Floor
25 Farringdon Street
London EC4A 4LP
Tel: 071 832 3085

Contact point for projects over £20 million:
European Investment Bank
London Office
68 Pall Mall
London SW1Y 5ES.
Tel: 071 839 3351
Fax: 071 930 9929

EIB Headquarters:
A McDonaugh
European Investment Bank
100 Boulevard Konrad Adenauer
L-2950 Luxembourg
Tel: INT.+ 352 43791
Fax: INT.+ 352 437704

5. EBRD: European Bank for Reconstruction and Development

See Chapter 31

6. EIF: European Investment Fund

Statutory Basis

The EIF will have legal personality and financial autonomy and will be established under public international law. This creation involves a series of legal steps which are currently being implemented. Firstly, at an Inter-Governmental Conference on 25 March 1993, the Member States agreed on the necessary amendment to the Statute of the EIB. As the Statute of the EIB forms part of the Treaty of Rome as amended, this amendment requires ratification by all Member States, in accordance with the Treaties. Secondly, on the basis of this amendment, the EIB Board of Governors will adopt the Statute of the Fund. Finally, by way of a Decision of the Council of Ministers, the EC will be entitled to join the Fund as a member and contribute to its capital.

Objectives

The EIF's main objectives will be to contribute towards strengthening the internal market and furthering economic and social cohesion.

Background

In its declaration on economic recovery in Europe, the Edinburgh Summit in December 1992 "invited ... the ECOFIN Council and the EIB to give urgent and sympathetic consideration to the establishment as quickly as possible of a European Investment Fund with 2 BECU of capital contributed by the EIB, other financial institutions and the Commission." This invitation resulted from work which had been begun, in close collaboration, by the EIB and the Commission and pursued by a working party of the EIB's Board of Directors. After the European Parliament had been consulted, an Inter-Governmental Conference held on 25 March 1993 approved an act amending the Protocol on the Statute of the EIB and empowering the Bank's Board of Governors to establish a European Investment Fund. The act is being submitted for ratification in accordance with each Member State's own procedures.

The EIF will operate on a self-sustaining basis as a separate legal entity, keeping accounts separately from the Bank. It will be managed on a day-to-day basis by the

EIB, under mandate. The following three bodies will administer and supervise the Fund:

i a Financial Committee will be responsible for the day-to-day management of the EIF. It will consist of three members, one of whom will represent the financial institutions;

ii a Supervisory Board will undertake general control of the Fund's operations, decide about operations exceeding a certain size, determine the commission rate on guarantees and the general conditions for equity participation. It will consist of seven members, two of whom will represent the financial institutions; and

iii a General Meeting consisting of the representatives of the shareholders. It will lay down general directives for the activities of the EIF, and ensure that they are implemented. It will also approve the annual accounts and the appropriation of net profits and, as the ultimate decision-making body of the Fund, it will decide on major issues such as the approval of applications for membership, capital increases etc.

The Audit Committee of the Fund will be responsible for certifying both the conformity of the accounts in respect of its assets and liabilities, and that the fund has operated within its Statute.

Programme Content

EIF support will mainly target SMEs, and major infrastructure projects forming part of TENS, which are designed to benefit EC activity and facilitate cross-border links. It will offer two main types of financial products.

i Financial guarantees

Loan guarantees, feasibility studies and interest rate subsidies are the three ways of furnishing financial support for TENs set out in the new Article 129c of the EECT, introduced by the Maastricht Treaty. The amount and nature of guarantees given will depend on the circumstances of the project. Variations in the risks involved will be reflected in different rates of guarantee commissions. Since this will be an open fund, guarantees may be provided not only for shareholders in the EIF but also for third parties. They would not generally cover more than half the project cost and could be given in participation with other guarantors. It is estimated that the Fund will be capable of providing guarantees worth up to 10 BECU given the level of initial subscribed capital.

ii Equity Participation

During its two-year start-up period, the EIF's activities would consist only of providing guarantees. It cannot take equity stakes until the completion of a further study and authorisation by a decision of the General Meeting. The Fund could, however, take small direct participations in TEN projects during the start-up phase. The targeting of SMEs reflects the objectives of both the new Titles XIII

(Industry) and XIV (Economic and Social Cohesion) introduced by the Maastricht Treaty.

It is anticipated that, when equity-taking operations commence, the EIF will provide equity or quasi-equity to SMEs only through competent intermediaries. The viability criterion will be an essential element in its approach to SMEs.

The EIF will be run on the basis of banking criteria. Its operations will be co-ordinated, where necessary, with other forms of Community assistance. The availability of EIF guarantees and equity participations should facilitate private financing for infrastructure projects by providing a partial or, in some cases, complete alternative to recourse to government guarantees or financing.

The Fund is scheduled to start operations sometime in 1994.

INFORMATION

William Stevens
Evca
Keiberpark
Minervastraat 6
Box 6
B-1930 Zaventem
Belgium
Tel: INT.+ 322 720 6010
Fax: INT.+ 322 725 3036

NON-FINANCIAL

1. PUBLICATIONS

The catalogue of official publications is published by:
The Office of Official Publications
2 rue Mercier
L-2985 Luxembourg
Tel: INT.+ 352 499 281

Reports and some other official publications are listed in HMSO Daily List in the UK and Iris Oifigiuil in Ireland and in many cases, are available at Stationery Office book shops or agents.

London
HMSO Bookshop
49 High Holborn
London WC1V 6HB
Tel: 071 873 0011

Mail Order:
HMSO Publications Centre
51 Nine Elms Lane
London SW8 5DR
Tel. 071 873 8463
Fax: 071 873 8200

Dublin
The Irish Stationery Office
Sun Alliance House
Molesworth Street
Dublin 2
Tel: 01 71 03 09

Mail Order:
Government Publications Office
4-5 Harcourt Street
Dublin 2
Tel: 01 61 31 11
Fax: 01 78 06 45

Many EC publications are available at the EC offices and Info-points listed in Appendix 2.

2. DATA-BASES

The Office for Official Publications published the fourth edition of the Directory of Public Databases in January 1993. It contains 46 databases available to the general public and includes the various products and services associated with them as well as the commercial partners responsible for their distribution.

A list of the databases can be found in Appendix 7.

3. COMMUNITY OFFICES AND INFORMATION POINTS

These are included in Appendix 2.

Appendix 1

Schedule of Grant and Other Assistance Programmes

ACE: co-operation in the field of economics

AGRICULTURAL STRUCTURES: diversification into non-agricultural activities

AIM: advanced informatics in medicine

AIR: R&D in agriculture, agro-industry and fisheries

ALTENER: promotion of renewable energy sources

ARCHITECTURAL HERITAGE: conservation and promotion of the EC's architectural heritage

ARION: study visits for educational specialists

AVICENNE INITIATIVE: science and technology co-operation with Maghreb and Mediterranean countries

BABEL: to promote cross-lingual television programmes

BIOMED I: biomedical and health research programme

BIOTECH: reinforcing basic biological knowledge

BRITE/EURAM II: for SMEs manufacturing or testing advanced materials

CADDIA: co-operation in and documentation for imports/exports in the agricultural market

CAMAR: management of agricultural resources

CARTOON: developing cartoon production capacity in Europe

CEDEFOP: concerted approach to vocational training

CHILDCARE: increase in child-care for parents in employment or training

COAL RESEARCH

COHESION FUND: environment and TEN infrastructures in Member States with a per-capita GNP of less than 90% of the EC average

COLLEGE OF EUROPE

COMETT II: co-operation between universities and industry in technology training

CONTROLLED THERMONUCLEAR FUSION: research into self-sustaining nuclear reactors

CONVERSION LOANS

CO-OPERATION IN SCIENCE AND TECHNOLOGY WITH ALA COUNTRIES

CO-OPERATION IN SCIENCE AND TECHNOLOGY WITH CEECs

COST: European co-operation in scientific and technical research

COUNCIL OF EUROPE SCIENTIFIC AND TECHNOLOGICAL PROGRAMME

CRAFT: co-operation in R&D for SMEs

DECOMMISSIONING OF NUCLEAR INSTALLATIONS

DELTA: meeting electronic distance learning needs

DOCDEL: electronic publishing and document delivery

DOCUMENTARY: promoting creative status of documentaries

DOSES: R&D of statistical expert systems

DRIVE II: vehicle safety in Europe

EAGGF: agricultural guidance and price guarantee fund

EAVE: European audio-visual entrepreneurs

EC COMMISSION TRAINEESHIPS

ECIP: EC investment partners

EC JAPAN CENTRE FOR INDUSTRIAL CO-OPERATION

ECLAIR: linkage of agriculture and industry research programme

ECOS: Eastern Europe city co-operation

EC SCIENCE AND TECHNOLOGY FELLOWSHIP PROGRAMME IN JAPAN

ECSC LOANS:
- to CEECs
- conversion loans
- housing loans
- industrial loans
- Paul Finet grants for education of children of miners or steel workers killed by occupational disease or industrial accident
- re-adaptation grants

ECSC SOCIAL RESEARCH PROGRAMMES:
- ergonomics for the steel and coal industries
- industrial hygiene in mines
- ECSC medical research programme
- research on safety in the ECSC industries
- technical control of nuisance and pollution for iron and steel works

EC STUDENT GRANTS: to permit students to study on an equal footing in other Member States

EIF: financial guarantees and equity participation

ENERGY TECHNOLOGY TRANSFER WITH LDCs

ENS: European nervous systems

ENVIREG: improving the environment in the most disadvantaged coastal areas

ENVIRONMENT PROGRAMME

ENVIRONMENTAL ACTION PLAN FOR CEECs

EQUAL OPPORTUNITIES: studies, seminars and projects for women

ERASMUS: exchange programme for students in higher education

ERGO: initiatives for long-term unemployed

ERGONOMICS PROGRAMME FOR THE STEEL AND COAL INDUSTRIES

ESCF: European Seed Capital Funds

ESPRIT: research in information

ESSI: software technology transfer programme

ETP JAPAN: training for executives in Japan

EURATOM LOANS

EUREKA: promoting cross-border R&D
- DIAGNOSTICS
- EUROAGRI: food industry
- EUROBOND: adhesives
- EUROCARE: preservation of the physical heritage
- EUROENVIRON: terrestrial environment
- EUROLASER: laser technology
- EUROMAR: marine environment
- EUROSURF: surface engineering
- EUROVOLTAIC: solar power
- FAMOS: flexible automation
- MAINE: maintenance of capital equipment

EURET: improving the effectiveness of transport systems

EURO AIM: association for an independent audio-visual market

EUROLEADERS: introducing a European dimension to the training of entrepreneurs

EUROMANAGEMENT: introducing a European dimension to the training of managers

EUROMARKETING: marketing assistance to SMEs

EUROPA CINEMAS

EUROPEAN ARCHITECTURAL PRIZE: for awareness of modern architecture

EUROPEAN BANK OF RECONSTRUCTION AND DEVELOPMENT

EUROPEAN CITY OF CULTURE: to bring peoples closer together

EUROPEAN CULTURAL MONTH: to bring cities in the CEECs and EC closer together

EUROPEAN DEVELOPMENT FUND: technical and financial assistance for developing countries:
- Lomé countries
- Overseas Countries and Territories

EUROPEAN FILM ACADEMY

EUROPEAN FILM DISTRIBUTION OFFICE

EUROPEAN INVESTMENT BANK:
- and CEECs
- and Mediterranean countries

EUROPEAN LITERATURE PRIZE: for a significant contribution to contemporary European literature

EUROPEAN NERVOUS SYSTEMS

EUROPEAN PARLIAMENT RESOLUTIONS PROJECTS:
- EC BAROQUE ORCHESTRA
- EC YOUTH OPERA
- EC YOUTH ORCHESTRA
- EUROPEAN POETRY FESTIVAL

EUROPEAN REGIONAL DEVELOPMENT FUND: reducing imbalances in the EC
- ARTICLE 10:
- ECOS: establishing co-operative links between regions
- RECITE: supporting co-operation networks

EUROPEAN SCIENCE FOUNDATION

EUROPEAN SCRIPT FUND

EUROPEAN SOCIAL FUND: job creation
- CHILDCARE
- ERGO
- EUROFORM: training to meet needs resulting from single market
- HANDYNET: mobility for the disabled
- HORIZON: professional and social integration for the handicapped
- LEDA: know-how for local employment development
- NOW: vocational training and employment for women
- TIDE: telecommunications for the disabled and elderly

EUROPEAN SPACE AGENCY

EUROPEAN TRANSLATION PRIZE: translation of contemporary literary works

EUROQUALIFICATION

EUROTECH CAPITAL

EUROTECNET II: development of technological training programmes

EVE: promoting European audio-visual works

FIGHT AGAINST DRUGS

FISHERIES AND AQUACULTURE PROCESSING

FISHERIES AND AQUACULTURE STRUCTURES: development of fisheries and fish farming

FLAIR: food science research programme

FORCE: promoting vocational training involving companies

FORESTRY GRANTS: promoting afforestation on agricultural land

FRAMEWORK PROGRAMMES

GRECO: promoting high quality television fiction

HANDYNET: mobility for the disabled

HELIOS II: assisting the rehabilitation of the disabled

HOUSING LOANS

HUMAN CAPITAL AND MOBILITY PROGRAMME

IMPACT: action for a European information services market

IMPROVEMENT OF PROCESSING AND MARKETING OF AGRICULTURAL PRODUCTS

INDUSTRIAL HYGIENE IN MINES

INDUSTRIAL LOANS

INSIS: promoting the use of new electronic technologies

INTERREG: for national border areas

IRIS: promoting vocational training for women

JEAN MONNET CHAIRS FOR PHARE COUNTRIES

JEAN MONNET FELLOWSHIPS: for full-time research at the European University Institute in Florence

JEAN MONNET PROJECT: creation of new academic posts to develop courses in European studies

JESSI: sub-micron silicon research programme

JOINT VENTURE PHARE PROGRAMME

JOULE II. non-nuclear energies

KALEIDOSCOPE: artistic and cultural events

KAROLUS: training officials on enforcement of EC legislation

KONVER: assistance to areas affected by reductions in military expenditure

LANGUAGE-BASED TRAINEESHIPS

LEADER: protection of rural areas

LEDA: local employment creation, especially for actors

LIBRARIES PROGRAMME

LIFE: implementing EC environmental policy

LIFE SCIENCES FOR DEVELOPING COUNTRIES

LINGUA: for improving the teaching of foreign languages

LINGUISTIC RESEARCH AND ENGINEERING

LUMIERE: the protection of the European film heritage

MANAGEMENT AND STORAGE OF RADIO-ACTIVE WASTE

MAP-TV: enhancing European audio-visual archives

MAST II: marine science and technology

MATTHAEUS: training for customs officials

MATTHAEUS-TAX: training for officials in indirect taxation

MEASUREMENT AND TESTING PROGRAMME

MED-CAMPUS: co-operation between HEIs in EC and Mediterranean countries

MEDIA: to stimulate the audio-visual industry

- BABEL
- Cartoon
- Documentary
- EAVE
- EURO AIM
- Euro Media Guarantees
- Europa Cinemas
- European Film Academy
- European Film Distribution Office
- European Script Fund
- EVE
- GRECO
- Lumière Project Association
- MAP-TV
- Media Business School
- Media Investment Club

- Media Salles: promoting cinema and European films
- SCALE: small countries achieve their audio-visual level in Europe
- SOURCES: stimulating creative European screen-writing

MEDIA BUSINESS SCHOOL

MEDIA INVESTMENT CLUB

MEDIA SALLES

MEDICAL RESEARCH PROGRAMME

MEDIUM-TERM FINANCIAL SUPPORT FOR CEECs AND NON-MEMBER STATES

MEDIUM-TERM FINANCIAL SUPPORT FOR MEMBER STATES: emergency aid with balance of payments problems

MINT: helping SMEs absorb new technologies

MONITOR: strategic analysis, forecasting and assessment in research and technology

- FAST: Forecasting and Assessment of Science and Technology
- SAST: Strategic Analysis in Science and Technology
- SPEAR: Support Studies for the Evaluation of R&D

NETT: promoting co-operation between industry and users of new environmental technology

NOW: help with qualification and employment of women

NUCLEAR FISSION SAFETY PROGRAMME

NUCLEAR SAFETY PROGRAMME IN THE CEECs

ORA: telematics systems for rural areas

PAUL FINET FOUNDATION

PERIFRA: for peripheral regions affected by trade concessions to CEECs, cut-backs in armaments production or the closure of military bases

PETRA II: work experience for 16- to 27-year-olds

PHARE: economic reconstruction of Eastern Europe, including:

- ACE
- Environmental Action Plan for CEECs
- Fight against Drugs
- Jean Monnet Chairs
- JOPP
- Nuclear Safety in CEECs
- Regional Energy Sector Programme
- Regional Environment Sector Programme
- Regional Industrial Property Programme

- Regional Quality Assurance Programme
- Regional Transport Programme
- Telecommunications Programme

PILOT/DEMONSTRATION PROJECTS IN THE IRON AND STEEL INDUSTRY

POVERTY 3: combating poverty among disadvantaged groups

PRISMA: preparing regional industry for the single market

PROMOTION OF SMEs' ACCESS TO MARKETS IN THIRD COUNTRIES AND EXPORT PROMOTION

PSEP: supporting the physical and social environment and the preservation of the countryside and wildlife

RACE II: research in advanced communications

READAPTATION GRANTS

RECHAR: conversion of coal closure areas

RECITE: regions and cities for Europe

REGEN: networks for transporting energy

REGIONAL ENERGY SECTOR PROGRAMME

REGIONAL ENVIRONMENT SECTOR PROGRAMME

REGIONAL INDUSTRIAL PROPERTY PROGRAMME

REGIONAL QUALITY ASSURANCE PROGRAMME

REGIS: assisting ultra-peripheral regions

RENEVAL: conversion of shipbuilding areas suffering job losses

RESIDER: conversion of areas dependent on a declining steel industry

RETEX: diversification in areas over-dependant on the textile industry

ROBERT SCHUMAN SCHOLARSHIPS: post-graduate research on EC matters

SAFETY IN THE ECSC INDUSTRIES

SAVE: to achieve the EC's energy efficiency goals

SCALE: improving small countries' audio-visual level in Europe

SPEC: providing support for local job creation

SPRINT: innovation and technology transfer

STA: science and technology fellowship in Japan

STAR: regional development of technology

STD 3: life sciences for developing countries

STEEL RESEARCH GRANTS

STOA: scientific and technological options assessment

STRIDE: regional development of science and technology

STRUCTURAL FUNDS: (all three have to be considered together)

- EAGGF Guidance Section
- European Regional Development Fund (ERDF)
- European Social Fund (ESF)

STUDIES AND TECHNICAL ASSISTANCE PROGRAMME

SUBSIDIES FOR TRANSNATIONAL MEETINGS BETWEEN EMPLOYEES' REPRESENTATIVES

TACIS: technical assistance to former Soviet Union

TECHNICAL CONTROL OF NUISANCE AND POLLUTION FROM IRON AND STEEL WORKS

TEDIS II: development of electronic data interchange

TELECOMMUNICATIONS PROGRAMME

TELEMAN: handling in nuclear and other hazardous environments

TELEMATICS: support for the establishment of TENs

- AIM
- DELTA
- DRIVE II
- ENS
- Libraries Programme
- Linguistic Research and Engineering
- ORA

TELEMATIQUE: advanced telecommunications in the least-favoured areas

TEMPUS: training for CEECs

TEMPUS-PHARE: trans-European mobility for university students

TEMPUS-TACIS: mobility for university students

THERMIE: pilot programme for new energy projects

TIDE: programme for the development of technology for disabled and elderly persons

TOWN-TWINNING

TPF: uptake of new technology by manufacturing firms

TRAINING IN RESTORATION TECHNIQUES

TRANSLATION OF CONTEMPORARY LITERARY WORKS

TRANSPORT INFRASTRUCTURE FUND: improvement of transport generally

VALOREN: improving the economic base of disadvantaged regions

VALUE II: the dissemination of the results of research

VENTURE CONSORT INNOVATION FINANCE SCHEME: growth of SMEs through cross-border venture capital syndicates

WNLEI: assisting women to create their own businesses

YOUTH FOR EUROPE: exchange activities for 15- to 25-year-olds

YOUTH WORKERS' EXCHANGE: study visits and work placements for 18- to 28-year-olds

Appendix 2

Useful Addresses

These include:

1. Main Commission Offices
2. European Parliament Offices
3. UK Government Departments
4. Irish Government Departments
5. Euro-Info Centres: UK
6. Euro-Info Centres: Ireland
7. Euro-Info Centres: Other Member States
8. EC Delegations to Non-Member States
9. EC Delegations to International Organisations

1. MAIN COMMISSION OFFICES

Commission of the European Communities
200 rue de la Loi
B-1049 Brussels
Tel.(exchange): INT.+ 322 299 1111

Commission of the European Communities
Batiment Jean Monnet
Rue Alcide de Gasperi
L-2920 Luxembourg
Tel: INT.+ 352 43011

"THE COURIER"
"The ACP-EEC Courier"
Commission of the European Communities
200 rue de la Loi
B 1049 Brussels
Tel: INT.+.322 299 1111

Office For Official Publications
Office For Official Publications of the EC
2 rue Mercier
L-2985 Luxembourg
Tel: INT.+ 352 499281
Fax: INT.+ 352 490003

CENTRE FOR THE DEVELOPMENT OF INDUSTRY
Centre for the Development of Industry
Rue de l'Industrie 26-28
B-1040 Brussels.
Tel: INT.+ 322 513 4100
Fax: INT.+ 322 511 7593

UK

England
Commission of the European Communities
Jean Monnet House
8 Storey's Gate
London SW1P 3AT
Tel: 071 973 1992
Fax: 071 973 1900/1910

Wales
Commission of the European Communities
4 Cathedral Road
Cardiff CF1 9SG
Tel: 0222 371631
Fax: 0222 395489

Northern Ireland
Commission of the European Communities
Windsor House
9-15 Bedford Street
Belfast BT2 7EG
Tel: 0232 240708
Fax: 0232 248241

Scotland
Commission of the European Communities
9 Alva Street
Edinburgh, EH2 4PH
Tel: 031 225 2058

IRELAND
Commission of the European Communities
39 Molesworth Street
Dublin 2
Tel: 01 71 22 44
Fax: 01 71 26 57

2. EUROPEAN PARLIAMENT OFFICES

Secretariat
The European Parliament
Plateau du Kirchberg
BP 1601
Luxembourg
Tel: INT.+ 352 43001

UK
The European Parliament Office
2 Queen Anne's Gate
London SWIH 9AA
Tel: 071 222 0411

IRELAND
The European Parliament Office
43 Molesworth Street
Dublin 2
Tel: 01 71 91 00

3. UK GOVERNMENT DEPARTMENTS

Department of Trade & Industry
Kingsgate House
66-74 Victoria Street
London SW1E 6SW
Tel: 071 215 5000

DTI Regional Offices:
DTI South-East
Bridge Place
88-89 Eccleston Square
London SW1V 1PT
Tel: 071 215 0574
Fax: 071 215 0875

DTI West Midlands
77 Paradise Circus
Queensway
Birmingham B1 2DT
Tel: 021 212 5000
Fax: 021 212 1010

DTI South-West
The Pithay
Bristol BS1 2PB
Tel: 0272 272666
Fax: 0272 299494

DTI East Midlands
Severns House
20 Middle Pavement
Nottingham NG1 7DW
Tel: 0602 506181
Fax: 0602 587074

DTI East
Building A
Westbrook Research Centre
Milton Road
Cambridge CB4 1YG
Tel: 0223 461939

Scotland
Scottish Trade International
120 Bothwell Street
Glasgow G2 7JP
Tel: 041 228 2869 (overseas trade)
Tel: 041 228 2843 (single market)
Fax: 041 221 3712

UK: DEPARTMENT OF THE ENVIRONMENT
Department of the Environment
2 Marsham Street
London
SW1P 3EB
Tel: 071 276 0900

EC Initiatives on Regional Planning, Urban Regeneration and Rural Development
Enquiries
Tel: 071 276 3936
Fax: 071 276 3936

DTI North-West
Sunley Tower
Piccadilly Plaza
Manchester M1 4BA
Tel: 061 838 5228
Fax: 061 228 3740

DTI Yorkshire & Humberside
25 Queen Street
Leeds LS1 2TW
Tel: 0532 443171
Fax: 0532 338301/2

DTI North-East
Stanegate House
2 Groat Market
Newcastle-upon-Tyne NE1 1YN
Tel: 091 235 7273

Wales
Welsh Office Industry Department
New Crown Building
Cathays Park
Cardiff CF1 3NQ
Tel: 0222 825527
Fax: 0222 823088

Northern Ireland
Industrial Development Board for Northern Ireland
IDB House
64 Chichester Street
Belfast BT1 4JX
Tel: 0232 233233
Fax: 0232 231328

Policy and procedures on ERDF Grants
N R Cartwright
(as left)
Tel: 071 276 3805

REGIONAL OFFICES OF THE DEPARTMENT OF THE ENVIRONMENT

Department of the Environment, North
Wellbar House
Gallowgate
Newcastle-upon-Tyne NE1 4TD
Tel: 091 232 7575 ext.2328
Fax: 091 261 8393

Department of the Environment, North West
Sunley Tower
Piccadilly Plaza
Manchester M1 4BE
Tel: 061 832 9111
Fax: 061 838 5790

Department of the Environment
Merseyside Task Force
Graeme House
Derby Square
Liverpool L2 7SU
Tel: 051 227 4111 ext.2585
Fax: 051 236 1199

Department of the Environment
Yorks. & Humberside
City House
New Station Street
Leeds LS1 4JD
Tel: 0532 438232 ext.2250/2318
Fax: 0532 444898

Department of the Environment
East Midlands
Cranbrook House
Cranbrook Street
Nottingham NG1 1EY
Tel: 0602 47612 ext.341
Fax: 0602 509159 ext.560

Department of the Environment
West Midlands
Five Ways Tower
Frederick Road
Edgbaston
Birmingham B15 1SJ
Tel: 021 626 2000 ext.2437/2413
Fax: 021 626 2404

Department of the Environment
South West
Tollgate House
Houlton Street
Bristol BS2 9DJ
Tel: 0272 218811 ext.8171
Fax: 0272 218269

Department of the Environment
South East
Charles House
375 Kensington High Street
London W14 8QH
Tel: 071 605 9000
Fax: 071 605 9249

Department of the Environment
London Regional Office
Millbank Tower
21-24 Millbank
London SW1P 4QH
Tel: 071 217 3000 ext.4588
Fax: 071 217 4586

The Scottish Office
Environment Department
St.Andrew's House
Edinburgh EH1 3DG
Scotland
Tel: 031 556 8400
Tlx: 727301

4. IRISH GOVERNMENT DEPARTMENTS

Department of Industry & Commerce
Kildare Street
Dublin 2
Tel: 01 61 44 44

Department of the Environment
O'Connell Bridge House
Dublin 1
Tel: 01 679 33 77

Department of Tourism, Transport & Communications,
Kildare Street
Dublin 2
Tel: 01 662 1444
Fax: 01 676 6154

Department of Enterprise & Employment
Davitt House
Adelaide Road
Dublin 2
Tel: 01 76 58 61

Department of Finance
Government Buildings
Lower Merrion Street
Dublin 2
Tel: 01 76 75 71

Department of Energy
Clare Street
Dublin 2
Tel: 01 71 52 33

Department of Agriculture & Food
Kildare Street
Dublin 2
Tel: 01 78 90 11

5. EURO-INFO CENTRES: UK

Northern Ireland
Euro-Info Centre
Local Enterprise Development Unit
LEDU House
Upper Galwally
Belfast BT8 4TB
Tel: 0232 491031
Fax: 0232 691432

Northern Ireland
Euro-Info Centre
Department of Economic Development
Industrial Science Division
17 Antrim Road
Lisburn BT28 3AL
Tel: 0846 665161
Fax: 0846 676054

Wales
Euro-Info Centre
Wales Euro Info Centre
University College Cardiff
Guest Building
PO Box 430
Cardiff CF1 3XT
Tel: 0222 229525
Fax: 0222 229740

Scotland
Euro-Info Centre
Atrium Court
3rd Floor
50 Waterloo Street
Glasgow G2 6HQ
Tel: 041 221 0999
Fax: 041 221 6539

Scotland
Highland Opportunity Ltd
Development Department
Highland Regional Council
Regional Buildings
Glenurquhart Road
Inverness IV3 5NX
Tel: 0463 702560
Fax: 0463 710848

England - South-East
Euro-Info Centre
Centre for European Business Information
11 Belgrave Road
London SW1V 1RB
Tel: 071 828 6201
Fax: 071 834 8416

Euro-Info Centre Kent
County Hall
Maidstone ME14 1XQ
Tel: 0622 694109
Fax: 0622 691418

Euro-Info Centre Thames Valley & Surrey
Commerce House
2-6 Bath Road
Slough SL1 3SB
Tel: 0753 577877
Fax: 0753 524644

Euro Info Centre - Isle of Wight Development Board
Bugle House
117-118 High Street
Newport
Isle of Wight PO30 1TP
Tel: 0983 826222
Fax: 0983 826365

London Chamber of Commerce
Euro-Info Centre
69 Cannon Street
London EC4N 5AB
Tel: 071 489 1992
Fax: 071 489 0391

Euro-Info Centre Brighton
Federation of Sussex Industries (FSI) and Chamber of Commerce
169 Church Road
Hove
East Sussex BN3 2AB
Tel: 0273 26282
Fax: 0273 207965

Euro-Info Centre - Southern Area
Civic Centre
Southampton SO9 4XP
Tel: 0703 832866
Fax: 0703 231714

England - East
Euro Info Centre East Anglia
112 Barrack Street
Norwich NR3 1UB
Tel: 0345 023114
Fax: 0603 633032

Euro-Info Centre
Exeter Enterprises Ltd
University of Exeter
Reed Hall
Exeter EX4 4QR
Tel: 0392 214085
Fax: 0392 264375

England - South West
Euro-Info Centre
Bristol Chamber of Commerce and Industry
16 Clifton Park
Bristol BS8 3BY
Tel: 0272 737373
Fax: 0272 745365

Yorkshire & Humberside
Yorkshire & Humberside Euro-Info Centre
Westgate House
100 Wellington Street
Leeds LS1 4LT
Tel: 0532 439222
Fax: 0532 431088

West Midlands
Euro-Info Centre
Birmingham Chamber of Industry & Commerce
75 Harbone Road
PO Box 360
Birmingham B15 3DH
Tel: 021 454 6171
Fax: 021 455 8670

Euro-Info Centre Nottingham
Nottinghamshire Chamber of Commerce
The Business Advice Centre
309 Haydn Road
Nottingham NG5 1DG
Tel: 0602 624624
Fax: 0602 856612

Manchester Chamber of Commerce and Industry
Euro-Info Centre
56 Oxford Street
Manchester M60 7JH
Tel: 061 236 3210
Fax: 061 236 4160

East Midlands
Euro-Info Centre
The Business Centre
10 York Road
Leicester LE1 5TS
Tel: 0533 559944
Fax: 0533 553470

North West
North West Euro Service Ltd
Liverpool Central Libraries
William Brown Street
Liverpool L3 8EW
Tel: 051 298 1928
Fax: 051 207 1342

North-East
Northern Development Company
Euro-Info Centre
Great North House
Sandyford Road
Newcastle-upon-Tyne NE1 8ND
Tel: 091 261 0026
Fax: 091 222 1779

6. EURO-INFO CENTRES: IRELAND

European Business Information Centre
Irish Trade Board
Merrion Hall
Strand Road
Sandymount
Dublin 4
Tel: 01 269 5011
Fax: 01 269 5820
Tlx: 93678 CTT EI

European Business Information Centre
Galway Chamber of Commerce and Industry
Hardiman House
5 Eyre Square
Galway
Tel: 091 62624/98127
Fax: 091 61963

European Business Information Centre
Cork Chamber of Commerce
CTT Office
67-69 South Mall
Cork
Tel: 021 509 044
Fax: 021 271 347

European Business Information Centre
Shannon Development
The Granary
Michael Street
Limerick.
Tel: 061 410 777
Fax: 061 315 634

European Business Information Centre
Sligo Chamber of Commerce
16 Quay Street
Sligo.
Tel: 071 61274
Fax: 071 60912
Tlx: 40223 CTT EI

European Business Information Centre
Waterford Chamber of Commerce
CTT Office
Western Industrial Estate
Cork Road
Waterford
Tel: 051 72639
Fax: 051 79220

7. EURO-INFO CENTRES: OTHER MEMBER STATES

Belgium
Euro-Info Centre
Rue Archimede 73 Archimedesstraat
B-1040 Bruxelles - Brussel
Tel: 32 2 235 38 44
Fax: 32 2 235 01 66

Denmark
Kommissionen for De Europaeieske Faellesskaber
Hojbrohus
Ostergade 61
Post-box 144
DK-1004 Kobenhaven K
Tel: 45 33 14 41 40
Fax: 45 33 11 12 03

France
Commission des Communautés Européennes
288 Bvd. St Germain
F-75007 Paris
Tel: 33 1 40 63 38 00
Fax: 33 1 45 56 94 17

Commission des Communautés Européennes
2 rue Henri-Barbusse
F-13241 Marseilles Cedex 01
Tel: 33 91 91 46 00
Fax: 33 91 90 98 07

Germany
Kommission der Europaischen Gemeinschaften
Zitelmann Strasse 22
D-53113 Bonn
Tel: 49 228 53 00 90
Fax: 49 228 53 00 950

Kommission der Europaischen Gemeinschaften
Kurfurstendamm 102
D-10711 Berlin
Tel: 49 30 896 09 30
Fax: 49 30 892 20 59

Kommission der Europaischen Gemeinschaften
Erhardtstrasse 27
D-80331 Munchen
Tel: 49 89 202 10 11
Fax: 49 89 202 10 15

Greece
Euro-Info Centre
2 Vassilissis Sofias
PO Box 11002
10674 Athina
Tel: 30 1 724 39 82
Fax: 30 1 724 46 20

Italy
Commissione delle Comunita Europee
Via Poli 29
I-00187 Roma
Tel: 39 6 699 11 60
Fax: 39 6 679 16 58

Commissione delle Comunita Europee
Corso Magenta 59
I-20123 Milano
Tel: 39 2 480 15 05
Fax: 39 2 481 85 43

Luxembourg
Commission des Communautés Européennes
Batiment Jean Monnet
Rue Alcide De Gasperi
L-2920 Luxembourg
Tel: 352 43 01 1
Fax: 352 43 01 4433

The Netherlands
Commissie van de Europese Gemeenschappen
Korte Vijverberg 5
Postbus 30465
2500 AB Den Haag
Tel: 31 70 346 93 26
Fax: 31 70 364 66 19

Portugal
Commissao das Comunidades Europeias
Centro Europeu Jean Monnet
Largo Jean Monnet 1-10
P-1200 Lisboa
Tel: 351 1 154 11 44
Fax: 351 1 355 43 97

Spain
Comision de las Comunidades Europeas
Calle de Serrano 41, 5a planta
E-28001 Madrid
Tel: 34 1 435 17 00
Fax: 34 1 576 03 87

Comision de las Comunidades Europeas
Edificio Atlantico
Av. Diagonal 407 bis Planta 18
E-08008 Barcelona
Tel: 34 3 415 81 77
Fax 34 3 415 63 11

8. EC DELEGATIONS TO NON-MEMBER STATES

Algeria
Commission des Communautés Européennes
7 rue Larbi Alik
16035 Hydra
Alger
Tel: 213 2 59 21 70
Fax: 213 2 59 39 47

Antigua and Barbuda
Commission of the European Communities
Second floor, Alpha Building
Redcliff Street
PO Box 1393
St John's
Tel: 1 809 462 29 70
Fax: 1 809 462 11 87

Angola
Commissao das Comunidades Europeias
Rua Rainha Jinga 6
Caixa Postal 2669
Luanda
Tel: 244 2 39 30 38
Fax: 244 2 39 25 31

Argentina
Comision de las Comunidades Europeas
Plaza Hotel
Florida 1005
Buenos Aires
Tel: 54 1 11 22 24
Fax: 54 1 31 34 374

Aruba
see Netherlands Antilles

Australia
Commission of the European Communities
18 Arakana Street
Yarralumia
ACT 2600
Canberra
Tel: 61 62 71 27 77
Fax: 61 62 73 44 45

Austria
Kommission der Europaischen Gemeinschaften
Hoyosgasse 5
A-1040 Vienna
Tel: 43 1 505 33 79
Fax: 43 1 505 33 797

Bangladesh
Commission of the European Communities
House CES (E) 19
Road 128 Gulshan
Dhaka 12
Tel: 880 2 88 35 64
Fax: 880 2 88 31 18

Barbados
Commission of the European Communities
James Fort Building
Hincks Street, PO Box 654 C
Bridgetown
Tel: 1 809 427 43 62
Fax: 1 809 427 86 87

Belize
Commission of the European Communities
PO Box 907
Blake Building (3rd floor)
Car, Huston & Eyre Street
Belize
Tel: 501 2 727 85
Fax: 501 2 727 85

Benin
Commission des Communautés Européennes
Avenue Roume, Batiment administratif
BP 910
Cotonou
Tel: 229 312 684
Fax: 229 312 5328

Botswana
Commission of the European Communities
North Ring Road 68
PO Box 1253
Gaborone
Tel: 267 31 44 55
Fax: 267 31 36 26

Brazil
Commissao das Comunidades Europeias
Q.1.7
Bloco A Lago Sul
Brasilia DF
Tel: 55 61 248 31 22
Fax: 55 61 248 07 00

Bulgaria
Commission of the European Communities
Interpred World Trade Centre
Block A 3rd floor
36 Dragan Tsankov Boulevard
1056 Sofia

Postal address:
Commission of the European Communities
PO Box 668
1000 Sofia
Tel: 359 2 73 98 41-5
Fax: 359 2 73 83 95

Burkina Faso
Bureau des Communautés Européennes
BP 352
Ouagadougou
Tel: 226 30 73 85
Fax: 226 30 89 66

Burundi
Commission des Communautés Européennes
Avenue du 13 Octobre
BP 103
Bujumbura
Tel: 257 22 34 26
Fax: 257 22 46 12

Cameroon
Commission des Communautés Européennes
Quartier Bastos
BP 847
Yaoundé
Tel: 237 22 13 87
Fax: 237 20 21 49

Canada
Commission of the European Communities
Commission des Communautés Européennes
Office Tower
Suite 1110
350 Sparks Street
Ottawa
Ontario KIR 7S8
Tel: 1 613 238 64 64
Fax: 1 613 238 51 91

Cape Verde
Commissao das Comunidades Europeias
Achada de Santo Antonio
CP. 122
Praia
Tel: 238 61 37 50
Fax: 238 61 34 67

Central African Republic
Commission des Communautés Européennes
Rue de Flandre
BP 1298
Bangui
Tel: 236 61 30 53
Fax: 236 61 65 35

Chad
Commission des Communautés Européennes
Concession Caisse Coton
Route de Farcha
BP 552
N'Djamena
Tel: 19 235 51 59 77
Fax: 19 235 51 21 05

Chile
Comision de las Comunidades Europeas
Avenida Americo Vespucio Sur 1835
Santiago 9
Tel: 56 2 228 24 84
Fax: 56 2 228 25 71

Postal Address:
Comision de las Comunidades Europeas
Casillia 10093
Santiago 9

China
Commission of the European Communities
Dong Zhi Men Wai Dajie 15
Sanlitun
100600 Beijing
Tel: 86 1 532 44 43
Fax: 86 1 532 43 42

Comoros
Commission des Communautés Européennes
BP 559
Boulevard de la Corniche
Moroni
Tel: 269 73 31 91
Fax: 269 73 22 22

Congo
Commission des Communautés Européennes
Avenue Lyautey
BP 2149
Brazzaville
Tel: 242 83 38 78
Fax: 242 83 60 74

Costa Rica
Comision de las Comunidades Europeas
Barrio Amon, 25m al Norte del Parqueo del INS - Centro Colon
Apartado 836
1007 San Jose
Tel: 506 33 27 55
Fax: 506 21 65 95

Cuba
see Mexico

Cyprus
Commission of the European Communities
Irish Tower 8th floor
242 Agapinor Street
Nicosia 137
Cyprus
PO Box 3480
Tel: 357 2 36 92 02
Fax: 357 2 36 89 26

Czechoslovakia
Commission of the European Communities
Hotel Diplomat, Suite 332/334
Evnopska 15
16000 Praha 6
Tel: 42 2 331 43 32/331
Fax: 42 2 331 43 65

Djibouti
Commission des Communautés Européennes
11, Boulevard du Marechal Joffre
BP 2477
Djibouti
Tel: 253 35 26 15
Fax: 253 35 00 36

Dominican Republic
Comision de las Comunidades Europeas
Calle Rafael Augusto Sanchez no 21
Ensanche Naco-Santo Domingo
Tel: 1 809 566 97 30-540 5837
Fax: 1 809 567 58 51

Egypt
Commission of the European Communities
6, Ibn Zanki Street
Zamalek
Cairo
Tel: 202 341 93 93/340 31
Fax: 202 340 03 85

Equatorial Guinea
Commission des Communautés Européennes
BP 779
Malabo
Tel: 29 44/29 45

Ethiopia
Commission of the European Communities
Tedla Desta Building, 1st floor
Africa Avenue (Bole Road)
PO Box 5570
Addis Ababa
Tel: 251 1 51 25 11/51 01 80/51 01 89
Tel: 251 1 51 01 29/51 26 72
Fax: 251 1 51 41 19
Hilton Business Centre Fax: 251 1 51 00 64

Finland
Commission of the European Communities
Pohoiseplanadi 31
PO Box 234
SF-00100 Helsinki
Tel: 358 0 65 64 20
Fax: 358 0 65 67 28

Gabon
Commission des Communautés Européennes
Quartier Batterie IV
Lotissement des Cocotiers
BP 321
Libreville
Tel: 241 73 22 50
Fax: 241 73 65 54

Gambia
Commission of the European Communities
10 Nelson Mandela Street
PO Box 512
Banjul
Tel: 220 27 777
Fax: 220 26 219

Ghana
Commission of the European Communities
The Round House 65
Cantonments Road
Cantonments
Accra
Tel: 233 21 77 42 01
Fax: 233 21 77 41 54 or
Ghana P & T No 77 26 42

Ghana
Postal address:
Commission of the European Communities
PO Box 9505
Kotoka Airport
Accra

Grenada
Commission of the European Communities
PO Box 5
St George's Old Fort
St George's
Tel: 1 809 440 35 61/440 49 58
Fax: 1 809 440 41 51

Guinea
Commission des Communautés Européennes
BP 730 Conakry
Corniche Sud
Madina Dispensaire
Conakry
Tel: 224 46 13 25
Fax: 224 44 18 74

Guinea Bissau
Comision de las Comunidades Europeas
Barrio da Penha
PO Box 359
Apartado 1113
Bissau Cedex
Tel: 245 25 10 71
Fax: 245 25 10 44

Guyana
Commission of the European Communities
72 High Street
Kingston
Georgetown
Tel: 592 2 640 04
Fax: 592 2 626 15

Haiti
Commission des Communautés Européennes
Delmas 60
Impasse Brave no 1
Port-au-Prince
Tel: 509 57 54 85
Fax: 509 57 42 44

Hungary
Commission of the European Communities
Berc utea 23
H-1016 Budapest
Tel: 36 1 166 44 87
Fax: 36 1 166 42 21

India
Commission of the European Communities
65 Golf Links
New Delhi 110003
Tel: 91 11 462 92 37
Fax: 91 11 462 92 06

Israel
Commission of the European Communities
The Tower
3 Daniel Frisch Street
Tel Aviv 64731
Tel: 972 3 696 41 66
Fax: 972 3 695 19 83

Jamaica
Commission of the European Communities
8 Olivier Road
Kingston 8
Tel: 1 809 924 63 33/4/5/6/7
Fax: 1 809 924 63 39

Japan
Commission of the European Communities
Europa House
9-15 Sanbancho
Chiyoda-Ku
Tokyo 102
Tel: 81 3 239 04 41
Fax: 81 3 261 51 94 or 81 3 239 93 37

Kenya
Commission of the European Communities
National Bank Building
Harambee Avenue
PO Box 45119
Nairobi
Tel: 254 2 33 35 92
Fax: 254 2 21 59 25

Lebanon
Commission des Communautés Européennes
PO Box 1640
Centre Saint Paul
Jounieh
Tel: 961 9 93 71 47/93 71 48
Fax: 961 9 93 71 54
Radio Telephone (Cyprus) 357 951 59 28

Indonesia
Commission of the European Communities
Wisma Dharmala Sakti Building, 16th floor
Jl. Jendral Sudirman 32
PO Box 55 JKPDS
Jakarta 10220
Tel: 62 21 570 60 76/570 60 68
Fax: 62 21 570 60 75

Ivory Coast
Commission des Communautés Européennes
Immeuble 'Azur'
Boulevard Crozet 18
01 BP 1821
Abidjan 01
Tel: 225 21 24 28/21 75/21 09 28
Fax: 225 21 40 89

Jamaica
Postal address:
Commission of the European Communities
PO Box 463
Constant Spring
Kingston 8

Jordan
Commission of the European Communities
Al Jahez Street No 15
Shmeisani
PO Box 926794
Amman
Tel: 962 6 66 81 91/66 81 92
Fax: 962 6 68 67 46

Korea
Commission of the European Communities
CPO Box 9553
109 lst ga Changehoog-Dong
Choong-Ku - Seoul
Tel: 82 2 271 07 81 3
Fax: 82 2 271 07 86

Lebanon
Commission des Communautés Européennes
PO Box 11-4008 Beirut
Immeuble Duraffourd
Avenue de Paris
Tel: 961 9 136 30 30/31/32

Lesotho
Commission of the European Communities
PO Box MS 518
Maseru 100
Tel: 266 31 37 26
Fax: 266 31 01 93

Liberia
Commission of the European Communities
34 Payne Avenue, Sinkor
PO Box 10-3049
1000 Monrovia 10
Tel: 231 26 22 78/26 26 87
Fax: 231 26 22 66

Madagascar
Commission des Communautés Européennes
Immeuble Ny Havana - 67 hectares
BP 746
Antananarivo
Tel: 261 2 242 16/275 27
Fax: 261 2 321 69

Malawi
Commission of the European Communities
Lingadzi House
PO Box 30102, Capital City
Lilongwe 3
Tel: 265 73 02 55/73 01 73
Tel: 265 73 05 93/73 38 90
Fax: 265 73 05 93

Mali
Commission des Communautés Européennes
Rue Guegau - Badalabougou
BP 115, Bamako
Tel: 223 22 23 56/22 20 65
Fax: 223 22 36 70 or
via the German Embassy
Tel: 223 22 32 99/22 37 15

Malta
Commission of the European Communities
Villa 'The Vines'
51 Ta'Xbiex Seafront
Ta'Xbiex/Malta GC
Tel: 356 34 51 11/34 48 91/34 48 93/3448 95
Fax: 356 34 48 97

Mauritania
Commission des Communautés Européennes
Ilot V, Lot no 24
BP 213
Nouakchott
Tel: 222 2 527 24/527 32
Fax: 222 2 53 524

Mauritius
Commission des Communautés Européennes
61/63 route Floreal 'La Mauvraie' Vacoas
PO Box 10 Vacoas
Tel: 230 686 50 61/50 62/50 63/36 74
Fax: 230 686 63 18
(also responsible for Mayotte, Réunion and Seychelles)

Mexico
Comision de las Comunidades Europeas
Paseo de la Reforma 1675
Lomas de Chapultepec CP.
11000 Mexico-Df
Tel: 525 540 33 45/46/47-202 86 22/202 84 90/202 79 98
Fax: 525 540 65 64
(also responsible for Cuba)

Morocco
Commission des Communautés Européennes
2 bis avenue de Meknes
BP 1302
Rabat
Tel: 212 7 76 12 17/76 12 46/76 12 48
Fax: 212 7 76 11 56

Mozambique
Commissao das Comunidades Europeias
Avenida do Zimbabwe 1214
CP. 1306
Maputo
Tel: 258 1 49 07 20/49 18 66/74 40 93
Tel: 258 1 49 02 71/49 02 66
Fax: 258 1 49 18 66

Namibia
Commission of the European Communities
Saniam Building, 4th floor
Independence Avenue
Windhoek
Tel: 264 61 351 34-22 00 99
Fax: 264 61 351 35

Netherlands Antilles
Commissie van de Europese Gemeenschappen
Scharlooweg 37
PO Box 822, Willemstad
Curacao
Tel: 599 9 61 84 88
Fax: 599 9 61 84 23
(also responsible for Aruba)

Niger
Commission des Communautés Européennes
BP 10388
Niamey
Tel: 227 73 23 60/73 27 73
Tel: 227 73 48 32/73 45 08
Fax: 227 73 23 22

Nigeria
Commission of the European Communities
4 Idowu Taylor Street
Victoria Island
PM Bag 12767
Lagos
Tel: 234 1 61 78 52/61 08 57
Fax: 234 1 61 72 48

Norway
Commission of the European Communities
Postboks 1643 Vika 0119 Oslo 1
Haakon's VII Gate No 6
N-0161 Oslo l
Tel: 47 22 83 35 83
Fax: 47 22 83 40 55

Pacific (Fiji)
Commission of the European Communities
Dominion House, 3rd floor
Private Mail Bag, GPO
Suva, Fiji
Tel: 679 31 36 33
Fax: 679 30 03 70

Pakistan
Commission of the European Communities
PO Box 1608, No 9 Street No 88
Sector G 6/3
Islamabad
Tel: 92 51 21 18 28/21 24 15/21 30 26
Fax: 92 82 26 04

Papua New Guinea
Commission of the European Communities
The Lodge, 3rd floor
Bampton Street
PO Box 76
Port Moresby
Tel: 675 21 35 44/21 35 04/21 37 18
Fax: 675 21 78 50

Peru
Comision de las Comunidades Europeas
Av. Paseo de la Republica 3755
5 piso
San Isidro
Lima 27
Tel: 51 14 40 30 97
Fax: 51 14 40 97 63

Philippines
Commission of the European Communities
Salustiana D. Ty Tower
Seventh floor, 104 Paseo de Roxas Street
corner Perea Street
Legaspi Village, Makati
Metro Manila
Tel: 63 2 812 64 21
Fax: 63 2 812 66 86

Poland
Commission of the European Communities
Aleja Vjazdowskie 14
Warzawa 00567
Tel: 48 22 21 64 01/21 64 02
Fax: 48 2 625 04 30

Russia
Commission of the European Communities
Stolovy perenlok 7a
121069 Moscow
Tel: 7 095 202 01 36/202 64 67/230 29 83
Fax: 7 095 202 76 05

Rwanda
Commission des Communautés Européennes
Avenue Deputé Kamuzinzi 14
BP 515
Kigali
Tel: 250 755 86/755 89/725 36
Fax: 250 74313

Sao Tome and Principe
Commission des Communautés Européennes
BP 132
Sao Tome
Tel: 239 12 217 80

Senegal
Commission des Communautés Européennes
Avenue Pompidou 57 (2e étage)
BP 3345
Dakar
Tel: 221 23 13 24/23 47 77
Tel: 221 23 79 75/23 60 64
Fax: 221 21 78 85

Sierra Leone
Commission of the European Communities
Wesley House
4 George Street
PO Box 1399
Freetown
Tel: 232 22 22 39 75/22 30 25/22 55 43
Fax: 232 22 252 12

Solomon Islands
Commission of the European Communities
Second floor, City Centre Building
PO Box 844
Honiaria
Tel: 677 227 65/220 73
Fax: 677 233 18 or 677 235 13 CCBSI

Somalia
Commission of the European Communities
Via Makka Al Mukarram no Z-A6/17 (km 4)
PO Box 943
Mogadiscio
Tel: 252 1 811 18/211 18/210 49
Fax: 252 1 211 18/210 49

Sudan
Commission of the European Communities
Floor 3, The Arab Authority for Agricultural
Investment and Development Building
Army Road, PO Box 2363
Khartoum
Tel: 249 750 54/751 48/753 93

Surinam
Commissie van de Europese Gemeenschappen
Dr S. Redmondstraat 239
PO Box 484
Paramaribo
Tel: 597 49 93 22/49 93 49/49 21 85
Fax: 597 49 30 76

Sweden
Commission of the European Communities
PO Box 16396
Hamngatan 6
S-11147 Stockholm
Tel: 46 8 6 11 11 72
Fax: 46 8 20 44 35

Tanzania
Commission of the European Communities
Extelcoms House, 9th floor
Samora Avenue
PO Box 9514
Dar es Salaam
Tel: 255 51 464 59/464 60/464 61/464 62
Fax: 255 51 467 24

Togo
Commission des Communautés Européennes
22 Avenue Nicolas Grunitzky
BP 1657
Lomé
Tel: 228 21 36 62/21 08 32/21 77 45
Fax: 228 21 13 00

Trinidad and Tobago
Commission of the European Communities
2 Champs Elysées
Long Circular
Maraval
PO Box 1144
Port of Spain
Tel: 1 809 622 66 28/622 05 91
Fax: 1 809 622 63 55

Turkey
Commission of the European Communities
Kuleli Sokak 15, Gazi Osman Pasa
06700 Ankara
Tel: 90 4 137 68 40/41/42/43
Fax: 90 4 137 79 40

Swaziland
Commission of the European Communities
Dhlan 'ubeka Building, 3rd floor
Corner Walker and Tin Streets
PO Box A.36
Mbabane
Tel: 268 429 08/420 18
Fax: 268 467 29

Syria
Commission of the European Communities
Chakib Arslane Street
Abou Roumaneh
Damascas
Tel: 963 11 24 76 40/24 76 41
Fax: 963 11 42 06 83

Thailand
Commission of the European Communities
Kiang Gwan House II
19th floor
140/1 Wireless Road
Bangkok 10330
Tel: 66 255 91 00
Fax: 66 255 91 14

Tonga
Commission of the European Communities
Maile Taha
Taufa'ahau Road
Nuku-Alofa
Tel: 676 238 20
Fax: 676 238 69

Tunisia
Commission des Communautés Européennes
BP 143 - 21 av. Jugurtha
Cite el Mahrajene
1082 Tunis
Tel: 216 1 78 86 00/78 61 40
Fax: 216 1 78 82 01

Uganda
Commission of the European Communities
Uganda Commercial Bank Building
Plot 12, Kampala Road, 5th floor
PO Box 5244, Kampala
Tel: 256 41 23 33 03/23 33 04
Tel: 256 41 24 27 01/23 37 08
Fax: 256 41 23 37 08

United States of America
Commission of the European Communities
2100 M Street, NW (7th floor)
Washington DC 20037
Tel: 1 202 862 9500/862 9501/862 9502
Fax: 1 202 429 17 66

United States of America
Commission of the European Communities
3 Dag Hammarskjold Plaza
305 East 47th Street
New York NY 10017
Tel: 1 212 371 3804
Fax: 1 212 758 2718

United States of America
Commission of the European Communities
44 Montgomery Street-Suite 2715
San Francisco CA 94104
Tel: 1 415 391 34 76
Fax: 1 415 391 36 41

Uruguay
Comision de las Comunidades Europeas
Edificio Artigas (1o piso)
Calle Rincon 487
Montevideo
Tel: 598 2 96 37 44/96 37 45
Tel: 598 2 96 31 66/96 31 80
Fax: 598 2 95 36 53

Vanuatu
Commission of the European Communities
Orient Investment Building
Ground floor
Kumul Highway
PO Box 422
Port-Vila
Tel: 678 225 01
Fax: 678 232 82

Venezuela
Comision de las Comunidades Europeas
Apartado de Correos 67076
Plaza Las Americas 10617
Avda Orinoco
Las Mercedes
Caracas 1060
Tel: 58 2 91 51 33
Fax: 58 2 91 88 76/91 11 14 (SPI)

Western Samoa
Commission of the European Communities
Ioane Viliamu Bldg, 4th floor
PO Box 3023
Apia
Tel: 685 200 70
Fax: 685 246 22

Former Yugoslavia
Commission of the European Communities
Kablarsku 29
Senjak 11040
Beograd
Tel: 38 11 64 86 66
Fax: 38 11 65 14 58

Zaire
Commission des Communautés Européennes
7l avenue des Trios Z
BP 2000
Kinshasa
Tel: 871 154 62 21
Fax: 871 154 62 21

Zambia
Commission of the European Communities
Plot 4899
Brentwood Drive
PO Box 34871
Lusaka
Tel: 260 1 25 07 11/25 11 40
Fax: 260 1 25 09 06

Zimbabwe
Commission of the European Communities
NCR House, 10th floor
Samara Rachel Avenue 65
PO Box 4252
Harare
Tel: 263 4 70 71 20/70 71 43/
Tel: 263 4 70 71 39/70 71 40/70 49 88
Fax: 263 4 72 53 60

9. EC DELEGATIONS TO INTERNATIONAL ORGANISATIONS

UN

Commission des Communautés Européennes
Case postale 195
37-39 rue de Vermont
CH-1211 Genève 20 CIC
Tel: 41 22 734 97 50
Fax: 41 22 734 22 36/734 23 31

Commission of the European Communities
3 Dag Hammarskjöld Plaza
305 East 47th Street
New York NY 10017
Tel: 1 212 371 38 04
Fax: 1 212 758 27 18

OECD

Commission des Communautés Européennes
12 Avenue d'Eylau
F-75116 Paris Cedex 16
Tel: 33 1 44 05 31 60
Fax: 33 1 44 05 31 79

Appendix 3

Part 1: The Directorates-General

The Directorates-General are the equivalent at the Commission of ministries or departments of state at the level of national government. As at national level, there are periodic re-definitions of responsibilities and the same unavoidable overlaps, so that different aspects of policy on a particular topic, such as, transport can be covered by several different D-Gs.

The internal organisation of the D-Gs varies considerably, depending on the size of the D-G and the range of matters in which it is involved, but each one is presided over by a Director-General with a personal cabinet consisting of a Deputy Director-General and a small team of advisers. The D-Gs are answerable to the Commission as a whole and each one is under the personal supervision of one of the Commissioners in the same manner as government departments are supervised by a Minister.

The current D-Gs are as follows:

DG I	External Economic Relations
DG 1A	External Political Relations Enlargement Task Force (TFE)
DG II	Economic and Financial Affairs
DG III	Industry
DG IV	Competition
DG V	Employment, Industrial Relations and Social Affairs
DG VI	Agriculture Veterinary and Phytosanitary Office
DG VII	Transport
DG VIII	Development
DG IX	Personnel and Administration
DG X	Audio-visual Media, Information, Communication and Culture
DG XI	Environment, Nuclear Safety and Civil Protection
DG XII	Science, Research and Development: Joint Research Centre
DG XIII	Telecommunications, Information Market and Exploitation of Research
DG XIV	Fisheries

DG XV	Internal Market and Financial Services
DG XVI	Regional Policies
DG XVII	Energy
DG XVIII	Credit and Investments
DG XIX	Budgets
DG XX	Financial Control
DG XXI	Customs and Indirect Taxation
DG XXII	Co-ordination of Structural Policies
DG XXIII	Enterprise Policy, Distributive Trades, Tourism and Co-operatives
	Consumer Policy Service
	Task Force for Human Resources, Education, Training and Youth
	EC Humanitarian Office
	European Foundation for the Improvement of Living and Working Conditions
	European Centre for the Development of Vocational Training (CEDEFOP).

Part 2 The Commissioners

The Current Commissioners, their portfolios and spokesmen are given below. The direct telephone numbers for their spokesmen's service are INT.+ 322 29 followed by the five digits in brackets. The fax numbers used are INT.+ 322 29 50143 or 60309.

President Jacques Delors (French)
President's Spokesman: Bruno Dethomas (52207)

Portfolios
Secretariat-General
Forward Studies Unit
Inspectorate-General
Legal Service
Monetary Matters
Spokesman's Service
Joint Interpreting & Conference Service
Security Office

Vice-Presidents (6)

Commissioner Henning Christophersen (Danish)
Commissioner's Spokesman: Troels Kroyer (60633)

Portfolios
Economic & Financial Affairs
Monetary Matters (with Jacques Delors)
Credit & Investments
Statistical Office

Commissioner Manuel Marin (Spanish)
Commissioner's Spokesman: Xavier Prats Monne (61230)

Portfolios
Co-operation & Development
Economic co-operation with Southern Mediterranean, Middle East, the Near East, Latin America and Asia
Lomé Convention
EC Humanitarian Aid

Commissioner Martin Bangemann (German)
Commissioner's Spokesman: Helmut Schmitt von Sydow (60435)

Portfolios
Industrial Affairs
Information Technology
Telecommunications

Commissioner Sir Leon Brittan (UK)
Commissioner's Spokesman: Peter Guildford (58562)

Portfolios
External economic affairs: (North America, Japan, China, CIS, Europe including CEEC)
Commercial Policy

Commissioner Karel Van Miert (Belgian)
Commissioner's Spokesman: Bruno Julien (56133)

Portfolios
Competition
Personnel & Administration
Translation & Information technology

Commissioner Antonio Ruberti (Italian)
Commissioner's Spokesman: Viviane d'Udekem d'Acoz (61919)

Portfolios
Science, R&D
Joint Research Centre
Human Resources
Education, training and youth

MEMBERS OF THE COMMISSION (10)

Commissioner Abel Matutes (Spanish)
Commissioner's Spokesman: Paula Laissy (53258)

Portfolios
Energy
EURATOM Supply
Transport

Commissioner Peter Schmidhuber(German)
Commissioner's Spokesman: Oliver Nette (60435)

Portfolios
Budgets
Financial Control
Fraud prevention
Cohesion Fund

Commissioner : Christine Scrivener (French)
Commissioner's Spokesman: Viviane d'Udekem d'Acoz (63062)

Portfolios
Customs & indirect taxation
Direct Taxation
Consumer Policy

Commissioner: Bruce Millan (UK)
Commissioner's Spokesman: Elizabetta Olivi (63081)

Portfolios
Regional Policy
Relations with the Committee of the Regions

Commissioner: Hans Van Den Broek (Dutch)
Commissioner's Spokesman: Nico Wegter (53069)

Portfolios
External Political relations
Common foreign and security policy
Enlargement negotiations

Commissioner: Joao de Deus Pinheiro (Portuguese)
Commissioner's Spokesman: Paula Laissy (53258)

Portfolios
Relations with European Parliament
Relations with Member States on transparency, communications and information

Culture & Audio-Visual policy
Official Publications Office

Commissioner : Padraig Flynn (Irish)
Commissioner's Spokesman: Gerard Kiely (53127)

Portfolios
Social Affairs & Employment
Relations with Economic & Social Committee
Immigration, home affairs and justice

Commissioner : René Steichen (Luxembourger)
Commissioner's Spokesman: Gerard Kiely (53127)

Portfolios
Agriculture and rural development

Commissioner: Ioannis Paleokrassas (Greek)
Commissioner's Spokesman: Bruno Julien (56133)

Portfolios
Environment, nuclear safety and civil protection
Fisheries

Commissioner: Raniero Vanni d'Archirafi (Italian)
Commissioner's Spokesman: Elizabetta Olivi (63081)

Portfolios
Institutional matters
Internal Market
Financial Services
Enterprise policy: small business and distributive trades

Appendix 4

List of Acronyms and Glossary of EC Terms

ACE	Action by the Community Relating to the Environment; or Action for Co-operation in the Field of Economics
ACELP	Advisory Committee on European Library Plan
ACFCI	Association of French Chambers of Commerce and Industry
ACNAT	Action by the Community Relating to Nature Conservation
ACP[1]	African, Caribbean and Pacific states
ACPM	Advisory Committee on Project Management
AER	Assembly of European Regions
AIM	Advanced Informatics for Medicine in Europe
ALA	Asian and Latin American Countries
ALTENER	Promotion of Renewable Energy Resources
ANDEAN PACT	Bolivia, Columbia, Ecuador, Peru and Venezuela
ANVAR	Agence Nationale de Valorisation de Recherche
ARION	Actleprogramma: Reizen met een Instructief Paracter voor Onderwijss (Study visits for education specialists)
AWP	Annual Work Programme
BABEL	Broadcasting Across the Barriers of European Language
BCR	Bureau Communautaire de Reference (Community Bureau of Reference)
BECU	Billion ECU

---

[1] Under Lomé IV, these are: Angola, Antigua, the Bahamas, Barbados, Belize, Benin, Botswana, Burkina Faso, Burundi, Cameroon, Cape Verde, the Central African Republic, Chad, Comoros, Congo, Djibouti, the Dominican Republic, Equatorial Guinea, Ethiopia, Fiji, Gabon, Gambia, Ghana, Grenada, Guinea, Guinea Bissau, Guyana & Heitio, Haiti, the Ivory Coast, Jamaica, Kenya, Kiribati, Lesotho, Liberia, Madagascar, Malawi, Mali, Mauritania, Madagascar, Mozambique, Namibia, Niger, Nigeria, Papua New Guinea, Rwanda, St Christopher & Nevis, St Lucia, St Vincent & Grenadines, Sao Tome & Principe, Senegal, Seychelles, Sierra Leone, Solomon Islands, Somalia, Sudan, Surinam, Swaziland, Tanzania, Togo, Tonga, Trinidad & Tobago, Tuvalu, Uganda, Vanuatu, Western Samoa, Zaire, Zambia and Zimbabwe

Benelux	Belgium, the Netherlands and Luxembourg customs union
BEP	Biomolecular Engineering Programme
BIC	Business Information Centre / Business Innovation Centre
BICEPS	Bio-informatics Collaborative European Programmes and Strategy (the forerunner of AIM)
BIR	Basic Information Report
BMFT	German Federal Ministry for Research And Technology
BNSC	British National Space Centre
BOS	Bi-monthly Operational Summary
BRAIN	Basic Research in Adaptive Intelligence and Neuro-computing
BRIDGE	Biotechnology Research for Innovation, Development and Growth in Europe
BRITE/EURAM	Basic Research in Industrial Technologies for Europe / European Research in Advanced Materials
CA	Concerted Action
CADCAM	Computer Aided Design/Computer Aided Manufacturing
CADDIA	Co-operation in Automation of Data and Documentation for Imports/Exports and Agriculture
CAMAR	Competitiveness of Agricultural and Management of Agriculture Programme
CAN	Committee of an Advisory Nature
CAP	Common Agricultural Policy
CCC	Consumers' Consultative Council
CCL	Common Command Language
CDI	Centre for the Development of Industry
CE	Communauté Europèene (EC)
CEC	Commission of the European Communities
CEDEFOP	European Centre for the Development of Vocational Training
CEEC	Central and Eastern European Countries
CEEP	European Centre of Public Enterprise; or Central and Eastern European Programme
CEMR	Council of European Municipalities and Regions
CEN	Comité Européen de Normalisation (The European Committee for Standardisation)

CENELEC	Comité Européen de Normalisation Electronique
CEPT	Confederation of European Posts and Telecommunications
CFC	Chlorofluorocarbons
CFSP	Common Foreign and Security Policy
CGC	Comité Consultatif de Gestion et Co-ordination (Management, Co-ordination and Advisory Committee)
CIS	Commonwealth of Independent States
CIT	Committee for Innovation & Technology Transfer
CODEST	Committee for Development of European Science and Technology
COMDOC	Community Document
COMECON	Council for Mutual Economic Assistance
COMETT	Community Programme in Education and Training for Technology
CONVER	see KONVER
CORDIS	Community Research and Development Information Service
COREPER	Committee of Permanent Representatives
COST	European Co-operation on Science & Technology
CRAFT	Co-operative Research Action for Technology
CRP	Communications Research Programme
CREST	Scientific and Technical Research Committee of the EC
CSF	Community Support Framework
CT	Community Transit
CUBE	Concentration Unit for Biotechnology in Europe
DELTA	Developing European Learning through Technological Advance
DES	Department of Education and Science (UK)
DG	Directorate-General (of the European Commission)
DIANE	Direct Information Access Network Europe
DoE	Department of the Environment (UK)
DOSES	Research and Development of Expert Statistical Systems
DRIVE	Dedicated Road Infrastructure for Vehicle Safety in Europe
DTI	Department of Trade and Industry (UK)
EAGGF	European Agricultural Guidance and Guarantee Fund
EAP	Environmental Action Programme

EAVE	European Audio-Visual Entrepreneurs
EBN	European Business and Innovative Centre Networks
EBRD	European Bank of Reconstruction and Development
EC	European Communities
ECB	European Central Bank
ECHO	European Community Host Organisation
ECHR	European Convention on Human Rights
ECIP	European Communities Investment Partners
ECJ	European Court of Justice
ECLAIR	European Collaborative Linkage of Agriculture and Industry through Research
ECO	European Co-ordination Office
ECOFIN	Council of Finance and Economic Ministers
ECOS	Eastern European City Co-operation Scheme
ECOSOC	Economic & Social Committee
ECP	European Co-operation Programme
ECSC	European Coal and Steel Community
ECSCT	European Coal and Steel Community Treaty
ECTS	EC Course Credit Transfer Scheme
ECU	European Currency Unit
EDF	European Development Fund
EDI	Electronic Data Interchange
EEA	European Economic Area; or European Environment Agency
EEC	European Economic Community
EECT	European Economic Community Treaty (referred to as the Treaty of Rome)
EEIG[2]	European Economic Interest Grouping
EFA	European Film Academy
EFDO	European Film Distribution Office

[2] An association of two or more natural or legal persons in two or more Member States formed for the purpose of developing the economic activities of its members: its purpose is not to make profits for itself. Council Regulation 2137/85/EEC (OJ 1985 No. l199/1)

EFL	English as a Foreign Language
EFTA	European Free Trade Association
EIB	European Investment Bank
EIC	Euro-Information Centre
EIF	European Investment Fund
EIS	Export Intelligence Service
EJOB	European Joint Optical Disability Project
ELWW	European Laboratories Without Walls
EMCF	European Monetary Co-operation Fund
EMF	European Monetary Fund
EMI	European Monetary Institute
EMS	European Monetary System
EMU	Economic and Monetary Union
ENS	European Nervous System
ENTP	European Network of Training Partnerships
ENVIREG	European Regional Fund for the Environment
EOI	Expression of Interest
EP	European Parliament
EPC	European Political Community; or
	European Political Co-operation
EPO	European Patent Office
EPOCH	European Programme on Climatology and Natural Hazards
ERASMUS	European Action Scheme for the Mobility of University Students
ERC	Exchange Risk Cover
ERDF	European Regional Development Fund
ERG	Exchange Risk Guarantee
ERM	Exchange Rate Mechanism
ESA	European Space Agency
ESARDA	European Safeguards R&D Association
ESCB	European System of Central Banks
ESCF	European Seed Capital Funds
ESCFN	European Seed Capital Funds Network

ESF	European Social Fund; or European Science Foundation
ESPRIT	European Strategic Programme for Research in Information Technology
ESSI	European Systems and Software Initiative
ETP	Executive Training Programme in Japan
ETSI	European Telecommunications Standards Institute
ETUC	European Trade Union Confederation
EUA	European Unit of Account
EURAM	European Research - Advanced Materials
EURATOM	European Atomic Energy Community
EUREKA	European Research & Co-ordination Agency
EURET	Research on Transport Systems
EUROFORM	Programme for the development of new qualifications and skills
EUROPOL	European Central Criminal Investigation Office
EUROSTAT	The Statistical Office of the EC
EUROTECNET	Network of Demonstration Projects on Vocational Training and New Information Technologies
EUROTRA	EC R&D Programme for a Machine Translation System of an Advanced Design
EVCA	European Venture Capital Association
EVE	Espace Video Européen
FAST	Forecasting and Assessment in Science and Technology
FEOGA	European Agricultural Guidance and Guarantee Fund (French Acronym for EAGGF)
FFR	Focused Fundamental Research
FIGF	Financial Instrument for the Guidance of the Fisheries Sector
FLAIR	Food-Linked Agro-Industrial Research
FOC	Fibre Optic Cable
FORCE	Formation Continue: (Development of Continuing Education in Firms)
FOREST	Forestry and Wood R&D
GATT	General Agreement on Tariffs and Trade
GCC	Gulf Co-operation Council

GDP	Gross Domestic Product
GNP	Gross National Product
GRECO	Groupement Européen pour la Circulation des Oeuvres (promoting high quality television fiction)
GSP	Generalised System of Preferences
HDTV	High Definition Television
HEI	Higher Education Institute
HELIOS	Action Programme for the Vocational and Social Integration of Handicapped Persons
HORIZON	Initiative for the Handicapped and Disadvantaged Persons
HTM	High Temperature Materials Programme (at JRC Petten)
IACS	Integrated Administration and Control System
IAP	Indicative Aid Programme
IBC	Integrated Broad-band Communications
ICP	Inter-University Co-operation Programme
ICT	Information and Communications Technology
IDA	Irish Development Agency
IDO	Integrated Development Operations
IGC	Inter-Governmental Conference
IMF	International Monetary Fund
IMO	Information Market Observatory
IMP	Integrated Mediterranean Programme
IMPACT	Information Market Policy Actions
INSIS	Inter-Institutional Services Information System
INTERREG	European Regional Fund for Border Areas
IPR	Intellectual property rights
IRDAC	Industrial Research and Development Advisory Committee
IRIS	Demonstration Projects on Vocational Training for Women
IRTE	Introduction of an Integrated Road Transport Environment
IRTU	Industrial Research and Technology Unit
ISDN	Integrated Services Digital Network
ISE	Integrated Service Engineering
ISERBS	Iron and Steel Employees' Readaptation Benefits Scheme

IT	Information Technology
ITB	Industrial Training Board
ITER	International Thermonuclear Experimental Reactor
ITT	Invitation to Tender
JEP	Joint European Project / programme
JESSI	Joint European Sub-micron Silicon Programme
JET	Joint European Torus
JOPP	Joint Venture PHARE Programme
JOULE	Joint Opportunities for Unconventional or Long-Term Energy Supply
JRC	Joint Research Centre (of the EC)
LAB	Legal Advisory Board
LDC	Less-Developed Country
LEADER	European Initiative for Rural Development
LEDU	Local Enterprise Development Unit
LEI	Local Employment Initiative
LIFE	Financial Instrument for the Environment
LINGUA	Action Programme on Modern Language Teaching
MAFF	Ministry of Agriculture, Fisheries and Food (UK)
MAGP	Multi-Annual Guidance Programme
MAGHREB	Countries: Algeria, Morocco and Tunisia
MAP-TV	Memory-Archives Programme TV
MASHREQ	Countries: Egypt, Jordan, Lebanon and Syria
MAST	Marine Science and Technology
MECU	Million ECU
MEDIA	Measures to Encourage the Development of the Audio-Visual Industry
MEDSPA	Protection of the Environment in the Mediterranean Region
MEP	Member of the European Parliament
MFN	Most Favoured Nation
MHR	Medical Health Research Programme
MIDA	Technical Assistance Bureau for Community Human Resources Initiatives
MINT	Managing the Integration of New Technology

MoD	Ministry of Defence (UK)
MONITOR	A Community Programme in the field of strategic analysis, forecasting and evaluation in matters of research and technology
MRC	Medical Research Council
MTFA	Medium-Term Financial Assistance
NAO	National Authorising Officer
NARIC	National Academic Recognition Information Centre
NCI	New Community Instrument
NCU	National Co-ordination Units
NERC	Natural Environment Research Council
NET	Next European Torus
NETT	Network for Environmental Technology Transfer
NGO	Non-Governmental Organisation
NMP	New Mediterranean Policy
NORSPA	Protection of Northern Coastal Zones
NOW	Training Measures for Women
NPCI	National Programme of Community Interest
NTB	Non-Tariff Barrier
NUTS[3]	Nomenclature of Statistical Territorial Units
NUTS I	64 regions in the EC;
NUTS II	167 basic administrative regions; and
NUTS III[4]	824 subdivisions of level II regions.
OCT[5]	Overseas Countries and Territories
ODA	Office Document Architecture; or

[3] Analysis of socio-economic problems at regional level requires a definition of "region" which helps to capture as clearly as possible the issues under examination at Community level. NUTS provides a uniform frame of reference for regional statistics, distinguishing between three levels of regional disaggregation.

[4] Full details of NUTS are published in Official Journal 1988 C 212.

[5] There are British, Dutch and French OCTs as follows: British: Anguilla, British Antarctic Territory, British Indian Ocean Territory, British Virgin Islands, Cayman Islands, Falkland Islands, Montserrat, Pitcairn, St Helena and the Turks & Caicos Islands. Dutch: Aruba, Bonaire, Curacao, Sabah, St Eustatius and St Martins. French: French Polynesia, French Southern and Antarctic Territories, Mayotte, New Caledonia, St Pierre and Miquelon, Wallis and Futuna Islands.

	Official Development Assistance
OECD	Organisation for Economic Co-operation and Development
OEEC	Organisation for European Economic Co-operation
OII	Open Information Interchange
OJ	Official Journal of the European Communities
OJ C	Official Journal - Information and Notices
OJ L	Official Journal - Legislation
OJ S	Official Journal - Supplement
OOPEC	Office for the Official Publications of the EC
OP	Operational Programme
ORA	Opportunities for Rural Areas (R&D)
OSI	Open Systems Interconnection
PABLI	Pages Bleues Information (electronic version of BOS)
PEP	Projects in Export Policy
PETRA	Partnership in Education and Training
PHARE	Assistance for the Economic Restructuring of CEEC
PIU	Project Implementation Unit
PPS	Purchasing Power Standard: a unit representing an identical volume of goods and services in different countries
PREST	Programme of Policy Research in Engineering Science & Technology
PRISMA	Preparing Regional Industry for the Single Market
PSEP	Physical and Social Environment Programme
RACE	Research in Advanced Communications in Europe
RDU	Research and Development Units
REC	Regional Environmental Centre
RECHAR	Programme for Restructuring of Coal-Mining Areas
REGEN	Programme for Energy Networks
REGIS	Programme for Ultra-Peripheral Areas
RENEVAL	Programme for shipbuilding areas
RESIDER	Programme for coal mining areas
REWARD	Recycling of Waste R&D
RIPP	Regional Industrial Property Programme

RMC	Research management Centre
RPFB	Russian Project Finance Bank
RTD	Research and Technological Development
RTP	Research and Technology Policy Division (DTI)
SAD	Single Administrative Document
SAST	Strategic Analysis in Science & Technology
SAVE	Specific Actions for Vigorous Energy Efficiency
SCA	Shared-Cost Action
SCALE	Small Countries Improve their Audio-Visual Level in Europe
SCRIPT	Support for Creative Independent Production Talent
SEA	Single European Act
SERC	Science and Engineering Research Council
SME [6]	Small and Medium-sized Enterprise
SOURCES	Stimulating Outstanding Resources for Creative European Screen writing
SPEAR	Support Studies for the Evaluation of Community R&D
SPEC	Support Programme for Employment Creation
SPES	Stimulation Plan for Economic Science
SPRINT	Strategic Programme for Innovation and Technology Transfer in Europe
STA	Science & Technology Agency (fellowship in Japan)
STABEX	Stabilisation of Export Earnings for Agricultural Commodities
STAR	Special Technology Action for Regional Development
STD3	Life Sciences for Developing Countries
STEP	Standard for Exchange of Product Data or Science and Technology for Environmental Protection
STMS	Short term Monetary Support
STOA	Scientific and Technological Options Assessment
STP	Science Training Programme (in Japan)

[6] A SME is a company which has less than 500 employees, a net annual turnover of less than 38 MECU and is not more than one-third owned by a parent company or any other organisation larger than a SME. Larger shareholdings may, however, be held by investors such as banks or venture capital funds.

STRIDE	Science & Technology Research into Innovative Developments in Europe
TAC	Total Allowable Catch
TACIS	Technical Assistance in the CIS and Georgia
TAO	Technical Assistance Office
TED/TEDIS[7]	Tenders Electronic Daily
TELEMAN	Research Programme on Remote Handling in Nuclear Hazardous and Disordered Environments
TELEMATIQUE	Programme to promote use of advanced telecommunications services by SMEs
TEMPUS	Trans-European Mobility Programme for University Studies
TEN	Trans-European Network
TFHR	Task Force, Human Resources
TFE	Enlargement Task Force
TGP	Transitional Guidance Programme
THERMIE	Energy Demonstration Programme
THTP	Transnational High-Technology Projects
TIE	Technology International Exchange
TIDE	Technology Initiative for the Disabled and Elderly
TIP	Technology Integration Project
TPF	Technology Performance Financing
TTWA	Travel-to-work area
TVA	Taxe sur valeur ajoutée (VAT by another of its ten different names)
UETP	University-Enterprise Training Partnerships
UKAEA	United Kingdom Atomic Energy Authority
UN	United Nations
UNCTAD	United Nations Conference on Trade and Development
UNICE	Union des Industries de la Communauté Européene (Union of Industries of the European Community)

[7] TEDIS is the on-line version of the OJ S Series consisting of a directory of invitations to tender for public works and supply contracts from the Member States, the ACP countries, non-associated countries carrying out projects financed by the EDF and under GATT, Sweden, Japan and the USA etc.

VALOREN	Development of certain regions of the EC by exploiting indigenous energy potential
VALUE	Valorisation and Utilisation for Europe
VAT	Value Added Tax
VER	Voluntary Export Restraint
VSLI	Very Large Scale Integration
VTS	Vessel Traffic Services
WAGR	Windscale Advanced Gas-Cooler Reactor
WAS	World Aid Section
WDA	Welsh Development Agency
WEU	Western European Union
WHO	World Health Organisation
WIPO	World Intellectual Property Organisation
WNLEI	Women's Local Employment Initiative
YEB	Youth Exchange Bureau
YEC	Youth Exchange Centre
YIP	Youth Initiative Project
YFE	Youth For Europe

Appendix 5

The Presidency

Article 146 of the EEC Treaty states:
"The Council shall consist of a representative of each Member State at ministerial level, authorised to commit the government of that Member State.

The office of President shall be held in turn by each Member State in the Council for a term of six months, in the following order of Member States:

1993	January/June	Denmark	July/December	Belgium
1994	January/June	Greece	July/December	Germany
1995	January/June	France	July/December	Spain
1996	January/June	Italy	July/December	Ireland
1997	January/June	Netherlands	July/December	Luxembourg
1998	January/June	UK	July/December	Portugal."

Article 147 provides:
"The Council shall meet when convened by its President on his own initiative or at the request of one of its members or of the Commission."

Title V of the Maastricht Treaty gives the Presidency a pivotal role in the operation of the Common Foreign and Security Policy of the Community.

Article J.5 states:

"1. The Presidency shall represent the Union in matters coming within the common foreign and security policy.

2. The Presidency shall be responsible for the implementation of common measures; in that capacity it shall in principle express the position of the Union in international organisations and international conferences.

3. In the tasks referred to in paragraphs 1 and 2, the Presidency shall be assisted by the previous and next Member States to hold the Presidency. The Commission shall be fully associated in these tasks."

The indications are that the Presidency is going to become even more important as the provisions on the common foreign and security policy start acquiring some meaning. It will therefore be vital to anticipate the long-term policy priorities of the various Member States, even before they assume their place in the Troika under Article J.5.3, rather than - as in the past - waiting until they assume the Presidency.

Appendix 6

ECU Rates of Exchange

The ECU, which was introduced on 1 January 1979, is made up of a basket of currencies comprising, in differing proportions, the national currencies of the Member States. The proportions as at 1 January 1994 are:

German Mark	30.10%
French Franc	19.00%
UK Pound Sterling	13.00%
Italian Lira	10.15%
Dutch Guilder	9.40%
Belgian Franc	7.60%
Spanish Peseta	5.30%
Danish Krone	2.45%
Irish Punt	1.10%
Portuguese Escudo	0.80%
Greek Drachma	0.80%
Luxembourg Franc	0.30%

As at 1 January 1994 1 ECU =

41.42 Belgian / Luxembourg Francs
7.69 Danish Krone
1.90 German Marks
278.00 Greek Drachmas
154.83 Spanish Pesetas
6.68 French Francs
0.81 Irish Punt
1876.28 Italian Lira
2.14 Dutch Guilders
196.71 Portuguese Escudos
0.78 UK Pound Sterling
1.19 US Dollar
1.59 Canadian Dollar
126.23 Japanese Yen
1.67 Swiss Francs
8.33 Norwegian Krone
9.48 Swedish Krona
6.68 Finnish Markka
13.38 Austrian Schillings
1.80 Australian Dollar
2.16 New Zealand Dollar

Appendix 7

Directory EC Public Databases

ABEL:
a bibliographical database which can be used to search, select and order documents from the OJ.

AGREP:
a factual database containing the publicly-financed research projects in agriculture, forestry, fisheries and foodstuffs that are being conducted in the Member States.

BACH:
contains statistical data on aggregate company accounts.

BIOREP:
a factual database containing a permanent inventory of biotechnology research projects undertaken in the Member States.

CCL-TRAIN:
the training database that enables users to become familiar with on-line information retrieval and more particularly, with use of the common command language (CCL).

CELEX:
the computerised inter-institutional documentation system for Community Law.

COMEXT:
the database for statistics on the EC's external trade and trade between the Member States.

CORDIS:
Community research and development information service.

CORDIS RTD-ACRONYMS:
the CORDIS database covering acronyms relating to Community RTD activities.

CORDIS RTD-COMDOCUMENTS:
the CORDIS database covering the Commission documents relating to Community RTD activities, a valuable source of advance information on proposed programmes.

CORDIS RTD-NEWS:
brings comprehensive, up-to-the minute coverage of all Community RTD activities.

CORDIS RTD-PARTNERS:
RTD partner search service whose purpose is to catalyse RTD-related activities ranging from joint proposals to the commercial exploitation of the research results.

CORDIS RTD-PROGRAMMES:
database on research and technological development programmes, covering all RTD programmes and initiatives financed by the Community.

CORDIS RTD-PROJECTS:
database covering RTD projects wholly or partly financed by the Community.

CORDIS RTD-PUBLICATIONS:
database covering the publications resulting from Community programmes of research and technological development.

CORDIS RTD-RESULTS:
contains information resulting from research and development in science, technology and medicine. covering research projects in both private and public sector organisations, funded nationally, internationally or privately.

CRONOS:
a statistical database containing macroeconomic data in the form of time series covering all aspects of the economic and social situation in the Member States.

DOMIS:
a directory of sources and services available in Europe relating to information on materials, mainly intended for users working in industry, research or administration. It provides details of the specialist sources existing in the materials field.

ECDIN:
a factual database on chemical products liable to react with the environment.

ECHO NEWS:
a full text database: the on-line version of "ECHO Facts for Users" published fortnightly by ECHO, a service provided by the D-G for Information Technologies and Industries and Telecommunications.

ECLAS:
the database of the Commission Central Library, containing bibliographical references covering all aspects of European integration.

ECU:
latest daily ECU rates in main currencies.

EMIRE:
the on-line version of the "European employment and industrial relations glossaries", a set of twelve volumes giving an introduction to the national employment law and industrial relations systems.

EPISTEL:
designed to disseminate information on Parliament's work to accredited journalists and other opinion formers, as well as to supply MEPs with news which has appeared or is to appear in the printed media.

EPOQUE:
European Parliament on-line query system.

ESPRIT:
the on-line version of the publication "ESPRIT, the project synopses" contains references to current ESPRIT projects.

EURISTOTE:
database of institutes and researchers on European integration.

EUROCONTACT:
a factual database set up by the Commission to help European organisations find partners with whom they can participate in the various research programmes.

EUROCRON:
statistical data in tabular form, covering the main sectors of the economies of the Member States.

EURODICAUTOM:
a terminological database containing scientific and technical terms; and acronyms and abbreviations.

EUROFARM:
a statistical database containing, in tabular form, the results of Community surveys of the structure of agricultural holdings.

EUROLIB-PER:
a collective catalogue of periodicals in the libraries belonging to the EUROLIB group.

HTM-DB:
a factual database on the mechanical properties of high-temperature materials and methods of assessing these properties.

I'M GUIDE:
detailed information on electronic information products and organisations such as Data-base and CD-ROM producers, host organisations, brokers and publishers, together with network access details.

INFO 92:
an information system on the completion of the internal market and its social dimension.

MISEP:
a bibliographical database created as part of the MISEP programme providing a network for the Member States and the Commission to exchange information about measures taken in Member States concerning employment, and the fight against unemployment in so far as they are covered in articles in the quarterly "Policies Bulletin" or described in the BIRs for each country.

OVIDE:
an information and communication service primarily for the use of members, officials and agents of the European Parliament.

RAPID:
intended to give rapid access to press releases and information from the Spokesman's Service of the Commission.

REGIO:
Eurostat's database for regional statistics; it covers the main aspects of economic and social life in the Community: demography, economic accounts, employment etc.

REM:
the results of radioactivity readings in the environment taken in several European countries following the Chernobyl accident and relating particularly, to the air, fall-out and foodstuffs.

SABINE:
a system of databases specialising in the storage, retrieval and management of nomenclatures ("metadata", or data on data).

SCAD:
a Community system for access to documentation comprising references to Community acts and related preparatory documents, publications of the Community institutions, articles from periodicals with a Community interest and statements and opinions from both sides of industry.

SESAME:
a documentary database containing descriptions of research, development and technology projects in the energy sector under programmes managed by D-Gs XII or XVII or various Member States.

TED:
Tenders Electronic Daily, an the on-line version of the OJ S series consisting of a directory of invitations to tender for public works and supply contracts from the Member States, ACP countries associated with the EC, non-associated countries carrying out projects financed by the EDF or under GATT, from EFTA, Japan and the US etc.

THESAURI:
an analytical directory of structured vocabularies for information retrieval.

XIII MAGAZINE:
on-line version of XIII Magazine, written by journalists, independent experts and representatives of EC institutions and other organisations active in communications and information technologies.

Appendix 8

Continuous Updating Service

Retaining clients automatically receive immediate briefings concerning all changes or anticipated changes in the programmes in which they are interested. The cost of this service depends on which programmes are involved and which other PACE services the client requires.

On 1 January 1995 PACE will launch "PACE GRANTS NEWS", a monthly newsletter about EC Grants and Other Assistance Programmes which will be available on subscription. The subscription will be £240 (350 ECU or US$400) for 12 issues, but there will be a special price of £120 (175 ECU US$200) for subscriptions taken out before 31 December 1994.

To order, please call one of the numbers below or fill in the subscription form on the following page, and return it to:

Public Affairs Consultants Europe Ltd
3 Chiltern Business Centre
Garsington Road,
Oxford OX4 5NG

Tel: 0865 (INT.+44 865) 770099
Fax: 0865 (INT.+44 865) 770011

or

Public Affairs Consultants Europe Ltd
Rue de la Presse 4
1000 Brussels.

Tel: (02) (INT.+32 2) 217 80.80
Fax: (02) (INT.+32 2) 218 31.41

PACE GRANTS NEWS SUBSCRIPTION FORM

Please enrol me for a subscription for 12 issues of "PACE GRANTS NEWS" commencing ...

Name ______________________

Position ______________________

Organisation ______________________

Address ______________________

____

____

Post Code ____________ Country ____________

Tel No: ____________ Fax No: ____________

Any Special Instructions ______________________

☐ I enclose a cheque payable to PACE

☐ Please send me an invoice

☐ Please debit VISA/ACCESS Card No:

Expiry Date ______________________

In the Name of ______________________

Card Billing Address ______________________

____

____

Signature ______________________

If you are dissatisfied with "PACE GRANTS NEWS" after receiving the first three issues, you may return it and cancel your subscription and we will refund your money.

"PACE GRANTS NEWS" IS ZERO-RATED FOR VAT PURPOSES

INDEX

TABLE OF EUROPEAN COMMUNITY PRIMARY LEGISLATION - TREATIES

SECONDARY LEGISLATION - COUNCIL DECISIONS

COMMISSION DECISIONS

DIRECTIVES

REGULATIONS

RESOLUTIONS

Public Affairs Consultants Europe Ltd. (PACE) are part of a network operating in all the Member States of the European Union. They have been involved with the Commission's "New Approach to the Harmonisation of Technical Regulations" since 1989 and also:

* Monitor the European Union legislative programme on behalf of businesses, trade associations, national regional and local bodies, voluntary organisations and other special interest groups

* Organise action programmes to protect or promote these interests

* Undertake research, prepare reports and briefing materials on EU matters including access to funding

* Provide speakers for lectures and seminars and organise in-house training sessions on EU matters

* Publish books and journals about the European Union including:

  "Maastricht and the UK"

  "Help from Brussels, the PACE Guide to EC Grants and Other Assistance"

  "An Introduction to the European Union"

  "PACE Grants News" (monthly)

  "The Social Chapter"

Public Affairs Consultants Europe Ltd
3 Chiltern Business Centre
Garsington Road
Oxford OX4 5NG
Tel: 0865 (INT.+44 865) 770099
Fax: 0865 (INT.+44 865) 770011

Rue de la Presse 4
1000 Brussels.
Tel: (02) (INT.+32 2) 217 80.80
Fax: (02) (INT.+32 2) 218 31.41